Brücken über dem Abgrund

Amy Colin/Elisabeth Strenger (Eds.)

Brücken über dem Abgrund
Auseinandersetzungen mit jüdischer
Leidenserfahrung, Antisemitismus und Exil
Festschrift für Harry Zohn

Bridging the Abyss
Reflections on Jewish Suffering,
Anti-Semitism, and Exile
Essays in Honor of Harry Zohn

Wilhelm Fink Verlag

Herausgegeben mit Unterstützung des Österreichischen Kulturinstitutes, New York, und des Österreichischen Bundesministeriums für Auswärtige Angelegenheiten (Kultursektion)

Umschlagabbildung: Seidenmalerei von Sabine Colin

Die Deutsche Bibliothek - CIP-Einheitsaufnahme

Brücken über dem Abgrund: Auseinandersetzungen mit
jüdischer Leidenserfahrung, Antisemitismus und Exil;
Festschrift für Harry Zohn = Bridging the abyss / Amy Colin;
Elisabeth Strenger (eds.).- München: Fink, 1994
 ISBN 3-7705-2950-2
NE: Colin, Amy D. [Hrsg.]; Zohn Harry: Festschrift; Bridging the
abyss

ISBN 3-7705-2950-2
© 1994 Wilhelm Fink Verlag, München

Inhaltsverzeichnis

Teil Zwei — Part Two
Exilerfahrungen — Exile Experience

I. *"Einmal Exil, immer Exil"*
"Once in Exile, Always in Exile"

II. *Stefan Zweig und sein Freundeskreis*
Stefan Zweig and his Friends

III. Brücken im Bau:
Dichtung und Übersetzung als
Vermittlungsversuch zwischen Kulturen

Building Bridges:
Literature and Translation as Cultural Mediation

Vorwort

Das zwanzigste Jahrhundert neigt sich dem Ende zu. Als würde sich die verflossene Zeit mit all ihren Problemen und Kämpfen noch einmal aufbäumen, um den Anbeginn einer neuen Zeit zu verhindern, sind in den letzten Jahren jene dunklen Mächte der Vergangenheit wiedererwacht, die Europa bereits in zwei Weltkriege gestürzt haben: Wie ein Lauffeuer breiten sich Nationalismus, Rassismus und Fundamentalismus aus, schüren den Haß zwischen den Menschen und steigern ethnische Konflikte zu gewalttätigen Auseinandersetzungen. Krieg, wirtschaftliche Misere, soziale Not haben eine nicht mehr aufzuhaltende Völkerwanderung ausgelöst, die Westeuropäer als Bedrohung der eigenen politischen Stabilität empfinden. Ihre Angst vor dem Zustrom von Flüchtlingen ist jäh in Fremdenfeindlichkeit umgeschlagen und hat im vereinten Deutschland zu furchterregenden Morden an ausländischen Bürgern geführt.

Noch vor wenigen Jahren war die Bundesrepublik ein Land, das stets Flüchtlingen zu helfen suchte und Ausländern die Chance bot, sich in Deutschland eine neue Existenz aufzubauen. Die Einwanderer leisteten ihrerseits einen wertvollen Beitrag zur Entwicklung der Wirtschaft und Kultur. Das Aufflammen des deutschen Neo-Faschismus und der Fremdenfeindlichkeit löste eine Welle von Sympathiebekundungen für die Opfer der Gewaltakte aus, machte indes auch die Hoffnung zunichte, man habe die Phantome der Vergangenheit für immer gebannt.

Nirgends wird die Frage nach den Ursachen und Auswirkungen von Vorurteilen, Rassismus und Antisemitismus dringender zu beantworten sein als im vereinten Deutschland. Denn diese Frage ruft die schmerzliche Erinnerung an die Zeit der braunen Barbarei, an den Massenmord wach. Die Shoah Erfahrung bestimmt die Perspektive, aus der Deutsche wie Ausländer die gegenwärtigen politischen Entwicklungen in der Bundesrepublik betrachten. Aber verleiten solche Vergleiche unterschiedlicher Zeiten nicht zu falschen Schlußfolgerungen? Auf den Schauplatz des Geschehens sind neue Akteure getreten. Die Szene hat sich völlig verändert. Selbst die Opfer tragen andere Namen: Ausländer, Asylanten, Wirtschaftsflüchtlinge. Zu den Betroffenen gehören auch Juden, obwohl deren Zahl in Deutschland verschwindend klein ist. Aber die häufigen Schändungen jüdischer Gräber signalisieren, daß der Antisemitismus noch lange nicht überwunden ist. Hat sich die "Judenfeindschaft" verselbständigt? Lebt sie auch dort noch weiter, wo es kaum noch oder gar keine Juden mehr gibt? Hat der alte Antisemitismus in Deutschland

lediglich neue Wortführer und Zielscheiben gefunden? Verbirgt er sich
nun hinter der Maske der Fremdenfeindlichkeit? Wenn Antisemitismus
eine Form des Menschenhasses ist, der sich auf Juden richtet, weil sie in
den Augen der Nichtjuden seit Jahrhunderten die Andersartigkeit par
excellence verkörpern, dann wird die Analyse des Judenhasses einen
Einblick in die Ursachen und Folgen der heutigen Ausländerfeindlichkeit
gewähren können.

In Walter Benjamins geschichtsphilosophischen Thesen heißt es, der
Engel der Geschichte blicke stets zurück in die Zeit und sehe nur eine
Kette von Katastrophen, Berge von Trümmern, die man Vergangenheit
nennt. Gerne würde der Engel Halt machen, den Betroffenen helfen oder
zumindest die Toten begraben, aber er kann es nicht, denn ein vom
Paradiese unablässig wehender Wind, der Fortschritt heißt, trägt ihn fort
in die Zukunft. Zwar haben wir Menschen eine gewisse Ähnlichkeit mit
dem Angelus Novus, den Paul Klee malte und Walter Benjamin beschrieb, aber wir können dennoch — zumindest gedanklich — bei den
Trümmern der Geschichte verweilen, um die Ursachen der Tragödien zu
deuten und auf diese Weise vielleicht das Chaos der Gegenwart zu
begreifen.

Der Band *Brücken über dem Abgrund* geht den ursächlichen Zusammenhängen zwischen Macht, Rasse und *Gender* in unterschiedlichen politischen und literarischen Konstellationen von der Antike bis zur
Gegenwart nach. Im Mittelpunkt der Betrachtungen stehen die
vielschichtigen Folgen antisemitischer Vorurteile und die Reaktion der
Juden und Jüdinnen auf die ihnen entgegengebrachte Feindschaft. Die im
ersten Teil des Bandes vereinten Essays analysieren den Antisemitismus
als konstitutiven Faktor der Identitätsbildung. Denn Judenfeindschaft
zwingt zur Standortbestimmung. Die Antisemiten grenzen ihr Ich vom
Anderen ab, um eine innere Stabilität zu gewinnen, die lediglich ein
Trugbild ist. Die Ausgegrenzten denken ihrerseits über die aufge-
zwungene Andersartigkeit nach, stählern die Waffen, mit denen sie um
die politische und gesellschaftliche Gleichstellung, um Integration oder
die Gründung eines eigenen Staates kämpfen. Das Los der jahrzehntelang
verfolgten Juden war schwer; aber das Schicksal der Jüdinnen war
doppelt schwer, denn sie mußten Widerstände innerhalb wie außerhalb
ihrer Gemeinde überwinden, sich nicht nur mit Antisemitismus, sondern
auch mit Frauenfeindlichkeit auseinandersetzen.

Exilerfahrungen jüdischer Emigranten und Emigrantinnen von Joseph
Roth bis Stefan Zweig und Mimi Grossberg sowie deren unterschiedliche
Versuche, zwischen heterogenen Kulturen zu vermitteln, bilden den
Fokus des zweiten Teils dieses Bandes. Die Einsichten dieser Schriftsteller
und Schriftstellerinnen aus der Zeit des Zweiten Weltkrieges weisen
heutigen Flüchtlingen einen Weg, die Schwierigkeiten des Exildaseins

zumindest seelisch und geistig zu verarbeiten. Hilde Domins Worte, "einmal Exil, immer Exil", treffen für die meisten dieser Autoren zu, denn ihre Heimat wurde ihnen zur Fremde, aber die Fremde nicht zur Heimat. Anders erging es dem angesehenen jüdischen Literaturwissenschaftler Harry Zohn, der für seine Leistungen als Germanist 1960 das Verdienstkreuz der Bundesrepublik Deutschland und 1984 das Ehrenkreuz für Wissenschaft und Kunst der Republik Österreich erhalten hatte.

Harry Zohn kam 1923 in Wien zur Welt, einer Stadt, die ihn nachhaltig prägen sollte. Er wuchs in einer gläubigen jüdischen Familie auf, genoß sowohl eine religiöse als auch eine säkularisierte Erziehung und entdeckte früh sein Interesse für Literatur. Bereits im Gymnasium pflegte er mittelhochdeutsche Gedichte aufzusagen, las Chajim Nachman Bialik sowie Karl Kraus und verfolgte die politischen Ereignisse mit wachsender Besorgnis. "In meiner Kindheit spielte Wien alle Farben — jedenfalls rot, schwarz und braun —, ... zur Zeit des 'Anschlusses' war ich 14 Jahre alt und stand sozusagen erst an der Schwelle des Verstehens meines doppelten Erbtums, des österreichischen und des jüdischen, an der Schwelle des Selbstverständnisses."[1] schreibt Harry Zohn. Die Haßliebe seiner Schulkameraden sollte er früh zu spüren bekommen. Antisemitische Äußerungen, aber auch Schlägereien und Anpöbelungen gehörten zum Alltag. "Da man es den 'arischen' Schülern nicht mehr zumuten konnte die Schulbank mit den nunmehr zu 'Untermenschen' degradierten Juden zu drücken"[2], wurde das Gymnasium zur Judenschule erklärt und fungierte später als Sammelstelle für die zu deportierenden Juden. Es handelt sich um das ehemalige Sperlgymnasium, das Sigmund Freud viele Jahre vor Harry Zohn besucht hatte.

Im März 1938 hörte Harry Zohn im Radio die historische Rede des Kanzlers Schuschnigg; Zohns Eltern hatten während der von Schuschnigg angesagten Volksabstimmung für ein freies, unabhängiges Österreich demonstriert. Wohl spürten sie die drohende Gefahr, in der sich deutsche wie auch österreichische Juden befanden, aber sie ahnten "die Exzesse der kochenden Volksseele, das tiefe Braun des sprichwörtlich *goldenen* Wiener Herzens"[3] nicht. Wie zum Hohn war jener Frühling mild und schön; er schien den Umbruch zu begünstigen, berichtet Harry Zohn. "Es folgten Tage und Wochen der Furcht, Verwirrung und Verzweiflung, mit dem markerschütternden Dröhnen der deutschen Bombergeschwader und dem tierischen Gebrüll 'Sieg Heil!' im Ohr."[4] Als Jude konnte sich Harry Zohn nicht mehr auf die Straße trauen, denn jüdische Bürger wurden verhaftet und mißhandelt. Zur allgemeinen Volksbelustigung zwangen die Nazis meist ältere Juden — Frauen wie Männer, Rabbiner, Lehrer, Ärzte, Juristen — mit Bürsten, manchmal sogar mit Zahnbürsten die Parolen der

Vaterländischen Front von den Mauern und Trottoirs zu entfernen. Manche jüdische Mitbürger konnten noch rechtzeitig flüchten, andere begingen Selbstmord, die meisten wurden deportiert und ermordet. "Verzweifelt standen die Juden Schlange vor ausländischen Konsulaten, um ein Visum zu ergattern, und war das einmal erreicht, mußten nachgerade sadistische Schikanen der Behörden ertragen werden, beispielsweise die mit großen Schwierigkeiten verbundene Erlangung der steuerlichen 'Unbedenklichkeitserklärung'"[5]. Zohns Schwestern gelang es, nach England auszuwandern. Aber Harry Zohn blieb in Wien, wo er die *Kristallnacht* erlebte. Die Familie hatte sich in eine Werkstatt geflüchtet, hielt sich den ganzen Tag versteckt, bis sie "im Schutz der Dunkelheit an brennenden Synagogen, eingeschlagenen Schaufenstern und johlenden Menschenmengen vorbei nach Hause schleichen konnte"[6]. Bald darauf kündigte man ihnen die Wohnung; sie zogen zu einer befreundeten Familie. Am 10. November wurde Harry Zohn benachrichtigt, daß die Bemühungen seiner Schwestern, ihm eine Einreisebewilligung für England zu verschaffen, geglückt waren. Trotz seiner schweren Grippe und hohen Fiebers reiste der vierzehnjärige Zohn allein nach England. Es war der 2. Februar 1939. Seine Eltern kamen im Frühsommer nach, aber die meisten ihrer Angehörigen konnten Österreich nicht mehr verlassen; sie wurden deportiert und starben im KZ.

> Der Reisepaß, mit dem ich aus Wien auswanderte, war der des Deutschen Reiches, komplett mit Hakenkreuz und dem Roten J, das ein Schweizer Polizeipräsident zur Kennzeichnung der Juden angeregt hatte. Für mich aber galten die Worte Ernst Waldingers: "Wenn ich auch nicht die alten Psalmen summ'/Ich wandle auf der Ahnen Tränenspur ... /Ich bin ein Sohn der deutschen Sprache nur/Ich bin kein Deutscher, wohl ist mir darum." Diese Entwurzelung hatte schließlich zur Festigung meines Selbstverständnisses und meiner jüdischen Identität beigetragen.[7]

heißt es in Harry Zohns autobiographischen Erinnerungen. Zunächst verbrachte er einige Zeit im Ramsgate Hostel, durfte weder arbeiten, noch die Schule besuchen. Bald darauf sollte der Teenager das harte Leben in der Emigration kennenlernen. Denn die britische Regierung stufte alle deutschsprachigen Ausländer — ob Juden oder Deutsche — als *enemy aliens* ein und internierte sie. Um dem zu entgehen, leistete Harry Zohn wie auch viele andere Jugendliche kriegswichtige Arbeit in der sogenannten *Chiltern Emigrants Farm Training Colony*, wo sie in Baracken bei eisiger Kälte schlafen und im Schweine-oder Kuhstall, beim Schneiden der Hecken, Bauen der Zäune und Ebnen der Wege helfen mußten. Harry arbeitete in einem Steinbruch, erkrankte aber und wurde zum Barackendienst beordert. Er hielt es nicht lange aus. Im Frühjahr 1940 gelang es seinen Eltern und ihm, ein amerikanisches Einreisevisum zu erhalten.

> Wir schifften uns Anfang Mai in Liverpool ein, und zwar auf einem kleinen Schiff namens Baltrover, das "nicht für es gebaut war" — um ein Wort Morgensterns zu zitieren, d.h. nicht für den Transatlantikverkehr, sondern als Vergnügungsdampfer in der Ostsee fungiert hatte. Wegen der ständigen Gefahr eines Angriffs deutscher Unterseeboote mußte das Schiff in einem Konvoi zickzack fahren, was eine Überfahrt von drei Wochen bedeutete, während derer mein Vater und ich fast ständig seekrank waren...[8]

berichtet Harry Zohn. Das Schiff lief in Boston ein, wo sie niemanden kannten. Dennoch ließen sie sich in dieser Stadt nieder. Leicht sollte es Harry Zohn auch hier nicht haben; er arbeitete zunächst als Tellerwäscher und Speisenträger, wurde dann aufgrund der Wiener Schulzeugnisse in einer High School als *senior* eingestuft, die er ein Jahr später mit Auszeichnung absolvierte. Ab Herbst 1941 war er Werkstudent der Suffolk Universität und ging 1946 an die Clark Universität. Er wollte zunächst Journalist werden, entschloß sich dann aber, Germanistik zu studieren. Denn er liebte die deutschsprachige Literatur und wollte sich 'ganz einfach seine Muttersprache nicht rauben lassen.'[9] Im Jahre 1947 erhielt er ein Stipendium der Harvard Universität, das ihm ermöglichte, seinen Magister und sein Doktorat in vier Jahren abzuschließen. Der Doktorvater Karl Viëtor schlug das Dissertationsthema vor: "Stefan Zweig als Mittler in der europäischen Literatur". Und Harry Zohn nahm es begeistert an, denn er verspürte eine Wahlverwandschaft mit diesem österreichischen Schriftsteller — ein Gefühl, das seine Freundschaft mit Friderike Maria, Zweigs erster Frau, noch wesentlich vertiefte.

Während der Arbeit an der Dissertation war Harry Zohn zugleich als Assistent in Harvard tätig; nach Abschluß des Doktorats im Jahre 1951 wurde er an die Brandeis Universität berufen, eine unter jüdischer Ägide gegründete Hochschule. Seit 1967 ist er Professor für neuere deutsche Literatur an dieser Hochschule, deren Abteilung für Germanistik er viele Jahre lang geleitet hat. Goethes Wort, "Wo ich nütze, ist mein Vaterland" ist Harry Zohns Devise. Deshalb konnte er im amerikanischen Exil eine neue Heimat finden. Wien wurde ihm dennoch nicht fremd. Immer wieder fährt Harry Zohn nach Österreich, hält Vorlesungen, nimmt an Symposien teil und gehört zu den aktivsten amerikanischen Germanisten, die sich unermüdlich für das Studium der europäischen, insbesondere österreichischen Kultur in den USA einsetzen. "Ich kann jedenfalls von mir sagen, daß ich mir weder mein angestammtes jüdisches noch mein angeborenes Wiener Erbe habe rauben oder 'vermiesen' lassen."[10] Wien bedeutet für Harry Zohn nicht nur die österreichische Kultur, sondern auch der jüdische Beitrag an ihrem Aufblühen. Zu den bedeutenden österreichischen Juden, mit denen sich Harry Zohn verbunden fühlt, zählen Stefan Zweig, Arthur Schnitzler, Karl Kraus, aber auch die Komponisten Gustav Mahler und Arnold Schönberg. Auch seine Freundschaften mit Mirjam und Naëmah Beer-Hofmann, Franz Mittler, Franzi Ascher-Nash, Felix Pollak, Friedrich Torberg, Hertha Pauli, Alfred Farau, Robert Rie, Mimi Grossberg, Ernst Křenek, Otto Zausmer, Theodor Kramer, Irene Harand, Frank Zwillinger, Max Knight, Joseph Fabry, Ernst Waldinger, Robert Stolz und Max Schönherr verbinden ihn mit seinem doppelten Erbe.

Der angesehene Germanist Harry Zohn hatte ehrenvolle Ämter inne: Er war Präsident des Massachusetts Chapter der AATG (American Association of Teachers of German) und der American Translators Association, Vizepräsident der Stefan Zweig Gesellschaft und Direktor der Goethe Society of New England. Manche dieser Ämter bekleidet er immer noch: Er ist Vizepräsident der Schnitzler Gesellschaft, Mitglied des österreichischen und amerikanischen PEN Clubs sowie des PEN Centers for German-Speaking Writers Abroad und Mitbegründer wichtiger literaturwissenschaftlicher Zeitschriften und Gesellschaften. Die zahlreichen Veröffentlichungen Harry Zohns umfassen Monographien, Artikeln, Einleitungen, Editionen, Übersetzungen. Durch seine Schriften über Theodor Herzl, Karl Kraus, Kurt Tucholsky, Arthur Schnitzler, Stefan Zweig, Gershom Scholem, Walter Toman, Jacob Burckhardt, Martin Buber, Sigmund Freud, Marianne Weber, Alex Bein, Nelly Sachs, Brigitte Fischer, André Kaminski, Fritz Molden, Manès Sperber, u. v. a. wurde er zum geistigen Mittler zwischen der deutsch-österreichischen, jüdischen und amerikanischen Kultur. "Vorbildlich für mich wurde ein Passus in Stefan Zweigs 1937 erschienener Essaysammlung *Begegnungen mit Menschen, Büchern, Städten*. Dort schreibt Zweig, es sei sein Bestreben, 'auch das Fremdeste zu verstehen, immer Völker und Zeiten, Gestalten und Werke nur in ihrem positiven, ihrem schöpferischen Sinne zu bewerten und durch solches Verstehenwollen und Verstehenmachen demütig, aber treu unserem unzerstörbaren Ideal zu dienen: der humanen Verständigung zwischen Menschen, Gesinnungen, Kulturen und Nationen.' In einer Studie über Stefan Zweig warf ich die Frage auf, ob solches Mittlertum als eminent jüdische Eigenschaft zu werten sei und gelangte zu eir.er behutsamen, bedingten Bejahung ..."[11], heißt es in Harry Zohns Erinnerungen.

Aber das Geheimnis dieses kulturellen Mittlertums liegt in seiner reichen Übersetzertätigkeit verborgen. Zu den fünfunddreißig Werken, die er aus dem Deutschen ins Englische übertrug, zählen Sigmund Freuds *Delusion and Dream* (1956), Jacob Burckhardts *Judgements on History and Historians* (1958), Theodor Herzls *The Complete Diaries* (4 Bde.) und *Zionist Writings* (1973), Walter Benjamins *Illuminations* (1973) und *Charles*

Baudelaire (1973), Gershom Scholems *From Berlin to Jerusalem* (1980), André Kaminskis *Kith and Kin* (1988), Alex Beins *The Jewish Question: Biography of a World Problem* (1989) sowie Manès Sperbers *The Unheeded Warning* (1991) und *Till My Are Closed With Shards* (1994). Harry Zohns Übertragungen sind eine besondere Leistung, denn seine Muttersprache ist Deutsch; die Zielsprache, Englisch, hatte er erst als Heranwachsender gelernt. Diese rege Übersetzertätigkeit ermöglichte es Harry Zohn, seine versunkene Welt der österreich-jüdischen Literatur in seine neue Welt des amerikanischen Englisch zu übertragen. Auf diese Weise überwand er die Isolation des Emigrantendaseins, steigerte die Exilerfahrung zur Grunddimension seines Schaffens und schuf die geistige Brücke zwischen den heterogenen Kulturen, die ihn prägten. Harry Zohns kuturelles Mittlertum gab die Anregung zum Titel der vorliegenden Festschrift, die seinen siebzigsten Geburtstag würdigt. Im Namen aller Gratulanten wünschen wir Harry Zohn, auch in Zukunft solche Brücken über dem Abgrund zu bauen.

Amy Colin
Pittsburgh, Dezember 1993

Anmerkungen

1 Harry Zohn: "Ich stamme aus Wien ...", Wiener Vorlesung, Herbst 1993; unveröffentlichtes Typoskript, S. 5.

2 Harry Zohn: "Als der Adolf über uns kam. Betrachtungen eines *Thirty Eighters*". In: *Das Jüdische Echo*, Oktober 1989, Band 37, Nummer 1, S. 29.

3 Ebd.

4 Ebd.

5 Ebd. S. 30.

6 Zohn: "Ich stamme aus Wien...", (Anm. 1), S. 12.

7 Anm. 2, S. 31.

8 Gespräch mit Harry Zohn, Dezember 1993; vgl. Zohn: "Als der Adolf über uns kam", (Anm. 2), S. 29-30.

9 Gespräch mit Zohn, Anmerkung 7.

10 Zohn: "Ich stamme aus Wien ...", (Anm. 1), S. 14.

11 Ebd. S. 6.

Foto von Harry Zohn

Preface

The twentieth century is drawing to a close. Yet the problems and struggles of the past are once again rearing their ugly heads as though to prevent the start of a new era. Those dark powers, which already cast Europe into two world wars, overshadow the present. Like brush fires, nationalism, racism, and fundamentalism are spreading, inflaming hatred between peoples, and turning ethnic conflicts into violent battles. War, economic poverty, social duress have caused an unstoppable migration that West Europeans view as a threat to their political stability. Their fear of a wave of refugees has turned into a hateful xenophobia, which in united Germany has led to the horrific murders of foreigners.

Just a few years ago, the Federal Republic of Germany was a country that consistently sought to help refugees and offered foreigners the opportunity to build a new life for themselves. The immigrants, for their part, made a valuable contribution to the development of Germany's economy and culture. The rise of neo-Fascism and xenophobia has prompted declarations of sympathy for the victims of recent violence, but at the same time has destroyed the hope that the phantoms of the past had been exorcised once and for all.

The search for the causes and effects of prejudice, racism, and anti-Semitism is nowhere so pressing as in united Germany, for these questions awaken the painful memory of brown barbarism, of mass murder. The Shoah experience determines the perspective from which the German as well as the outsider observe the current developments in the Federal Republic. But might not such comparisons of historically disparate times lead us to false conclusions? New actors have stepped onto the world stage. The scene has changed completely. Even the victims have different names: foreigner, asylum seeker, economic refugee. Sometimes we find among the victims Jews living in Germany, although their number is becoming ever smaller. Much more common than attacks on Jewish citizens is the desecration of Jewish graves. These outbursts of hatred and revenge signal that anti-Semitism is nowhere near being overcome. Anti-Semitism still thrives where there are hardly any more Jews. Indeed, the old anti-Semitism seems to have found new spokespersons and targets in Germany. Is it now hiding behind the mask of xenophobia? If Anti-Semitism is a form of hatred that is directed towards Jews, because for centuries, they have personified otherness *par excellence* in the eyes of non-Jews, then the analysis of anti-Semitism can provide insight into the causes and effects of today's xenophobia.

In his philosophical reflections, Walter Benjamin describes the angel of history as looking backward in time and seeing only the chain of catastrophes and mountains of rubble, that we call the past. The angel would gladly pause and help the survivors, or at least, bury the dead, but it cannot, because a wind called progress blows steadily from paradise, carrying it away into the future. Although we share a certain similarity with the *Angelus Novus* painted by Paul Klee and described by Benjamin, we can, at least in thought, linger by the rubble of history to interpret the sources of these tragedies and perhaps in this way comprehend the chaos of the present.

The book, *Bridging the Abyss*, explores the interrelations among power, race, and gender in varying political and literary constellations from antiquity to the present. It focuses on the many-layered effects of anti-Semitic prejudice and the reaction of Jewish men and women to this antagonism. The essays collected in the first part of this volume analyze anti-Semitism as a constitutive factor in creating identity. Anti-Semitism forces one to declare one's position, for Anti-Semites set boundaries that separate their I from the Other, thereby achieving the illusion of an inner stability. Those that are on the other side of the boundary reflect on this difference that has been imposed upon them; they sharpen the weapons with which they fight for political and social equality, integration, or the establishment of their own state. The fate of Jews who have been persecuted for decades is ponderous, but the fate of Jewish women is twice as difficult, for they have had to overcome obstacles created by discrimination within as well as without their community.

Exile, as experienced by Jewish émigrés, from Joseph Roth to Stefan Zweig and Mimi Grossberg, forms the focus of the second part of the volume. The insights of these writers indicate a way to process the difficulties of exile to today's refugees, at least intellectually. Hilde Domin's words, "Once exiled, always exiled," speak to most of these authors' experiences for their homeland became a strange land, while adopted foreign lands never quite became their homeland. It was different, however, for Harry Zohn, the respected literary scholar, whose accomplishments and contributions to his native culture were recognized by receiving the *Verdienstkreuz* of the Federal Republic in 1960 and Austria's *Ehrenkreuz für Wissenschaft und Kunst* in 1984.

Harry Zohn was born in 1923 in Vienna, a city that influenced him deeply. He grew up in an observant Jewish family where he enjoyed the advantages of both a religious and secular education. Early on he discovered his interest in literature. While attending Gymnasium his literary tastes ranged broadly — one could find him reciting Middle High German poems or reading Chajim Nachman Bialik and Karl Kraus. His preoccupation with literature did not prevent him from following the political developments of the day with growing unease. Reflecting on his youth, he wrote:

> In my childhood, Vienna bet on all colors — in any case, red, black, and brown — ... at the time of the *Anschluss* I was fourteen years old and stood, so to say, for the first time on the threshold of understanding my double heritage, the Austrian and the Jewish, on the threshold of self-knowledge...[1]

The love-hate relationship he had with his schoolmates made itself felt early on. Anti-Semitic remarks, but also fights and roughing-up were everyday occurrences. "Because one couldn't impose upon Aryan pupils to share a desk with Jews who had been degraded to *Untermenschen*,"[2] the *Gymnasium* was declared a Jewish school and was used later as a collection center for Jews awaiting deportation. This school was the former Sperlgymnasium, which Sigmund Freud had attended years before.

In March 1938, Harry Zohn heard Chancellor Schuschnigg's historic speech on the radio. Zohn's parents had demonstrated for a free and independent Austria at the *Volksabstimmung* called by Schuschnigg. They suspected what the fate of the Jews might be at the hands of Nazi barbarism, but they could not really imagine "the excesses of the boiling *Volksseele*, the deep brew of the proverbial 'golden' Viennese heart."[3] As though in mockery, that spring was mild and lovely — it seemed to favor the upheaval, Harry Zohn reported. He recalled that, "days and weeks of fear followed, confusion and despair, with the bone-numbing drone of the German bomber squadrons and the bestial *Sieg Heil!* roaring in the ears."[4] As a Jew, Harry Zohn did not dare to go out because Jewish citizens were being arrested and harassed. To entertain the people, the Nazis forced mostly older Jews, women as well as men, rabbis, teachers, doctors, lawyers to clean the slogans of the Patriotic Front from the walls and sidewalks with brushes, sometimes even toothbrushes. Some Jews could flee in time, others committed suicide, most were deported and murdered. "Desperately, Jews stood in line outside embassies, to somehow get a visa. Once the visa was obtained, they had then to deal with the sadistic chicanery of the bureaucrats to get the necessary papers to emigrate, for example the *Unbedenklichkeitserklärung* that certified proper payment of taxes."[5] Harry Zohn's sisters were able to emigrate to England, but he stayed in Vienna, where he experienced *Kristallnacht*. The family had taken refuge in a workshop where they remained in hiding the entire day, until, "under cover of darkness they could sneak home past burning synagogues, smashed shop windows and shouting crowds."[6] Soon thereafter, they lost their apartment and had to move in with friends. On November 10, Harry Zohn learned that his sisters had succeeded in getting him an entry permit for England. In spite of having influenza and a high fever, the fourteen-year old travelled alone to England. It was February 2, 1939. His parents followed in early summer, but most of their relatives could no longer leave Austria — they were deported and died in concentration camps.

In his memoirs, Harry Zohn writes:

> The passport with which I emigrated from Vienna was issued by the German Reich, complete with a swastika and the Red J that a Swiss police commissioner had initiated as a way to designate Jews. For me, however, the words of Ernst Waldinger were more important: "Even though I don't hum the old psalms, I wander in my ancestors' trail of tears ... I am a son of German only / I am no German, and I am glad of it.[7]

This uprooting actually served to strengthen his self awareness and his Jewish identity. Upon his arrival in England, Harry Zohn lived at Ramsgate Hostel. He was allowed neither to work nor to attend school. Soon thereafter, the teenager was to experience the hard life of a refugee, for the British government designated all German-speaking foreigners, whether Jewish or German, as enemy aliens and interned them. To avoid internment, Harry Zohn, along with many other youths, did work vital to the war effort at the Chiltern Emigrants Farm Training Colony. Here they slept in often ice-cold barracks and worked in pigsties and cow stalls, trimmed hedges, built fences and levelled roads. Harry worked in a stone quarry, but when he became ill he was assigned to barrack duty. He could barely cope. In Spring 1940 he and his parents were able to get a visa for the United States. Of that journey, he reports:

> We boarded the ship at Liverpool in the beginning of May. It was a small ship named the Baltrover, that "wasn't built for it," to cite Morgenstern, that is, not for transatlantic crossings, but had served as a pleasure steamer in the Baltic. Because of the constant threat of a German submarine attack, the ship had to sail in a zig-zag pattern, making the crossing last three weeks, during which my father and I were always seasick.[8]

The ship landed in Boston where they knew no one. Still, they settled in this city. Harry Zohn would not have an easy time here either — he worked first as a dishwasher and busboy. When he finally entered high school, it was as a senior because of his Viennese school records. He graduated one year later. Beginning in Fall 1941 he was a work-study student at Suffolk University. In 1946 he went to Clark University. At first, he wanted to become a journalist, but then decided to study German literature, for he loved literature written in German, and did not want "to have his mother tongue simply stolen from him."[9] In 1947 he received a scholarship for graduate study at Harvard and he was able to complete his Master's degree and PhD in four years. His dissertation advisor, Karl Viëtor, suggested his thesis: "Stefan Zweig as Mediator in European Literature." And Harry Zohn took up this topic enthusiastically, since he felt an affinity with this Austrian writer — a feeling that his friendship with Friderike Maria, Zweig's first wife who was then living in Connecticut, deepened even further.

While he worked on his dissertation at Harvard, Harry Zohn was a teaching fellow. After receiving his Ph.D. in 1951, he took a position at Brandeis University. Since 1967 he has served as Professor of Modern German Literature at Brandeis. For many years he chaired the Department of Germanic and Slavic Languages. Goethe's words, "Where I can serve, there is my homeland" is Harry Zohn's motto. For that reason he could find a new home in his American exile, yet Vienna did not become a foreign land for him. "In any case, I can say about myself, that I didn't allow my Jewish heritage (by virtue of origins) nor my Viennese heritage (by virtue of birth) to be stolen from me or ruined for me."[10] Vienna means more than Austrian culture for Harry Zohn. Vienna also means the Jewish contribution to her cultural achievements. Among the illustrious Austrian-Jewish figures to whom Harry Zohn feels connected number Stefan Zweig, Arthur Schnitzler, Karl Kraus, and the composers Gustav Mahler and Arnold Schoenberg. His friendships with Mirjam and Naëmah Beer-Hofmann, Franz Mittler, Franzi Ascher-Nash, Felix Pollak, Friedrich Torberg, Hertha Pauli, Alfred Farau, Robert Rie, Mimi Grossberg, Ernst Křenek, Otto Zausmer, Theodor Kramer, Irene Harand, Frank Zwillinger, Max Knight, Joseph Fabry, Ernst Waldinger, Robert Stolz and Max Schönherr bind him to his double heritage.

As a respected Germanist, Harry Zohn has held important positions in many professional organizations. He served as the President of the Massachusetts Chapter of the AATG and the American Translators Association, Vice President of the Stefan Zweig Gesellschaft and Director of the Goethe Society of New England. Currently he still holds various prominent positions: Vice President of the Schnitzler Gesellschaft, member of the Austrian and American PEN Clubs, of the PEN Centers for German-Speaking Writers Abroad. He has participated in founding significant professional organizations and critical journals. Harry Zohn's many publications include monographs, articles, introductions, editions, translations. Through his writings on Theodor Herzl, Karl Kraus, Kurt Tucholsky, Arthur Schnitzler, Stefan Zweig, Gershom Scholem, Walter Toman, Jacob Burckhardt, Martin Buber, Sigmund Freud, Marianne Weber, Alex Bein, Nelly Sachs, Brigitte Fischer, André Kaminski, Fritz

Molden, Manès Sperber among others, he has become an intellectual mediator between the German-Austrian, Jewish, and American cultures. Harry Zohn reflects on his cultural role in his memoirs:

> A passage in Stefan Zweig's collection of essays, *Encounters with People, Books, Cities* that appeared in 1937 has been a model for me. Zweig writes here, it is his aim to understand even that which is most foreign, always to evaluate peoples and times, figures and works only in their positive, their creative capacity, and through this desire to understand and make understandable to serve humbly but loyally our indestructible ideal: that of humane understanding between people, perspectives, cultures, and nations. In a study of Stefan Zweig I posed the question, whether this role as mediator is to be evaluated as an eminent Jewish trait and found the answer to be a careful, conditional, Yes.[11]

But the secret of his own capacity for this cultural mediation lies in his rich contributions as a translator. The thirty-five works that he has translated from German into English include Sigmund Freud's *Delusion and Dream* (1956), Jacob Burckhardt's *Judgements on History and Historians* (1958), Theodor Herzl's *The Complete Diaries* (4 Volumes) and *Zionist Writings* (1973), Walter Benjamin's *Illuminations* (1973) and *Charles Baudelaire* (1973), Gershom Scholem's *From Berlin to Jerusalem* (1980), André Kaminski's *Kith and Kin* (1988), Alex Bein's *The Jewish Question: Biography of a World Problem* (1989), and Manès Sperber's *The Unheeded Warning* (1991) and *Till My Eyes Are Closed With Shards* (1992). Harry Zohn's renderings are a special accomplishment since his native tongue is German and the target language for his works is English, which he first learned as a young man. This intense activity as a translator has made it possible for Harry Zohn to convey something of the vanished world of Austrian-Jewish literature to his new American milieu. By this means, he overcame the isolation of the immigrant existence. He has been able to transform the experience of exile into the basis of his creativity and to build the intellectual bridge between the heterogeneous cultures that formed him. Harry Zohn's role as a cultural mediator inspired the title of this collection of essays honoring his contributions on the occasion of his seventieth birthday. In the name of all friends and colleagues, we wish Harry Zohn future opportunities for building many more such bridges over the abyss.

Amy Colin   Translated by Elisabeth Strenger
Pittsburgh, December 1993   Waltham, December 1993

Notes

[1]   Harry Zohn: "Ich stamme aus Wien ...," lecture held in Vienna, Fall 1993; unpublished typescript, p. 5.

[2]   Harry Zohn: "Als der Adolf über uns kam. Betrachtungen eines *Thirty Eighters*." In: *Das Jüdische Echo*, October 1989, Vol. 37, Number 1, p. 29.

[3]   Ibid.

[4]   Ibid.

[5]   Ibid., p. 30.

[6]   Zohn (Note 1), p. 12.

[7]   Note 2, p. 31.

[8]   Conversation with Harry Zohn, December 1993; cf. Zohn (Note 3), pp. 29-30.

[9]   Conversation with Zohn (Note 7).

[10] Zohn, (Note 1), p. 14.

[11] Ibid., p. 6.

Sabine Colin: Seidenmalerei, Herbst 1993

Teil Eins — Part One

Macht, Rasse, Gender
Von der politischen Wirklichkeit
zur literarischen Metamorphose

Power, Race, and Gender
From Political Realities
to Literary Metamorphosis

I.

Antisemitismus und kein Ende?

Still Anti-Semitic After All These Years?

Julius H. Schoeps

Vom Antijudaismus zum Antisemitismus: Zur Struktur, Funktion und Wirkung eines Vorurteils[1]

I.

Das Verhältnis der Juden zu den Völkern ist heute von dem Trauma Auschwitz her bestimmt. Nicht nur im jüdischen Denken und Fühlen hat der "Holocaust" tiefe Narben hinterlassen. Der Untergang der europäischen Judenheit, der von der Welt geduldete, durch Schweigen und durch mangelnde Hilfsbereitschaft unterstützte Massenmord an den Juden Europas wirkt nach, wird jüdische und nichtjüdische Existenz auch in Zukunft noch beeinflussen. Die Angst vor der Wiederkehr des Grauens, die Angst, das Unvorstellbare könnte wieder Wirklichkeit werden, sitzt tief. Verdrängen läßt sich diese Angst nicht, und zwar schon deshalb nicht, weil vieles bis heute ungeklärt blieb. Wie hatte es dazu kommen können, daß eine Kulturnation im Herzen Europas der Barbarei verfiel? War es nur die logische Konsequenz der biologisch begründeten Rassenideologie, die sich zu einer Art Rassenmythologie gesteigert hatte? Oder waren es schlicht die Wahnideen eines Verrückten, der Subalterne aller Ränge und Schichten dazu gebracht hatte, fabrikmäßig zu morden?

Fest steht nur, daß seit der Zeit der Zerstörung des Tempels im Jahre 70, seit der Zeit der Verbannung und gewaltsamen Zerstreuung, es das Problem der Juden unter den Völkern gibt, einer Minderheit, deren Angehörige durch Religion, Geschichte und Tradition irgendwie zusammengehalten werden, obwohl sie in Sprache, Sitten und Kultur weitgehend voneinander geschieden und sich an die Bedingungen ihrer jeweiligen Wohnländer angepaßt haben. In seiner lesenswerten Untersuchung *Die Judenfrage. Biographie eines Weltproblems* hat der 1988 verstorbene Jerusalemer Historiker Alex Bein die Ansicht vertreten, es seien wahrscheinlich die Juden selbst gewesen, die die Voraussetzungen der sogenannten "Judenfrage" geschaffen hätten.[2] Sie seien als Volk nicht untergegangen, wären bei ihrer Identität geblieben und hätten es

gewissermaßen abgelehnt, die "Spielregeln" der Völkergeschichte anzuer-
kennen. Trotz des völligen Zusammenbruchs ihrer staatlichen Existenz
und ihres religiösen Zentrums, trotz des so offensichtlich scheinenden
Beweises ihrer eigenen Machtlosigkeit und der Machtlosigkeit ihres
Gottes, hätten sie an ihrer Religion und Lebensweise festgehalten. Aber,
so Bein, vermutlich ist es gerade diese Haltung, mit der sich viele
Nichtjuden im Grunde bis heute nicht haben abfinden können. Diese
Haltung ist es, die auf Unverständnis stößt.

Gewiß hat es zu allen Zeiten Menschen gegeben, die den Juden positiv
gegenüberstanden, aber Normalfall ist doch Ablehnung gewesen. Wer
sich um eine wirkliche Antwort auf die Frage bemüht, was letztlich
hinter der Ablehnung gegenüber den Juden steckt, muß den Mut haben,
Fragen so radikal wie nur möglich zu stellen. Das Phänomen der
Judenfeindschaft ist nicht zu begreifen, wenn man es nur von außen
analysiert und interpretiert. Die Judenfeindschaft hat immer auch mit
einem selbst zu tun, mit dem eigenen "Ich". Es fällt deshalb auch schwer,
sich dieser Problematik überhaupt zuzuwenden. Sie ist lästig. Wenn man
diesen Fragen wirklich auf den Grund geht, fühlt man, wie die eigene
Identität ins Wanken geraten könnte. Und das ist bekanntlich etwas, vor
dem die meisten Angst haben und was die wenigsten wollen.

Antisemitismus, wie die Judenfeindschaft in ihrer modernen Ausprägung genannt wird, allein und ausschließlich als eine Krisen-
erscheinung der kapitalistischen Gesellschaft zu deuten, führt zu Fehlein-
schätzungen. Denn eine solche Interpretation ist zwar modern, aber sie
greift letztlich, trotz bestimmter Einsichten, zu kurz und wird dem
Phänomen nicht gerecht. Die Judenfeindschaft hat nämlich — und das ist
der Kern der folgenden Überlegungen — ihre Wurzeln in religiösen
Überzeugungen, und zwar in der christlich-jüdischen Differenz, genauer
in der traditionellen Ablehnung des Judentums durch das Christentum
und die christliche Welt.

II. Judenhaß als Folge christlicher Indoktrination

Die Vorstellung, Gott hätte die Juden verflucht und verworfen, weil sie
Jesus nicht als Messias anerkannten und seine Kreuzigung veranlaßten,
diese Vorstellung bestimmte das christliche Judenbild durch die Jahrhunderte — und bestimmt es weitgehend auch noch heute. So führt selbst
nach 1945 der Bruderrat der Evangelischen Kirche Deutschlands (EKD)
in der Schrift "Wort zur Judenfrage" das Argument ins Treffen: "Indem
Israel den Messias kreuzigte, hat es seine Erwählung und Bestimmung
verworfen"[3].

Nicht die soziale Wirklichkeit, sondern die Anschuldigungen der
Kirchenväter von Origines über Augustinus und Johannes Chrysostomus
bis hin zu Hieronymus schufen das Stereotyp: das von Generation zu
Generation weitergegebene Zerrbild des Juden. Als Urtypus des Sünders

und Frevlers immer wieder nachgezeichnet und mit neuen Farben ausgemalt, wirkt der Jude als abschreckendes Beispiel. Mit dem Katechismus nimmt es das Kind auf und durch die Predigt der Erwachsene in der Kirche. Jede Skulptur und jedes Gemälde über Kreuzigung und Leiden des Heiland und der Märtyrer, mit dem die Kirchen ausgeschmückt sind, erinnert daran und verdeutlicht es. Im Lied, im Märchen, aber auch im Passionsspiel — überall taucht dieses Bild auf, das nicht nur die seit altersher im Umlauf befindlichen antijüdischen Vorurteile bündelt, sondern (und ich bin mir der Brisanz dieser Aussage durchaus bewußt) auch als eine verdeckte Aufforderung an den Betrachter verstanden werden kann, sich gegen die Juden abzusetzen und sich ihrer handgreiflich zu erwehren.

Der an verschiedenen Stellen des Neuen Testamentes formulierte Gottesmordvorwurf ist über die Jahrhunderte präsent geblieben und hat die Einstellung gegenüber den Juden bestimmt. Es gibt kein antijüdisches Argument, "das länger benutzt, häufiger vorgebracht, hartnäckiger beibehalten und tiefer internalisiert wurde" (Stefan Lehr). Der Vorwurf des Gottesmordes hat Haßgefühle ausgelöst, Vorurteile gezeugt und das Verhältnis zwischen Christen und Juden nachhaltig vergiftet. Im Verlauf der Jahrhunderte stereotyp wiederholt hat dieser Vorwurf den Juden im Volksbewußtsein zum Dämon stilisiert und ihn die Gestalt des Ahasver annehmen lassen, des ruhelosen Weltenwanderers. Man sah in ihm den blutsaugenden Vampir, den bocksfüßigen Teufel, den geschwänzten Satan — er wurde die Personifikation allen Unheils, die Inkarnation des Bösen schlechthin.

Das von den Kirchenvätern geschaffene Bild vom verworfenen und deshalb verderbten Juden ist Grundlage aller späteren Anfeindungen geworden. Dieses Bild erfuhr seine besondere Ausprägung durch die Fremdheitsgefühle, die die Juden bei den Nichtjuden bis zum heutigen Tage auslösen. Das hat zweifellos zum einen mit der religiös-nationalen Absonderung der Juden zu tun, die seit der Antike unverändert auf Ablehnung und Mißtrauen stößt, zum anderen mit dem unbeirrbaren Glauben an die Einzigkeit des unsichtbaren Gottes und insbesondere dem Anspruch auf Auserwählung, der bis heute von der Umwelt als hochmütiger Aberglaube, als Gottlosigkeit, wenn nicht sogar als Betrug angesehen wird.

Es gibt für die Ablehnung des Anspruchs der Auserwählung durch die nichtjüdische bzw. christliche Welt eine sehr frühe jüdische Selbsterklärung in einem kalauernden *Midrasch,*[4] der sich eines Wortspieles bedient: Am Sinai sei die *sina* auf die Völker der Welt herabgestiegen. Dies meint, die Auserwählung der Juden zum Thoraempfang habe den Neid, den Haß und die Wut anderer Völker hervorgerufen, da sie nicht zum Thoraempfang ausersehen wurden. Zweifellos ist dies ein alter und auch starker Realgrund für die Judenfeindschaft, der

bis heute anhält: der Glaube, Gott habe mit Abraham und dessen
Nachkommen einen Bund geschlossen, einen Bund der auf dem Sinai
durch Moses erneuert worden sei und Israel dadurch das auserwählte
Volk Gottes und von Gott als ein Werkzeug zum Segen der Menschheit
vorgesehen wurde.

Über zweitausend Jahre hat man alles getan, "um das wirkliche Bild
des Juden dem von der Kirche geformten möglichst anzugleichen" (Alex
Bein). Die christliche Welt empfand die Existenz von Juden und des
Judentums als eine Belästigung, als etwas Unerträgliches. Selbst ein so
bedeutender protestantischer Theologe wie Karl Barth konnte sich Zeit
seines Lebens von dem Gefühl der Abneigung nicht freimachen. Gegenüber Friedrich-Wilhelm Marquardt bemerkte er einmal in einem Brief,
daß er bei der Begegnung mit Juden, immer eine "völlig irrationale
Aversion" herunterzuschlucken habe.[5] Ein Kommentar erübrigt sich.

Letztlich ist es immer das gleiche Bild, das über die Jahrhunderte
vermittelt wird — der Jude als "Antichrist", den es — um der eigenen
Selbstvergewisserung willen — zu bekämpfen gilt. Die Mittel, die sich
Kirchenfürsten und Politiker dazu aussannen, gleichen sich auf eine
seltsam fatale Weise. Obgleich Jahrhunderte dazwischen liegen, ähneln
zum Beispiel die Bestimmungen des I. Laterankonzils von 1215 den
spanischen Gesetzen des 16. Jahrhunderts und den Nürnberger Gesetzen
der Nazis (Gesetz "zum Schutz des deutschen Blutes und der deutschen
Ehre" vom 15. September 1935) des 20. Jahrhunderts. Es ist ganz offensichtlich, daß sich bestimmte Vorstellungen, wie man sich von den Juden
abgrenzen könne, über Jahrhunderte gehalten haben.[6] So erfuhr das
Verbot der Eheschließung zwischen Juden und Christen 1935 nur in der
Wortwahl eine Abänderung. Es lautete nun, "Eheschließungen zwischen
Juden und Staatsangehörigen deutschen oder artverwandten Blutes sind
verboten". Das im Jahre 1215 erlassene Verbot, Dienstboten in jüdischen
Häusern zu beschäftigen, besagte in der Version von 1935, "Juden dürfen
weibliche Staatsangehörige deutschen oder artverwandten Blutes unter
45 Jahren nicht in ihrem Haushalt beschäftigen"[7].

Selbst der gelbe Stern ("Judenstern"), der den Juden zum Zwecke der
Markierung angeheftet wurde, war nicht eine Erfindung der Nazis,
sondern hatte eine uralte kirchliche Tradition. Bereits auf dem Lateran-
konzil von 1215 war verfügt worden, Juden müßten durch besondere
Kleidung oder Abzeichen erkennbar sein. Diese Politik der Markierung,
die darauf abzielte, die Juden in den christlichen Ländern vom Rest der
Bevölkerung zu unterscheiden, ist von den Nazis wieder aufgenommen
und sowohl als Mittel der Kennzeichnung als auch der Demütigung
benutzt worden. Wie es dazu kam, daß sie die Farbe "gelb" wählten,
darüber läßt sich nur mutmaßen. Wahrscheinlich wußten sie — als
beflissene deutsche Bildungsbürger vielleicht sogar aus Goethes Farben-
lehre, daß diese Farbe negativ besetzt ist. Bekannt war ihnen jedenfalls,

daß seit altersher die Farbe zur Kennzeichnung aller Geächteten benutzt wird, der Dirnen und Ketzer, der Schänder von Hostien – und eben auch der Juden.

III. Säkulare Judenbilder und Bedrohungsängste

Mit dem Ende des 18. und mit dem Beginn des 19. Jahrhunderts begann eine Entwicklung, die für Juden zu einer tödlichen Bedrohung werden sollte. Der Emanzipationsprozess brachte ihnen zwar schrittweise die rechtliche Gleichstellung, nicht aber die ersehnte gesellschaftliche Anerkennung, um die sie mit jeder Faser ihres Seins kämpften. Im Gegenteil: Je mehr Rechte sie erhielten, je mehr sie sich an die Umgebungsgesellschaft in Kleidung, Sprache, Gestik und Verhalten anpaßten, desto bösartiger wurde die Ablehnung, auf die sie stießen. Rabiate Antisemiten entwickelten Abgrenzungsstrategien, die nicht nur den Emanzipationsprozeß rückgängig zu machen versuchten, sondern darüber hinaus auch darauf abzielten, den Juden als Juden zu markieren. "Jeder Jude", so heißt es bei Eduard Drumont, "den man sieht, jeder Jude, der sich offen als solcher zeigt, ist verhältnismäßig wenig gefährlich ... Der unbestimmbare und nicht deutlich zu erkennende Jude – das ist der gefährliche Jude ..."[8]

Wie kann man aber jemanden identifizieren, der sich äußerlich nicht mehr von seinem Gegenüber unterscheidet? Gibt es dafür überhaupt Möglichkeiten? Antisemiten haben sich geradezu einen Sport daraus gemacht, anhand von Namen Juden zu markieren. In der Studie *Der Name als Stigma*[9] des Kölner Linguisten und Kulturwissenschaftlers Dietz Bering kann man nachlesen, mit welcher Raffinesse hier verfahren wurde. Zahllos waren in der Zeit der Weimarer Republik die Witze, Verse und Spottlieder, in denen ein jüdisch klingender Name wie Cohn, Hirsch oder Katz zur Zielscheibe der Verhöhnung und Verachtung gemacht wurde. (Beispiele: "Mit meinem Hund hab ich e Zustand im Geschäft! Zuerst hatt ich einen Komis, der hieß Katz, natürlich hat der Hund den Katz immer gebissen. Dann hab ich den Katz entlassen und einen genommen, der hieß Eckstein, da war's noch schlimmer!" Oder: "Über allen Gipfeln Ozon. Unter allen Wipfeln sitzt Kohn").

Joseph Goebbels, der Propagandaminister der Nazis, hat die Namenswaffe virtuos benutzt, um mit seinen Angriffen auf den Berliner Polizeivizepräsidenten Bernhard Weiß, den er bei jeder sich bietenden Gelegenheit mit dem Namen "Isidor" titulierte,[10] den Antisemitismus in der Bevölkerung anzufachen. Instinktiv wußte Goebbels, daß er mit seinen Attacken einen Punkt traf, der bei jedem Menschen konstitutiv ist: Der Name hat mit der jeweiligen Identität eines Menschen zu tun, und der gezielte Angriff auf diesen ist der Versuch der Persönlichkeits-

destruktion, die in der Zeit der Weimarer Republik systematisch
betrieben wurde, um die Juden zu stigmatisieren und ihre Ausgrenzung
aus der Gesellschaft vorzubereiten.

Motor und Auslöser der Aus- und Abgrenzungskampagnen seit
Beginn des letzten Jahrhunderts waren ganz offensichtlich tiefsitzende
Bedrohungsängste, die vom einsetzenden Modernisierungsprozeß und
den damit verbundenen sozio-ökonomischen Umwälzungen hervorgerufen wurden — und nicht nur die Gesellschaft als Ganzes, sondern
auch das Individuum selbst, jeden einzelnen, jede einzelne also
beeinflußte, ob sie es wollten oder nicht. Zudem verloren im neunzehnten
Jahrundert die Kirchen und damit auch die christliche Religion
zunehmend an Boden und Überzeugungskraft. An ihrer Stelle traten
Vernunftglaube und die Wissenschaft, die für die Neuerer eine Alternative darstellten. Das traf aber nicht für die Masse der Bevölkerung zu.
Sie litt darunter, daß scheinbar festgefügte Ordnungen nicht mehr galten
und jahrhundertealte bis dahin als gültig empfundene Bilder und Vorstellungen als obsolet empfunden wurden.

Im Zuge des Übergangs von der ständisch-feudalen zur bürgerlich-
kapitalistischen Gesellschaft hatten mehr Menschen Schwierigkeiten ihr
seelisches Gleichgewicht auszubalancieren. Verantwortlich dafür wurde
alles und jedes gemacht. Das wirkte sich natürlich auch auf die Juden
aus, von denen man meinte, sie seien die eigentlichen Drahtzieher des
Geschehens und steckten hinter allen Ungereimtheiten und Problemen,
mit denen man täglich konfrontiert würde. Die Pogrome des Jahres 1819,
die in die Geschichtsschreibung als die sogenannten Hep-Hep-Krawalle
eingingen, sind nicht plötzlich und unerwartet ausgebrochen. Sie waren
in Wort und Schrift vorbereitet worden, und zwar von Intellektuellen wie
dem Philosophen Johann Gottlieb Fichte und den heute weitgehend
vergessenen, aber damals durchaus einflußreichen Universitäts-
professoren Jakob Friedrich Fries und Friedrich Rühs, die notorische
Judenfeinde waren.

Gierig wurden demagogische Parolen aufgegriffen, wie die des
extremen Antisemiten Hartwig von Hundt-Radowsky, der sich selbst
"Grattenauer der Zweite" nannte. In seinem 1819 in Würzburg erschiene-
nen "Judenspiegel", bei dem ein deutlich pornographisch-aggressiver
Unterton erkennbar war, hatte er angeregt, Jüdinnen ins Bordell zu
stecken, jüdische Männer zu kastrieren, sie in Bergwerken nur noch unter
Tage arbeiten zu lassen oder sie an die Engländer zu verkaufen, die sie
in ihren überseeischen Kolonien als Sklaven vermarkten sollten. Hundt-
Radowskys Forderungen, die Juden auszurotten oder sie zumindest aus
Deutschland zu vertreiben, war qualitativ eine neu erreichte Stufe der
Judenfeindschaft, die als eine Frühform des modernen Vernichtungs-
antisemitismus gelten kann.

Aber kehren wir zurück zu der uns beschäftigenden Ausgangsfrage, ob und inwieweit traditionell christlich-religiöse Überzeugungen bzw. Restbestandteile christlicher Theologie sich im 19. Jahrhundert mit scheinbar nicht-religiösen Phänomenen verbunden haben. Der im Gefolge der Französischen Revolution von 1789 und im Zuge der Befreiungskriege sich entwickelnde deutsche Nationalismus verkörperte zwar die liberale Idee der Selbstbestimmung und den demokratischen Gedanken der Volkssouveränität, hatte aber auch eine versteckte heilsgeschichtliche Dimension, die sich in den Überzeugungen niederschlug, das Christentum sei eine deutsche Religion und von einem verdeutschten Christentum oder verchristlichtem Deutschtum würde die Befreiung ausgehen.

Der zu Beginn des 19. Jahrhunderts aufkommende, auf Herder und Fichte zurückgehende, neue romantische Volksbegriff, dazu die patriotischen Predigten von Ernst Moritz Arndt ("Einmüthigkeit der Herzen sey eure Kirche, Haß gegen die Franzosen eure Religion, Freyheit und Vaterland seyen die Heiligen, bei welchen ihr anbetet!"), sowie die vom Turnvater Jahn geprägte Auffassung, das deutsche Volk sei das ursprüngliche, das unverfälschte, das "heilige Volk" lassen in nuce christliches Sendungsbewußtsein und Heilsgewißheit erkennen, jene Strukturelemente also, die seit dem letzten Jahrhundert integrale Bestandteile des deutschen Nationalismus geworden sind.

Es war nur noch ein kleiner Schritt die überkommene theologische Antithese Judentum-Christentum in die Antithese Judentum-Deutschtum umzudefinieren. Das tradierte Judenbild, das Stereotyp des dämonisch-antichristlichen Juden erfuhr im ausgehenden 18. und zu Beginn des 19. Jahrhunderts die entsprechende Umdeutung oder — vielleicht besser — Modernisierung. Der Jude war jetzt nicht mehr der Anti-Christ, der von Gott Verdammte, sondern der Wucherer, der Preistreiber, der Bankrotteur, der Todfeind, eine Gefahr für die wirtschaftliche und politische Existenz Deutschlands und der Deutschen schlechthin.

Ziel der christlichen Judenfeindschaft war bis zum Beginn der Neuzeit die Diffamierung, allenfalls Ausgrenzung, nicht aber die Vernichtung der Juden. Sie galten als ein von Gott verfluchtes Volk, das zur Knechtschaft verurteilt und über die Welt verstreut war. Aber man glaubte auch, die Juden könnten sich jederzeit von dem göttlichen Fluch lösen, wenn sie die Taufe nahmen und zum Christentum übertreten würden. Die zu Beginn des neunzehnten Jahrhunderts aufkommenden Rassenlehren ließen diesen Ausweg jedoch nicht mehr zu. Die religiöse Verfluchung und die Verwerfung durch Gott wurde durch den Topos des nicht veränderbaren Rassencharakters ersetzt, der im Falle der Juden als minderwertig erklärt wurde. Der Jude war nun nicht mehr eine vage Vorstellung, sondern "körperliche Wirklichkeit, ein feststehender Menschentyp, rassenmäßig bestimmt und in seinen Eigenschaften definierbar ..." (A. Bein)

Neben deutschtümelnden Patrioten wie dem Turnvater Jahn und dem sich völkisch gebärdenden Schriftsteller Ernst Moritz Arndt hat nicht unerheblich zur Durchsetzung antisemitischer Rassenlehren die sogenannte wissenschaftliche Religionskritik beigetragen, die sich zwar gegen die Religion als solche, aber im Grunde insbesondere gegen die Juden und das Judentum richtete. Der Linkshegelianer Bruno Bauer zum Beispiel war ein ausgemachter Judenfeind und entwickelte sich im Verlauf seines Lebens zu einem Doktrinär des deutschen Konservativismus und zu einem Anhänger abstruser Rassenlehren. Bauer war es, der in Deutschland als einer der ersten vom "Racentypus" sprach, der eine "Raceneigentümlichkeit" konstatierte und einen scharfen Trennstrich zwischen Juden und Nicht-Juden gezogen wissen wollte. "Die Taufe", so bemerkte Bruno Bauer einmal, "macht den Juden nicht zum Germanen"[11].

Das von den Judenfeinden gezeichnete Bild des Juden war zweifellos das Spiegelbild der Zeit und ihres Bewußtseins. Man attackierte die Juden, ahnte gleichzeitig jedoch, daß es ein Angriff auf das eigene Denken war, ein Angriff auf das Menschsein überhaupt. Zunehmend war erkennbar, daß das Christentum an Einfluß auf das Leben verlor. Andererseits war nicht zu übersehen, daß die Menschen die im Kirchenglauben gebotenen Erklärungsmodelle beizubehalten gewillt waren und sich von tradierten Feindbildern im Denken und Handeln beeinflussen ließen. Der Text eines Flugblattes der Wiener 1848er Revolution macht deutlich, daß man sich dieser Doppelbödigkeit durchaus bewußt war. Hellsichtig wird in diesem prophezeit, was die Juden in einer ungläubig gewordenen Welt zu erwarten hätten: "Die Christen, die keinen Christenglauben mehr haben, werden die wütendsten Feinde der Juden sein ... Wenn das Christenvolk kein Christentum und kein Geld mehr hat ... dann, ihr Juden, laßt Euch eiserne Schädel machen, mit den beinernen werdet ihr die Geschichte nicht überleben"[12].

IV. Erlösung und Vernichtung

Der Übergang der religiösen Judenfeindschaft zum modernen Antisemitismus läßt sich sehr gut am Fall Richard Wagner exemplifizieren. Wagner, der sein musikalisches und publizistisches Werk als eine Einheit ("Gesamtkunstwerk") verstand, war der Typus des Judenhassers, bei dem sich christliches Denken mit rassistisch-völkischen Motiven vermengte. Ihm ging es nicht mehr allein um die Ausgrenzung der Juden, sondern um deren Vernichtung. In seiner 1850 erschienenen Kampfschrift *Das Judentum in der Musik* hatte Wagner dem Juden nicht nur jede Befähigung zu künstlerischer Schöpfung abgesprochen, sondern ihn darüber hinaus als parasitär, dunkel-dämonisch und mit dem ahasverischen Fluch bela-den charakterisiert. "Aber bedenkt", so der letzte Satz des Wagnerschen Pamphlets, "daß nur eines eure Erlösung von dem auf euch lastenden Fluche sein kann: die Erlösung Ahasvers — der Untergang!"[13]

Mit seinem *Parsifal*, der als ein "Bühnenweihfestspiel" konzipiert war, präsentierte Wagner der Welt nicht nur die Idee eines "arischen Christus", sondern auch die düstere Vision der "Weltvernichtung," der "Welt-Aufhebung", die der Wiederkehr Christi vorangehen sollte. Wagner und seine Anhänger waren fest davon überzeugt, daß die Selbst-Vernichtung der Juden dem Erwachen der Deutschen vorangehen müßte. In immer neuen Variationen hat Wagner sich immer wieder mit diesem Thema befaßt, das von manchen heutigen Wagnerverehrern verdrängt von anderen sogar überhaupt bestritten wird.

Richard Wagners "Heilslehren" haben nicht nur die bürgerliche Kultur des wilhelminischen Deutschland beeinflußt, sondern in erheblichem Maße auch zur Ausbildung der rassistischen "Weltanschauung" beigetragen, die dann letzten Endes in der sogenannten "Endlösung der Judenfrage" explodiert ist. Der Münchener Literaturwissenschaftler Hartmut Zelinsky hat in einer lesenswerten Dokumentation und in zahlreichen Aufsätzen nachgewiesen, wie Hitler und die Nazis das Werk Wagners und Bayreuth vereinnahmt und zu Propagandazwecken mißbraucht haben.[14] Einer der vielen Belege dafür ist eine Äußerung von August Kubizek, dem Jugendfreund Hitlers, der in seinen nach 1945 veröffentlichten Erinnerungen versicherte, daß dieser "in Richard Wagner ... viel mehr als nur Vorbild und Beispiel [suchte]. Ich kann nur sagen: er eignete sich die Persönlichkeit Richard Wagners an, ja er erwarb ihn so vollkommen für sich, als könnte dieser ein Teil seines eigenen Wesens werden"[15].

Wer sich die Mühe macht, Notizen Hitlers vor dem Münchener Putsch und sein Bekenntnisbuch *Mein Kampf* mit Wagners *Mein Leben* zu vergleichen, dem fällt auf, wie sehr Hitler auf zentrale Wagnersche Begriffe wie Wiedergeburt, Reinheit, Reinerhaltung des Blutes, Blutsvermischung, Göttin der Not, Verfallserscheinungen der Menschheit, weltbewegende Idee, germanische Revolution oder germanischer Staat zurückgegriffen hat. Ganze Passagen über Juden und Antisemitismus, urteilt Hartmut Zelinsky, würden wie Wagner-Paraphrasen wirken und deutlich machen, wie sehr Hitler in Wagner nicht nur ein Genie, sondern den Propheten seiner großgermanischen Träume und antijüdischen Wahnvorstellungen gesehen hat.

Das Geheimnis des Erfolges, den Hitler und die Nazis bei ihren Anhängern hatten, hängt wohl damit zusammen, daß die von ihnen propagierte völkische Ideologie letztlich einen christlich-religiösen Kern hatte. Die Menschen fühlten sich durch die NS-Propaganda und die liturgischen Handlungen (Feiern für die Märtyrer der Bewegung, Aufmärsche in Nürnberg, die Schaffung "deutscher Weihestätten") angesprochen. Sie glaubten sich durch Hitler verstanden und im Nationalsozialismus wie in einer Kirche aufgehoben. Die Ansicht beginnt sich deshalb heute auch zunehmend durchzusetzen, daß der Hitlersche Nationalsozialismus eine echte Glaubensbewegung war, eine Bewegung, die sich alle mythologischen Funktionen einer Religion zu eigen gemacht hatte. Unbedingtes Bekenntnis und totale Unterwerfung waren erforderlich. Von Anfang an stilisierte sich Hitler in der Rolle des "erlösenden Führers" (wahrscheinlich bis er selbst daran glaubte) und genoß es, daß er als "Messias aller Deutschen" gefeiert wurde.

Zahlreich finden sich in den Reden und Texten Hitlers und seiner Anhänger Stellen, die gnostischer und apokalyptischer Natur sind. Da ist die Rede von gut und böse, hell und dunkel. Dem jüdischen Dämon steht der arische Lichtmensch gegenüber. Da findet sich der Topos vom "Dritten Reich" und Anspielungen auf die Apokalypse des Johannes. In *Mein Kampf* heißt es: "So glaube ich heute im Sinne des allmächtigen Schöpfers zu handeln: Indem ich mich des Juden erwehre, kämpfe ich für das Werk des Herrn"[16]. Deutlicher als mit diesen Worten kann eigentlich nicht belegt werden, wie sehr Christentum und Nationalsozialismus eine quasi symbiotische Beziehung eingegangen sind. Mit der Formulierung, "Indem ich mich des Juden erwehre, kämpfe ich für das Werk des Herrn" hat sich Hitler mit der Rolle des Erlösers und Retters identifiziert, desjenigen also, der die Deutschen aus der Not befreien und ans Licht führen will.

Auf die Verschmelzung von Politik und Religion im Nationalsozialismus fielen nicht nur ein Großteil der Bevölkerung herein, sondern bezeichnenderweise auch zahlreiche christliche Theologen. Der damals in Bonn lehrende Neutestamentler Ethelbert Stauffer zum Beispiel forderte im Zeichen der Begegnung von Kreuz und Hakenkreuz, jeder gläubige Christ müsse auch ein überzeugter Nationalsozialist sein. Nicht viel anders argumentierte sein Kollege, der Tübinger Neutestamentler Gerhard Kittel, einer der Wortführer der "Deutschen Christen." Wie viele andere namhafte Theologen in den Jahren nach 1933 hatte auch Kittel sowohl die Segregationspolitik der Nazis gerechtfertigt als sich auch voll hinter die NS-Judenpolitik gestellt.[17] Dabei ging er von der Überzeugung aus, das Christentum sei seinem Wesen nach antijüdisch, folglich müsse ein jeder aufrechte Christenmensch verpflichtet sein, die NS-Juden-Politik in Wort und Schrift zu unterstützen.

Antijüdische Stereotypen prägten vor und nach 1933 in zunehmenden Maße auch die Sprache. Da Sprache sowohl Vorstellungen und Gedanken des einzelnen Menschen als auch das Bewußtsein und die Denkweise ganzer Epochen bestimmen kann, sind die von Theologen, Politikern, Literaten und Publizisten jahrhundertelang verwendeten Klischees zur Beschreibung der Juden besonders aufschlußreich. So bezeichneten sie seit der zweiten Hälfte des neunzehnten Jahrhunderts die Juden als "Schädlinge", die den "Volkskörper" "zersetzen" und "vergiften". Oft wurden die Juden mit Bazillen", "Trichinen", aber auch mit "Ratten" und "Schmeißfliegen" verglichen. In der Zeit des Nationalsozialismus besonders beliebt, und noch heute gerne verwendet, ist das Bild des "Parasiten," das suggeriert, der Jude lebe auf Kosten anderer, erschleiche sich durch Schmeichelei und Unterwürfigkeit Vorteile, ohne wirkliche produktive Arbeit zu leisten.

Hitler und seine Anhänger hatten das Bild des "Parasiten" verinnerlicht. In den Juden sahen sie eine parasitäre Rasse, die nur auf Kosten der "Wirte" und nur von der Ausbeutung anderer Völker und Rassen leben kann. Goebbels, Formulierungen Richard Wagners aufnehmend, faßte 1937 auf dem Nürnberger Parteitag die verschiedenartigen Vorstellungen vom Juden in folgenden Worten zusammen: "Sehet, das ist der Feind der Welt, der Vernichter der Kulturen, der Parasit unter den Völkern, der Sohn des Chaos, die Inkarnation des Bösen, der plastische Dämon des Verfalles der Menschheit"[18].

Mit Sicherheit haben die aus dem Arsenal der Biologie stammenden Sprachbilder mit dazu beigetragen, die letzten moralischen Hemmungen, den inneren Widerstand gegen Unrecht und Verbrechen bei Millionen von Menschen zu schwächen. Vermutlich hat sogar, wie Alex Bein annahm, das Bild vom Juden in nicht geringem Maße die Methoden des organisierten Judenmordes mitbestimmt. So wie man im Mittelalter in ihnen den Antichristen und Satan erschlug und auf dem Scheiterhaufen verbrannte, so war die Methode des Vergasens in den Mordlagern Hitlers die logische Konsequenz, nachdem sich die Vorstellung von den Juden als Parasiten endgültig durchgesetzt hatte. Waren die Juden tatsächlich Schmarotzer, Bazillen und Ungeziefer, so war nicht nur geboten, sie auszurotten, es lag auch nahe, bei dieser Ausrottung das Mittel anzuwenden, mit dem man Bazillen und Ungeziefer vertilgt — nämlich Giftgas.

V. Antisemitismus ohne Juden

Nach 1945 hat man lange Jahre in Deutschland geglaubt, der Antisemitismus sei überwunden. Bis in die frühen siebziger Jahre war man davon überzeugt, das Wissen um den organisierten Massenmord hätte die Deutschen geläutert, hätte quasi eine kathartische Wirkung zur Folge gehabt. Das mag im Einzelfall so gewesen sein. Der eine oder andere hat vielleicht wirklich nichts vom ganzen Ausmaß des Schreckens gewußt. Andererseits läßt sich heute die gebetmühlenartig vorgetragene Behauptung nicht mehr aufrechterhalten, man sei nicht über das informiert gewesen, was mit den Juden geschah. Die Behauptung war und ist eine beliebte, zur Entlastung gerne benutzte Argumentionsfigur, die eigentlich nur den einen Zweck hat, Schuldgefühle und schlechtes Gewissen zu kaschieren.

Das antisemitische Vorurteil ist nach wie vor vorhanden. Die empirischen Untersuchungen der Sozialforscher belegen, daß in der bundesdeutschen Bevölkerung 15% offen antisemitisch eingestellt sind und bei weiteren 30% der Antisemitismus in Latenz feststellbar ist.[19] Das bemerkenswerte an diesen Zahlen sind nicht so sehr die Zahlen als solche, sondern der Sachverhalt, daß der Antisemitismus nicht lebender Juden bedarf, um sich zu artikulieren. Ein rechtsradikaler Skinhead, der "Juden raus" brüllt und Grabsteine auf jüdischen Friedhöfen mit antisemitischen Parolen beschmiert, kennt meist weder einen Juden, noch weiß er irgendetwas vom Judentum. Das hindert ihn aber nicht, sich als Antisemit zu begreifen.

Der Antisemitismus hat ganz offensichtlich eine psycho-soziale Funktion. Eine Bevölkerung, konfrontiert mit Problemen irgendwelcher Art, bedarf nach wie vor des Sündenbocks, um sich abzureagieren. Das war früher nicht anders als heute, nur mit dem Unterschied, daß lebende Juden kaum mehr zur Verfügung stehen, an denen sich die aufgestauten Neid-, Haß- und Frustrationsgefühle entladen könnten. Begriffe wie "Jude" und "Judentum" haben sich verselbständigt; sie sind gewissermaßen zu Metaphern des Bösen geworden. Pöbelnde Skinheads benutzen sie bewußt oder unbewußt, aber auch durchaus ehrbare Politiker, wenn sie sich in bestimmten Situationen hilflos fühlen und überzeugt sind, einen Schuldigen dafür finden zu müssen.

Juden spielen in der Gesellschaft des Nach-Holocaust-Deutschlands zahlenmäßig kaum noch eine Rolle, dennoch ist die Abneigung gegen sie nach wie vor fest verwurzelt. Dafür ist zweifellos das jahrhundertealte, gezeichnete Zerrbild verantwortlich, das im Unbewußten eingebrannt, nicht mehr der realen Erscheinung des Juden bedarf, um Wirkung zu haben. Es führt ein Eigenleben, das unbestimmbar geworden ist. Ludwig Börne meinte bereits 1816, die Abneigung gegenüber den Juden entspringe "einer angeerbten Gespensterscheu"[20] und habe seine Wurzeln in der magisch-mystischen Vorstellungswelt der christlichen Bevölkerung. Ähnlich argumentierte der Odessaer Arzt Leon Pinsker sechzig Jahre später, der den Antisemitismus als eine "Gespensterfurcht" diagnostizierte, als eine Art erblicher Angstneurose, die sich jeder rationalen Begründung entziehe und die er für nicht heilbar hielt.[21]

Für uns Heutigen stellt sich die folgende Frage: Wenn das Bild vom Juden freischwebend ist, das antijüdische Vorurteil sich also verselbständigt hat und ein integraler Bestandteil der deutschen Kultur geworden ist, kann man dann überhaupt noch etwas tun? Es reicht da sicher nicht aus, jährlich eine "Woche der Brüderlichkeit" zu veranstalten. Sie ist eine zum Ritual erstarrte Veranstaltung, die der Selbstbeschwichtigung dient, von der aber die Öffentlichkeit so viel wie keine Notiz mehr nimmt. Auch Filme, Bücher und Theaterstücke, die eher Kultur widerspiegeln als diese wirklich beeinflussen, verändern nicht bestimmte

Bewußtseinskonstellationen. Ein eingefleischter Antisemit hört im übrigen nicht plötzlich auf, ein Antisemit zu sein, wenn man es von ihm fordert. Warum sollte er auch? Jeder Psychoanalytiker kann bestätigen, daß ein Antisemit mit einem Vorurteil besonders zufrieden ist: Weder wünscht er, davon befreit zu werden, noch ist er für diesbezügliche Aufklärungs-bemühungen zugänglich.

Mit den üblichen Mitteln des Aufklärens ist dem Antisemtismus nicht beizukommen. Vielleicht ist eine denkbare Möglichkeit das christlich-jüdische Verhältnis zu retheologisieren und von Vorurteilen zu befreien. Einiges ist in den letzten Jahren auf diesem Feld geschehen. Es gibt beispielhafte Synodalbeschlüsse und Konzilerklärungen, die Hoffnungen erwecken, gleichzeitig aber auch die Grenzen theologischer Arbeit aufzeigen. Der Synodalbeschluß der evangelischen Kirche im Rheinland ("Wir bekennen betroffen die Mitverantwortung und Schuld der Christen-heit in Deutschland am Holocaust") vom 11. Januar 1982 stieß zum Beispiel auf den Widerspruch der Professoren der Theologischen Fakultät der Universität Bonn, denen die 8-Punkte-Erklärung der Synode zu weit-gehend war und sich deshalb gegen diese Erklärung ausgesprochen haben.

Der notwendige innerchristliche Erneuerungsprozeß wird nur dann wirklich zum Ziel führen, wenn man als Protestant oder Katholik nicht davor zurückschreckt, das christliche Selbstverständnis von Grund auf zu überdenken. Hier liegt aber auch das eigentliche Problem. Wird nämlich der Antijudaismus aus den kirchlichen Dokumenten gestrichen, auf die Judenmission als dem Christentum auferlegte Verpflichtung verzichtet und vielleicht sogar die christliche Verantwortung für die Leidens-geschichte der Juden eingestanden, insbesondere auf den industriell-organisierten Völkermord in diesem Jahrhundet, dann könnte die Situa-tion eintreten, daß es kein Christentum mehr ist, jedenfalls keines, das mit dem ursprünglichen noch etwas zu tun hat. Nicht wenige Geistliche und Laien fühlen sich deshalb durch theologische Erneuerungsbemühun-gen in ihrem Glauben und in ihrer Identität bedroht und weigern sich vehement, den geforderten oder herbeigewünschten Paradigmenwechsel im christlich-jüdischen Verhältnis zu akzeptieren.

Mag sein, daß die Bekämpfung des Antisemitismus ein aussichtsloses Unterfangen ist. Die gemachten historischen Erfahrungen sind derart, daß man fast daran glauben möchte. Aber auch wenn wir die Aussichtslosig-keit akzeptierten, sollten wir aus der uns auferlegten Verpflichtung zur Humanitas und zur Toleranz uns dennoch bemühen, Vorurteile zu be-kämpfen, wo immer wir sie antreffen. Die Einsicht, daß der Bekämpfbar-keit des Antisemitismus Grenzen gesetzt sind, ist zwar bitter, darf uns aber nicht hindern, das Wort zu erheben, wo Unrecht geschieht und Vorurteile in ihren militanten Ausprägungen das Bewußtsein und das Handeln von Menschen bestimmen. Unabdingbare Voraussetzung, damit dies überhaupt eine Chance hat, ist freilich radikale Aufklärungsarbeit und w i r k l i c h e s Wollen — in der Familie, im Religionsunterricht, in der Schule, in den Hörsälen der Universitäten, aber auch am Arbeitsplatz. Ob damit etwas bewirkt werden kann? Sicher ist das nicht. Aber — wir haben keine andere Wahl.

Anmerkungen

1 Wir danken dem R. Piper Verlag für die Genehmigung zum Wiederabdruck dieses Essays.

2 Über Wort und Begriff "Judenfrage" vgl. Alex Bein: *Die Judenfrage. Zur Biographie eines Weltproblems.* Stuttgart 1980, Bd. 1, S. 3 ff.

3 Abgedruckt bei Gerhard Czermak: *Christen gegen Juden. Geschichte einer Verfolgung.* Nördlingen 1989, S. 259 f.

4 *Midrasch* (hebräisch: Auslegung, Deutung); *Midraschot* ist die in den *Midraschim* gesammelte rabbinische Literatur, die den Bibeltext deutet. Sie besteht aus lehrhaften, religionsgesetzlichen Erklärungen (*Halacha*) und erzählenden Passagen (*Haggada*). Vgl. *Der große Brockhaus.* Wiesbaden 1979, Bd. 7, S. 557.

5 Karl Barth an Friedrich Wilhelm Marquardt, 5. September 1967. In: Karl Barth: *Briefe 1861 – 1868.* In: Ders.: *Gesamtausgabe.* Hg. v. Jürgen Fangmeier und Heinrich Stoevesandt. Zürich 1975, Bd. 5, S. 420-421.

6 Es gibt kaum eine antijüdische Maßnahme, die nicht ihr exaktes Vorbild in der Kirchengeschichte gehabt hätte. Vgl. die von Raoul Hilberg (*Die Vernichtung der europäischen Juden.* Berlin 1982, S. 15 f.) zusammengestellte Tabelle, in der die kanonischen und die nazistischen antijüdischen Maßnahmen einander gegenüber gestellt sind.

7 Abgedruckt in: *Verfolgung, Vertreibung, Vernichtung. Dokumente des faschistischen Antisemitismus 1933 bis 1942.* Hg. v. Kurt Pätzold. Leipzig 1983, S. 113.

8 Eduard Drumont: *La France juive.* Paris 1943, Bd. 1, S. 322.

9 Dietz Bering: *Der Name als Stigma. Antisemitismus im deutschen Alltag 1812 – 1933.* Stuttgart 1987.

10 Vgl. Dietz Bering: *Kampf um Namen. Bernhard Weiß gegen Joseph Goebbels.* Stuttgart 1991, S. 229 ff.

11 Bruno Bauer, *Staats- und Gesellschaftslexikon.* Hg. v. Hermann Wagener. Berlin 1859-1867, 23 Bde., hier Bd. 7, S. 12.

12 *Flugblatt 1848.* Wien, Stadtbibliothek, E 50395.

13 Richard Wagner: *Gesammelte Schriften und Dichtungen.* Leipzig 1911, Bd. V, S. 85.

14 Insbesondere sind zu nennen: Der "Plenipotentarius des Untergangs oder der Herrschaftsanspruch der antisemitischen Kunstreligion des selbsternannten Bayreuther Erlösers Richard Wagner. Anmerkungen zu Cosima Wagners

Tagebüchern 1869-1883". In: *neohelicon* IX, 1, Budapest-Amsterdam, 1982, S. 145-76; *Richard Wagner. Ein deutsches Thema. Eine Dokumentation zur Wirkungsgeschichte Richard Wagners 1876 — 1976.* Hg. v. Hartmut Zelinsky. Berlin und Wien 1983; "Richard Wagners Kunstwerk der Zukunft und seine Idee der Vernichtung". In: *Von kommenden Zeiten. Geschichtsprophetien im 19. und 20. Jahrhundert.* Hg. v. Joachim H. Knoll und Julius H. Schoeps. Stuttgart/ Bonn 1983, S. 84-106; "Das erschreckende 'Erwachen' und wie man Wagner von Hitler befreit." In: *Neue Zeitschrift für Musik,* September 1983, S. 9-16; "Die deutsche Losung Siegfried oder 'innere Notwendigkeit' des Judenfluchs im Werk Richard Wagners." In: Udo Bermbach: *In den Trümmern der eigenen Welt — Richard Wagners — Der Ring der Nibelungen.* Hamburg 1989, S. 201–249.

[15] August Kubizek: *Adolf Hitler, mein Jugendfreund.* Graz und Stuttgart 1953, S. 84.

[16] Adolf Hitler: *Mein Kampf.* München 1926, S. 70.

[17] Vgl. Leonore Siegele-Wenschkewitz: "Protestantische Universitätstheologie in der Zeit des Nationalsozialismus". In: *Antisemitismus.* Hg. v. Günter Brakelmann und Martin Rosowski. Göttingen 1989, S. 52-76.

[18] Vgl. Bein (Anm. 1), Bd. 1, S. 361.

[19] Vgl. Alphons Silbermann: *Sind wir Antisemiten? Ausmaß und Wirkung eines sozialen Vorurteils in der Bundesrepublik Deutschland.* Köln 1982; *Antisemitismus nach dem Holocaust. Bestandsaufnahme und Erscheinungsformen in deutschsprachigen Ländern.* Hg. v. Alphons Silbermann und Julius H. Schoeps. Köln 1986.

[20] Ludwig Börne: *Sämtliche Schriften.* Hg. v. Inge und Peter Rippmann. Dreieich 1977, Bd. 1, S.137.

[21] Vgl. Julius H. Schoeps: "Leon Pinsker. Autoemancipation. Ein Mahnruf von 1882". In: *Beter und Rebellen. Aus 1000 Jahren Judentum in Polen.* Hg. v. Michael Brocke. Frankfurt/Main 1983, S. 223-236. *Die Kirchen und das Judentum. Dokumente von 1945 bis 1985.* Hg. v. Rolf Rendtorffs und Hans Hermann Henrix. Paderborn und München 1988.

Frank Stern

From the Liberation of the Jews to the Unification of the Germans:
The Discourse of Antagonistic Memories in Germany[1]

I.

It was freedom! Then someone came toward me. A man from town, with a rucksack on his back.... The first human face I had seen in my newly gained freedom: the enemy. I saw many, many more faces standing behind him: men, women, children, a vast throng. They walked through their streets, rode on their streetcars, led their lives behind their windows — just as always.... Now we were to walk and ride together once again. We would visit each other's homes, I would buy at their shops, and we would meet at the theater. As if nothing had happened. As if they hadn't stood up from their office desks and stepped out of their living rooms in order to sweep the sidewalks clean of us. Now they returned to their offices and houses, and their sidewalks were open again.... There was no return. I knew at that moment that things could never work out again. The hatred, the rifle butts and gas had separated our lives and theirs. Our eyes would never be able again to meet. Even if a good will should arise from the depths of their hearts and move forward to meet our longing: to be one of them — the last word had been spoken about them, about us. Things would never be alright ever again. (Lotte Paepcke)[2]

A short time before the Federal Republic of Germany was founded, the U.S. High Commissioner John McCloy addressed a convention of the reestablished Jewish communities in the country. Germany's relation to the Jews, he stressed, would be the "real touchstone" of the new German democracy.[3] These words were spoken in 1949, and decades later this remark has not lost its historical relevance. For Germany's relation to the Jews can still be seen as the important touchstone of German democracy.

Recent German history, particularly after unification, illustrates that the experience of the Jewish people with German politics and culture in the twentieth century is less on the German agenda today than ever before. On the other hand, the brutal nature of this experience is, and will remain for generations to come, on the Jewish agenda. I refer later to this phenomenon, which defines a discourse of antagonistic memories.[4]

II.

Jews and things Jewish in German political culture seem to boil down to the following essentials: most Germans feel that Germany has acknowledged its guilt and responsibility for the past, it has paid off its moral and material debt, and proven its democratic character in the decades since 1945.[5] Germany, its politicians have said, had a special responsibility towards the Jewish people and the State of Israel. But now, they claim, Germans and Jews are passing through a process of reconciliation. The historical lesson has been learned, and normalization — so it seems — is uppermost on the agenda. It would not be difficult to cite numerous official statements which substantiate such conceptions.

But does this attitude satisfy the historian of contemporary Jewish history, of recent intellectual and political developments, of German arts and culture as they have emerged in the last decades, and led, finally, to the rebirth of the German national state in our fin de siècle? Has Auschwitz received its place in the history, culture, mentality, and everyday life of the Germans as they themselves see it? Is German "normalcy" in fact normal? Is the Jewish chapter of German history turning out to be just another negligible episode in the process of German normalization?

Germany's recent rise to influence and power forces us to reconsider just what the impact of the Holocaust on German historical consciousness has been. What has confronted us in the last few years are contextual and structural changes in German historical consciousness. It is not the cultural critic but the historical process itself that deconstructs and reconstructs this collective consciousness today. Against this background, we need a clearer picture of the role, content, and functions of Jews and things Jewish in German historical consciousness as it has developed since the liberation of the concentration camps.

Primo Levi closes his last book *The Drowned and the Saved* with the following reflections:

> Let it be clear that to a greater or lesser degree all were responsible, but it must be just as clear that behind their responsibility stands that great majority of Germans, who

> accepted in the beginning, out of mental laziness, myopic
> calculation, stupidity, and national pride, the "beautiful words" of
> Corporal Hitler, followed him as long as luck and the lack of
> scruples favored him, were swept away by his ruin, afflicted by
> deaths, misery and remorse, and rehabilitated a few years later as
> the result of an unprincipled political game.[6]

After 1945, it took German political culture exactly four years to turn
from a perception of responsibility and guilt to the conception of collective shame as stated by Theodor Heuss, the first President of the Federal
Republic.[7] The decades thereafter were characterized by Germany's
ambitious enterprise to reconcile itself with its own past while using the
Jews and things Jewish as a medium for this historical reconciliation. The
Jews had their particular place not only in German political culture, in
collective memory, and historical consciousness, but also in Germany's
political and international shifts toward national identity, sovereignty,
and cultural respectability. A few key events and developments illustrate
this shift. When the Federal Republic was founded in 1949, the Cold War
was at its height. Denazification and reeducation activities, which were
conscientiously pursued by the Allies in the immediate postwar years,
particularly by the American Office of Military Government in Germany,
yielded when Germany became the major ally in the West's confrontation
with Communism. The fierce fight of many American officials and
intellectuals for a new German democracy and against anti-Semitism as
the main focus of German antidemocratic traditions did not fit into the
mainstream of the desire for rollback or containment policies.[8] By 1947
the disengagement of many had begun, with many of them leaving their
positions in Washington or in the American administration in Germany,
and returning to academic life. Denazification, as John H. Herz wrote in
1948, which had begun with a bang, ended with a whimper.[9]

In the first postwar years we can easily retrospect, that there existed
a historic triangle — of Americans, Germans, and Jews.[10] The Jews living
in the late 1940s in Germany, be it the 15,000 German Jews or the more
than 230,000 displaced persons in Jewish camps mostly in the American
zone of occupation, looked first of all to their American liberators and
guardians and mistrusted the German administration and society.[11] This
was also the way most Germans perceived the Jews, who were seen as
siding with the victors, their former enemy. For millions of Germans
Hitler had lost, but he had not just lost the war; he had lost the war
against the Jews. The German imagery of Jews and things Jewish entailed
two aspects: first, the allies made public the atrocities committed by
Germans against the Jews. What had been known or whispered about
could now be seen on posters and on the movie screen. Second, when the
allied documentary "Death Mills" was shown to thousands and thousands

of Germans or when the population of Weimar was led through the walls of corpses in Buchenwald, most turned their heads away. This became a recurring feature, millions turned their heads away in order not to see what they already knew. Primo Levi describes this reaction: "How many had the possibility of knowing everything, but chose the more prudent path of keeping their eyes and ears (and above all their mouths) well shut."[12]

The atrocities were kept at an emotional and cognitive distance, making it easier to adjust to the German postwar existence. Hitler, and thus Germany, it could be understood, had lost the war against the Jews. These perceptions combined with two other images of the Jews: first, the returning Jews, the survivors, insisted on their former rights, claiming them with the assistance of Allied authorities; and second, thousands of Jewish displaced persons received food and care parcels, that is, elementary goods that destitute Germans themselves so badly needed. Resentments built up within the German population, and the traditional economic anti-Jewish sentiment once more adjusted to postwar realities. It is apparent that a newly structured, multi-layered image of the Jews and things Jewish characterized German consciousness in the early postwar period and lasted for years to come. German historical consciousness, therefore, was not dependent just on pictures of wartime atrocities, or guilt consciousness, or a lingering bad conscience, as we are often told. It is important to note the relevance of these various images, which reveal more than just the continuities of German cultural anti-Semitic traditions. Rather, these images reflect deeper strata of German opinions, attitudes, and behavior towards the Jews.

Popular images of the Jews are not necessarily expressions of overt anti-Semitism. Usually they are ambivalent and expand from prejudiced notions and open hostility to social and cultural distance, on the one hand, and, on the other, to admiration, closeness, religious affection, and even identification. Except for openly racist images, most images of Jews reflect ambiguous patterns of thought and of emotions based on the cultural and religious heritage of western civilization. Even more importantly, they are influenced by the given cultural and social context. Concerning Jews, it is not always important what one believes but what one is led to believe and what one is expected to voice in public according to widely held popular attitudes and normative social expectations.

The literary historian Hans Mayer has described this intricate pattern in his book *Outsider* when he analyzes the German image of Jews, women, and homosexuals as central examples.[13] When talking about anti-Semitism, as well as about problems of race and gender, we ought to analyze the metamorphoses of related images more than just the stereotypical results.

The complex relationships of such images and their ambivalent changes influence the metamorphosis that took place in postwar German
attitudes towards Jews. In the decades since 1945, "imagining the Jews"
has become one of the main features of German thinking. The attempted
German genocide of the Jews became the catalyst, however, not of facing
the moral challenge of historical guilt and collective responsibility, but of
imagining the Jews as a rather abstract part of West German political culture. These postwar images of the Jews were stronger than the confrontation with the living — as the failure of the vast majority of the Germans
after 1945 to stand up to their collective responsibility shows.

In the late 1940s and throughout the 1950s the postwar German
government and people did not ask for forgiveness for the Nazi crimes,
nor did they invite the surviving Jews and their children to return to
Germany. Something else happened and is still happening. A kind of
collective allusion to the former Jewish presence became characteristic of
the public remembrance of the past. Imagining the Jews had and still has
to fit into the evolving German national identity, which is largely void of
any real Jewish presence. In short, the public German discourse on Jews
and things Jewish is primarily a discourse among Germans and not a
discourse between Germans and Jews.[14] Even where Germans are haunt-
ed by their own memory, they do not want to be troubled by live Jews
bearing witness from generation to generation about perpetrators, victims,
and survivors. Live Jews are some kind of "stranded objects"[15] on the
shore of German memory, strangers to their *Heimat*, their homeland, as
the following words of a Jew who had lived in Germany in the postwar
years may illustrate:

> I perceived my presence — as well as that of the other German
> Jews — to be a kind of piece on exhibit in a museum, a museum
> which it was preferable to avoid. We had survived and become
> obsolete, at least in this country, a country that had not become
> our own.[16]

In this context it is most instructive to see what kind of legitimating use
German politicians and academics made of some of the returning Jewish
émigrés in the 1950s. Consider, for instance, the following words, spoken
in honor of a returned scholar, newly appointed as a university rector,
who was addressed in these terms:

> In an exemplary illustration of reconciliation, you have returned
> to the fatherland and resumed your position at this university. So
> much loyalty requires loyalty in response. It is for that reason that
> we see your election to the highest academic office at this our

Johann Wolfgang Goethe University as the crowning act of our own obligation to *Wiedergutmachung* (restitution).[17]

The two central figures of speech which characterize a recurrent philosemitic pattern — not to mention the embarrassing return of the German "fatherland" in this speech — are "reconciliation" and "restitution." As if any returning Jew could serve as a deputy for the murdered Jews. It was not to his credit that the newly appointed rector refrained from any critical response. Instead, he climbed up into the ranks of the traditional ivory German "Mandarins" as if he had never been forced to leave Germany, as if he had never been one of the most sophisticated proponents of the Frankfurt School of critical thought. I refer to Max Horkheimer.

III.

The more we move away from 1945, the more it becomes obvious that there is no such thing as a shared collective western memory of the Holocaust.[18] Particularly within the German-Jewish context, there exist only contrary and even antagonistic memories. Many oral history sources and publications, not only in Germany,[19] show that what is receding quickly into the depths of history for one side remains a burning remembrance for the other.[20]

The place of the Jews in the minds of Germans is not constant but is part of the flow of time and a function of those issues that are moving into the very center of German historical consciousness. A German perception of the Jews was central after 1945 and the following decades whenever Germany's political culture was distinctly defined by its relation to the past, the Holocaust being the central event of this past. It has become less and less central since the 1960s as Germany has developed into a major European power, a development that has gone hand in hand with Germany's endeavor to cope once and for all with the legacy of the past by stepping "out of Hitler's shadow." The centrality of the Jews and the Holocaust in German historical consciousness has been fading away with the increasing advance of German images of national identity, which have focused on the country's economic success and cultural traditions.[21]

The conservative politician Franz Josef Strauss made the point perfectly clear when he remarked: "A people who has produced these economic achievements has a right not to want to hear any more about Auschwitz."[22]

Beginning in the immediate postwar period, yet another element developed in the complex pattern of imagining the Jews. In addition to the image of the Jew as victim, a memory of the Jewish contribution to

German culture and science was revived and elevated. This development is important insofar as the early postwar period also represents the cultural background for the development of a relatively new phenomenon in attitudes concerning Jewish topics. Analysts attached to the American Military Government in Germany called this phenomenon a "new philosemitism."[23]

This new philosemitism as it evolved after May 1945 had three aspects. First, there was the notion, which rapidly spread in the German population, that in any dealings with Allied institutions and officials, it could be useful to show an emphatically pro-Jewish attitude. It became common practice, for instance, to refer to former Jewish friends and neighbors. Millions of Germans, it now appeared, had "helped" the Jewish victims. In fact, there were more "Jewish friends" reported as "helped" than the number of Jews who had ever lived in the German Reich. Second, philosemitism was an attitude based on humanistic and, in particular, Christian concepts. In turning away from anti-Semitic stereotypes, this new approach reached out to the absolutized opposite. Jews and things Jewish became romanticized and even idolized. Every Jew came to be seen as some close relative of G. E. Lessing's esteemed Jewish character in *Nathan the Wise*; every Jewish child was supposed to be a genius; and every Jewish woman turned out to be the beautiful Jewess. Third, before long, pro-Jewish attitudes and values were politically instrumentalized. It proved to be useful for West German politicians and the young Federal Republic to build on this kind of philosemitism, to affirm the new democratic character of Germany by formally referring to her pro-Jewish stance. Philosemitism, thus, became a compelling mixture of political opportunism and utility. It was a pragmatic means to prove something that was still difficult to prove otherwise, namely Germany's new democratic character. The Adenauer administration realized very soon that integration of the country into the West could be achieved more easily if it were based on a new political norm defined by agreements with Jewish survivors and the State of Israel. Obviously, McCloy, the U.S. High Commissioner, was both understood and misunderstood when he stated that the relation to the Jews could be viewed as a touchstone of democracy. He had meant to encourage a cultural change in the direction of western democratic and humanistic values and not just formal pro-Jewish confessions. Yet, when during the 1950s anti-Semitic scandals in Germany upset the American public, the Bonn government could now conveniently refer to its official pro-Jewish position. As things turned out, the heart of the matter was not collective shame or responsibility but political utility, as Konrad Adenauer pointed out in 1966:

> We had done the Jews ... so much injustice, we had committed so many crimes against them, that somehow these had to be

expiated, there had to be recompense if we wished once more to
gain respect and standing among the world's nations. Moreover,
the power held by the Jews, even today, especially in America,
should not be underestimated.[24]

He voiced this view, of course, only after retiring and not while in
office. Philosemitism became closely linked to the conservative temper of
the fast-evolving Federal Republic. It helped to whitewash the Yellow
Badge and became for many Germans, and, in particular, for official
institutions one form of denazifying themselves. In 1963, the philosopher
Ernst Bloch warned that philosemitism "itself implied something akin to
an outgrown, yet immanent form of anti-Semitism."[25]

The late 1940s and the 1950s were marked by anti-Semitic continuities
which led to the anti-Semitic wave of 1959-60, but official German politics
were deeply imbued with philosemitic modes of behavior. The images of
the Jews then in circulation were double-faced: anti-Semitic clichés combined with a philosemitic appreciation of everything Jewish. Lessing's
Nathan the Wise appeared numerous times on stage and projected the Jew
in his philosemitic aspect. He was well-educated, represented a form of
the Jewish religion that smacked of Protestantism, was well situated
economically, and he lived in a period untainted by the mass murder
organized by the Germans. This Jew had nothing to do with the Jewish
displaced person or other Jewish survivors but, by contrast, offered a
kind of psychological mirror for the presumably newly tolerant and all-
understanding German.

At the end of the 1950s, Anne Frank became the symbolic younger
sister of Nathan.[26] Millions wept over her fate and thousands of young
Germans identified with her. Obviously it was easier to deplore the cruel
fate of one innocent child than to accept the historical responsibility for
the murder of the anonymous six million. Besides, as it was insinuated,
she had simply "died" in a camp. In contemplating her death, there was
no need to remember the gas chambers. And one could also ask: "Hadn't
her father in fact survived?" In the end, this was a way to remember one
victim instead of the others.

The bureaucratic facts about the systematic, well organized program
of genocide entered the German public sphere for the first time with the
Eichmann trial of 1961 in Jerusalem. In response to the anti-Semitic wave
of the late 1950s, and in reference to the publicity of the trial in and
outside Germany, school curricula were changed and a broader public
had to confront its own past in the media. The challenge the trial posed
to German historical consciousness was juxtaposed with an intensification
of the officially ordained philosemitism and an idealized and romanticized image of the new Jew, who showed strength and worked the soil:
namely, the Israeli, particularly the Kibbutznik. Israeli female singers

soon followed and were a hit in Germany — a popular culture phenomenon which combined ingeniously with the traditional image of the beautiful Jewess.

With the advent of the figure of the sun-burned Israeli, the image of the Jews became, so to say, modernized. In 1965, the establishment of diplomatic relations with Israel contributed to the formalized institution of the special German-Jewish relationship.[27] Official diplomatic relations with the Jewish State became a regular function of Germany's international relations, a move which seemed to normalize what otherwise could not be normal only twenty years after the liberation of the last survivors in 1945.

After 1967, the official philosemitic taboos were partially cracked. A younger generation of Germans questioned their parents and their past in the Third Reich. Their more recent past in the reconstruction period of Germany was also questioned, including the nature and content of mainstream historical consciousness. Workshops on anti-Semitism in many universities opened new perspectives and centered on anti-Semitism as a form of racism. Others within the student generation discovered international solidarity against imperialism. The United States became the main object of disapproval, but after the Six Day War in the Middle East a new "victim of imperialism" — this time an Israeli brand of it — was discovered. This new Palestinian victim, it seemed to many young Germans, was a victim of the Jewish survivors, themselves the former victims of Nazi politics. The ploy is obvious: the new solidarity with the victim's victim created an emotional and cognitive distance to both the Jews murdered by Germans and the survivors living in and outside Germany. In the eyes and minds of the younger generation, the parents' dead Jewish neighbor or the later object of philosemitic bathos was replaced by the victimized Palestinian. This shift in intellectual consciousness influenced the agenda of the German left and the peace movements. At times, the overt political anti-Zionism concealed a latent cultural anti-Semitism.

In the 1970s, emotional and intellectual distance was broadened still further. The search for new German identities now referred more readily to *Heimat*, homeland, in terms of ethnic and regional identities, on the one hand, and, on the other, to philosemitic stereotypes which could easily slide into anti-Zionist and anti-Israeli sentiment. This complex perception of the Jews and Israel was shaken up in 1979 when the TV mini-series *Holocaust* stirred up millions of Germans. As had happened before with such works as Lessing's *Nathan the Wise*, Anne Frank's *Diary*, Rolf Hochhuth's *The Deputy*, or Peter Weiss's *Investigation*, the discussion of the German crimes against the Jews took place more readily in the cultural and aesthetic sphere than in the realm of politics. The English term "Holocaust" now became the code word for what had happened a generation before. It helped to avoid speaking in German about annihilation, destruction, mass murder. The necessary psychological distance could be created by using the English term. And since then the term "Holocaust" has become well established in German political culture and can be found in the media and on book covers. This distance is measurable by the semantics that have been favored: Auschwitz is far in the "East," well outside Germany, "Holocaust" is conveniently a foreign term; and, as it is usually said, crimes have been committed "in the name of Germany" but not by Germans. Most of the real German perpetrators have vanished from collective consciousness, the very rare trials of the 1970s and 1980s being more or less a nuisance.

The 1970s and the 1980s were the decades that saw the anonymization of the crimes Hitler and the Nazis perpetrated, so to speak, not the Germans. Bitburg and the Historians' Debate indicated shifts in historical consciousness which relativized the relevance of the Holocaust as well as the impact of the Jewish critique of both events. All these examples, as Saul Friedländer wrote after Bitburg, "attest to a constant seesaw between learning and forgetting, between becoming briefly aware of the past and turning one's back on it. A near automatic process."[28]

With the unification of the two Germanys the postwar period has definitely come to an end. Imagining the Jews seems now to be pushed to the margins of political culture. And yet it is clear that this distance is difficult for the Germans, as became obvious in the unification process. The third rise of Germany as a forceful economic and political power in our century was necessarily accompanied by changes in collective identification and historical self-understanding. May 8, the day commemorating victory over Nazism in 1945, no longer played any role whatsoever by the time May 8, 1990 came around. How different this was from May 8, 1985, when German president Richard von Weizsäcker made his much-quoted speech urging remembrance as the debates about Bitburg raged. Then, public discourse was still determined by the pre-1945 past. Five years later, however, the debate about the problems and future form of German unity overlay and submerged all remembrance. The new key word became "normalization."

In 1990, the wording of the preamble to the unification treaty between the two German states became an obvious sign of this normalization. The Jewish community in Germany called for a clear and unequivocal formula referring to German crimes under Nazism and the resulting responsibilities of a unified Germany. But the Federal Government and the parliament refused to include such language. To be sure, speeches by Chancellor Helmut Kohl and President Richard von Weizsäcker did mention a general sense of German responsibility for what had occurred in the past, but because this past was not specified it seemed to have wider connotations than just the Third Reich. Indeed, the preamble, by consciously and deliberately omitting all references to crimes against Jews and other peoples, can be read as Germany's reconciliation with its own past. Its main theme is continuity, referring back to 2,000 years of German history and virtually ignoring the Nazi period. From this perspective, the establishment of a new united Germany lies at right angles to the debate surrounding the founding of the two German states in 1949. At that time, the demands of the representatives of surviving Jews were initially ignored, but later became politically relevant, at least in Bonn, largely due to pressure from the United States and the engagement of German liberals. In 1990, however, the former Allies stripped themselves of their rights with respect to Germany. Relations between Germany and its Jewish inhabitants were no longer a criterion for evaluating the German state: the Federal Republic no longer wished to be judged by its relation to the Nazi past. Official German historical consciousness has taken a sharp turn toward the future, guided by a highly selective version of a reinterpreted past. The upsurge of xenophobic right-wing violence, the open or silent acclamation of vast strata of the populace, and, particularly the reluctance of the leading political parties, politicians, and police to react forcefully prove that one major lesson of the past has been forgotten. Indeed, polls indicate that, for the younger generation of Germans, there is a clear relationship between ignorance of the Holocaust and hatred of non-Germans: strong feelings of nationalism, authoritarian attitudes, and lack of knowledge about the Holocaust correlate with a high level of antagonism toward foreigners.[29] Thus, one has to be careful to register only social problems as unemployment, housing shortages, and the influx of foreigners at the root of violent right-wing extremist activities. Although there exists scapegoatism we are witnessing a fundamental revival of German ethnicism and nationalism in the very center of German political culture. As a result, the conservative mainstream is shifting to the right while the extreme right, in fact, is more and more overlapping with this conservative mainstream. The elections of 1993 and the election year 1994 illustrate such development.

The "normalization" that has accompanied German unification, by excluding the crimes of World War II and the Holocaust from the nation's self-understanding, has obscured the challenge that the Jewish legacy and the State of Israel pose for German identity. We are farther away from German-Jewish reconciliation today than ever before in the postwar period. Never since 1949 have Jews in Germany felt so isolated as they do now.

Other recent examples for shifts in national consciousness in the field of culture include the official reasonable way with the film *Europa, Europa,* and the selective, and — in terms of the number of visitors — highly successful representation of Jewish history in a monumental exhibition in Berlin during the spring of 1992. The film *Europa, Europa* was considered harmful for the German image abroad, since it dealt with the Holocaust and thus it was not presented as the German contribution to the Oscar competition. In the Berlin exhibition the Holocaust was mentioned only in passing, and the Jews were again depicted as strangers, as exotic flowers in a non-Jewish garden, flowers that can best be admired from a distance.

At the same time, one sees a good deal about Jewish history on German TV, and the book stores are full of publications on Jewish topics. One recognizes something resembling a rejection of memory, on one hand, and a revitalized interest in Jews and things Jewish, on the other. How do these two tendencies happen to appear at the same time? They seem to originate in two intellectual developments: first, the naive *Betroffenheit*, this specific German "state of speechless embarrassment"[30] of parts of the younger generation when it comes to the remembrance of the Holocaust. As Ian Buruma describes it: "One way out of this state is to confess. Not only does confession relieve the pressure of guilt, but it can lift the confessor to a higher moral plane, to the point, almost, of being able to identify with the victims of the sins." This *Betroffenheit* has "resulted in a wave of interest in Jewish matters, especially in Berlin." Second, one detects a state of mind that combines most fittingly with an emotional and intellectual nostalgia about the lost and dead Jewish culture. "The Jewish past has become almost folkloric, a lost paradise," as Ian Buruma puts it. "It is as though German public opinion needs the moral approval or castigation of famous Jews before it can make up its mind about anything, especially about the state of being German." This wave of interest in things Jewish is doubtless a passing phenomenon, a complex repercussion of traditional postwar philosemitism, and it calls back the shadow of a Jewish presence in the new and regained German *Heimat*. Besides, one has to be careful not to overestimate the impact of this new wave of interest outside Berlin or Frankfurt. Such nostalgia, as Michael Kammen pointed out in another context in his *Mystic Chords of Memory*, represents a highly selective history. It is a way of "dis-remembering" — it is "history without guilt," and void of any appropriate feeling of collective responsibility.[31]

In a more specific context the question of a German Holocaust memorial is still unsolved. The debate over a central site in Berlin continues although most participants assume that such a memorial has to be close to the Brandenburg Gate and remnants of the headquarters of the Nazi regime. The question has been widely discussed whether it should really be a Holocaust memorial or, rather, a memorial dedicated to all victims of war and terror. This, of course, would transform almost all Germans into victims and thus contribute to the relativization of German historical responsibility. One can assume that this debate will continue in the German media, at least until 1995, the fiftieth anniversary of the downfall of the Third Reich. This debate has evolved into an almost macabre intervention by German officials in the inauguration of the Holocaust Museum in Washington. The German government, worried that the museum will damage Germany's image, offered millions of dollars to have a post-World War II Germany exhibit included in the museum. What goes on in the minds of German politicians when they seriously propose such an offer? Does the memory of the Holocaust carry a price? Germany's chief government spokesperson contended that "it would have been very good if people could see that in the meantime, there is another Germany."[32] When this failed, German organizations suggested that school curricula in America be altered to add the study of postwar Germany to the growing number of Holocaust history courses. A spokesperson of the American Jewish Committee responded that efforts to steer attention away from the Holocaust Museum would not help Germany's image. When a search for documents and other material for the museum was carried out all over Europe only "Germany," said a member of the Holocaust Museum council, "sought to influence how it would be portrayed in the exhibits."[33] The German government would be well advised to spend the money it intended to invest in Washington for a Holocaust Museum in Germany. What Germany most needs is not museums abroad to improve its image, but serious confrontations with the past in Berlin, Munich, Rostock, and in those 150 German cities where violent foreigner-hatred found an outlet between August 1992 and August 1993. Far more important than the image of Germany in other countries are the political and cultural realities of a country that has not yet learned to live with its past.

IV.

The immediate past that the majority of Germans talk about since 1990 are the forty-five years of communist rule in East Germany and not the period of Nazi terror. We are living through a *Zeitwende*,[34] a shift of time. After the opening of the files of the former East German secret service the term *Vergangenheitsbewältigung* (mastering the past), no longer refers so much to the Third Reich as it does to East Germany since 1945. Public opinion polls from 1991 and 1992 show that approximately 60% of the German population want to put the memory of the Holocaust behind them.[35]

One may ask, is there any way of slowing down this process? I believe there is. One has to beware of any kind of Jewish "appeasement" in what seems to be a determined German reordering of collective memory. Jews are not outsiders to the historical process but active agents in the rethinking of this history. By their presence, it becomes necessary in reconceptualizing the contemporary German-Jewish discourse to start with Auschwitz. For in the beginning of the German postwar period was Auschwitz, not Adenauer or Germany's integration into the West. One ought, therefore, to read the distinct contemporary traces of Auschwitz and pursue the real historical process in the relation of Germans and Jews since 1945.

I would like to stress, that Auschwitz — from this point of view — is not a metaphor but a German place, and as such it is not of merely passing interest to German history. It belongs centrally to the national history of the Germans as well as to the history of modern western culture. Current debates on the Holocaust in Germany, however, show a contrary tendency. What is developing is a myth of the new German innocence. Rudolf Augstein, editor of *Der Spiegel*, is one of those creating this new German innocence. In a commentary he stressed that there is no way of speculating, that the young Germans, who know Auschwitz only from their schoolbooks, may be forced to remember ("zur Erinnerung zwingen").[36]

Following this line of thinking, an ambiguous German historical consciousness is developing which promotes an emotional and intellectual distance from the Holocaust for the sake of a new German national identity and, ultimately, the creation of a new German national state. Conservative politicians are more than eager to recall dreams of the nation and national identity as a remedy for the ongoing crisis of unification (*Vereinigungskrise*). Many conservatives and national-minded Germans look forward to the future, while, in fact, remaining trapped in a selectively remembered past. Since the impact of the Holocaust cannot be negated, its meaning has to be changed and integrated in an almost harmless way into the new German national thinking.

This, though, is not a new phenomenon but developed already in the 1980s in German culture. Some movies of Rainer Werner Fassbinder contributed to this thinking, as did the highly popular TV serial *Heimat*.[37] On the day of her burial in Berlin (1992), Marlene Dietrich was denounced by some as a "traitress to the fatherland."[38] This sentiment would not have been voiced openly before 1989 or referred to in the media as a widespread attitude in parts of the German public.

The future will show the Jewish view of the past to be more and more antagonistic in the face of these evolving trends. Nothing brought this to the fore more clearly than the reactions by the German Government, German business, and the German peace movements before, during, and after the Gulf War. In a strange turnabout, Dresden was equated with Tel Aviv, on the one hand, and Berlin with Baghdad, on the other. Such a willful rearrangement of historical facts relativizes everything, so that Germans and Jews become similarly victimized. Drawing on recurring television footage of Israel's occupation a new image of the Jew was constructed. This time it was not *Nathan the Wise* or Anne Frank, not a Jewish Nobel prizewinner or a heroic Kibbutznik. Rather, what emerges is either the Jew who relentlessly and amorally haunts German memory the so-called "German hater" or the morally defunct Israeli, who is regarded as being no better than the Germans of the Third Reich.

In the unification process now under way, some German intellectuals project another image of the Jew. In a popular essay on Germans and Jews Konrad Löw stresses emphatically that the Jews "deprived many Germans of the joy of having self-confidence and therefore of a healthy national consciousness."[39] Indeed, some Germans cannot bring themselves to forgive the Jews for Auschwitz. Hans Jürgen Syberberg, for example, remarked in 1990: "The partition of the country as a punishment for Auschwitz has come to an end."[40] But in fact the clash of antagonistic memories has by no means come to an end. At the end of August 1992, while racist and anti-foreigner rioting was going on in about thirty German cities, a bomb was thrown at a Holocaust Memorial site in Berlin. From 1941 to 1944 thousands and thousands of Jewish citizens of Berlin were deported from there to the concentration campus in the East. This site has been vandalized several times since 1989. In September 1992, the Jewish cemetery in Berlin-Weissensee was desecrated, and right-wing extremists tried to set the Holocaust Memorial site at Ravensbrück on fire. When months later some of these extremists were caught, one of them simply said: "I hate foreigners and Jews." In short, foreigner-hatred and anti-Semitism are strongly related to each other in unified Germany. Yet, another fact has to be pointed out in this context: at the same time, that the rewriting of historical identity concentrates on the cultural mainstream, the right-wing extremists are busy burning houses of asylum seekers and of the Turkish minority. But they combine this with the burning of Holocaust memorial sites, which is nothing less than the practical side of the policies of Holocaust-denial. These events call to mind another remark by John McCloy from the speech quoted above:

> The moment that Germany has forgotten the Buchenwalds, and the Auschwitzes, that was the point at which everyone could begin to despair of any progress in Germany.

In conclusion, there is no coherent and simple notion of the Jews in the German mind throughout the postwar period. This notion changed in time. With the unification of Germany, it also changes in space. The decades since 1945 have witnessed a metamorphosis in the centrality of the image of the Jews, both in the very content and structure of the images, and in their place in Germany's political culture. This metamorphosis of the image of the Jews is part and parcel of the German endeavor to come to terms with the past, and to overcome the particular relevance of the Shoah for German identity and national consciousness. From the perspective of the early nineties, it is striking to decipher the contradictions that characterize the German imagining of the Jews since 1945. In the late forties, the early sixties, the late seventies, since Bitburg in the eighties, and in the time of the unification process we can observe periods of an intensification of dealing culturally with Jewish past and presence. This intensification is always connected, on the one hand, with Germany's rise within the western political sphere, and with remarkable shifts in the public debate about German identity on the other. Whenever clarity concerning German matters seemed to be reached the Jews and things Jewish lost their centrality in these periods. This process was paralleled by an intellectual curve that began with the tabooization of anti-Semitism after 1945, the privatization of anti-Semitic prejudice in the following years, and the evolving new philosemitism that became an official norm of West German political culture. The positive image and the negative image of the Jew coexisted in collective memory, and since the late sixties one can observe a decline of philosemitic modes of thinking and behavior which allows traditional anti-Jewish images to come to the fore.

The relevance of the place of the Jews in German historical consciousness underwent several shifts. It shifted from the reeducational center of postwar political culture, which was highly influenced by the Allies, to the political margins of German nation-building. In the fifties and sixties the churches and special institutions like the Societies for Christian-Jewish Cooperation and the yearly "Brotherhood Week" had to keep the memory of the Jews alive. In the 1960s and 1970s a new generation of intellectuals came close to a new working through of memory and then fell back, relativizing the impact of the Holocaust. In the 1970s and 1980s another shift took place when popular cultural images of the Jews led to an aestheticization of the Holocaust in different representations in literature, cinema, and television. Since the end of the eighties, the impact of the Jews in historical consciousness shifted temporarily to the political sphere, but now it appears to be held at stark distance. Jews appear as intruders to the making of the new German historical consciousness. Things Jewish were and are seen as representations of the past which no longer seemed to be relevant as building blocks of the new historical discourse. In short, the discourse on Jews in Germany was an inherent cultural discourse shifting between these different spheres.

Toward the end of the twentieth century, German and Jewish collective memories fall away from one another more than ever before. The Jewish-German discourse is inherently antagonistic. The future German historical consciousness, I would contend, will reorder the European map. On this map, Auschwitz will be for most Germans just another site of World War II, while for the Jews and, no doubt, for others it will forever remain a place of historical singularity and centrality. But, whatever view the Germans may hold, others will not forget that millions of innocent people were condemned to live, suffer, and die "inside the vicious heart."[41]

Notes

1 This article is a revised version of a published lecture given at the Robert A. and Sandra S. Borns Jewish Studies Program: *Jews in the Minds of Germans in the Postwar Period. The 1992 Paul Lecture.* (Bloomington, 1993), and refers to another recent publication by the author: *German Unification and the Question of Antisemitism.* New York 1993.

2 Lotte Paepcke: *Ich wurde vergessen. Bericht einer Jüdin, die das Dritte Reich überlebte.* Freiburg, Basel, Vienna 1979, p. 120f.

3 *The New York Times* (9. 8. 1949), *Die Neue Zeitung* (8. 1. 1949), *Allgemeine Wochenzeitung der Juden in Deutschland* (8. 1. 1949); see also *Proceedings of the Heidelberg Conference on the Future of Jewish Communities in Germany*, ed. by the American Jewish Committee. New York 1949; Thomas Alan Schwartz: *America's Germany. John J. McCloy and the Federal Republic of Germany.* Cambridge 1991, p. 175f.

4 See for this context Frank Stern: "Antagonistic Memories. The Post-War Survival and Alienation of Jews and Germans." In: *International Yearbook of Oral History and Life Stories* 1 (1992), p. 21f.

5 See as an example for this kind of reasoning the book by the Bavarian lawyer Klaus Michael Groll: *Wie lange haften wir für Hitler? Zum Selbstverständnis der Deutschen heute.* Munich 1990.

6 Primo Levi: *The Drowned and the Saved.* London, New York 1988, p. 170.

7 Theodor Heuss in a speech given at a festive occasion of the Society for Christian-Jewish Cooperation in Wiesbaden, December 1949. In: Theodor Heuss: *An und über Juden. Aus Schriften und Reden 1906-1063.* Düsseldorf 1963, p. 122.

8 See Frank Stern: *The Whitewashing of the Yellow Badge. Antisemitism and Philosemitism in Postwar Germany.* Oxford, New York 1992.

9 John H. Herz: "The Fiasco of Denazification in Germany." In: *Political Science Quarterly* 63 (1948), p. 569f.

10 See Frank Stern: "The Historic Triangle: Occupiers, Germans and Jews." In: *Tel Aviver Jahrbuch für deutsche Geschichte* 19 (1990), p. 47f.

11 See Yehuda Bauer: *Out of the Ashes. The Impact of American Jewry on Post-Holocaust European Jewry.* Oxford, New York 1989; Micha Brumlik: *The Situation of the Jews in Today's Germany. The 1990 Paul Lecture.* Bloomington 1991.

12 Levi (Note 4), p. 4.

13 Hans Mayer: *Außenseiter.* Frankfurt/Main 1981.

[14] See Christiane Schmelzkopf: *Zur Gestaltung jüdischer Figuren in der deutschsprachigen Literatur nach 1945*. Hildesheim 1983; Heidy M. Müller: *Die Judendarstellung in der deutschsprachigen Erzählprosa. 1945-1981*. Hanstein 1984; Anat Feinberg: *Wiedergutmachung im Programm. Jüdisches Schicksal im deutschen Nachkriegsdrama*. Cologne 1988; and for the general context James E. Young: *Writing and Rewriting the Holocaust*. Bloomington, Indiana 1988.

[15] On the level of film analysis see Eric L. Santner: *Stranded Objects. Mourning, Memory, and Film in Postwar Germany*. New York 1990; Gertrud Koch: *Die Einstellung ist die Einstellung. Visuelle Konstruktionen des Judentums*. Frankfurt/Main 1992.

[16] A. Kronheim: "'Der Name klingt doch jüdisch ...' — Erinnern aus dem Nachkrieg." In: *Ausstellungskatalog, Zehn Brüder waren wir gewesen ... Spuren jüdischen Lebens in Neukölln*. Berlin 1988, p. 471.

[17] Cited in Rolf Wiggershaus: *Die Frankfurter Schule. Geschichte. Theoretische Entwicklung. Politische Bedeutung*. Munich 1988, p. 497.

[18] See the contributions to this problem in: *Probing the Limits of Representation. Nazism and the "Final Solution"*, ed. by Saul Friedländer. Cambridge 1992.

[19] See Alvin H. Rosenfeld: *A Double Dying. Reflections on Holocaust Literature*. Bloomington 1988; Lawrence L. Langer: *Holocaust Testimonies. The Ruins of Memory*. New Haven 1991.

[20] See Selma Leydesdorff: "Das gebrochene Schweigen: Lebensgeschichten von Überlebenden des jüdischen Proletariats in Amsterdam." In: *Bios. Zeitschrift für Biographieforschung und Oral History* 2 (1988), p. 25.

[21] See Harold James: *A German Identity 1770-1990*. London 1989. Concerning unification see also his article "Germans and their Nation." In: *German History* 2/9 (1991), p. 136f.

[22] Cited in Wolfgang Benz: "Antisemitism in East and West Germany after Reunification." In: *The Danger of Antisemitism in Central and Eastern Europe in the Wake of 1989-1990*, ed. by Yehuda Bauer. Jerusalem 1991, p. 28.

[23] *Trend. A Weekly Report of Political Affairs and Public Opinion*, ed. by the Office of Military Government for Bavaria: Information Control Division, Number 23 (11. 11. 1946). In: National Archives Washington, Register Number 7/37-1/1.

[24] *Deutschland Berichte* 1/2 (January 1966).

[25] Ernst Bloch: "Die sogenannte Judenfrage." In: *Frankfurter Allgemeine Zeitung*, 3. 14. 1963.

[26] See for the American context Alvin H. Rosenfeld: "Popularization and Memory: The Case of Anne Frank." In: *Lessons and Legacies. The Meaning of the Holocaust in a Changing World*, ed. by Peter Hayes. Evanston Illinois 1991, p. 243f.

[27] See Lily Gardner Feldman: *The Special Relationship Between West Germany and Israel*. Boston, London, Sydney 1984.

[28] Saul Friedländer: "Some German Struggles with Memory." In: *Bitburg in Moral and Political Perspective*, ed. by Geoffrey H. Hartman. Bloomington 1986, p. 32.

[29] M. Brusten and B. Winkelmann: "The Understanding of the Holocaust and its Influence on Current Perspectives of German Youths: An Overview of Quantitative Research on Attitudes of Students." In: *Soziale Probleme* 3 (1992), p. 20.

[30] This and the following quotes see Ian Buruma: "The Ways of Survival." In: *New York Review of Books*, 7. 16. 1992.

[31] See Michael Kammen: *Mystic Chords of Memory. The Transformation of Tradition in American Culture.* New York 1991, p. 535.

[32] *Washington Post*, 3. 30. 1993.

[33] Ibid.

[34] The term *Zeitwende* was coined in the forties by Richard Koebner, historian and Jewish émigré from Breslau who taught at the Hebrew University of Jerusalem. See Richard Koebner: *Geschichte, Geschichtsbewußtsein und Zeitwende. Vorträge und Schriften aus dem Nachlaß.* Gerlingen 1990, p. 147f.

[35] David A. Jodice: *United Germany and Jewish Concerns. Attitudes Toward Jews, Israel, and the Holocaust. The American Jewish Committee. Working papers on Contemporary Anti-Semitism.* New York 1991, p. 3; *EMNID-Umfrage*, published in: *Spiegel Spezial* 2 (1992).

[36] *Der Spiegel*, 4. 27. 1992.

[37] See Saul Friedländer: *Reflections of Nazism. An Essay on Kitsch and Death.* New York 1984.

[38] See *Die Zeit*, 4. 2. 1992.

[39] Konrad Löw: *Im heiligen Jahr der Vergebung. Wider Tabu und Verteufelung der Juden.* Zürich 1991, p. 85.

[40] *Frankfurter Allgemeine Zeitung*, 8. 24. 1990.

[41] Meyer Levin: *In Search: An Autobiography.* New York 1950, p. 232.

Andrei S. Markovits

The Politics of Memory:
The Predicament of German-Jewish Relations in the former Bundesrepublik and in Post-Wall Deutschland[1]

I.

Fifty-five years ago an event occurred in the heart of Europe, among the nation of poets and thinkers, which initiated the greatest tragedy ever befalling the Jewish people in its lengthy history. This tragedy is what has come to be known as the Holocaust, more recently still as the Shoah, an event which the Nazis with eerie precision called *die Endlösung* ("the final solution"). It is not the fact that roughly one third of the Jewish people were murdered which renders this event unparalleled in the annals of human brutality. (Indeed, in purely quantitative terms that measure the percentage of people murdered and maimed, the Holocaust represents "merely" the third most disastrous calamity befalling the Jewish people; the destruction of the First Temple with the ensuing forced departure to Babylon caused many deaths; the destruction of the Second Temple by the Romans and the subsequent wars culminating in the tragedy of Massada[2] were also devastating.)

It is not so much the "quantity" of the killings that renders the Shoah unique, rather, it is its finality, its intended completeness — its character of the *Endlösung*, a state-sponsored, state-approved, state-directed policy of *systematic* mass extermination of one particular people all over the world — which made it unprecedented. For the Nazis, the Jews in New York, Sidney, Buenos Aires or Mexico City were as much a lethal enemy which had to be eradicated as Jews in Berlin, Amsterdam, Warsaw, Bialystok or Budapest. The Nazis failed in the implementation of their endeavor only because Germany lost the war; but I am still frightened and amazed as to how successful they were: in barely seven years (1938-1945) they killed six million Jews. It all started with that classical anti-Semitic expression of mass politics which the world has come to know from its Russian origins as "pogrom," an event which the Nazis labeled with their customary cynical euphemism and bureaucratic penchant:

Kristallnacht. This marked the beginning of what was to become the first mechanized, completely systematic and bureaucratized annihilation of human beings in history. It was, and still remains, a unique event.

Kristallnacht represented a major step in the Nazis' avowed mission to roll back the universalizing project of the French revolution. (One of the Nazis' mottos was not by chance: "We are against everything since 1789.") The French Revolution liberated the Jews and rendered them — at least formally, that is politically — into citizens, *citoyens.* The French Revolution and the Enlightenment de-particularized Jews (among others, by physically de-ghettoizing them) thereby universalizing them into politically accepted and formally equal human beings in the public realm as citizens.

Starting with the Nuremberg Laws, continuing with *Kristallnacht,* then the Wannsee Conference and culminating in Auschwitz, the Nazis created a logical chain that reversed the universalistic achievements of the French Revolution: first, the stripping of political rights; then of economic rights; then of social rights; and ultimately of physical rights.[3] Paradoxically, the Nazis actually adhered to a universalizing principle in their re-particularization of the Jews: namely that of the universality of death and unconditional destruction. All Jews, universally, had to be destroyed, not only Polish, Hungarian, or German Jews.

It is on one hand frightening, on the other very telling of the altered *Zeitgeist,* that in the last few years the things I just delineated are not only subject to constant revision and re-interpretation (as part of legitimate scholarship) but that they are increasingly seen by a growing and sophisticated public as essentially untrue, a hoax, and a myth perpetrated by the Jews, their devious allies, and obsequious servants. In the wake of the fashionable relativization of everything which some post-modern epistemologies demand (and many right-wing power holders welcome) we have reached the sad spectacle where we rejoice when a French Holocaust denier, a certain Jean-Claude Pressac, formerly an avid follower of the notorious Holocaust denier Robert Faurisson, publishes a detailed technical book (completely devoid of human content) as to how exactly the gas chambers and ovens worked in Auschwitz-Birkenau.[4] Of course there is absolutely nothing wrong with having a study like this based on new archival material from the former Soviet Union. Indeed, such meticulous research should be welcomed, particularly if it is based on hitherto inaccessable data. But to see this book as a godsend, a *deus ex machina,* which now definitively "proves" the existence of the Holocaust is frightening. What the reaction to this book bespeaks is that we have reached a point where it is becoming increasingly necessary to "prove" the existence of the Holocaust as a precondition for any further debate. This is a very sobering fact barely fifty-five years after *Kristallnacht.*

I will divide the main body of my essay into two parts: First, I will offer an overview of the Federal Republic's dealing with the Nazi past, the Holocaust and *Kristallnacht* between 1949 and 1989/90; and second, I will analyze the changes that have informed the Germans' dealing with their past since the fall of the Berlin Wall on *Kristallnacht* in 1989 and German unification on October 3, 1990.[5]

II. The Bundesrepublik Phase: 1949-1989

Comparatively speaking, one has to give the Bundesrepublik much credit for dealing with the past at all, for showing some contrition, for providing some restitution and reparation for past wrongs, no matter how incomplete and inadequate.[6]

This is important because very few countries apologized, let alone atoned, for their past wrongs:

— The Turks have never apologized for the genocidal massacres of the Armenians. Indeed, they have yet to acknowledge them.

— The Japanese are only now issuing oblique and opaque statements as to their war crimes in Asia with — as is evident — serious domestic consequences.

— The French, perceive the Algerian episode — and even the legacy of World War II — as still fraught with controversy and conflict as was evident during the trial of Klaus Barbie and subsequent debates concerning the roundup of Jews by the French police during the war.

— The Americans have yet to "overcome" the Vietnam episode in which they, too, committed atrocities. Certainly no reparation or restitution has been forthcoming on our part vis-à-vis Vietnam, quite the contrary: economic boycott and political isolation of Vietnam have been our steadfast response with very few changes in sight. We **did** have the MyLai trial and the sentencing of Captain Medina and Lieutenant Kelly, a stellar moment in the history of our democracy.

The sad fact is that few, if any, countries have punished their officers on a voluntary basis for crimes committed against an enemy. Almost invariably, these acts of contrition, if forthcoming at all, are the result of a defeat. Concretely, they are imposed in some fashion "from above"; "from the outside" and "by the victors" instead of being the voluntary creation of genuine responses on the part of the perpetrators and guilty. Thus, moments such as the MyLai trial in the United States and the Israeli justice system's condemning reaction to the country's indirect, though no less explicit, involvement in the massacres at Sabra and Shatila testify to rare moments of moral fortitude and inner strength which, tellingly, only liberal democracies with their openness and built-in criticism are able to muster.

In the case of Germany, too, the issue of dealing with the atrocities committed by Germany in the name of Germans during World War II — indeed the war itself — was imposed "from the outside" and "from above." Thus, it is undoubtedly a significant datum for a proper understanding of postwar German politics, history and culture to emphasize the fact that National Socialism was not defeated by the German people, that for whatever reason Nazism as a political rule remained legitimate in Germany until its complete defeat from the outside. In notable contrast to the Italian case, where Italian partisans executed Mussolini and the Italian people actively participated in fascism's demise and eventual defeat, no such developments occurred in Germany.

This does not mean that a majority of Germans were active in national socialist politics. It merely connotes that Nazism as a political rule enjoyed at least a functioning tacit approval, a compliance among the vast majority of the German people which made the system work to the bitter end. It does not so much imply an active and participatory Nazism as it does a passive and compliant one. The absence of a successful indigenous revolt against National Socialism on the part of the German people says much more about a culture of *Mitläufer* than it does about a culture of fanatics.

One can discern three responses to the national socialist past in the three successor states to the Third Reich. In Austria's case, the title of a much-read book best summarizes Austria's "exit option" concerning its responsibilities for its complicity with the Third Reich: *Anschluß: The Rape of Austria* says it all.[7] The myth developed in which the big, bad Germans "raped" helpless little Austria. This myth was instrumental in the formulation of the Moscow Declaration of 1943 in which the Allies declared Austria as Hitler's first victim. Moreover, the continuation of this myth and its structural legacy contributed to Austria's becoming neutral in 1955 and thus furnishing an impressive tangible result of the Cold War's first (albeit brief) détente in 1955.

The myth of the German rape helped exonerate and exculpate Austria in the eyes of the global public. Most important, however, it absolved the Austrian people from a sense of collective responsibility for its actions during the Third Reich. Paradoxically, it was the otherwise infamous Waldheim Affair that changed Austria's sense of complacency and self-righteousness, at least to some extent.[8] It took Austria forty years after Auschwitz to assume at least a semblance of responsibility for its complicity in the Third Reich's murderous machinery.

If Austria got off the hook by declaring itself the victim of Nazi Germany by virtue of a political and military rape, then the German Democratic Republic (GDR) pleaded innocence by claiming to be the victim of capitalism. The GDR's exculpatory argument went as follows:

Fascism (the German left [West or East] rarely, if ever, using the words "National Socialism" which are much more specific to the Third Reich, and preferring the much more generic "fascism" instead) was a product of capitalism. With the GDR being socialist and having "overcome" and "transcended" capitalism, it thus embodied the "good" Germany, the "moral" Germany, the legacy of social democracy and communism, the tradition of workers and peasants but not of capitalists. Thus, with everything good claimed by the Germany east of the Elbe river, all evil seemed to have been miraculously relegated to the country's western part. End of story!

This exculpatory mechanism was arguably one of the very few policies advocated by the East German government that enjoyed real legitimacy among the people. The dividends were high: Nobody had to deal with the difficult past. Everybody was offered a quick and wholesale absolution for past wrongs. There developed a state-sanctioned exoneration from above which met with the East Germans' approval.

This led to many bizarre distortions. Among them, for example, was the widespread belief (especially among East Germany's children) that it was the East German People's Army in collaboration with the Red Army that defeated Hitler's fascism. Among the most shameful consequences of this state-sanctioned absolution was the fact that Jews were never recognized *qua* Jews as victims, only *qua* their political opposition to the regime as antifascists. Given this frame of mind it is not surprising that at the Buchenwald concentration camp memorial every conceivable nationality is listed among the victims of that terrible camp except Jews. This wholesale exculpation also led to the East German government's active support for groups and people whose sole purpose had been the destruction of the state of Israel. The government's vicious anti-Zionism often assumed tones which were hardly different from the most vitriolic anti-Semitic attacks voiced by the Nazis barely forty years before. This absolution also offered the East Germans one of the few areas in which they could genuinely feel superior to their West German cousins. The West Germans might have had the cars, the houses, the vacations, and all the material comforts afforded by a successful consumer society; but, unlike the East Germans, they had not "overcome" Germany's fascist past. Hence, it was the East Germans, no matter how poor and drab, who claimed to be the morally superior Germans, the democratic Germans, the non-Nazi Germans.

Not until the collapse of the Communist regime in the fall of 1989 and the establishment of the first, and last, legitimately elected East German government in the spring of 1990 did East Germany have anything to say about the Holocaust beyond the hackneyed clichés of Communist dogma. Not by chance, among the East German parliament's first declarations was a belated admission of culpability and responsibility concerning East

Germany's involvement in the machinery of the Third Reich. This statement of culpability also included an apology to the Jewish people and to the state of Israel coupled with a pledge to provide reparations and restitution to both. This, of course, became a moot point in rapid order because, unbeknownst to the legislators at the time, East Germany ceased to exist barely ten months later.

For better or worse, the Federal Republic of Germany saw itself from its very inception in 1949 as the successor to the Third Reich. This bore advantages as well as disadvantages. Pertaining to the former, the new republic had somehow to confront the burdens of the past. There were no exit options, no cop-out mechanisms as in the case of Austria and the GDR. As to the advantages of being the sole heir to the Third Reich, the Federal Republic could claim to be the only "real" Germany, the legitimate successor to all previous Germanies, not only the Third Reich but the Weimar Republic and the Kaiserreich. In other words, the FRG avoided the complications associated with ruptures. The country's very identity was based on a clear claim to continuity.

How did the Federal Republic deal with the past, in particular with the Nazi regime's systematic murder of six million Jews? I suggest that it did so with a mixture of silence, cover-up, monetary reparations, and compartmentalization.

Silence: Until the first significant Auschwitz trial in Frankfurt (1963) and the advent of the New Left and the student revolts of 1968, there occurred very little public discussion of the Nazi past. Some political activists on the left, some trade unionists, and a few Protestant clergymen, such as the recently deceased Hellmut Gollwitzer, spoke about the genocide of the Jews perpetrated by Germans, but on the whole there was silence. No active denial, just passive silence.

Cover-up: The Federal Republic's *raison d'être* constitutes a legacy of World War II and its aftermath. Thus, that era of German history cannot be separated from the Cold War and its ramifications on European politics. With the Soviet Union and communism replacing National Socialism and Japanese military fascism as the West's main enemy, former foes developed into the closest allies and former friends became mortal enemies. In the case of the Federal Republic this shift in alliances entailed a major change in policies which now emphasized reconciliation and forgiving instead of the earlier pursuit of justice. Concretely, this meant that virtually all measures of de-nazification which had been so ambitiously designed at the end of the war by the Allies all but halted. The end result was that excepting the very top of the Nazi power elite, none of the Third Reich's major players were as much as reprimanded, let alone punished, for their heinous deeds.

Thus, a massive de facto (if not necessarily *de jure*) cover up occurred as a consequence of the Cold War which permitted a high continuity in personnel in virtually all key institutions of the country: the state bureaucracy, the judiciary, industry, the professoriate, and party elites (not including those of the Social Democratic and Communist parties, which the Nazi regime persecuted with a special vengeance).

Monetary reparations: Two dimensions are noteworthy in this context: First, restitution to individual victims of Nazi rule and second, collective reparation to the Jewish people via financial support to the state of Israel. Three things are worthy of mention with regard to reparations.

1. The central role of Konrad Adenauer who — for pragmatic and instrumental reasons — truly believed that the Germans needed to make a grand and tangible gesture of reconciliation to the Jews for the Holocaust.

2. The fact that this peculiar financial arrangement helped both Israel and Germany. The former got much-needed cash and goods. The latter bought respect among the community of nations, especially its recently acquired Western allies with whom it formed various organizations, such as the North Atlantic Treaty Organization (NATO) and the European Economic Community (EEC). Both of these organizations proved essential in weaning the new Bundesrepublik from its less than attractive past.[9]

3. By reaching this arrangement with Israel on a collective basis and with Jews on an individual basis, the Germans succeeded in monetarizing the complex issue of coming to terms with the past. By paying billions of Deutschmarks to the Jews and Israel, the West Germans clearly did more than anybody else. Yet, demanding (perhaps even unfair) as this may sound this monetarization developed into a convenient substitute, a legitimate replacement for the real "Trauerarbeit" (labor of mourning) which would have been appropriate and absolutely necessary for the German people to come to terms with the enormity of the crimes committed in its name by the previous regime. In other words "guilt-geld" became an expedient replacement for *Trauerarbeit*.

Compartmentalization: The Federal Republic compartmentalized the Holocaust by bracketing it as an aberration in German history. Of course, atrocities and horrors were committed; and yes, the Nazis were criminals and their Third Reich was a reprehensible regime. But — so this argument maintained — all of these were the deeds of a small, fanatical, deranged group of criminals who somehow succeeded in seducing, misleading, and bamboozling the otherwise upright German people into following them on their criminal and devious journey of death and destruction. In other words, instead of offering a systemic analysis of and explanation for the Holocaust and its perpetrators, West German elites compartmentalized the Shoah as an aberration, an accident, as something that was extraneous to the desired continuity of German history and thus to the legitimation of the Federal Republic.

Enter 1968: This period changed things in a number of ways — on the whole for the better. The events of 1968 democratized Germany both "from below" via the student movement and "from above" via the Social-Liberal coalition. Suddenly the past became a major topic in universities, political parties, parliaments, the media — in short, the public. Even though often couched in the obfuscatory and generic term of "fascism" instead of the more precise and historically specific "National Socialism," there ensued for the first time a real confrontation with the past. By the late 1960s, the silence about the past had finally been broken. No matter how inadequately, obliquely, and sometimes even erroneously West Germany's citizens got to confront the Nazi past, "1968" forced them to do so on a larger scale than at any other time since the end of the war. It was this legacy of democratization as well as contrition that led to what still remains the most moving public act on the part of a German postwar leader, namely Willy Brandt's kneeling at the memorial to the martyrs of the Warsaw Ghetto uprising. It was also the democratizing legacy of "1968" which by the early 1980s changed the term *Kristallnacht* to the much more accurate and politically correct *Reichspogromnacht* which in the meantime has become the term of choice for this momentous event among politically sensitive Germans.

Lest we extol "1968" and its legacy, it is only appropriate that we mention some of its less fortunate sides concerning German-Jewish relations. Foremost among them has been the left's vehement anti-Israelism which, on many an occasion, assumed anti-Semitic dimensions.[10] Much of the student left, as well as the world of the so called "new social movements," created a milieu and culture in which hatred of Israel was *de rigueur*, a required *Glaubensbekenntnis*. In this context Jews were approved but Israelis despised. Indeed, the latter were somehow seen as the new Germans, the new Prussians with Moshe Dayan being a reincarnation of Erwin Rommel, the legendary "desert fox." If the Israelis in their efficiency and militarism had become the new Germans, then the Palestinians developed into the new Jews. Thus, this milieu developed a grotesque distortion in which the Israelis were tantamount to Nazis and the Palestinians were identified with their Jewish victims.[11]

This frame of mind led to harmless but telling manifestations such as making the *kefiya*, the Palestinian checkered headscarf, the garment of choice in this milieu. Alas, it also led to many more harmful developments and ugly episodes such as, for example, the training of German terrorist groups in Palestinian camps; the Entebbe episode where barely two decades after Auschwitz Germans (in this case leftists) once again "selected" Jews from others on a highjacked El Al airliner for the sole purpose of killing them; and the wanton statements by Hans-Christian Stroebele, one of the Green party's leaders, during the Gulf War in which he welcomed the bombardment of Israel by Iraqi SCUD missiles as just punishment for crimes committed by the Jews against the Palestinians.[12]

Mention should also be made in this context of the incident surrounding Rainer Werner Fassbinder's play *Garbage, the City and Death* in 1985 which featured a confrontation between the two contradictory legacies of "1968": the ugly one in the writing of a viciously anti-Semitic play by one of 1968's most important and internationally acclaimed cultural legacies in Germany, namely the director Rainer Werner Fassbinder; and the empowering one which witnessed the Jewish community's first direct involvement in the activities of the Federal Republic's civil society by occupying the theater's stage and preventing the play's performance. Instead of appealing to the state's protective powers and waiting for its beneficence, Jewish citizens took matters into their own hands, thus asserting for the first time their collective presence in an act of political defiance and dissent.[13]

Despite its ugly sides of left-wing anti-Semitism, "1968" meant on the whole a fundamental democratization of West German public life. Above all, it embodied the belated republicanization of German life. "1968" signified the West German public's profound Westernization. It also meant a definite democratization of many aspects of public and private life in the Federal Republic. Lastly, it also entailed a significant degree of denationalization of West Germany's political culture in the sense that it rendered collective identification with "republic," "democracy," and "constitutionalism" as important as attachment to "nation," "Volk," and "state." It is precisely because of its quintessentially "bundesrepublican" qualities that "1968" has been so vehemently attacked in the changed political climate of the post-wall Deutschland.

Two cathartic events deserve brief mention. The first concerned a sappy Hollywood soap opera entitled *Holocaust*. First aired as a mini-series/docu-drama on American television (NBC) in 1978, it reached the Federal Republic with the customary six-to-eight months delay. After many acrimonious discussions and vicious attacks on the movie's "sensationalism" and "Hollywood kitsch," the series was eventually broadcast on the Federal Republic's third chanel which — being the

German equivalent of the American PBS — prides itself on attracting a selective, more sophisticated audience. Still, millions watched all four episodes. More important still was the fact that millions stayed up after each episode to watch the open-ended panel discussions that followed each of the installments. A nation-wide debate and soul searching engulfed the Federal Republic in February 1979 in which the Holocaust and the German people's role was discussed on a scale never previously experienced in the history of the Bundesrepublik. The personalization of the Holocaust achieved by depicting the tragedy of one Jewish family resulted in greater awareness and compassion among millions of Germans than had any of the numerous documentaries which had regularly been shown in the preceding thirty years of the Federal Republic's existence.[14]

The second cathartic event was Federal President Richard von Weizsäcker's memorable speech delivered to the German parliament and people on May 8, 1985 in commemoration of the fortieth anniversary of the end of World War II and the defeat of national socialism. In this speech, which, with Willy Brandt's kneeling in Warsaw, must be gauged as one of the most morally courageous acts on the part of a German public figure since 1945, the president unmistakably placed Auschwitz into the realm of German responsibility if not guilt. "All of us," von Weizsäcker said, "whether guilty or not, whether old or young, must accept the past. We are all affected by its consequences and liable for it.... We must understand that there can be no reconciliation without remembrance."[15] Alas, this sentiment was not shared by the general public. Barely a year after Weizsäcker's memorable speech, public opinion polls showed that less than 12 percent of the Federal Republic's citizens agreed with Weizsäcker's exhortation to remember, repent, and resolve.

Telling of the unresolved complexity of German history's meaning even in contemporary politics is the fact that May 8 remains a highly charged and exceedingly ambivalent symbol. To some, it is a day of defeat and occupation; to others, a small minority to be sure, it is a day of liberation; to most, it is a day fraught with such complexity, difficulty, and ambiguity that it begs for silence and forgetting.

The 1980s were a decade of mixed results. On the positive side, West Germans became aware in increasing numbers of what the Holocaust really was. The words "Holocaust" and "Shoah" entered the German vernacular, as did *Reichspogromnacht*. Indeed, at the fiftieth anniversary of *Kristallnacht* in 1988, Federal chancellor Helmut Kohl attended services at the Jewish synagogue in Frankfurt. In general, this anniversary received much attention in the media and in hundreds of German cities, towns, and villages. Some people even wanted to make the anniversaries of *Reichspogromnacht* into an official day of national remembrance and atonement.

On the negative side, there occurred the travesty of President Ronald Reagan's ceremonious visit to the Bitburg cemetery in which lay the bodies of over forty soldiers of the *Waffen SS*, specifically members of the notorious "Das Reich" division which was responsible for the annihilation of the French town Oradour-sur-Glane in 1944.[16] More worrisome still was the controversy over the so-called *Historikerstreit* (the historians' debate) in which — for the first time in the history of the Federal Republic — academically legitimate historians, such as Ernst Nolte, Andreas Hillgruber, Thomas Nipperdey, Klaus Hildebrand, and Michael Stuermer, engaged in a clear exculpatory relativization of the Nazis' crimes against the Jewish people. While each of these authors emphasized different epistemological and methodological concerns in his argumentation, the collective effect of the whole was unmistakable: the Holocaust perpetrated by the Germans was but one of many atrocities committed by many peoples during the twentieth century. Mass extermination was thus an unpleasant, but common, side effect of the modernization process. As such, Auschwitz was qualitatively no different from the Gulag, Cambodia's killing fields, or any of the other numerous atrocities littering this century's history. Whereas the historians pursuing this argument in no way denied the Holocaust's existence, the thrust of their contentions and the weight of their professional positions created an atmosphere of acceptability for a discourse in which the real Holocaust deniers could flourish.[17]

The miraculous events of 1989 relegated *Kristallnacht/Reichspogromnacht* into little more than a marginal (and burdensome) curiosity in recent German history. With the fall of the Berlin Wall on exactly the fifty-first anniversary of *Kristallnacht*, the cunning of history made certain that henceforth this ignominious yet so important event would become ghettoized as a "Jewish holiday" in the new Germany. A new, much more joyous occasion, would surely displace *Kristallnacht* from the calendar of memory for most Germans. With World War II genuinely ending on November 9, 1989, the new Deutschland would have little use for troublesome reminders of the *Kristallnacht* type. November 9th, 1938 would become but one of four November 9ths which have indelibly shaped German history: November 9, 1918, the end of the *Kaiserreich* and the beginning of Germany's first (and ill-fated) experiment with democracy; November 9, 1923, Hitler's rise to national prominence via his "beer hall putsch"; November 9, 1938, *Kristallnacht/Reichspogromnacht*; and November 9, 1989, the fall of the Berlin Wall.

III. The Deutschland Phase: 1989 - ?

The old Bundesrepublik is dead. The changes wrought by the demise of the German Democratic Republic and the ensuing geographic expansion of Federal Republic entail more than a quantitative change. The new Deutschland is also qualitatively a different entity from the old Bundesrepublik. The judgment is still pending whether this massive change is one for the better or worse. Fact is, however, that its enormity is evident in every aspect of German and European politics.

Two important features which defined the old Bundesrepublik are currently subject to major discussion in Germany and Europe and will undoubtedly be redefined in the years to come. The first pertains to the Federal Republic's lack of an independent foreign policy; and the second centers on the Federal Republic's subordinate role as a military power. Both were manifestations of the Federal Republic's lack of total sovereignty and autonomy, and a concomitant deference to and dependence on the political leadership of the United States in the global arena and France in the European theater. This structural arrangement formed the core of that quintessentially bundesrepublican trait aptly characterized by the adage "economic giant but political dwarf." This syndrome vanished on November 9, 1989. With the unification of Germany came full sovereignty. The only remaining question is how will the metamorphosis of the political dwarf into a political adult, change things in Germany and Europe? Will this adult necessarily become a giant? If so, will it be a gentle giant or a bully? Does it have to become a giant even against its will? Or could it manage its growing process so that it develops into a balanced way? The end of the Bundesrepublik and the beginning of Deutschland mean nothing more than a process of normalization. But given Germany's troubled history, this normalization process may be anything but normal. At the heart of this immensely complex transition period is the interaction of power and democracy in the new Deutschland.

Three outcomes are possible which — for brevity's sake — I label "optimist," "pessimist," and "realist." The "optimist" argument runs as follows: The Bundesrepublik has been such a successful political, economic, and social arrangement that for the first time in German history, democracy and power are compatible. Forty years of wealth and successful parliamentary rule have created a climate of democracy and a culture of tolerance which have all but extirpated any longings for authoritarianism of any kind, let alone for National Socialism. In addition to deeply anchoring democracy in the fabric of the Federal Republic's political culture and institutions, the Bundesrepublik has — at least in the optimist view — also rendered German power benign, if not innocuous. The country's thorough Westernization should offer a guarantee against the recurring of any past ideologies and longings which in former times did not exactly strengthen democracy's presence in Germany. With the Federal Republic inextricably tied to Western Europe, the United States and a host of international associations, the risk of a "free-floating," hence adventurous, Germany is minimal. The Federal Republic's immense success in organizing capitalism through a tight web of relationships among labor, capital, and the state have created a climate of moderation which none of the "players" want spoiled. To the optimists, the new Deutschland is merely a slightly bigger and more complicated Bundesrepublik in which the interaction of democracy and power will remain as compatible as in the former Federal Republic thus posing no threat to anybody.

For the pessimists, the Federal Republic's successes have not allayed the deep problems which have caused the nightmares of modern German history. Basically characterizing the Bundesrepublik as a fair-weather success story, the pessimists remain skeptical as to the compatibility of power and democracy in the new Deutschland. Seeing the relationship between power and democracy as mutually contradictory in the German case, the pessimists believe that the Bundesrepublik's democratic stability and economic abundance were possible precisely because of the country's limited power. But with the current Germany becoming one of the "players," it is only a matter of time in the pessimists' view when the logic and exigencies of power will undermine those of democracy. In other words, if the optimists are confident that the transformation from political dwarf to political adult person will yield benign results for German democracy as well as European stability, the pessimists fear the danger of a German bully whose actions will be inimical to the Bundesrepublik's successful democratic discourse. To the pessimists the depth of the Bundesrepublik's democratic order remains ephemeral since it was not attained by the German people but was imposed (albeit successfully) from the outside. The pessimists' imagery of the new Deutschland is best summarized by Raoul Hilberg's telling imagery. Queried by a reporter of the *Frankfurter Rundschau* how he assessed the new Germany, Hilberg responded that Germany to him was like a reformed alcoholic who, since unification, has once again attained access to a liquor store.

The realists, in turn, draw on elements from the optimists as well as the pessimists. With the optimists, they believe that the new Deutschland will remain democratic. Moreover, still in line with the optimists, the realists predict that Deutschland's newly attained importance and power will not significantly alter the Bundesrepublik's democratic achievements even though it might limit some on the margins. With the pessimists, the realists share a judgment that Deutschland will become much less Western than the Bundesrepublik had been. In terms of geopolitical engagements and cultural preferences, Deutschland will inevitably develop much more into a European — specifically Central European — power than had been the case with the Bundesrepublik. While the realists see a continuity on matters of democracy between the Bundesrepublik and Deutschland, they most definitely perceive changes on matters of power, even if they do not expect these changes to affect adversely the country's democratic fabric. To the realists the new Germany's increased autonomy and sovereignty is part of an inevitable process of normalization which by definition entails significant, though not necessarily detrimental, changes.[18]

How will the changes from Bundesrepublik to Deutschland affect the Jews? Only a few tentative points can be offered. Most obviously, the Jews are in the process of losing their function of helping to legitimate the Bundesrepublik internationally, something which they did more twenty-five years, but which never quite disappeared until now. Germans will become less guilt-ridden as well as responsible vis-a-vis Jews meaning that the Jews, too, will become "normalized". This, in turn, means that Jews will become even more abstracted and "musealized" than they had already been in the Bundesrepublik. There will be even more synagogues without congregants, just as one can expect a proliferation of museums and exhibits without the context of real existing and current experience. This means that the Germans will never be able to come to terms with the Holocaust no matter how good their intentions have been or might still be. This is because coming to terms with any past — let alone with one burdened by the heinous magnitude of the Shoah — necessitates real, material, physical, concrete presence of the victim on a scale a good deal larger than the roughly 40,000 Jews currently living in Germany. Coming to terms with one's past cannot be thought and abstracted. It has to be experienced on a daily basis. For that there are simply not enough Jews in contemporary Germany. Fifty-five years after Kristallnacht that may not be such a bad thing.

Notes

[1] This essay is dedicated to the memory of my dear friend Laci Rozsa, whose warmth and modesty will always move me. It is based on a lecture delivered at the University of Pittsburgh on November 7, 1993. The lecture, entitled "Kristallnacht in Post-Wall Germany: Will its Memory be Ghettoized?" commemorated the 55th anniversary of Kristallnacht. This commemorative event was sponsored by the University of Pittsburgh and the Holocaust Center of Greater Pittsburgh.

2 For a fine example of this argument, see Steven T. Katz: *Historicism, The Holocaust, and Zionism*. New York 1992.

3 Tellingly, the Nazis reversed the process of emancipation so pointedly presented by T. H. Marshall in his seminal *Citizenship and Social Class and Other Essays*. Cambridge 1950, in which the author identifies the emancipatory struggles of the eighteenth century as focussed on the "political"; those of the nineteenth century as concentrated on the "economic"; and those of the twentieth century as centered on the "social," hence reversing T. H. Marshall's model.

4 See Jean-Claude Pressac: *Les crématoires d'Auschwitz; la machinerie du meurtre de masse*. Paris 1993.

5 For a detailed delineation of the qualitative differences between the old Bundesrepublik and the new Deutschland, see Michael Huelshoff, Andrei S. Markovits, and Simon Reich, eds., *From Bundesrepublik to Deutschland: German Politics after Unification*. Ann Arbor, Michigan 1993; also Andrei S. Markovits: "Aus der Bundesrepublik wurde Deutschland. Die politische Klasse hat versagt." In: *Gewerkschaftliche Monatshefte*, Vol. 44, Number 8, 1993, pp. 473-477.

6 I find it important to come clean on this issue in the following sense. By being an American Jew of Central European origins and a child of Holocaust survivors and a Holocaust-ravaged family, my criteria for German contrition, reparation, and restitution are completely unreasonable and unfair. In a sense, whatever the Germans did, are doing, or might have done will always remain inadequate for me. In a sense, the Germans simply cannot win with me. There is nothing wrong with my having such impossibly exacting standards as long as they are explicitly stated and clearly understood as informing my approach and analysis.

7 Gordon Brook-Shepherd: *Anschluß: The Rape of Austria*. London 1963.

8 See Richard Mitten: *The Politics of Antisemitic Prejudice: The Waldheim Phenomenon in Austria*. Boulder, Colorado 1992.

9 For a superb treatment of the topic of reparations in the context of German-Jewish relations and the relations between Israel and the Federal Republic of Germany, see Lily Gardner Feldman: *The Special Relationship between West Germany and Israel*. Boston 1984.

10 For the most extensive study of this topic, see Martin W. Kloke: *Israel und die deutsche Linke: Zur Geschichte eines schwierigen Verhältnisses*. Frankfurt 1990.

11 See Andrei S. Markovits: "Germans and Jews: An Uneasy Relationship Continues." In: *The Jewish Frontier*, April 1984, pp. 14-20.

12 See Andrei S. Markovits and Philip S. Gorski: *The German Left: Red, Green and Beyond*. New York 1993.

[13] For an analysis of the Fassbinder controversy, see Andrei S. Markovits: "Rainer Werner Fassbinder's *Garbage, the City and Death*: Renewed Antagonisms in the Complex Relationship Between Jews and Germans in the Federal Republic of Germany." In: *New German Critique*, Fall 1986, pp. 146-163.

[14] For a detailed comparative study of *Holocaust* reception in the Federal Republic of Germany and Austria, see Andrei S. Markovits and Rebecca S. Hayden: "*Holocaust*, Before and After the Event: Reactions in West Germany and Austria." In: *New German Critique*, Winter 1980, pp. 53-80.

[15] See Richard von Weizsäcker: *A Voice from Germany: Speeches by Richard von Weizsäcker*, trans. by Karin von Abrams. New York 1987.

[16] For a detailed account of the Bitburg affair, see *Bitburg in Moral and Political Perspective*, ed. by Geoffrey Hartman. Bloomington, Indiana 1986; and Ilya Levkov, ed.: *Bitburg and Beyond: Encounters in American, German and Jewish History*. New York 1987.

[17] For the historians' debate, see Peter Baldwin, ed., *Reworking the Past: Hitler, the Past and the Historians' Debate*. Boston 1990; also Ernst Reinhard, ed., *"Historikerstreit": Die Dokumentation der Kontroverse um die Einzigartigkeit der nationalsozialistischen Judenvernichtung*. Munich 1987; Reinhard Kuehnl, ed., *Vergangenheit, die nicht vergeht: Die "Historiker-Debatte". Dokumentation, Darstellung und Kritik*. Cologne 1987; Dan Diner, ed., *Ist der Nationalsozialismus Geschichte? Zu Historisierung und Historikerstreit*. Frankfurt/Main 1987; and Hilmar Hoffmann, ed., *Gegen den Versuch, Vergangenheit zu verbiegen*. Frankfurt/Main 1987.

[18] For a more detailed presentation of the "optimists," "pessimists," and "realists," see Andrei S. Markovits and Simon Reich: "Should Europe Fear the Germans?" In: *From Bundesrepublik to Deutschland: German Politics after Unification*, ed. by Michael Huelshoff, Andrei S. Markovits, and Simon Reich. Ann Arbor, Michigan 1993, pp. 271-289.

Jehuda Reinharz

Zionism and the Austrian Left
Before World War I

I. Historical Developments

Socialist and labor Zionist groupings emerged in Russia and Austria during the turbulent years that bridged the nineteenth and twentieth centuries. At the Seventh Zionist Congress, in 1905, they were no longer represented merely by individual delegates, but appeared as organized factions in the World Zionist Organization. Jewish labor parties arose out of the same anomalous situation that produced Zionism itself, as well as all other modern Jewish ideologies. Since Jews were both a dissident religious minority and a "depressed" group, the liberal leaders of Western Jewries found they could not rely solely on religious toleration and civic emancipation to solve the Jewish problem. They had to develop programs of cultural, social, and economic amelioration. The late nineteenth-century leftist ideologues, who were primarily concerned with social and economic issues, also realized that they could not deal with the problems of Eastern and East-Central European Jewries without confronting the issues of emancipation and anti-Semitism. Because liberals and leftists focused on different aspects of the same anomalous general-Jewish situation, as it developed in different regions at different periods, they shaped their views in response to characteristically different gentile counterparts or adversaries.

The debate between Zionists and the liberal leaders of Western Jewry centered on "assimilationism" — a term coined by the Zionists. It was based on the Western liberals' assumption that Jews, once emancipated, should not differ from their fellow-countrymen in anything other than their "religion" which was to be redefined in the narrowly ecclesiastical sense of Western churches and reshaped in the style of the locally prevalent Christian denomination.

In practice, the non-Zionist West did not, or could not, fully abide by the logic of this assumption. For Jewish emancipation, followed by a remarkably successful intellectual acculturation, economic advance, and — to a certain extent — social assimilation was countered by the rise of new, increasingly virulent forms of Jew-hatred. Until the emergence of Zionism, Jewish modernists adjusted to the anomaly in practice, while evading it intellectually, within a general ideology of liberalism. Excluded from German Masonic orders, student *Korps* or *Burschenschaften*, Jews formed their own parallel societies, but conducted them — in theory at least — as "nonsectarian" bodies. In addition, the local Jewish community, nominally organized for purely cultic functions, actually performed a considerable variety of intracommunal welfare services. Special agencies, like the *Alliance Israélite Universelle*, were active on an international scale, conducting a range of cultural, economic, and political projects no less comprehensive than those later envisioned by the Zionists; but they presented these activities in the guise of "philanthropic" assistance to their "coreligionists." These quite evidently ethnic functions veiled their national character under the publicly acceptable titles of general philanthropy and of a special responsibility for the need of one's own church.

Western Jewish philanthropy, extended to the Jewish community in Palestine, made possible Zionist and non-Zionist cooperation. Yet, at the same time, it gave cause for disputes over strategic and tactical theories. Although the roots of disagreement were ideological, such cooperation became possible in practice when reciprocal, or one-sided, concessions covered up underlying differences.

Leftist Zionism arose in a confrontation with socialist or social-revolutionary Jewish ideologies, primarily in the Russian and Austro-Hungarian empires. It had to contend with a Jewish opposition, usually dominant among the local left-oriented elements, that did not propose to reshape the Jewish community as a Western-style religion purged of ethnic attributes, regarded Jewishness, whether religious or ethnic, as an historical irrelevancy and a present-day encumbrance. That Jews were at once a religiously and ethnically defined community, a faith-group and a nationality, was not a matter of debate in Eastern and East-Central Europe. The question at issue was how this undisputed fact was to be dealt with in practice.

In the multinational Austro-Hungarian empire, the ethnic quality of the Jewish situation was enhanced by the additional factor of an ethnically divided electorate. The curial system permitted a number of Jewish representatives to be chosen even under the conditions of a highly restricted, as well as easily manipulated franchise.[1]

The liberal Jewish deputies, spokesmen for the established community leadership, adopted a singular policy: in a parliament where all other deputies grouped themselves according to ethnic interests and openly defended them, Jews alone took the mandate of their Jewish electors as instructions to submerge their ethnic identity. They were like the editor of the *Neue Freie Presse* about whom Herzl ironically remarked, "He belongs to a species which I have never seen: he is an Austrian."[2] Similar to the editor, they needed a neutral identification with the state in order to deny the existence of a Jewish people.

But there was no "Austrian" national formation with which to identify directly. The political establishment of the Dual Monarchy was based on a compact through which the German-speaking population, dominant over the empire as a whole, generally recognized Magyar dominance in Hungary and the dominance of Polish conservative aristocrats in Galicia. The Jews demonstrated that they were Austrian primarily by identifying with the German-speaking liberals; but also by joining the "club," or bloc, of Polish deputies, if elected in Galicia.[3] Similarly, German-speaking Jewish notables sided politically with the dominant Magyars in Hungary. But under this multicolored camouflage of "Austrian" neutrality, the Jewish deputies nonetheless defended special Jewish interests.

Thus, the theory that Jews were simply a religious sect, indistinguishable in all other respects from their fellow countrymen, was combined with patently ethnic practices by Jewish liberals. When Jewish nationalists arose, they sought to widen the functions and democratize the structure of the ethnic community, although it was already constituted on a fairly wide ethnic base. Consequently, Jewish "nationalism" expressed itself not so much in practice as in theories of Jewish social policy.[4] In this respect, Jewish nationalism differed from the Jewish establishment.

Viewing the activities of Jewish organizations as humanitarian aid in an openly ethnic, rather than coreligionist perspective, the nationalist program radicalized and politicized the whole range of already existing functions which had emerged due to the anomalous Jewish situation. Not only emigration was to be properly directed, so that it would produce an autonomous, concentrated settlement in a Jewish homeland. Local welfare and political activities too, in the view of the nationalists, were to be critically reviewed in terms of the principle of auto-emancipation. The aim of cultural reform was no longer the introduction of European culture into the Jewish ghetto in whatever language was convenient. Instead, Hebrew, the national language, or Yiddish, the folk language, were to be cultivated as the organ of a distinct cultural individuality. The aim of vocational reform was no longer to remove complaints against Jewish usury and make Jews acceptable in Gentile society. Instead, vocational retraining programs, producers', consumers', and credit cooperatives, as well as political and trade union struggles were proposed as a means of gaining the rights and protect the interests of oppressed Jewish workers. The social integration sought was to be one that solidified and activated an inner Jewish, autonomous consensus, not one that established Jews as a fully absorbed part of Gentile society. And Jewish political activity was to serve openly Jewish ends, whether it was directed toward the international problem of Jewish migration or the local problems inherent in each country's domestic politics.

Views like these were held not only by Zionists, who were most clearly and comprehensively committed to them. Eastern European Jewry also produced a variety of nationalist movements which pursued strategies that differed from the Zionists' goals. Hence they disagreed on the issue of Palestine as the proper place for concentrated Jewish resettlement. The question as to whether minority rights in the Diaspora rather than the solution of the Jewish problem in emigration should be the nationalist aim was another question often debated. Moreover, Eastern Europe produced a Jewish socialist movement which was strongly and explicitly concerned with the Jewish problem as an ethnic problem. Its approach to issues of Jewish social policy was based on presumptions similar to those of the Zionists than of Western Jewish liberals. In 1897, the very year when Herzl founded the World Zionist Organization, the Bund (*Algemeyner Yidisher Arbeter Bund in Lite, Poyln un Rusland*), a Jewish, social democratic, general labor organization was also founded.

Socialist Zionist parties arose within a political sphere whose polar antipodes were the *Bund*, on one side, and the World Zionist Organization, on the other. Jewish workers' groups and radical intellectuals, who felt attracted toward both organizations, but were unable to accept either fully, formed new parties suspended in dynamic tension between organized Zionism and organized Socialism and seeking to unite both ideas in an original synthesis.

The Austrian socialist movement had to face the nationality issue at its Brunn convention of 1899, when the South Slavs presented a proposal to reorganize Austria as a federation of **nations**, not of territories. The principle of "exterritorial" (or, as it was later called, "personal") national autonomy would be adopted, granting members of all ethnic groups throughout Austria the right to belong to national entities that autonomously administered their linguistic and cultural affairs. The party gave qualified recognition to this view in a novel compromise, later explained and elaborated as a new socialist nationality theory by Otto Bauer and Karl Renner. The party proposed to reorganize Austria as a democratic federation of **territories** constituted, as far as possible, on nationally homogeneous lines; but autonomous **regions** for each major nationality comprised within larger territorial units dominated by another nationality were to be designated and serve as the base for **unions** organized over the whole area of the federation to administer the national affairs of each ethnic group. As for the Social Democratic party itself, an earlier convention at Vienna in 1897, had already organized it as a federation of the socialist parties of the constituent nationalities of all Austria, without reference to territories.

It was quite obvious, and explicitly stated by the authors of the new policy, that these reforms included no solution to the Jewish question and were not to be applied to the Jews. The countrywide national unions of the Brünn program were based on autonomous national **regions**, not on the personal national identification of scattered **individuals**. Essentially, they were a method to bring some dispersed national minorities, like the Germans in Bohemia or Bukovina, under the protection of a national entity based on a territory where they were dominant. They were not intended for a minority like the Jews, scattered throughout the Empire.

Whatever the intentions of its authors, the Bauer-Renner theory admirably served the purposes of the *Bund* in Russia and Poland, especially if construed as justifying the principle of exterritorial autonomy in the form originally propounded by the South Slavs. The Bundists most committed to a Jewish "national" line (which they always carefully distinguished from a "nationalistic" line) could not rest content with their first formulas that took up the struggle for Jewish civil and political rights. A generation of Zionist critics of Jewish liberalism had stamped this kind of thing as a species of bourgeois assimilationism. Not only Zionists but socialists now talked — however vaguely — of national political **self-determination** and of national **cultural rights** as essential elements in any nationalities' program.

Nevertheless, it required a long and tedious internal discussion before the *Bund* could define its position on these matters. In 1899, the third *Bund* convention confined its Jewish demands to civil equality, and ignored national rights. The fifth convention, in 1903, split so evenly over the Jews' right to foster their own nationality and claim cultural autonomy that no resolution was adopted and the entire debate was dropped from the published account of the proceedings. Not until the sixth convention, in 1905, was a program of Jewish cultural autonomy finally accepted.[5]

The *Bund* was primarily interested in another feature of the Austrian model: the federal structure of the Social Democratic party, based on countrywide constituent parties of the several nationalities. Attempts on behalf of Jewish autonomous labor organization to adopt this principle met with sharp opposition in Congress Poland, the semiautonomous Russian province annexed at the Congress of Vienna. The Polish Socialist Party (P. P. S.) strongly opposed a separate Jewish labor organization in its area, and insisted that if any such body arose, it should at least support the Polish demand for full territorial autonomy for Russian Poland. In regard to the All-Russian Social Democratic Party, founded a year after the *Bund*, a different situation prevailed at first. The *Bund* played a decisive role in founding the Russian party, supplied some of its foremost leaders, and was one of its most successful exponents of mass action — largely confined to the centers of dense Jewish settlement in northern Russia. Under these circumstances, the *Bund* was conceded autonomy for the purpose of organizing the Jewish workers. In the beginning, there was not much argument about this.

But by 1903, the opposition to Jewish separatism had spread, affecting the second congress of the Russian Social Democrats. The *Bund* proposed to reorganize Russian social democracy as a federation, with its constituents being the socialist parties of the various Russian nationalities **without reference to the territories where they lived**. The latter point was of immediate concern, for the *Bund* was beginning to extend its activities to South Russian Jewish communities; there it encountered the same kind of opposition from the P. P. S. in Congress Poland. The Bundists were fully aware of the general hostility likely to be provoked by such demands. Accordingly, they declared their "federative statute" for the all-Russian party to be a "basis for negotiation" not an "ultimative" demand.[6] But their efforts were of no avail. They were so sharply rebuffed that the *Bund* was forced to leave the all-Russian party it had so significantly helped to create.

Other conflicts at that time completely broke up the unity of the Russian Social Democrats, which could no longer be reestablished until 1906. The *Bund* was among the parties then invited to rejoin and help reconstitute the all-Russian party. The *Bund*'s demands were now slightly altered. It no longer spoke of a federal organization of Russian social democracy, since in any case socialist parties of various nationalities were recognized by invitation to the reunion convention. It no longer asked to be recognized as the **only** socialist party entitled to organize Jews, but pleaded for its right to organize in all Russian territories. The *Bund* was not promoting a program of Jewish national cultural autonomy. Not daring to insist on the adoption of these principles by the all-Russian party, the *Bund* asked only that its own right to advance them be recognized. In the end, the *Bund* rejoined the all-Russian party with only partial satisfaction of its demands, such as its right to organize Jewish workers. Moreover, the assembly avoided giving any sanction to the *Bund*'s national cultural program by declaring that it had not yet considered this question.

The vacillations and hesitations of the *Bund* on Jewish national issues are easily understood if one considers the hostile attitude of other Russian radicals to the notion of a Jewish nationality. Although pogroms and open anti-Semitism were no longer condoned or encouraged for tactical reasons as they had been by Russian radicals in the 1880s, Bundists encountered sometimes an opposition that gave them a sense of special hostility oriented against them as **Jews**; for even Russian progressives were ambivalent toward the Jews' civil rights struggle, in particular their demand for national autonomy. In European socialist circles of that time anti-Semitism was viewed as an instrument deliberately employed by reactionaries precisely in order to win popular and labor support away from the left. But despite the leftist condemnation of anti-Semitism, leftists and liberal progressives to expose themselves to anti-Semitic attacks by fighting for Jewish causes too vigorously. Compared to the Social Revolutionaries and liberals, the Russian Social Democrats showed themselves particularly reserved in this respect.

In the eyes of nationally-inclined Jewish workers, the *Bund's* distinct handicap was that it felt compelled, at great cost, to find a place in the ranks of social democracy. Under such pressure, the *Bund* was unable to fight uncompromisingly for a more satisfactory attitude toward Jewish interests even on elementary issues like civil rights and anti-Semitism. Progressives and labor elements in the Zionist camp found much to criticize in the WZO, sharing in many cases the attitude of the *Bund*. A few years after 1897, when the WZO and the *Bund* were founded, such circles began to group themselves in various socialist Zionist formations.

II. "Autoemancipation" and Other Zionist Struggles

We have noted the ideological embarrassment of Jewish liberals and leftists forced by Diaspora conditions to conduct an ethnic policy. This problem posed inherent ideological difficulties for Zionists as well. The most clearly distinctive feature of Zionism in Eastern Europe was not the slogan of "autoemancipation," for this expressed an emotional attitude shared by other nationalists and, in some sense, by Bundists as well. What singled out Zionists was their doctrine that an exodus from Diaspora countries to Zion was the way to realize autoemancipation. Such a doctrine, if construed with rigid and simplistic consistency, would preclude Zionists from any concern with the domestic politics of the countries they planned to leave. Leftist anti-Zionists took just such a simplistic view of Zionism, attacking it as a defeatist, reactionary movement which diverted the Jewish masses from the barricades of the social revolution.

But Zionism was no more committed to a single principle than any other ideological movement. The rather complex compromises with cultural Zionism involved in formulating the Basel Program are a case in point. The fact that Herzl's early adherents included men with a strong commitment to both socialism and ethnic politics also had significant effects.

Noteworthy among them was Nathan Birnbaum, the most prominent pre-Herzlian Austrian Zionist. In his varied career, he ultimately went from liberal Zionism to traditionalist anti-Zionism. By the late 1890s, his increasingly intimate identification with the folklore, language and vital interests of the Eastern European masses had turned him into a socialist and Yiddishist. While Birnbaum naturally was suspicious and resentful of so meteoric a newcomer as Herzl, he saw in him a man with a dynamic political style who could be used to break the hold of the bourgeois establishment that dominated Hovevei-Zionism, as well as all other Jewish communal institutions. Together with his followers like Saul Raphael Landau, a young Galician student activist and Zionist journalist, he hoped to remold Zionism according to his own strategy. The revived Zionist organization initiated by Herzl was helpful in achieving these goals. The group of Zionist leftists also comprised the French Dreyfusards, Bernard Lazare (Lazare Marius Bernard), and Jacques Bahar. As newcomers to Jewish nationalism, like Herzl, they had no preconceived designs, but later their sympathies aligned them with the Austrian radicals.

Herzl, for his part, was interested in the support of Lazare and Bahar and in Landau's rather than Birnbaum's technical cooperation because he felt he could use such men in molding Zionist policy and organization according to his own design. Given the narrow compass of early inner-Zionist politics, confined as it was to a small group of men, this was a situation bound to end in bitter personal clashes. Apart from personalities, there were also strategic and tactical disagreements, centering on the issue of involvement in Diaspora politics.

At the time of Herzl's appearance, Austrian Zionists were engaged in controversy with a variety of antagonists in their immediate environment. They were opposed to the Jewish *Reichsrat* deputies who conducted a pro-German "Austrian," instead of an ethnic Jewish policy. They were critical of the Jewish magnates who maintained control of Jewish institutions by means of a restricted community franchise. They were sharply opposed to official anti-Jewish discrimination. They were up in arms against Polish and German anti-Semitic politicians, who pretended that there were no Jewish proletarians, and that all Jews were bourgeois oppressors of the autochthonous workers and peasants. They were hardly less critical of Social Democratic leaders, for some of them, although being Jewish, also ignored the existence of the Jewish poor and Jewish workers, and who refused to commit their party to a firm and open stand against anti-Semitism. Landau, who became the editor of *Die Welt*, Herzl's new Zionist journal, wanted to devote this organ to a militant attack on all these fronts, as well as to the main goal: propaganda for a charter to resettle Zion. By contrast, Birnbaum had more understanding for Herzl's view that Zionists must maintain neutrality on local issues. Consequently, he favored the idea of a Jewish People's Party, similar to other Austro-Hungarian nationality parties, in which Zionist and non-Zionist ethnic militants would join in action on Diaspora issues.

Herzl's approach to these matters may well be called simplistic, but it was certainly far from rigid. The compelling tactical reasons that made him try to suppress cultural questions (even though the Basel Program specified them as Zionist concerns) applied equally well to domestic politics in the Diaspora (to which Zionists did not commit themselves in Basel). The issues involved here could divide Zionists no less dangerously than their differences over culture. It is easy to see why Herzl wholeheartedly adopted at least one strategy of the Diaspora ethnic politicians. It is the attack on the undemocratic plutocracy that controlled the Jewish community. For Herzl could not act on behalf of the Jews in the diplomatic sphere if the community repudiated him. But he did not restrict himself entirely to those Diaspora issues where Zionism as such was under attack. He also was ready to use *Die Welt* to support the linguistic concession offered by the Austrian government to the Czechs, in pointed contrast to the liberal Jewish leaders who supported the German parties in their determined opposition. His main reasons, other than the joy of defying the Jewish establishment, were tactical: he hoped to gain sympathy for Zionism from the government by demonstrating his usefulness.

But this was one case where Landau, who tried to conduct Jewish ethnic politics through *Die Welt*, broke with Herzl's editorial policy. The line Landau favored was one of complete neutrality on this and other disputes between Austro-Hungarian Gentile nationalities. He wanted the Jews to be recognized as an independent political interest, and not subordinated to any other national bloc.

Another source of irritation was Herzl's rather equivocal attitude to the publication in *Die Welt* of attacks on anti-Semitism. He welcomed such attacks when levelled against Social Democrats who failed to disavow Jew-hatred, but he was sometimes less than enthusiastic about complaints regarding anti-Jewish discrimination by public officials. In his view, anti-Semitism would not be ended by Jewish agitation against it, but by the exodus Zionism would ultimately organize; and for this end, Zionism needed an understanding with the authorities, who were anti-Semites themselves.

Two opposed interests heightened the friction. Herzl's efforts to set up Zionist financial instruments and gain the support and confidence of substantial investors aroused acute suspicions among the radicals. Herzl for his part was cool to their efforts at labor organization and strongly rebuffed their attempts to obtain labor representation in the WZO.

Herzl frequently expressed his personal sympathy for oppressed workers, certainly for the Jewish poor. His antipathy toward the wealthy Jewish employers and community leaders, who were the main objects of radical attack, was equally open. But, considering the legal complications which already hindered the effective functioning of the Zionist executive,

even in relatively liberal Vienna, Herzl thought it essential to avoid
Zionist involvement in European domestic politics. Above all, he rejected
any Zionist association with socialism, for it was precisely the suspicion
of such a connection that he knew would shut certain doors to him in
high quarters. He did not hide his displeasure when Max Nordau made
a speech in Vienna leaning too far toward the socialists. He was at pains
on several occasions to explain away incidents which betrayed radical
sentiments among Zionist congress delegates, directed especially against
the Russian and Turkish autocrats.

Given these circumstances, it is not surprising that the most active
radicals, Birnbaum, Landau, Lazare, and Bahar, soon left the WZO.
Birnbaum remained active for a while, and Landau for a longer period,
in radical nationalist formations outside the Herzlian Zionist movement.
No opponents earned angrier and more contemptuous epithets from
Herzl's pen than these men and their associates. They, for their part,
joined in a chorus of criticism levelled against the Zionists by their
opponents. Not only traditionalists and liberals, but ethnically-oriented
critics conducted this polemic since the beginning of Zionism. The latter
foemen not only shared the Zionist mythos of autoemancipation, but
claimed to be its most authentic protagonists. It was the very point of
their attack on the Zionists to charge that the Hovevei-Zionists and the
WZO had betrayed the spirit of autoemancipation.

Such a tone was frequently taken in the circles from which the *Bund*
arose. Julius Martov's dictum that "a class which cannot fight for its
freedom does not deserve freedom," echoes the Marxist slogan that the
workers' liberation must be won by the workers themselves. It even more
clearly evokes overtones of the Zionist cry of "autoemancipation," for the
"class" in question is pointedly identified with the Jewish ethnic group.
Moreover, while making the proud claim that they themselves were the
fighters who would achieve Jewish autoemancipation, the socialists
coupled this boast with reproaches to other Jews who shamefully failed
the task:

> Upon us, the Jewish proletariat, fell the unpleasant fate of being
> exploited by the lowest, most shameless bourgeoisie in the world.
> Robbed not only of political rights, like all the Russian
> bourgeoisie, but also of civil rights, our bourgeoisie does not seek
> ways to better its lot but simply waits for the gracious kindness
> of the Russian government. It does not even occur to our
> bourgeois intelligentsia that only through energetic independent
> action can Jews expect any improvement of their position.[7]

The "bourgeoisie" referred to here implicitly includes the Hovevei-Zionist
movement. After the emergence of Herzlian Zionism, Bundist propa-

ganda, now issued in the name of a countrywide movement, took occasion to make this point explicit:

> The Zionists kowtow and lick the hand of the slaughterer of the whole Jewish people, the Czarist autocracy, the atrocious, thieving Czarist autocracy that made paupers, beggars, sick, weak, and feeble wretches out of the Jews.... You tell us to hide in a corner so that, God forbid, no one should notice and trample on us; keep our heads bowed as lowly as possible, so we should not catch anyone's eye; speak quietly, like a beggar at the door; beg for mercy and kindness.... That's how the Zionists talk, the same Zionists who always yell about national and personal self respect, national pride and self consciousness and other such jabber and keep attacking "slavery within freedom"! ... If the West European Jewish bourgeoisie is sunk in "slavery within freedom," then you, the Zionist Russian bourgeoisie, are sunk in a still bigger pile of muck — in "slavery within slavery."[8]

A similar critique of Zionism developed among populist, progressive intellectuals. In an open letter from "A Jew to the Jews," published as a Russian pamphlet in 1892 by the populist Fund of the Free Russian Press in London, Chaim Zhitlowsky scolded the Jewish intelligentsia for neglecting their own people. Zhitlowsky, who in the course of his variegated, mercurial career, was also a brilliant founder and paradoxical leader of both Zionist and anti-Zionist nationalist labor factions, elaborated his own program through a critical appreciation and analysis of the Hovevei-Zionist alternative.

Zionism, he noted, was "a sheer utopia" in its positive program; but, in other respects, it was "a national movement ...not incapable of certain progressive elements," and its "critique of the present situation [was] ... in accord with the simple truth" at many points:

> The Hovevei-Zionists criticize the Jewish position on two main points, which are indeed the most serious. The first point is the ethical degeneration of the Jewish people, a consequence of an urban commercial life; the second point is the severe decline in autonomous national activism among the Jews, who place all their hopes for reform and improvements on influential intercessors in high quarters.[9]

But, owing to its utopian character, Zionism could not be the instrument for either of the remedies correctly indicated by its analysis. Instead, it degenerated into a reactionary force striving "to preserve among the people the mystique of religious nationalism and, with its own hands, pulling chestnuts out of the fire for the future Jewish landlords and kulaks in Palestine." The solution of the Jewish problem had, therefore, to be undertaken by the radical intelligentsia through a revised populist tactical approach. First they had to organize the Jewish masses, together with all Russian workers and peasants, in order to accomplish the revolutionary seizure of political rights. Then, after the revolution, they had to organize the mass of Jews for rural resettlement in Russia, for the "return to the soil" implied in their view the end of anti-Semitism. Finally, as producers rather than parasites, the Jews would no longer be under the pressure to assimilate, but would be recognized as a family among equal nationalities in Russia.

The rise of Herzl caused Simon Dubnow, a liberal constitutionalist, to develop in a series of articles, the most extensive critique and elaborate alternative to Zionism which had ever been written by a non-Zionist nationalist. His "Letters on Old and New Judaism" published in *Voskhod* from 1897 on engaged in arguments with various schools of Zionist thought. In these letters Dubnow laid bare the "utopian" character of Zionism and expounded his own "autonomist" proposals, elaborated on the basis of the nationalities theory of the Austrian Social Democrats.

In the sixth letter, originally published in 1898, he offered the following analysis of Herzl's recently concluded Congress:

> Political Zionism is thus a web of fantasies: the dream of the creation of a Jewish state guaranteed by international law, the dream of colonizing a great part of the Jewish people, and the dream of finding the solution of the Jewish problem in this manner.
>
> What remains of the Basel Program in practice? I believe only the second and third [sub] paragraphs of the Program: the "organization of the Jews" and the "strengthening of the national consciousness." These principles, which are also included in [Dubnow's] theory of autonomism, together with the gradual extension of the settlement of Palestine, will be the outstanding results of the Zionist effort. To this end, however, the Zionists must become sober, and understand that the "return to Judaism" [proclaimed in Herzl's Congress address] is the chief goal and not a means for the (illusionary) establishment of a Jewish state. Otherwise the failure of political Zionism may cause even greater spiritual disillusionment than the despair brought about by the failure of assimilation.[10]

Thus, at the turn of the century, radical but ethnically oriented critics outside the WZO had established a canon for the progressive nationalist attack on official Zionist policy. It condemned Herzlian neglect of the political struggle in the Diaspora, demanded immediate action to improve the social and economic position of the Jewish masses, and tended to defend the right of the Jews to preserve their national, cultural individuality in perpetuity in the Diaspora. All these themes also occur in the polemics against the official line conducted by the Democratic Faction within the World Zionist Organization.

III. "Gegenwartsarbeit" A Bridge Between Zionism and the Left?

Within the Zionist orbit, programs of Diaspora activity were referred to as *Gegenwartsarbeit*, that is, actively concerned with "immediate," rather than "ultimate," Jewish problems. Such a program was obviously timely, in view of the halting progress of Herzlian diplomacy toward the ultimate goal. Consequently, Herzl's followers, as well as the internal opposition, formulated pertinent proposals. Herzlians stressed the generally accepted Zionist assumption that Jews could pursue a true "**national** policy" only in relation to Zion. In the Diaspora, there could be only Jewish "**social** policy."

> For us Zionists, who strive towards a radical solution of the Jewish problem and regard all immediate policy (*Gegenwartspolitik*) as only a means to an end, a "way station," **Jewish social policy remains as before only a provisional program** (*Gegenwartsprogramm*)), which we break down into the **special problems of the spiritual, economic, and corporal advancement** of the Jewish people.

On this basis, it was argued that Zionist Diaspora activities must be restricted to the "forum internum" — that is, such Diaspora politics as Zionists conducted should be confined to the "conquest of the communities."[11] But within these limits a fairly elaborate program of Zionist social reform and welfare activities in the Diaspora was outlined.

The internal Zionist opposition viewed the matter in a rather different light. Like Dubnow and other nationalist critics outside the WZO, these Zionists held Herzl responsible for neglecting Diaspora affairs, and they proposed a *Gegenwartsprogramm* as a major reform in Zionism. In contrast to Herzl who had antagonized men like Birnbaum and Lazare, they hoped to attract not only such veteran progressive Zionists, but also the progressive Jewish youth. Through activity in local Diaspora affairs, they decentralized and democratized the Herzlian Zionist organization.

As Martin Buber's presentation of *Gegenwartsarbeit* shows all these positions were derived from a theory which, like Dubnow's or Ahad Ha'am's, placed primary emphasis on the reestablishment of Jewish solidarity and consensus. The Zionist interest in *Gegenwartsarbeit*, he said, was not produced because of the fading prospects of achieving the Herzlian ultimate goal. In fact, faith in the future goal made work on the tasks of the present possible. The rational, objective necessities of Zionism had the primary effect of arousing enthusiasm among disoriented Jews. The actual tasks of Zionism, however, had not fully satisfied the subjective needs of young progressives until the movement reached its present, new stage. A new, reflective Zionism, understanding the objective and subjective significance of the movement as one, had now attained the level of historical self-determination.

> Inward and outward awareness complemented each other: we became more autonomous vis-à-vis the movement. We went our separate ways; but **one** idea united us: we share in a movement where political action represents only the indispensable ultimate consequence, requiring the strictest and tightest centralization, and where organization and agitation are only widely ramified and indispensable instruments, which must be relatively decentralized and be entrusted to those specifically qualified. The essence and soul of the movement, however, we see in the transformation of national life (*Volksleben*), in the education of a truly **new** generation, in the development of the Jewish people (*Stamm*) into a strong, united, autonomous, healthy, and mature community (*Gemeinschaft*). That is, in those processes which, at the moment, are inadequately expressed by the slogan of "advancement" (*Hebung*) conveyed to us by the London [fourth Zionist] congress.[12]

Following the London congress, Austrian Zionists held a convention at Olmuetz (Olomouc) on March 24-25, 1901, at which the Herzlian and opposition members established a unified territorial organization for the whole Austrian monarchy. Berthold Feiwel, of the emerging Democratic Faction, introduced a proposal for Diaspora activities which was adopted by the convention. It developed in greater detail lines of action familiar to Austrian Zionists before Herzl, and more recently revived in a Zionist party platform which had been prepared on the occasion of communal elections. Under the heading of economic advancement, it proposed to establish Zionist employment exchanges, vocational training in the crafts, planning and control of communal social welfare work, trade unions, and producers', consumers', and credit cooperatives. Under the heading of cultural advancement, it called for the creation of adult education centers (Toynbee Halls), reading rooms and libraries, mobile libraries and newspaper exchanges, courses, lecture series, educational publications and services, Hebrew language and Jewish art societies, and clubhouses. Under the heading of corporal advancement, it promoted the establishment of athletic and gymnastic societies, medical services, and medical and recuperative centers.

Another line of nationalist Diaspora activity discussed at that time was Zionist participation, through a Jewish ethnic party, in general elections and political affairs. The pre-Herzlian Austrian Zionists had committed themselves to this line; indeed, Diaspora nationalists had contended with strict Hovevei-Zionists within the movement over primacy for local ethnic politics or for Palestine resettlement in the Zionist program. In September 1900, Adolf Stand, a veteran leader of Galician Zionists, proposed to Herzl that the movement put up candidates in the elections to the Austrian parliament which were about to be held. It was decided to maintain, however, the policy of not presenting Zionist candidates. Instead, other candidates were to be asked to indicate their sympathy for Zionist aims in order to earn Jewish support. Only after the call for elections to the first Russian Duma in 1905, and the broadening of the franchise in Austria in 1907, did Zionists participate as an ethnic party in general elections and politics.

In WZO debates at the turn of the century, Zionist radicals joined in opposition to the Herzlian policies which had estranged men like Birnbaum and Lazare. Among those closely associated with the group that founded the Democratic Faction was Nachman Syrkin, the stormy petrel of the movement, whose socialist views, fully developed in his 1898 essay, "The Socialist Jewish State," were often and vigorously proclaimed at the early Zionist congresses. In Russia, the potential popular strength of the Zionist opposition was largely concentrated in newly organized study circles and workers' organizations similar to those of the socialists. These societies maintained contact with the WZO through a center for correspondence conducted by Dr. Jacob Bernstein-Kohan, a Russian member of the Zionist Action Committee, a man whose brother was a famous revolutionary and political prisoner. Bernstein-Kohan was kept under surveillance by the authorities because of his reputed radical connections.

In spite of these bonds and affinities, outright socialism found scarcely more room in the Democratic Faction than earlier in the WZO. From the beginning, that is the earliest discussions about founding a progressive Zionist students' and workers' faction, Nachman Syrkin tried in vain to gain support in the Democratic Faction for his socialist Zionist theory and strategy. He proposed two separate plans of activity, both to be conducted according to socialist-Zionist principles. In Palestine, or another suitable territory, a Jewish socialist commonwealth was to be created by cooperative settlements of immigrant workers. In the Diaspora, Zionists were to cooperate with the social democratic revolutionary parties, on condition that the latter abandoned their hostility to Jewish nationalism. When these proposals were rejected, Syrkin attempted to create a socialist-Zionist movement of his own, in direct rivalry with the emerging Democratic Faction. The Faction itself considered proposals to pursue the economic advancement of the Jewish masses through training, cooperative institutions and similar nonpolitical methods in the Diaspora. But in the end, it lost its specific progressive coloration completely, merging into the common front of practical Zionists concerned with the Uganda issue.

Notes

[1] Marsha L. Rozenblit: *The Jews of Vienna 1867-1914.* Albany 1983. William A. Jencks: *The Austrian Electoral Reform of 1907.* New York 1974.

[2] Theodor Herzl: *Diaries,* ed. by Raphael Pata, trans. by Harry Zohn. New York 1960, Vol. 1, p. 1626.

[3] C. A. Macartney: *The Habsburg Empire 1790-1918.* New York 1969.

[4] Anna Drabek, Wolfgang Häusler, Kurt Schubert, et. al.: *Das Österreichische Judentum. Voraussetzungen und Geschichte.* Vienna and Munich 1974, pp. 103-140.

[5] See Haim S. Kasdan: "Der Bund bis dem Finftn Tsuzemanfor." In: *Di Geshikhte fun Bund,* ed. by Aaronson, Gregori, et al. New York 1960, Vol. 1, pp. 156, 180-181; Grigori Aaronson: *Di Natsionale un Organizatsionele Frage,* Vol. 2, pp. 499-500.

[6] Ibid., pp. 180-181.

[7] "Der vendpunkt in der geshikte fun der yidishe arbeterbavegung, 1895." In: *YIVO Historishe Shriftn* 3, 1939, p. 650.

[8] I. S. Hertz: "Der Bund un di Andere Rikhtungen." In: *Di Geshikhte fun Bund,* Vol. 1, p. 351.

[9] Haim Zhitlovsky: "A Yid tsu Yidn." In: *Gezamelte Shriftn,* Vol. 6 (1917), pp. 49-51.

[10] Simon Dubnow: *Nationalism and History: Essays on Old and New Judaism.* Philadelphia 1958, p. 164.

[11] Philipp Menczel: "Jüdische National and Realpolitik." In: *Die Welt* 5, Number 4, January 25, 1901.

[12] Martin Buber: "Gegenwartsarbeit." In: *Die Welt* 5, Number 6, February 8, 1901, p.4.

Marion Kaplan

Schwesterlichkeit auf dem Prüfstand: Feminismus und Antisemitismus in Deutschland, 1904–1938[1]

I. Der Jüdische Frauenbund zwischen Judentum und Feminismus

Deutsche Jüdinnen waren aufgrund ihres ethnisch/religiösen Erbes und ihres Geschlechts gesellschaftlich doppelt gefährdet: als Jüdinnen waren sie Diskriminierungen seitens der Nichtjuden ausgesetzt und als Frauen wurden sie in ihren eigenen jüdischen Gemeinden wie Bürger zweiter Klasse behandelt. Während jüdische Männer das Wahlrecht in Deutschland bereits Jahrzehnte zuvor erhalten hatten, mußten Jüdinnen warten, bis das deutsche Frauenstimmrecht im Jahre 1918 gesetzlich verankert wurde. Das war für jüdische Frauen ein säkularer Sieg, denn bei jüdischen Gemeindewahlen war ihnen immer noch die politische Stimme verwehrt. In der zweiten Hälfte des neunzehnten Jahrhunderts hatten deutsche Frauen bescheidene Verbesserungen ihrer sozialen und politischen Lage erzielt, z. B. Stellungen im Lehrberuf (1860-80) und Beamtentum (1880-90) gefunden; an diesen Fortschritten hatten jüdische Frauen nicht teil, weil die antisemitische Einstellung ihrer Umwelt, sie daran hinderte. Dennoch profitierten deutsch-jüdische Frauen im Deutschen Kaiserreich von den politischen und wirtschaftlichen Erfolgen der jüdischen Männer sowie der Feministinnen, insbesondere von der Zulassung der Frauen zu Hochschulstudien, zur Ausübung akademischer Berufe und politischer Betätigung. Um die Jahrhundertwende war es jüdischen Mittelschichtsfrauen zunehmend möglich, ihre Fähigkeiten jenseits von Heim und Familie einzusetzen. Sie waren in der Frauenbewegung sowie in den jüdischen Wohlfahrtseinrichtungen tätig, konnten zudem eine Hochschulausbildung und den Zugang zu einer Berufskarriere erhalten.

1904, anläßlich der Konferenz des *International Council of Women*, gründeten Jüdinnen aus der deutschen Frauenbewegung und Mitglieder der orthodoxen jüdischen Frauenvereine unter der Leitung von Bertha Pappenheim[2], einer begeisterten Feministin und gläubigen Jüdin, den *Jüdischen Frauenbund* (JFB). Bertha Pappenheims Organisation, deren Vorsitzende sie jahrelang war, gewann eine breite Anhängerschaft: 50.000 Frauen; etwa 20 Prozent aller Jüdinnen über dreißig. Bis 1938 sollte der

JFB eine entscheidende Rolle in der jüdischen Gemeinde spielen und bis
1933 eine wichtige Funktion in der deutschen Frauenbewegung erfüllen.

Der Frauenbund verknüpfte feministische Zielsetzungen — "Für Frauen-
arbeit und Frauenbewegung"[3] — mit einem ausgeprägten Gefühl für das
Judentum. Zu seinen Aufgaben zählten: 1. Die Stärkung des jüdischen
Gemeinschaftsgefühls; 2. die Unterstützung der bürgerlichen Frauen-
bewegung und ihrer Ziele; 3. die Förderung der Frauen in jüdischen
Gemeinden, vor allem ihre Gleichberechtigung mit den Männern; 4. die
Berufsausbildung jüdischer Frauen; 5. die Bekämpfung der Immoralität,
insbesondere des Mädchenhandels. In der Unterstützung der bürgerlichen
Frauenbewegung unterschied sich der JFB von anderen vorher oder zur
gleichen Zeit bestehenden jüdischen Frauenorganisationen.[4] Seine
Forderungen waren im wesentlichen reformistisch, nicht nur von der
Stellung der Frau im Judentum geprägt, sondern auch von der Situation
von Juden und Frauen in Deutschland und damit von der Allgegenwart
des Antisemitismus und der Unnachgiebigkeit des Antifeminismus. Um
politisch Einfluß zu gewinnen, ließ sich der JFB auf traditionelle liberale
Strategien ein. Gleichzeitig entwickelte er jedoch eine eigene Alternative
zur "Männermacht", indem er eine Organisation "von Frauen für Frauen"
aufbaute.

Der JFB spiegelte die sozio-ökonomische Lage deutscher Jüdinnen
wider, die größernteils der Mittelschicht angehörten.[5] Sie waren
Hausfrauen, die keiner Erwerbsarbeit nachgingen, weder eine akade-
mische Ausbildung noch Bindungen an die Welt der Intellektuellen oder
Arbeiter hatten. Der Eintritt in die Organisationen der Akademikerinnen
oder in Arbeiterinnenvereine kam für sie nicht in Frage. Der JFB bot
diesen Mitgliedern die Möglichkeit, mit gleichgesinnten Frauen zusam-
menzukommen, Frauen, die denselben religiösen wie kulturellen Background hatten. Repräsentantinnen der jüdischen Arbeiterklasse waren im
JFB nicht vertreten, obwohl diese meistens die Adressatinnen der sozialen
Dienstleistungen des JFB waren. Die jüdische Arbeiterklasse setzte sich
aus osteuropäischen Juden und ihren Familien zusammen, die in mehre-
ren aufeinanderfolgenden Wellen nach Deutschland eingewandert waren.
Diese Juden waren meist im Kleinhandel oder in der Leichtindustrie
beschäftigt. Nicht nur Arbeiterinnen, auch jüngere Frauen blieben dem
Bund fern. In der Kriegs- und Nachkriegszeit, als die Bevölkerung unter
den Wirtschaftskrisen litt, gelang es dem JFB nicht, junge Frauen zum
Eintritt in die Organisation zu bewegen. So waren in den dreißiger Jahren
nur wenige junge Gesichter unter den Verwitweten und alternden Mitgliedern zu finden.[6] Obwohl der Gegensatz zwischen orthodoxem Judentum und Feminismus unüberbrückbar zu sein schien und zu Spannungen
im Leben und Wirken der JFB Mitglieder führte, war keine dieser Frauen
bereit, ihren jüdischen Glauben zugunsten einer radikalen feministischen
Position aufzugeben oder gar die jüdische Herkunft zu verleugnen.[7] Dies

war ein generelles Dilemma der damaligen Mino-ritäten, die sich ihrer andersartigen Umwelt anpassen, aber dennoch ihre ethnische Besonderheit nicht aufgeben wollten. Der Verlust der jüdischen Identität wäre für sie ein zu hoher Preis für die soziale Anerkennung gewesen. So begrüßten sie zwar die Akkulturation, nicht aber die totale Assimilation. Diese Haltung war bei Juden in Deutschland nicht ungewöhnlich. Viele Juden hatten ihre Emanzipation als Chance begriffen, 'als Juden in die Reihen der anderen Bürger' aufgenommen zu werden und nicht als Aufforderung, lediglich die Nichtjuden nachzuahmen.[8] Tatsächlich läßt das Ausmaß jüdischer Organisations- und Gemeindeaktivitäten einen sehr positiven Gemeinschaftsgeist erkennen, der vom Antisemitismus häufig verstärkt, aber nicht von ihm verursacht wurde. Gerade diese Vitalität der jüdischen Gemeinde, die auch in ihrer deutschen Umgebung eine gewisse Unabhängigkeit bewahren konnte, machte letztendlich viele Juden für die Realitäten Nazideutschlands blind.

Doch die jüdischen Feministinnen waren ebensowenig gewillt, Frauenziele für die jüdische Solidarität zu opfern. Sie beharrten auf beiden Positionen, und ihre Kampagnen zeigen, welche politischen und gesellschaftlichen Hürden sie in Deutschland zu überwinden hatten. Innerhalb der jüdischen Gemeinde kämpfte der JFB um die Gleichberechtigung der Frauen, ihre Berufsausbildung und versuchte, dem Mädchenhandel ein Ende zu bereiten. Zur Unterstützung der Berufsausbildung für Frauen richtete der JFB Arbeitsvermittlungen ein, Berufberatungszentren, Abendkurse zur Verbesserung beruflicher Fähigkeiten und mehrere Schulen, die Kurse in den traditionell weiblichen Bereichen Hauswirtschaft, Kinderpflege, elementare Gesundheitsfürsorge und Sozialarbeit anboten. Die jüdischen Feministinnen bestanden darauf, daß Hausarbeit genauso anzuerkennen sei wie andere Arbeit, lehnten aber die Haltung ab, die Frau gehöre *ausschließlich* ins Haus. Die Berufstätigkeit wurde als Mittel zur ökonomischen, psychologischen und emotionalen Unabhängigkeit angesehen, und der JFB rechnete damit, daß die erwerbstätigen Frauen zunehmend ein politischer Faktor würden. Es bereitete den Mitgliedern des JFB Sorge, daß sich das Berufsprofil der deutschen Juden so auffällig von dem aller anderen Deutschen unterschied. Ein Ergebnis jahrhundertelanger Diskriminierung sowie beschränkter Möglichkeiten der Berufswahl war die Konzentration der Juden im Handel. Im Jahre 1925 waren beispielsweise fünfunddreißig Prozent der Jüdinnen im Handel beschäftigt und drei Prozent in der Landwirtschaft, während es bei nichtjüdischen Frauen vierzehn bzw. vierunddreißig Prozent waren.[9] Angesichts des extremen Antisemitismus während und nach dem Ersten Weltkrieg engagierten sich jüdische Organisationen, darunter auch der JFB für eine Politik der Umschulung der jüdischen Mitbürger, die angeleitet wurden, Berufe zu ergreifen, die typisch für die deutsche Bevölkerung der damaligen Zeit waren. So suchten junge Männer Arbeit in der Industrie, im Handwerk und in der Landwirtschaft, während jüdische Mädchen hauswirtschaftliche Berufe ergriffen.

Der JFB bekämpfte die gewerbsmäßige Prostitution sowie den Handel mit jüdischen Frauen aus Osteuropa, die ins Ausland gelockt, in die Prostitution gezwungen und häufig an Bordelle verkauft wurden.[10] Um Kupplern das Handwerk zu legen, richtete der JFB in Bahnhöfen und Häfen Anlaufstellen für alleinreisende Frauen ein, bot bedürftigen jungen Frauen und weiblichen Reisenden Essen, Unterkunft, finanzielle Hilfe und Information. Er organisierte außerdem gesellige Abende für junge Frauen in Deutschland, um "sie von der Straße fernzuhalten" und ihren Sinn für die jüdische Gemeinschaft zu stärken. Als Teil eines "vorbeugenden Programms" unterstützte der JFB berufs- und allgemeinbildende Institute für jüdische Mädchen in Osteuropa und schickte Lehrerinnen und Krankenschwester dorthin. Er gab auch Broschüren heraus, die vor den Gefahren des Mädchenhandels warnten. Der JFB arbeitete mit nationalen und internationalen Wohlfahrtsorganisationen zusammen und gründete in Deutschland das erste jüdische Heim für gefährdete Mädchen, ledige Mütter und uneheliche Kinder. Das Eintreten für eine Verbesserung der Lage lediger Mütter und die Sorge um die jüdischen Prostituierten (die "irrenden jungen Schwestern") waren die radikalsten Angriffe des JFB auf die Normen der eigenen, jüdischen Gesellschaft.

Bertha Pappenheim hielt der jüdischen Gemeinde vor, sie mache sich der Komplizenschaft schuldig, wenn sie nichts gegen Verbrechen dieser Art unternähme. Da man gegen Juden den Vorwurf erhoben hatte, am Prostitutionsnetz beteiligt zu sein, forderte Bertha Pappenheim jüdische Gemeinden auf, sich aktiv im Kampf gegen den Mädchenhandel einzusetzen. Auf diese Weise hoffte sie, dem Argwohn und Antisemitismus unter den Gegnern des Mädchenhandels entgegenzuwirken. Da Bertha Pappenheims Ansicht nach extreme Armut und Unterdrückung der osteuropäischen Juden die hauptsächlichen Ursachen für deren Verstrickung im Prostitutionsnetz waren, setzte sie sich für eine Verbesserung der wirtschaftlichen und sozialen Lage der jüdischen Frauen ein. Die Aktionen des JFB waren keine einfache Rettungsmission und kein Kreuzzug gegen das Laster. Als Feministinnen wollten die JFB Mitglieder die Aufmerksamkeit der Mitmenschen auf die sexuelle Unterdrückung der Frau lenken, die traditionellen Geschlechterrollen hinterfragen und die Stellung der Frauen im Judentum verbessern.

Der Kampf um politische Mitsprache in der jüdischen Gemeinde war die schwierigste Aufgabe des JFB. Der JFB bestand darauf, daß Frauen in jeder Hinsicht am Gemeindeleben beteiligt werden sollten, und zwar nicht nur als "Ehrendamen" oder Mitarbeiterinnen von "Festkomitees". Als die Frauen nach dem Ersten Weltkrieg in Deutschland das Wahlrecht erhielten, erwarteten die Jüdinnen das gleiche Recht und hofften auf die Unterstützung der jüdischen Gemeinde. Sie wurden bitter enttäuscht und mußten den Kampf um politische Gleichberechtigung allein fortsetzen.[11] Sie veranstalteten öffentliche Versammlungen, eine Frauen-Stimmrecht-woche, warben für ihre Ziele in jüdischen Zeitungen und führten gerichtliche Auseinandersetzungen. Gegen Ende der zwanziger Jahre hatten sie in sechs der sieben wichtigsten deutschen Städte (in denen mehr als die Hälfte aller deutschen Juden lebten) und in verschiedenen Gegenden Süd- und Westdeutschlands das Gemeinde-Wahlrecht errun-gen.[12] Die Mehrzahl der jüdischen Frauen war also wahlberechtigt. Sie hatten dadurch zwar weder Macht noch Einfluß, aber wenigstens die formale Gleichberechtigung gewonnen.

Diese Kampagnen zur Verbesserung des gesellschaftlichen Status und der Lebensbedingungen von Frauen, aber vor allem der Frauenbund selbst mit seinen 485 Lokalen und 20 Bezirksvereinen gab seinen Mit-gliedern ein Gefühl von Solidarität und Stärke; er lehrte sie, sich selbst zu helfen und auf diese Weise Selbstachtung zu gewinnen. Die JFB Mit-glieder, die für ihre bedürftigeren Schwestern die eine oder andere soziale Verbesserung erreicht hatten, wurden aufgrund ihrer öffentlichen Tätigkeit emanzipierter. In Interviews, die 40 Jahre nach der Auflösung des JFB mit ehemaligen Mitgliedern geführt wurden, ist immer noch ein uneingeschränkter Enthusiasmus zu spüren. Er zeugt von der Bedeutung des JFB für die persönliche Entwicklung dieser Frauen, die durch Arbeit für andere Frauen sich selbst verwirklichen und Selbstvertrauen ge-winnen konnten.

II. Die Grenzen schwesterlicher Solidarität

Der *Jüdische Frauenbund* arbeitete, mit anderen Frauenorganisationen zusammen. Die Mitglieder des Vorstandes, aber auch andere einzelne Repräsentantinnen des JFB nahmen an Konferenzen des *Deutschen Staats-bürgerinnenverbandes*, des *Weltbundes für Frauenstimmrecht*, der inter-nationalen Organisationen gegen den Mädchenhandel und der deutschen und internationalen *Abolitionistischen Föderation* teil. [13] Der JFB, der sich selbst für einen "wichtigen Faktor" in der deutschen Frauenbewegung hielt — eine Selbsteinschätzung, mit der andere nicht unbedingt überein-stimmten — akzeptierte den *Bund Deutscher Frauenvereine* als Modell. So schrieb Bertha Pappenheim: "Die deutsche Frauen-bewegung hat den zögernden, unsicheren Vorstößen der jüdischen Frauen Richtung und Vertrauen gegeben."[14]

Der BDF bejahte die konventionellen Vorstellungen, daß es zwischen den Geschlechtern fundamentale Unterschiede gibt, die sie dazu be-stimmen, jeweils wichtige, aber unterschiedliche Funktionen zu erfüllen.

Auch der Frauenbund glaubte, die mütterlichen Instinkte der Frau, ihre Aufopferungsbereitschaft, ihre Milde und Geduld seien eine Ergänzung zum Tatendrang und Unternehmungsgeist des Mannes. Wie der BDF betonte auch der JFB stets die Pflichten und Aufgaben der Frau und stellte nicht die Fragen der Gleichberechtigung in den Mittelpunkt der Diskussionen, die ein zentrales Anliegen des anglo-amerikanischen Feminismus war. Die Mitglieder des JFB stellten den *Status quo* der Frauen allerdings indirekt in Frage, in dem sie traditionell akzeptierte Werte und Rollenvorstellungen bekämpften. Auch taktisch verhielt sich der JFB ähnlich wie der BDF. Beide lehnten die politische Agitation ab und wählten unaufdringlichere Methoden. Sie reichten Petitionen ein, veröffentlichten Informationen und klärten die nicht organisierten Frauen über die Ziele des Feminismus auf. Bis auf ein paar Ausnahmen waren sie meistens bürgerliche Damen, die auf die öffentliche Meinung bedacht waren und jede Radikalität scheuten, um Feindseligkeiten zu vermeiden.

Von 1907 bis 1933 gehörte der JFB dem *Bund Deutscher Frauenvereine* an, der 1921 etwa 220.000 Mitglieder stark war; diesem Verband war auch der *Deutsch-Evangelische Frauenbund*, der 1928 ungefähr 200.000 Mitglieder zählte, von 1908 bis 1918 angeschlossen. Bertha Pappenheim, die von 1914 bis 1924 im Vorstand des BDF amtierte, vertrat die Ansicht, jüdische Frauen, die in deutschen Organisationen arbeiteten, könnten dem Antisemitismus durch persönlichen Kontakt entgegenwirken. Die Zusammenarbeit mit deutschen Feministinnen war daher für Bertha Pappenheim ein Mittel, gegen Vorurteile anzukämpfen, aber auch ein Beweis, daß eine Freundschaft zwischen Juden und Deutschen möglich sei.

Bei aller Gemeinsamkeit vertrat der JFB in der Abtreibungsfrage eine andere Meinung als der BDF. Der JFB sah die eugenische Indikation nicht als zwingenden Grund für eine Abtreibung an. Er stützte sich auf das Argument, es gäbe "keinen wissenschaftlichen Nachweis, mit Hilfe dessen man mit Sicherheit die Wertigkeit des Neugeborenen analysieren könne"[15]. Diese ablehnenden Äußerungen über die eugenische Indikation sollte sich später angesichts des Gebrauchs, den die Nazis davon machten[16], als prophetisch erweisen.

Auch in Fragen von Frieden und Pazifismus, Hauptanliegen der internationalen Frauenbewegung, gab es nach anfänglicher Übereinstimmung mit dem BDF später entschiedene Differenzen. Während des Ersten Weltkriegs setzte sich der JFB für das "Vaterland" ein. Der JFB trat dem *Nationalen Frauendienst* bei, einer vom BDF gegründeten Organisation des freiwilligen Hilfsdienstes von Frauen im Kriege.[17] Nach dem Krieg schloß sich die jüdische Organisation der Friedensbewegung an, während der BDF eine mehr nationale Haltung vertrat. Führende Mitglieder des JFB waren Pazifistinnen. Das Nachrichtenblatt der Organisation brachte regelmäßig Ankündigungen und Berichte über Friedenskonferenzen und Veranstaltungen der *Internationalen Frauenliga für Frieden und Freiheit*.[18] 1927 legte der JFB seinen Mitgliedern nahe, in die WILPF (*Women's International League for Peace and Freedom*) einzutreten. Das war ein radikaler Schritt angesichts der internationalen Haltung der Liga und des gekränkten deutschen Nationalstolzes, unter dem auch manche Mitglieder des BDF litten.[19] Außerdem sandte der Frauenbund inoffizielle Beobachterinnen zu Abrüstungskonferenzen und ließ Petitionen zirkulieren, die sich für die Abrüstung aussprachen. Das Argument des JFB lautete: eine Frauenbewegung müsse auch eine Friedensbewegung sein, sonst nütze sie nichts; es bestünde eine "natürliche Verbindung zwischen Mutterschaft und Frieden".[20]

Der JFB unterhielt Beziehungen zu den Friedensbewegungen, um auch der eigenen Bevölkerung helfen zu können. So unterstützte er die *Liga der jüdischen Frauen* (einer Sektion der WILPF), die "den Antisemitismus als Feind des Weltfriedens" bekämpfte.[21] Im Jahre 1920 protestierte der deutsche Zweig der WILPF in einem offenen Schreiben gegen den deutschen Antisemitismus. Dieser, vom pazifistischen Standpunkt verfaßte Brief, der sich an die *Internationale Liga* wandte, führte religiöse, patriotische und feministische Argumente gegen den Antisemitismus ins Treffen.[22] 1926 verabschiedete der WILPF eine Resolution gegen den Antisemitismus. So fühlten sich die Mitglieder des Frauenbundes nicht nur in ihrer "Frauenposition", sondern auch als Jüdinnen gerechtfertigt, die Liga und die Friedensbewegung zu unterstützen.

Einige der wichtigsten JFB Aktivistinnen, die späteren Vorsitzenden der Organisation sowie viele andere prominente Mitglieder, machten ihre ersten politischen Erfahrungen im BDF.[23] Ottilie Schönewald, die letzte JFB Vorsitzende, gab sogar zu, daß "das deutsche Element [in der Geschichte des JFB] aus politischen oder vielleicht psychologischen Gründen heruntergespielt worden ist ... der JFB war Teil der deutschen Frauenbewegung und muß in diesem Kontext verstanden werden".[24] Es ist bemerkenswert, daß der JFB den BDF als Verbündeten im Kampf gegen den Antisemitismus ansah und sich an ihn um Hilfe wandte, als er beispielsweise von der Initiative erfuhr, in Leipzig eine antisemitische Frauenorganisation zu gründen. Während der Wirtschaftskrise in Deutschland, die zu einem Aufflammen des Antisemitismus führte, schrieb Agnes von Zahn-Harnack, die neugewählte Vorsitzende des BDF, umgehend an den JFB und erklärte, weder sie noch der BDF würden Angriffe auf Juden oder das Judentum dulden.[25] Ab 1930 wirkte der BDF wesentlich bei der "Aufklärungsarbeit" mit, die der JFB wie auch andere deutsch-jüdische Organisationen betrieben, um dem Fanatismus Einhalt zu gebieten. Der JFB lud Vertreterinnen nichtjüdischer Frauen- und Jugendorganisationen zu Vorträgen und geselligen Abenden und zu Führungen durch die Synagogen ein. Agnes von Zahn-Harnack leitete ein solches "Aufklärungsarbeitstreffen". Repräsentantinnen der katholischen Frauenorganisation, Theologinnen und führende Feministinnen waren anwesend. Zahn-Harnack schlug dem JFB vor, doch christliche Frauen zu Diskussionen und Festtagsfeiern sowie Gottesdiensten in den Synagogen einzuladen und bemerkte: "Der Kampf gegen den Antisemitismus muß von den christlichen Frauen ausgehen."[26] Der JFB bereitete Schriften vor, die jüdische Ethik, Geschichte und Sitten erklärten, und verteilte sie an seine Gäste.[27] Oft verglich er die Emanzipation der Juden und der Frauen miteinander und betonte, jede dieser Gruppen hoffe zwar, sich in die herrschende Gesellschaft einzufügen, habe aber doch ein Bewußtsein der eigenen besonderen Qualitäten entwickelt, die sie zu erhalten bestrebt seien. Aufgrund der Überlegung, rassische und geschlechtliche Diskriminierungen würden sich gegenseitig verstärken, vertrat der JFB die Ansicht, deutsche und jüdische Frauen sollten sich gegen den Antisemitismus einsetzen, da Juden und Feministinnen denselben Kampf um Gleichberechtigung führten. Für beide Gruppen sei eine offene, liberale, pluralistische Gesellschaft lebensnotwendig. Der JFB forderte die Frauenbewegung auf, den Antisemitismus zu bekämpfen, "nicht für uns, sondern für die Idee von einem deutschen Geist, an den wir alle glaubten".[28] Als die NSDAP immer mehr Anhänger gewann, publizierte der BDF *Gelbe Blätter* und Pamphlete, die hauptsächlich gegen die Nazis gerichtet waren. Aber der BDF suchte häufiger die Rechte der Frauen als die der Juden zu sichern und maß den eigenen Interessen eine größere Bedeutung zu als der Bekämpfung des Rassismus. Er übersah indes, daß auch er vom Nationalsozialismus bedroht war.[29] Trotzdem verschaffte es dem JFB eine gewisse Genugtuung, daß der BDF den Nazis offiziell feindlich gesonnen war. Der letzte Aufruf des BDF vom März 1933 an die deutschen Frauen, sie sollten nur Parteien wählen, die die Rechte der Frauen und Rechtsstaatlichkeit anerkannten, war in großen Buchstaben quer über die Titelseite des JFB-Nachrichtenblattes abgedruckt.[30]

Aber die Führung des JFB erkannte auch, wie wenig Verständnis manche BDF Mitglieder für jüdische Sitten und Gebote, wie den Partikularismus hatten. Er reargierte besonders empfindlich auf die Mißachtung der jüdischen Gepflogenheiten und auf eine allmähliche Zunahme des Antisemtismus im BDF. Obwohl JFB und BDF in Fragen der Geschlechts- und Klassenzugehörigkeit immer noch ähnliche Interessen vertraten, teilten mehr und mehr BDF Mitglieder die negativen Einstellungen zum Judentum, die in Deutschland zur damaligen Zeit vorherrschend waren. Sie reichten von einer liberalen Unduldsamkeit gegenüber den jüdischen Besonderheiten[31] bis hin zum unterschwelligen oder sogar offenen Antisemitismus.

Üblicher und verbreiteter als offener Haß oder offene Sympathiebekundung für Juden war das, was wir den gemäßigten Antisemitismus genannt haben, dieses vage Gefühl des Unbehagens gegenüber Juden, das diesen bei weitem nichts zuleide tun wollte, aber möglicherweise mit dazu beigetragen hat, Aversionen, die Deutsche andernfalls Nazis gegenüber gehabt hätten, zu neutralisieren.[32]

Nur wenige Juden waren Ziel persönlicher Angriffe, doch praktisch waren alle mit Antisemitismus konfrontiert und hielten es für etwas, das es im Leben nun einmal gab.[33] Es waren weniger die Universitäten, sondern vor allem die rechten politischen Parteien, die Kirchen und bestimmte Ränge der Beamtenschaft und Armee,[34] die einen offenen Antisemitismus vertraten. Trotz dieses von der Regierung tolerierten Antisemitismus wie auch der Zunahme rechter antisemitischer Organisationen, (die 1920 über 200.000 Anhänger hatten), waren die deutschen Juden davon überzeugt, daß sie ihren Platz in Deutschland hatten und ein deutsch-jüdisches Zusammenleben möglich sei.

Die Mitglieder des jüdischen Frauenbundes teilten diese Meinung. Und doch waren sie sich der Distanz bewußt, die sie von den Schwestern im BDF trennte. Sogar die nichtjüdischen Frauen, die sich erboten, dem JFB in seinem Kampf gegen den Rassismus beizustehen blieben zurückhaltend. Wie ein JFB-Mitglied bemerkte:

> Wir lebten unter anderen, saßen zusammen in demselben Klassenzimmer, besuchten zusammen die Universität, trafen einander bei gesellschaftlichen Anlässen — und waren uns völlig fremd. War es ihre Schuld? Unsere? Schwer zu sagen, aber auch bedeutungslos. Es war eine Tatsache — die sich mit der Zeit verhängnisvoll auswirkte — daß diejenigen, die sich für uns einsetzen wollten, nichts von uns wußten.[35]

Mitglieder des JFB hatten das Gefühl, ihre liberalen feministischen Schwestern würden sie nur akzeptieren, wenn sie ihr Jüdischsein "versteckten". Wie eine der führenden Frauen im JFB feststellte, "werden jene jüdischen Frauen geschätzt, die möglichst wenig merken lassen, daß sie Jüdinnen sind".[36] Das war richtig: der BDF mied, was er für "Sektierertum" hielt. Im Sinne des deutschen Liberalismus förderte er die Integration der Juden, reagierte jedoch mit Unbehagen auf Juden, die sich dieser Homogenisierung widersetzten. Bertha Pappenheim nannte die jüdischen Frauen, die direkt in den BDF eintraten (und so ihre jüdische Identität hintansetzten) die "Halben". Allmählich wurde die mangelnde Sensibilität, bzw. die antisemitische Einstellung unter den Mitgliedern des BDF auch nach außen hin offenbar. So versäumte es die Führung des BDF bei Aktionen, bei denen sie sich um die Mitwirkung der evangelischen und katholischen Frauen bemühte, den JFB heranzuziehen. Bertha Pappenheim empfand dies als Kränkung. Die Auseinandersetzung mit dem BDF verlief für sie so unbefriedigend, daß sie sich während des

Ersten Weltkrieges aus dem *Nationalen Frauendienst* zurückzog. Ein anderes Beispiel ist die offensichtlich am Antisemitismus gescheiterte Wahl Alice Salomons zur Vorsitzenden des BDF.

In seiner Haltung gegenüber der politischen Entwicklung der Weimarer Republik hielt der BDF in den Augen seiner jüdischen Anhängerinnen zu lange an seiner vorgeschobenen Neutralität fest. In den Anfangsjahren der Weimarer Republik hatte die Einstellung der BDF-Spitze, die für die *Demokratischen Partei* eintrat, dem JFB keinerlei Schwierigkeiten bereitet. Denn die meisten Juden unterstützten die liberale, mittelschichts-orientierte *Deutsche Demokratische Partei*. 1918 gegründet, umfaßte diese Partei vor allem Geschäftsleute und Akademiker, unterstützte die Weimarer Verfassung und lehnte den Antisemitismus ab, da er mit Vor-stellungen von Vernunft, Toleranz und individueller Freiheit nicht zu vereinbaren war. Nach 1930, mit zunehmender Polarisierung in der Politik, fiel der Großteil der jüdischen Wählerstimmen an die *Sozial-demokratische Partei*, beziehungsweise an die *Katholische Zentrumspartei*, die sich für die religiösen Rechte von Minderheiten und gegen Rassismus einsetzte. Mitte der zwanziger Jahre hatten rechte Politiker langsam Führungspositionen eingenommen. Da fand sich der JFB in zunehmenden Maße isoliert. Aufgrund des Argumentes, der BDF müsse "über den Parteien" stehen, um die große Masse seiner Anhängerinnen zu halten — von denen viele sogar noch mehr rechts als die Führung standen — lud der BDF konservative und rechte Abgeordnete, deren Parteien zum großen Teil offiziell antisemitisch waren, zu seinen politischen Debatten ein. Die angebliche Notwendigkeit, "neutral" zu sein — hinter der sich häufig eine antisemitische Haltung verbarg — führte in der Praxis zur Einladung rechtsextremer Redner seitens des *Deutschen Staatsbürgerinnen Verbandes*, einer Tochterorganisation des BDF. Einer dieser Nazis hielt einen Vortrag über das Thema "Was sollten die Frauen von den National-sozialisten erwarten?" Die deutschen Frauen schickten dem JFB eine Entschuldigungsnote, in der sie um Verständnis baten: "Ihr versteht, daß wir diese Entscheidung nach ernsthafter Diskussion getroffen haben"[37]. Gegen Anfang der dreißiger Jahre mußten sogar die Frauen, die am uner-schütterlichsten zu den Jüdinnen in der deutschen Frauenbewegung standen, zugeben, daß in den dem BDF angegliederten Vereinen "stille, unterschwellige Strömungen" zu spüren waren. Diese "mystischen, irrationalen Strömungen", die nicht ausdrücklich antisemtisch waren, lehnten die feministische Bewegung als zu rational ab. Nach Ansicht der jüdischen Feministinnen richteten sich aber diese Strömungen nicht nur gegen die Frauenbewegung, sondern auch gegen Juden und bedrohten die eigene Zusammenarbeit mit der "vorurteilslosen" Frauenbewegung sowie den Feminismus selbst.[38]

Offenbar war dem JFB die ambivalente Position der Juden in Deutsch-land klar. In gewisser Weise war er selbst ja ein typisches Beispiel dafür.

Einerseits versuchte er, eine gut funktionierende Zusammenarbeit mit dem BDF aufrecht zu erhalten, um Ziele des Feminismus zu unterstützen, um als Teil der deutschen Bewegung akzeptiert zu werden und dem wachsenden Antisemitismus entgegenzuwirken. Andererseits bot er jüdischen Frauen, die — bei aller Achtung für ihr deutsches Erbe und den deutschen Feminismus — empfindsam auf das Ausgeschlossensein und den Antisemitismus reagierten, den passenden Rahmen. Der *Jüdische Frauenbund* bildete eine separatistische Alternative: Trotz mancher Affinitäten blieb er unabhängig von der männlichen jüdischen Führung und der deutschen Frauenbewegung, da JFB-Anhängerinnen ein ambivalentes Verhältnis zu beiden Organisationen hatten.

III. Der jüdisch-feministische Kampf ums Überleben

Der Mahlstrom, den die Machtergreifung der Nazis auslöste, machte jede Möglichkeit jüdischer Frauen zunichte, sich für die Arbeit in der deutschen Frauenbewegung oder in der jüdischen Gemeinde zu entscheiden. Die Zeit der braunen Barbarei zwang sie, immer neue Strategien des bloßen Überlebens zu finden. Im Juni 1933 löste sich der *Bund Deutscher Frauenvereine* von selbst auf, um nicht Opfer der Gleichschaltung zu werden — einem Prozeß, bei dem die gesamte Spitze einer Organisation durch aktive Nationalsozialisten ersetzt und alle Mitglieder gezwungen wurden, an Naziprogrammen mitzuwirken. Der JFB war ein paar Tage zuvor aus der deutschen feministischen Organisation ausgetreten; der BDF hatte den Rückzug dieses Frauenbundes mit "tiefstem Bedauern" akzeptiert.[39]

Vielleicht hatten Jüdinnen erwartet, daß die deutschen Feministinnen ein Gefühl schwesterlicher Verbundenheit und Loyalität für sie bewahren würden; sie sollten bitter enttäuscht werden. Wie Paula Ollendorf, ein führendes JFB-Mitglied, berichtet, fanden ihre früheren Freundinnen und BDF Kolleginnen, mit denen sie jahrelang zusammengearbeitet hatten, gleich nach Hitlers Machtergreifung "dumme Ausreden", um "nicht mit Juden erwischt zu werden". Eine dieser Kolleginnen, eine "alte Kämpferin" für die Berufsausbildung von Frauen und ein bekanntes Mitglied der *Demokratischen Partei*, bat Paula Ollendorf und Martha Parker, ihr beim Nachweis zu helfen, daß sie immer eine nationale Gesinnung gehabt habe. Parker berichtet:

> Ich lachte und sagte, sicher, ich kann dir das bezeugen, aber das würde wenig nützen. Paula konnte darüber nicht lachen — sie meinte: "Es ist aller Bankrott." Ich sagte, es sei der Bankrott Deutschlands und sie antwortete, ihrer sei es auch.[40]

Natürlich gab es Ausnahmen, doch auch Ottilie Schönewald, die letzte
Vorsitzende des JFB, litt unter dem Mangel an Solidarität seitens ihrer
nichtjüdischen Schwestern:

> Wo waren die deutschen Frauen damals? Wenn sie kurz nach dem
> 9. November 1938 dieselben Worte für mich gefunden hätten wie
> in ihren Briefen heute (1955), sie hätten mir soviel bedeutet. Kaum
> eine unserer deutschen sogenannten Freundinnen ... fand den Weg
> zu uns. Dies war unglücklicherweise nicht ein persönliches, nur hie
> und da auftretendes Phänomen. Ja, Angestellte ... und Arbeiter, die
> Leute in meinem Wahlkreis, die Armenunterstützung erhielten,
> scheuten sich nicht, ihre Zuneigung zu zeigen ... sie wußten, wo sie
> uns finden konnten, und das am hellichten Tag. Und soweit ich
> weiß, hat das keinem von ihnen geschadet.[41]

Die fehlende Frauensolidarität hinderte die Schönewald nicht daran, 1935
der Vorsitzenden der neuen Nazi-Frauenorganisation, Gertrud Scholtz-
Klinck, ein Schreiben zu übersenden, in dem sie gegen die Rede des
Kölner Gauleiters protestierte. Vor Tausenden von Kindern hatte dieser
erklärt: "Juden müssen sterben, wenn die Menschheit in Frieden leben
will." Ottilie Schönewald erhielt keine Antwort. Ihr Schritt war ein
mutiger, wenn auch vergeblicher Versuch, sich auf die Solidarität unter
Müttern zu berufen.[42]

Zwischen 1933 und 1938 schloß sich der *Jüdische Frauenbund* mit anderen jüdischen Organisationen zum Kampf ums Überleben zusammen.
Dieser Kampf spielte sich auf verschiedenen Ebenen ab: man verhinderte
das Auseinanderfallen der jüdischen Gemeindeorganisationen, stellte die
Fortdauer jüdischer Bräuche sicher, half Bedürftigen und bereitete Juden
auf die Emigration vor. Während der Hitlerjahre konzentrierte sich der
JFB auf die Sozialarbeit und nicht so sehr auf die Durchsetzung feminis-
tischer Ziele. Der JFB forderte zwar weiterhin die Gleichstellung der
Frauen innerhalb der jüdischen Gemeinde, setzte seine Dienstleistungen
für Frauen fort und vertrat die Interessen von Frauen vor der neu-
gegründeten jüdischen Zentralorganisation, der *Reichsvertretung der
deutschen Juden*, doch die Bedürfnisse der jüdischen Gemeinden in
Deutschland nahmen gegenüber rein feministischen Zielen den Vorrang
ein. Der extrem frauenfeindliche Charakter des "Dritten Reichs" machte
zudem den Feminismus wirkungslos und riskant.

Noch 1933, als die soziale, gesetzliche, politische und letztendlich
physische Ächtung der Juden begann, schlugen die "Aufklärungs-
kampagnen" des JFB in den defensiven Versuch um, den Antisemitismus
durch "Selbstzucht" der Jüdinnen abzubauen. Diese Bemühungen, "bei
Frauen und Mädchen eine Schlichtheit in der äußeren Erscheinung" zu
fördern, war schon seit dem Ersten Weltkrieg eine Antwort des JFB auf

die Feindseligkeit der Nichtjuden gewesen. Wie in den früheren JFB Kampagnen gegen den Mädchenhandel und in den Versuchen, das "unrepräsentative" Berufsprofil zu ändern, trat auch in diesen neuen Bestrebungen eine Haltung zum Vorschein, die auf der Vorstellung beruhte, Selbstdisziplin sei der Schlüssel zum Akzeptiertwerden und zur Selbstverteidigung. Der Ausspruch, "Stiefkinder müssen doppelt artig sein"[43], bringt dies besonders deutlich zum Ausdruck. Alle Juden, besonders die Frauen, wurden ermahnt, durch einen schlichten Lebensstandard dem Neid und den Ressentiments der Antisemiten vorzubeugen. Jüdische Zeitungen und Organisationen empfahlen den jüdischen Frauen eindringlich, Kleidung und Verhalten zu vermeiden, die Anstoß erregen könnten, und warnten "Frauen, die sich mit glitzernden Juwelen behängen", daß sie den Feind nur aufhetzten.[44] Diese Warnun-gen hatten zum Ziel, ein negatives Cliché zu bekämpfen, das in den Köpfen der Antisemiten wie der jüdischen Männer existierte; aber sie trugen im Grunde zur Verbreitung dieses Stereotyps der jüdischen Frau bei und unterstützten dabei zwei weitere Vorurteile: Zum einen die übertriebene Vorstellung von der Zahl der jüdischen Frauen, die unter der Last ihres Geschmeides zusammenbrachen und zwar zu einer Zeit zunehmender Arbeitslosigkeit und eines Boykotts jüdischer Geschäfte); und zum anderen den Irrtum, Bescheidenheit könne den Antisemitismus beschwichtigen. Als Jüdinnen und Frauen doppelt gefährdet, zeigten die Mitglieder des Frauenbundes eine charakteristische Eigenheit unterdrückter Minderheiten, nämlich sich selbst die Schuld für erlittene Repressalien zu geben.

Mit seinen Hilfsmaßnahmen zur Stützung der jüdischen Gemeinde hatte der Frauenbund bescheidene Erfolge erzielt. Er arbeitete mit zentralen jüdischen Wohlfahrtsorganisationen zusammen, stellte ehrenamtliche Helferinnen für einige der Sozialfürsorgeämter und übernahm die Verantwortung für jüdische Schulen und Institutionen.[45] Außerdem gründete der JFB zusätzlich eigene neue Ortsgruppen, zog neue Mitglieder an (viele davon kamen aus der aufgelösten deutschen Frauenbewegung und den Organisationen berufstätiger Frauen) und knüpfte engere Verbindungen zu anderen nationalen und internationalen jüdischen Frauenorganisationen. Durch seine kulturellen Aktivitäten und sein Nachrichtenblatt bemühte sich der JFB, seine Mitglieder bzw. Leserschaft über jüdische Sitten, Geschichte und Religion zu informieren. Der JFB hatte dies immer schon getan, aber in Jahren der braunen Barbarei bekamen seine Bemühungen eine neue, psychologische Dimension. Seine kulturellen und religiösen Aktivitäten gaben der jüdischen Minderheit, die sich mit so viel Ablehnung konfrontiert sah und jegliche Hoffnung zu verlieren schien, neuen Lebensmut.

Materielle Unterstützung leistete der Frauenbund, indem er anderen jüdischen Gruppen half, Geld, Kleidung und Brennmaterial zu sammeln.

Als immer mehr Juden ihr Einkommen verloren, versuchte der JFB den jüdischen Mittelschichtsfrauen und deren Familien zu helfen, sich an einen niedrigeren Lebensstandard zu gewöhnen. Er verstärkte die Hilfsprogramme für Hausfrauen, richtete Kurse ein, in denen Kochen, Flicken, Nähen, Krankenpflege und häusliche Reparaturarbeiten unterrichtet wurden, und verfaßte ein eigenes Kochbuch für Juden, die Schwierigkeiten hatten, koscheres Fleisch zu kaufen, weil Hitler das Schächten verbieten ließ. Der JFB ermunterte sie, sich gegenseitig zu helfen und organisierte in verschiedenen Städten Gemeinschaftsküchen, "Spielkreise" für Kinder, Vermittlung von Haushaltshilfen und Gesprächsnachmittage. Der Frauenbund betonte wiederholt, welche entscheidende Rolle den Frauen dabei zufiele, im Heim eine Harmonie herzustellen.

Die letzte große Aufgabe des JFB war die Vorbereitung der Frauen auf die Emigration. 1935 nahmen die Nürnberger Gesetze den Juden die Bürgerrechte und verboten Ehen und außereheliche Geschlechtsverkehr zwischen Juden und "Ariern". Die "Gesetze zum Schutz deutschen Blutes und deutscher Ehre" zeigten dem JFB, daß die Auswanderung nötig war. Daher verstärkte der JFB seine Bemühungen, Mädchen in Berufe umzuschulen, die den Asylorten angemessen waren. Das JFB-Nachrichtenblatt widmete dem Prozeß und den Problemen der Emigration von Frauen ganze Nummern; JFB-Mitglieder begleiteten auch Kinder auf die Reise ins Ausland, brachte sie in Sicherheit, kehrten dann aber wieder nach Deutschland zurück, um ihre Arbeit fortzusetzen.

Nach der *Kristallnacht* (November 1938) wurde der Frauenbund auf Anweisung der Nazis aufgelöst. Seine finanziellen Mittel und seine Einrichtungen gingen an die Reichsvertretung über, die führenden JFB-Mitglieder schlossen sich dem Mitarbeiterstab dieser Organisation an. Obwohl die Frauen viele Möglichkeiten zum Auswandern hatten, arbeiteten sie weiter für die jüdische Gemeinde. Diejenigen, die nicht zur nationalen Führung gehörten, leisteten weiter, zusammen mit anderen Juden aus ihrer Gemeinde, Sozialarbeit. 1942 wurden viele der führenden Frauen des JFB deportiert. Sie fielen der Hitlerschen "Endlösung des Judenproblems" zum Opfer. Hannah Karminski, die frühere geschäftsführende Sekretärin des JFB, schrieb einer Freundin über den letzten Besuch bei Cora Berliner, der früheren stellvertretenden Vorsitzenden des JFB:

> C. und unsere anderen Freundinnen nahmen Bücher mit. Sie einigten sich über die Auswahl. Meines Wissens nahm C. Faust I und eine Anthologie mit. Als ich sie am letzten Tag kurz vor ihrer Deportation besuchte, saßen sie im Hof in der Sonne und lasen Goethe.[46]

Anmerkungen

Abkürzungen

ALBI	Archiv des Leo Baeck Institutes, New York
AZDJ	*Allgemeine Zeitung des Judentums* (Berlin)
BJFB	*Blätter des Jüdischen Frauenbundes: Für Frauenarbeit und Frauenbewegung*
LBIYB	*Leo Baeck Institute Yearbook* (London)
ZDSJ	*Zeitschrift für Demographie und Statistik der Juden* (Berlin)

[1] Dieser Beitrag ist die stark gekürzte Fassung von "Sisterhood under Siege. Feminism und Anti-Semitism in Germany 1904-1938". In: *When Biology became Destiny: Women in Weimar and Nazi Germany*. Hg. v. Renate Bridenthal, Alina Grossmann und Marion Kaplan. New York 1984. Eine Übersetzung ins Deutsche von Sibylle Koch-Grünberg erschien in: *Feministische Studien*, Heft 1, 1984, S. 128-139; die vorliegende Fassung ist eine von Amy Colin neu bearbeitete Übersetzung ins Deutsche. Mit freundlicher Genehmigung der Autorin.

[2] Bertha Pappenheim, die erste Patientin, die Joseph Breuer nach der Methode der kathartischen Psychotherapie vom Dezember 1980 bis Juni 1982 behandelte, ist als Fall *Anna O.* recht bekannt. Diese Krankengeschichte ist in Freuds und Breuers *Studien über Hysterie* veröffentlicht worden. Siehe Ellen Jensen: "Anna O, — A Study of Her Later Life". In: *The Psychoanalytic Quarterly*, 39 (1970), S. 269-93. Dieser Artikel enthält eine Bibliographie psychoanalytischer Stellungnahmen zu Anna O. und Bertha Pappenheim. Bevor sie den JFB gründete, schrieb sie einige Theaterstücke und Pamphlete mit feministischen Themen und übersetzte Mary Wollstonecrafts *A Vindication of the Rights of Women*. Bezüglich weiterer Informationen siehe M. Kaplans Kapitel über Bertha Pappenheim in *The Jewish Feminist Movement in Germany: The Campaigne of the Jüdischer Frauenbund, 1904-1938*. (Connecticut 1979).

[3] "Für Frauenarbeit und Frauenbewegung" ist der Untertitel des JFB-Frauenblattes, *Bätter des Jüdischen Frauenbundes* (BJFB). Januar 1928, S. 1, und *Jahrbuch der Frauenbewegung* (1912).

[4] In dem Essay "Die Jüdischen Frauenvereine in Deutschland", ZDSJ, 10 (Januar 1914), S. 2-5, und 10 (Februar 1914), S. 7-23, beschreibt Jacob Segall die dem JFB vorausgehenden Organisationen.

[5] Um 1870 gehörten etwa 60 Prozent der deutschen Juden der Mittel- und Oberschicht an. Weitere 25 Prozent sind der unteren Mittelschicht zuzurechnen. Monika Richarz (Hrsg.), *Selbstzeugnisse zur Sozialgeschichte im Kaiserreich. Jüdisches Leben in Deutschland.* Stuttgart 1979, S. 24.
1933 ließen sich nur 8,7 Prozent der deutschen Juden der Rubrik "Arbeiter" zuordnen, bei den nichtjüdischen Deutschen waren es dagegen 46, 4 Prozent.

Volkszählung. Die Bevölkerung des Deutschen Reiches nach der Volkszählung 1933. Berlin 1936, Heft 5, S. 25 und 27.

[6] Das entspricht auch einem demographischen Trend: In den dreißiger Jahren waren mehr als 50 Prozent der deutschen Juden über 40 Jahre alt. Erich Rosenthal: "Jewish Population in Germany 1910-1939". In: *Jewish Social Studies* 6 (1944), S. 234-47.

[7] Auch heute fordern Frauen, die sich für Feministinnen und gläubige Jüdinnen ansehen, eine größere Gleichberechtigung innerhalb der jüdischen Gemeinde und – im Gegensatz zum JFB – eine stärkere Mitwirkung im jüdischen religiösen Ritual. Siehe z. B. Susan Dworkin: "A Song for Women in Five Questions". In: *Moment* (Mai/Juni 19175), S. 44; Sally Priesand: *Judaism and the New Woman.* New York 1975; und neuere Nummern der Zeitschrift *Lilith.*

[8] Donald L. Niewyk: *The Jews in Weimar Germany.* Baton Rouge/London 1980, S. 99-100; Zitat aus Hannah Arendt: *The Jew as Pariah.* New York 1978, S. 68.

[9] Heinrich Silbergleit: *Die Bevölkerungs- und Berufsverhältnisse der Juden im Deutschen Reich.* Berlin 1930, S. 109.

[10] Zum Mädchenhandel und der Kampagne des JFB siehe Kap. 4 von M. Kaplans Buch *Die jüdische Frauenbewegung in Deutschland.* Übers. v. Hainer Kober. Hamburg 1981, p. 153-180.

[11] *BJFB,* August 1927, S. 6-7; Februar 1928, S. 1-2.

[12] BJFB, Februar 1928, S. 1.

[13] *BJFB,* Juli 1929. S. 13; August 1926, S. 3-4.

[14] *BJFB,* Juli 1936, S. 8.

[15] *BJFB,* Januar 192, S. 4.

[16] Vgl. Gisela Bock: "Racism and Sexism in Nazi Germany". In: *When Biology became Destiny: Women in Weimar and Nazi Germany.* Hg. v. R. Bridenthal, A. Grossmann, M. Kaplan. New York 1984.

[17] *AZDJ,* 18. Mai 1915, S. 2; ebd., 14 Mai 1915, S. 1; *BJFB,* April 1936, S. 9-10.

[18] BJIB, August 1926, S. 4.

[19] Vgl. *Israelisches Familienblatt,* 15. Dezember 1927, S. 8.

[20] *BJFB,* November 1931, S. 8.

[21] *BJFB,* August 1926, S.4. Interview mit Dora Edinger, früheres Mitglied des JFB, 1975.

[22] *Israelisches Familienblatt,* 28. Oktober 1920, S. 3.

[23] Vgl. die Memoiren von Ottilie Schönewald; ebenfalls die Interviews mit Lilli Liegner, Klara Caro und Dora Edinger (alle frühere JFB-Leiterinnen).

[24] *Schönewald Collection, ALIBI,* IV, 14 (geschrieben 1957 oder 1958).

[25] AZDJ, Dezember 26, 1919. S. 1.

[26] *BJFB,* Dezember 1931, S. 7-8.

[27] *BJFB,* Dezember 1931, S. 7-8.

[28] *BJFB,* Dezember 1930, S. 7.

[29] *BJFB,* Dezember 1930, S. 5-7; September 1932, S.4-5.

[30] Dies war im Juni 1932 der Fall, als Mitglieder des geschäftsführenden Ausschusses des BDF, u.a. Zahn-Harnack, darauf bestanden, nur gegen die Naziangriffe auf Frauen Einwände zu erheben. Die Mehrheit jedoch war der gleichen Meinung wie Emma Ender: "Der Nationalsozialismus ist im Kampf gegen Juden und Frauen groß geworden." Evans, a.a.O., S. 255.

[31] *BJFB*, März 1933, S. 1.

[32] Reinhard Rürup: "Jewish Emancipation and Bourgeois Society", *LBIYB*, (1969), S. 80.

[33] Niewyk, a.a.O., S. 80.

[34] Ebd. S. 86, 112.

[35] Ebd. S. 55.

[36] Rahel Straus: *Wir leben in Deutschland. Erinnerungen einer deutschen Jüdin 1880–1933.* Stuttgart 1962, S. 266.

[37] *BJFB*, Dezember 1930, S. 5-6.

[38] Bezüglich weiterer Informationen über den *Deutsche Staatsbürgerinnen Verband*, siehe *BJBF*, Februar 1931, S. 13. Bezüglich der jüdischen politischen Bindungen siehe Niewyk, a.a.O.

[39] *BJFB*, Juli 1933. S. 1-2, Zitat aus: *Central Verein Zeitung*, Oktober 1931.

[40] *BJFB*, Juni 1933, S. 11-12.

[41] Paula Ollendorff Collection, *ALBI*, 3060, Nr. 15.

[42] *Schönewald Collection.* IV, 8.

[43] Ebd.

[44] Ludwig Holländer, geschäftsführender Direktor einer deutsch-jüdischen Schutzorganisation, zitiert von Peter Gay in "Encounter with Modernism: German Jews in German Culture, 1888 – 1914," In: *Midstream*, February 1975, S. 60.

[45] *Israelisches Familienblatt*, 7. Februar, 1918, S. 10; *AZDJ*, 16. September 1921, S.2; Adolf Asch: *Memoiren*, ALBI, S. 3.

[46] "Letters from Berlin," *LBIYB*, 1 (1957), S. 312.

Sander L. Gilman

Sounding too Jewish: The Discourse of Difference

I.

In his most recent novel Philip Roth evoked the specter of what it means to sound too Jewish. Projecting his anxiety about the formation of an American-Jewish literary identity on to his image of England, Roth has his unnamed protagonist tell the following anecdote. He has seen a commercial on British television in which a "youngish middle-aged, rather upper class English actor" begins to remove his make-up having just performed Charles Dickens's Fagin:

> To relax after the performance he lights up one of these little cigarillos, contentedly he puffs away at it, talking about the flavor and the aroma and so on, and then he leans very intimately into the camera and he holds up the cigarillo and suddenly, in a thick, Faginy, Yiddish accent and with an insinuating leer on his face, he says, "And, best of all, they're *cheap*."[1]

The protagonist's immediate response is to phone an Anglo-Jewish friend to ask him about the commercial. He is admonished that he will "get used to it." "It" being British anti-Semitic representations of the Jew. But the protagonist worries about such insults, as well as being criticized for making "such a fuss about being Jewish."

It is, of course, not *being* Jewish which is the problem here, but *sounding* Jewish, indeed sounding *too* Jewish against which Roth's figure protests. The "Faginy, Yiddish" accent marks the stage Jew as different, as not really belonging to cultivated British society with its Oxbridge accent. Roth's protagonist protests by calling his Anglo-Jewish friend and *speaking* with him in his American-accented English. He must sound different, but this difference is in no way represented in Philip Roth's text. Philip Roth writes a clear, mid-Atlantic literary language, undifferentiated from the language of most other contemporary American writers. Indeed if Martin Amis's recent novel, *London Fields*, with its American-Jewish novelist-protagonist is any indication, it is the language of modern socially critical fiction, even in British ears. And yet the fear of sounding different, sounding too Jewish (which may well mean sounding too "New Jersey" in the ear of Roth's imagined British listener) haunts Philip Roth's work.

Roth's critique of the British image of the Jew mirrors the anxiety which his protagonist has about his command of his own language, not the Yiddish-accented language of the anti-Semite's image of the Jew, but the language of high culture, the literary language of the Anglophone novelist. Jews, according to Roth, compulsively tell stories: "With the nigger it's his prick and with the Jew it's his questions. You are a treacherous bastard who cannot resist a narrative..." (93) It is the Jewish author's command of the language of the narrative, the language in which the questions are asked, which is drawn into question.

The meaning of Roth's Jewish character's complaint that the anti-Semitic stereotype of the Jew is represented as sounding too Jewish is one which needs further contextualization. The creation of the image of the Jew who is identifiable as different because he or she sounds "too Jewish" provides a model through which we can see the structure of the image to create an absolute boundary of the difference of the Jew even as this boundary historically shifts and slides. Jews sound different because they are represented as being different. Jewish authors have felt compelled to respond to this image of difference, and to create a counter image of the Jew who sounds Jewish, for within their creation of texts, Jewish authors are Jews who sound Jewish.

What does it mean to sound too Jewish? I have argued in my study *Jewish Self-Hatred* that there is a long tradition of representing the "hidden" language of the Jew as a signifier of specific difference.[2] And that the difference represented is always an attempt to present the qualities of the Jew (usually negative, but sometimes, indeed, positive) as separate from the referent group. The image of the "Jew who sounds Jewish" is a stereotype within the Christian world which represents the Jew as possessing all languages or no language of his or her own; of having a hidden language which mirrors the perverse or peculiar nature of the Jew; of being unable to truly command the national language of the world in which he/she lives or, indeed, even of possessing a language of true revelation, such as Hebrew.

II.

The stereotype of the Jews' language is rooted in the earliest history of the rise of Christianity (or rather in the separation of the early Church from Judaism) and is mirrored in a static manner in a series of texts — the Gospels, or, as the early Christians referred to them "The New Testament" — which were generated dynamically over time.[3] As early as Eusebius and Athanasius (in the fourth century CE) these texts become the central canon of Christianity as the so-called "pseudo-Gospels" (such as the Gospel of Nicodemus) are removed. In the Gospels, Christians are given a representation of the Jew who sounds Jewish and a direct message about the inherent difference of the Jew. It is in the continuity of the Gospels at the center of Christianity — not in the theology or indeed in the practice of the Church — that the representation of the Jew who sounds Jewish is preserved. And it is to this central stereotype that Western (that is, Christian or secularized) society turns when it needs to provide itself with a vocabulary of difference for the Jew.

This can be understood by comparing four analogous passages from the Gospels. Let us turn to the Gospels in their canonical order and read one passage, the last words of Christ in all of them. Matthew, the first gospeler, represents a Christ whose final *ipsissima verba* are as follows: "And about the ninth hour Jesus cried with a loud voice, saying, 'Eli, Eli, Lama Sabachthani?' that is to say, My God, My God, why hast thou forsaken me?" (27: 46) Mark has Christ "at the ninth hour... [crying] with a loud voice, saying 'Eloi, Eloi, Lama Sabachthani? which is, being interpreted, My God, My God, why hast thou forsaken me?" (15: 34). The significance of this lies in the presentation of Christ as speaking Aramaic, the language of the Jews: his words need to be translated into Greek, Latin, or English for the Christian reader to understand. The reader is thus made aware of the foreignness of Christ's language — he speaks the language of difference; he is a Jew who sounds Jewish. Placed in the mouth of Christ, the "hidden" language of the Jews is the magical language of difference. It generates a positive image of difference.

But in the second and later set of passages, Christ speaks in an unmediated manner. No Aramaic haunts his language. There is no need for translation. We, the imagined readers, — whether we understand Greek, Latin or English — can understand his words directly. His language is our language. If we take the parallel passage from the Gospel of Luke we can trace the same course with very different results. Christ is taken to Calvary and there he is crucified. "And when Jesus had cried with a loud voice, he said, Father, into thy hands I commend my spirit: and having said thus, he gave up the ghost." (23: 46) In John, the last of the Gospels which narrated the life of Jesus, Christ is taken to Golgotha and there "he said, It is finished: and he bowed his head, and gave up the ghost." (19: 30) In Luke and John there is no need for translation or interpretation. The language of this passage is completely transparent to the reader, who understands that Christ speaks the same language as he or she does. This "lucanization," according to Morton Scott Enslin, "reflects a marked sameness of tone, their smoothness and freedom from the little idiosyncrasies which stamp the man himself...."[4] His language needs no translation; it is transparent, familiar not foreign. The later Gospels provide a verbal sign of difference between the image of the

Jews and that of the early Christians represented in the text — Jews who were at the time becoming Christians in a world in which the valorized language was Greek.

This movement in the Gospels from the image of Christ as a Jew who sounds Jewish to that of the Christian, whose discourse is separate and distinct from that of the Jew, becomes clearest in the writings which codified the views of the early Church. In Acts, Peter's first speech to his fellow Jews in Jerusalem is recounted in a manner that differentiates between Greek, the language of his readers (now feeling themselves as "Christians"), and the representation of the Jews' discourse. He writes, for example, "And it was known unto all the dwellers at Jerusalem; insomuch as that field is called in their proper tongue, Aceldama, that is to say, The field of blood." (1: 19) But the utterances of Jesus in Acts never needs this type of translation. His language is consistently accessible.

A similar movement of the text is to be found in the recounting of the defense of the first Christian martyr, Stephen. The movement away from the "hidden" language of the Jews reveals itself to be more than a rejection of the language of the Jews. It is also an appropriation of the discourse of the Jews which Stephen reveals to the reader as having been misused by the Jews themselves. By stripping away the polluting nature of the "hidden" language of the Jews Stephen reveals to the reader that the very discourse of the Jews was never really their own.

Stephen, a Greek-speaking Jew, had begun successfully to evangelize among the Jews. He was prosecuted by Jewish priests who brought false witnesses to accuse him of blasphemy. His defense is quite extraordinary. He begins by recounting to his Jewish accusers a synoptic history of the Jews as represented in the Torah from the appearance of God to Abraham though the building of the Temple to — the coming, death, and resurrection of Christ:

> Ye stiffnecked and uncircumsized in heart and ears, ye do always resist the Holy Ghost: as your fathers did, so do ye. Which of the prophets have not your fathers persecuted? and they have slain them which showed before of the coming of the Just One; of whom ye have been now the betrayers and murderers... But he, being full of the Holy Ghost, looked up steadfastly into heaven, and saw the glory of God, and Jesus standing on the right hand of God... (Acts 7: 51-55)

The entire story of the Jews is reduced to a preamble to the coming of Christ. The sense of continuity between the "real" Jews of the past and the "new" Jews of the early Church, between the "true" Jewish experience actually written "on the heart" and not merely inscribed on the skin, becomes his defense. The act of circumcision, which had become the sign of the special relationship between the (male) Jew and God becomes a false sign, a sign written on the body of the hypocrisy of the hidden language of the Jew. The continuity between the Torah and the Gospels, the Christian demand that the Jews of the Torah prefigure (and thus are replaced by) the Christian experience removes the discourse of the Jews about their own history from their own control. As St. Augustine stated in his manual for new converts to Christianity: "the New Testament is concealed in the Old; the Old Testament is revealed in the New."[5] The Torah suddenly becomes the Old Testament. The "hidden" language of the Jews disappears from the tradition of the early Church even though it is preserved in what now comes to be called the "New" Testament as a sign of the difference of Christ's nature from that of the Jews. The successful separation of the "Church" from the "Synagogue" is indicated in the latest of the Gospels, Revelations, as well as in the Pauline epistles, where the separation between the divine discourse of the Church and the corrupt discourse of the Jews is absolute.

The rhetoric of European anti-Semitism can be found within the continuity of Christianity's image of the Jew. It is Christianity which provides all of the vocabularies of difference in Western Europe and North America, whether it is in the most overt "religious" language or in the secularized language of modern science. For it is not merely that the Jew is the obvious Other for the European, whether the citizen of the Roman Empire or of the Federal Republic of Germany. Anti-Semitism is central to Western culture because the rhetoric of European culture is Christianized, even in its most secular form. This perpetrated made the negative image of difference of the Jew found in the Gospel into the central referent for all definitions of difference in the West.

"Racial" or "scientific" anti-Semitism of the late nineteenth century is thought to have formed a radical break with the "medieval" religious tradition of Jew-hating, due to its self-confessed atheism. But this is not true. The nature of the secularization of religious models within the biological sciences of the nineteenth century is misunderstood. The basic model of the Jew found within "religious" contexts is merely secularized in the course of the eighteenth and nineteenth centuries. In both models the special language and related discourse of the Jew reflects the continuity of the image of the Jew. This is related to the continued presence at the heart of the self-definition of the Christian world of the Gospels with their complex and shifting image of the Jew.

The early Christians found proof of the inferiority of the Jews in their refusal to accept Jesus as the Messiah and convert to Christianity. This blindness and intractability became the definition of those psychological limitations of the Jew which precluded the Jew from ever becoming a truly "cultured" member of Western society. The perversity of the Jew's nature in betraying Christ over and over again throughout history (remember the central trope of Christianity is the regular reenactment of the crucifixion) becomes the biologically determined quality of the Jew which leads to the Jew's heartless role in the rise of capitalism (or communism — take your pick). The Jew's role in literally destroying the life of Christians, whether through the ritual use of Christian blood or the mass poisoning of wells which lead to the Black Death becomes the Jew's biological role as the transmitter of diseases such as syphilis (and, according to at least one commentator in Chicago in 1988, AIDS[6]).

The image of the Jew who sounds too Jewish is the counter-image of the hidden language of the Jew. The language used by the Jew reveals or masks the Jew's corrupt nature. But the informed listener hears the Jew hidden within no matter whether this difference is overt or disguised. The image of the "hidden" language and corrupt (and corrupting) discourse of the Jews is reflected within the tradition of Jews dealing with their internalized sense of difference. Thus the memory of language is thus never neutral for Jews, especially German Jews. The ancient Western tradition labels the language of the Jew as corrupt and corrupting, as the sign of the inherent difference of the Jew. This tradition sees the Jew as inherently unable to have command of any "Western," that is, cultural language. The Jew is not only "not of our blood," as Monsignor Joseph Frings of Cologne expressed it in 1942, but also "does not speak our language."[7] The Jews' language reflects only the corruption of the Jews and their discourse, a corruption that is made manifest in the essential Jew's language from the eighteenth century to the present, Yiddish. It is against this view that Jewish writers — Jewish because they internalize the label of "Jew" — must establish dominance over the language and discourse of their culture. The image of the language of the Jews and the idea of a "Jewish" language and discourse is central to any self-definition of the Jew in the Christian West.

We can take a specific example from the 1940s, the most recent period when the Jews were simply labelled as unable to command the language of their "host" nations. The stigma of being Jewish was central to the definition of all German "Jews," no matter what their prior religious, ethnic, or cultural self-definition. Theodor Adorno, writing in 1945, juxtaposes in two aphorisms his view that "Anti-Semitism is the rumor about the Jews" and "Foreign words are the Jews of language."[8] Jews are the product of language, and language becomes like the anti-Semite's image of the wandering or cosmopolitan Jew. The language of the anti-Semite here defines the nature of the Jew and his/her discourse. Thus, the Jew becomes the agent who uses corrupt language, while the corrupt discourse becomes the embodiment of the nature of the Jew. Adorno ironically sees the act of the passing of rumors as defining the reality of the Jews in Germany; but he also sees the nature of language (within the historic German demand for a "pure" language) as creating a category of exclusion and stigma. The interchangeability of these two categories reflects the interchangeability of the image of the Jew as possessing a unique, corrupting, and corrupt discourse embodied in the Jew's language — whether in the Jews' use of the language of culture or that special language of the Jews, Yiddish. For language purists of the 1920s and 1930s the most corrupt version of German was *mauscheln*, the language ascribed to the Eastern Jew who attempted to speak German.

The Jewish survivors of the Shoah were quite aware of the barbaric result of the incarnation of this idea of the Jews' language in the fascist image of the bestial, non-human Jew. Jewish writers who were forced or felt themselves driven to write in these languages had to deal with the problem of writing in a language in which their own sense of control of that medium was undermined by the image of the languageless, base Jew. After the Shoah this image of the Jew remained quite alive in the rhetoric of the language in which the non-Jew wrote about Jews. How can one capture memory in a tongue that you are supposed not to command? Is it not unauthentic to write in the language of the murderers, at least about victims and the survivors? The Jew, and the language of the Jew, is therefore what the non-Jew says the Jew is. For the non-Jews, language is assumed to be authentic, at least when it represents the Jew.

This is the problem with Jean-Paul Sartre's comment that:

> Jewish authenticity consists in choosing oneself as Jew — that is, in realizing one's Jewish condition. The authentic Jew abandons the myth of the universal man; ... he ceases to run away from himself and to be ashamed of his own kind.... He knows that he is one who stands apart, untouchable, scorned, proscribed — and it is as such that he asserts his being.[9]

Such a definition of Jewish "authenticity," with all of its evocation of Christian suffering and martyrdom, may be fine for a Frenchman who does not find himself labeled as a Jew, but for the Jew who is so labeled, so a sense of the "authentic" limits the range of Jewish response to the model of sacrifice presented in the Gospels. What Sartre — hardly a Christian thinker — incorporates into the model of the Jew is the model of particularist humility in the face of suffering. This does not permit Jews much range to create a discourse appropriate for themselves.

III.

This debate and the hidden language of the Jews has recently resurfaced in a new guise. In the Federal Republic of Germany during the 1950s and 1960s, there had been a traditional, liberal approach (e.g., in the writing of Ralf Dahrendorf) which tended to see the path of German history as having taken a special turn which lead to the exploitation of anti-Semitism as a political platform and, eventually, if not inexorably, to the Shoah. The literary image of the Shoah at this time (as in the works of Alfred Andersch) was of a world of destruction in which the German served as the agent of destruction, destroying not only (not even primarily) Jews but other "good" Germans. Indeed, the Jew was quite often represented as mute or as passive in this liberal tradition. Or indeed, as in the central works of Günther Grass such as *The Tin Drum*, as possessing a "special" or "hidden" language which marked them as different.[10] The cultural difference of German Jews or perhaps better of Jews in the Federal Republic of Germany, the difference of having to deal in 1989 with their growing invisibility as well as their past, has gone unnoticed in this cultural tradition. These German authors, as many of their contemporaries, had no problem with dealing with dead Jews, or old Jews, for as Henryk Broder has noted, there seems to be a "incurable love of German intellectuals for dead or half-dead Jews"[11] and, one might add, to distant Jews (they all read Ephraim Kishon). But the idea of a negative symbiosis,[12] a need for Jews in contemporary Germany to struggle with their invisibility as living, contributing members of contemporary society is impossible for them to understand.

The recent German critical response to Günther Grass's "borrowing" or rather misuse of a page from Edgar Hilsenrath's *Night*, an autobiographical novel of the Shoah, reflects the current sense that Jewish writers are little more than a source for German post-modern literary work. In his novel of 1979, *The Meeting at Telgte*, Grass mines Hilsenrath's account of the murder of Jews in the Shoah for an image of death completely separate from the experience of the immediate past.[13] Hilsenrath the novelist is made mute, his language is stolen from him, and the German critics speak of playful incorporation! This borrowing was noted in 1987 by Christoph Sieger in the notes to the critical edition of the novel as well as by Andreas Graf in an essay in the *Deutsche Vierteljahresschrift* in 1989.[14] Both of these critics seem to see in Grass's "borrowing" only a post-modern playfulness with categories of "reality" and fictionality." Unlike D. M. Thomas's plagiarism in *The White Hotel*, the criticism of contemporary West German critics on Grass's "borrowing" from Hilsenrath has certainly not made the front page of any newspaper in Germany.[15] And it most probably will not. For the treatment of Grass's borrowing is seen as a legitimate literary undertaking. Grass's purposeful confusion of "reality" and "narrativity" is stressed by Graf, the subtitle of whose essay is "on the ironic interchange between literature and reality." Might I suggest another reading. For all of the questions raised by Thomas's use of Kuznetsov it was acknowledged that he maintained the context of Kuznetsov's description of Babi Yar, Thomas's novel is ultimately about the Holocaust. Günther Grass's "borrowing" is placed in quite a different context. Grass isolates this text and displaces it into the seventeenth century, with an evocation of the post World-War II era and the *Gruppe 47*. He thus brackets the world which Hilsenrath inhabited. This violation of the Jew's authenticity, of the voice of the Jew narrating his own experience within the literary world of contemporary fiction is marked by Grass's borrowing. The Jew not only vanishes, his voice becomes the authentic voice of the German experience of the seventeenth century or the immediate post-war era.

The English translation of Hilsenrath's first novel appeared before the German edition which was published in former West Germany only with great difficulty. The novel received a wide readership solely when it came out as a paperback. By contrast, Grass's novel was widely advertised and widely discussed (if rarely read) as soon as it appeared. Grass manages to incorporate and thus make invisible, not only his source, but certainly as important, the context out of which this source springs, the post-war German Jews struggle to establish their own identity in German culture. Grass's visible Jews are marked by the flaw of the hidden language ascribed to the Jews; his hidden Jew, Edgar Hilsenrath, marks the invisibility of the Jew in the literary world of post-war Germany. As certainly as Markus and Matern represent the visible Jew with his contaminated discourse in the world of the Danzig Trilogy, so does Hilsenrath function in Grass's work as the hidden Jew, representing the Jew within post-war "high" culture, neither seen nor heard. For even when they are seen — as in the popularity of Hilsenrath's novel *The Nazi and the Barber* — they are relegated to the world of the past, a world completed and closed. They are not acknowledge as part of the world of the present, taking their themes out of their own experience but casting them in the discourse of the high culture in which they live. Thus the *Spiegel* review of Hilsenrath's latest novel evokes "the Jew Werfel" and his novel of the Armenian massacre; in other words, a dead Jew is evoked to categorize the living author.

What has become central is the question as to whether or not the Jew in contemporary Germany, so long the marker of what the German was not, still plays any role in contemporary German thought or whether he has been replaced by other categories of difference, such as the Turk.[16] But it is clear that these two images are related. The far right associates the public image of the "foreigner" with the image of the "Jew." Graffiti in Turkish neighborhoods in West Berlin, such as "Zyklon B" or "off to

Auschwitz" directly evoke the Shoah. Jewish inhabitants of West Berlin understand comments such as "Just wait until we've gotten rid of [Heinz] Galinski — because then your time here has come as well" not merely as threats against the Turks but also as threats against themselves as "foreigners."[17] It is clear from contemporary neo-conservative historians that the role of the Jew has shifted. The German wishes to shed the burden of the past, in which the Jew was the central icon of difference. How does the history of anti-Semitism function in a world devoid of Jews, or at least, a world in which the Jew is no longer heard? And how does this unheard Jew respond? And this especially with the rise of a public discourse of anti-Semitism in the light of the heightened expectations of German reunification. Deprived of the Shoah as the central marker of an self-defined "authentic" discourse about Jewish difference, the contemporary West German Jew must seek other models. There has been a necessary shift from the earlier model, in which Jews internalized the extraordinary visibility given to them within the culture of the Diaspora. The process of internalization is now linked to the marginal invisibility of the Jews. Thus the need for new German-Jewish periodicals such as *Semit* and *Babylon* which provide a "new language" for the German Jew — not the language of the official, post-Shoah discourse of the Jewish community under Heinz Galinski but a new language, a unique language — now modeled on the language of the "new" Jewish left in the United States. This recent growth in the awareness of the need to generate a discourse which is "their own" has lead younger, liberal German-Jews to evolve their own "authentic" discourse. Based on the model of American periodicals such as *Tikkun*, whose attempt to revivify the role of self-identified Jews within the left (where there had been a long tradition of repressing any Jewish identity, except as an ethnic marker) has resulted in a "new" manner for Jews to speak. While the old left borrowed its vocabulary from the old, often anti-Semitic European left, it in fact returns to the older, *Bundist* model of cultural and political activism merging this with a political critique of contemporary Israeli politics rather than Zionism as an ideology. Here, too, a model for the appropriate language of the Jew responds to the idea of the special language of the Jew in a context of European Socialism in which the "Christian" roots are difficult but not impossible to trace.

IV.

Yet the myth of the "hidden" language of the Jew is not a "German" or a "German-Jewish" problem. In post-Shoah America — the image of the "hidden language" of the Jew — the absence of the center in the Jew's character as reflected in his/her ability to command truly the discourse of the world in which he/she dwells — can be found in artifacts of higher culture from Geoffrey Wolff's 1979 autobiographical study of his father's life[18] to Bernard Wasserstein's 1988 biography of the Hungarian Jew Trebitsch Lincoln.[19] The image of the "talking" Jew — the post-Shoah manifestation of an internalized metaphor of the Jews' hidden language can and does materialize in contemporary Jewish culture throughout the Diaspora. Its roots lie in a Jewish internalization of the Christian image of the Jews' innate difference. One can turn to the intense competition for acceptance between the German-Jewish and Eastern European-Jewish communities in the United States for one salient example. In 1939 Karl A. Menninger recounted his own middle-Western, Christian discomfort at hearing the editor of *The New York Times*, Arthur Sulzberger tell "a story involving the imitation of the Jewish accent of Dr. [A. A.] Brill [the pioneer Eastern European-Jewish psychoanalyst], which I thought was in very bad taste. As a matter of fact, it was the second time he had told it in my presence, and he admitted that he had told it in his office when he made a speech to the employees a few days ago. He is such a cultivated, dignified fellow that it is amazing to hear him come out with this ridicule of the accent of other Jews ..."[20] Menninger supplies his own reading of Sulzberger's reason for distinguishing between his discourse and that of someone whom Menninger sees as a "fellow Jew." Menninger comments that Sulzberger was "timid about being known to be a Jewish newspaper owner." (284) That is, he was anxious about his discourse, the discourse of the journalist being identified as a hidden Jewish discourse. The charge that the media was in the hands of the Jews had first been lodged in Germany in the mid-nineteenth century. The force of this charge had been exacerbated by the public response of the American media to the rise of the Nazis. Sulzberger's fear of the Jew within was articulated by him in his identification of the discourse of the Eastern Jew as aberrant, at a time in 1939 when, in Germany as well as in the United States, the anxiety of all Jews, even extremely acculturated one such as Sulzberger, about their status as members of the dominant culture was high.

When we turn to the most recent past, we can find in the realm of American popular culture a real "Jew who sounds Jewish" — the comic Jackie Mason — whose discourse marked him as different surely as did that of A. A. Brill (and Arthur Sulzberger). The career of Jackie Mason, the last of the "borscht belt" comics, had an extraordinary rebirth during 1987. An act designed for the Catskills which had brought Mason to fame during the 1960s (including a much publicized spat with the TV power Ed Sullivan) led to bankruptcy in 1983. Suddenly this same act became the vehicle which brought him stardom (again) in the late 1980s. Mason understood what had happened: "The Jewish people took me for granted, the young people saw me as an anachronism, then I went to Broadway where I never ever thought I'd succeed." And the reason for his invisibility was his *mauscheln*:

> People said I was too Jewish — and I even suffered from anti-Jewish prejudice from Jews themselves. There was a profound rejection problem: the reverse discrimination of Jews against other Jews who talk like me in show business. I think they were ashamed and embarrassed about my accent, that I was somehow symbolic of the whole fear that Jews would be discriminated against again.[21]

For Jackie Mason, the move to Broadway provided a neutral space in which *mauscheln* was no longer associated with a "Jewish" environment; that is, the audience (Jewish or not) no longer identified with the comic as a representative of the self.

During the fall of 1989 Jackie Mason starred in an ill-fated "sit-com" entitled *Chicken Soup* on ABC. It was canceled on November 8, 1989, even though it was the 13th highest rated network television show. *USA Today*, a good barometer of middle-class opinion, thought "Mason's ethnic shtick wouldn't play to the masses."[22] The use of the Yiddishism in this very phrase placed the discourse of this Jew who sounds Jewish beyond the pale of polite language, the language of middle-class comedy. We have seen in the past decades, as Henry L. Gates, Jr. has recently noted, that the representation of the African American on American television has moved from that of Amos and Andy to Dr. Clifford Huxtable, from the representation of the African American sounding too "black" to one possessing the dominant discourse of American culture.[23] For Jews, the seeming lack of movement from the Jackie Mason of the 1960s to the Jackie Mason of the 1980s was offensive. The Jewish Defense League picketed the ABC studio in New York and "Dan Bloom, a Jewish children's book author from Alaska tried organizing a grass-roots campaign against the show ... He didn't like the Jewish stereotypes portrayed." Bloom observed: "I ... got the feeling he offended many Jews in America. They've heard this type of humor in their homes, but in the public living rooms of America for everybody to hear it seemed embarrassing."[24] Gates quotes W. E. B. Du Bois' saying of 1921 that "the more highly trained we become, the less we can laugh at Negro comedy." The Jew who sounds Jewish, for some American Jews, represents the hidden Jew within, the corrupt Jew of the Gospel, the mark of difference which offends even after the Jew is integrated into the mainstream of American culture.

The question of Mason's discourse was not limited to the reception of his television program. Mason's role as a "Jew who sounds Jewish," a Jew

visibly marked by his discourse, had become a source of comment during
September and October of 1989. In the campaign for mayor in New York
City, Mason backed the Republican candidate Rudolph W. Giuliani, who
had made a special effort to attract the traditionally Democratic Jewish
voters to support him rather than the African-American Democratic
candidate, David N. Dinkins. Guiliani's desire for Jewish support in this
contest was articulated by Mason in September 1989 when he stated in
an interview in *The Village Voice*:

> there is a sick Jewish problem of voting for a black man no matter
> how unfit he is for the job. All you have to be is black and don't
> curse the Jews directly and the Jew will vote for a black in a
> second. Jews are sick with complexes.[25]

Mason's comment about the nature of African-American/Jewish relations
lead to a firestorm of accusations about Mason's "racism" and forced
Mason to withdraw from his public role in Giuliani's campaign. What
was most interesting was the subsequent revelation that Mason had
earlier called Dinkins "a fancy *shvartze* with a mustache" during a late
August meeting with four reporters from *Newsweek*.[26] It is this
Yiddishism which generated a further debate about the visibility of the
hidden language of the Jews. The response to Mason, whether in his
political role as a supporter of Giuliani or in his role as a television actor
was that such a discourse was much "too Jewish." Mason was
self-consciously seen as a Jew because his discourse (whether his comic
or his "racist" discourse) set him apart of the accepted image of the Jew.
His image violated the conventional (media) wisdom about the way that
Jews were supposed to sound: they were not supposed to sound
different, they were supposed to sound "liberal." The question of a
hidden language, a language which was "too Jewish" focussed the image
of Jackie Mason as a Jew, but in a pejorative sense. The term "Jew" came
to be understood in a public perception that Jews have a hidden, shared
code in talking about African Americans. Thus the *Newsweek* reporters
refrained from breaking the story about the use of Mason's Yiddishism
until *The Village Voice* published the story about the "Jewish complex."
The *Newsweek* reporters discussed breaking the story after their meeting
with Giuliani and Mason on August 31 because of "Mr. Mason's use of
'*schvartzer*.'"[27] They decided not to use the material at all. One can
speculate that it was the question of attributing a hidden language, a
language which marked Mason as a Jew, which caused their hesitation
to release the interview. Indeed, when the question of releasing this
material was broached in another context, the removal of the use of the
Yiddishism became central to the use of the interview. The liberal sensi-

tivity to the claim that Jews sound different is a marker that this charge
is alive and well in modern American society.

The extent of the power of the Jews' hidden language in the 1980s may
well reveal itself in a piece which appeared this past summer in *Esquire*
— not the natural locus for texts dealing with this question. The novelist
Daphne Merkin, an associate publisher at Harcourt Brace Janovich,
comments on her inner life as the child of a Shoah survivor:

> Floating always among us was an awareness of the importance of
> avoiding, if one could help it, "too Jewish" an appearance, the
> dread stigma of "too Jewish" a voice. My sisters, accordingly,
> emerged with carefully modulated accents that sounded vaguely
> foreign, a mix of German and British. I, by some cruel twist of
> fate, developed an accent that sounded unmistakable, harshly
> "New Yawk." My mother and sisters wanted to know why I
> talked as if I came from Brooklyn, but somehow I must have
> wanted to shed all vestiges of the dominant culture and get back
> to the lusty Jewish core ... Can racial self-hatred be passed along,
> like a bad gene?[28]

Merkin's comments on the fantasy of self-hatred, on the rejection of the
Jewish core, of "the prominent nose, darker coloring, or intensity of gaze
I associated with being Jewish." For Merkin, the return to the "lusty
Jewish core" is the act of talking with a "Jewish" accent — here, the accent
of the urban environment, of New York. This is not an accidental
association. It is not merely that more Jews live in New York than in
Jerusalem, but that there is a traditional association between the idea of
the American city and that of the Jew. For the nineteenth- and early
twentieth-century mind, cities are places of disease and the Jews are the
quintessential city dwellers.[29] For the turn-of-the-century Vienna
psychiatrist Richard Krafft-Ebing, the Jew is the ultimate "city person"
whose sensibilities are dulled.[30] And for Henry James, returning to the
haunts of his childhood in 1907, this city of Jews — New York — is the
deathbed of the English language, the "East side cafes" have become the
"torture rooms of the living idioms."[31] After the Shoah the "hidden"
language of the Jews in New York continues to be represented in the
language of the immigrant-survivor (the mixed dialects of Merkin's
sisters as well as literary figures such as the protagonist of Saul Bellow's
Mr. Sammler's Planet). Merkin attempts to set herself apart from this
tradition by merging her language with the general culture, but the
discourse of her attempt at acculturation, the language of "New Yawk"
is also marked as a language of Jews, but of American Jews not of the
European survivor. The image of the city of Jews haunts Adolf Hitler's
image of Vienna, the city in which he first learns to "see" the Jew and,

therefore, becomes aware of the "hidden" difference in this language of the Jew — even when he or she is speaking "good" German. Merkin attempts to makes the acculturation of her Jewish discourse into a positive marker; one can, however, note that the "Jewish American Princess" speaks a similar "jargon." Debbie Lukatsky and Sandy Barnett Toback in their *Jewish American Princess Handbook* (1982) append a glossary of "Jewish Jargon" to the volume.[32] "Jewish" terms such as "Chuppa" ("Marriage canopy. More decorative than symbolic") and "shagits" ("blond haired, blue eyed forbidden fruit who ends up marrying a shiksa") compete with terms such as "Guilt" ("Jewish hereditary disease. Symptoms including a churning stomach and feelings of deep-seated anxiety. Highly contagious, especially when the Princess spends too much time in the company of her mother") and "money" ("the ultimate aphrodisiac [Credit cards acceptable]"). Such lists were standard in all of the anti-Semitic literature of the late nineteenth and early twentieth centuries, when West European Jews were no longer marked by a "special" accent, as they came to speak German, French, or English. The lists pointed to the inherent hidden language of the Jew, his or her cultural difference and corruption. This legend of the Jew who sounds Jewish now takes on new meaning for Jews in the 1980s.

Merkin brings her piece to a close with the realization that:

> there is no sign that the world has grown more fond of the Jews, so there is no sign I will ever be free of a certain fascination with the darker impulses at work in myself and others ... There is some kind of relief in being able to recognize the aggressor, even identify with him for a while, and then walk on. Like tipping one's hat at one's enemy, it may not be a grandstanding gesture, but it's definitely a civilized one. (85)

The true civilized gesture in Merkin's piece, however, lies not in its message, but in its medium. Her essay on the seduction of the Other who is one's self was written in a completely acculturated style and appeared in *Esquire*, a popular "men's" magazine with intellectual pretensions. Merkin's act of writing frees her from her sense of self-hatred in proving that she really is a member of the cultural elite of "New Yawk."

The discourse concerning the internalization of difference appears throughout contemporary Jewish writing. Daniel Landis, director of the National Education Project of the Simon Wiesenthal Center in Los Angeles, wrote in a recent issue of *Tikkun* that the very abuse of the metaphor of the Shoah by Jews and Christians alike reflects the essence of the "self-hating" Jew:

> There really are Jews who have internalized the anti-Semitism of
> the societies in which they live, and who feel angry at the parts
> of themselves that are distinguishably Jewish. The self-hating Jews
> have a quandary. On some level they identify as Jews, but they
> simultaneously deny an essential part of that definition; either
> peoplehood, religious culture, or the Jews' historical relationship
> to the land of Israel. The Israel/Nazi analogy relieves the
> self-hating Jews of this tension: they can be good prophetic Jews
> by opposing exclusivistic Jews, fanatical Judaism, and the "Fascist"
> Jewish state.[33]

The discourse of the "self-hating Jew" becomes the marker of the
"corrupt" (and "corrupting") locus of where the "real" Jew, the evil Jew
lurks. Landes's need to "define" the Jew in a narrow manner which
includes himself (evidently not a "self-hating Jew") but excludes others is
striking. The pure internalization of a negative image — as in the case of
those Italian "Jews" who literally discovered their "Jewishness" with the
promulgation of the Fascist racial laws in 1938 — is not a possibility for
Landes. It is the rejection of some intrinsic quality of "Jewishness" —
which would include a contemporary political definition which puts their
discourse, their generation of a corrupting metaphor "beyond the Pale."

Phillip Lopate, one of the literary editors of *Tikkun*, presented a similar
argument — but in a very different context.[34] He is — if the subsequent
exchange with Jehuda Bauer in *Tikkun* is any indicator — precisely the
sort of "self-hating Jew" whom Landes condemns. In a long piece on
"Resistance to the Holocaust" Landes critiques the "kitsch" aspects of the
Shoah, seeing it as an event in world history and bemoans the special,
indeed central, status given to it by many contemporary Jews in the
United States and Israel. He notes that his first exposure to this
"Shoah-ization" (my word — not his) of the discourse of modern Jewry
came in a "large communal seder in Houston, about 1982":

> ... the introduction of references to the Holocaust in every second
> or third prayer seemed to have a different function. For many of
> the people at that seder in Texas, the Shoah *was* the heart of their
> faith; it was what touched them most deeply about being Jewish.
> The religion itself — the prayers, the commentaries, the rituals, the
> centuries of accumulated wisdom and tradition — had shriveled
> to a sort of marginally necessary preamble for this negative
> miracle.

This is the negative, corrupt discourse of the Jew — the replacement of a
"true" language of difference (in the prayers, commentaries, etc.) with a
false center — the metaphor of the Shoah. But what is the "real" reason for

this substitution, indeed what is the "real" hidden language which marks the "true Jew" according to Lopate:

> The importance of the Shoah for such assimilated Jews must be considered within the broader framework of the erosion of Jewish group memory in the modern period. By group or "collective" memory, I mean simply all the customs, rituals, ceremonies, folkways, *Yiddishkeit*, cuisine, historical events, and so on that used to be the common inheritance of every Jew.

This is an extraordinary leap, one which must be contrasted with that of Merkin and Landes.

The real Jew is the Eastern Jew, whose "*Yiddishkeit*" (and Lopate stresses the authenticity of this experience by employing the "real" language of the Jews, Yiddish) is the mark of the Jews' "hidden" language. This is Merkin's "New Yawk," the goal which she, as the child of Shoah survivors seeks — the authenticity of the *shtetl's* "never-never world" transported into Shalom Aleichem's "New Yawk." (It is also the counter-image of Philip Roth's "Faginy, Yiddish" image of the Jew employed by the British anti-Semite.) It is an intact world, a world with shared experiences, which excludes the "acculturated" survivors of the Shoah. For here Lopate reveals his hidden agenda. These Jews gathered around the seder table in Houston are not assimilated — they have not disappeared into the mass culture of the American experience. They may well be acculturated, like many of the Western and some of the Eastern European Jews who died in the Shoah, but their participation in a seder indicates their self-identification as part of a cultural sub-group. Lopate's definition of the Jew, like that of Landis, postulates a "good" Jew who sounds Jewish (Lopalte, Landis) and a "bad" Jew who sounds Jewish (the object of their investigation). Their act of writing "proves" to the reader their command of the "good" discourse of the Jew.

Let us conclude this survey of the post-Shoah continuation of the myth of the Jews' "hidden" language with a comment from the Indian poet Nissim Ezekiel. Ezekiel is an Anglophone Jewish poet who abandoned his mother tongue of Marathi to write poetry and drama in the dominant literary language of the Commonwealth, English. But in a culture where "English" is a co-terminus with "Christian." In an interview he was asked whether having "been a Jew in India, sent first to a Catholic, then to a Presbyterian school made him conscious of a sense of physical frailness" and whether the question of identity was a problem for him?[35] He answered:

> Yes, it did create a problem. I did have a feeling of things loaded against myself, with no prospect of getting strength and

confidence. My background did make me an outsider; but it's too
easy to talk of being an outsider. I don't want to remain negative:
I feel I have to connect, and turn the situation to the positive.

But he noted that "the notion of being a world poet" makes him

feel a little empty, rootless. One needs some sense of belonging.
But there is a trap in identifying one's audience in terms of
specific geographic location. I write my poems for anyone who is
likely to enjoy them in any part of the world, in any time...

This view of literature as a "safe space" in which even the Jews' language
can be heard is echoed in his "Minority Poem" from the early 1980s:

In my room, I talk
to my invisible guests:
they do not argue but wait

Till I am exhausted
then they slip away
with inscrutable faces.

I lack the means to change
their amiable ways,
although I love their gods.

It's the language that really
separates, whatever else
is shared ...[36]

Nissim Ezekiel's attempt to bridge this perceived gap between his Jewish
culture and the cultures among which he lives is to be found in his
Latter-Day Psalms, his rewriting of a series of biblical texts into the
language of modern Anglo-Indian poetry. His deeply felt attempts to
capture the world of Bene-Israel life in poems such as his "Jewish
Wedding in Bombay" still places the voice of the Anglophone-Jewish
writer into the position of the poet per se. There is nothing "Jewish" about
his language, even though his themes may evoke the difference and
separateness of the Jew. For Nissim Ezekail's poetic idiom, in marked
contrast to the parodied language of his *Very Indian Poems in Indian
English*, are written in the language of Anglophone high culture. It is in
the international world of letters, of Anglophone ("Christian") high
culture that the Jew — whether in Houston, "New Yawk" or Bombay, all
find a space which is seemingly neutral. But it is of course only

seemingly so. For the trap is that high culture in Germany and in the United States provides a medium for Jews to "escape" the label of being unable to control the language in which they write and think, but it also lends it credibility. For "high" culture is indeed on one level the secularized fetishism of the text as practiced by Christianity.

The roots of our contemporary sense of the centrality of books is rooted in the centrality of the Book (taken over and refashioned from Judaism) which dominates the so-called Judeo-Christian world. The discourse of Western culture never completely lacks the claim that Jews cannot be part of "true" culture. One can think about Gore Vidal's attack on Norman Podhoretz in the 1986 as being more concerned with their "Jewish" identities (i.e., Israeli politics) than their "American" cultural identities.[37] "High" culture does not provide the bulwark against the charge of being different; indeed it provides, as Sacan Bercovitch has so cogently argued, a set of definitions for difference which seem to be more and more concrete.[38] These ideological limits are present within the image of the Jew in Western high culture from the very beginnings of Christianity through to the present day. They appear in an infinite series of variations and permutations but they exist within all of Western culture.

Notes

[1] Philip Roth: *Deception*. New York 1990, p. 109.

[2] Sander L. Gilman: *Jewish Self-Hatred: Anti-Semitism and the Hidden Language of the Jews*. Baltimore 1986.

[3] See Rosemary Reuther: *Faith and Fatricide: The Theology Roots of Antisemitism*. New York 1974.

[4] Morton Scott Enslin: *Christian Beginnings*. New York 1938, p. 421.

[5] Augustine: *The First Catechetical Instruction*, trans. by Joseph P. Christopher. Westminster, Maryland 1946, p. 134.

[6] Ann Marie Lipinski and Dean Baquet: "Sawyer Aide's Ethnic Slurs Stir Uproar." In: *Chicago Tribune*, 1 May 1988, p. 1; Anthony Lewis: "A Dangerous Poison." In: *The New York Times*, 31 July 1988, p. E:25; and Cheryl Deval: "Sawyer Won't Fire Aide over Ethnic Slurs." In: *Chicago Tribune*, 5 May 1988, p. 1.

[7] Cited by Saul Friedländer: *Kurt Gerstein: The Ambiguity of Good*, trans. by Charles Fullman. New York 1969, pp. 148-149.

[8] Theodor Adorno: *Minima moralia: Reflexionen aus dem beschädigten Leben*. Berlin 1951, p. 200.

[9] Jean-Paul Sartre: *Anti-Semite and Jew*, trans. by George J. Becker. New York 1965, pp. 136-37.

[10] See Sander L. Gilman: "Jewish Writers and German Letters: Anti-Semitism and the Hidden Language of the Jews." In: *The Jewish Quarterly Review* 77, 1986/7, p.119-148.

[11] Henryk M. Broder: "Die unheilbare Leibe deutscher Intellektueller zu toten und todkranken Juden." In: *Semit* 3, 1989, p. 29.

[12] The term is from Dan Diner: "Negative Symbiose: Deutsche und Juden nach Auschwitz." In *Babylon* 1, 1986, pp. 9-10.

[13] Compare the passages in Günther Grass: *The Meeting at Telgte*, trans. by Ralph Mannheim. New York 1979, p. 35 and Edgar Hilsenrath: *Night*, trans. by Michael Roloff. New York 1974, pp. 278-79.

[14] Günter Grass: *Das Treffen in Telgte*, ed. by Christoph Sieger. In: *Werkausgabe in Zehn Bänden*, ed. by Volker Neuhaus. Frankfurt a. M. 1987, vol. 6, pp. 37-38 and Andreas Graf: "ein leises 'dennoch': Zum ironischen Wechselbezug von Literatur und Wirklichkeit in Günter Grass' Erzählung Das Treffen in Telgte." In: *Deutsche Vierteljahresschrift für Literaturwissenschaft und Geistesgeschichte* 63, 1989, pp.282-94.

[15] D. M. Thomas: *The White Hotel*. New York 1981. On the "borrowing" see Lady Falls Brown: "The White hotel: D. M. Thomas's considerable debt to Anatoli Kuznetsov and Babi Yar." In: *South Central Review* 22, 1985, pp. 60-79; Yevgeny Yevtushenko: "Babi Yar." In: *The Holocaust Years: Society on Trial*, ed. Roselle Chartock and Jack Spencer. New York 1978, pp.36-45; James E. Young: *Writing and Rewriting the Holocaust: Narrative and Consequences of Interpretation*. Bloomington, Indiana 1988. George Levine: "No Reservations: The White Hotel." In: *New York Review of Books*, 28 May 1981, pp. 20-23; Mary F. Robertson: "Hystery, Herstory, History: 'Imagining the Real' in Thomas's The White Hotel." In: *Contemporary Literature* 25, 1984, pp. 452-477; Ellen Y. Siegelman: "The White Hotel: Visions and Revisions of the Psyche." In: *Literature and Psychology* 33, 1987, pp. 69-76. See also D. W. Thomas: "On Literary Celebrity." In: *The New York Times Magazine*, 13 June 1982.

[16] See the special issue of *New German Critique* 46, 1989 on *Minorities in German Culture* in which the Jew is but one of a growing list of "minorities" that play a defining cultural difference in the Federal Republic.

[17] These examples are cited in a letter from Y. M. Bodemann (Berlin) printed in the *SICSA Report* 3, 1989-90, p. 3.

[18] Geoffrey Wolff: *The Duke of Deception: Memories of My Father*. New York 1979.

[19] Bernard Wasserstein: *The Secret Lives of Trebitsch Lincoln*. New Haven, Connecticut 1988.

[20] Howard J. Faulkner and Virgina D. Pruitt, ed., *The Selected Correspondence of Karl A. Menninger, 1919-1945*, New Haven, Connecticut 1988, p. 282.

[21] Glenn Collins: "Jackie Mason, Top Banana at Last." In: *The New York Times*, 24 July 1988, Section 2, p. 1 and 14.

[22] "Highly Touted 'Soup' Goes Down the Drain." In: *USA Today*, 8 November 1989, pp. 1D-2D.

23 Henry L. Gates, Jr.: "TV's Black World Turns — But Stays Unreal." In: *The New York Times*, 12 November 1989, Section 2, p 1 and 40.

24 *USA Today*, op. cit.

25 Cited in *The New York Times*, 28 September, 1989, p. B1.

26 Cited in *The New York Times*, 2 October, 1989, p. B1.

27 Cited in *The New York Times*, 14 October, 1989, p. 28.

28 Daphne Merkin: "Dreaming of Hitler." In: *Esquire*, August 1989, pp. 75-83.

29 Richard Krafft-Ebing: *Psychopathologia Sexualis: A Medico-Forensic Study*, rev. trans. by Harry E. Wedeck. New York 1965, p. 24.

30 Compare Otto Binswanger: *Hysterie*. Vienna 1904, p. 82.

31 Henry James: *The American Scene*. London 1907, pp. 129-131.

32 Debbie Lukatsky and Sandy Barnett Toback: *Jewish American Princess Handbook*. Arlington Heights, Illinois, 1982, pp. 142-43.

33 Daniel Landes: "Anti-Semitism Parading as Anti-Zionism." In: *Tikkun*, May-June 1989, pp. 85-88.

34 Phillip Lopate: "Resistance to the Holocaust." In: *Tikkun* May-June 1989, pp. 55-65. The debate with Bauer is included in the same issue, pp. 65-70.

35 John B. Beston: "An Interview with Nissim Ezekiel." In: *World Literature Written in English* 16, 1977, pp. 87-94.

36 Nissim Ezekiel: *Collected Poems 1952-1988*. Delhi 1989, p. 236.

37 See Norman Podhoretz: "Vidal's Outburst: An Ominous New Stage in Anti-Semitism." In: *The Washington Post*, 8 May 1986; Edwin M. Yoder: "Is Distaste for Israeli Policy Anti-Semitism?" In: *Los Angeles Times*, 22 May 1986; William Safire: "Vidal, Waldheim, Grant." In: *The New York Times*, 19 May 1986.

38 Sacvan Bercovitsch, ed., *Reconstructing American Literary History*, Cambridge, Mass. 1986, p. 34.

Evelyn Torton Beck

From *KIKE* to *JAP*:
How Misogyny, Anti-Semitism, and Racism Construct the *Jewish American Princess*[1]

I.

The stereotyping of the Jewish American woman as the JAP, which stands for Jewish American Princess, is an insult, an injury, and violence that is done to Jewish women. The term is used widely by both men and women, by both Jews and non-Jews. When gentiles use it, it is a form of anti-Semitism. When Jews use it, it is a form of self-hating or internalized anti-Semitism. It is a way of thinking that allows some Jewish women to harm other Jewish women who are just like them except for the fact that one is okay — "she's **not** a JAP." The other is not okay — "she's too JAPie." The seriousness of this term becomes evident when we substitute the words "too Jewish" for "too JAPie," and feel ourselves becoming considerably less comfortable.

When I speak on college campuses, young women frequently tell me that when someone calls them a Jew they are insulted because they know it's being said with a kind of hostility, but if someone calls them a JAP they don't mind because they frequently use this term themselves. They think the "J" in JAP really doesn't mean anything — it's just there. While everyone seems to know what the characteristics of a "Jewish American Princess" are, no one ever seems to think about what they are saving when they use the term. How is it that you don't have to be Jewish to be a JAP? If this is so, why is the word "Jewish" in the acronym at all? Words are not meaningless unless we choose to close our ears and pretend not to hear.

This subject is frequently trivialized, but when it is not, when we take it seriously, it makes us extremely tense. Why is that? I think it's because it takes us into several "war zones." It brings us in touch with Jew-hating, or anti-Semitism. It brings us in touch with misogyny, or woman-hating. And it brings us in touch with class-hatred, old money vs. nouveau riche. (Jews have classically been seen as intruders in the United States and have been resented for "making it.") It also puts us strongly in touch with racism. It is no accident that the acronym JAP is also the word used for our worst enemies in World War II — who were known as "the Japs." During World War II, posters and slogans saying "Kill Japs" were everywhere. It was a period in which slang terms were readily used in a pejorative way to identify many different minorities: "Japs," "Kikes," "Spics," "Wops," "Chinks" were commonplace terms used unthinkingly. And women were — and, unfortunately, still are — easily named "bitches," "sluts," and "cunts."

In such a climate, negative stereotypes easily overlap and elide. For example, in the popular imagination, Jews, "Japs," women and homosexuals have all been viewed as devious, unreliable, and power hungry. What has happened in the decades following World War II is that the "Japs," whom we de-humanized when we dropped our atom bomb on them, have subliminally merged in the popular imagination with "kikes" and other foreign undesirables. (The fact that in the 1980s Japan poses a serious economic threat to the United States should not be overlooked either.) While efforts to eradicate slurs against ethnic minorities have made it not okay to use explicitly ethnic epithets, women still provide an acceptable target, especially when the misogyny is disguised as supposedly "good-natured" humor. In this insidious and circuitous way, the Jewish American woman carries the stigmas of the "kikes" and "Japs" of a previous era. And that is very serious.

The woman, the Jewish woman as JAP has replaced the male Jew as the scapegoat, and the Jewish male has not only participated, but has, in fact, been instrumental in creating and perpetuating that image. I want to show how some of the images of Jewish women created in American culture by Jewish men provided the roots of the "Jewish American Princess." But first I want to provide a context for understanding the development of this image. I want to look at anti-Semitism in the United States, and at misogyny, and show how the merging of anti-Semitism and misogyny creates the Jewish American Princess.

Between 1986 and 1987 there was a 17 percent rise in anti-Semitic incidents in this country. Of these incidents, 48 percent occurred in the Northeast, and the highest rates of increase were in New York State; California, particularly Los Angeles, and Florida. These are all areas where there are high concentrations of Jews. On November 9 and 10, 1987, the anniversary of *Kristallnacht*, the Night of Broken Glass, when Goebbels staged a mass "spontaneous pogrom" in Austria and Germany in 1938, swastikas were painted on entrances to synagogues in a number of different cities in the United States: Chicago, Yonkers, and others dotted across the country. Windows were smashed — not simply of Jewish-owned stores, but of identifiably Jewish businesses, such as kosher meat markets, a kosher fish store, a Jewish book store — in five different neighborhoods, particularly in a Chicago suburb largely populated by Holocaust survivors. Having grown up in Vienna and having lived under the Nazis, the horror of that night resonated for me in a way that it might not for those who are much younger. But that these pogrom- like episodes happened on the eve of *Kristallnacht* cannot have been an accident, and the timing of these incidents should not be lost upon us.

In response to these attacks many members of the Jewish community wanted to hide the facts, and one member of the Jewish community in Chicago actually said, "The swastikas could have meant general white supremacy; they were not necessarily aimed at Jews." They just "happened" to be placed on synagogues, right? In the same way, it just "happens" that the word "Jewish" is lodged in the very negative image of this hideous creature known as the Jewish American Princess. Anyone who is aware of Jewish history and knows about the ridicule, defamation, and violence to which Jews have been subject will not be able to write this off so easily.

The Jewish American Princess phenomenon is not new; I (as well as other Jewish feminists) have been talking about it for at least ten years now, but only recently has it been given wide public attention. One reason for this is that it is beginning to be seen in the light of increased anti-Semitism and racism, particularly on college campuses. Dr. Gary Spencer, who is a male professor of sociology at Syracuse University (and it is unfortunate that his being male gives him credibility over women saying the same things) closely examined the library and bathroom graffiti of his school and interviewed hundreds of students on his campus and has concluded that JAP-baiting is widespread, virulent, and threatening to all Jews, not "just" Jewish women (which we gather might have been okay or certainly considerably less serious).

Spencer discovered that nasty comments about "JAPS" led to more generally anti-Semitic graffiti that said among other slogans, "Hitler was right!" "Give Hitler a second chance!" and "I hate Jews." He also discovered that there were certain places in which Jewish women — JAPS — were not welcome: for example, certain cafes where Jewish women were hassled if they entered. He also found that certain areas of the University were considered "JAP-free zones" and other areas (particular dorms) that were called "Jew havens." At The American University in Washington, D.C., largely Jewish residence halls are called "Tokyo Towers," making the racial overtones of JAP explicit. But let the parallels to Nazi occupied Europe not be lost upon us. Under the Nazis, movements of Jews were sharply restricted: there were many areas which Jews could not enter, and others (like ghettos and concentration camps) that they could not leave.

What I want to do now is to show how characteristics that have historically been attributed to Jews, primarily Jewish men, have been reinterpreted in terms of women: how misogyny combined with Jew-hating creates the Jewish American Princess. And I want you to remember that Jewish men have not only participated in this trashing, but they have not protected Jewish women when other men and women have talked about "JAPs" in this way. And this fact, I think, has made this an arena into which anyone can step — an arena that becomes a minefield when Jews step into it.

Jews have been said to be materialistic, money-grabbing, greedy, and ostentatious. Women have been said to be vain, trivial and shallow; they're only interested in clothing, in show. When you put these together you get the Jewish-woman type who's only interested in designer clothes and sees her children only as extensions of herself. The Jew has been seen as manipulative, crafty, untrustworthy, unreliable, calculating, controlling, and malevolent. The Jewish Princess is seen as manipulative, particularly of the men in her life, her husband, her boyfriend, her father. And what does she want? Their money! In addition, she's lazy — she doesn't work inside or outside the home. She is the female version of the Jew who, according to anti-Semitic lore, is a parasite of society; contradictorily, the Jew has been viewed both as dangerous "communist" as well as non-productive "capitalist." The cartoon vision of the Jewish American Princess is someone who sucks men dry: she is an "unnatural mother" who refuses to nurture her children (the very opposite of the "Jewish mother" whose willingness to martyr herself makes **her** ludicrous). And she doesn't "put out" except in return for goods; she isn't really interested in either sexuality or lovingness. We live in a world climate and culture in which materialism is rampant, and Jewish women are taking the rap for it. The irony is they are taking the rap from non-Jews and Jewish men alike — even from some Jewish women.

Another way in which Jewish women are carrying the anti-Semitism that was directed in previous eras at Jewish men is in the arena of sexuality. Jews have been said to be sexually strange, exotic. There are many stereotypes of Jewish men as lechers. The Jewish American Princess is portrayed as both sexually frigid (withholding) and as a nymphomaniac. Here we again see the familiar anti-Semitic figure of the Jew as controlling and insatiably greedy, always wanting more, combining with the misogynist stereotype of the insatiable woman, the woman who is infinitely orgasmic, who will destroy men with her desire. Like the Jew of old, the Jewish woman will suck men dry. But she is worse than "the Jew" — she will also turn on her own kind.

There are physical stereotypes as well: the Jew with the big hook nose, thick lips, and frizzy hair. The Jewish American Princess has had a nose job and her hair has been straightened, but she too has large lips (an image we immediately also recognize as racist). Jews are supposed to be loud, pushy, and speak with unrefined accents. Jewish American Princesses are said to come from Long Island and speak with funny accents: "Oh my Gawd!" The accent has changed from the lampooned immigrant speech of previous generations, but assimilation into the middle class hasn't helped the Jewish American Princess get rid of her accent. It doesn't matter how she speaks, because if it's Eastern and recognizable Jewish, it's not okay.

I also want to give you some idea of how widespread and what a moneymaking industry the Jewish American Princess phenomenon has become. There are greeting cards about the "JAP Olympics," with the JAP doing things like "bank-vaulting" instead of pole-vaulting. Or cross-country "kvetching" instead of skiing. In this card the definition of the Yiddish term "kvetch" reads: "an irritable whine made by a three-year-old child or a JAP at any age." So in addition to the all-powerful monster you also have the infantilization of the Jewish woman. And there are the Bunny Bagelman greeting cards: Bunny has frizzy hair, big lips, is wearing ostentatious jewelry — and is always marked as a Jew in some way. One of her cards reads, "May God Bless you and keep you . . . rich!" Or Bunny Bagelman is a professional, dressed in a suit carrying a briefcase, but this image is undermined by the little crown she incongruously wears on her head bearing the initials "JAP." There is also a Halloween card with a grotesque female figure; the card reads, "Is it a vicious vampire? No, it's Bunny Bagelman with PM syndrome!" In analyzing these kinds of cartoons, you begin to see how sexism is absolutely intertwined with anti-Semitism.

Such attacks devalue Jewish women and keep them in line. An incident reported by Professor Spencer at Syracuse University makes this quite evident. At a basketball game, when women who were presumed to be "JAPs" stood up and walked across the floor at half-time (and it happened to Jewish and non-Jewish women), 2,000 students stood up, accusingly pointed their fingers at them, and repeatedly yelled, "JAP, JAP, JAP, JAP, JAP" in a loud chorus. This was so humiliating and frightening that women no longer got out of their seats to go to the bathroom or to get a soda. This is a form of public harassment that is guaranteed to control behavior and parallels a phenomenon called "punching" at the University of Dar El Salaam, Tanzania. Here, when women were "uppity" or otherwise stepped out of line, huge posters with their pictures on them were put all over campus, and no one was to speak to them. If you spoke to these women, you were considered to be like them. This is a very effective way of controlling people.

The threat of physical violence against Jewish women (in the form of "Slap-a-JAP" T-shirts and contests at bars) is evident on many Eastern college campuses. A disc jockey at The American University went so far as to sponsor a "fattest JAP-on-campus" contest. That this kind of unchecked verbal violence can lead to murder is demonstrated by lawyer Shirley Frondorf in a recent book entitled *Death of a "Jewish American Princess": The True Story of a Victim on Trial* (Villard Books, 1988). Frondorf shows how the murder of a Jewish woman by her husband was exonerated and the victim placed on trial because she was someone who was described by her husband as "materialistic, who shopped and spent, nagged shrilly and bothered her husband at work" — in other words, she was a JAP and therefore deserved what she got. This account demonstrates the dangers inherent in stereotyping and the inevitable dehumanization that follows.

One of the most aggressively sexual forms of harassment of Jewish women, which amounted to verbal rape, were signs posted at a college fair booth at Cornell University that read, "Make her prove she's not a JAP, make her swallow." Part of the mythology is that the Jewish woman will suck, but she won't swallow. So you see that as the degradation of woman **as woman** escalates, the anti-Semitism also gets increasingly louder. In a recent Cornell University student newspaper, a cartoon offered advice on how to "exterminate" JAPS by setting up a truck offering bargains, collecting the JAPS as they scurried in, and dropping them over a cliff. While the word "Jew" was not specifically mentioned, the parallels to the historical "rounding up" of Jews and herding them into trucks to be exterminated in the camps during World War II can hardly be ignored. This cartoon was created by a Jewish man.

This leads me directly to the third thing I want to discuss, namely, how and why Jewish men have participated in constructing and perpetuating the image of the Jewish American Princess as monster. How is it that the Jewish Mother (a mildly derogatory stereotype that nonetheless contained some warmth) has become the grotesque that is the Jewish American Princess, who, unlike the Jewish Mother, has absolutely no redeeming features? Exactly how the Jewish Mother (created entirely by second generation American men who had begun to mock the very nurturance they had relied upon for their success) gave birth to the Jewish American Princess is a long and complex story. This story is intertwined with the overall economic success of Jews as a class in the United States, the jealousy others have felt over this success, and the discomfort this success creates in Jews who are fearful of living out the stereotype of the "rich Jew." It is also a likely conjecture that middle-class American Jewish men view the large numbers of Jewish women who have successfully entered the work force as professionals as a serious economic and ego threat.

We find the origins of the Jewish American Princess in the fiction of American Jewish males of the last three decades. In the 50s, Herman Wouk's *Marjory Morningstar* (née Morgenstern) leaves behind her immigrant background, takes a new name (one that is less recognizably Jewish), manipulates men, has no talent, and is only interested in expensive clothing. The postwar Jewish male, who is rapidly assimilating into American middle-class culture and leaving behind traditional Jewish values, is creating the Jewish woman — the materialistic, empty, manipulative Jewish woman, the Americanized daughter who fulfills the

American Dream for her parents but is, at the same time, punished for it. It looks as if the Jewish woman was created in the image of the postwar Jewish male but viewed by her creator as grotesque. All the characteristics he cannot stand in himself are displaced onto the Jewish woman.

In the 60s, Philip Roth created the spoiled and whiny Brenda Potemkin in *Goodbye, Columbus* at the same time that Shel Silverstein created his image of the perfect Jewish mother as martyr. Some of you may remember this popular story from your childhood. A synopsis goes something like this:

> Once there was a tree and she loved the little boy. And he slept in her branches, and loved the tree and the tree was happy. And as the boy grew older, he needed things from her. He needed apples, so she gave him apples, and she was happy. Then she cut off her branches because the boy needed them to build a house. And she was happy. Then finally he needed her trunk because he wanted to build a big boat for himself. And she was happy. The tree gave and gave of herself, and finally the tree was alone and old when the boy returned one more time. By now, the tree had nothing to give. But the boy/man is himself old now, and he doesn't need much except a place on which to sit. And the tree said, "An old stump is good for sitting and resting on. Come boy and sit and rest on me." And the boy did, and the tree was happy.

This "positive" entirely self-**less** mother, created as a positive wish fantasy by a Jewish man, very easily tips over into its opposite, the monstrous woman, the self-absorbed JAP who is negatively self-less. She has no center. She is only clothes, money, and show.

In concluding, I want to bring these strands together and raise some questions. Obviously Jews need to be as thoughtful about consumerism as others, but we need to ask why the Jewish woman is taking the rap for the consumerism which is rampant in our highly materialistic culture in general. We need to think about the image of the Jewish American Princess and the father she tries to manipulate. What has happened to the Jewish Mother? Why has she dropped out of the picture? If (as is likely true of all groups) some middle-class Jewish women (and men) are overly focused on material things, what is the other side of that? What about the middle-class fathers who measure their own success by what material goods they are able to provide to their wives and children and who don't know how to show love in any other way? Someone who doesn't know how to give except through material goods could easily create a Child who comes to expect material goods as a proof of love and self-worth, especially if sexist gender expectations limit the options for women. We need to look more closely at the relationship between the "monster" daughter and the father who helped create her.

This brings up another uncomfortable subject—incest in Jewish families. We have to look carefully at the image of the "little princess" who sits on Daddy's lap and later becomes this monstrous figure. (My father thought it appropriate for me to sit on his lap until the day he died, well into his eighties, and I do not believe he was unusual in his expectations.) There are enough stories of incest in which we know that the father who sexually abuses his daughter when she is a child becomes quite distant when she reaches adolescence and may continue to abuse her in psychological ways. And the JAP image is a real form of psychological abuse. We need to look at these things to understand that this phenomenon is not trivial, and to understand how it undermines all Jewish women and particularly harms young women coming of age. It cannot do Jewish men such good either to think of their sisters, daughters, mothers, and potential girlfriends with such contempt.

Last, I want to say that we have many false images of Jewish families. There is violence in Jewish families, just as there is violence in families of all groups. It is time to put the whole question of the Jewish American Princess into the context of doing away with myths of all kinds. The Jewish family is no more nor less cohesive than other families, although there is great pressure on Jewish families to pretend they are. Not all Jewish families are non-alcoholic; not all Jewish families are heterosexual; not all Jews are upper or middle class; and not all are urban or Eastern. It's important that the truth of Jewish women's (and also Jewish men's) lives be spoken. Beginning to take apart this image of the Jewish American Princess can make us look more closely at what it is that we, in all of our diversity as Jews, are; what we are striving towards; and what we hope to become.

Notes

[1] Evelyn Torton Beck: "From *Kike* to *JAP*." In: *Sojourner: The Woman's Forum*, September 1988, pp. 18-20. Reprinted by author's permission.

II.

Worte als Waffen

Words as Weapons

Ritchie Robertson

"Herr Peregrinus":
Persona, Race, and Gender in Heinrich Heine's
Die Harzreise

The "I" who addresses us in Heine's works is peculiarly elusive. Hence the concept of "persona," or literary mask, has proved exceptionally productive in analyzing his works. This applies not only to the dazzling bravura performance of *Ideen. Das Buch Le Grand*, where the identities of Heine himself, the Graf vom Ganges, and a Venetian knight are bewilderingly superimposed on one another, but also to *Die Harzreise*, which on a superficial reading might seem to present a unitary "I" that can be identified with the biographical Heine.[1] In his letters as well as his published works, Heine constantly assumes or imagines other identities. "Ich bin stolz darauf, ein Perser zu seyn," he writes in 1824; in 1825: "Ich will ein Japaner werden"; and in 1829, in a downcast mood: "ach, ich möchte ein Kätzchen seyn!"[2] In real life, too, Heine loved to adopt roles. *Die Harzreise* includes a patronizing account of the narrator's meeting with an apprentice tailor, who is presented as an instance of the German "Volk." By telling with charming ignorance how the Duke of Brunswick has been captured in the Holy Land, the tailor supposedly demonstrates the timeless, tradition-bound character of the uneducated German people, who believe that they are still living in the age of the Crusades. Yet the "tailor" was in fact a commercial traveller named Carl Dörne, who was also good at role-playing. On reading about himself in the version of *Die Harzreise* published in 1826 in Gubitz's periodical *Der Gesellschafter*, Dörne sent in an essay called "Reise von Osterode nach Clausthal. (Seitenstück zu H. Heines *Harzreise*)," where, after describing Heine's appearance, he recounted their meeting as follows:

> Der Fremde sah mich mit einem sardonischen Lächeln von der
> Seite an, nannte sich Peregrinus und sagte, er sey ein Cosmopolit,
> der auf Kosten des türkischen Kaisers reise, um Rekruten an zu
> werben. "Haben Sie Lust?" fragte er mich. — "Bleibe im Lande
> und nähre dich redlich!" erwiderte ich, und dankte sehr. Um
> indessen Gleiches mit Gleichem zu vergelten, gab ich mich für

einen Schneidergesellen aus und erzählte dem türkischen
Geschäftsträger: daß ich von B. komme, woselbst sich ein
Gerücht verbreitet, daß der junge Landesherr auf einer Reise
nach dem gelobten Lande von den Türken gefangen sey, und ein
ungeheures Lösegeld bezahlen solle. Herr Peregrinus versprach,
sich dieserhalb bei dem Sultan zu verwenden, und erzählte mir
von dem großen Einflusse, den er bei Sr. Hoheit habe.[3]

This little incident deserves some scrutiny. In Dörne's description,
Heine presents himself as a cosmopolitan, a person of no fixed abode or
nationality. His sobriquet "Peregrinus" means "pilgrim" or "wanderer,"
evoking the persona of the rootless, homeless, permanently exiled Jew.
But Heine couples this persona with the compensatory fantasy of
exercising influence upon the Sultan of Turkey, in whose realms Jews
were protected. Moreover, such an allusion to the Orient evokes the
figure of the Chevalier de Geldern, the great-uncle portrayed in Heine's
Memoiren. The Chevalier had travelled extensively in the Near East,
ascended Mount Moriah, and became the leader of a Bedouin robber
band. In this fantasy (as in others quoted above) the Orient figures as a
realm of freedom where the Jew can escape the restrictions imposed on
him in Western Europe and attain power and influence.

At the time of his Harz journey, Heine was particularly bitter about
the resurgence of anti-Semitism.[4] He was embittered not only by the
"Hep-hep" riots of 1819 and the gradual restriction of Jews' civil rights in
Prussia and other German states, but also by the rise of German
nationalism. Thanks to the propagandistic efforts of Fichte, Arndt, and
Jahn, nationalists had constructed a definition of Germanness that
excluded even assimilated Jews like Heine. Fichte's *Reden an die deutsche
Nation* classified German, along with Greek, as an "Ursprache." Its native
speakers were able to commune with the deepest roots of their being in
a manner impossible for those descendants of Germanic tribes who, like
the French, had adopted versions of Latin — and impossible also, by
implication, for Jews who spoke German. The anti-Semitic historian
Friedrich Rühs declared that nothing short of conversion could enable
Jews to become citizens of a Christian state, and spoke with especial
severity of people who (like Heine) had distanced themselves from
traditional Judaism without accepting Christianity:

> ... es kommt nicht darauf an, daß einzelne Mitglieder sich über
> die strengen Vorschriften wegsetzen, das Ansehn der Rabbiner
> und des Ceremonialgesetzes, worin das Wesen des Judentums
> besteht, nicht mehr anerkennen, die Bande zerissen haben, die
> ihnen lästig waren, und die Hauptlehre der jüdischen Religion
> von der Zukunft des Messias für lächerlich erklären: auf diese

kann durchaus gar keine Rücksicht genommen werden; sie bilden ein Mittelding zwischen Juden und Christen, das sich eine eigne Art von völlig unhaltbarer natürlicher Religion, eine moralische Religion der Convenienz und des Vortheils, in thörigstem Dünkel zusammengesetzt hat, eine eigne Secte, die kein Staat anerkennt und die nur eine stillschweigende Duldung genießt.[5]

Brentano's satire *Der Philister vor, in und nach der Geschichte*, read to the "Christlich-deutsche Tischgesellschaft" in March 1811, denounced the Jews as the murderers of Christ, described them as "diese von den ägyptischen Plagen übriggebliebenen Fliegen," and remarked that they could be caught with "Ekel und Humanität und Aufklärung," thus associating them with the supposedly discredited values of the Enlightenment.[6] 1815 saw the highly successful Berlin production of C. B. Sessa's comedy *Unser Verkehr*, a coarse and distasteful satire on the attempts by a Jewish family to enter German society despite the strong German-Jewish dialect ("Mauscheln") which they persist in talking. Even Heine's admired E. T. A. Hoffmann was not free from anti-Semitism, though he had many Jewish friends including Eduard Hitzig (whom Heine mocks in "Jeuda ben Halvey") and the painter Philipp Veit, a grandson of Moses Mendelssohn. In *Die Brautwahl* Hoffmann presents two unpleasant Jewish characters, the old Jew Manasse and his quasi-assimilated nephew Baron Benjamin Dümmerl; the latter, despite his wealth and his mysteriously acquired title, is "ein unausstehlicher Bengel" whose substantial nose ("ansehnliche Nase") becomes the object of a practical joke.[7]

Heine was well aware of these tendencies. In his correspondence he refers resentfully to the efforts of German nationalists like Rühs to deny a German identity to Jews like himself. In a letter written on 7 March 1824 from "Verfluchtes Nest-Göttingen" to his friend Rudolf Christiani, Heine mocks the absurdities of the nationalists, then goes on to reflect:

> Ich weiß, daß ich einer der deutschesten Bestien bin, ich weiß nur zu gut, daß mir das Deutsche das ist, was dem Fische das Wasser ist.... Ich liebe sogar im Grunde das Deutsche mehr als alles auf der Welt, ich habe meine Lust und Freude dran, und meine Brust ist ein Archiv deutschen Gefühls, wie meine zwey Bücher ein Archiv deutschen Gesanges sind.[8]

There was no secure "Jewish" identity for Heine to fall back on — he felt ambivalent about the scholarly efforts of the "Verein für Cultur und Wissenschaft des Judentums," though he served as its deputy secretary, and the Jewishness represented by his Hamburg relatives was for him tainted by commercialism.

Heine's ambivalent feelings about Germany and about Jewishness reappear in *Die Harzreise*. His persona is not just a literary device; it does not only undergo the psychological development traced by Jeffrey Sammons; it is also a means of constructing a fictive "racial" identity which does not quite conform to any available version of Germanness or Jewishness but is related to them in tense and complex ways.

Consider, for example, Heine's satire on German pedantry. The narrator has himself been immersed in the study of law at Göttingen. He needs the walking tour to recover from this enforced tedium, and as soon as he emerges on to the highway and inhales the fresh morning air he starts to feel better. Many Germans, however, carry an atmosphere of narrow-minded pedantry with them wherever they go. These include the Göttingen schoolboy who despises another for not knowing the genitive of *mensa*; the well-fed citizen of Goslar who interprets nature teleologically, maintaining that trees are green because green is good for people's eyes; and the young merchant who is moved by a magnificent sunset to exclaim: "Wie ist doch die Natur im allgemeinen so schön!" (DHA VI, 119) Even the Brocken embodies German pedantry by the thoroughness with which it enables one to survey the surrounding landscape from its summit. Unimaginative pedantry is not portrayed as exclusively a "German" trait — its most single-minded exponent is Saul Ascher, a leading figure of the Berlin Enlightenment (and, as Heine fails to mention, the author of a courageous pamphlet opposing German nationalism). Thus, Heine collapses the anti-Semitic distinction between "German" and "Jewish" identity, but reveals his ambivalence towards his Jewishness by delivering the Jews a decidedly back-handed compliment: they prove their Germanness by being as pedantic and unimaginative as the Germans.

The narrator himself is free from pedantry. He makes it abundantly clear that for him Göttingen is an alien environment. He feels more at home out in the country, chatting to miners and workmen, especially to children, who in his opinion form an intermediate link between adults and animate nature:

> Die Kinder, dacht' ich, sind jünger als wir, können sich noch erinnern, wie sie ebenfalls Bäume oder Vögel waren, und sind also noch im Stande, dieselben zu verstehen; unsereins aber ist schon alt und hat zu viel Sorgen, Jurisprudenz und schlechte Verse im Kopf. (DHA VI, 91)

Unlike the over-rational Saul Ascher, who is puzzled by things that any child can understand, the narrator appreciates folk poetry and folk tales, and comprehends the unchanging rural life from which they sprang. It should be noted, though, that instead of rhapsodizing about some creative "Volksseele," Heine locates the people's creativity firmly in the material conditions of their lives. He points out that if material possessions are handed down for generations, their owners will readily become so familiar with them as to credit the cupboard and the stove with a life of their own. One cannot invest material objects with much emotion if one often moves house, if one's maid keeps moving the furniture around, and if one's possessions are merely commodities that one has recently bought and will soon replace. In these reflections, Heine anticipates the sensitive critique of commodification put forward eighty years later by Georg Simmel in *Die Philosophie des Geldes*.

Are we to suppose, then, that the narrating persona in *Die Harzreise* identifies himself with what is best in the German character, its intuitive sympathy with nature and ordinary people, while remaining free from the faults, like pedantry, to which the Germans are prone? Does *Die Harzreise* turn on a contrast between, let us say, Philistinism and Romanticism? No, Heine's fiction is far more complicated than that. For a variety of reasons, his persona is complex, fragile, and unstable.

The narrator constantly affirms his fondness for nature. The opening verses contrast the affectations of town society with the simple beauty of the countryside. Stressing nature's simplicity, the narrator draws a contrast with the artificial landscape descriptions of E. T. A. Hoffmann: "Der selige Hoffmann würde die Wolken buntscheckig bemalt haben" (DHA VI, 91). And yet, as Klaus Pabel has pointed out, Heine's landscape descriptions exhibit considerable artifice.[9] They make insistent use of the vocabulary of art:

> Wie ein guter Dichter, liebt die Natur keine schroffen Uebergänge. Die Wolken, so bizarr gestaltet sie auch zuweilen erscheinen, tragen ein weißes, oder doch ein mildes, mit dem blauen Himmel und der grünen Erde harmonisch correspon-direndes Colorit, so daß alle Farben einer Gegend wie leise Musik in einander schmelzen, und jeder Naturanblick krampfstillend und gemüthsberuhigend wirkt. (VI, 91)

Here a landscape is described as a skillful composition, carried out by Nature, the supreme poet. By combining the language of poetry, painting, and music, Heine implies that nature can perform a synthesis of the arts beyond the power of any actual artist, who must remain confined to a single medium. And by demonstrating his ability both to appreciate and to analyze natural beauty, Heine distances himself not only from the unresponsive Philistines but also from any naive or straightforward response to landscape. He transcends the opposition between Philistinism and Romanticism.

A more fragile superiority is conferred by the narrator's dreams. On the one hand, they show how hard it is to shake off the atmosphere of his Göttingen studies. The first dream is set in the law section of the Göttingen University Library, where various law professors pay homage to Themis, the goddess of justice; the third extends the attack on pedantry by introducing Saul Ascher, the personification of rationalism, whose ghost undertakes to demonstrate from Kant the non-existence of ghosts. On the other hand, both dreams disclose the power of the narrator's imagination to defeat the overweening pride of pedantry and rationality. The law professors are first captivated by the sexuality of the gigantic Themis, then thrown into confusion by her lament for "Prometheus," i.e. Napoleon, whose confinement on St. Helena reveals the complicity of the legal profession with the injustice carried out by the Holy Alliance. The narrator escapes from the resulting chaos into an adjacent room with pictures of the Belvedere Apollo and the Medici Venus: from the trivial or dishonest antics of the lawyers into the timeless calm of classical art. By creating such confusion, the dream illustrates the destructive, punitive power of the imagination, while the classical statues remind us that the imagination can also create permanent objects of beauty. Dionysian chaos counterbalances Apolline order. The second dream, however, shows that the narrator can in turn become the victim of his imagination. Fairy-tale motifs combine with "Tagesreste" from the previous day's journey to bring him face to face with his beloved in the form of a marble statue. Like Pygmalion, or like the hero of Eichendorff's *Das Marmorbild*, he brings the statue to life. In doing so, however, the narrator has pressed the creative power of art too far and assumed the power that belongs only to God:

> Es war mir, als hörte ich, wie Gott rief: "Es werde Licht!" blendend schoß herab ein Stral des ewigen Lichts; aber in demselben Augenblick wurde es wieder Nacht, und Alles rann chaotisch zusammen in ein wildes, wüstes Meer. (VI, 98)

The dream returns the narrator to the time before creation, when the Earth was without form and void; but he is also fleeing from the ghosts of the dead (fit punishment for his blasphemous attempt to create life) who themselves are whipped on by a harlequin. This harlequin, the narrator realizes, is himself. Here, as often in Heine, the persona is split, this time into a victim and an avenger. As a punishment for trying to usurp God's creative powers, the would-be artist is confronted with an image of himself as a mere uncreative entertainer. Thus the narrator's commitment to art can be dangerous — it may end by disclosing a world in which nature is reduced to chaos, human life to the ghosts of the dead, and art to clowning.

Does the narrator's sympathy with the German people offer a firmer basis for the identity he is constructing? Hardly, for his attitude to the people is detached and sometimes, as in the encounter with the supposed tailor, downright condescending. The "Unterthanstreue" of the miner who takes him down the Carolina mine is praised in equivocal terms: "Andere Völker mögen gewandter seyn, und witziger und ergötzlicher, aber keines ist so treu, wie das treue deutsche Volk" (VI 95). Moreover, we soon learn that the miner's loyalty is to the Duke of Cambridge. The kingdom of Hanover was in personal union with the crown of Britain, and Adolphus Frederick, Duke of Cambridge, the youngest son of George III, had been its "Generalstatthalter" since 1814. "German loyalty" thus seems naively misplaced; Heine implies that it takes no account of the nationality of the merits of the Germans' rulers. The narrator represents himself as behaving so affably to the miners that they invite him to join their community. On the other hand, Carl Dörne reports of Heine "Er hatte überhaupt eine hofmännische Kälte an sich, die mich immer in einiger Entfernung von ihm hielt" (VI, 531). Courtly coldness implies a foreign bearing, which might be French or British: for example, the "britisierende, eingefrorene Wesen" of the minister in Eichendorff's *Ahnung und Gegenwart*.[10] Heine's affinity with the German people seems to be only a fragile literary construct.

The narrator shows much more detachment when he encounters spokesmen for German nationalism. This theme first appears in the opening description of Göttingen, where the traditional student societies, with their Germanic names, are jokingly derived from the barbarian invasions and their barbarous duelling is described. These rowdy *Landsmannschaften* differed from the nationalist *Burschenschaften*, founded in 1815 and banned soon afterwards, whose members wished to reform student behavior. Heine himself, when studying in Bonn and full of enthusiasm for German medieval culture, had joined the *Burschenschaft* "Allgemeinheit" in November 1819; the society was officially prohibited in June 1820. In Göttingen he also joined a *Burschenschaft*, but was expelled from it in December 1820 for obscure reasons which were probably connected with anti-Semitism.[11] During his second period of residence in Göttingen he took part in the activities of the *Landsmannschaft* "Guestphalia." Heine's expulsion left a trauma which finds expression in the Brockenhaus episode, where several *Burschenschaftler* appear. One of them, the student from Greifswald dressed in pseudo-medieval costume, serves to typify nationalism, not only because the tiny University of Greifswald had a notably reactionary student association, as Jost Hermand points out in his invaluable edition, but also because it had been attended by the fervent nationalist Ernst Moritz Arndt. Arndt, like the Greifswald student, recommended that Germany should be divided into thirty-three *Gauen* on the medieval model. Another representative of medievalism appears earlier: the elderly man who, having travelled round the world and made and lost a fortune, is now on his way back to Quedlinburg, the site of his family vault. Quedlinburg is also the burial place of the Emperor Heinrich I. This person, whose age and weariness are repeatedly emphasized, represents the defunct German Emperor. His lost fortune alludes to the dissolution of the Holy Roman Empire in 1806 — an event that inspired Heine's remark: "Wir leben in einer bedeutungschweren Zeit: tausendjährige Dome werden abgebrochen, und Kaiserstühle in die Rumpelkammer geworfen" (VI, 100). Behind this observation lies a historical event — the demolition of the Goslar Cathedral and the removal of its Imperial throne. Later, the narrator reflects on the vain ambition of the medieval Emperors who ruined themselves and their Empire by their desire for the title of Holy Roman Emperor.

Heine's ambivalence towards German traditions may be illustrated by his contrasting treatment of two national legends, Faust and Hermann. The Faust legend, described as "die große, mystische, deutsche National-tragödie vom Doctor Faust" (VI, 116), is hallowed for him by its popular character and its association with Goethe. Although, or because, the visit to Goethe that concluded Heine's Harz journey seems to have gone wrong, the text is full of allusions to Goethe.[12] Its very title is a tribute to the author of "Harzreise im Winter." The legend that Heine treats unfavorably is that of Hermann (Arminius) who defeated three Roman legions in the Teutoburger Wald in 9 CE. Its best-known version in Heine's day was Klopstock's trilogy of Hermann dramas (Kleist's *Die Hermannsschlacht* had been published only in 1821). The Greifswald student ist "ein deutscher Barde" (VI, 123; this was Klopstock's fanciful term for primitve German poets) and is at work on a heroic poem about Hermann's victory, about which Heine's narrator gives him ironic advice. Twenty years later, in *Deutschland: Ein Wintermärchen*, Heine is yet more sarcastic about Varus' defeat:

> Hier schlug ihn der Cheruskerfürst,
> Der Hermann, der edle Recke;
> Die deutsche Nationalität,
> Die siegte in diesem Drecke. (IV, 114)

The German identity constructed by Heine's narrator in *Die Harzreise* is, then, a highly qualified one. At first sight, Jewishness seems to play little part in it. Jews are mentioned mainly as money-grubbing business-men. The narrator observes that if it rained thaler, the children of Israel would gladly scoop up this silver manna. Apostrophizing a newly-made thaler, he foretells that after centuries of circulation it will be gathered to Abraham's bosom: "Abraham" suggests a Jewish money-lender, just as a

typical purchaser of used furniture is shortly afterwards called "Isaak."
The narrator emphatically distances himself from this mercenary spirit by
remarking that he is always absent when money is being made. This recalls Heine's dislike for the commercialism of his Hamburg relatives.
Slightly earlier, however, we find a more equivocal allusion to the Jews.
Affecting to be shocked by the Hanover Catechism's juxtaposition of
Christian doctrine and the multiplication table, the narrator remarks that
"we" in Prussia avoid such a clash when attempting to convert the "Leute,
die sich so gut aufs Rechnen verstehen" (VI, 91). On closer inspection, this
jest rebounds against the Christians; for if the multiplication table
contradicts the doctrine of the Trinity, as the narrator mock-piously
complains, then so much the worse for Christianity and so much the
better for the Jews, whose matter-of-fact outlook at least secures them
from absurdity. Similarly, in Die Bäder von Lucca, the common-sensical
Hirsch-Hyacinth represents the good side of Hamburg commercialism.
Besides, money-grubbing is not confined to Jews: it is the Philistines of
Göttingen (so called in contrast to students, but also, by implication, in
contrast to Jews) who present their clean bills and dirty faces, and appear
(in a parody of God's promise to Abraham) as numerous as "Sand, oder
besser gesagt, wie Koth am Meer" (VI, 84). If the narrator poses as a
Protestant Prussian, therefore, it is only as a stalking-horse for a
damaging blow against Christianity.

An unmistakably personal allusion to the narrator's Jewishness occurs
at the very end of the travel narrative. Standing on the summit of the
Ilsenstein, on which a cross has been erected for the safety of travellers,
he is overcome by giddiness and only saves himself by clutching the
cross. This alludes to Heine's own conversion to Christianity in the
summer of 1825. It was a purely nominal conversion, intended to secure
Heine from the restrictions on academic employment imposed on
unbaptized Jews. He said that he would never have converted if the law
had permitted him to steal silver spoons; and his regret is recorded in the
anecdote of how a visitor discovered him weeping and exclaiming, "Allen
Meschumodim soll zu Muthe sein wie mir."[13]

The identity constructed by the narrator not only combines German
and Jewish elements in an unstable solution. It is also a gendered
identity, poised among several available models of masculinity. The
narrator, for example, distances himself firmly from the brutish whoring
practiced by some Göttingen students, like the two he sees emerging with
a prostitute from the "myrtle bowers" at Rauschenwasser. Since the
barbarity of such students has already been lampooned, this brutish
sexuality is firmly associated with German traditionalism. Moreover,
myrtle was a standard rococo symbol for amorous dalliance. By using it
so sarcastically, Heine distances himself also from this conventional
language, implying that it is now affected and dishonest. Thus one

characteristically German form of sexuality is defined as physical grossness disguised by rococo affectation.

The new-style student life of the *Burschenschaften* has its own sexual character, represented by the coarse sentimentality of the Greifswald student:

> "O, verständest Du mich, ich bin ein Liebender, ich bin ein Glücklicher, ich werde wieder geliebt, und, Gott verdamm' mich! es ist ein gebildetes Mädchen, denn sie hat volle Brüste, und trägt ein weißes Kleid und spielt Clavier!" (VI, 124)

In contrast to the promiscuity of the Göttingen *Landsmannschaften*, this fellow looks forward to a future of Biedermeier domesticity, married to a young lady with the standard female accomplishments. Heine makes this domestic idyll sound scarcely more appetizing than the goings-on in the "myrtle bowers."

The narrator distances himself most of all from the maudlin sentimentality of the two students who express their feelings in Ossianic rhapsodies. This is a different, but equally spurious, rhetoric. It is discredited by Goethe's use of it in *Die Leiden des jungen Werther* to convey Werther's ineffectual passion for Lotte. Heine always treated Werther's passion with disrespect, notably in *Zur Geschichte der Religion und Philosophie in Deutschland*, where he quotes Lessing's demand that Goethe should undercut his novel by adding a cynical epilogue (VIII, 69).[14] Here, the two students' effusions also allow Heine to discharge his homophobia, which a few years later found such unbridled expression in his polemic against Platen. He indicates their homosexuality by comparing them to classical statues (recalling not only Greek homosexuality but also the homosexual neo-classicist Winckelmann), and by juxtaposing sentimental clichés with physical disgust: shut into a cupboard by a rowdy fellow-student, the two vomit over each other while continuing their Ossianic declamations.

In contrast to all these sexual deviations, the narrator credits himself with gallant romantic adventures, like the stolen kiss in Goslar, and with an unhappy love affair which is referred to occasionally and with the minimum of self-pity. He also values family life, as embodied by the mining community, and is fond of children. His emotional history is largely confined to the inset poems, particularly the long three-part poem ("Auf dem Berg steht die Hütte") about a romance with a miner's daughter. Heine thus links gender with genre. The proper language for emotion is the simple language of the folk-song. Prose is an unsuitable medium for expressing such feelings, whether it be the overstrained prose of Werther's Ossian, the comic grossness of the Greifswald student, or the sensual novels of Clauren (Carl Gottlieb Samuel Hein) to which Heine, here and in other works, refers with prudish disgust. These unattractive versions of sexuality are identified as characteristically German. By contrast, the gallant sexuality of the narrator is that of somebody continually on the move, who will not abandon his wandering life for the restrictions of domesticity or a fixed identity. Given that Die Harzreise is saturated in reminiscences of Goethe, this aspect of the persona recalls Faust's "Bin ich der Wandrer nicht? der Unbehauste?"[15] Indeed, the verse dialogue between the poet and the miner's daughter is clearly modelled on the scene in Faust where Gretchen questions her lover about his belief in God. But the persona's rootlessness also suggests the Jewish identity which enables him to empathize with German life but not to find a secure home there. Once again we have the cosmopolitan "Herr Peregrinus."

The development of the narrator's gender identity culminates in his walk down the Ilse valley. He takes the legend of Princess Ilse as a pretext for fusing landscape and femininity in the personifications of the three rivers — Ilse, Bode, and Selke — and compares himself to Paris, who had to award the apple to the most beautiful of three goddesses. Before that, however, comes the poem beginning "Ich bin die Prinzessin Ilse." Ilse appears as a charming temptress. Like the water-nixie in Goethe's "Der Fischer," she allures men and makes them forget their martial duties. The temptress figure fascinated Heine. She can be traced through his works from "Die Lorelei" via Herodias in Atta Troll to Die Göttin Diana. Her erotic charm is enhanced by her identification with nature. It thus exercises a particular spell for the kind of poet who, like the persona here, has a special affinity with nature. Here the poem spoken by Ilse is followed by the narrator's reflections:

> Unendlich selig ist das Gefühl, wenn die Erscheinungswelt mit unserer Gemüthswelt zusammenrinnt, und grüne Bäume, Gedanken, Vögelgesang, Wehmuth, Himmelsbläue, Erinnerung und Kräuterduft sich in süßen Arabesken verschlingen. Die Frauen kennen am besten dieses Gefühl, und darum mag auch ein so holdselig ungläubiges Lächeln um ihre Lippen schweben, wenn wir mit Schulstolz unsere logischen Thaten rühmen ... (VI, 133)

In this passage the narrator distances himself from the arid, over-rational kind of masculinity that prides itself on logical prowess. This continues the earlier satire on pedantry but interprets it in terms of gender. Masculine rationality is contrasted with the more intuitive kind of masculinity that responds to nature and emotion, mixing them up with a fine disregard for logical categories. The latter identity is that of the poet as defined in this text: Ilse pursues "den träumenden Dichter" (VI,

131). But the poet's intuitive qualities, by rendering him susceptible to the seductions of temptresses like Ilse and Lorelei, put him in danger. He may fall victim to their destructive, emasculating charms; or, like Werther, he may be driven by unrequited love to suicide. *Die Harzreise* ends with the narrator avoiding both these temptations. The story about the aloe, which flowers once a century with a crack caused by the bursting of its pod, leads up to the narrator's assurance that if the woman he is addressing hears the sound of a shot, it will not be his suicide but his love bursting into poetry.

This illustrates how *Die Harzreise* provides fictional responses to real-life trauma. The trauma of unrequited love which haunts the text, appearing especially in the narrator's second dream and in the poem beginning "Heller wird es schon im Osten," is resolved by transmuting it into poetry. Similarly, Heine's real identity-crisis, in which a German identity seemed unattainable and a Jewish identity undesirable, is resolved by elaborating a fictional identity which maintains a critical distance from both. As the episode of the cross indicates, however, this fictitious identity is vulnerable; it bears the scar of Heine's apostasy from Judaism. And in remaining aloof from various forms of communal living, exemplified by the brutality of German student societies, the banal domesticity of the *Burschenschaftler*, and the commercialism of the Hamburg Jews, the persona defines himself as a perpetual wanderer and thus, despite conversion, more deeply Jewish than any of the Jewish figures mentioned in the text.

Notes

[1] See Jeffrey L. Sammons: *Heinrich Heine: The Elusive Poet*. New Haven and London 1969.

[2] Heinrich Heine: *Säkularausgabe*. Berlin 1970ff, Vol. XX, pp. 148, 215, 359.

[3] Heinrich Heine: *Historisch-kritische Ausgabe der Werke*. Hamburg 1973ff, Vol. VI, p. 530. Future references to this edition are given in the text by volume and page number.

[4] See especially Michael Werner: "Heinrich Heine. Über die Interdependenz von jüdischer, deutscher und europäischer Identität in seinem Werk." In: *Juden im Vormärz und in der Revolution von 1848*, ed. by Walter Grab and Julius H. Schoeps. Stuttgart and Bonn 1983, pp. 9-28.

[5] Fridrich [sic] Rühs: *Über die Ansprüche der Juden an das deutsche Bürgerrecht*. Berlin 1816, pp. 5-6.

6   Clemens Brentano: *Werke*, ed. by Friedhelm Kemp. Munich 1963-8, Vol. II, p. 966.

7   E. T. A. Hoffmann: *Die Serapions-Brüder*. Munich 1963, pp. 563, 573.

8   Heine: *Säkularausgabe*, Vol. XX, p. 148.

9   Klaus Pabel: *Heines "Reisebilder": Ästhetisches Bedürfnis und politisches Interesse am Ende der Kunstperiode*. Munich 1977, p. 100.

10 Joseph von Eichendorff: *Werke*. Munich 1970-88, Vol. II, p. 121.

11 See Eberhard Galley: "Heine und die Burschenschaft." In: *Heine Jahrbuch* 11, 1972, pp. 66-95.

12 See Jost Hermand: "Werthers Harzreise." In his: *Von Mainz nach Weimar*. Stuttgart 1969, pp. 129-51.

13 Michael Werner, ed., *Begegnungen mit Heine*. Hamburg 1973, Vol. I, p. 149.

14 Cf. the poems "Die Tendenz" ("Girre nicht mehr wie ein Werther ..."). In: *Neue Gedichte* and "Der weiße Elefant" ("Er ist ein vierfüßiger Werther geworden") in: *Romanzero*.

15 J. W. Goethe: *Faust*, line 3348.

Gerald Stieg

Karl Kraus gegen Martin Heidegger[1]

De systèmes prétendus philosophiques qui ne sont
qu'une poésie obscure et mal écrite ... (Stendhal)

I.

Zu den Gemeinplätzen über die unüberschreitbare Bedeutung von
Heideggers Denken gehört das ökologische Argument: "Seine Diagnose
der Entfremdung und Verknechtung des Menschen in einer verwüsteten
Umwelt war prophetisch und ist weder an Ernsthaftigkeit noch Kohärenz
überholt worden."[2] So George Steiner, (gewiß kein bedenkenloser
Heidegger-Diener). Dem ist mit aller Energie zu widersprechen: Er hatte
darin zumindest einen Vorgänger, der alle seine Zaubersprüche gegen
den Geist der Technik mit größter Genauigkeit vorweggenommen hatte.
Es schiene mir der Mühe wert, an der nur auf den ersten Blick
befremdlichen Parallele Heidegger/Kraus die Methode Heinrich Heines
in seinem Buch *Zur Geschichte der Religion und Philosophie in Deutschland*
(*De l'Allemagne*) aufzunehmen und die Sprache der deutschen Philosophie
ins Idiom Voltaires zu übersetzen.[3] Leider tun die meisten französischen
Philosophen das Gegenteil: Sie versuchen, ihre Sprache dem "Jargon der
Eigentlichkeit" anzupassen und damit das kaum Verständliche endgültig
unverständlich zu machen. Es ist kein Zufall, daß der Widerstand gegen
die Heidegger-Idolatrie in Frankreich nicht dort zu suchen ist, wo man
ihn erwarten sollte, nämlich bei der intellektuellen Linken, sondern bei
jenen, die sich um die französische Übersetzung der Werke Ludwig
Wittgensteins und überhaupt der Philosophie des "Wiener Kreises"
bemüht haben. Ihr Schulhaupt, Jacques Bouveresse, hat den Sachverhalt
in einem Vortrag so formuliert:

> Niemand wagt Heidegger gegenüber den notwendigen Schritt der
> Übersetzung ins Banale. Was Karl Kraus 1934 in *Dritte*
> *Walpurgisnacht* getan hat, nämlich die Übersetzung der
> Rektoratsrede in die Sprache der nationalsozialistischen
> Gewalttätigkeit, ließe sich auf den Großteil der Texte Heideggers
> anwenden.[4]

Es wäre also keineswegs abwegig, sogar die als sakrosankt erklärten Thesen von *Sein und Zeit*, z. B. die Paragraphen 35-38 (Gerede, Neugier, Zweideutigkeit, Verfallen und Geworfenheit) und den berühmten Abschnitt über das "Man"(§ 27)[5] ins Idiom der *Fackel* zu übersetzen. Anders gesagt, Karl Kraus hat das, was Heine post festum mit Kant, Fichte und Hegel vollzogen hat, antizipierend mit Heidegger vorgenommen. Heine ist überzeugt von der Gefährlichkeit der deutschen Philosophie ("Kantianer, Fichteaner und Naturphilosophen"):

> Lächelt nicht über den Phantasten, der im Reiche der Erscheinungen dieselbe Revolution erwartet, die im Gebiet des Geistes stattgefunden. Der Gedanke geht der Tat voraus, wie der Blitz dem Donner. Der deutsche Donner ist freilich auch ein Deutscher und ist nicht sehr gelenkig und kommt etwas langsam herangerollt; aber kommen wird er, und wenn ihr es einst krachen hört, wie es noch niemals in der Weltgeschichte gekracht hat, so wißt: der deutsche Donner hat endlich sein Ziel erreicht.... Es wird ein Stück aufgeführt werden in Deutschland, wogegen die Französische Revolution nur wie eine harmlose Idylle erscheinen möchte.... Und die Stunde wird kommen.[6]

Und die Stunde ist 1933 gekommen. Karl Kraus hat sich damals auf die Suche nach den Philosophen gemacht, die die nationalsozialistische Revolution im "Reiche der Erscheinungen" durch ihre jeweilige Revolution im "Gebiete des Geistes" vorbereitet hatten, auf die Suche nach den "Worthelfern der Gewalt"[7] also. Unter ihnen fand er den "Denker Heidegger"[8].

II. Schweigen und Reden

An zwei einschneidenden Daten der Geschichte des 20. Jahrhunderts hat Karl Kraus mit Schweigen reagiert: 1914 und 1933. Vom 10. Juli 1914 bis zum 5. Dezember 1914 (bzw. 19. November 1914) und von Ende Dezember 1932 bis Oktober 1933 (*Fackel* 888), respektive Juli 1934.

In beiden Fällen war er dem Verdacht ausgesetzt, selbst "Worthelfer" der losgelassenen Gewalt zu sein. Vor 1914 galt er den Liberalen und "Linksradikalen" als Verräter eigener Ideale zugunsten der aristokratischen "Reaktion". Mit "Franz Ferdinand und die Talente" und "Sehnsucht nach aristokratischem Umgang" (beide Juli 1914) schien Kraus unverhohlen "rechtsradikal" geworden zu sein:

> Sie haben geglaubt, ich sei ein Revolutionär, und haben nicht gewußt, daß ich politisch noch nicht einmal bei der Französischen

Revolution angekommen bin, geschweige denn im Zeitalter
zwischen 1848 und 1914, und daß ich die Menschheit mit
Entziehung der Menschenrechte, das Bürgertum mit Entziehung
des Wahlrechts, die Juden mit Entziehung des Telephons, die
Journalisten mit Aufhebung der Preßfreiheit und die
Psychoanalytiker mit Einführung der Leibeigenschaft regalieren
möchte.[9]

Mag auch satirische Übertreibung am Werk sein, das Programm hat
Ähnlichkeiten mit dem nationalsozialistischen, und Kraus findet sich 1933
— nicht völlig zu Unrecht — von der noch existierenden liberalen Presse
als "geistiger Ahne" Hitlers denunziert. 1914 wie 1933 kann er in einer
bestimmten Optik als "Worthelfer" der sich etablierenden Gewalt gesehen
werden.

Er antwortet zunächst mit SCHWEIGEN, und als er das Schweigen
bricht, reflektiert er die Bedeutung des Schweigens:

Wer Taten zuspricht, schändet Wort und Tat und ist zweimal
verächtlich. Der Beruf dazu ist nicht ausgestorben. Die jetzt nichts
zu sagen haben, weil die Tat das Wort hat, sprechen weiter. Wer
etwas zu sagen hat, trete vor und schweige! ("In dieser großen
Zeit", Dezember 1914).[10]
... [Das Schweigen] war bloß die Sorge, den Abscheu gegen das
andere Wort, gegen jenes, das die Tat begleitet, sie verursacht und
ihr folgt, gegen den großen Wortmisthaufen der Welt, jetzt nicht
zur Geltung bringen zu können und zu dürfen. Und das
Schweigen war so laut, daß es fast schon Sprache war
("Schweigen, Wort und Tat", Dezember 1915).[11]

Im Oktober 1933 hat Kraus diesem SCHWEIGEN eine Gedichtgestalt
gegeben, im schmalsten aller *Fackelhefte*:

Man frage nicht, was all die Zeit ich machte.
Ich bleibe stumm;
und sage nicht, warum.
Und Stille gibt es, da die Erde krachte.
Kein Wort, das traf;
man spricht nur aus dem Schlaf.
Und träumt von einer Sonne, welche lachte.
Es geht vorbei;
nachher war's einerlei.
Das Wort entschlief, als jene Welt erwachte.[12]

Was Karl Kraus 1914 und 1933 seinem "Schweigen" folgen ließ, gehört zu den Ehrenmalen des europäischen Geistes und der deutschen Sprache. Angesichts historischer Täterschaft von Untaten vertrat er das Menschenrecht der gemarterten Kreatur und hat sich nicht geschämt, manches eigene Wort zurückzunehmen oder zumindest seinen zweideutigen Interpreten den Mund zu schließen.

Wie anders Heidegger!

Es geht mir hier nicht darum, das historische Material auszubreiten, das es nunmehr zur Genüge gibt. 1933 hat Heidegger als Universitätspolitiker eine Rede[13] gehalten, deren entscheidende Stellen Kraus benützt (d. h. "übersetzt") hat, um 1933 (!) den "Denker" als "Worthelfer der Gewalt" zu entlarven. Kraus bezieht sich ironisch auf Goethes "Klassische Walpurgisnacht":

> Daß für den Aufbau und insbesondere den "ideologischen Überbau" eines Lebens ..., daß für derlei die Philosophie nicht müßig zu sein hat, versteht sich von selbst, und so leicht wie eine, die zu einer richtiggehenden Walpurgisnacht gehört, "Denn wo Gespenster Platz genommen,/Ist auch der Philosoph willkommen."[14]

Mephistopheles hat zwei Vorsokratiker bereit (Thales und Anaxagoras), eine Finte der Literaturgeschichte, wenn man bedenkt, daß Heidegger mindestens bis zu den Vorsokratikern zurückgeschritten ist. Karl Kraus vollzieht eine hochsatirische "Rettung" Wagners und Nietzsches vor dem Ehrenamt eines "Treuhänders des nationalsozialistischen Gedankens"[15] und überantwortet diese Rolle Heidegger, Benn und Spengler. Heidegger gehört zu jenen "Handlangern ins Transzendente, die sich in Fakultäten und Revuen anstellig zeigen, die deutsche Philosophie als Vorschule für den Hitler-Gedanken einzurichten. Da ist etwa der Denker Heidegger, der seinen blauen Dunst dem braunen gleichgeschaltet hat und klar zu erkennen beginnt, die geistige Welt eines Volkes sei

> ... die Macht der tiefsten Bewahrung seiner **erd- und bluthaften Kräfte** als Macht der **innersten Erregung** und **weitesten Erschütterung seines Daseins.** ("Rektoratsrede")[16]

Karl Kraus vollzieht auf ein paar Seiten der *Dritten Walpurgisnacht* eine Rückübersetzung des "blauen" Dunstes deutscher Philosophie in "Worthilfe der Gewalt" mittels eines Wortspiels:

> Das Bekenntnis zu Blut- und Erdverbundenheit, mit dem sich jetzt diese abgründigen Worthelfer der Gewalt beeilen, könnte vielleicht an jene Gefahr der Verbindung denken lassen, die zwar

nicht in der Philosophie, aber in der Medizin als Tetanus bekannt ist, und so wäre die Psychose auf einen nationalen Starrkrampfanfall zurückzuführen, dem alles ausgesetzt ist, was exerzieren und dozieren oder beides zugleich kann.[17]

Heideggers Aufruf zum dreifachen Dienst (Arbeitsdienst, Wehrdienst, Wissendienst ist für Kraus: "Wehrdienst des Geistes") beschwört die drei "Bindungen", die dem "deutschen Wesen **gleichursprünglich**" sind. Karl Kraus "übersetzt" das "fragende, ungedeckte Standhalten inmitten der Ungewißheit des Seienden im Ganzen"[18] ganz im Geiste Heines in das, was es ist, kaum verhüllte Nazipropaganda, "Wehrdienst des Geistes". (Für dergleichen ungeistige Gleichungen hatte er seit' dem Ersten Weltkrieg einen untrüglichen Spürsinn).

Natürlich wußte Heidegger, was er da redete und schrieb. Es folgte der Machtübernahme des Nationalsozialismus, es ging ihm nicht voran. Kraus brach 1914 sein Schweigen unter anderem so:

> ... in dieser Zeit, in der eben das geschieht, was man sich nicht vorstellen konnte, und in der **geschehen** muß, was man sich nicht mehr **vorstellen** kann, und könnte man es, es geschähe nicht — ; ... in dieser lauten Zeit, die da dröhnt von der schauerlichen Symphonie der Taten, die Berichte hervorbringen, und der Berichte, die Taten verschulden: in dieser da mögen Sie von mir kein eigenes Wort erwarten.... In den Reichen der Phantasiearmut, wo der Mensch an seelischer Hungersnot stirbt, ohne den seelischen Hunger zu spüren, wo Federn in Blut tauchen und Schwerter in Tinte, muß das, was nicht gedacht wird, getan werden, aber ist das, was gedacht wird, unaussprechlich.[19]

Der deutsche "Denker" Heidegger hat 1933 in seiner Rektoratsrede und einigen anderen noch weniger verschlüsselten Verlautbarungen offenen Götzendienst der Gewalt betrieben. Dem folgt philosophisches Schweigen.

Kraus hat schließlich die Veröffentlichung der *Dritten Walpurgisnacht* zurückgehalten, um nicht den Zorn der Nazis gegen unbeteiligte Opfer herauszufordern. Sie erschien 1952 als ewiges Mahnmal für alle von Heidegger bis Waldheim, die nichts gewußt haben, nur ihre Pflicht taten und weiter behaupten, daß niemand so etwas habe voraussehen können usw. Heideggers "Rektoratsrede" von 1933 ist in Deutschland im Jahre 1983 neu aufgelegt worden, versehen mit einem "Rechenschaftsbericht" über das "Rektorat 1933/34" aus dem Jahre 1945[20]. Vermutlich wäre sie auch heute noch in Archiven verschollen, hätte nicht 1982 in Frankreich eine zweisprachige Edition stattgefunden[21]. Heideggers "Rechtfertigung" von 1945 stimmt weitgehend mit dem "Spiegel-Gespräch" von 1966

überein, das erst nach dem Tod des Philosophen 1976 veröffentlicht
werden durfte.[22] Es ist eine jämmerliche Geschichte des Schweigens und
Verschweigens, deren miese Gestalt ihren tragischen Höhepunkt in der
Begegnung von Paul Celan und Heidegger gefunden hat.[23] Doch vorher
schon (z. B. im Briefwechsel mit Herbert Marcuse)[24] war der Grundton
gegeben.

Daß jemand vor dem Grauen schweigt, ist natürlich, erst recht dann,
wenn er spürt, daß sein eigenes Denken mit dem historischen Grauen in
einem unheimlichen Verwandtschaftsverhältnis steht. Daß es selbst dem
Wortgewaltigsten die Rede verschlägt, liegt in der Natur von Denken und
Sprache. Karl Kraus ist einer der großartigsten Zeugen dieses Phänomens,
Heidegger einer der beschämendsten des Gegenteils: der Denker als
Worthelfer der Gewalt. Und nie hat er das Schweigen darüber gebrochen,
auch nicht um der Hoffnung eines Dichters willen:

> ... einer Hoffnung, heute,
> auf eines Denkenden
> kommendes (un-
> gesäumt kommendes)
> Wort
> im Herzen, (Celan, *Todtnauberg*)[25]

Gerhart Baumann hat in seinen *Erinnerungen an Paul Celan* Heideggers
Schweigen so gerechtfertigt: "Der betagte Denker trug die ungeheure Last
des 'unsühnbaren Irrtums' und 'einer Schuld', ohne darüber ein Wort zu
verlieren, — ein Schweigen, das als Herausforderung ausgelegt werden
konnte."[26] (Baumann ist sich nicht bewußt, daß das Vokabular von
Schuld und Sühne Heidegger wesensfremd ist.) Angesichts der *Dritten
Walpurgisnacht* klingt folgende Rechtfertigung besonders hohl: "Der
Nachkomme, der aus dem Abstand ungefährdet zu urteilen vermag,
kommt leichter zu seinem Recht, aber liegt darin immer ein *Verdienst*?"[27]

Fünfundfünfzig Jahre nach Karl Kraus, der, so weit ich sehe, weder in
der französischen noch in der deutschen Diskussion des Falles Heidegger
auch nur die geringste Rolle spielt, entdeckte die französische
Öffentlichkeit durch Victor Farias Buch *Heidegger und der
Nationalsozialismus*, was man schon längst wußte, nicht aber wahr haben
wollte. Farias Werk löste in Frankreich ein Erdbeben aus.[28] Daß man
plötzlich Zeitungstitel wie "Heil Heidegger" (*Libération*) oder gar
Heidegger mit Hitlerschnurrbart und Parteiabzeichen als Titelkonterfei
der alles eher als exklusiven Zeitschrift *Lire* erblicken konnte, gehört zu
den Mysterien einer alchimistischen Hochzeit zwischen Journalismus und
Esoterismus. Was seit den fünfziger Jahren, nicht zuletzt im Namen
Johann Peter Hebels und Albert Schweitzers, Robert Minder[29] gegen eine
chinesische Mauer der Erkenntnisverweigerung absolut vergeblich

versucht hatte, war plötzlich in Frankreich Alltagsthema. Der Nazi Heidegger![30]

III. Das absolut Verschwiegene

Aber es gab auch weiterhin versuche, Heidegger reinzuwaschen. Argumente wie "Wir haben ohnehin alles gewußt", "Die Heideggergegner reagieren wie die Nazis: Laßt uns ihn verbrennen!", "Die Verwundung des Denkens" durch Heideggers Position hätte durch kein klärendes oder entschuldigendes Wort von seiner Seite geheilt werden können", usw. Die heillose Kurzsichtigkeit solcher Weißwäscherei zeigt sich an einem Satz wie dem folgenden: "Ohne Heideggers furchtbares Schweigen würden wir das Gebot nicht verspüren, das sich an unser Verantwortungs-bewußtsein richtet, die Notwendigkeit, Heidegger so zu lesen, wie er sich selbst nicht gelesen hat." Als was? Als Nazi? "Wenigstens hat er dies nicht beansprucht. Oder vielleicht hat er es beansprucht und sich deswegen, wie ich vermute, in SCHWEIGEN gehüllt. Vielleicht hat er beansprucht, daß er bereits auf seine Weise gesagt hat, ohne sich dabei zu bequemen Sätzen verleiten zu lassen, was sich im Nationalsozialismus korrumpieren mußte."[31] Die "bequemen Sätze" wären in solcher Optik z. B. die der weitgehend unbekannten *Dritten Walpurgisnacht*, wo ein Experte sondergleichen das Gerede aufs Maß der Vernunft reduziert, nämlich auf seine geistige Nichtigkeit. Karl Kraus ist unzweifelhaft ein Schüler Nietzsches: in der Umwertung der Werte (Stichwort Sexualethik, eine Sache, die Heidegger so fremd zu sein scheint wie Hitler selbst) sucht er seinesgleichen nach Nietzsche, aber diese Umwertung macht Halt vor dem Respekt vor dem Kreatürlichen aller Art. Nietzsche war Antisemit wie Karl Kraus. Dieser jeweilige Antisemitismus vollzog sich in dialektischen Krämpfen, die sowohl Kraus wie Nietzsche essentiell davon ausschlossen, direkte "Worthelfer der Gewalt" zu werden. Der listige Heidegger hat diese "Frage", er, der die "Frage als Frömmigkeit des Denkens" herumgereicht hat, nie gestellt. Hier herrscht verneinendes SCHWEIGEN.

Deutschnationalismus und Antisemitismus bei Heidegger? Ich greife fast willkürlich aus der *Gesamtausgabe* Heideggers den Band 53 heraus (erschienen 1984). Er trägt den Titel "Hölderlins Hymne 'Der Ister'"[32] und enthält die im Sommersemester 1942 in Freiburg gehaltene Vorlesung über Hölderlin und Sophokles. Ich wähle diesen Band nur willkürlich, denn wer möchte Heideggers Betrachtungen über die "Donau" vom Jahre 1942 übergehen, wenn man weiß, daß der Philosoph zu den größten Hindernissen für den Nationalsozialismus den Widerstand der christlichen Kirchen und das erstehende österreichische Selbstbewußtsein gerechnet hat (Löwith).[33] Karl Kraus gehörte zu den unbedingtesten Vertretern des österreichischen Widerstands, und sei es im Namen des katholischen Dollfuß.

Heideggers "Auslegung" der "Ister"-Hymne gehört zu jenen typischen Textvergewaltigungen, deren er sich nicht nur an Hölderlin, sondern auch an Rilke und Trakl schuldig gemacht hat. Potenziert ist hier die Vergewaltigung durch eine mehr als eigenwillige Interpretation des ersten Standchors aus der *Antigone* des Sophokles. Selbst die hochnationalistische Deutung Hölderlins durch Wilhelm Michel (*Das Leben Friedrich Hölderlins*, Bremen 1940) sieht in der Hymne zumindest teilweise eine "Rüge"[34], also eine Variation der für Hölderlin charakteristischen Deutschlandschelte. Pierre Bertaux hatte schon 1936 in einer politisch-historischen Konstellation von höchster Brisanz auf den durchaus eklektischen Charakter Hölderlins[35] verwiesen, in dem logischerweise der Bibel eine zentrale Stelle zukam.

Heidegger, gebürtig aus der Gegend, in der die Donau ihre Quellen hat (die allerdings nur im Oberlauf Danubius hieß; Ister war dem Unterlauf zum schwarzen Meer hin vorbehalten), verkürzt die abendländische Tradition schroff auf ein deutsch-griechisches "Gespräch", aus dem aller Orient, vor allem natürlich der jüdische ausgeschlossen sind. Doch selbst innerhalb der Geschichte des deutschen Klassizismus, die von Winckelmann bis Goethe und Schiller ein dezidiertes Antichristentum ist, fühlt sich Heidegger nicht heimisch. Er spielt die Karte Hölderlin gegen die Weimarer Klassik, aber die Karte ist gezinkt. Kraus hat Hölderlin abgesehen von satirischen Effekten (Idiotima; journalistische Lyriker, die nicht Irre gehen wollten) zweimal verwendet: einerseits als Zitat — die Deutschlandschelte aus dem *Hyperion* im Ersten Weltkrieg, mit einer satirischen Pointe "ökologischer Natur" — andererseits als Emblem des Lyrikers schlechthin neben Goethe und Trakl.[36] Was Heidegger mit Hölderlin betrieb, war ihm absolut fremd, so fremd, daß selbst der Hölderlin-Mißbrauch in seiner engeren Umgebung (Rilkes "Kriegs"-Hymnik) nur zu privaten Sticheleien Anlaß gab.[37] Es gibt kein Zeichen, daß ihm Trakls Begegnung mit Hölderlin auch nur bewußt geworden wäre. Umgekehrt gibt es keinen Zweifel daran, daß Trakl mit Hölderlin in einem griechisch-biblischen Code verkehrt. Hölderlin gehört nicht zu Kraus' "klassisch aufgeräumtem Geisteshorizont" (Ludwig von Ficker).[38] Für Celan ist Hölderlin durch den Mißbrauch vom "Kriegsalmanach" des Inselverlags von 1915 bis zu Heidegger geradezu "Feindsprache" geworden.

Der Heidegger von 1942, den uns seine Apologeten als inneren Emigranten und Widerstandskämpfer aufreden wollen, betreibt sein esoterisches Geschäft auf eine ganz besondere Art. Versuchen wir eine Übersetzung aus dem Geist von Heine und Kraus: laut Heidegger braucht der Mensch, um "heimisch zu werden", einen "Durchgang durch das Fremde"[39] und eine Auseinandersetzung mit der Fremde. Selbst

Nietzsche hat die Sache falsch verstanden (Primat des Römertums), ganz zu schweigen vom falschen Ausgangspunkt des deutschen Klassizismus, der im Griechentum die "Vollendung des Menschentums" sah. Für Heideggers Hölderlin sieht das so aus:

> **Das** Fremde freilich, durch das hindurch die Heimkehr wandert, ist kein beliebiges Fremdes im Sinne des bloßen unbestimmt Nicht-Eigenen. Das auf die Heimkehr bezogene, d.h. mit ihr einige **Fremde**, ist die **Herkunft** der Heimkehr und ist das gewesene Anfängliche des eigenen und Heimischen. Dieses Fremde des geschichtlichen Menschentums der Deutschen ist für Hölderlin das Griechentum.[40]

Schon vorher als Schlußfolgerung des Kapitels "Das Heimischwerden die Sorge der Dichtung Hölderlins":

> Die Zwiesprache der Hymnendichtung Hölderlins mit den fremden Dichtern ist **jedem Zufall** enthoben. Ihre Einzigkeit und Eindeutigkeit entspringt auch nicht einer gerade herrschenden "historischen" Bildung oder der persönlichen Vorliebe. Die beiden Dichter, die der Sorge Hölderlins im Zeitraum seiner Hymnendichtung entsprechen und antworten, sind zwei Dichter des fremden und alten Landes der Griechen: Pindar und Sophokles.[41]

Das ist wohl in Heideggers Augen ein Kapitel der *Geschichte des Seins*, aus der die Geschichte des Augenblicks (1933-1942) die *Bibel*, das *Alte Testament* und erst recht seine laut Nietzsche potenzierte Form des *Neuen Testaments* endgültig ausgeschlossen zu haben schien. Man braucht nicht ein Anhänger des Nazareners und seiner Geschichte zu sein, um darauf zu verweisen, daß Hölderlin Christus kennt und Nietzsche sein wahnwitziges Werk *Ecce Homo* mit "Dionysos gegen den Gekreuzigten" beschließt. Karl Kraus und Nietzsche sind einander in vielen Spielformen des "aristokratischen" Antisemitismus nahe. Bei Heidegger scheint jede Auseinandersetzung mit diesem Substrat der negativen Geistesgeschichte zu fehlen. Als Spezialist des NICHTS tut er so, als wäre es nicht da. Das Denken spielt sich auf deutsch und griechisch ab.

Bei Nietzsche hatte man wenigstens Recht auf wüste Ausfälle gegen das jüdisch-demokratische Denken, z. B. den egalitären Anspruch des dialektischen (sokratischen) Denkens an sich, wo jeder kraft seiner Intelligenz argumentiert. Nietzsche argumentiert in dieser Sache wie Heidegger, Pinochet, Stalin, Hitler und jeder Hausherr, der auf sich hält. Die Intelligenz ist plebeisch, die Macht aristokratisch. Denken gegen Sein. 1942, als Heidegger über Hölderlins "Donau" und Sophokles *Antigone* nachdenkt, zwei politisch höchst bedenkenswerte Gegenstände, gerade in diesem historischen Augenblick, fällt ihm folgendes ein:

> Wir wissen heute, daß die angelsächsische Welt des Amerikanismus entschlossen ist, Europa, d. h. die Heimat, und d. h. den Anfang des Abendländischen, zu vernichten. Anfängliches ist unzerstörbar. Der Eintritt Amerikas in diesen planetarischen Krieg ist nicht der Eintritt in die Geschichte, sondern ist bereits schon der letzte amerikanische Akt der amerikanischen Geschichtslosigkeit und Selbstverwüstung.[42]

Von deutscher Selbstverwüstung ist natürlich keine Rede — und wird **nie** die Rede sein.

Heidegger tut so, als kreise sein Denken ausschließlich um den "Herd" seiner Europa-Idee, die er in Athen zu sehen glaubt. Mitten in seinen pseudoetymologischen Behauptungen über die griechische POLIS erlaubt er sich polemische Spitzen gegen dümmere Kollegen, die "Alles" Griechische als "politisch" bestimmt gesehen hätten, ja schlimmer noch: "Die Griechen erscheinen in den meisten 'Forschungsergebnissen' als die reinen Nationalsozialisten."[43] (Nicht nur Forscher, sondern auch ein Dichter wie Benn, ein anderer "Worthelfer der Gewalt", haben im "Dritten Reich" eine "klassische Walpurgisnacht" mit spartanischem Akzent gesehen. Heidegger, der hier plötzlich Farbe bekennt, rät den Kollegen zur Mäßigung: "Dieser Übereifer der Gelehrten scheint gar nicht zu merken, daß er mit solchen 'Ergebnissen' dem Nationalsozialismus und seiner geschichtlichen Einzigartigkeit durchaus keinen Dienst erweist, den dieser außerdem gar nicht benötigt."[44]

Wozu reden, wenn die Taten Zeugnis geben. Leider hat Kraus, als er die *Dritte Walpurgisnacht* verfaßte, dieses Kleinod der deutschen Philosophie noch nicht vor Augen gehabt. Auf Heideggers verschlagen-verschwiegene Art wird mit solchen Seitenhieben verdeutlicht, daß die wahre Philosophie, die der "geschichtlichen Einzigartigkeit" des Nationalsozialismus gerecht wird, seine eigene ist. (Es ist hier nicht ganz unnütz, die Protagonisten des deutschen Revisionismus, die die Einzigartigkeit des Dritten Reichs leugnen möchten, sowohl auf Kraus als auf Heidegger zu verweisen, denen diese Einmaligkeit sehr wohl bewußt war.) Worin aber besteht diese "Einmaligkeit", wenn nicht in der bewußten und rabiaten Leugnung eines entscheidenden Teils der von Heidegger ständig berufenen und den "Amerikanern" aberkannten "abendländischen Tradition"? Was bei Nietzsche noch als wortgewaltige Fehde Zarathustras mit Jerusalem[45] und dem "verjudeten" Plebejer Sokrates ausgetragen wurde, ist bei Heidegger einem SCHWEIGEN verfallen, das einer totalen Verneinung gleichkommt. Ein kurzer Blick in Hölderlins *Hymnik*, die von Heidegger zu einem exklusivem Gespräch mit den alten, vorsokratischen

Griechen erklärt wird, zeigt, daß selbst an den "Quellen der Donau", von "Patmos" ganz zu schweigen, Hölderlin ein "Gespräch" mit einem ganz anderen "Fremden", nämlich "Asien" und seinen "Propheten und Patriarchen" führte. Heideggers berühmter Wahrheitsbegriff, die gewalttätige Übersetzung des griechischen "aletheia" mit "Unverborgenheit", gehört in diesen Kontext. Die Frage nach der "polis", dem Politischen also, führt zu folgendem Ergebnis: "Ist dem so, dann sieht es so aus, als müßten wir griechischer denken als die Griechen selbst. Es sieht nicht nur so aus, es ist so. Denn wir selbst müssen in bezug auf uns selbst künftighin deutscher denken als alle bisherigen Deutschen ..."!!![46] Der Komparativ des Nationalen! Was anders verbirgt sich dahinter als der Komparativ von "wahr": griechischer und deutscher ist wahrer als jede andere — fremde — Form von Wahrheit. Die "geschichtliche Einzigartigkeit" des Nationalsozialismus ist eine Stufe der "Entbergung des Seins," eine Wahrheit *sui generis*.

Heideggers Hölderlin-und Sophoklesinterpretation enthält nicht die geringste Spur von Antisemitismus. Doch liegt in der Verschweigung ein deutlicher Wille zur Verneinung des ganz Fremden, das mit dem Deutschen nichts zu tun hat. "Deutscher" denken als deutsch heißt im Klartext der *Dritten Walpurgisnacht*: "Deutschland erwache! Juda verrecke!"

Bleiben wir noch einen Augenblick bei Heideggers Wahrheitsbegriff! Seine Übersetzung von "aletheia" durch "Unverborgenheit" — die Geschichte der Übertragung dieses Worts ins Französische gehört ins Wörterbuch des Grotesken[47] — paßte im Grunde viel besser auf ein bibel-griechisches Wort, nämlich "APOKALYPSE". Es ist ein zentrales Wort der Kraus'schen Satire. Die "Fackel der Wahrheit" hat durch und durch apokalyptischen Charakter. *Die letzten Tage der Menschheit* und *Dritte Walpurgisnacht* sind bewußte "Apokalypsen", Enthüllungen der "Wahrheit des Seins". Natürlich steht hinter diesem Wahrheitsbegriff notwendigerweise eine ethische, richtende Instanz. Die Metaphorik, die in der Brenner-Enquête über Kraus von 1913[48] oder in Elias Canettis *Karl Kraus, Schule des Widerstands*[49] herrscht, ist geprägt von der Vorstellung des Jüngsten Gerichts: der "Hohepriester der Wahrheit" (Trakl) ist "abgestiegen zur Hölle, zu richten die Lebendigen und die Toten" (Kokoschka); er "steht an der Schwelle des jüngsten Gerichts" (Loos). Es liegt auf der Hand, daß die beiden Begriffe der "Wahrheit" radikal unvereinbar sind. Doch muß hier auf eine fundamentale Gemeinsamkeit verwiesen werden, die allen "Wahrheitsbesitzern" eignet: Robert Musil hat sie in seinen Tagebüchern präzis festgehalten:

> Lange vor den Diktatoren hat unsere Zeit die geistige Diktatorenverehrung hervorgebracht. Siehe George. Dann auch Kraus und Freud, Adler und Jung. Nimm noch Klages und Heidegger dazu. Das Gemeinsame ist wohl ein Bedürfnis nach

Herrschaft und Führerschaft, nach dem Wesen des Heilands. Gibt
es auch gemeinsame Züge der Führer? Z. B. Feste Werte, bei
denen sich trotzdem Verschiedenes denken läßt.[50]

Musil hat den distanziert strukturalistischen Blick auf das Phänomen, er
scheint kein Urteil über die "festen Werte", bei denen man sich das
Verschiedenste denken kann, abgeben zu wollen. Immerhin schlägt er
drei Kategorien vor: George, den Dichter-Propheten; die vier
"apokalyptischen" Tiefenpsychologen; die zwei deklarierten Feinde der
Vernunft. Es dürfte dies eines der ganz wenigen Dokumente sein, wo
Freud, Kraus und Heidegger auf einen Nenner gebracht sind.

Daß es einen gemeinsamen Nenner zwischen Kraus und Heidegger
gibt, gilt es im folgenden herauszuarbeiten. Der gemeinsame Nenner
bedeutet nicht Identität oder gar Tautologie in dem Sinn, wie einer der
radikalsten Heidegger-Kritiker in Frankreich das "Wahrheitsproblem"
wortspielend eingekreist hat: "Die Aletheia ist die Apokalypse der
Wahrheit. Aber eine Theaterapokalypse."[51] In der "Unverborgenheit" ist
jeder Unterschied von "wahr und falsch", jede Spur einer "adaequatio ad
res" ausgelöscht. Ebenso wie Heideggers "Entbergungen" nichts mit dem
traditionellen Anspruch auf wissenschaftliche oder philosophische
"Wahrheit" zu tun haben (wollen), ebenso entschlägt sich sein Denken
jeden moralischen Anspruchs. Robert Minder notierte: "zu Rechenschaft
der 'Welt' gegenüber fühlt der Führer und Verführer der Jugend sich
nicht verpflichtet. Moralische Indifferenz — ein Grundübel in den Augen
Hebels — gehört vom Wesen her zur Philosophie Heideggers."[52]
Heideggers Schweigen steht im Zeichen dieser Indifferenz.

IV. Die Frage nach der Technik

Wer Heidegger sagt, sagt Schwarzwald: "Heidegger hatte bewußt den
Gang seines Denkens mit der Landschaft seines Herkommens bleibend
verknüpft; nie sah er sich gezwungen oder bewogen, die angestammte
Heimat zu verlassen, immer schon war er zum Bleiben entschlossen." (G.
Baumann[53] um ihn vom "ewigen Juden" Celan abzugrenzen). (Die
Legende will sogar, daß Heidegger den Ruf nach Berlin aufgrund des
Rates eines Schwarzwaldbauern abgelehnt habe). Als Celan 1967 in
Freiburg eine Lesung halten sollte, reagierte Heidegger, zu dessen
"bevorzugten" Lektüren Celans *Mohn und Gedächtnis*, also die *Todesfuge*,
gehört haben sollen, so: "Schon lange wünsche ich, Paul Celan kennen zu
lernen. Er steht am weitesten vorne und hält sich am meisten zurück....
Es wäre heilsam, P. C. auch den Schwarzwald zu zeigen."[54] So eine
kleine Kur auf einer Almhütte ist gut für geistig "Gefährdete" wie Celan.
(Aufgrund einer mündlichen Mitteilung von Jean Bollack kann ich hier

folgende Ungeheuerlichkeit einführen: Heideggers Sohn Hermann hat in einem Brief an Gisèle Celan 1980 behauptet, sein Vater habe erst nach Celans Tod erfahren, daß dieser Jude gewesen sei! Auch habe man die Hoffnung auf ein Wort des Denkenden im *Hüttenbuch* einfach als Wunsch nach brieflichem Kontakt gedeutet ... Ernst Jünger hat im *Schwarzwald bei Todtnauberg* folgende Epiphanie erlebt:

> Schlicht wie ein Bauer, aber wie einer aus dem Märchen, der sich nach Belieben verwandeln kann. "Schatzhäuser im tiefen Tannenwald." Etwas vom Fallensteller war auch dabei. Das war der Wissende — der, den das Wissen nicht nur reich macht, sondern auch fröhlich, wie Nietzsche es von der Wissenschaft verlangt. In seinem Reichtum war er unangreifbar, ja ungreifbar — selbst wenn die Büttel kommen sollten, um ihm den Rock zu pfänden — das verriet ein listiger Seitenblick. Er hätte einem Aristophanes behagt.[55]

Indem ich dies lese, fühle ich mich notgedrungen als ein Büttel, der dem armen Denker den Rock pfänden will. Daß er Aristophanes "behagt" hätte, liegt auf der Hand. Man stelle sich Heidegger an Stelle des Sokrates in den *Wolken* vor: der Lacherfolg wäre verzehnfacht. Doch Jünger wird ernst:

> Martin Heideggers Vaterland ist Deutschland mit seiner Sprache; Heideggers Heimat ist der Wald. Dort ist er zu Hause — im Unbegangenen und auf den Holzwegen. Sein Bruder ist der Baum.
>
> Wenn Heidegger die Sprache ergründet, sich in ihr Wurzelwerk vertieft, dann leistet er mehr, als, wie Nietzsche sagen würde, "unter uns Philologen" gefordert wird. Heideggers Exegese ist mehr als philologisch, auch mehr als etymologisch: er faßt das Wort, wo es noch frisch, in voller Keimkraft im Schweigen schlummert, und hebt es aus dem Humus des Waldes empor.[56]

Ein Freiburger Kollege, der Historiker Hermann Heimpel, sieht es anders:

> Sagte er von einem Kollegen "der Jude", verkannte er sich selbst. Freilich, er konnte damals sein Pathos in klingende Schellen verwandeln, und der Jugend-Bewegte war es gewohnt, rollenden Feuern starke Sprüche nachzurufen — wie im Haß gegen die Urbanität. Wald-gefesselt. Der Schwarzwald hat seine dunklen Seiten.[57]

Der Antipode zu Jüngers Wald-Idolatrie ist seit "Alte Meister" Thomas Bernhard, demzufolge Heidegger, der "Schwarzwaldphilosoph"[58], die Philosophie total "verkitscht" habe.

In Heideggers Philosophie der Technik ist etwas vom "Schwarzwaldsterben" vorweggenommen. Daß es dabei oft kitschig zugeht, ist unbestreitbar, soll aber bei einer so ernsten Frage nicht das Entscheidungskriterium sein. Doch muß man sich deswegen unwidersprochen folgenden Gedankengang gefallen lassen ("Hebel der Hausfreund")? Heidegger kann nicht an Goethes berühmtem Wort vorbei, Hebel habe das Universum "verbauert". Es folgt eine lange Liste der "Fragwürdigkeiten" der Modernität, die so endet:

> Wir irren heute durch ein Haus der Welt, dem der Hausfreund fehlt, jener nämlich, der in gleicher Weise und Stärke dem technisch ausgebauten Weltgebäude **und** der Welt als dem Haus für ein ursprünglicheres Wohnen zugeneigt ist. Jener Hausfreund fehlt, der es vermöchte, die Berechenbarkeit und Technik der Natur (??) in das offene Geheimnis einer neu erfahrenen Natürlichkeit der Natur zurückzubergen. Dieser Hausfreund verbauert allerdings das Universum. Aber dieses Verbauern hat die Art jenes Bauens, das auf ein ursprünglicheres Wohnen des Menschen hinausdenkt.
>
> Dafür braucht es Bauende, die wissen, daß der Mensch durch die Atomenergie nicht leben, sondern höchstens umkommen, das heißt sein Wesen verlieren muß ... Demgegenüber bedenken die eigentlich Bauenden, daß das bloße Leben, das man lebt, noch kein Wohnen ist. Denn der Mensch "wohnet", wenn er wohnt, nach dem Wort Hölderlins "dichterisch ... auf dieser Erde"[59].

Diese für Heidegger typische Assoziationskette, die auch seinem Technikessay immanent ist, konstruiert einen Bogen vom "Bauern" zum "Wohnhaus des Dichters". Hebel wird durch diesen etymologischen Schwindel auf die gleiche sakrale Ebene wie Hölderlin "erhoben". Der Sakralisierung des Führers und des Volkes folgt die Sakralisierung deutschester und griechischster Poesie. Zu den etymologischen Finten Heideggers gehört folgende Wortspielerei: "Causa, casus, gehören zum Zeitwort cadere, fallen, und bedeutet dasjenige, was bewirkt, daß etwas im Erfolg so oder so ausFÄLLT."[60] Hier ist der Ort, ein Kraus'sches Wortspiel einzuführen, das in seinem Wesen Heidegger sicher gefallen hätte:

> *Lyrik der Deutschen*
> Wer kann, ist ihr Mann und nicht einer, der muß,
> sie irren vom Wesen zum Scheine.

Ihr lyrischer FALL war nicht Claudius,
aber Heine.[61]

Dem "Wesen der Technik" als "Herausforderung" stellt Heidegger eine
Reihe von archetypischen Figuren gegenüber: die Windmühle (ihr
Gegenstück ist das Wasserkraftwerk im Rhein), "das Feld, das der Bauer
vormals bestellte, wobei bestellen noch hieß: hegen und pflegen. Das
bäuerliche Tun fordert den Ackerboden nicht heraus."[62] (Robert
Minder[63] hat gezeigt, daß Heideggers Vokabular, wenn es um das
Bauerntum geht, direkt aus der Blut-und Bodenideologie Walter Darrés
abgeleitet ist, z. B.: das Wort von der "Hege" ("In diesem Wort
(="Hegehof") kommt das Hegende an Blut und Boden unmißverständlich
zum Ausdruck") oder von den Bauern als "Hörigen (ihrer) Herkunft,
nicht Knechte(n) von Machenschaften" ("Der Feldweg"). Gegenstück zu
diesem Tun sind einerseits der Kohle- und Erzbergbau ("Entbergung" des
Erdreichs als "Erzlagerstätte"), andererseits "Ackerbau als motorisierte
Ernährungsindustrie".[64] Da darf auch der Wald nicht fehlen:

> Der Forstwart, der im Wald das geschlagene Holz vermißt und
> dem Anschein nach noch wie sein Großvater dieselben Waldwege
> begeht, ist heute von der Holzverwertungsindustrie bestellt, ob er
> es weiß oder nicht. Er ist in die Bestellbarkeit von Zellulose
> bestellt, die ihrerseits durch den Bedarf an Papier herausgefordert
> ist, das den Zeitungen und illustrierten Magazinen zugestellt
> wird. Diese aber stellen die öffentliche Meinung daraufhin, das
> Gedruckte zu verschlingen, um für eine bestellte Meinungs-
> herrichtung bestellbar zu werden.[65]

Wenn man von der Sprache und dem Umstand absieht, daß Heidegger
weder die Waffenindustrie noch die Massenvernichtung von Menschen
unter das "herausgeforderte Entbergen des Seins"[66] rechnet (das
Schweigen darüber ermöglicht zukünftiger Philosophie ein Absatzgebiet),
fühlt man sich geradezu in die Nähe der *Fackel* gerückt, die die rasche
Verwandlung von Bäumen in Zeitungsblätter lange vor 1914 als Symptom des "Fortschritts" diagnostiziert und im Schlußakt der *Letzten Tage
der Menschheit* einen "toten Wald" zur Sprache gebracht hat. *Die Welt ohne
Blatt* (Juni 1920), eine Satire über die Folgen der Rationierung des Papiers
für die Wiener Presse, wiegt zentrale Texte Heideggers durch Präzision
und Witz auf, nicht zuletzt den besten, den Kraus einem Zitat verdankt:
eine von der Papiernot betroffene Zeitung erklärt ihre Inserate als ein
"aus wirtschaftlichen Notwendigkeiten erwachsendes **Naturprodukt**". [67]
Zahllos sind die Texte Kraus', die man mit der Existentialanalyse
Heideggers in *Sein und Zeit* (über das "Man", das "Gerede", die "Neugier")
und seiner sich an Platons Wortschöpfung "Idee" messendem "Ge-stell"

(= Wesen der Technik) in Parallele setzen könnte. Bevor wir eine knappe Anthologie bieten, muß der Unterschied in der Konzeption des "Wesens" des technischen Fortschritts herausgearbeitet werden. Heideggers Einführung des "Ge-stells" mit seiner Serie von etymologischen Assoziationen (stellen, bestellen) läuft darauf hinaus, die Kantsche Dialektik von Zweck und Mittel zu überholen. Die Vorsilbe Geleitet dabei das Denken über Ge-birg, Gemüt, Ge-stell[68] zum Ge-schick: das Wesen der Technik wird dabei zu einem Ge-schick des Seins, zu einer ge-schickten Gefahr. Gefährlich ist die besondere Erscheinungsform der "Wahrheit" (Entbergung), die der Technik eignet. Der Hauptvorwurf besteht darin, daß die technische Herausforderung zum Ziel hat, das "Verborgene" zum verfügbaren "Bestand" im Sinn von "Lagerbestand" ("Stock") zu machen. Obwohl sich Heidegger 1942 gegen den Umstand wehrt, daß "das gedankenlose Zusammenwerfen (s)eines Denkens mit Rilkes Dichtung bereits zur Phrase geworden ist"[69], wage ich die Gedankenlosigkeit, den tieferen Sinn der "Frage nach der Technik" auf einige Verse der "Siebenten Duineser Elegie" zu reduzieren:

> ... Wo einmal ein dauerndes Haus war,
> schlägt sich erdachtes Gebild vor, quer, zu Erdenklichem
> völlig gehörig, als ständ es noch ganz im Gehirne.
> Weite Speicher der Kraft schafft sich der Zeitgeist, gestaltlos
> wie der spannende Drang, den er aus allem gewinnt.
> Tempel kennt er nicht mehr.[70]

In seinem Rilke-Essay "Wozu Dichter?" — in dürftiger Zeit — von 1946 mildert Heidegger die Verurteilung des "tief unwahren Wortes" vom Offenen. Dagegen findet sich dort ohne Anführungszeichen (!) der folgende Satz: "Die bildlosen Gebilde der technischen Produktion schlagen sich vor das Offene des reinen Bezugs."[71] Ein überaus typisches Zeichen für Heideggers Umgang mit Gedichten: Aneignung durch schlampige Paraphrase!

Klage um den Verlust des "Ursprünglichen," des "Anfänglichen", des "Heiligen", die durch "Speicher" ("Bestand", "Lager") ersetzt sind, denen jede "Unmittelbarkeit", "Eigentlichkeit" abgeht, die also Triumphe der "Vermittlung" darstellen, des "Man", des "Zeitgeistes".

Die Nähe zu Kraus ist unüberhörbar, aber auch jene zu Marx' Begriff der "Entfremdung", der in Brechts Gedicht *Nachdenkend über die Hölle* eine an Rilke und Heidegger gemahnende Wendung nimmt:

> ... Und Obstmärkte
> Mit ganzen Haufen von Früchten, die allerdings
> Weder riechen noch schmecken.[72]

Lagerhausbestände? Heidegger hat 1935 in seiner *Einführung in die Metaphysik,* in der er den Begriff der "Werte" kritisierte, geschrieben:

> Dies alles nennt sich Philosophie. Was heute vollends als Philosophie des Nationalsozialismus herumgeboten wird, aber mit der inneren Wahrheit und Größe dieser Bewegung (nämlich mit der Begegnung der planetarisch bestimmten Technik und des neuzeitlichen Menschen) nicht das Geringste zu tun hat, das macht seine Fischzüge in diesen trüben Gewässern der "Werte" ...[73]

Halten wir fest, daß Heidegger zunächst sogar "**der** Bewegung" geschrieben hatte und daß er den eben zitierten Satz unverändert in die späteren Auflagen seit 1953 übernommen hat. Er sah sich selbst in der Tat wie schon oben angedeutet als der "wahre" Denker der Bewegung, die hier als Begegnung mit der Technik definiert wird. Man wird hier vielleicht einen Widerspruch entdecken: wie kann die "Heimkehr" ins "Anfängliche", "Ursprüngliche", in die "Schwarzwaldheimat" der hegenden und pflegenden Bauern mit dem technologischen und Rüstungsboom des Dritten Reichs zusammenstimmen? Kraus hält dafür die Formel "elektrisch beleuchtete Barbaren"[74] bereit, denn er sieht im Nationalsozialismus nicht einen "Aufbruch", eine "Gegenbewegung" zu den "Gefahren" des "Gestells", sondern die konsequente Vollendung der Logik der Technik, betrieben von den "Untergangstern"[75] des Abendlandes, zu deren Worthelfer sich Heidegger hergegeben hat.

1930 hat Karl Kraus in einer Glosse das "Wesen" des geschichtslosen "Amerikanismus" mittels eines Zitates konzentriert:

Der Fordschritt

(Der standardisierte Mensch.) Henry Ford hat kürzlich hundert Millionen Dollar für die Errichtung einer Schule gestiftet, die er die Schule der Zukunft nennt. "Ich habe so lange Autos fabriziert," erklärte er, "bis ich den Wunsch bekam, nunmehr Menschen zu fabrizieren. Die Losung der Zeit ist Standardisierung." — Die erste Musterschule Fords, die ihre Tätigkeit bereits begonnen hat, nimmt nur Knaben im Alter von 12 bis 17 Jahren auf. Verpönt sind Sprachen, Literatur, Kunst, Musik und Geschichte. — Die Lebenskunst müssen die Schüler lernen, sie müssen verstehen, zu kaufen und zu verkaufen" — Endlich einmal eine tabula rasa mit Vorwänden, die dem einzigen und wahren Lebenszweck vielfach hinderlich waren![76]

In diesem Ford-Zitat sieht Kraus eine Bewegung auf die Spitze getrieben, die für ihn paradigmatisch war: die Verwechslung von Zweck und Mittel. Anfang 1915, im Angesicht des Krieges, fand er die aphoristische Form für den Sachverhalt:

> Es gibt eine Idee, die einst den wahren Weltkrieg in Bewegung setzen wird: Daß Gott den Menschen nicht als Konsumenten und Produzenten erschaffen hat. Daß das Lebensmittel nicht Lebenszweck sei. Daß der Magen dem Kopf nicht über den Kopf wachse. Daß das Leben nicht in der Ausschließlichkeit der Erwerbsinteressen begründet sei. Daß der Mensch in die Zeit gesetzt sei, um Zeit zu haben und nicht mit den Beinen irgendwo eher anzulangen als mit dem Herzen.[77]

Schon 1909, fast gleichzeitig mit *Apokalypse*, hatte er im satirischen Essay *Der Fordschritt* geschrieben: "Wir verdanken ihm, daß wir schneller vorwärts kommen. Aber wohin kommen wir? Ich selbst begnügte mich, es als das dringendste Bedürfnis zu empfinden, zu mir zu kommen."[78] Es wäre leicht, hier eine wahre Anthologie zu dieser Frage vorzulegen, deren Kern die Verkehrung von "Zweck und Mittel" ist — eine Verkehrung, die ihren Grund darin hat, daß die Raum-Zeiterfahrung und -beherrschung durch Technik und Wissenschaft das "natürliche" menschliche Maß, das heißt das "kreatürliche" Maß überschritten hat. Der Erhöhung der Geschwindigkeit entspricht die rapide Ausdehnung des Raums und die Vervielfältigung der Kräfte: im Prinzip ein für den "natürlichen" Menschen durch und durch "magischer Vorgang". Die Metapher der Magie hat Kraus auch in Anschluß an Goethe immer wieder benützt: da ist einerseits die Ballade vom "Zauberlehrling," andererseits der 5. Akt von *Faust II*, der — genau gelesen — die "Frage nach dem Wesen der Technik" und der industriellen Revolution schon gestellt hatte. Nach der brutalen Vernichtung der idyllischen Überreste eines anderen Daseinsgefühls (Philemon und Baucis) stellt sich der erblindende Faust die Frage:

> ... Könnt' ich Magie von meinem Pfad entfernen,
> Die Zaubersprüche ganz und gar verlernen,
> Stünd' ich, Natur, vor dir ein Mann allein,
> Da wär's der Mühe wert, ein Mensch zu sein. (V 11404 ff.)

Das Opfer des technischen "Wunders" ahnt:

> ... Denn es ging das ganze Wesen
> Nicht mit rechten Dingen zu. (V 11404 ff.)

1965 hat Gershom Scholem einen neuen israelischen Computer in einer Rede getauft, und zwar als "Golem" und dabei bedauert, daß das Weizmann Institut seinen Vorschlag eines Instituts für experimentelle Dämonologie und Magie abgelehnt habe zugunsten der Konstruktion des Golem. "Ich sage dem Golem und seinem Schöpfer: Wachset in Frieden und zerstört nicht die Welt! Schalom."[79]

Es leuchtet ein, daß in der "Frage nach der Technik" zumindest in einem Punkt ein Konsensus zwischen Heidegger und Kraus besteht, nämlich in der Diagnose der "Gefahr". Aber es scheint sogar in der Frage nach der Rettung aus der Gefahr eine Parallele vorzuliegen: Heidegger sieht das "Rettende" in der Dichtung (Hölderlins und der alten Griechen). Über die Etymologie beschwört er die ursprüngliche Identität der "techne" als "poiesis" (Hervorbringen) und entläßt uns in seinen Mythos.

Kraus' *Theriak* — ich nehme hier den Titel von Uwe Dicks Gedichtfolge auf[80] — bleibt bei aller Beschwörung von "Natur und Ursprung" das Rezept eines treuen Sohns der "Aufklärung" und erst recht der "Klassik". Dies zu zeigen, ist hier nicht der Ort, Adorno/Horkheimer verdanken ihre "Dialektik der Aufklärung" nicht zuletzt dem Autor der *Letzten Tage der Menschheit*. Er hält an der Möglichkeit von individueller Schuld und Verantwortung fest.

V. Wer spricht?

"Im Wesen der Sprache eines geschichtlichen Volkes liegt es, gleich einem Gebirge zumal in die Ebene und in das Flache auszulaufen und zugleich mit seltenen Gipfeln in sonst unzugängliche Höhen hinaufzuragen."[81] Kraus sprach von "jenen Gipfeln, wo Ruh ist"[82]. Sind diese Gipfel und die Wege zu ihnen vergleichbar? Heidegger zieht aus seiner Metapher den richtigen Schluß, daß Übersetzung nicht "Verflachung" sein darf, die sich dem "beliebigen Meinen und dessen Verständnis-Horizont"[83] anpaßt. Wer wollte ihm da widersprechen? Fragwürdiger ist schon die Behauptung, daß eine als "unrichtig" erkannte Übersetzung ebendarum "wahrer"[84] sei. Heideggers Feindseligkeit gegen die "angelsächsische Welt des Amerikanismus" betrifft auch die englische Sprache, die von ihm nur unter dem Gesichtspunkt der "Nützlichkeit" der "technisch-praktischen Verkehrszwecke" gesehen wird im Gegensatz zum "Sprach-geist der (natürlich alt-) griechischen Sprache"[85]. Amüsante und erhellende Gegenbeispiele: Karl Kraus hat das Deutsche dank dem Lateinunterricht gelernt,[86] Elias Canetti "weiß, was ein Tiger ist", durch ein Gedicht von Blake[87]. Der literarische Paradigmawechsel des 18. Jahrhunderts geschah im Namen Shakespeares, der sogar Herder das "griechische Wesen" in germanischer "Schaube" zu vertreten schien. Doch

für den "klassischen Humanismus" hat Heidegger nur Verachtung über
wie für das *Neue Testament*.

> Wir lernen die griechische Sprache, damit das verborgene Wesen
> unseres eigenen geschichtlichen Anfangs für uns sich in die
> Klarheit unseres Wortes finde ... Wir dürfen (!) die griechische
> Sprache nur lernen, wenn wir sie aus wesentlicher geschichtlicher
> Notwendigkeit um der eigenen deutschen Sprache willen lernen
> müssen.[88]

Man vergleiche dazu oben den Komparativ "deutscher und griechischer"!
Den Schluß aber: "Denn auch diese (die deutsche) müssen wir erst
lernen," hätte Karl Kraus gewiß unterschrieben. Sein Aphorismus "Die
deutsche Sprache ist die tiefste, die deutsche Rede die seichteste."[89]
scheint dem Sprachdenken Heideggers nicht unverwandt. Im Sprach-
erlernen und im Übersetzen gilt für Heidegger: "Die Sprache lernen heißt
hören lernen ... Das Horchen und Gehorchenkönnen ist die Grund-
bedingung für das echte Lesen des echten Wortes."[90]
   Also Gehorsam: Sprachgehorsam! Karl Kraus, der das Deutsche zur
"gedankenreichsten Sprache" erklärt, fragt sich rhetorisch: "Welch ein Stil
des Lebens möchte sich entwickeln, wenn der Deutsche keiner anderen
Ordonnanz gehorsamte als der Sprache!"[91] Noch näher bei Heidegger:
"Sie ist schon in ihrer zugänglichsten Region wie eine Ahnung des
höchsten Gipfels, den sie erreicht hat ..."[92] Der allerdings heißt nicht
Hölderlins Hymnen, sondern Goethes *Pandora*. Und Karl Kraus ist ein
unbedingter Vertreter des goethischen Symbols, dem Heidegger im
Zeichen von Hölderlins "Nennen"="Entbergen" den Krieg erklärt. Kraus
beschließt seinen Essay mit dem Ruf: "Der Mensch lerne, ihr zu
dienen!"[93]
   Wozu aber führt nach Kraus der wahre Sprachgehorsam? Zum
Zweifel! "Der Zweifel als die große moralische Gabe, die der Mensch der
Sprache verdanken könnte und bis heute verschmäht hat, wäre die
rettende Hemmung eines Fortschritts, der mit vollkommener Sicherheit
zu dem Ende einer Zivilisation führt, der er zu dienen wähnt." [94]
   Bei Heidegger dagegen führt der angebliche Gehorsam gegenüber der
griechischen und deutschen Sprache zu ihrer Vergewaltigung. Es ist
erstaunlich, wie leichtfertig George Steiner in *Après Babel* diese
Gewalttätigkeit des "Be-Greifens" verteidigt[95]. Der Mythos Hölderlin, vor
allem die Sophokles-Übersetzungen, hat da ganze Vorarbeit geleistet. Wer
wagt heute die Seins-Entbergung anzuzweifeln, über die Goethe und
Schiller in Lachen ausgebrochen waren. Und Heidegger profitiert davon
so: bei Hölderlin lautet der Anfang des Chores aus *Antigone*: "Ungeheuer
ist viel. Doch nichts/Ungeheurer als der Mensch." Heidegger macht
daraus: "Vielfältig das Unheimliche, nichts doch/über den Menschen

hinaus Unheimlicheres ragend sich regt."[96] (Hölderlin: 9 Worte; Heidegger: 13; Sophokles: 7!) Gewiß, alle Übersetzer inklusive Hölderlin übersetzen "pelei" ungenau mit "ist", doch braucht es kein besonders ausgeprägtes Stilgefühl, um zu begreifen, daß mit der Wagnerimitation "ragend sich regt" ein Kulissen-Gipfel erreicht ist. Sophokles wird an die Kandare von Heideggers Sprachwillkür genommen. Daß diese technisch gesprochen aus Stabreimen, Assonanzen und etymologischen Phantasien zusammengezimmerte Sprache eine internationale Wirkung entfalten konnte, gehört zu den mannigfaltigen Triumphen der Magie im technisch-wissenschaftlichen Zeitalter.

Je näher die Worte Kraus' und Heideggers einander zu sein scheinen, desto ferner stehen einander die Dinge. "Die einzige Verbindung", die Kraus anstrebte, war die von "Wort und Wesen"[97], eine Formel, die furchtbar heruntergekommen ist zu Titeln wie "Wort und Wesen in Südtirol" usw. Zu den auffallendsten Parallelen im Wortschatz neben dem "Sprachgehorsam" gehört das Bild vom "Haus der Sprache"[98]. Nach Heidegger ("Humanismusbrief"[99]) kommt im "Denken das Sein zur Sprache ... Die Sprache ist das Haus des Seins. In ihrer Behausung wohnt der Mensch. Die Denkenden und die Dichtenden sind die Wächter dieser Behausung." Die Kombination "Volk der Denker und Dichter", im Ersten Weltkrieg abgewandelt zu "Henker und Richter", eine Formel, die im Zweiten auf ihren "Gipfel" gelangte, wird von Heidegger im Herbst 1946 völlig unbefangen als magische Formel für die Deutschen weiter-verwendet. Denn noch im "Spiegel-Gespräch" von 1966 gibt er kund, daß man nur auf deutsch denken kann, ja daß die Franzosen, wenn sie zu denken anfangen, es auf deutsch tun.[100] Er hat in Kraus beinahe einen Bundesgenossen: "'Volk der Dichter und Denker': seine Sprache vermag es, den Besitzfall zum Zeugefall zu erhöhen, das Haben zum Sein. Denn größer als die Möglichkeit, in ihr zu denken, wäre keine Phantasie."[101] Wer spricht? Die deutsche Sprache? "Von Rache sprech' ich, will die Sprache rächen/ an allen jenen, die die Sprache sprechen."[102] Über Heidegger geht in Frankreich die Anekdote um, seine Frau habe schwatzhafte Franzosen während eines Vortrags des Magiers mit dem Satz "ES spricht!" zum Schweigen gebracht.

Mir scheint, daß Paul Celan in seinem Heidegger-Gedicht einen wesentlichen Racheakt des poetischen Denkens aus der Sprache gesetzt hat: ein Wort wie "Waldwasen" — Heideggers wagnerisierendes Reden verbunden mit der etymologischen "Apokalypse" (Wasen=Schindanger) — widerspricht der Bewohnbarkeit des Heideggerschen "Hauses" absolut.

Kraus war sich seines "geschichtlichen Ortes" bescheidener bewußt als Heidegger: "Ich bin nur einer von den Epigonen,/ die in dem alten Haus der Sprache wohnen."[103] In der "Behausung" dieser seiner Gottheit waren viele Wohnungen, nicht nur für Deutsche und Griechen, sondern auch für Juden, Engländer, Neger und Chinesen. Darum lohnt es nicht mehr, der letzten Verwechslung noch ausdrücklich nachzugehen: das Ursprüngliche (Anfängliche) kennt nur die "Rasse des Menschen".[104]

Anmerkungen

[1]   Dieser Essay erschien unter dem Titel "Kraus und Heidegger". In: *Wespennest. Zeitschrift für brauchbare Texte und Bilder*, Nummer 90 (1993), S. 29-40.

[2]   Steiner, George: *Martin Heidegger*, übers. v. G. Stieg. Paris 1981, S. 201.

[3]   Heinrich Heine: *Zur Geschichte der Religion und Philosophie in Deutschland*. In: Ders.: *Sämtliche Werke*. München 1964, Bd. 9, S. 242ff.

[4]   Zitiert nach einem Vortrag über "Heidegger und Kraus" im Österreichischen Kulturinstitut Paris, Dezember 1991 (übers. v. G. Stieg).

[5]   Martin Heidegger: "Das alltägliche Selbstsein und das Man". In: Ders.: *Sein und Zeit*. Tübingen 1967 (11. unv. Aufl.), S. 167-180 und S. 126-130.

[6]   Heine, (Anm. 3), S. 284.

[7]   Karl Kraus: *Die Dritte Walpurgisnacht*. München 1952, Sigle DW. Eine "Vorfassung" erschien Ende Juli 1934 als *Fackel* 890-905 unter dem Titel "Warum die Fackel nicht erscheint" (315 Seiten!). Albrecht Betz hat in seinem Aufsatz "'Die Worthelfer der Gewalt' in der *Dritten Walpurgisnacht*". In: Gilbert Krebs und Gerald Stieg (Hrsg.), *Karl Kraus et son temps*. Paris-Asnières 1989, S.155-171, nachgewiesen, daß Karl Kraus für die "Fälle" Heidegger, Spengler und Benn das in Paris erscheinende *Neue Tagebuch* (Juli-1933) als Quelle benutzt hat.

[8]   DW, S. 58.

[9]   *Fackel* 400-403, S. 92.

[10]   *Fackel* 404, S. 2.

[11]   *Fackel* 413-417, S. 25.

[12]   *Fackel* 888, S. 4.

[13]   "Die Selbstbehauptung der deutschen Universität", 27. Mai 1933.

[14]   DW, S. 55.

[15]   Ebd. S. 58.

[16]   Ebd. S. 58 ("Rektoratsrede", S. 14).

[17]   Ebd. S. 59.

[18]   Ebd.

[19]   *Fackel* 404, S. 1.

[20]   Heidegger: *Die Selbstbehauptung der deutschen Universität. Das Rektorat 1933-1934*. Frankfurt/Main 1983.

[21]   Heidegger: *L'auto-affirmation de l'Université allemande, édition bilingue*. Hg. v. Gérard Granel. Paris 1982.

[22]   Das "Spiegel-Gespräch" von 1976 findet sich in: *Antwort. Martin Heidegger im Gespräch*. Pfullingen 1988, S. 81-114.

23 Gerhart Baumann: *Erinnerungen an Paul Celan*. Frankfurt/Main 1986.

24 Bernd Martin: *Heidegger und das "Dritte Reich". Ein Kompendium*. Darmstadt 1989, S. 155.

25 Paul Celan: *Gesammelte Werke* in fünf Bänden. Frankfurt/Main 1983, Bd. 2, S. 255.

26 Baumann, l. c., S. 75.

27 Ebd. S. 76.

28 Victor Farias: *Heidegger et le nazisme*. Paris 1987. (1989 Ausgabe im "Livre de poche").

29 Robert Minder: *Heidegger und Hebel oder die Sprache von Meßkirch*. In: Ders.: *Dichter in der Gesellschaft*. Darmstadt o. J., S. 210-264.

30 G. Stiegs Essay "Heidegger und Kraus", der in der Zeitschrift *Wespennest* erschien, enthält eine ausführliche Auseinandersetzung mit der französischen Heidegger-Rezeption, u. a. mit Jacques Derrida (Derrida: "Heideggers Schweigen". In: *Antwort*, l. c., S. 158-159).

31 Ebd.; vgl. auch Derrida, l. c., S. 160.

32 Heidegger: *Hölderlins Hymne "Der Ister"*. In: *Gesamtausgabe, II. Abteilung: Vorlesungen 1923-1944*, Frankfurt/Main 1984, Bd. 53, Sigle Ister.

33 Vgl. Karl Löwiths Äußerungen in: Martin, l. c., S. 154.

34 Wilhelm Michel: *Das Leben Friedrich Hölderlins*. In: *Werke*. Darmstadt 1963, S. 518.

35 Pierre Bertaux: *Hölderlin. Essai de biographie intérieure*. Paris 1936, S. 329ff, 348, 352.

36 Kraus' Äußerungen über Hölderlin zeugen von geringem Interesse für den Dichter. Bezeichnend ist, daß Kraus die in *Fackel* 462 (Oktober 1917) abgedruckte und von ihm auch öffentlich gelesene "Scheltrede" auf die Deutschen aus dem "Hyperion" durch einen Leser (!) kennengelernt hat. Andere Erwähnungen: *Fackel* 657, S. 186, *Fackel* 743, S. 82, *Fackel* 917, S. 67.

37 Kraus: *Briefe an Sidonie Nádherny von Borutin*. München 1974, Bd. 1, S. 118.

38 Ludwig von Ficker: *Denkzettel und Danksagungen*. München 1967, S. 119. Zu dieser Problematik vgl. auch Stieg: *Der "Brenner" und die "Fackel"*. Salzburg 1976, bes. S. 264-271. Ludwig von Ficker hat in den 50er Jahren "im Namen Trakls" freundschaftliche Beziehungen zu Heidegger unterhalten und leider dessen Deutungen abgesegnet.

39 Ister, S. 60.

40 Ebd. S. 67.

41 Ebd. S. 61.

42 Ebd. S. 68.

43 Ebd. S. 98.

44 Ebd.

45 Siehe dazu Dominique Bourel und Jacques Le Rider (Hrsg.), *De Sils-Maria à Jérusalem. Nietzsche et le judaïsme*. Paris 1991, bes. S. 21-46 (Philhellenismus und Antisemitismus), S. 47-66 (Spinoza). Leider ist der "Fall Heidegger" aus diesem Buch ausgeklammert und der "Fall Kraus" bloß in eine Fußnote verwiesen.

46 Ister, S. 100.

[47] Henri Meschonnic: *Le langage Heidegger*. Paris 1990, S. 316-320.

[48] *Rundfrage über Karl Kraus*. Innsbruck 1917. Zusammenfassung der in *Brenner* III, 18, 19, und 20, 1913 erschienenen Beiträge.

[49] Elias Canetti: *Das Gewissen der Worte*. München 1975.

[50] Robert Musil: *Tagebücher*. Hg. v. Adolf Frisé. Reinbek 1976, Bd. 1, S. 896.

[51] Meschonnic, l. c., S. 320.

[52] Minder, l. c., S. 250.

[53] Baumann, l. c., S. 75.

[54] Ebd. S. 59-60.

[55] Vgl. Ernst Jüngers Äußerungen in: Martin, l. c., S. 153-154.

[56] Ebd.

[57] Vgl. Hermann Heimpels Äußerungen in: Martin, l. c., S. 148.

[58] Thomas Bernhard: *Alte Meister*. Frankfurt 1985, S. 87.

[59] Heidegger: *Hebel der Hausfreund*. Pfullingen 1957, S. 24, Sigle Hausfreund.

[60] Heidegger: *Die Frage nach der Technik*. In: Ders.: *Vorträge und Aufsätze*. Pfullingen 1954, Teil 1, S. 8, Sigle Technik.

[61] *Fackel* 588-594, S. 87.

[62] Technik, S. 14.

[63] Minder, l. c., S. 250.

[64] Technik, S. 14.

[65] Ebd. S. 17-18.

[66] Ebd. S. 17.

[67] *Fackel* 544-545, S. 4.

[68] Technik, S. 19ff.

[69] Ister, S. 113.

[70] Rainer Maria Rilke: *Sämtliche Werke in zwölf Bänden*. Frankfurt/Main 1976, S. 711.

[71] Heidegger: "Wozu Dichter in dürftiger Zeit?" In: Ders.: *Holzwege*. Frankfurt/main 1950, S. 268.

[72] Bertold Brecht: *Gedichte*. In: *Gesammelte Werke*, Bd. 3. Frankfurt/Main 1967, S. 830.

[73] Heidegger: *Einführung in die Metaphysik*. Tübingen 1953, S. 152.

[74] DW, S. 11.

[75] Ebd. S. 65.

[76] *Fackel* 838-844, S. 50.

[77] *Fackel* 406-412, S. 96.

[78] *Fackel* 275-276, S. 38.

[79] Gershom Scholem: "Le Golem de Prague et le Golem de Rehovot". In: Ders.: *Le messianisme juif*. Paris 1974, S. 478.

[80] Uwe Dick: *Theriak. 13 Fügungen. Mit einem Essay von Eva Hesse*. München 1986.

[81] Ister, S. 76.

[82] *Fackel* 781-786, S. 97.

[83] Ister, S. 76.

[84] Ebd. S. 74.

[85] Ebd. S. 80-81.

[86] *Fackel* 423-425, S. 39-40. (Gedicht an den Lateinlehrer H. S. Sedlmayer).

[87] Canetti: *Die Provinz des Menschen. Aufzeichnungen 1942-1972.* München 1973, S. 29.

[88] Ister, S. 81.

[89] *Fackel* 406-412, S. 152.

[90] Ister, S. 81.

[91] *Fackel* 885-887, Ende Dezember 1932, S. 1-4.

[92] Karl Kraus: "Die Sprache". In: Ders.: *Die Sprache.* Hg. v. Heinrich Fischer. München 1954, Bd. 2, S. 437.

[93] Ebd. S. 438.

[94] Ebd. S. 437.

[95] George Steiner: *Après Babel.* Paris 1978, S. 298ff.

[96] Ister, S. 71.

[97] *Fackel* 508-513 (April 1919), S. 80; "Wort und Wesen — das ist die einzige Verbindung, die ich je im Leben angestrebt habe."

[98] "Bekenntnis". In: *Fackel* 443-444, S. 28.

[99] Heidegger: *Brief über den Humanismus.* Frankfurt/Main 1949 (ursprünglich "Brief" an Jean Beaufret, 1946!), S. 42.

[100] *Antwort,* l. c., S. 107-108.

[101] "Die Sprache", (Anm. 92), S. 438.

[102] "Bekenntnis", l. c., S. 28.

[103] Ebd.

[104] Der Begriff stammt vom *Brenner*-Mitarbeiter Carl Dallago, der im *Brenner,* IV, 6, 1913, S. 245-257), ausgehend vom "Fall Kraus", der vom Rasseantisemiten Lanz von Liebenfels als "Retter des Ariergermanentums" beansprucht worden war, jegliche Form von Rassismus aufs schärfste ablehnte.

Edward Timms

Karl Kraus and the Struggle for Rights

"Considering the defectiveness of our laws," wrote Jonathan Swift in an exemplary formulation, "it is possible that many great abuses may be visibly committed which cannot be legally punished.... I am apt to think that it was to supply such defects as these that satire was first introduced into the world."[1] Kraus's career is framed by similar assumptions. The program of *Die Fackel*, as defined in July 1900, was to remedy deficiencies in the legal system. Kraus was to act as self-appointed public prosecutor (*Ankläger*, F 45: 20). Looking back over his career in 1919, he described it as an "administration of justice extending over twenty years" (F 51418: 51). And his polemics of the 1920s are cast in a forensic mode, with an explicit appeal to readers "schooled in criminology" ("kriminalistisch vorgeschult," F 771-6: 102). Walter Benjamin, writing in the *Frankfurter Zeitung* in 1930, even emphasized that every aspect of Kraus's work without exception was conceived "within the sphere of law" ("in der Sphäre des Rechts").[2] Benjamin's formulation is suggestive, but it ignores that Kraus's attitude towards the law had undergone dramatic fluctuations at different stages in his career. It also fails to elucidate the German-Jewish subtext which gives Kraus's stance its underlying significance.

Kraus conceived the law in dynamic terms as a "struggle for rights" — "Kampf ums Recht" (F 657-67: 150) or "Rechtskampf" (F 827-33: 39), deriving such concept from the jurist Rudolf von Ihering's lecture *Der Kampf ums Recht*, delivered in 1872 while he was Professor of Law at the University of Vienna. The lecture, one of the most influential legal texts of the late nineteenth century, was frequently reprinted during the following decades. Kraus was probably introduced to it when he registered as a student at the Vienna Law Faculty in December 1892. At that stage he showed so little enthusiasm for the Law as a discipline that within eighteen months he switched to the Faculty of Philosophy. And later in life, he emphatically denied that his legal studies had helped to shape his polemical style (F 679-85: 59). Despite these disclaimers, however, there can be little doubt that Ihering's principles left their imprint upon Kraus's polemical strategy.

Ihering's philosophy of law was crucial to Kraus's writings, for the Viennese jurist did not conceive of law as a static system of rules, but as the dynamically evolving product of a struggle between competing interest groups. The health of a legal system depended not on the wisdom of professional jurists, but on the active participation of public-spirited citizens. The individual who enforced his rights through the courts was not motivated simply by self-interest. He was also serving the whole community by affirming the rule of law as a universal principle. The participation of the citizen in the struggle for justice thus had a double function: it enabled him both to affirm his own personality and to discharge his duty to society. Ihering detected among Austrians of the late nineteenth century a reluctance to stand up for their rights. He urged every citizen to become "guardian and executor of the law within his own sphere" ("Wächter und Vollstrecker des Gesetzes innerhalb seiner Sphäre").[3] This affirmative view of the law was to have a profound effect on Kraus's writings, both his early social satire and his later political polemics.

I. Popular Accusation

During the early years of *Die Fackel*, Kraus's attitude towards the courts was predominantly critical, and the "defectiveness" of the Habsburg legal system formed a prime target of his polemics, which bear the mark of Ihering's theory. In fact, the early programme of *Die Fackel* is explicitly defined in Ihering's terms: "Weil unser öffentlicher und mündlicher Strafprozeß die Popularklage nicht kennt, habe ich ja zum Zwecke der *öffentlichen, schriftlichen Popularklage* die "Fackel" gegründet" (F 46: 20). The concept of "Popularklage" derives from a passage in *Der Kampf ums Recht* where Ihering pays tribute to an institution, known in Roman Law as *actiones populares*, which entitled any public spirited citizen to appear in court and call offenders to account.[4] The principle which Ihering espoused in theory Kraus adopted in practice, speaking out fearlessly as a self-appointed public prosecutor against miscarriages of justice as well as other social abuses.

The mode of "popular accusation" structured much of Kraus's early writing. Reacting against the oppressiveness of Habsburg institutions, his satire before 1914 was primarily directed against the judiciary. In *Sittlichkeit und Kriminalität* (1908) he attacked the enforcement of morals by reactionary judges operating an anachronistic legal code. He recognized that the authoritarian legislation of the nineteenth century was losing its validity in a period of rapidly changing social and sexual moeurs. The failure to adapt legal precedents to new cultural norms was attributed not only to the hypocrisy of bourgeois society, but also to the constitutional chaos of the multinational empire. Disputes between national factions hindered the introduction of more enlightened legislation (as Kraus notes in May 1904). Consequently, court decisions which were technically "correct" ("richtig") became as objectionable as judgments which were manifestly "faulty" ("falsch," F 163: 9).

Kraus's essays were widely read, not least by aspiring lawyers. An article published in 1924 in the progressive law journal, *Das Tribunal*, recalled that in earlier days public prosecutors used surreptitiously to read *Die Fackel* in court, concealed behind their piles of legal briefs. Kraus came to be regarded as "judge of the judges" ("Richter über die Richter"), creating through *Die Fackel* a "revolutionary tribunal" ("Revolutions-tribunal" F 649-56: 112). Kraus's attitude to the law, however, was ideo-logically ambiguous. At times his attacks on judges may have appeared revolutionary. But his writings also betrayed a certain sympathy with the Josephinist tradition, which assigned the ultimate authority to an enlightened elite, rather than to the democratic consensus. Kraus, even in his most radical phase, had little sympathy with the Marxist view that the courts represent a repressive system of class justice. And he offended both socialists and democrats through the critique of the jury system which forms one of the leitmotifs of his writings.

Kraus's experience in the Bahr-Bukovics case of 1901 had taught him that Austrian juries could not be relied on to grasp questions of legal principle. During the first decade of *Die Fackel* the prejudices of jurors formed almost as significant a theme as the arrogance of judges. Kraus's critique culminated in July 1913 as he published one of his most cogent early contributions (F 378-80: 1-10). Aligning himself with the conservative jurist Heinrich Lammasch, Kraus incisively exposed the inadequacies of the jury system. Trial by jury presupposed an educated electorate and a consensus about moral norms. The system was unworkable in a state riven by faction, where the verdict could depend on whether a juror is "Jew or Christian, anti-Semite or freemason, Czech or German, Austro-German or Pan-German, landlord or janitor, coffee-house owner or customer, hammer or anvil" ("ob einer Jud oder Christ, Antisemit oder Freimaurer, Tscheche oder Deutscher, Deutsch-nationaler oder Alldeutscher, Hausherr oder Hausmeister, Cafetier oder Stammgast, Hammer oder Amboß ist" F 378-80: 8). A jury system that is dependent on property rights, not education, subordinates complex judicial and ethical questions to the verdict of butchers and grocers. Ignorance of the law, according to a celebrated axiom, may be no defence against punishment, but, as Kraus scathingly concludes: "Unkenntnis des Gesetzes schützt nicht vor Strafe, reicht aber nicht aus, das Urteil zu fällen" (F 378-80: 1-10).

Kraus's critique of the Habsburg legal system left him with an insoluble dilemma. His satire on the courts exposed what has aptly been described as a "Legitimationskrise."[5] But during his conservative phase around 1912 he found it difficult to conceive of a viable alternative. His radical commitment to the struggle for rights was at odds with his desire for what he termed, "eine Befestigung des konservativen Willens," (F 354-6: 70). In October 1915 he noted with satisfaction that not only parliamentary government but also trial by jury had been suspended for the duration (F 406-12: 104). This satisfaction was shortlived, however, for the crisis of World War I precipitated new forms of legal tyranny by military prosecutors who abused their emergency powers. In the threatened frontier areas of Austria-Hungary, martial law was enforced during the war years with a ruthless disregard for civil liberties, especially for the rights of dissenting minorities. Kraus soon realized that if military courts were permitted to operate without restraint, the rule of law itself was at risk.

Kraus's growing awareness of this danger was reinforced by the campaign in the *Arbeiter-Zeitung* against the iniquities of military justice. He himself vigorously supported such campaign, for which he gave Friedrich Austerlitz particular credit (F 501-7: 108). By the end of the war, when Kraus himself was under investigation by the military authorities, it had become clear to him that the courts and the constitution, whatever their deficiencies, were fundamental to the defence of freedom. Between 1915 and 1918 he completely revised his views about the virtues both of parliamentary government and of a democratic legal system. And he emerged from World War I as the committed advocate of legal reform.

II. The Rehabilitation of Justice

In 1919 the legislators of the new republic embarked on a dynamic programme of constitutional and judicial reform. Within a year the privileges of the old elite were swept away by new legislation which guaranteed the democratic rights of all citizens. The abolition of the death penalty in 1919 was a significant milestone. It marked a decisive break with the punitive principles of the past and a shift towards remedial conceptions of justice, as advocated by the liberal jurist Hans Kelsen. Court procedures were made more democratic by extending the system of trial by jury so that all citizens had the right to act as jurors. And a new Constitutional Court was established to strengthen civil rights against arbitrary political action.

An effective legal system presupposes a consensus about basic values. It was the conflict of ideologies during the late Habsburg Empire which undermined the authority of the courts. In the years 1918-1920, however, a new consensus emerged which expressed itself through the enlightened legislation of the coalition government. The redrawing of political frontiers eliminated the clash between nationalities which had frustrated earlier attempts at reform. Under the pressures of political emergency,

Social Democratic leaders like Karl Renner, Otto Bauer and Robert Danneberg joined hands with prominent Catholics like Ignaz Seipel and Jodok Fink to lay the foundations for a democratic republic. The constitution they created and the laws they passed had an enduring value, for they satisfied a need for social reconstruction which was recognized by politicians in both camps.

These reforms created the basis for a new democratic order with which Kraus was able to identify. He continued to campaign against anachronistic laws and pedantic judges, arguing that the Social Democrats should have introduced even more radical reforms in order to remove some of the "fossils" ("Fossilien") from the Austrian judiciary (F 640-8: 38). But in important respects the satirist could now feel that he had the courts on his side. He particularly welcomed the Press Law of 1922, which was piloted through Parliament by Friedrich Austerlitz. By making it mandatory to distinguish paid advertisements from editorial comment and objective reportage. This law fulfilled one of Kraus's lifelong aims. It also enshrined in Paragraph 23 (the *Berichtigungsparagraph*) the citizen's right to oblige editors to print formal corrections of misleading news items, a paragraph which Kraus was to invoke on many occasions.

During the debate about the new Press legislation Kraus explicitly aligned himself with the public prosecutor, insisting on "obedience to the law" ("Befolgung des Gesetzes" F 601-7: 65). In *Die Fackel* of June 1923, Kraus welcomed the successful implementation of these reforms as a "rehabilitation of justice" (F 622-31: 13-20). During the 1920s the satirist's attitude towards the courts thus underwent a radical transformation. We now repeatedly find the scourge of judicial malpractice siding with the courts, rather than pitting his wits against them. Time and again he endorsed the administration of justice, so often ridiculed during the late Habsburg era, as the one institution capable of setting the situation to rights, when all other forces in the state have failed: "ich gebe mich der Zuversicht hin, daß die Justiz über allen versagenden Mächten dieses Gemeinwesens ihrer eigentlichen Bestimmung, zum Rechten zu sehen, gerecht werden wird" (F 717-23: 130-1).

This change of attitude is evident in Kraus's growing fondness for litigation. The court actions which he instigated during the first twenty years of *Die Fackel* were relatively infrequent and never central to his strategy. His humiliating defeat in the 1901 libel suit initiated by Hermann Bahr and Emmerich Bukovics undermined his confidence in the ability of the courts to support his satirical crusade. In this case the jury had found against him and the judge had imposed a fine (F 69: 1-22). During the following dozen years Kraus had shown no great desire for litigation. Kraus conducted his two most protracted pre-war polemics against Maximilian Harden and Alfred Kerr exclusively in print, not through the courts. Even when he did legal action, the outcome (as in the case against Fritz Wittels) might pass unrecorded in *Die Fackel*.

After 1918 Kraus transformed his strategy. By conducting his campaign of "popular accusation" not only in writing, but actually in the courts he became the living embodiment of Ihering's theory: the citizen committed to the struggle for justice. The number of legal suits Kraus initiated between 1919 and 1936 runs well into three figures. Time and again he reprints in *Die Fackel* the transcripts of court actions, often at great length, presenting the legal verdicts of the courts are seen as validating the ethical judgments of his polemics. In January 1920 he devoted almost forty pages of small print to two cases arising from his critique of patriotic propaganda (F 521-30: 9-47). The favorable outcome of these actions strengthened Kraus's conviction that in the democratic climate of the 1920s the satirist could become the ally of the public prosecutor.

This strategy acquired further momentum when Oskar Samek, a specialist in Press Law, became Kraus's lawyer. At that time, Samek who was in his early thirties, had just started his career. He quickly gained Kraus's confidence and was subsequently to become one of his most loyal friends and effective allies. Samek's exceptional dedication sustained the satirist through countless court actions during the following fifteen years. Some, like the campaign against Bekessy, were to be triumphantly successful. Others, like Kraus's second crusade against Alfred Kerr, proved inconclusive. The attempt to establish that Kerr, a professed pacifist, was in fact the author of a sequence of xenophobic poems, resulted in a protracted series of court actions. The patience of Kraus's most loyal readers must have been exhausted when they found themselves confronted in September 1928 with a mammoth number of *Die Fackel* devoted exclusively to his litigious polemics with Kerr (F 787-94: 1-208).

Kraus's reliance on the courts struck contemporary observers as excessively legalistic. Franz Werfel was one of several opponents who accused the satirist of vindictiveness. Not only Werfel's poems, but also his play *Paulus unter den Juden* (1926) allude to his polemics against Kraus. His dramatic legend, set in Jerusalem shortly after the death of Christ, ascribes the cult of law to a sterile Judaic tradition, destined to be superseded by the Christian ethos of love. Although contemporary reviewers (including D. J. Bach in the *Arbeiter-Zeitung*) praised Werfel's play, both Kraus and Freud vehemently objected to it. Freud denounced Werfel's self-indulgent religiosity in an exchange of letters which reduced the playwright to a stammering apology.[6] Kraus, by contrast, seized on Werfel's repudiation of the primacy of law. Werfel's play sets the figure of Rabbi Beschwörer, a fanatical adherent of Judaic Law, against St. Paul, the inspired apostle of Christ. Werfel ridiculed the Rabbi in terms which Kraus construed as a coded attack on his own position. Rejecting Bach's positive review as having missed the main point of Werfel's argument, Kraus quotes key scenes from the play, in order to expose the tendentiousness of the author's attitude towards Judaism and the Law.[7]

Werfel's portrayal of Rabbi Beschwörer prompted Kraus to write a striking passage which clarifies his attitude towards the law. Yet far from repudiating the implied identification, Kraus's text actually affirms his own role as law-giver among the Jews:

> Ich weiß, die Juden haben es schwer mit mir, und es grenzt wirklich schon an Fanatismus, daß ich nicht davor zurückscheue, nebst den Sprachgesetzen auch noch die Strafgesetze befolgt zu wünschen, ja den letzten armseligen Rest einer ramponierten Autorität gegen eine korrupte Freiheit mobil zu machen. Es ist die alte Beschwerde, daß ich innerhalb der Literatur, die so gern leben und leben lassen möchte, den starren Rechtsbegriff verkörpere.... Im allgemeinen komme ich ja mit Polemik und Satire in meinem Beruf aus, aber für gewisse Sonderfälle des freiheitlichen Lebens behalte ich mir eben die Maßnahmen jenes dürftigen kriminalistischen Schutzes vor, den die fragwürdigste Staatsgewalt dem Steuerzahler gewährt (F 759-65: 108).[8]

Kraus here acknowledges that the law has a double value for the Jews, both timely and archetypal. It is an element in their cultural heritage which in his view has lost none of its relevance; indeed, it has gained a new significance in the contemporary political situation. Traditionally the calling of the prophet or rabbi was to "give the Jews a hard time," that is: to set for them higher ethical standards than for their non-Jewish contemporaries. This is one aspect of Kraus's self-appointed role. But he also shows great political insight in linking Jewish attitudes towards the law with the crisis of liberal society. In a situation where freedom is being corrupted and authority undermined, there are compelling political reasons for upholding the "rigid rule of law." To understand Kraus's position, we must take into account the special significance of the law for German-speaking Jews, above all the laws governing their rights as citizens in the post-World War I period.

III. Citizens and Migrants

During the First Republic, Austrian citizenship was a problematic concept. The collapse of Austria-Hungary in November 1918 deprived millions of Habsburg subjects of their status under international law: the *allgemeines österreichisches Staatsbürgerrecht* guaranteed by the Austrian *Staatsgrundgesetze* of 1867.[9] For formerly subject peoples, Czechs and Slovaks, Poles and Slovenes, the acquisition of a new nationality may have been a matter for rejoicing. But the proclamation of the successor states plunged the widely scattered German-speaking communities of the Habsburg crown into confusion. Were inhabitants of Lemberg or Czernowitz, who had traditionally owed allegiance to Vienna, now to be defined as Poles or Romanians? Or could they reassert their identity as German-Austrians? A mass migration to the territories of the new republic was out of the question. The resources of Vienna, already overstrained by refugees could not cope with a further influx. The food situation was desperate, and the indigenous population were themselves threatened with starvation.

Faced with this emergency, the National Assembly rushed through a new law on 5 December 1918 regulating citizenship (*Staatsbürger-rechtsgesetz*). Citizenship was to be restricted to those currently living within the territories of German-Austria. But they were entitled to citizenship only if their legal place of domicile (*Heimatrecht* or *Zuständigkeit*) was in one of the territories previously governed from Vienna. This excluded those whose domicile had been in the Hungarian half of the Monarchy, because Hungarian and Austrian citizenship had been quite distinct under the constitution of the Dual Monarchy. Hence Hungarians resident in Vienna had been classified as foreign citizens.[10] The law of December 1918 also specifically denied citizenship to people from the so-called "refugee areas" (*Flüchtlingsländer*), Galicia, Dalmatia, and Istria.[11] This provision had special bearing on the situation of the Eastern Jews, especially those seventy thousand refugees from Galicia who had migrated to Vienna during the war. The demand that these Jewish refugees should be compulsorily repatriated was one of the dominant themes of Austrian politics in the years 1919-22. It featured prominently in the anti-Semitic press, and even the Social Democrats felt obliged to make concessions to the popular agitation.

The policy of repatriation proved hard to implement. In Hungary, Romania, Poland and the Ukraine there was fierce fighting for control of border territories, accompanied by violent pogroms. In November 1918, for example, there were anti-Semitic outrages in Lemberg (now Lvov) which were prominently reported in Vienna. Attempts were nevertheless made in the autumn of 1919 to return the refugees to their place of origin. Under pressure from anti-Semitic agitation, the Social Democratic Governor of Vienna and Lower Austria, Albert Sever, announced that train-loads of Galician refugees would be repatriated during September 1919. This move proved a fiasco, for an acute coal shortage paralyzed the transport system for several weeks and prevented any trains from leaving

Vienna.[12] It was only under the supervision of the League of Nations that a resettlement programme was finally carried out.

The Treaty of Saint-Germain, signed on 9 September 1919, contained a series of clauses designed to clarify the question of citizenship and protect the rights of minorities. According to Article 4 of the Treaty, all those with *Heimatrecht* within the frontiers of the new Republic were to be Austrian citizens. Those whose *Heimatrecht* was in an area which was formerly part of Austria-Hungary (but not in the territory of the new Republic) were excluded from Austrian citizenship and became citizens of the state in which their place of domicile now lies. However, there was a significant exception to this rule, Article 80, one of the most controversial in the whole Treaty. For this article made it possible for members of German-speaking minorities living in remote areas of the former Habsburg Empire to obtain Austrian citizenship by "option." The crucial criterion was that they should "speak the same language and belong to the same race" as the majority of the population.[13] This wording seems to have been designed to prevent a mass migration of Eastern Jews. But the criterion of "race" was never clearly defined.

Initially, Article 80 of the Treaty of Saint-Germain was interpreted rather liberally. A brochure by Dr. Lukas Langhoff, published in 1920 under the title *Staatsbürgerschaft und Heimatrecht in Österreich*, exemplifies this liberal interpretation. To establish that one "belonged to the Austrian people" ("Zugehörigkeit zum österreichischen Volke"), Langhoff argued, it would probably suffice to show that one had "completely adapted to Austrian conditions in one's family and civic life" ("sich mit Familien- und staatsbürgerlichem Leben ganz an Österreichs Verhältnisse angepaßt hat").[14] It was thus possible for assimilated German-speaking Jews from the eastern provinces, such as the novelist Joseph Roth, to opt for Austrian citizenship. Had it not been for Article 80 of the Treaty of Saint Germain, that most Austrian of authors would have been Polish. For the registration document which granted Roth Austrian citizenship in June 1921 records that he was "domiciled" ("zuständig") in Brody, his birthplace in Galicia.[15]

Towards the end of 1921, however, this liberal application of the "option" clause was blocked. Interior Minister Leopold Waber, backed by other members of the coalition government, who perceived themselves as *Großdeutsche*, put through a measure that made it impossible for any further Jewish migrants to opt for Austrian citizenship (the "Wabersche Optionspraxis").[16] This decision was based on a judgment of 9 June 1921 by the Austrian Administrative Court which interpreted the phrase about "race and language" in terms that excluded German-speaking Jews.[17]

The official Austrian census form of 1923 included a question about *Rassenzugehörigkeit*, thus taking a further step in the direction of making citizenship dependent on race. This marked a radical departure from the practice of the late Habsburg Empire, where nationality had been defined in terms of language, not of race. Admittedly, the concept of *Volkszugehörigkeit* had already been used in the Habsburg period by constitutional reformers to resolve conflicting national interests.[18] But in the political atmosphere of the early 1920s, the word *Rassenzugehörigkeit* acquired far more sinister implications. Kraus was not alone in registering his skepticism about this racial classification (F 622-31: 49). The issue, however, was regulated by another provision in the Treaty of Saint-Germain, (Article 3) under which the Austrian government guaranteed "complete protection of life and liberty to all inhabitants of Austria without distinction of birth, nationality, race, or religion." Article 3 represents an attempt by international law to set limits to discrimination against ethnic minorities.

There was, however, a further loophole in the otherwise well designed laws regulating citizenship. The possession of *Heimatrecht* in a community within the borders of the new republic provided the most secure basis of citizenship. Those who obtained citizenship by "option" had a more questionable legal status, for citizens without *Heimatrecht* were liable, if convicted of an offence, to be deported to their original place of abode, which might now be located in Poland or Romania. Such a device, popularly known as "der Schub," was one of the hazards of life for a significant minority of the population, not least for Jewish migrants.[19]

The picture is further complicated by the position of citizens born outside the Austrian Republic's territories who had acquired *Heimatrecht* before 1918. Kraus himself was born in Bohemia. His title to Austrian citizenship was based on *Heimatrecht*, acquired after his family settled in Vienna in the late 1870s. On paper his position appeared secure, but during the 1920s, a period when Jews without *Heimatrecht* were being deported from Vienna and resettled in Eastern Europe, he too must have been affected by the climate of insecurity. It was certainly no laughing matter for Kraus to find the right-wing *Wiener Stimmen* suggesting in the spring of 1921 that he too should board one of the trains to the East (F 568-71: 56). The anti-Semitic gibe had elements of polemical hyperbole. But with hindsight, we can see that those trainloads of Jewish migrants deported to the East during the early 1920s set a precedent. Kraus intuitively grasped that once the rights of citizenship are denied, there are no limits to tyranny. His involvements with the courts were often fiendishly complex and at times seem to assign a disproportionate importance to trivia. When we analyze his commitment to the rule of law, however, we finally reach the crude threat (dimly apprehended in May 1921) of the *Ostjudentransport* (F 568-71: 64).

Austrian Jews had reason to feel that their citizenship rights were less secure than those of their Christian compatriots. Indeed, the emphasis in Article 80 on being of "the same race and language" as the majority of the population was particularly unfortunate. It played into the hands of right-wing agitators who argued that there should be two categories of citizenship: full citizenship should be restricted to the dominant "Aryan" race, while members of ethnic minorities should be treated as second-class citizens and denied full civil rights. They also insisted that all recent Jewish migrants should be deported. "Hinaus mit den Ostjuden!" was the theme of a speech by Walter Riehl, the Austrian Nazi leader, in September 1920. Riehl, who was himself a lawyer, declared that if they could not solve the refugee problem by legal means, they would use brute force.[20] Other agitators exploited the refugee problem in order to call for the expulsion of *all* Jews from Austria: "Hinaus mit den Juden aus Wien und Österreich!"[21] The right wing particularly resented the acquisition of Austrian citizenship by "option." One of the first acts of the Nazi administration after the *Anschluß* was to declare that citizenship obtained under Article 80 of the Treaty of Saint-Germain was invalid. Thus in 1939 hundreds of Austrian Jews were deprived of their citizenship and declared stateless persons, no longer entitled to protection under the constitution.[22]

For right-wing extremists in the Nazi Party and for newspapers like *Der Volkssturm*, the newly founded Austrian state was itself a "Judenrepublik." They attacked both the constitution and the reformed legal code on the grounds that these were "Jewish" creations. The idea that civil law is a specifically Jewish invention may appear absurd. Yet the constitutional reforms which redefined Austria-Hungary as a secular state during the late nineteenth century were principally the work of jurists of Jewish origin, most notably Julius Glaser and Joseph Unger. Jews made an exceptional contribution to Austrian jurisprudence in the late Habsburg Empire.[23] During the First Republic they dominated the legal profession to an extraordinary degree. Statistical tables published in Vienna during the mid-1930s suggested that 85% of the city's lawyers were of Jewish origin.[24] These figures were exaggerated, but estimates by modern scholars still put the figure at over 60%.[25] For anti-Semites, the legal system itself appeared to be part of that "Jewish conspiracy" which had supposedly led to the defeat and humiliation of the German race.

One of the slogans of the Austrian National Socialists, prominently displayed at the University of Vienna in the 1920s, was *Volksrecht geht vor Staatsrecht*.[26] The concept of *Volksrecht* had been originally formulated to define those localized judicial systems within the Roman Empire that resisted the universalizing principles of Roman Law.[27] Austrian and German nationalists exploited this concept to support their claim that the rights enjoyed by the Aryan *Volk* should not be extended to inferior races.[28] The study of law at universities became polarized between nationalists and liberals. Hans Kelsen and his fellow progressive lawyers,

many of them Jews, argued that the principles of law should be
universal. But Nazi lawyers like Walter Riehl insisted that Jews should
be treated as aliens and subjected to discriminatory forms of
Fremdengesetzgebung. This distinction between *Fremdenrecht* and *völkisches
Recht* provided an allegedly legal basis for Nazi laws that discriminated
against the Jews from 1933 onwards.[29]

The enemies of democracy, in Austria as in Weimar Germany, also
denounced the republican constitution as a "Jewish" invention. This too
was not entirely a figment of the imagination. The constitution of the
Weimar Republic was the work of a Jewish lawyer, Hugo Preuss.
Although Catholics and Pan-Germans were well represented on the
committee that drafted the new Austrian constitution, Jewish members
were even more prominent. Otto Bauer was chairman of the committee
for constitutional reform, while Robert Danneberg played a decisive role
in establishing Vienna as a self-governing province. Hans Kelsen not only
advised the committee on the legal technicalities, but also later played a
preeminent role as President of the Constitutional Court. Kelsen's
adjudications, particularly on the question of the validity of divorce,
exposed him to virulent attack from both Catholic and anti-Semitic
factions. Moreover, it was not only the fanatics of the *Volkssturm* who
were dreaming of sweeping away the institutions of the "Jew Republic."
Leading figures at Vienna University, notably Othmar Spann, were
actively devising schemes for the suspension of individual liberties and
the establishment of a corporate state.[30] By 1930 Seipel himself was
campaigning against the constitutional principles which he had helped
to establish ten years earlier.[31]

Against this background, Kraus's preoccupation with the sphere of law
can be seen not as an obsession with an abstract ideal, but as a pragmatic
commitment to democracy. Less explicitly, it is a defence of Jewish
citizens against a double threat. The obvious danger emanates from anti-
Semitic thugs, like those who attacked Maximilian Harden and murdered
Walther Rathenau and Hugo Bettauer. Faced with a similar threat, Kraus
had no hesitation in asking for police protection. Moreover, he took Nazi
newspapers like Hitler's *Völkischer Beobachter* to court, when he found
himself threatened or defamed (F 800-5: 50). Kraus also exposed the more
oblique danger emanating from lawless Jews like Imre Bekessy, whose
criminal conduct compromised the position of their law-abiding fellow
citizens. Summing up his campaign against Bekessy in July 1926, Kraus
insisted that during a period of political upheaval ("Umsturz") it was
essential to uphold "basic laws of morality" ("moralische Grundgesetze,"
F 730-1: 4-5). The phrase conflated Kraus's moral crusade with an allusion
to the Basic Law of 1867, the *Staatsgrundgesetz über die allgemeinen Rechte
der Staatsbürger* which had abolished discrimination against the Jews and
established equal rights for all citizens.

In sum, Kraus's attitude towards the law underwent a fundamental transformation during the years separating the decline of the Habsburg Empire from the rise of National Socialism. In the Habsburg era, when legal institutions appeared to be virtually moribund, the thrust of his satire was directed against the oppressiveness of the law, above all against the enforcement of morals through the courts. He tended to take for granted the constitutional rights achieved during the late nineteenth-century liberal era, including the equality before the law attained by citizens of Jewish origin. Hence in this period, we characteristically find him attacking the legal system, ridiculing anachronistic verdicts, and condemning the prejudices of judges and juries. The more precarious situation after 1919 led to a change of direction. During the 1920s, we find him devoting his best energies to defending the law, above all the rights of citizenship. In some cases the satirist actually became the ally of the public prosecutor, insisting that the law should be enforced against those who threatened the stability of the Republic. The rule of law was emphatically endorsed as a protection for all citizens against anti-social forces which threatened their existence, above all for the German-speaking Jews. Thus Kraus can be seen as the most eloquent advocate of that "struggle for rights" propounded by Rudolf von Ihering, the great nineteenth-century jurist.

Notes

[1] Jonathan Swift: *The Examiner and Other Pieces*, ed. by Herbert Davis. Oxford 1957, Number 38 (26 April 1711), p. 141.

[2] Walter Benjamin: *Gesammelte Schriften*, ed. by Rolf Tiedemann and Hermann Schweppenhauser. Frankfurt/Main 1977, Vol. II. 1, p. 349.

[3] Rudolf von Ihering: *Der Kampf ums Recht*, 10th ed. Vienna 1891, pp. 45-49.

[4] Ibid., pp. 54-55.

[5] Reinhard Merkel: "Zum Verhältnis zwischen Strafrecht und Satire im Werk von Karl Kraus." In: *Literatur und Kritik*, Number 219-20 (November/December 1987), pp. 444-59, especially p. 446.

[6] See Paul Stefan Jungk: *Franz Werfel. Eine Lebensgeschichte*. Frankfurt/Main 1987, pp. 167-69.

[7] For the context of the passages quoted by Kraus (F 759-65: 106-7), see Franz Werfel: *Paulus unter den Juden*. Berlin, Vienna, Leipzig 1926, pp. 119-20, 155, 180.

[8] "I admit that I give the Jews a hard time, making no secret of my wish, which borders on fanaticism, that not only the laws of language but also the laws of the criminal code should be obeyed. Indeed, I wish to mobilize the final pathetic remnants of ruined authority against corrupted freedom. It is the old complaint

that in a literature which thrives on give and take I represent the rigid rule of law.... In general, polemic and satire suffice for my professional needs, but in certain cases of exceptional licentiousness I reserve the right to invoke the protection of the criminal law, however inadequate that protection may be and however problematic the political authority which grants it to the taxpayer."

[9] Edmund Bernatzik, ed., *Die österreichischen Verfassungsgesetze*. Leipzig 1906, p. 367.

[10] Gerald Stourzh: "The Multinational Empire Revisited: Reflections on Late Imperial Austria." In: *Austrian History Yearbook* 23, 1992, p. 12.

[11] "Wie wird man Staatsbürger?" In: *Arbeiter-Zeitung*, 9 December 1918, p. 1.

[12] See reports in the Viennese press in Autumn 1919, especially *Der Abend*, 6 October 1919, p. 2.

[13] *The Treaty of Peace between the Allied and Associated Powers and Austria, together with Other Treaties, Agreements, etc.* London 1921, p. 36-37.

[14] Lukas Langhoff: *Staatsbürgerrecht und Heimatrecht in Österreich*. Vienna 1920, p. 22.

[15] See the document dated 8 June 1921 conferring Austrian citizenship on "Herrn Josef Roth ... nach Artikel 80 des Staatsvertrages von St. Germain." Leo Baeck Institute, New York.

[16] Heinrich Benedikt: *Geschichte der Republik Österreich*. Vienna 1954, p. 386.

[17] Jonny Moser: "Die Katastrophe der Juden in Österreich". In: *Studia Judaica Austriaca* 5, 1977,p p. 67-134, especially p. 91-2.

[18] Stourzh (Note 10), p. 19.

[19] See Franz Kobler: *Recht und Unrecht der Ausweisung dargestellt auf Grund der österreichischen Gesetzgebung und Praxis*. Vienna 1931, especially. pp. 31-35.

[20] Police Report of 1 Sept 1920, cited in F. L. Carsten: *Faschismus in Österreich*. Munich 1978, p. 68.

[21] *Der Volkssturm*, 13 June 1920, p. 95.

[22] Hans-Joachim Seeler: *Das Staatsangehörigkeitsrecht Österreichs*. Frankfurt/Main 1957, p. 48, p. 159.

[23] Franz Kobler: "The Contribution of Austrian Jews to Jurisprudence." In: *The Jews of Austria*, ed. by Josef Fraenkel. London 1967, p. 25-40.

[24] Georg Glockemeier: *Zur Wiener Judenfrage*. Leipzig and Vienna 1936, p. 77.

[25] Steven Beller: *Vienna and the Jews 1867-1838: A Cultural History*. Cambridge 1989, p. 20.

[26] *Die Stunde*, 1 Feb 1925, p. 6.

[27] Ludwig Mitteis: *Reichsrecht und Volksrecht in den östlichen Provinzen des Römischen Kaiserreichs*. Leipzig 1891.

[28] Helmut Nicholai: *Grundlagen der kommenden Verfassung: Über den staatsrechtlichen Aufbau des Dritten Reiches*. Berlin 1933.

[29] Helmut Nicholai: *Die rassengesetzliche Rechtslehre: Grundzüge einer national-sozialistischen Rechtsphilosophie*. Munich 1933.

[30] Othmar Spann: *Der wahre Staat*. Leipzig 1921.

[31] Ignaz Seipel: *Der Kampf um die österreichische Verfassung*. Wien 1930.

Amy Colin

Macht, Opfer, Selbstzerstörung: Jüdisches Frauenschicksal in Gertrud Kolmars *Nacht*

> Marinus: ... Warum tut Nero das?
> Nerva: Weil er w i s s e n will. Das
> Geheimnis ist eine Frau; ihre Mitte bleibt
> tagverborgen. (Gertrud Kolmar, *Nacht*)[1]

I.

Wenn die Geschichte Menschen überrollt, scheinbar geordnetes Dasein ins Chaos stürzt und den Sinn des Geschehenen jeglichem rationellen Verständnis verschließt, dann ist man geneigt, Parallelen zu vergangenen, von Kriegen und Umwälzungen markierten Epochen zu ziehen, um Licht ins Dunkel der Gegenwart zu bringen. Aber Vergleiche politischer Ereignisse aus unterschiedlichen Zeiten können trügerisch sein, denn sie verstellen den Blick für die Eigentümlichkeiten der neuen Situation, da sie Hier und Jetzt stets aus der Sicht der Vergangenheit darstellen. Manchmal sind sie verzweifelte Versuche, eine Richtung in dem von Gewalt und Haß überschatteten Leben zu finden und sagen dann mehr über den Schreibenden selbst als über dessen Zeit aus.

Auf der Suche nach einem Schlüssel zum Verständnis der ursächlichen Zusammenhänge zwischen Machtstreben, Aufopferung und Selbstzerstörung wandte sich die deutsch-jüdische Autorin Gertrud Kolmar im Jahre 1938, als das Schicksal der deutschen Juden bereits besiegelt war, der legendenumsponnenen Gestalt des römischen Kaisers Tiberius zu. In seiner Schreckensherrschaft sah sie wohl eine Vorwegnahme der Katastrophen, in die Europa, vor allem Deutschland später geraten sollte. Die fiktive Begegnung zwischen dem machtbesessenen Tiberius und einer jüdischen Waise namens Ischta, die er kaltblütig ermordet, um sie einer Gottheit zu opfern, steht im Mittelpunkt des faszinierenden, doch unveröffentlicht gebliebenen Theaterstückes *Nacht. Dramatische Legende in vier Aufzügen*.[2] Gertrud Kolmar hatte dieses Werk wenige Monate vor der

Kristallnacht, im Zeitraum zwischen dem 17. März und dem 15. Juni 1938 verfaßt.

Durch Zufall war ich auf dieses Drama gestoßen, als ich im Sommer 1991 im New Yorker Archiv des Leo Baeck Institutes dank dessen großzügiger Unterstützung meine Forschungen zu einem Buchprojekt über deutsch-jüdische Autorinnen fortsetzte. Da fand ich unter den Dokumenten und Briefen eines anderen Autors diesen Text, dessen Titel weder im Katalog noch im Computer angeführt war. Gertrud Kolmars Theaterstück, das Peter Wenzel aufbewahrt und nach dem Krieg Max Picard nach New York eingesandt hatte, ist in den USA bislang unentdeckt geblieben. In Deutschland machte erst die 1993 in Marbach organisierte Ausstellung zum Leben und Schaffen Gertrud Kolmars auf dieses Werk aufmerksam. Es gehört zu den zahlreichen Ungerechtigkeiten des literarischen Betriebes, daß Gertrud Kolmars *Nacht* Lesern nicht zugänglich ist.

Gertrud Kolmars Tiberius-Drama entwickelt ein Thema weiter, das die Lyrikerin bereits in zwei ihrer früheren Dichtungen angeschnitten hatte. Ihr ebenfalls unveröffentlicht gebliebenes Theaterstück *Cécile Renault* (1934-35)[3] und ihr Gedichtzyklus *Robespierre* (1934)[4] decken die psychischen Mechanismen auf, die Machthaber zur Gewalt, zum Mord treiben. Ähnlich wie Robespierre bot auch Tiberius ein eindrucksvolles Beispiel für dieses Phänomen. Von der Antike bis zur Gegenwart hat die komplizierte Persönlichkeit des römischen Kaisers zahlreiche Geschichtsschreiber und Schriftsteller beschäftigt. Für die römischen Apologeten war er ein Mensch von "engelhaftem Charakter"; für Tacitus hingegen ein machtbesessener Imperator; auch in späteren Jahrhunderten blieb Tiberius stets eine umstrittene Gestalt; so beschrieb ihn Theodor Mommsen als einen klugen Staatsmann, der an der Grausamkeit der Welt gescheitert war und deshalb selbst grausam wurde. Im Drama *Der Tod des Tiberius* (1851) hatte Ferdinand Adolf Gregorovius den cäsarischer Charakter von Tiberius evoziert; Egmont Colerus' Prosawerk *Die Nacht des Tiberius* (1920) schildert die Misanthropie des römischen Kaisers; die Erzählung *Wenn Götter lieben* (1907) von Richard Voss und der Roman *Christus und Tiberius* (1938) von Annie Neumann-Hofer stellen ihn als einen Antichristen dar.

In den dreißiger Jahren enstanden nicht nur Annie Neumann-Hofers und Gertrud Kolmars Werke, sondern auch Ernst Kornemanns umfassende Studie *Tiberius*[5], die allerdings erst 1960, posthum veröffentlicht wurde. Der deutsche Historiker hatte sich zum Ziel gesetzt, die "oft falsch oder unzureichend vollzogene Rettung" des römischen Reichsfeldherrn "zu besorgen", da er Tiberius nicht für "geisteskrank, sondern ... nur für einen innerlich schwer belasteten und gehemmten Menschen" hielt, "dessen Jugendleben der wärmenden Sonne entbehren mußte".[6] Tiberius sei ein Opfer seiner Mutter Livia und seines Beraters Sejan gewesen, die ihn beide als Instrument ihrer Machtgier mißbraucht hätten. Im Gegensatz zu Kornemann hielt der angesehene Nervenarzt Gregorio Marañón, dessen Buch *Tiberio. Historia de un resentimiento* (1939)[7] zu den weitverbreitetsten Werken über den römischen Kaiser zählt, den römischen Staatsmann für einen Psychopathen, der zum Mörder wurde. Durch diese Deutung des von Ressentiments gezeichneten Tiberius hoffte Marañón einen Einblick in die Psychosen moderner Machthaber wie Hitler, Mussulini und Franko zu vermitteln.

Niemand fand treffendere Worte, um dieses, in den dreißiger Jahren neu erwachte Interesse für Tiberius zu erklären, als Marañón selbst. "Ist nicht die Tatsache einer Betrachtung wert, daß eine neue Geschichte des Tiberius just in dem Jahr erscheinen mußte, da jene große Umwälzung einsetzte, die der Welt unter dem Vorwand des Krieges ein neues Gesicht geben wird?"[8], schrieb Marañón 1941 im Vorwort zur zweiten Auflage seines Buches und fügte hinzu: "Immer wenn uns Späteren der Boden schwindet, wenn wir nicht wissen, wo unser Fuß beim nächsten Schritt Halt finden soll, blicken wir zurück in die Geschichte, und die beispielhafte Gestalt des von Ressentiments geängsteten Kaisers lebt wieder auf."[9] Nach Ansicht von Marañón gab es noch einen weiteren Grund, weshalb die Tiberius-Epoche für das Verständnis der im Zeichen der braunen Barbarei stehenden Zeit so relevant erschien:

> Tiberius und seine Epoche verkörpern die Weltstunde, in der die heidnische Welt untersank und die christliche Welt heraufkam. Ehe nach dem Sturz der Götter Gott ins allgemeine Bewußtsein trat, vergingen viele Jahre, die schlimmere Verwüstungen anrichteten als Kriege und Katastrophen: Verwüstungen in den Seelen. Die Menschen wußten, daß die Götzenbilder, an die sie sich in Stunden der Angst geklammert hatten, gestorben waren; aber noch wußten sie nicht, an welche neuen überpersönlichen Mächte sie sich halten sollten. Daher die düstere Trostlosigkeit einer Menschheit, deren Repräsentant Tiberius war.[10]

Gerade dieser krasse Widerspruch zwischen der untergehenden römischen Welt verrohter Sitten wie fehlender Ideale und der neu aufkommenden christlichen Denkweise, in deren Mittelpunkt der unbedingte Glaube an Gott stand, mußte Gertrud Kolmar wie auch allen anderen Schriftstellern und Historikern der dreißiger Jahre besonders zeitnah erscheinen. Auf die Bühne der Geschichte waren zwar neue Akteure getreten; die Gewänder, die sie trugen, waren modern; auch das Szenenbild hatte sich völlig verändert. Aber die Orientierungslosigkeit, die Angst und Aggression der Menschen angesichts des drohenden Unterganges waren die gleichen geblieben. Das politische Ziel, die Demokratie in Deutschland sowie in einigen anderen europäischen Ländern zu konsolidieren, war in die fernste Ferne gerückt.

Die düstere Trostlosigkeit einer Menschheit, die Hitlers Auftieg ermöglicht hatte, hält Gertrud Kolmars Theaterstück fest. Als Allegorie ihres eigenen Schicksals nimmt ihr Drama das tragische Ende jener gläubigen europäischen, vor allem deutschsprachigen Juden vorweg, die vor Hitlers Schergen nicht geflüchtet sind, weil sie die Shoah als Jahwes Strafe verstanden, ihr Schicksal göttlicher Fügung überließen oder anderen Menschen in Not helfen wollten. *Nacht* verknüpft diese jüdische Thematik mit dem Gedanken an die Möglichkeiten und Grenzen der Vermittlung zwischen heterogenen Kulturen. Es stellt die Auswirkungen der *Gender*[11] Unterschiede auf die von Mißverständnissen geprägten Deutungsversuche der Handlung dar, die einzelne Gestalten im Stück unternehmen. Diese Ideen- und Motivkonfigurationen konstituieren sich in einem Spannungsfeld, dessen Pole Fiktionalität und Geschichte sind. Denn Gertrud Kolmars barockartig wirkendes Drama verwebt Legenden mit geschichtlich überprüfbaren Informationen, neue, von der Lyrikerin erfundene Episoden mit biographischen Daten. Wie das Motto ihres Stückes, ein Zitat aus den *Annalen* von Tacitus[12], zeigt, hatte die Lyrikerin wichtige Quellen über Tiberius' Leben gekannt. Der historische Kontext, in den Gertrud Kolmar ihr Stück einbettet, eröffnet einen Weg zum Verständnis ihrer Gedankenwelt und bildet den Übergang zu meinen sich anschließenden interpretatorischen Ausführungen, deren Kristallisationspunkt die Manifestationsformen der kulturell und *Gender* bedingten Differenzen in der Deutung der Opfer- und Selbstaufopferungsthematik sind.

II.

Der römische Feldherr Tiberius (42 v. u. Z. bis 37 n. u. Z.)[13] war ein Sohn der Livia Drusilla und des Flottengenerals Tiberius Claudius Nero, der Julius Cäsar zunächst gedient und viele Auszeichnungen von ihm empfan-gen hatte, dann aber zur Partei seiner Mörder übergetreten war. Nach dem Tod des Diktators — während der kriegerischen Auseinandersetzungen der rivalisierenden Parteien — mußte Tiberius, von Octavian, dem späteren Kaiser Augustus, verfolgt, nach Neapel fliehen, konnte jedoch später nach Rom zurückkehren.[14] Als Kind erlebte Tiberius, der auch wie sein Vater Nero hieß, zunächst die Verbannung der Eltern und dann ihre Scheidung. Augustus hatte nämlich Tiberius' Vater Nero gezwungen, ihm Livia trotz ihrer erneuten Schwangerschaft "abzutreten"[15]. Unter dem Einfluß von Livia, die man als Inbegriff der Tugend und Schönheit betrachtete[16], sorgte Augustus für Tiberius' Erziehung, vertraute ihm wichtige Ämter an, schickte ihn als Quästor nach Rhodos, nahm ihn später nach Spanien mit und ernannte ihn zum Reichsfeldherrn. Er machte Tiberius zum zweit mächtigsten Mann im

Römischen Imperium. Zu jener Zeit war Tiberius mit Vispania glücklich verheiratet, die seinen Sohn Drusus II. zur Welt brachte. Aber Tiberius mußte sein Glück und seine Seelenruhe Staatsinteressen opfern. Auf Wunsch von Augustus und Livia ließ er sich nämlich von Vispania scheiden, obwohl diese ein zweites Kind von ihm erwartete, und heiratete Julia, eine aus Augustus' Ehe mit Scribonia stammende Tochter. Für Augustus war die Heirat zwischen seiner verwitweten Tochter Julia, die er vergötterte, und Tiberius ein Schachzug, der die Machtstellung der eigenen wie auch Livias Familie sichern sollte. Tiberius' Ehe mit Julia, die sich vielen Ausschweifungen hingab und nächtliche Orgien feierte, verlief jedoch unglücklich; Julia verschmähte Tiberius als Mann und schrieb einen berühmt gewordenen Brief an ihren Vater, in dem sie ihre Verachtung für den Gatten zum Ausdruck brachte; dieses Schreiben verletzte Tiberius zutiefst.

Das sollte nicht das einzige Mißgeschick sein, das Tiberius widerfuhr. Trotz seiner so wichtigen Stelle im Römischen Reich stand Tiberius stets im Schatten von Lucius und Cajus; dies waren Julias Kinder aus der Ehe mit Agrippa. Augustus, der seine Enkel über alles liebte, hatte sie, die noch Kinder waren, und nicht den erfahrenen Feldherrn Tiberius zu seinen Nachfolgern bestimmt. Manche Historiker behaupten, Tiberius hätte auch unter der großen Popularität seines Bruders Drusus I. gelitten. Nach dem plötzlichen Tod von Drusus übertrug sich die Liebe des Volkes und des Kaisers auf dessen Sohn Germanicus, den Tiberius ebenfalls als Rivalen empfand.

Tiberius' gekränkter Stolz und sein Gefühl, stets Augustus' zweite Wahl zu sein, hatten wohl seinen jähen Entschluß bestimmt, alle Ämter niederzulegen und sich als Privatmann auf die Insel Rhodos zurückzuziehen. Er widersetzte sich damit den Wünschen von Augustus, der ihm diesen Schritt viele Jahre lang nicht verzeihen konnte. In der damaligen Zeit war Rhodos der Sitz bedeutender griechischer Rhetoriker. Tiberius, der mit der griechischen Sprache, Literatur und Philosophie eng vertraut war, verkehrte mit ihnen, betrieb geschichtliche und astronomische Studien, hörte Philosophievorlesungen und befaßte sich auch mit der damals populären Astrologie und Wahrsagerei der Chaldäer. Er kümmerte sich um Kranke und empfing die Besuche sowohl griechischer Freunde als auch römischer Abgesand-ten. Als der Schutz der Mitregentenschaft ihm nicht mehr zustand, zog er sich ins Innere der Insel zurück, um sich keinen Demütigungen auszusetzen. Er fühlte sich in der Abgeschiedenheit auf seiner Lieblingsinsel Rhodos glücklicher als in Rom. Seine Bewunderung für die stoische Philosophie verstärkte seinen Hang zum Alleinsein. Zu den wenigen Freunden, die er auf Rhodos hatte, zählte Nerva, der Tiberius ins Exil gefolgt war, ihm bis zu Schluß treu blieb und mit ihm sogar nach Capri zog.

Nach Tacitus' und Juvenals Berichten soll Tiberius die zwölf höchst-gelegenen Villen, die er auf Rhodos besaß, jeweils einer anderen Gottheit geweiht haben. In diesen Villen pflegte er sich mit chaldäischen Astrologen zu treffen, die ihm Horoskope erstellten und Auskunft über seine Zukunft gaben. Obwohl ihn stets eine Schar von Astrologen umgab, vertraute er nur seinem einstigen Sklaven Thrasyllus, der ein guter Freund wurde. Viele Geschichten über Tiberius stammen aus dieser Zeit.

> Der Astrolog vom Dienst — berichtet die Legende — stieg jeden Abend auf einem Steilpfad, der hart am Abgrund hinführte, zur Wohnung des Kaisers hinauf, um sich mit ihm zu bereden und die Vorzeichen auszulegen; wenn Tiberius in dem Horoskop einen Betrug argwöhnte, mußte ein kräftiger Sklave, der dem Chaldäer beim Rückweg mitgegeben wurde, den Unseligen über die Klippen ins Meer stürzen. Das erste Mal, als an Thrasyllus die Reihe kam, befragte ihn Tiberius nach seiner Zukunft; jener prüfte den Stand der Gestirne und tat erbleichend seinem Herren kund, daß ihm eine große Gefahr drohe. Der Kaiser schöpfte Trost aus seiner Treue, küßte ihn, und von Stund an waren sie Freunde.[17]

Im Grunde hoffte Tiberius, durch die Sterndeuterei zu erfahren, ob es ihm beschieden sei, Alleinherrscher zu werden. Aber Augustus, der bereits im Jahre 2 n. u. Z. Julia wegen ihres ausschweifenden Daseins verbannt hatte, lehnte zunächst Tiberius' Gesuch um die Rückkehr nach Rom ab. Als Lucius und Cajus plötzlich starben, gelang es der Kaiserin Livia, ihren Gatten zu überreden, Tiberius' Selbstverbannung ein Ende zu setzen. Im Jahre 2 n. u. Z. kehrte Tiberius nach Rom zurück, lebte zunächst weiterhin in Abgeschiedenheit, errang jedoch bald wieder seine ursprüngliche Stellung. "Um des Staates willen" nahm ihn Augustus, der keine Nachfolger mehr zu haben schien, wieder auf, adoptierte ihn und stattete ihn noch einmal mit tribuzinischer Gewalt aus. Durch seine Verdienste um die Eroberung Germaniens, die Niederwerfung des Aufstandes in Pannonien und die Wiederherstellung der Ordnung im Donauraum gewann Tiberius schließlich das Vertrauen seines Stiefvaters wieder.[18]

Auf Livias Drängen wählte Augustus ihren Sohn zu seinem Nachfolger, zwang ihn jedoch Germanicus zu adoptieren, damit dieser später Kaiser werden konnte. Nach dem Tode von Augustus im Jahre 14 n. u. Z. wurde Tiberius Alleinherrscher. In den folgenden Jahren sollte ein Streit zwischen Tiberius und Germanicus entbrennen. Aber Germanicus, der die Feldzüge in Germanien leitete und Generalstatthalter im Osten war, starb kurz darauf. Seit dem Jahre 19 n. u. Z. regierte Tiberius gemeinsam mit seinem eigenen Sohn Drusus II., der 22 n. u. Z. die *tribunicia potestas* erhielt, aber ein Jahr später ebenfalls starb. Es heißt, Tiberius habe den Tod dieses Sohnes nie verwunden. Nach der

Niederwerfung des Sklavenaufstandes in Italien und der Revolten in Thrakien zog sich der Kaiser auf die Insel Capri zurück und überließ die Führung der Staatsgeschäfte seinem Berater Sejan, der als Sinnbild des machtgierigen und perfiden Intriganten in die Geschichte eingehen sollte.

Schicksalsschläge, Enttäuschungen, Machtkämpfe hatten den einst weitsichtigen Staatsmann und mutigen Reichsfeldherrn Tiberius in einen von Haß und Wahnvorstellungen besessenen Tyrannen verwandelt, der von unermeßlicher Rachsucht getrieben wurde. Ressentiments und Verfolgungsängste schufen einen unüberbrückbaren Abgrund in seinem Herzen, trieben ihn dazu, alle potentiellen Gegner kaltblütig auszuschalten und selbst deren Freunde, Bekannte und Kinder umbringen zu lassen. Einige der Untaten seien hier erwähnt: Gemeinsam mit Livia soll Tiberius die Ermordung von Agrippa Postumus, einem Enkel von Augustus, ausgeheckt haben. Tiberius erschwerte die Bedingungen der Verbannung Julias und ließ Asinius Gallus, Vispanias zweiten Gatten, verfolgen und einsperren. Unter dem Einfluß von Sejan, verbannte er im Jahre 29 n. u. Z. Agrippina, die Witwe von Germanicus, auf die Insel Pandataria (Santa Maria) und ihren Lieblingssohn Nero auf die Insel Ponza; beide gingen elend zugrunde. Aggrippinas Sohn Drusus III., der wegen angeblichen Ehebruchs verurteilt worden war, starb an Hungersnot im Kerker. Aus Rache für die angebliche Vergiftung seines Sohnes Drusus II. ließ Tiberius schließlich auch seinen langjährigen Berater Sejan töten, begnügte sich jedoch nicht mit seiner Ermordung, sondern befahl seinen Schergen, auch alle Freunde, Bekannte, selbst die Kinder von Sejan umzubringen. Da das römische Gesetz es verbot, Jungfrauen zum Tode zu verurteilen, mußte der Henker Sejans Tochter vergewaltigen, ehe er sie erwürgte.[19]

Da Tiberius selbst weder an Götter noch an Gott glaubte, schreckte er nicht einmal davor zurück, die Anhänger neuer oder fremder Glaubensrichtungen zu verfolgen. Jahrzehntelang war das Römische Reich den unterschiedlichsten Religionen offen gegenübergestanden und hatte selbst die Götter der eroberten Völker ins Parthenon aufgenommen. Tiberius aber ließ die Anhänger des Isis Kultes und die Druiden ans Kreuz nageln; er zwang die 4.000 in Italien lebenden Juden, nach Sardinien zu ziehen, wo sie dem sicheren Tod ausgesetzt waren.[20]

Die Folge seiner Schreckensherrschaft war eine geistige Leere, die sich im Römischen Reich allmählich ausbreitete. Sie bedingte eine innere Unsicherheit der Menschen und rief Haßgefühle hervor, die in Intrigen, Machtkämpfe und gegenseitiges Zerfleischen umschlugen. Gewaltsam klammerten sich die Römer an Wahnideen, die letztlich den Untergang ihres Reiches herbeiführten statt ihn aufzuhalten. Es sollten viele Jahre vergehen, ehe die Menschen einen neuen Halt finden konnten. Aber gerade in dieser Zeit völliger Orientierungslosigkeit war am äußersten Rande des Römischen Imperiums eine neue Glaubensrichtung entstanden,

die einen tiefen Einschnitt in der Entwicklung der Menschheit markieren
sollte. Es ist die Lehre Jesu Christi. Allerdings dauerte es Jahrzehnte, ehe
sich das Christentum über ganz Europa ausdehnte und breite Bevölke-
rungsschichten beeinflußte. Die Kreuzigung Christi fiel zwar in Tiberius'
Lebensspanne, fand jedoch nicht unter seiner Herrschaft statt. Dieser
Vorfall, der sich in Jerusalem zur Zeit des Kaisers Augustus ereignete,
wurde in Rom kaum zur Kenntnis genommen. Kriege, Triumpfe, Machtkämpfe, Intrigen, Querelen bezüglich der Erbfolge, all dies beschäftigten
Augustus und vor allem seinen machthungrigen Nachfolger Tiberius weit
mehr als das Entstehen einer neuen Religion, deren Anhänger er ohnedies
verfolgen ließ. Daher überrascht die Auffassung mancher Schrifsteller
nicht, der Skeptiker Tiberius sei ein Antichrist gewesen. Er blieb bis zum
Ende seines Lebens eine Art abergläubischer Agnostiker. Als er im Jahre
37 n. u. Z. starb, hatte er alles seinem Machtstreben geopfert. Der Satz,
den Robespierre in Gertrud Kolmars Theaterstück *Cécile Renault* spricht,
"Nun bin ich allein. Allein ... Nun habe ich alles zum Opfer gebracht.
Auch mein Andenken bei der Nachwelt."[21] trifft auch für Tiberius zu.

III.

Da Gertrud Kolmars Stück unveröffentlicht ist, soll der Inhalt ihrer
dramatischen Legende hier kurz skizziert werden. *Nacht* hält jenen
Zeitpunkt in Tiberius' Leben fest, als dieser, während der Selbstverbannung auf Rhodos, alle Götter und Sterne befragt, ob ihm Ruhm
und Ehre vergönnt seien, ob er wohl eines Tages nach Rom werde
zurückkehren können. Tiberius, dem das Orakel die Erfüllung seines
Wunsches versprach, will Sicherheit über den Wahrheitsgehalt einer
solchen Prophezeihung und über die Existenz der Götter haben. Ein
chaldäischer Priester, den Tiberius um Rat fragt, schlägt ihm vor, der
Göttin Ischtar, jener von den Babyloniern verherrlichten Liebesgöttin, die
aber auch als Kriegsgöttin betrachtet wurde, einen Tempel zu bauen und
ihr ein Tieropfer entgegenzubringen. Daher läßt Tiberius seinen stummen
Sklaven eine schwarze Ziege hoch oben ins Gebirge zum Treffpunkt mit
dem alten chaldäischen Priester bringen. Gertrud Kolmar, die an dieser
Stelle auf Tiberius-Legenden anspielt, läßt den Römer, der an Ischtars
Macht und der Glaubwürdigkeit des Priesters zweifelt, den stummen
Diener beauftragen, auf ein Zeichen hin den alten Priester ins Meer zu
stürzen. Aber der Chaldäer kann nicht nur die Zukunft weissagen,
sondern auch Gedanken lesen, und so errät er Tiberius' Mordabsicht. Da
erklärt er dem Römer, Ischtar nehme das furchtbare Menschenopfer an,
doch wolle sie nicht das Blut eines alten Mannes, sondern ein junges
Menschenleben. Obwohl Tiberius meint, den Priester zu durchschauen,
läßt er ihn fortziehen.

Allein, auf dem einsamen Berg zurückgeblieben, grübelt Tiberius weiter über den Sinn der Prophezeihung nach. Da erblickt er ein Mädchen. Es ist die Jüdin Ischta, die ihm gesteht, die Ziege losgebunden und versteckt zu haben. Sie fleht ihn an, die Ziege nicht zu schlachten, da sie ihr einziger Besitz sei. Die schicksalhafte Begegnug zwischen Tiberius und der Jüdin ist die Schlüsselszene dieser dramatischen Legende. Ischta lebt mit einem alten jüdischen Gelehrten Oreb in einer Höhle. Der alte Jude, der einst sehr reich war, hatte gesündigt und anderen Göttern gedient. Als er sich seines Frevels bewußt wurde, bestrafte er sich selbst, zog sich auf Rhodos zurück, um weitab von allen Menschen ein Leben im Sinne des jüdischen Glaubens zu führen. Nur Ischta, eine Waise, die er gerettet und erzogen hatte, durfte ihn begleiten und bei ihm bleiben. Nach ihrer Ansicht hatte Gott Oreb verziehen und ihm Weisheit geschenkt. Wie Ischta Tiberius berichtet, hatte Oreb sie die jüdischen Gebote gelehrt und ihr biblische Geschichten erzählt.

Tiberius, der an der Existenz göttlicher Kräfte Zweifelnde, fühlt sich von dem jüdischen Glauben an einen einzigen unsichtbaren Gott angezogen und beschließt, den alten Juden in seiner Höhle aufzusuchen. Er bringt dem kranken Mann Nahrung, die Ischta zum Teil ablehnt, weil die Lebensmittel nicht koscher sind. So erfährt Tiberius von den Speisegewohnheiten der Juden. Im Gespräch mit Oreb lernt er einiges über die Bibelgeschichten, die ihn zum Nachdenken anregen, ihn jedoch nicht überzeugen. Das Schicksal Itzchaks[22] (Isaak), der geopfert werden soll, aber im letzten Augenblick von Gott gerettet wird, beflügelt seine Phantasie und legt ihm den Gedanken nahe, ein Experiment zu wagen. Als sich der Jude in die Höhle zurückzieht und sich ein zweites, seltsames Gespräch zwischen Ischta und Tiberius entspannt, spielt der Römer mit dem Gedanken, die gläubige Jüdin zu ermorden, um zu sehen, ob Gott sie in letzter Minute retten würde, so wie er einst Itzchak gerettet hatte. Für Tiberius wäre ein solches Eingreifen der letztgültige Beweis für Gottes Existenz. Sollte aber Ischta sterben, dann wäre ihr Tod die Bestätigung der Machtlosigkeit oder Inexistenz Gottes. Ischta fühlt, daß Tiberius sie töten will und bleibt dennoch bei ihm. Sie vertraut Gott. Wenn sie Rettung verdient habe, so werde Gott sie retten, erklärt sie Tiberius. Wenn sie gesündigt habe, so müsse sie jetzt sterben.

Im letzten Aufzug erscheint Kaiserin Livia. Sie bringt Tiberius die Botschaft, Augustus habe ihm verziehen und gestatte ihm, wieder nach Rom zurückzukehren. Aber Tiberius will auf Rhodos bleiben und gesteht ihr, das Orakel habe gesagt, er werde Unsterblichkeit, Macht und Ruhm auf einem Felsen im Meer erlangen. Die Mutter zweifelt an der Richtigkeit dieser Deutung, kann aber ihren Sohn nicht überreden, nach Rom zurückzukehren. Erst als sie ihm vom Tod des Lucius berichtet, den sie vergiften ließ, ändert Tiberius seine Meinung. Da erkennt Tiberius plötzlich, daß nicht die Götter, sondern die Mutter und ihre politischen

Ränkespiele ihm zu Ruhm und Unsterblichkeit verhelfen und beschließt deshalb, gemeinsam mit Livia nach Rom zurückzukehren.

IV.

Ein Paradox markiert Struktur und Thematik dieses Theaterstückes, das die Stimmen heterogener Völker orchestriert, ihre Sprach- und Denkweisen in ein metaphernreiches, multilinguales Deutsch übersetzt, aber letztlich den Abgrund zwischen den Kulturen aufzeigt. Römer, Chaldäer, Griechen und Juden treten in diesem Stück auf, führen Gespräche mit-und übereinander, können sich jedoch nicht verständigen. Der Sprachduktus der einzelnen Gestalten ist auf die kulturellen Traditionen abgestimmt, die sie repräsentieren. Ein emphatischer, gefühlsbeladener Ton, Mißtrauen gegenüber allem Fremden, Skepsis kennzeichnen die Dialoge der Römer. Visionär ist die Sprache des chaldäischen Priesters. Alttestamentarisch sind die Bilder, die Ischta und der greise Jude verwenden. Wohl vermag Gertrud Kolmar die Eigenart der antiken Völker in eine Sprache zu übertragen, die von einer ganz anderen Denk- und Vorstellungswelt geprägt ist; wohl vermag sie, Leser und Leserinnen unserer Tage den Zusammenprall disparater Welten in plastischen Bildern vor Augen zu führen; aber die eigenen Zeitgenossen hatte sie nicht erreichen können. Die Botschaft ihres Stückes verklang ins Leere. Die Lyrikerin hatte nicht einmal die Chance, ihr Drama zu veröffentlichen.

Gerade diese schicksalhafte Spannung zwischen Übersetzbarkeit und Unübersetzbarkeit, Lesbarkeit und Unlesbarkeit heterogener kultureller Traditionen steht im Mittelpunkt dieses Dramas, wird zum Motor der Handlung, bestimmt das Denken und Tun der einzelnen Gestalten. Bereits die einleitende Szene, ein Gespräch zwischen den römischen Freunden von Tiberius, evoziert die Schwierigkeit, fremde Völker und Sitten zu begreifen, die mißglückten Versuche, zwischen disparaten Kulturen zu vermitteln, selbst wenn man deren Unterschiede erfaßt, sowie die Vielfalt der Interpretationsmöglichkeiten ein und desselben Phänomens. Am Beispiel einer Auseinandersetzung über unterschiedliche künstlerische Darstellungen der Götter zeigt Gertrud Kolmar, wie Unwissenheit der Römer zur Verachtung des Andersartigen führt und jegliche Möglichkeit des Umdenkens zunichte macht. Die Römer fühlen sich von den auf Rhodos vorherrschenden chaldäischen Götterdarstellungen, den Tiergestalten mit menschlichem Kopf oder Körper, zutiefst abgestoßen. Das Fremdartige dieser Statuen flößt ihnen Mißtrauen ein und läßt sie Verdacht schöpfen, diese Götter könnten den Römern nicht wohl gesinnt sein. Nach Vorstellung der römischen Freunde ist Göttlichkeit unabdingbar mit ästhetischer Schönheit verbunden. Das Schöne und Sublime in einem darzustellen, ist ihrer Ansicht nach letztlich die Aufgabe der Kunst. Einzig Nerva begreift, daß die sogenannten Barbaren das Nichterfaßbare des Göttlichen, das jenseits des Menschlichen steht, wiederzugeben versuchen und sie gerade deshalb Götter als Tiere mit menschlichen Körperteilen gestalten. Aber seine Deutung überzeugt die Römer nicht.

Ebenso unverständlich wie die fremden Gottheiten erscheint den Römern das Verhalten ihres Freundes Tiberius. Sie behaupten, das Exil habe ihn verändert. Auf meisterhafte Weise evoziert Gertrud Kolmar an dieser Stelle die Konsequenzen des Exils und die Art und Weise, wie dessen Wirkung auf die Persönlichkeit des Verbannten mißverstanden wird. In den Augen seiner römischen Freunde hatte Tiberius im Verlauf der sieben im Exil verbrachten Jahre allmählich die Merkmale der auf Rhodos lebenden Völker angenommen und war kein Römer mehr. Das Exil habe auch auf sie selbst eingewirkt, beklagen die Freunde, obwohl sie sich lange nicht so intensiv wie Tiberius mit den Glaubensrichtungen und Gewohnheiten der ethnischen Stämme auf dieser Insel befaßt hätten.

> **Marinus**: ... Griechen, Punier, Chaldäer ... Wenn wir einst wieder Rom erblicken, werden wir selbst dann noch Römer sein? ... Tiberius Nero ist es schon heut' nicht mehr.[23]

Die Frage, ob sie selbst noch Römer sein werden, legt den Gedanken nahe, das Exil habe zur Selbstentfremdung geführt. Dies impliziert die Vorstellung, das Fremde habe unmerklich die eigene, scheinbar homogene Identität der Römer verändert, die ihnen nun so unheimlich vorkommt wie die Kultur der andersartigen Völker. Den Abgrund zwischen den Kulturen hatten die Römer somit nicht überbrückt, sondern internalisiert.

Zwischen den Zeilen ihres Dramas schreibt die Dichterin eine andere Interpretationsmöglichkeit der Auswirkung des Exils auf Tiberius' Persönlichkeit ein: Sie führt dem Leser vor Augen, wie eine bewußt vollzogene, physische, d. h. geographische Entfernung von Rom im Falle von Tiberius in psychische Distanz umgeschlagen und, anders als bei seinen Freunden, eine gewisse Offenheit gegenüber dem Fremdartigen bedingt habe. Daher huldigt Tiberius sowohl römischen Gottheiten als auch Melkart, dem Gott der Punier und Sidonier. Der eigentliche, biographisch überlieferte Grund für Tiberius' Entscheidung, sein gekränkter Stolz, wird hier nicht erwähnt[24]. Gertrud Kolmar weist lediglich auf die große Isolation von Tiberius hin, der die Gunst des Kaisers eben nicht genießt. In ihrem Drama sind Tiberius' unstillbarer

Wissensdurst und die Faszination, die Rätsel des Lebens auf ihn ausüben, der Motor seiner Beschäftigung mit fremden Kulturen.

Indem die Dichterin Tiberius die Götter und Wahrsager nach der ihm beschiedenen Zukunft ständig befragen läßt, deutet sie die innere Orientierungslosigkeit und Unsicherheit der Hauptgestalt ihres Stückes an. Da der Römer keinen Halt in sich selbst finden kann, projiziert er die eigenen Zweifel nach außen, mißtraut den Menschen wie den Göttern. Daher erscheint Tiberius in Gertrud Kolmars Darstellung keineswegs als ein Psychopath oder geisteskranker Mörder, sondern eher als ein Suchender, der Rätsel entschlüsseln, vor allem das Geheimnis der Zukunft erfassen will und wohl gerne an Götter glauben würde, aber kein Vertrauen zu ihnen hat und sich vor Enttäuschungen fürchtet. Diesen Gedanken illustriert eine Szene des zweiten Aktes: Auf der Spitze des Berges, allein vor dem von Sternen beleuchteten Himmel, kurz vor Ankunft des chaldäischen Priesters, ruft Tiberius alle Götter an, ihm doch ein Zeichen ihrer Existenz zu geben. Er ist bereit, jedem Gott zu huldigen, den es gibt. "Götter! ... hier wachse ich euch entgegen ... Auf meinen Wirbel setzt euren rechten Fuß, setzt den linken mir ins Genick; der Nacken des Claudiers, der nie einem Todbestimmten sich beugte, neigt sich, Unsterbliche, euch! Seid! Seid!"[25]

Tiberius sucht konkrete Beweise, um an der Existenz Gottes oder der Götter zu glauben und damit die erwünschte Sicherheit über den Wahrheitsgehalt der Prophezeihung zu erlangen. Als skeptischer Rationalist ist er gezwungen, die Kunst der Interpretion zu lernen, um die Glaubwürdigkeit der chaldäischen Priester, ihrer Wahrsagungen und Deutungen der göttlichen Zeichen einschätzen zu können. So führt die Dichterin ihre Leserschaft unmerklich ins Zentrum der Gedankenwelt ihres Stückes.

Einen Einblick in die Wirkung von Kultur und *Gender* auf die hermeneutische Perspektive der einzelnen Gestalten gewähren die sich anschließenden Gespräche, die Tiberius zunächst mit Nerva, dann mit dem chaldäischen Priester und schließlich mit der Jüdin Ischtar führt. Gertrud Kolmar verknüpft hierbei den Hinweis auf die Kunst der Interpretation mit der biblischen Vorstellung, Gott würde die Wißbegierde, deren Instrument die Hermeneutik ist, bestrafen. Dabei projiziert die Dichterin einen Gedanken der Bibel, Gott habe die Menschen wegen ihrer Wißbegierde aus dem Paradies vertrieben, auf die römische Denkweise. So läßt sie Nerva seinen Freund Tiberius vor seinem Wissensdurst warnen, da die Götter ihn strafen, ja umbringen werden. Eine solche Vorstellung assoziiert die Bemühungen um eine adäquate Deutung nicht nur mit Bestrafung, sondern auch mit Tod und Zerstörung.

Der Dialog mit Nerva ist auch in anderer Hinsicht entscheidend, denn er offenbart Möglichkeiten und Grenzen der Hermeneutik am Beispiel der Prophezeihung: Während Tiberius die Zukunft aus der Stellung der

Gestirne zu erraten sucht, blickt Nerva in die Seele seines Freundes, beobachtet dessen Handlungen, lauscht seinen Worten. Auf diese Weise vermag der treue Freund, die Schreckensherrschaft Tiberius' vorauszusagen. Ein Gespräch der beiden Freunde ist in diesem Zusammenhang besonders aufschlußreich: Tiberius erklärt Nerva, die Wege der Menschen seien verschieden; sie würden sich manchmal kreuzen, aber ihre Zielrichtung sei stets eine andere. Nicht einmal die Götter würden sich da einmengen. An dieser Stelle erwähnt Tiberius Helios, der dem verleumdeten Sohn die Zügel des Sonnenwagens anvertraute:

> **Nerva:** Der Sonnensohn versengte die Welt. Wo seines Wagens Gluträder sie berührt, lohte und schrie die gemarterte Erde. Jedem gebührte sein Weg: So zünden, so brennen kannst du nicht wollen
> ...
> **Tiberius:** (schweigt)
> **Nerva:** Nero. Du willst es also.
> **Tiberius:** Ich antworte nicht.
> **Nerva:** Dein Schweigen antwortet, daß du es willst.[26]

Während Nerva sogar das Schweigen seines Freundes zu deuten weiß, versteht Tiberius nicht einmal sich selbst. Er glaubt, er folge den Weisungen der Gestirne, er tue, was er tun müsse; aber dieser Glaube ist lediglich die Selbsttäuschung eines Mannes, der Menschlichkeit, Verzeihung, Erbarmen nicht kennt.

Anders als Nerva stellt der alte chaldäische Priester die dunklen Absichten Tiberius' nicht als geheime Wünsche des Römers, sondern als Prophezeihungen der Gottheit dar. Diese Weissagungen beruhen indes nicht auf einer Deutung der Gestirne am Himmel; sie sind das Ergebnis einer genauen Beobachtungsgabe des Priesters, der die Gestik und Handlungsweisen von Tiberius aufmerksam verfolgt und die potentiellen Konnotationen seiner Worte richtig interpretiert.

> **Tiberius:** Und du erkundetest das Geheimnis des Abgrundes und der Sterne.
> **Der Priester:** Ich drang in mein eigenes Wesen an kundiger Führer Hand. Meine Heimat ist Chaldäa.
> **Tiberius:** Dir war der Himmelsbogen versprochen, der Erdkreis Rom.
> **Der Priester:** Einst wirst du beide im Rund deines Stirnreifs fassen, Herr der Welt.
> **Tiberius:** Nicht diesen Namen für mich.
> **Der Priester:** Ich gab ihn dir, weil so deine Seele dich nennt.
> **Tiberius:** Was weißt du von meiner Seele?
> **Der Priester:** Nichts weiß ich; alles weiß Ischtar.[27]

Wie Gertrud Kolmars Text andeutet, ist feine Selbstbeobachtung die Grundlage jeglicher genauen Interpretation der Psyche anderer Menschen. Nur weil der Priester in die Geheimnisse der eigenen Seele gedrungen war, konnte er zum Menschenkenner werden. Sein Einfühlungsvermögen rettet ihm das Leben, denn er erkennt rechtzeitig, daß Tiberius mit dem Gedanken spielt, ihn umzubringen.

> **Der Priester**: Weh! Was hast du getan?
> **Tiberius**: Ich schwieg und lauschte: was tat ich?
> **Der Priester**: (mit eindringlichem Flüstern) Furchtbares hast du beschlossen ... ein furchtbares Opfer hast du der Göttin gelobt ... sie nimmt es an ... sie fordert ... nicht die schwarze Ziege ... kein Tier ... anderes Blut ... ein anderes ... Du ... Töte mich nicht! Ein Greuel, wenn du den Priester mordest ... Sie will nicht den grauen Bart, die dürren Glieder ... das Junge, Kräftige will sie ...[28]

An dieser Stelle läßt Gertrud Kolmar jedoch die Möglichkeit der göttlichen Offenbarung offen. So bleibt es unklar, ob der Chaldäer Tiberius' Mordgedanken dank der Verfinsterung des Mondes oder seiner eigenen Menschenkenntnis errät. Wie Tiberius' Selbstgespräch zeigt, führt er das Wissen des Priesters nicht auf Ischtars Einfluß, sondern auf dessen Fähigkeit zurück, Gedanken zu lesen.

Einen weiteren Einblick in die chaldäische Kunst der Interpretation gewährt die Deutung eines Feuerzungen-Traumes, den Tiberius im Tempel des Melkart hatte. Die Feuerzungen rufen: "I. und S. Ein T. Und A."[29] Tiberius versteht den Sinn des kryptischen Traumes nicht, aber der chaldäische Priester assoziiert die scheinbar bedeutungslosen Buchstaben mit dem Namen der Göttin Ischtar; er liest sie als Anagramm für Ischtar. Aufgrund dieser Deutung zieht er den Schluß, Ischtar habe Melkart verdrängt und Tiberius erhört; sie werde ihm zum Ruhm verhelfen.

In Gertrud Kolmars Theaterstück tritt die Voraussage des Priesters nur deshalb ein, weil sie Tiberius' verborgenen Wunsch nach Macht wiedergibt, ihn auf diese Weise bestätigt und den Kampf des Römers um die Alleinherrschaft nicht nur unbewußt motiviert, sondern auch legitimiert. Das Drama verknüpft hierbei Sigmund Freuds Gedanken, der Traum sei eine Wunscherfüllung, mit einer Grundidee der antiken Traumdeutung: Es ist die Vorstellung, der Traum könne eine Prophezeihung beinhalten. In seinem bahnbrechenden Werk *Die Traumdeutung* (1900)[30] hatte sich Freud jedoch von antiken Traumbüchern distanziert, gerade weil sie die Wunscherfüllung nicht berücksichtigten und Symbole willkürlich mit Bedeutungen assoziierten. Dabei hatte er die Wirkung der Sprache auf das menschliche Denken und Handeln unterschätzt. Denn die antiken Traumauslegungen als Weissagungen trafen oft nur deshalb ein, weil die Menschen an sie glaubten, sich bewußt oder unbewußt der Prophezeihung entsprechend verhielten und sie — ohne es zu ahnen — in die Tat umsetzten. Wie die Propheten hatten auch die Traumdeuter bekanntlich alles getan, damit ihre Wahrsagungen in Erfüllung gingen. Indem Gertrud Kolmars Stück die Auflösung der scheinbaren Gegensätze zwischen der antiken und modernen Traumdeutung zeigt, wirft es ein neues Licht auf Freuds Traumlehre und verdeutlicht, wie sich die beiden interpretatorischen Traditionen wechselseitig ergänzen und beeinflussen.

Durch die Darstellung der Begegnung zwischen Tiberius und Ischta deckt Gertrud Kolmar weitere fatale Folgen kulturell und *Gender* bedingter Mißverständnisse auf, aber auch das schicksalhafte Zusammenwirken von Libido- und Todestrieb in Freuds Sinne. Kraß ist der Gegensatz zwischen der römischen und jüdischen Denkweise. Tiberius und Ischtar sind weltenweit voneinander entfernt. Sie versinnbildlichen den polaren Gegensatz zwischen Mann und Frau. Der einst tapfere Feldherr ist ein finsterer, phallozentrischer Egoist, der mit Mordgedanken spielt. Sein eigentlicher Name, Nero, stammt vom griechischen "ner" ab, der Bezeichung eines mutigen Mannes, aber suggeriert zugleich — durch die Anspielung auf die Farbe "schwarz" (ital. nero) — den Gedanken, Tiberius sei eine Gestalt der Nacht, des Todes. Seine Misanthropie beeinflußt seine Deutung der Gestalt Ischtas, die in diesem Stück als Symbol der humanen Denkweise erscheint. Unschuld, Liebe, unbedingter Glaube an Gott, Vertrauen und Zuversicht kennzeichnen ihr Wesen. Tiberius fühlt sich zwar von Ischtas Schönheit angezogen, beschließt aber, sie umzubringen, da er meint, sie sei das ideale Menschenopfer für Ischtar. Gerade Tiberius' pervers anmutender Gedankengang zeigt, wie Libido hier in Besitzgier umschlägt, deren extreme Manifestationsform das Ermorden eines Menschen ist, den man zu beherrschen glaubt. Gertrud Kolmar läßt Tiberius seinen Entschluß, Ischta zu opfern, auch auf andere falsche Deutungen von Indizien stützen: die Ähnlichkeit der Namen Ischtar und Ischta; der Umstand, daß die Jüdin noch eine Jungfrau ist, was den bildnerischen Darstellungen der Göttin Ischtar entspricht; Ischtas Wunsch, ihrem zukünftigen Sohn den Namen Ner zu geben; Tiberius interpretiert Ner als Abkürzung des eigenen Namens und damit als Beweis, das Ischta ihm gehöre. Vergeblich versucht Ischta Tiberius den Sinn von Ner, der hebräischen Bezeichung für Licht (Kerze), zu erklären. Tiberius hört zwar ihre Worte, legt sie aber stets in seinem eigenen Sinne aus. Gerade der Umstand, daß Ischta das Licht in sich tragen werde, erscheint ihm als ein weiterer Beweis, sie sei das ideale Opfer für Ischtar, die man für die Schwester des Sonnengottes hielt.[31]

Auch Ischta fühlt sich vom fremden Mann angezogen und will zunächst mit ihm gehen, ihm dienen. Der alte Mann, für den sie bislang gesorgt hatte, liegt im Sterben und hat sie fortgeschickt. Aber Ischta will nicht mehr zurück in die Stadt, zu sehr hat sie sich vom bunten Treiben der Menschen entfernt. Sie will mit Tiberius fortziehen, doch plötzlich hat

sie das Gefühl, eine Sünde zu begehen; Gott wolle es nicht einmal, daß
sie Tiberius anschaue:

> **Ischta**: ... der Heilige will nicht, daß ich dich anschaue. ... Sprach
> er zu dir und forderte mich wie Itzchak, Abrahams Sohn? Hörtest
> du seine Stimme? Er mag dich gürten, wo du ihn nicht gekannt,
> wie er Kyros, seinen Gesalbten, gürtete, daß er die Völker schlug.
> Und wenn du mich gelobtest um deines Sieges willen, wie Jiftah
> der Richter sein Kind ... aber er wußte es nicht ... (verstummt)?
> **Tiberius**: (nach einer Weile) Ich opfere dem, der da annimmt.
> Dem Ewigen Jisraëls oder Ischtar. Dem — der ist.[32]

Warum sich Ischta mit einem Male schuldig fühlt, bleibt zunächst unklar;
die potentiellen Konnotationen des Textes öffnen indes einen Denkraum,
in dem sich eine scheinbar paradoxe Weiblichkeitsvorstellung entfaltet.
Einerseits wird sich Ischta eines Liebesgefühls für den fremden Mann,
also ihrer eigenen Erotik bewußt, muß dies jedoch aufgrund ihrer
jüdischen, orthodoxen Erziehung als Sünde ablehnen; denn ihrer Ansicht
nach ist es die Aufgabe der Frau, Gattin und Mutter zu sein. Andererseits
identifiziert sich die Jüdin mit männlichen Gestalten. So versteht Ischta
die Lage, in der sie sich befindet, als ein Zeichen Gottes, er habe sie als
Opfer gefordert, wie er einst Itzchak verlangt hatte. Ischta wiederholt
auch unbewußt, die Handlungsweise ihres Vorbilds Oreb, der zunächst
fremden Göttern gedient hatte, ehe er sich selbst fand. Auch sie will einem
Fremden dienen. Als Tiberius Ischta auffordert, zu fliehn ("Flieh' und
lebe"), erwidert sie ihm: "Herr, ich bin deine Sklavin"[33]. Diese Antwort,
die scheinbar eine völlige Unterwerfung der Frau signalisiert, kann
jedoch auch als Folge der Identifikation Ischtas mit Oreb verstanden
werden und würde in diesem Falle ein Akt der Gleichstellung mit dem
Mann sein. Gerade der freie Entschluß Ischtas, die Sklavin von Tiberius
zu sein, erfährt in Gertrud Kolmars Text noch eine weitere, religiöse
Deutung. Denn Ischta glaubt, ihre Entscheidungen seien letztlich nicht
Ausdruck ihres eigenen Willens, sondern der Wunsch Gottes. Ischta sieht
sich in der Rolle von Jiftahs (Jephthahs) Tochter. Der Richter Jiftah hatte
Gott ein Menschenopfer gelobt, wenn die Juden im Kampf gegen die
Ammoniter siegen würden: "... so soll, was mir aus meiner Haustür ent-
gegengeht, ... dem Herrn gehören, und ich will's als Brandopfer
darbringen...." heißt es in der *Bibel* (Richter 11: 31). Jiftah ahnte nicht, daß
es sein einziges Kind, seine Tochter, sein würde. Obwohl der Richter
zutiefst enttäuscht war, daß Gott die Tochter nicht retten ließ, blieb er
dennoch gläubig. Religiöse Juden deuteten Jiftas Tat als Ent-scheidung
Gottes, dessen Willen sich im Schwur des Richters offenbarte. Wie
Bibelexegeten immer wieder betonen, ist die Tragödie Jiftahs und seiner
Tochter ein Beweis für ihren unerschütterlichen Glauben an Gott.[34]

Ähnliche Ansichten vertritt auch Gertrud Kolmar in ihrem Drama: So läßt sie Ischta betonen, Tiberius sei lediglich das Werkzeug Gottes, auch wenn er es selbst nicht weiß. Wenn sie Rettung verdient habe, werde Gott sie retten. Sollte sie aber sterben, so sei dies die Strafe für ihre Sünde. Wenn sie aber unschuldig sei und dennoch ihr Leben opfern müsse wie Jiftahs Tochter es ihres Vaters Schwur wegen getan hatte, dann sei dies der Wille Gottes. Gertrud Kolmar läßt somit Ischta ihr eigenes Schicksal im Sinne der Juden der Antike deuten, die sich selbst und nicht Gott die Schuld am eigenen Unglück gaben. Aber selbst wenn es keine Schuld gab, die sie büßen sollten, akzeptierten sie dennoch ihr Schicksal, weil sie es als Gottes Entscheidung ansahen. Für Tiberius aber, der die biblische Geschichte und die Traditionen der Juden nicht begreift, ist Ischtas Tod ein Beweis, daß es weder Ischtar noch Jahwe gibt. Er fühlt sich in seiner Skepsis allen Gottesvorstellungen gegenüber bestätigt.

Gertrud Kolmars Drama zeigt letztlich, wie beide Gestalten so in ihren Gedanken verfangen sind, daß sie die Bedeutung, die der andere dem gleichen Zeichen zuweist, nicht verstehen können. Ein Buchstabe markiert die semantische Differenz zwischen Ischta und Ischtar, Ner und Nero, doch dieser Buchstabe deckt einen Abgrund auf, den keine Übertragungs- und Deutungskunst mehr überbrücken kann. Mit den ungewöhnlichen Mitteln ihrer Kunst zeigt Gertrud Kolmar zugleich, wie Tiberius' Versuch, das Geheimnis der Zukunft zu entschlüsseln, zur Vernichtung eines anderen Rätsels führt, das in der Gestalt Ischtas versinnbildlicht wird. Denn für Gertrud Kolmar stellt die Frau ein Geheimnis dar. "Das Geheimnis ist eine Frau; ihre Mitte bleibt tagverborgen."[35] heißt es in diesem Stück.

Am Schluß ihrer dramatischen Legende weist Gertrud Kolmar noch einmal auf die Vielfalt der Deutungsmöglichkeiten hin. Als Tiberius seiner Mutter vom Orakel erzählt, das ihm Ruhm und Würde auf einem Felsen im Meere prophezeite, antwortet ihm Livia, woher er denn wisse, daß Rhodos gemeint sei. Sie bezweifelt die Richtigkeit dieser wörtlichen Interpretation. Um dies Tiberius zu erklären, erzählt sie ihm eine Geschichte: Die Söhne von Tarquinius hätten das Orakel von Delphi völlig mißverstanden, als sie meinten, ihre eigene Mutter küssen zu müssen, sobald sie nach langer Seefahrt die Küste Italiens erreicht hätten. Wohl lautete das Orakel, wer die Mutter zuerst küßt, werde Herrscher werden, Brutus aber küßte die Mutter Erde und wurde Herrscher.

Für Tiberius aber ist gerade die hermeneutische Ambiguität, die dem Orakel mehrfachen Sinn zuschreibt, ein Beweis für die Stichhaltigkeit einer einzigen Deutung, nämlich seiner eigenen Vorstellung von der Abwesenheit der Götter. Nicht sein Opfer, die Ermordung Ischtas, sondern der Tod Lucius und die Ränkespiele Livias, ermöglichten es Tiberius, der Nachfolger von Augustus zu werden. Da es für Tiberius keinen Gott und keine Götter gab, um seine Untat zu rächen, brauchte er

keine Schuldgefühle zu fürchten. Bezeichnenderweise endet das Stück mit
dem Hinweis auf Livia und Tiberius, die in die Nacht gehen, wohl ein
Sinnbild für die Schreckensherrschaft, die sie im Römischen Reich
begründen werden.

Indem Gertrud Kolmars Stück Tiberius' Menschenopfer als sinnlosen
Mord entlarvt, wendet sie sich bewußt gegen alle Verbrechen, die um
"höherer Zwecke" willen begangen werden. Die zeitgeschichtlichen
Anspielungen sind nicht zu übersehen. Denn zu solchen Untaten zählt
auch die "Endlösung", die von den Nazis als "Erlösung" der Menschheit
verstanden wurde; in ihrer Perversität hatten die braunen Barbaren der
Massenvernichtung der Juden eine heilsgeschichtliche Dimension verliehen. Zwar läßt die Dichterin Tiberius durch die Ermordung Ischtas
eine Erlösung von Zweifeln an der Existenz Gottes erhoffen, aber sie
macht auch die Unterschiede zwischen dem Römer und den Nationalsozialisten deutlich: Denn Tiberius' Tat ist nicht von Antisemitismus
bestimmt. Den Gedanken an die Ermordung einer Jüdin als eine Form
der Erlösung führt Gertrud Kolmar nicht auf einen christlich geprägten
Antisemitismus zurück, wie er von Otto Weininger und vielen anderen
Judenhassern vertreten wurde. Bewußt klammert sie die in ihren Tagen
weitverbreitete Vorstellung vom Antagonismus zwischen Judentum und
Christentum aus. Sie zeigt auch nicht, wie das Christentum des
Judentums bedarf, um zu einer Selbstdefinition zu gelangen. Dennoch
fügt sie in ihren Text eine klare politische Botschaft ein, die zur
Zeitgeschichte Stellung nimmt: Gerade indem Gertrud Kolmar das
dramatische Geschehen in einen nicht christlichen Kontext aus der
römischen Antike verlegt, deckt sie andere Ursachen der verbrecherischen
Denkweise Tiberius' wie ihrer eigenen Zeitgenossen auf: Es sind
psychologische Gründe, die zu solchen Untaten führen — Gründe, die im
ewigen Egoismus und in der Machtbesessenheit der Menschen wurzeln.
In diesem Zusammenhang unterminiert Gertrud Kolmar auch ein Haupt-
argument der Antisemiten ihrer Zeit, die immer wiederkehrende
Beschuldigung, die Opfer der angeblichen jüdischen Ritualmorde im
ausgehenden neunzehnten Jahrhundert seien christliche Mädchen
gewesen. Gerade deshalb ist in Gertrud Kolmars Drama eine jüdische
Waise das Opfer eines Ritualmordes, der von einem Römer begangen
wird.

Durch den Mord an Ischta bringt Tiberius das Weibliche und das
Jüdische zugleich um. Seine Tat ruft den Gedanke an die schicksalhafte
Verkettung von Weiblichkeit und Judentum wach — eine Vorstellung, die
geschichtlich weit zurückreicht. Im positiven Sinne hatte man die Emanzi-
pation der Juden und der Frauen immer wieder miteinander verglichen.
Im negativen Sinne hatten manche Antisemiten ihre haßerfüllten
Vorstellungen von der sogenannten unmoralischen Natur der Frauen auf
jüdische Männer projiziert, denen sie Perversität vorwarfen[36]. Die Wech-

selwirkung von Judenhaß und Frauenfeindlichkeit fand ihren Niederschlag auch in Weiningers *Geschlecht und Charakter*, wo es unter anderem heißt, die Voraussetzung für die Erlösung Welt sei die Überwindung des Weiblichen wie des Jüdischen.[37] Ähnliche Vorstellungen waren auch für die dreißiger Jahre kennzeichnend. Gertrud Kolmar deutet nur indirekt auf diesen Kontext hin und betont hingegen explizit die psychologischen Motive, die Tiberius' Verbrechen bedingen, das Umschlagen der Libido in einen Zerstörungstrieb.

Das Motiv des Opfers und der weiblichen Selbstaufopferung birgt in Gertrud Kolmars dichterischer Gestaltung eine weitere entscheidende Kritik an der eigenen Gesellschaft und Zeit. Wie Christine von Braun in ihrem Essay "Antisemitismus und Misogynie"[38] gezeigt hat, wurde durch den Säkularisierungsprozeß der christliche Opfertod, der ein konstitutiver Bestandteil der Heilsbotschaft ist, verweiblicht. So trat in der Malerei wie in der Literatur des achtzehnten Jahrhunderts das Motiv der Frau auf, deren Tod dem Geliebten oder gar der Menschheit Erlösung bringt. Die Nationalsozialisten hatten diese Vorstellungen aufgegriffen und die totale Opferbereitschaft der Frauen für das Ganze, fürs Vaterland, für den Sieg gefordert. In dieser Art von Selbstaufopferung hatte die Frau ihre Selbstverwirklichung zu finden. Gerade gegen diese Konzeption des Opfers wendet sich Gertrud Kolmars Theaterstück. Ischta opfert sich hier nicht für ein Volk, nicht fürs Ganze. Ihre Selbstaufopferung hat nichts mit den perversen Ideen der Nationalsozialisten, nichts mit der christlichen Heilsgeschichte zu tun. Ischtas Selbstaufopferung entspringt der jüdischen, der biblischen Denkweise.[39] Ihre Tat ist kein wehrloses sich zur Schlachtbank führen lassen, sondern ein freiwilliger Schritt, auch wenn die Jüdin sie als Erfüllung einer Forderung Gottes deutet. Ihre Tat ist ein Zeichen des unbedingten Glaubens an Gott, des Vertrauens in Gott, aber auch ein Mittel, die Zugehörigkeit zum Judentum und dessen geschichtlich bedingten Selbstverständnisses zu beweisen. Aber gerade deshalb erinnert sie nicht nur an die *Bibel*, sondern auch an Iphigenies Selbstaufopferung, das einer Gemeinschaft zur Konsolidierung ihrer Identität und ihres Selbstbewußtseins verhalf. Ischtas Entscheidung, freiwillig in den Tod zu gehen, ist letztlich auch ein Akt der Stärke, des Mutes einer Jüdin, die konventionelle, gesellschaftlich und religiös bedingte Werteinschätzungen der Frau hinterfragt. Ischta erscheint dadurch viel mächtiger als Livia, die alle Fäden in der Hand zu haben scheint und selbst den Kaiser in seinen Entscheidungen beeinflußt. Während Ischta die humane Denkweise eines Oreb weiterführt und in seinem Sinne handelt, verkörpert Livia die phallozentrische Frau, die um der Macht willen zu Morden bereit ist. Durch die Gegenüberstellung dieser beiden Gestalten deutet Gertrud Kolmar an, extreme Gegensätze dieser Art kennzeichneten nicht nur die Männer-, sondern auch die Frauenwelt.

Obwohl Gertrud Kolmar der jüdischen Vorstellung vom Unglück als Gottes Strafe und dem Selbstaufopferungsmotiv entscheidende Bedeutung zuweist, deutet sie zugleich die politische Sinnlosigkeit von Ischtas Tat an. Denn Ischtas Opfer beeinflußt Tiberius nicht, menschlich oder sogar gläubig zu werden. Ischta bewirkt im Grunde das Gegenteil. Sie bestätigt Tiberius in seinem Unglauben und Menschenhaß, die viele weitere Opfer fordern sollten; zu diesen zählten auch die Juden. Bewußt scheint Gertrud Kolmar hier einen anderen, weniger bekannten geschichtlichen Hinweis auszuklammern, der Ischtas Opfer einen politischen Sinn verliehen hätte. Als Kaiser hatte Tiberius nämlich Menschenopfer für religiöse und rituelle Zwecke generell verbieten lassen. Gertrud Kolmar nimmt keinen Bezug darauf; gerade dieser Umstand unterstreicht die Zweifel der Dichterin an der politischen Notwendigkeit der Selbstaufopferung. Die Gegenüberstellung der religiösen, psychologischen und menschlichen Bedeutung der Selbstaufopferung versus deren politischen Wirkungslosigkeit verleiht indes Gertrud Kolmars Drama eine figurative Offenheit, die zum Nachdenken anregt und die Wirkung des Dargestellten steigert.

Interessanterweise hatte gerade Freud, in seiner Studie über Moses[40], an der er zwischen 1934 und 1938 arbeitete, ebenfalls Zweifel an dem Sinn der Selbstaufopferung der Juden angemeldet. Die Schuld, die sie stets sich selbst statt Gott zuwiesen, erklärte er als Folge des Gedankens der Auserwähltheit, die eine entscheidende Rolle in der Identitätskonstitution der Juden als Volk spielte. Es wäre schwieriger gewesen, auf diese von Moses vermittelte Vorstellung zu verzichten und damit eine Schlüsseldimension des Judentums aufzugeben, als sich schuldlos zu empfinden und Gott die Schuld zuzuschreiben.

Freud zog die Konsequenz; als ihm die Flucht nach England ermöglicht wurde, verließ er Wien. Auch Gertrud Kolmar erwog im Jahre 1938 die Auswanderung aus Deutschland. Wie aus ihrer Korrespondenz hervorgeht, hatte sie einige Vorbereitungen getroffen, um das Land zu verlassen.[41] Doch obwohl Gertrud Kolmar bereits 1934 genau wußte, welches Schicksal die Juden in den sogenannten Säuberungslagern erwartete, nutzte sie die ihr gebotene Möglichkeit schließlich doch nicht aus. Die Dichterin, die sich ihr Leben lang für andere geopfert hatte, blieb in Berlin, um ihren kranken Vater zu pflegen. Der neunzigjährige Vater wurde deportiert. Kurze Zeit darauf wurde auch sie deportiert und starb im Konzentrationslager.

Hätte Gertrud Kolmar in diesem Stück eine Parallele zwischen Hitlers und Tiberius' Untaten gezogen, dann wäre ihr ganzes Unterfangen fragwürdig gewesen. Denn Tiberius hatte keine systematisch organisierte Ermordung ganzer Geschlechter auf dem Gewissen. Die Shoah, der Mord an sechs Millionen Juden, ist einzigartig in der Geschichte der Verbrechen. Aber Gertrud Kolmar vermeidet bewußt solche Vergleiche. Im Mittelpunkt ihres Stückes stellt sie keine generellen Betrachtungen über die Mörder-Opfer Beziehung und keine Analyse der eigenen Zeit aus der Sicht der Vergangenheit, sondern den fundamentalen Unterschied zwischen Menschenopfer als Mord und der jüdischen Selbstaufopferung. Vielleicht war die Niederschrift dieses Dramas der Weg Gertrud Kolmars, über die eigene Zeit und den Scheideweg zu reflektieren, an dem sie selbst im Jahre 1938 stand. Vielleicht identifizierte sie sich mit Ischta und handelte — bewußt oder unbewußt — wie diese. In manchen ihrer Briefe schreibt Gertrud Kolmar von einer Schuld, die sie tragen müsse. Vielleicht empfand sie, ihre Liebesbeziehung zu nichtjüdischen Männern, die Abtreibung des Kindes, ihr Leben in der Einsamkeit als Schuld.[42] Vielleicht hatte sie das Bedürfnis, für die eigene Lebensweise zu büßen.

> Wie viele von denen, die heute in bloßen Anblicken eines für sie viel zu großen Schicksals zusammenklappen, haben sich denn gefragt, ob sie nicht irgendeine Strafe verdient haben, nicht irgendeine Sühne leisten müssen? Ich war nicht schlimmer in meinem Trachten und Tun als andere Frauen. Aber ich wußte, daß ich nicht lebte, wie ich gesollt, und war immer bereit zu büßen. Und alles Leid, das über mich kam und über mich kommen mag, will ich als Buße auf mich nehmen und es wird gerecht sein.[43]

Aber vielleicht wollte Gertrud Kolmar das Los jener gläubigen Juden teilen, die wie Jeftahs Tochter freiwillig in den Tod gingen, weil sie dies für den Willen Gottes hielten. Sie war überzeugt, dieser Weg in die äußerste Ausgrenzung, in den Tod sei ihr von "innen her" bestimmt. Gerade als Verfolgte fühlte sie sich stärker und fand die Kraft, anderen Menschen zu helfen, ihnen einen Halt zu geben.[44] Gertrud Kolmar war eine der *Gerechten*[45]. Sie verstand jedoch auch, daß ihre christliche Um- und Nachwelt ihre Selbstaufopferung so wenig begreifen würde wie Tiberius das Verhalten Ischtas. Sie erfaßte zugleich, daß die National-sozialisten nicht nur die Juden, sondern alles und alle, ihrer sinnlosen Machtgier zu opfern bereit waren. Das "Unheimliche in der Kultur" war nicht allein das Erwachen ungehemmter Todes- und Zerstörungstriebe, sondern die unmöglich gewordene Vermittlung zwischen andersartigen Völkern, der Abgrund zwischen Deutschen und Juden.

Anmerkungen

[1] Gertrud Kolmar: *Nacht. Dramatische Legende in vier Aufzügen*, S. 4. Leo Baeck Institut (New York). Abdruck der Zitate mit freundlicher Genehmigung des Kösel Verlages.

[2] Ebd.

[3] Vgl. *Marbacher Magazin. Gertrud Kolmar 1894 - 1943*. Hg. v. Johanna Woltmann. Marbach 1993, S. 96.

[4] Ebd.; vgl. auch Gertrud Kolmar: *Weibliches Bildnis. Gedichte*. München 1987, S. 322, 762.

[5] Ernst Kornemann: *Tiberius*. Stuttgart 1960. Kornemann hatte viele Jahre lang an diesem Buch gearbeitet. Manche seiner Betrachtungen über Tiberius erschienen bereits in seinem Werk *Staten, Völker, Männer*. Leipzig 1934.

[6] Ebd. S. 12.

[7] Gregorio Marañón: *Tiberio. Historia de un resentimiento*. Buenos Aires 1939; Ders.: *Tiberius Geschichte eines Ressentiments*. Übers. v. Karl August Horst. München 1952.

[8] Ebd. S. 5.

[9] Ebd.

[10] Ebd.

[11] Der Terminus *Gender*, der in der amerikanischen und britischen Literaturtheorie häufig verwendet wird, läßt sich nicht adequat ins Deutsche übersetzen. So bedeutet der Begriff "Gender Studies" keineswegs "Geschlechtsstudien"; "Gender" Studien untersuchen die Auswirkungen der durch Konvention etablierten Unterschiede zwischen Mann und Frau auf unterschiedliche Lebens- und Wissensbereiche: Gesellschaft, Politik, Literatur, Philosophie, Rechtswissenschaften, usw.

[12] Das Zitat aus den *Annalen* von Tacitus, das Kolmar als Motto ihres Stückes wählt, verweist auf Tiberius' Interesse für Wahrsager.

[13] Die vorliegende geschichtliche Darstellung beruht auf den Berichten von Tacitus und den geschichtlichen Werken von Marañón und Kornemann.

[14] Livia war fünfzehn Jahre alt, als sie Tiberius Claudius Nero heiratete. Ihr Sohn Tiberius kam ein Jahr später zur Welt.

[15] Livia wurde Kaiserin und Ehefrau eines Mannes, der häufig ihrem Rat folgte, sich nie von ihr trennte, sie jedoch immer wieder betrog.

[16] In der damaligen Zeit war die Institution der Ehe nicht bloß ein Mittel, den erwünschten Statussymbol zu erlangen, sondern auch ein geschickter Schachzug, zwei politisch entfremdete Familien zu vereinen, um die Macht der einen oder anderen zu konsolidieren. Livia gehörte zur Familie der Claudier, die jahrzehntelang von den Juliern, den Verwandten von Augustus, verfolgt wurden. Die Eheschließung zwischen Augustus, der ein Oktavier war, und Livia trug nicht

zur Versöhnung der Claudier und Julier bei, denn der gegenseitige Haß war zu groß. Die Konflikte zwischen den beiden Familien sollten Tiberius' Leben überschatten und seine späteren politischen Entscheidungen beeinflussen. Denn nach Ansicht von Tacitus und vielen anderen Historikern hatte die herrschsüchtige Livia ihren Sohn Tiberius stets zur Durchsetzung ihrer machtpolitischen Interessen benutzt.

[17] Marañón, (Anm. 7), S. 219-220.

[18] Tiberius machte sich einen Namen als Feldherr, sicherte die Grenzen des Imperiums und leistete einen wichtigen Beitrag zur Errichtung einer gerechteren Verwaltung und Finanzordnung im Donauraum.

[19] Aber selbst die eigene, schwer kranke Mutter ließ Tiberius fallen, sobald er sie nicht mehr brauchte. Für Tiberius sollte die Mutter lediglich ein Instrument seiner Rachsucht werden.

[20] Zu Verfolgungen der einzelnen Religionen, vor allem der Juden und Isis-Anhänger unter Tiberius vgl. Horst R. Moehring: "The Persecution of the Jews and the Adherents of the Isis Cult at Rome A. D. 19". In: *Novum Testamentum. An International Quarterly for New Testament and Related Studies Based on International Cooperation.* Hg. v. W. C. van Unnik und J. W. Doeve. Leiden 1959, Bd. 3, S. 93-304. P. W. Barnett: "'Under Tiberius all was Quiet'". In: *New Testament Studies. An International Journal.* Hg. v. Matthew Black und R. McL. Wilson. Cambridge 1975, Bd. 21, S. 564-571; dieser Artikel weist vor allem auf Sejans Antisemitismus hin. P. S. Davies: "The Meaning of Philo's Text about the Gilded Shields". In: *The Journal of Theological Studies*, April (1986), Bd. 37, S. 109-114; dieser Aufsatz setzt sich mit einem nicht geklärten Konflikt zwischen Rom und Jerusalem auseinander.

[21] *Marbacher Magazin*, (Anm. 3), S. 97.

[22] Es ist interessant, daß Kolmar Isaak mit dem jüdischen Namen Itzchak benennt.

[23] *Nacht*, S. 2.

[24] Augustus hatte Tiberius' Stolz verletzt, da er nicht ihn, den erfahrenen Feldherrn, sondern zwei Kinder, Lucius und Cajus, als Erben der kaiserlichen Macht einsetzte. Diese Kränkung hatte Tiberius bestimmt, nicht nur ins Exil zu gehn, sondern auch seine Aufmerksamkeit anderen Kulturen zuzuwenden.

[25] Ebd. S. 12.

[26] Ebd. S. 6.

[27] Ebd. S. 10.

[28] Ebd. S. 15.

[29] Ebd. S. 9.

[30] Sigmund Freud: *Die Traumdeutung* (1900). In: *Die Freud-Studienausgabe.* Hg. v. Thure von Uexküll und Ilse Grubrich-Simitis. Frankfurt/Main 1989, Bd. 2.

[31] Bezüglich weiterer Informationen über die Göttin Ischtar vgl. Marie-Thérèse Barrelet: "Les déesses armées et ailées". In: *Syria. Revue d'art oriental et d'archéologie.* Paris 1954, S. 221-260; Hartmut Schmökel, "Zur kultischen Deutung des Hoheliedes". In: *Zeitschrift für die alttestamentarische Wissenschaft*, (1952), Bd. 64, S. 149-155; Mary K. Wakeman: "Feminist Revision of the Matriarchal Hypothesis". In: *Anima. An Experimental Journal*, Bd. 7, Nr. 2, 1981, S. 83-96. Vgl. auch Samuel T.

Lachs: "Hadassah that is Esther". In: *Journal for the Study of Judaism in the Persian, Hellenistic and Roman Period.* Dezember 1979, Bd. 10, S. 219-220; der Autor dieses Aufsatzes führt den hebräischen Namen Esther auf den babylonischen Namen Ischtar zurück; dies legt den Gedanken nahe, die babylonische Gottheit habe auch für die alten Hebräer eine Rolle gespielt.

[32] *Nacht*, S. 31.

[33] Ebd.

[34] "... der Geist des Herrn kam auf Jephthah" (Richter 11:31); vgl. *The Anchor Bible Dictionary.* Hg. v. David Noel Freedman. New York 1922, Bd. 3, p. 680-683; *Judges: The Anchor Bible*, kommentiert von Robert Bolin. New York 1975, p. 209-210; *Dictionary of the Bible.* Nashville 1962, S. 821. In einem der Fruchtbarkeitskulte aus dem Nahen Osten, die mit Jiftahs Geschichte zusammenhängen, weinen Frauen für den babylonischen Gott Tammuz, der von den Feinden getötet wurde; zu den Trauernden zählt auch seine Frau Ischtar; in einer mittelalterlichen Legende heißt es, die Tochter des Richters Jiftah sei nicht umgebracht worden, sondern habe sich in die Berge zurückgezogen, wo sie einen Orden der Jungfrauen gegründet habe. Die um Tammuz weinenden Frauen hätten Ischta ins Gebirge begleitet. Vielleicht waren Gertrud Kolmar diese Zusammenhänge zwischen Jiftahs Tochter und Ischtar bekannt.

[35] Vgl. Anm. 1.

[36] Sander L. Gilman: *Difference and Pathology. Stereotypes of Sexuality, Race, and Murder.* Ithaca 1985; Christina von Braun: "Antisemitismus und Misogynie. Vom Zusammenhang zweier Erscheinungen". In: *Von einer Welt in die andere.* Hg. v. Jutta Dick und Barbara Hahn. Wien 1993, S. 181-182.

[37] Otto Weininger: *Geschlecht und Charakter.* Wien 1917, S. 449-50.

[38] Christina von Braun, (Anm. 34), S. 185-190.

[39] Es war eine weit verbreitete Sitte der Antike, Gott oder den Göttern ein Brandopfer zu geloben, um einen Sieg herbeizuführen. Es ist jedoch umstritten, ob Menschenopfer bei den Römern und Juden der damaligen Zeit üblich waren. Nachweisbar sind lediglich die Selbstaufopferungen der Juden (vgl. die Geschichte der Makkabäer) wie der Römer. Zur Geschichte des Opfer-Kultes in der Antike vgl. Leonhard Rost: *Studien zum Opfer im Alten Israel.* Stuttgart 1981; Rolf Rendtorff: *Studien zur Geschichte des Opfers im Alten Israel.* Neukirchen-Vluyn 1967; S. C. Gayford: *Sacrifice and Priesthood.* London 1953; Friedrich Schwenn: *Die Menschenopfer bei den Griechen und Römern.* Gießen 1915. Ischtas Selbstaufopferung hat nichts mit der christlichen Deutung des Todes Christi als des Sühne-Opfers für die Sünden der Menschheit zu tun. Ischta ist keine Erlösergestalt. Vgl. auch Opfer, *Brockhaus Enzyklopädie.* Wiesbaden 1971, Bd. 17, S. 753-54.

[40] Freud: "Der Mann Moses und die monotheistische Religion: Drei Abhandlungen" (1939). In: *Fragen der Gesellschaft. Ursprünge der Religion. Die Freud-Studienausgabe*, Bd. 9. Frankfurt/Main 1980.

[41] *Marbacher Magazin*, S. 109.

[42] Ebd. S. 23, 31, 106.

[43] Kolmar: *Briefe an die Schwester Hilde (1938-43).* München 1970, S. 186.

44 Vgl. Hilde Wenzel: "Nachwort". In: Gertrud Kolmar: *Weibliches Bildnis. Gedichte*, (Anm. 4), S. 781.

45 Vgl. jüdische Legende von den Gerechten in jeder Generation, deren Tugenden die Juden vor der Vernichtung retten. Siehe auch bekannte literarische Umdeutung der Legende in: André Schwarz-Bart: *Le Dernier des justes*. Paris 1959.

Elisabeth Strenger

Nelly Sachs and the Dance of Language[1]

The Hasidic tales collected by Martin Buber constituted part of Nelly Sachs's initial significant intellectual and poetic contact with Jewish culture. The following anecdote, entitled "Silence and Speech," evokes the historical reasons Sachs had for maintaining the struggle for her poetic voice, at first as the memorializer, then as the singer, of her people:

> A man had taken upon himself the discipline of silence and for three years had spoken no words save those of the Torah and of prayer. Finally the Yehudi sent for him. "Young man," he said, "how is it that I do not see a single word of yours in the world of truth?" "Rabbi," said the other to justify himself, "why should I indulge in the vanity of speech? Is it not better just to learn and to pray?" "If you do that," said the Yehudi, "not a word of your own reaches the world of truth. He who only learns and prays is murdering the word of his own soul..."[2]

In her own poetry, Nelly Sachs locates the poetic voice in the throat, *die Kehle*, at times, more specifically — the nightingale's throat. In the nightingale, we recognize the romantic icon of Brentano and Eichendorff's poetry and also the Baroque emblem of the German metaphysical poets. One is reminded especially of Friedrich von Spee's devotional "Trutz Nachtigall." The conscious use of the nightingale reveals Sachs's continuing interest in the Baroque and Romantic poetic traditions. In addition to these intertextual possibilities, the throat, as a physiognomic feature, signifies the frailty of the voice and of the material aspect of life. This constellation of associations, juxtaposed with the biographical incidence of Nelly Sachs's loss of voice occasioned by a Gestapo interrogation ("Fünf Tage lebte ich ohne Sprache unter einem Hexenprozeß."[3]), underscores her dual vulnerability as a Jewish woman and her awareness of that vulnerability.

As a German Jew, exile and exodus determined the poles of Nelly Sachs's experience of culture and history. Her fate exemplifies how question of identification was intensified for all Jews writing in the German cultural context. The equation was solved differently by each individual: either the Jewish or German side is weighted with varying degrees of assimilation or commitment to Judaic tradition in response to historical, political, or personal pressures. The Nuremberg laws forced a realignment, a re-evaluation of points of orientation. The content of German culture, now radically shifted to a position of "otherness," was called into question. In Nelly Sachs's case, this shift manifests itself in her rejection of the literary norms of German Romanticism and her subsequent exploration of Hasidic mysticism and the adaptation of its ontological and semiotic systems.

Sachs's metamorphosis into a Jewish poet acknowledges her continuous development of Jewish issues and motifs that exist in a symbiotic relationship with the German language, for, as a modernist poet, her poetry's formative theme is language and its ability to bear meaning. The German language was discredited as a system encouraging meaning because it had been the language of the disruptive oppressors. She developed a strategy for salvaging her means of expression and communication — her system of metaphors, which is, in effect, a re-invention of language. Her system affirms the existence of bonds between words and their meanings, while opening up a new range of meanings, and it challenges words to describe what has been termed the indescribable.

To reject completely the German language would imply the loss of her poetic voice and the structuring element of her personal and cultural experience. For Sachs, inspired by the theological and linguistic precepts of Kabbalistic and Hasidic mysticism, the agent that initiates and sustains the creation and the creative process is language. Her poetic and semiotic experiments are conducted in German, on German, and through these she attempts to transform the language of the oppressors ("die Jäger") and reclaim it on behalf of the oppressed ("die Gejagten"). Two pieces that illustrate the process by which she appropriates and reshapes German as a medium to express the Jewish experience are "Chassidische Schriften" (1949) from the collection *Sternverdunkelung* and the scenic poem "Der magische Tänzer" (1955). "Chassidische Schriften" represents the initial stage of this process where she begins to develop a metaphoric system based primarily on the *Book of the Zohar*, one of the central Kabbalistic texts from thirteenth-century Spain. The dramatic poem "Der magische Tänzer" (1955) with its evocation of Kleist's *Über das Marionettentheater* reveals the deeply problematic relationship between the German and Jewish cultural spheres. It questions the possibility of reconstituting the language and posits two extensions to the traditional poetic medium: silence and dance.

Within the Jewish mystical tradition we find a perception of human language that emphasizes the ambivalence of language itself as a possible system of access to divine understanding. Human language is opposed to the immanent Creative, Divine Word. Medieval German Hasidism delivers perhaps the most unequivocal faith in the power of language. In this movement with its belief in mystic ascent, as Gershom Scholem describes, "the emphasis is no longer on the approach of the mystic himself to God's throne, but on that of his prayer. It is the word, not the soul, which triumphs over fate and evil."[4] But when commenting on Jewish mysticism's relationship to language, Scholem asks, "how can words express an experience for which there is no adequate simile in this finite world of man?" There is a strong sense that we can only know by analogy or association. The Kabbalistic tradition also operated within metaphors — these being the only means by which to "name" the "deus absconditus": "that which is infinite, that which is not conceivable by thinking. At best these are words with close approximations."[5] Sachs extends the limitations of language so that it can form a bridge between experiential "Bezogenheit" and the place in which language has its source — the place before language.[6]

Fashioning one's own language is in keeping with the great Jewish mystic traditions, from the secret passwords for protection on ecstatic journeys to the *Zohar's* artificially reproduced Aramaic. So too Nelly Sachs seeks to transform her language into one that can express the inexpressible. Her transformed language includes non-verbal communication strategies. Her highly visual metaphors become emblems in the reader's eye. The human body itself is pressed into service — gestures and dance are summoned to convey meaning both to the reader, and, in prayer, to God.

A consideration of the physical, sensual aspect of her imagery and communicative strategy, as represented by description and inclusion of gesture, leads to the observation of how verbal and non-verbal communication merge in the image of having the word, or sign, inscribed upon the body. Even in transcendant poems describing mystic projections, the reader finds Sachs's attention on the intersection between the material and spiritual. In the "Magischer Tänzer," the body becomes the word: first in dance, and then, finally, when the heart is torn from the body. Unmediated communication via the body takes place as the Hasidic mystic completes his journey to the place before language.

If we continue to interpret Sachs's poetry as attempts at transcending the strictures of the material world, we will only focus on the abstract qualities of her metaphorical system which, as Ruth Dinesen points out, is one of the obstacles to her critical reception.[7] At the core of her transcendant impulses lies an acute awareness and understanding of the materiality that constitutes the human experience of one's surroundings, of history, and of self. In the reading and the speech of bodies are found occasions not only for vertically channelled contact between the divine and human spheres, but her poems also record the touching between bodies as a means of establishing lateral bonds, or community. Sometimes the simple human or animal gestures echo contact between man and God. A mother stroking her child's hip in "Ein totes Kind spricht" parallels Jakob's encounter with the angel: "And there was one that wrestled with him until daybreak who, seeing that he could not master him, struck him in the socket of his hip... (Gen. 32:26). Sachs's lines transform the blow to the hip:

> Die Mutter löste ihre Hand aus der meinen,
> Damit es mich nicht träfe.
> Sie aber berührte noch einmal leise meine Hüfte—
> Und da blutete ihre Hand—[8]

Feminist questions, on the identification of a woman through her body and with her body, arise in relation to certain aspects of Sachs's poetry. She concretizes the body in her poetry, and though this body is not always a feminine body, hers, the poet's, is, and feminist implications, especially in evaluating the link between biography and poetry should not be overlooked.[9] Johanna Bossinade began the feminist exploration of Sachs's work. She discusses the importance of the feminine identity for her poetics in terms of Freud's theory of the female wound, the wounded female. She too has noted that many of Sachs's images of separation or loss are opposed to metaphors of maternal security or "Geborgenheit."[10]

Throughout her oeuvre we find the cosmos, that same starry realm that represents the patriarchal promise to Abraham, associated with feminine terms: the milky way, if we wish, becomes the mother's milk way. We find umbilical cords binding us to the divine in the form of crystalline wombs. And pervasive is the blood, not always the blood of victims or death, but the blood of exuberant, painful, beginning life. Sachs gives birth to language renewed, and this metaphorical feminine presence is far more pervasive than is warranted by traditional Jewish mysticism and the limited role it ascribes to the *Shekinah*, that feminine manifestation of God.

Sachs lets her body, the body, be heard, but not in a manner easily accounted for by a single theoretical model. And for Sachs, it is not just a question of what the body says, but what the body hears. What experiences does the body react to, testify to? Mystics transcend the body, but the locus of their experience remains the body, and their bodies are said to bear signs of light or blood in response to that experience. It is significant that the strongest statements we have about Sachs and the production of her poems is that she felt them burning within her. One can read these either as the signs of a changing woman's body or the searing ecstasy of a mystic. Her epoch has seen the fragility of the body — she writes against this thoughtless, horrific waste. Her epitaphs for the Holocaust's nameless victims collected in *Wohnungen des Todes* contain detailed descriptions of their bodies or gestures, of their physical existence, as well as testimonies to their spiritual presence.

The poem "Chassidische Schriften" serves as a significant marker in Nelly Sachs's quest to transform language. Blomster, Klingman and Weissenberger[11] have viewed this poem as a poetic/mystic manifesto and have discussed it in terms of how systematic her analysis and integration of Kabbalism and Hasidism have been. Sachs's mysticism is not a system of abstractions. She poetically transforms personal memory into an evocation of the cosmos and fate of a people. In this poem, she seeks to produce her own Hasidic text: a mystical contemplation on the opening passages of the Kabbalistic *Book of the Zohar*. But whereas the *Zohar*'s author was inspired to seek for the layers of illumination contained within each word of the Creation narrative, Sachs's meditation telescopes the entire Torah as it moves from Creation through Exodus.

The poem's epigram reads: "Es heißt: die Gebote der Thora entsprechen der Zahl der Knochen des Menschen, ihre Verbote der Zahl der Adern. So deckt das ganze Gesetz den ganzen Menschenleib." It invites us to contemplate the convergence of word and body although the dynamics of this convergence remain a mystery, a mystery which the poem goes on to invoke as the space in which all is whole and intact, and for which all creatures long.

The epigram is echoed within the poem: "Und die Knochen leben die magische Zahl der Gebote/ und die Adern bluten sich zu Ende." The poet's eye transgresses the boundaries of the body, passes through the permeable barrier of skin. The skeletal and bleeding body, the bones and open veins, transcend their conventional association with death to connote life as well, a life encompassed by, or more accurately stated, circumscribed by the Laws of the Torah. The body, an object of death and genocide in the *Wohnungen des Todes*, functions here primarily as the living symbol of a god's covenant with his people. The gender specific sign of circumcision is replaced by the whole inscribed body. In a fashion reminiscent of Christianity's saints who bore stigmata as signs of mystical union, the body becomes the sign of God's Covenant with his people. It can be "read" according to Kabbalistic numerology and one perceives the possibility of an unmediated experience of divinity.

The poem places the reader at the beginning of creation as light is born of darkness in the protective, nurturing matrix of the universe. The entire process is distilled into the elemental images of night, stars, water and sand that we find recurring in Sachs's poetry. The agent which initiates and sustains the creation is language: "und das Wort lief aus / ... Namen bildeten sich / wie Teiche im Sand." In as much as man participates in the naming activity he participates in creation, as Blomster has elaborated in his essay on Sachs's theosophy of the creative word.

In this poem, darkness and light have universal significance, but Sachs expresses her hopeful belief in transformation when she imagines the night giving birth to the stars. Dark and light are not in perpetual conflict, rather one can engender the other. Similarly she transforms the image of the stone, (hard, lifeless matter and symbolic of exile in the barren desert), into a petrified darkness that still contains the promise of divine movement and light. Even threatening quicksand becomes a metaphor for the potential for change on the most elemental level.

In conjunction with the final images of fertile seeds and stars, sand assumes yet another dimension inspired by the Bible (Genesis 22:17). God promises Abraham, "I will shower blessings on you, I will make your descendants as many as the stars in heaven and the grains of sand on the seashore." The poem closes with the image of another stigmatized figure: Jacob, whose injured hip bore the trace of his encounter with his deity. No longer the Jew victimized by history, Jacob is the emblem for an Israel which continues to sleep with the stars that betoken the promise to engender a people.

If we can "read" God's presence in or on our bodies, then the possibility exists that we might reverse the direction of communication in accordance with the mystics' belief that the path to God is the reversal of the path from God. For the Psalmist David, for the Hasidic pious, and for Nelly Sachs, the body could then speak back to God, in dance.

Hellmut Geißner has attempted to describe the nature of dance as it is understood and applied by Nelly Sachs according to anthropological categories of ritualistic dance.[12] He defines it as "enthusiasmic" dance which is at once inward and outward turning, seeking both to conjure the god and to join with him. Such an ethnographical definition ignores both the communal and personal/psychological aspects of dance. These other forces operating on dance are represented in Sachs's work by Hasidic dance and by the expressive/interpretative dance of her childhood. Only when one considers dance within this triad of contexts can one understand the complex dynamics of dance as an act of communication.

Critical interpretations measure carefully the weight of autobiography in her works. Bahr describes her symbolic autobiography: "Sie wollte hinter ihrem Werk verschwinden, wollte anonym bleiben."[13] Her individuality may have been suppressed, but not her humanity. Of the few facts that can be gleaned from her self-representations, her autobiographical sketches or references in letters, the most consistently mentioned by biographers and critics is her fascination with dance. She expresses her feelings especially pointedly in a letter to Walter Berendsohn (January 25, 1959):

> Da ist in erster Linie die Musik meines Vaters, die er oft stundenlang des Abends nach seinem Beruf auf dem Klavier phantasierte und die ich mit Hingegebenheit und gänzlicher Fortgerissenheit von Kindheit auf im Tanz begleitete.... Denn sie (die Tanz und Musikgedichte von ihrer Jugendzeit) sind ganz aus

dieser gemeinsamen Atmosphäre erwachsen, die meinen Vater und mich so gut wie wortlos und doch im Innersten verband ... (Der Tanz) ist Mein innerstes Element. Nur durch die Schwere des Schicksals, das mich betraf, bin ich von dieser Ausdrucksweise zu einer anderen gekommen: dem Wort! Mein Interesse für den Mimus und jene musikalische Art des Dichtens, die sich zuweilen wie lautlos über alle Grenzen beugt, beruht auf dieser meiner innersten Veranlagung.[14]

Note the change to the present and the discussion of her later scenic poetry: as a mature poet she still feels that dance is her natural element, not the word. In the scenic poem "Magischer Tänzer" dance is the return to cosmic harmony, harmony with the breath which animates the universe. Again in her correspondence Sachs states:

Aber in meinem Vater hatte ich auch in dieser Hinsicht den besten Lehrer, da er selber lange vor seiner Zeit jenen rhythmischen Takt der Bewegung mit dem des Atems in Verbindung brachte und für damalige Zeit ganz revolutionäre Ideen hatte, die es jedem Menschen gestatteten, einen natürlichen und verloren gegangenen Rhythmus wieder zu gewinnen.[15]

Besides the desire to recover a lost harmony, a desire strongly associated with nostalgic attachment to her father, Sachs's autobiographical reflections on dance contain another mystical aspect which illuminates her relationship to language. Of her dancing as her father played she writes: "Ich folgte ihm weit hinweg, um die Fernen zu erreichen, beugte mich hinaus in ein sprachloses Gebiet."[16]

One more piece of biographical evidence suggests that dance had not lost its attraction as a means of personal expression for the mature poet. Lili Simon reports Ingeborg Drehwitz's anecdote that tells of Sachs dancing with abandon when she saw the Berlin Tiergarten again for the first time after twenty-five years. She had returned to Germany to receive the Friedenspreis des Deutschen Buchhandels, Frankfurt, 1965.[17] In light of her constant experimentation with mime and movement that accompanied her poetic endeavors, we cannot easily dismiss this interest's childhood origins.

Theorists of dance and of its essential component — movement — emphasize the developmental aspects of kinesthetic awareness. Kinesthetics has been defined as:

the sensual discrimination of the position and movement of body parts based on information other than visual, auditory, verbal.... Sensors in muscles, tendons, joints, as well as the vestibular

apparatus of the inner ear ... provide a constant, though
subliminal, knowledge of the arrangement of body parts. This
awareness is enhanced by the sense of touch — the contact and
pressure sensors.[18]

In infancy, kinesthesis and physical contact with the external environment
are instrumental in helping the individual "begin to conceptualize the
world as an orderly and understandable place."[19]

Conceptualization then is grounded in movement. Isadora Duncan and
the proponents of dance education/dance therapy insisted that the
relationship between movement and the conceptualization of the self and
the world extends throughout one's life. Isadora Duncan writes in her
essay "Dancing in Relation to Religion and Love": "a child can understand
many things through the medium of the body which would be
impossible for it to comprehend by the medium of the written or spoken
word."[20]

Beyond the tactile exploration of one's own body, movement is
incorporated early into a pattern of communication strategies. For infants
there are the touches, gestures and facial expressions of caregivers. This
stage of kinesthesis is found in many moments in Nelly Sachs's poetry:
the cow licking her calf, the mother stroking her child's hip, the old
women combing their hair. These gestures, seen as either direct
expression of emotion or as symbolic, establish the communal matrix onto
which language (verbal communication) is grafted.

The power of Hasidic dance is best observed in its communal
implications. For the Hasid, dance is much more than the expression of
a single individual's encounter with God; the message the dancer conveys
to his pious observers is an equally important function. Through dance,
the hasid teaches and inspires. The Hasidic Tales contain many reports
of the infectiousness of dance; strangers, passersby, skeptics are drawn
into a communal ecstacy. Their oral tradition also tells of rabbis who
communicated their enlightenment through dance: The Baal Shem Tov,
founder of Eastern European Hasidism, danced with the Torah, and when
he set it down in the midst of the dance one of his disciples proclaimed,
"Now our master has laid aside the visible, dimensional teachings, and
has taken the spiritual teachings into himself."[21] And of a nameless,
pious grandfather is remarked, "You may believe me: he has made all his
limbs so pure and so holy, that with every step he takes, his feet
accomplish holy unifications."[22]

Nelly Sachs emblematizes the Hasidic dancer in her scenic poem "Der
Magische Tänzer." The stage directions for the first scene describe
impoverished surroundings hung with laundry. Marina, who has devoted
her life to David, the former stage-dancer turned mystic, struggles to
support him by taking in washing. The scene's opening dialogue between

Marina and her neighbor is about a head of cauliflower. This portrayal of quotidian life reminds one of the lack of disjuncture between daily and mystical/religious experience advocated by the Eastern European Hasids.

The figure of David gives the impression of being a large wounded bird ("den Eindruck eines großen angeschossenen Vogels"), and in this posture are suggested his vulnerability as a hunted object, his ungainliness and his interrupted flight. His metaphoric association with the bird indicates that he is not completely earthbound, he occupies a space between the material and celestial realms. David sits with his head dropping down until it hangs between his knees in the contemplative position of the early Merkabah or throne mystics. After fasting this position was required for the soul's mystic journey through the gates to the throne of God. It is a position many religions have in common: it influences the blood's progress to the brain — induces physical and psychological "symptoms." The rushing heard in the ears, the play of light against the eyelids, the changing body temperatures are all translated into different aspects of the ecstatic experience.

In the first scene the entire onus of David's functioning (as a subject as well as an object of our gazes, as someone who interprets or configures reality as well as someone who invites interpretation) is placed on his postures, gestures and movements. He is speechless, and the only way he communicates his mystical experience is through dance. His utterances during the second scene mark the stages of his spiritual journey through history and the cosmos. His seeking for the doorway into the night parallels experiences of the Merkabah mystics who confronted gatekeepers at each stage of their ascendancy to God's throne.

An ironic juxtaposition to this silent yet expressive figure is created by the figure of the neighbor, who is represented by a marionette with a built in tape for a voice. Through this figure Sachs dehumanizes the subject. This dehumanization is appropriate for the neighbor who, completely focussed on material reality, is lacking in sympathy for David's ecstatic re-enactment among the clotheslines of King David's dance before the Ark. This David's Ark is Marina's keepsake chest. Of course, the saint appears as crazed to the neighbor, to someone representing society's norm, just as King David's dance was derided by his wife, Michal.

For the second scene, the stage is transformed by lighting techniques into a crystalline globe in which the figures of David and Marina are encased. The crystalline globe creates the effect of a cosmic womb and indicates the return to a pre-creation state. The visualization of the womb pierced by light parallels the *Book of the Zohar's* Creation myth in which the male ray enters the female womb.

David's somnambulistic dance continues and a cosmic wind, the breath of the universe, sets the clotheslines into movement. The magic dancer, portrayed by a marionette, appears and the stage retains an enormous amount of kinetic energy until the piece concludes. David's somnambulism indicates the movements of one who has no self-consciousness.

The marionette's presence on stage and David's unself-conscious movements stand in an interesting relationship to Heinrich von Kleist's critical musings *Über das Marionettentheater*. This connection may serve as yet more evidence of Sachs's continuing connection to the German Romantic literary heritage. The most striking parallel with Sachs's understanding of dance is the reason given for preferring marionettes over the self-conscious, hence distorted movements of dancers, because they have the advantage of being antigravitational, or defying some of the rules of materiality. Kinetic energy overcomes considerations of mass and gravity:

> Zudem ... haben diese Puppen den Vorteil, daß sie antigrav sind. Von der Trägheit der Materie, dieser dem Tanze entgegenstrebendsten aller Eigenschaften, wissen sie nichts: weil die Kraft, die sie in die Lüfte erhebt, größer ist, als jene, die sie an der Erde fesselt.[23]

Dance, pure movement, for Kleist and Sachs presents the possibility of transcending materiality. Sachs's dancer takes on some of the characteristics of Kleist's marionettes in order to problematize the paradox of achieving transcendence of the body, through the body.

The magic dancer serves as guide along the mystical journey; he assists in preparing David for his ecstatic encounter. In a stark counterpoint to the scene of cultic, ritual preparations in Euripides' *Bacchae* where Dionysius suggests transformative actions to Pentheus, who dons the costume of a Bacchante, the magic dancer, by means of naming, shapes David's perception of the process in which he is engaged. Urged to burst from his skin, David flings off his coat; a belt is perceived as a tonguing snake. While the magic dancer's kinetic energy dismantles the world projected on the hanging linens and unravels the meridians hence negating the distinctions, divisions and confinements imposed by man upon the geos, David continues stripping until, in his shredded undergarments, he bares his chest.

The mention of the snake, its mouth open, winding about David's waist introduces the thematic of Eden and the Fall of Man which figures in Kleist's deliberations on the causes of man's loss of physical grace: "Anmut und Grazie." This loss is associated with Adam and Eve's shame upon becoming conscious of their nakedness. If we superimpose a mystic's reading of this scriptural passage, the awareness of nakedness represents a distinct separation from God. Kleist couches the idea of retracing our steps to God in satirical wit: "Mithin sagte ich ein wenig zerstreut, müßten wir wieder von dem Baum der Erkenntnis essen, um in den Stand der Unschuld zurückzufallen? Allerdings antwortet Herr C; das ist das letzte Kapitel von der Geschichte der Welt."

David continues his dance, unwinding the confining threads, unravelling the cocoon so that he can undergo his final metamorphosis. The butterfly, that royal sign, Sachs's metaphor of transformation, is here embodies in David's dance. The concluding gesture of his dance is to tear the heart from his bared chest. With this, the interior becomes the exterior, expression occurs through the body, since the living heart, not the work, becomes the bearer of the self, and ultimately, of meaning.

For Nelly Sachs, the human capacity to communicate, to express, to configure reality includes both verbal and non-verbal languages. The rhythmic movement of dance can overreach the body's boundaries of space, time, and gravity. Jewish mystical voices cry out over the uninitiated language of the German oppressors. Sachs's German dances in a new rhythmical ascendance to spiritual freedom. She explores and acknowledges the paradoxical nature of the mystic journey to God: the body is both the starting point of that journey and the vehicle through which the goal of transcendence is attained.

> On every sabbath eve Rabbi Hayyim of Kosov, the son of Rabbi Mendel, danced before his assembled disciples. His face was aflame and they all knew that every step was informed with sublime meanings and effected sublime things. Once while he was in the midst of dancing, a heavy bench fell on his foot and he had to pause because of the pain. Later they asked him about it. "It seems to me," he said, "that the pain made itself felt because I had interrupted the dance."[24]

Notes

[1] This paper was presented at the International Conference on Walter Benjamin and Nelly Sachs held at the University of Michigan, Ann Arbor in February, 1992.

[2] "Silence and Speech" in Martin Buber, trans. and ed., *Tales of the Hasidim: The Later Masters*. New York 1959, p. 228.

[3] Erhard Bahr: *Nelly Sachs*. Frankfurt/Main 1980, p. 39f.

[4] Gershom Scholem: *Major Trends in Jewish Mysticism*. New York 1941, p. 101.

[5] Ibid., pp. 12-13.

[6] Ibid., p. 4.

[7] Ruth Dinesen: "Verehrung und Verwerfung: Nelly Sachs – Kontroverse um eine Dichterin." In *Akten des VII. Internationalen Germanisten-Kongreßes*, ed. by Albrecht Schöne. Tübingen 1986, Vol. 10, pp. 130-137.

[8] *Fahrt ins Staublose: Die Gedichte der Nelly Sachs*. Frankfurt/Main 1961, p. 13.

[9] The foundations for further study have been laid by Ruth Dinesen's monumental work: *Nelly Sachs. Eine Biographie*. Frankfurt/Main 1992.

[10] Johanna Bossinade: "Fürstinnen der Trauer: Die Gedichte von Nelly Sachs." In: *Jahrbuch für Internationale Germanistik*, Vol. 16/i, 1984, pp. 133-157.

[11] A.W. Blomster: "Theosophy of the Creative Word." In: *Germanic Review*, Vol. 44, 1969, pp. 211-227; Ulrich Klingman: *Religion und Religiosität in der Lyrik von Nelly Sachs*. Frankfurt/Main 1980, p. 107; Klaus Weissenberger: *Zwischen Stein und Stern: Mystische Formgebung in der Dichtung von Else Lasker-Schüler, Nelly Sachs und Paul Celan*. Bern 1976.

[12] Hellmut Geißner: "Sprache und Tanz." In: *Das Buch der Nelly Sachs*, ed. by Bengt Holmqvist. Frankfurt/Main 1968.

[13] Bahr, p. 30.

[14] Ibid., p. 32.

[15] Ibid., p. 33.

[16] These lines (cited by Holmqvist, 26) reveal a striking parallel to an anthropological observation of dance's function: Through dance, primal peoples "touch unknown and unseen elements, which they sense in the world around them." Jamake Highwater: *Dance Rituals of Experience*. New York 1985, p. 27.

[17] Lili Simon: "Nelly Sachs: Dichterin der großen Trauer." In: *Neue Deutsche Hefte*, Vol. 35, 1988, pp. 687-704.

[18] Carol-Lynne Moore and Kaoru Yamamoto: *Beyond Words: Movement Observation and Analysis*. New York 1988, p. 60.

[19] Ibid., p. 70.

[20] "Dancing in Relation to Religion and Love," In: *Art of the Dance*, ed. by Seldon Cheney. New York 1969, p. 122. The American Dance Therapy Association defines dance therapy as "the psychotherapeutic use of movement as a process which furthers the emotional and physical integration of the individual." Cited by Moore and Yamamoto, p.168.

[21] Buber: "The Early Masters." p. 53.

[22] Ibid., p. 171.

[23] Heinrich v. Kleist: *Sämtliche Werke und Briefe*, Vol. III. Munich 1982, p. 342.

[24] Buber: "The Later Masters," p. 98.

Teil Zwei — Part Two

Exilerfahrungen

Exile Experience

I.

"Einmal Exil, immer Exil"

"Once in Exile, Always in Exile"

Edward K. Kaplan

God in Exile:
Abraham Joshua Heschel, Translator of the Spirit

I.

> Dark is the world to me, for all its cities and stars. If not
> for my faith that God in His silence still listens to my
> cry, who could stand such agony? (Heschel, "On
> Prayer," 1970)[1]

What is the meaning of exile to a person of prayer? How does human
alienation relate to the divine? Does Jewish theology provide models
appropriate to the horrors and displacements of our century?

Both before and after World War Two, Abraham Joshua Heschel (1907-
1972), who emigrated to the United States in 1940 from his native
Warsaw, sought to convey his compelling confidence in God's presence.[2]
Heschel's diverse books, monographs, essays, and speeches launch us
upon a spiritual voyage, often rocked with lulling, rhythmical swells, yet
also storm-tossed and vehement. His masterful English prose throbs with
intimate holiness for which most of us only yearn. Abounding in
metaphors and vivid comparisons, his style seduces our craving for
harmony while his philosophical polemics challenge our minds. Our faith
may be incited by Heschel's fearless dedication to piety and compassion,
or we may reject his trust in the Almighty.

Heschel wrote little about his life in Europe, nor did he share the
details of his several emigrations. But about twenty-five years after his
arrival on our shores, he defined himself as a survivor in his inaugural
lecture as Harry Emerson Fosdick Visiting Professor at the Union
Theological Seminary:

> I speak as a member of a congregation whose founder was
> Abraham, and the name of my rabbi is Moses.
>
> I speak as a person who was able to leave Warsaw, the city
> in which I was born, just six weeks before the disaster began. My
> destination was New York, it would have been Treblinka. I am a

brand plucked from the fire, in which my people was burned to death. I am a brand plucked from the fire of an altar of Satan on which millions of human lives were exterminated to evil's greater glory, and on which so much else was consumed: the divine image of so many human beings, many people's faith in the God of justice and compassion, and much of the secret and power of attachment to the Bible bred and cherished in the hearts of men for nearly two thousand years.[3]

Addressing Christian theologians and divinity students, Heschel identifies with our biblical ancestors, Abraham and Moses, who heeded God's message and fathered the Jewish people. His message reminds Jews, Christians, and Moslems that we are all members of Abraham's congregation and that our common response to Hitler's war against humanity was more than physical. Religious people must cooperate to revive "the divine image of so many human beings, many people's faith in the God of justice and compassion, and much of the secret and power of attachment to the Bible." Heschel as "a brand plucked from the fire" bears urgent witness to the potential sanctity of all mankind.

While educating our sensitivity to the living God, Heschel's approach to religious belief and practice is authentically modern in its confrontation with despair. He insists that pain and anguish are necessary for true insight to occur: "We must first peer into the darkness, feel strangled and entombed in the hopelessness of living without God, before we are ready to feel the presence of His living light."[4] The apologist's insistence on a "meaning beyond absurdity" implies a precarious ordeal of raw and horrible alienation.

II. Awe and Consternation

Heschel's interpretation of Jewish tradition includes his historical and personal experience, although his writings rarely evoke the circumstances of their author's development.[5] Not until he completed his final book, *A Passion for Truth*, delivered to the publisher just weeks before his death in December 1972, did he define the irremediable tensions within his spirit.

While Heschel's confidence in the living God did not waver, his perception of the world might swing from prayerlike ecstasy to dismay at human corruption. He tamed this devastating contradiction in terms of polarity, a dynamic coexistence of contraries. Two Hasidic extremists, "two teachers," as he called them, the violently judgmental Mendl of Kotzk and the compassionate Baal Shem Tov, provide the model:

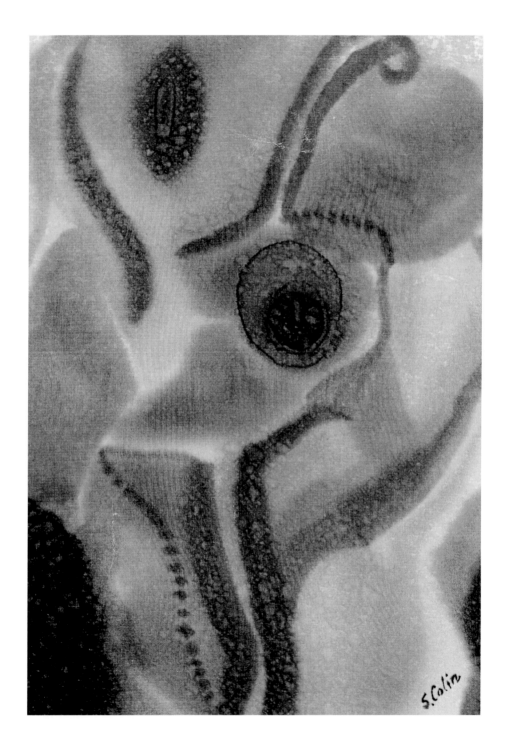

Sabine Colin: Seidenmalerei, Herbst 1993

One may look upon the world with enthusiasm and absorb its wonder and radiant glory; one may also see and be shocked by its ugliness and evil. The Prophet Isaiah heard the seraphim proclaim, "The whole earth is full of His glory" (Isaiah 6:3); Job, however, maintained that "the earth is given over to the power of the wicked" (9:24). Reb Mendl drew closer to Job than to the seraphim.

The Baal Shem adopted the perspective of the seraphim; the world was filled with glory, evil being but an instrument of the good, capable of conversion to good. The Kotzker did not want to listen to angels; what he heard and saw was a world dominated by falsehood.[6]

Heschel's sensitivity embraces two opposing but equally authentic perspectives: dismay at the pervasiveness of deceit, self-deception, and acquiescence to evil, awe at the persistence of divine concern and human compassion. Through his Hasidic models, he conceptualized this contradiction as rational judgment versus love and faith.

In a very strange way, I found my soul at home with the Baal Shem Tov but driven by the Kotzker. Was it good to live with one's heart torn between the joy of Mezbizh [home of the Baal Shem] and the anxiety of Kotzk? To live both in awe and consternation, in fervor and horror, with my conscience on mercy and my eyes on Auschwitz, wavering between exaltation and dismay? Was this a life a man would choose to live? I had no choice: my heart was in Mezbizh, my mind in Kotzk.[7]

For those outside the Hasidic idiom, the Kotzker might represent our helplessness in face of moral chaos. It is significant that Heschel's last book compares the Kotzker and Søren Kierkegaard, two religious radicals who could not bear the discrepancy between God and social practice, the Absolute and the fallible. Heschel responds directly to our compromises with faith, an implicit abandonment to metaphysical absurdity, and the trivialization of the spirit by conventional Christianity and Judaism.

III. Geographic and Internal Emigrations

Heschel's several emigrations within Europe before World War Two provide a historical correlative to his theological categories. Before settling in the United States, he had undergone several exiles, cultural and metaphysical, integrating within his vast sympathy several Jewish subcultures. An affirmative personality, he maintained traditions others might have repudiated as they entered the modern world.

Abraham Heschel's name changes trace a sage of cultural emigration. His full name was Abraham Joshua Heschel Heschel, for he was named after his father's great-great grandfather, the revered rebbe of Apt (Opatow, Poland), Avraham Yehoshua Heschel (1748-1825). In Warsaw, he was called "Avrohom Yehoshua Hesh'l Hesh'l" in its Yiddish spelling; in Vilna, he was known as "Avrohom Hesh'l"; as a university student in Berlin he became "Abraham Heschel," with the Germanic spelling of his family name — while his Polish passport still read "Abraham Heszel." When "Abraham Heszel" entered New York harbor in March 1940, he had absorbed the substance of Hasidism, secular Yiddish culture, liberal Jewish *Wissenschaft*, and German academia. He did not use his middle name "Joshua" (in the English spelling) until some time later. In America, he published his first articles under the name "Abraham Heschel," and then, after achieving renown, he reappropriated his distinguished Hasidic name, deprived of the repeated "Heschel." He published his influential books as "Abraham Joshua Heschel."[8]

But let us return to the first of these cultural identities. Heschel was born in 1907 in Warsaw, scion of aristocratic Hasidic dynasties on both his mother's and his father's sides. As a future rebbe he was tutored by traditional scholars, and he mastered the classic Jewish texts, Bible, Talmud, Maimonides, the Zohar, Hasidic tradition, oral and written. Around 1925 he left Warsaw to prepare himself for the German university at the secular, Yiddish-language *Real-Gymnasium* (Natural Science and Mathematics Gymnasium) in Vilna — the "Jerusalem of Lithuania" — where he received his diploma in June 1927. He had emancipated himself from the limiting aspects of his Hasidic community without relinquishing its spirit.

Language formed his expanding identity as a modern European Jew. As a child he spoke Yiddish and mastered Hebrew and Aramaic texts. To prepare himself for Vilna he had to learn Polish. To matriculate at the University of Berlin, he had to master German. In each society he remained essentially a stranger: in Hasidic Warsaw as a boy and adolescent, he was driven by a thirst for secular, as well as sacred, learning. At the left-wing, non-religious *Real-Gymnasium*, he remained an observant Jew whose name proclaimed his Hasidic *yichus* (pedigree). In Berlin, he enrolled simultaneously at the *Hochschule für die Wissenschaft des Judentums*, the liberal rabbinical seminary, and the University of Berlin.

During his ten years in Berlin, Heschel became a Jewish intellectual and academic scholar. Writing yielded the fullest integration of his cultural disparities: while practicing scientific reflection he published Yiddish poems depicting the spiritual and ethical hypersensitivity of a Jew intoxicated with God.[9] In 1933 he earned the doctorate in philosophy from the Friedrich Wilhelm (now Humboldt) University with a dissertation on *Das prophetische Bewußtsein* (Prophetic Consciousness).[10] That same year he published his first book in Warsaw, a collection of Yiddish poems, *Der Shem ham'forash: Mentsh* (Mankind: God's Ineffable Name). Heschel taught Talmud to advanced students at the *Hochschule für die Wissenschaft des Judentums* and he edited a series on Jewish subjects for the prominent artistic and literary publishing house, the Erich Reiss Verlag. In 1935 he published a popular biography of Maimonides in elegant and picturesque German.[11]

Heschel in Berlin had joined the massive revival of Jewish learning which challenged the Nazis.[12] He met Martin Buber around 1930, and by 1935 Heschel had established close communication with him.[13] In March 1937, invited by Buber who was preparing to emigrate to Palestine, Heschel moved to Frankfurt-am-Main as co-director, with Ernst Kantorowicz, of the *Mittelstelle für jüdische Erwachsenenbildung* (Central Organization for Jewish Adult Education). There and at the *Jüdisches Lehrhaus* Heschel advanced Buber's program for spiritual renewal which began to flourish in Germany, quite ironically, in defiance of the racist government's severe restrictions on Jewish professional, economic, and educational opportunity.

While teaching and preparing curricular materials for Germany's relatively assimilated Jews, Heschel had realized the necessity to emigrate. He started an intricate correspondence with Julian Morgenstern, President of Hebrew Union College in Cincinnati, Ohio, the Reform rabbinical seminary, seeking a visa to the United States.[14] But the quotas were filled.

These were excruciating months for Heschel as for all European Jews. On 28 October 1938, Heschel was expelled from Germany to the Polish border, with about eighteen thousand other Jews holding Polish passports. Remaining at the border almost two weeks, he obtained a post teaching Bible and Jewish philosophy at the *Instytut Nauk Judaistycznych* (Institute for Jewish Studies) in Warsaw, a modern academy founded in 1928 by Moses Schorr and Mayer Balaban. In July 1939 Heschel was able to leave for London, where his older brother Jacob, an Orthodox rabbi, had emigrated with his family in February. After nine months of transit Heschel obtained a non-quota visa, allowing him to enter the United States.

IV. God in Exile

This sketch of Heschel's life in Europe only hints at the agonies he endured both before and after Germany invaded Poland on 1 September 1939, six weeks after he reached London. By the time he emigrated, Heschel had defined himself as a prophetic thinker — not only as a scholar of prophetic consciousness.[15] In February 1938, he confronted Europe's moral bankruptcy in a speech entitled "Versuch einer Deutung." Heschel's first interpretation of Nazism underlies his American theology and its ethical foundation.[16]

Here are the circumstances of the event. Martin Buber had been invited to address a group of Quaker leaders by Rudolf Schlosser (1880-1944), a German Quaker and pacifist. But Buber had a severe bout of influenza that evening and he designated Heschel to take his place.[17] Among those present were Amalie and Rudolf Schlosser and the widow of Franz Rosenzweig. Heschel, as "Buber's assistant," impressed them as "a very serious young man, with strong inner concentration, [who] attempted to fathom the meaning of this new persecution of the Jewish people."[18]

His theological mind fitfully interpreted the increasing attacks against Jewish civilization that, in Warsaw, Vilna, and Berlin, was his own. Heschel's speech is at once eloquent, prophetic in its bold questioning of divine purpose, and somewhat abstract. It opens dramatically with a symbolic scene:

> Carried over the gates of the world in which we live are the weapons of the demons. It is happening in our time that the peoples are forging their sickles into swords and their scythes into spears. And by inverting the prophetic words entirely, the peoples turn away from the words that come from Zion. It is our lot that we must face that world. We learn how the vision of the prophets is fulfilled in the distortion of the two characteristics of the human face, the likeness to the Creator and the mark of Cain, of which the latter shows more and more clearly and threatens to wipe out the former more and more thoroughly.[19]

Heschel formulates devastating judgments, fearlessly and relentlessly. Somewhat reminiscent of Buber, who also spoke in solemn and biblical terms, he painfully confronts the theological implications of the terror against the Jews that would subsequently be known as "the Holocaust."

Heschel declares that God speaks through historical events and insists that religious people are ultimately responsible for exposing the emergency's true meaning. Well aware he is that his audience is composed of Quakers who heroically saved Jews, and others, from the ravages of disease, poverty, and persecution. They would certainly understand his prophetic view:

> It is a basic fact of the world that HE, the invisible, is in the habit of emerging from His distance and concealment to announce His opinion to mankind. There are two kinds of proclamations given

to mankind: the proclamation through the word to the human spirit and the proclamation through history to human life. The prophets gained their wisdom either through the event of revelation or through [mankind's] desecration of the world. And the people either received the words from the mouths of the prophets or they received punishment from the "weapons of Divine fury."

Ironically, the people victimized by Nazi persecution are the most morally prepared to fathom its significance: "No human community among our contemporaries has observed the true face of the present time as closely as those who remain faithful to HIM. The events of this hour, as God's action, affect primarily and immediately the people of this belief." He cites a dictum from "Rabbi Baal Shem, the founder of Hasidism": "If a person sees something evil, he should know that it is shown to him so that he may realize his own guilt — repent for what he has seen."

The Nazi terror — whose full extent the world could only begin to recognize four or five years later — serves a judgment on contemporary civilization as a whole. Religion, too, has failed. For trivialization of belief had diminished our moral sense:

At the beginning of this era there was blasphemy. The sanctuaries of this world — justice, peace, belief — were abused and desecrated. And then desecration degenerated to a level without precedence.

We have long neglected to consider the Name in earnest. We have trifled with the Name, using it lightly, bearing it lightly. Now judgment is upon us.

Through the millenia, His voice has wandered throughout the world. How it was trapped and imprisoned in the temples! How it was misunderstood and distorted, cheated and disfigured! — And now we behold how this voice gradually withdraws, grows faint and is muted.

For a believer, this was a grim diagnosis. God is in exile! Heschel's theology views the Transcendent as imprisoned even "in the temples." People had lost contact with ultimate truth and replaced "His Name" with idols. The present was no different from Bible times, when God hid the divine face and withdrew divine compassion from humankind.

Nevertheless, Heschel ends his speech with hope, with a paradoxical interpretation of events. He trusts that spritually aware people may recover their ability to address God. Prayer is a solution within the reach:

In view of the unprecedented profanation of the holiest of all values we are often moved by the question as to whether and how we can or may utter the Name.

It occurs sometimes that the Name erupts from our heart like a cry. Then this happens not just as an event within us but as a miracle before us: that this word is there, mighty and holy, the Name of One who is more than cosmos and eternity, and we cannot grasp it, and we know that this word is infinitely more than our life and our heart from which it has erupted. In such tension our prayer matures, and the right to call Him by His name.

If we face reality courageously, prayer may arise and release us from immobilizing despair. An active faith can infuse the unpredictable with new energy. The very tension between the world's horror and our yearning for deliverance can awaken prayer — which can save us.

Heschel's historical analysis is thoroughly realistic. He ends by recognizing that the Jews must leave Germany. Yet even at the brink of despair, in February 1938, he trusts God. His theological understanding of his people's forced emigration provides unshakable hope:

> Perhaps we are all now going into exile. It is our fate to live in exile, but HE has said to those suffering: 'I am with him in his oppression.' The Jewish teachers tell us: Wherever Israel had to go in exile, the Eternal went with them. The divine consequence of human fate is for us a warning and a hope.

These words of faith ring like a bell in the wilderness. Heschel's perspective, derived from the Zohar, that "the *Shechinah* [the divine Indwelling] lies in the dust,"[20] justifies his commitment — then and for the rest of his life — to redeem God's presence from worldly corruption. Rudolf Schlosser was so deeply impressed that, at great personal risk, he distributed hundreds of mimeographed copies of Heschel's speech in Germany.

V. Translating the Jewish Soul

This brief, intense period of Abraham Joshua Heschel's emigration years — from 1938 before he was expelled from Germany, returned to Warsaw, remained on a transit visa in London, and emigrated in 1940 to the United States — had nurtured a theology of exile which demands a commitment to sanctify humanity and redeem the Holy Name. In the United States, translation, in more than just its literal sense, became Heschel's only means of rescuing his — and his people's — soul in agony. Within two years of his emigration, by dint of disciplined effort and his remarkable linguistic gifts, he mastered the new language. As a consummate stylist in English he pursued his prophetic mission, eventually developing a rhetorical strategy to evoke the reality of God through the category of the "ineffable."[21]

First, he would "translate" and expand papers he had already prepared in Germany and Poland. Two essays in particular — one written in Hebrew, the other in German — condense Heschel's European legacy: "Al mahut ha-teffilah" (The Essence of Prayer) and "Das Gebet als Äusserung und Einfülung" (Prayer as Expression and Empathy). Both publications fell into enemy hands before they could be circulated. "Prayer as Empathy and Expression" appeared in the 1939 issue of the *Monatsschrift für Geschichte und Wissenschaft des Judentums*, tragically, its final issue, confiscated and destroyed by the Nazis. Heschel had contributed "The Essence of Prayer" to the Jubilee Volume to honor Mayer Balaban, the Polish-Jewish historian, a senior colleague at the Warsaw Institute of Jewish Science. The Nazis destroyed that book before its publication.[22] Heschel's first writings in English build upon these formulations, remarkable for their insight but still groping for a system.

During his five years at the Reform Hebrew Union College in Cincinnati, Heschel strategically placed articles in professional journals. These beautifully-styled reflections elaborate the subtle dynamics of spiritual inwardness that only a devoted practitioner of prayer could grasp: "An Analysis of Piety" in *The Review of Religion* (March 1942) of Columbia University was followed by "The Holy Dimension" in *The Journal of Religion* (April 1943) of the University of Chicago, and "Faith" in *The Reconstructionist* (November 1944). Heschel integrated these articles into his first major theological work in English, *Man Is Not Alone: A Philosophy of Religion* (1951). Heschel's national reputation was launched by Reinhold Niebuhr, America's most influential Protestant theologian, who correctly predicted: "He will become a commanding and authoritative voice not only in the Jewish community but in the religious life of America."[23]

How do we reconcile Heschel's apparent preoccupation with "mystical" concerns while human lives, in addition to religion, were threatened with annihilation? After all, he was one among thousands of escapees whose family, friends, and cultural foundations were decimated. Given his direct experience of Nazi Germany between 1933-1938, and the fact that two of his sisters and his mother died in the Warsaw ghetto, and another sister and her husband in Treblinka, why would he choose to translate Jewish spirituality? Was the recent immigrant avoiding direct action?

During the early 1940s, Heschel did in fact make several unsuccessful attempts to convince American Jews to aid their European brethren. But as an immigrant, he had no status.[24] Realizing that his influence depended only upon his writings, in March 1943 he published in English a revision of his 1938 Frankfurt speech, now entitled "The Meaning of This War," in the *Hebrew Union College Bulletin*. The next year an expanded version appeared in the British periodical, *Liberal Judaism*.[25] Rendered all the more urgent by the outbreak of war, it opened thus:

> Emblazoned over the gates of the world in which we live is the escutcheon of the demons. The mark of Cain in the face of man has come to overshadow the likeness of God. There have [sic] never been so much guilt and distress, agony and terror. At no time has the earth been so soaked with blood. Fellow-men turned out to be evil ghosts, monstrous and weird. Ashamed and dismayed to live in such a world, we ask: Who is responsible?[26]

Heschel had transformed his somewhat abstract German speech into English syntax and even more dramatic imagery. Having mastered a new language, these "translations" tragically confirm views he had formulated in 1938.

Even after the outbreak of world war, Heschel still judged all humanity responsible. A historical — and not a transcendent — process was at work. What was in 1943-44 almost recognized as the extermination of European Jewry was not a mutation:

> Our world seems not unlike a pit of snakes. We did not sink into the pit in 1939, or even in 1933. We had descended into it generations ago, and the snakes have sent their venom into the bloodstream of humanity, gradually paralyzing us, numbing nerve after nerve, dulling our minds, darkening our vision. Good and evil, that were once as real as day and night, have become a blurred mist. In our everyday life we worshiped force, despised compassion, and obeyed no law but our own unappeasable appetite. The vision of the sacred has all but died in the soul of man....

The outbreak of war was no surprise. It came as a long expected sequel to a spiritual disaster. Instilled with the gospel that truth is mere advantage and reverence weakness, people succumbed to the bigger advantage of a lie — "the Jew is our misfortune" — and the power of arrogance — "tomorrow the whole world shall be ours," "the people's democracies must depend upon force." The roar of bombers over Rotterdam, Warsaw, London, was but the echo of thoughts bred for years by individual brains, and later applauded by entire nations. It was through our failure that people started to suspect that science is a device for exploitation; parliaments pulpits for hypocrisy, and religion a pretext for a bad conscience.[27]

Heschel struggled to rescue a fundamental human sensitivity. As he had proclaimed in 1938, humanity was not alone in exile. The divine itself was imprisoned and crying for redemption. God was inseparable from historical experience. Authentic religion — with a real God who demands everything — provides both terrifying challenges and metaphysical opportunities:

The greatest task of our time is to take the souls of men out of the pit. The world has experienced that God is involved. Let us forever remember that the sense for the sacred is as vital to us as the light of the sun. There can be no nature without spirit, no word without the Torah, no brotherhood without a father, no humanity without attachment to God....

The martyrdom of millions [in this very hour[28]] demands that we consecrate ourselves to the fulfillment of God's dream of salvation. Israel did not accept the Torah of its own free will. When Israel approached Sinai, God lifted up the mountain and held it over their heads, saying: "Either you accept the Torah or be crushed beneath the mountain."

The mountain of history is over our heads again. Shall we renew the covenant with God?[29]

VI. Exile and Redemption

The year 1945 marked a decisive turning point in Heschel's ability to translate the spirit of Judaism. His articles of the early 1940s had defined his mission as a new American. He became a naturalized citizen in May 1945 during his last semester at Hebrew Union College in Cincinnati.[30] The following academic year he joined the faculty of the Jewish Theological Seminary of America, the Conservative rabbinical college in

New York, where he remained, devoting over twenty-five years of teaching, writing, and social activism to rescuing the soul of history's spectators.

In another speech — this time delivered in Yiddish — Heschel consolidated his American identity. On 7 January 1945, four days before his thirty-eighth birthday, he addressed the annual conference of the Yiddish Scientific Institute (Yivo) on East European Jewish piety.[31] The paper was published in Yiddish in the *Yivo Bleter* (March-April 1945), and translated into English, probably by Shlomo Noble, for the *Yivo Annual of Jewish Social Science* (1946). Then Heschel himself revised and expanded the English for his first American book, *The Earth is the Lord's. The Inner Life of the Jew in East Europe*,[32] graced with exquisite woodcuts by Ilya Schor, another Jewish refugee from Poland. Perhaps Heschel's most widely reprinted essay, *The Earth is the Lord's* translates his Yiddish soul into the idiom of those who shared his exile. The writer had mastered the art of evoking the delicate and passionate feelings of sensitive observant Jews in order to nurture a yearning for God.

Heschel's first two "American" books chant the refugee's kaddish in an authentic, but borrowed tongue. In 1950 *The Earth is the Lord's* responds to our spiritual poverty and the moral obtuseness — of Jews and gentiles — which allowed Hitler's genocide to proceed. His lyrical portrait, selective to be sure, strives to resurrect the inwardness of Jews who experienced God's vital presence in their normal community activities. The following year, *The Sabbath: Its Meaning for Modern Man* evokes the weekly experience of holiness, the day of rest and worship, which should awaken a foretaste of Heaven.

The Earth is the Lord's is more than a lamentation; it calls for commitment and action. Religious reality is essential to the human condition, and Biblical history judges the present while leading us to the future. God's exile is ours as well. For Heschel, inner piety is inseparable from prophetic activism. In the chapter entitled "Kabbalah," as he recalls the evil haunting Jews in seventeenth- and eighteenth-century Eastern Europe, he echoes his 1938 response to the expulsion of Jews from Germany:

> Man's good deeds are single acts in the long drama of redemption, and not only the people of Israel, but the whole universe must be redeemed. Even the Shekhinah itself, the Divine Indwelling, is in exile. God is involved, so to speak, in the tragic state of this world; the Shekhinah "lies in the dust." The feeling of the presence of the Shekhinah in human suffering became indelibly engraved in the consciousness of the East European Jews. To bring about the restitution of the universe was the goal of all efforts.[33]

So long as God remains in exile, we are responsible. At the same time, Heschel viewed exile as a source of energy, painful, unforeseeable, but not ultimately defeating. To be a Jew was to share God's exile, but sharing also in holy consolation, while taking initiative for fulfilling God's messianic dreams. Moral activism — and not cynicism or despair — should be thrust forward by a concrete, agonizing and yet elevating "feeling for the presence of the Shekhinah in human suffering."

Heschel remained envigorated by this sense of urgency, for exile and redemption were the systole and diastole of his militant faith: "Judaism is the track of God in the wilderness of oblivion. By being what we are, namely Jews; by attuning our own yearning to the lovely holiness of this world, we will aid humanity more than by any particular service we may render."[34] We must not forget, despite our comforts, whose exile we still share: "We are God's stake in human history. We are the dawn and the dusk, the challenge and the test."[35]

Notes

[1]   A.J. Heschel: "On Prayer." In: *Conservative Judaism*, Vol. 25, Number 1, Fall 1970, p. 7. This numinous talk summarizes his vision of personal and public worship and moral responsibility. The passage emerges from *Man Is Not Alone*. New York 1951, p. 147: "Dark is the world to me, for all its cities and stars, if not for the breath of compassion that God blew in me when he formed me of dust and clay, more compassion than my nerves can bear. God, I am alone with my compassion within my limbs. Dark are my limbs to me; if not for Thee, who could stand such anguish, such disgrace?"

[2]   See Fritz A. Rothschild's necrology, "Abraham Joshua Heschel (1907-1972): Theologian and Scholar." In: *American Jewish Yearbook*, 1973, pp. 533-44; Samuel H. Dresner's introduction to A. J. Heschel, *The Circle of the Baal Shem Tov. Studies in Hasidism*. Chicago 1985; Edward K. Kaplan: "Abraham Joshua Heschel." In: Steven T. Katz, ed., *Interpreters of Judaism in the Late Twentieth Century*. Washington, D.C. 1993, pp. 131-50, with an annotated bibliography.

The most complete bibliography can be found in Fritz Rothschild's comprehensive anthology (the 1975 revision), *Between God and Man*. New York, orig. 1959, with an important analysis of Heschel's system. John C. Merkle's detailed analysis, *The Genesis of Faith: The Depth Theology of Abraham Joshua Heschel*. New York 1985, also contains a bibliography and evaluates all the important criticism.

[3]   Heschel: "No Religion is an Island." In: *Union Seminary Quarterly Review*, Vol. 21, Number 2, 1966, pp. 117-134. Reprinted in Kasimow, Harold and Byron L. Sherwin, eds., *No Religion Is An Island. A.J. Heschel and Interreligious Dialogue*. New York 1991.

4　Heschel: *God In Search of Man*. New York 1955, p. 140. See Edward K. Kaplan: "Mysticism and Despair in Abraham J. Heschel's Religious Thought." In: *Journal of Religion*, Vol. 57, 1977, pp. 33-47.

5　The most notable exception is a passage from *Man's Quest for God*. New York 1954, in which Heschel describes how, as a young student in Berlin, he almost forgot to recite his evening prayers (pp. 96-100).

6　*A Passion for Truth*. New York 1973, p. 34. During that period, Heschel also wrote in Yiddish a two-volume book, *Kotsk: in gerangl far emesdikeyt* (*Kotzk: The Struggle for Integrity*). Tel Aviv 1973, as yet to be translated. See the important article of Jeffrey Shandler: "Heschel and Yiddish: A Struggle with Signification." In: *The Journal of Jewish Thought and Philosophy*, Vol. 2, 1993, pp. 245-99, and esp. pp. 285-94 for a comparison of the English and Yiddish versions.

7　Heschel: *A Passion for Truth*, (see note 6), op. cit., p. xiv.

8　His brother Jacob, and Orthodox rabbi, anglicized his family name as "Heshel," without the German "sch," when he emigrated to London in 1939.

9　Heschel's first poem appeared in the anthology *Varshever shriftn* (1926/27), published by the Literarn-klub baym farayn fun yidishe literatn un zhurnalistn in Varshe (Warsaw Writers and Journalists Club, which later became the PEN Club). His first significant sequences of verse appeared in the New York Yiddish periodical *Zukunft*, December 1929 and November 1930. See Jeffrey Shandler, (note 6), op. cit.

10　Heschel: *Die Prophetie* was published in Cracow by the Polska Akademja Umiejetnosci (Polish Academy of Sciences) in 1936 and distributed in Berlin by the Erich Reiss Verlag. The same text appears with a different title page carrying the title of his dissertation, *Das prophetische Bewußtsein*, with the dates of his oral examination (23 February 1933) and final "Promotion" (11 December 1935).

11　Heschel: *Maimonides: Eine Biographie*. Berlin 1935; *Maimonide*, trans. into French by Germaine Bernard (Paris: Payot 1936). The English translation, *Maimonides. A Biography*, trans. by Joachim Neugroschel, was published in 1982 by Farrar, Straus & Giroux.

12　For the background see Ernst Simon, "Jewish Adult Education in Nazi Germany as Spiritual Resistance." In: *Leo Baeck International Yearbook*, Vol. 1, 1956, pp. 68-104.

13　Edward Kaplan telephone conversation with A. J. Heschel, 20 February 1972. Other information on Buber and Heschel from Martin Buber: *Briefwechsel aus sieben Jahrzehnten*. Vol. II: 1918-1938, Heidelberg 1973; Vol. III: 1938-1965, Heidelberg 1975.

14　See Michael Meyer: "The Refugee Scholars Project of the Hebrew Union College." In: Bertram W. Korn, ed., *A Bicentennial Festschrift for Jacob Rader Marcus*. New York 1976, pp. 359-75. Heschel's correspondence with Julian Morgenstern, courtesy of the American Jewish Archives, Cincinnati Campus, Hebrew Union College-Jewish Institute of Religion.

15 Among the numerous reviews of Heschel's dissertation, *Die Prophetie*, appearing in Europe; see H. Wheeler Robinson in *The Journal of Theological Studies*, January 1937, pp. 181-82, and H. Bacht, S. J. in *Biblica*, Vol. 20, 1939, pp. 202-206.

16 The original German text is printed in Margarethe Lachmund, ed., *Begegnung mit dem Judentum. Ein Gedenkbuch. (Stimmen der Freunde [Quäker] in Deutschland)*. Vol. 2, Bad Pyrmont 1962, pp. 11-13.

17 Martin Buber to Ernst Simon, 2 March 1938. In: *Briefwechsel*, Vol. 2 (op. cit.), letter no. 594, p. 658.

18 Lachmund, (see note 16) op. cit., p. 11.

19 "Die Welt in der wir leben, trägt das Wappen der Dämonen an ihrem Eingang. Es geschieht in unseren Tagen, daß die Völker ihre Sicheln zu Schwertern umschmieden und ihre Winzerhippen zu Speeren. Und in voller Umkehrung der prophetischen Worte wenden sich die Völker ab von der Weisung, die von Zion ausgeht. In dieser Welt Antlitz schauen, ist unser Los. Wir erfahren, wie die Vision der Propheten in ihrer Verzerrung erfüllt wird. Von beiden Merkmalen des menschlichen Antlitzes, der Ebenbildlichkeit mit dem Schöpfer und dem Kainszeichen an der Stirn, tritt das zweite immer deutlicher hervor und droht das erste immer gründlicher zu verwischen."

20 Heschel: *The Earth is the Lord's*. New York 1950, p. 72; "The Mystical Element in Judaism." In: Louis Finkelstein, ed., *The Jews: Their History, Culture, and Religion*. New York 1949, p. 610 (in vol 1. of the 2-volume edition, in vol. 2 of the 4-volume paperback edition). I have spelled *Shekhinah* in the standard form.

21 Edward K. Kaplan: "Language and Reality in Abraham J. Heschel's Philosophy of Religion." In: *Journal of the American Academy of Religion*, Vol. 41, 1973, pp. 94-113; and "Abraham J. Heschel's Poetics of Religious Thinking." In: John C. Merkle, ed., *Abraham Joshua Heschel. Exploring His Life and Thought*. New York 1985, pp. 103-19.

22 Heschel eventually published "Al mahut ha-tefillah" in the Hebrew monthly *Bitzaron*, Vol. 3, Number 5, 1941, pp. 346-53. This and many other bibliographical items are available thanks to the efforts of Fritz A. Rothschild, *Between God and Man* (see note 2).

23 Reinhold Niebuhr: "Masterly Analysis of Faith." In: *New York Herald Tribune Book Review*, Vol. 118, 1951, p. 12.

24 See interview with Heschel (translated from Yiddish) cited by Samuel H. Dresner in his introduction to *The Circle of the Baal Shem*, (see note 2), p. xxv.

25 Heschel: "The Meaning of this War." In: *Hebrew Union College Bulletin*, Vol. 2, Number, 3, 1943, pp. 1-2, 18. The expanded version in: *Liberal Judaism*, Vol. XI, Number 10, 1944, pp. 18-21 is reprinted as the final chapter of Heschel's *Man's Quest for God*, pp. 147-51, from which the following quotations are taken. Expressions in square brackets are found in the 1944 version.

26 *Man's Quest for God*, (see note 5), p. 147.

27 Ibid., p. 149.

[28] Deleted in *Man's Quest for God* (1954).

[29] Ibid., pp. 150-51.

[30] Certificate of Naturalization, no. 6475263, dated 28 May 1945, U.S. District Court, Southern District, Cincinnati, Ohio.

[31] *Newsletter of the YIVO*, Number 7, 1945, p. 5. See Jacob Neusner: *Stranger at Home. "The Holocaust," Zionism, and American Judaism*. Chicago 1981, pp. 82-85 on the significance of Heschel's speech. See especially Jeffrey Shandler: "Heschel and Yiddish," (see note 6), op. cit., pp. 268-84 for a detailed analysis of this transition in the texts.

[32] The publisher's preface concerning the Holocaust is omitted from subsequent editions. Now published by Farrar, Straus & Giroux, as is *The Sabbath. Its Meaning for Modern Man*. New York 1951.

[33] Heschel: *The Earth is the Lord's*, p. 72. This chapter anticipates Heschel's entire theology and summarizes his germinal article, based on his interpretation of the Zohar, "The Mystical Element in Judaism." In: Louis Finkelstein, ed., *The Jews: Their History, Culture, and Religion*, (see note 20), op. cit., pp. 602-23.

[34] Heschel: *The Earth is the Lord's*, (see note 20), pp. 107-108.

[35] Ibid., p. 109.

Eberhard Frey

Exile Experience in Berthold Viertel's Poetry

"Wir gingen ins Exil wie entthrohnte Könige" (D 322).[1] With these provocative words, Berthold Viertel (1885-1953), director, writer and poet in exile, begins one of his brief autobiographical fragments. He compares himself and his fellow exiles from the Third Reich to "deposed kings" and then points out that "some of us" had indeed taken up residence on the French "Riviera" — famed playground of the world's surplus royalty — while others had to "swallow the bread of poverty and servitude": "Einige von uns hausten tatsächlich wie solche an der Riviera. Andere würgten das Brot der Armut und der Knechtschaft." But already in the next sentence Viertel hastens to remove himself from the inclusive "we" and "us" of the earlier statements by saying: " — Ich verließ kein Königreich. Meine Arbeit hatte bereits im Triebsand zerbröckelnder Verhältnisse begonnen. Sie blieb provisorisch" (D 322). Is he, or is he not a part of this group of exiles? Does he, or does he not have the right to feel like a "deposed king"? What are the realities behind Viertel's poetically insightful yet sweeping observations?

According to Joseph P. Strelka, to study literary works as "exile literature", i. e., as "literature written in exile", implies, almost by definition, the study of the consequences and impact of the author's exile situation upon his literary production.[2] Such consequences may range from subtle and momentary changes of perception or style or theme to complete reversals of topic and approach, and even total silence. In a previous article, "Stilwandlung in Berthold Viertels Gedichten,"[3] I have attempted to identify changes and developments in an exile author's literary works; and the changes, in the case of Berthold Viertel's poetry, are very obvious and drastic; but it will be more difficult to show to what extent such changes are clearly the consequence of the author's physical exile situation rather than of other inner and outer circumstances. This should be kept in mind as we proceed.

Viertel himself never resided on the Riviera — nor in the nearby fishing village of Sanary-sur-mer, where such well-established authors as Lion Feuchtwanger and Franz Werfel had hoped to weather the years of Nazi rule — but he had indeed spent some relatively prosperous years in sunny Santa Monica(-by-the-sea), working as a director in the major Hollywood film studios, when, eventually, those authors and other illustrious refugees such as Thomas and Heinrich Mann, Bertolt Brecht, and Alfred Döblin began to arrive in California, their final place of refuge. Like deposed kings in exile, these refugees had lost much of their public recognition, of their cultural and social environment and a large part of their audience, but, unlike most royalty, they could not rely on pensions or inherited family wealth. Franz Werfel, Lion Feuchtwanger, and Thomas Mann were very successful with translations of their works, and they attained some wealth and recognition. Other writers expanded their audience and their income indirectly by writing for the film industry, as Brecht and Salka, Viertel's wife, did with moderate degrees of success. Some, such as Alfred Döblin and Heinrich Mann, barely survived with the help of charitable donations from friends, relatives (e. g., Thomas Mann helped his brother Heinrich), the "European Film Fund" and other refugee organizations. The one-year $100-a-week screen writers contracts offered to about a dozen of these authors by large film studios could also be classified as charity. So much for the "wealth" and "poverty" of the literary "kings of exile."

As for the "servitude": hardly any of the known exile authors was able or willing to do menial labor in a factory or service job — even though their wives might sometimes feel compelled to do so. (Mrs. Jellinek and Mrs. Wechsberg, for instance, worked as seamstresses).[4] Berthold Viertel's own situation in Hollywood is probably the best example of what he had in mind when talking of "servitude" or "Knechtschaft." In 1928 he had come over from Germany on a three-year contract as a writer and director with the Fox Film Corporation. His weekly salary was to rise from $600 to $800 to $1000 in successive years, a sizable sum at that time. Yet, having to work in a rigid corporate studio system and to contend with constant intervention and censorship of his creative efforts caused him so much frustration that he left Fox prematurely, tried out other movie companies with little satisfaction, and finally, in 1932, found himself back in Europe with new, more independent film projects on his mind. There he soon was to get proof of the legitimacy of his exile status.

Viertel came to Berlin just in time to witness Hitler's rise to power. The new authorities in Berlin refused to grant the "Austrian Jew" a working permit to direct a film version of Hans Fallada's *Kleiner Mann, was nun?*, even though he had agreed to accept a German, non-Jewish director as a mandatory partner. Obviously, not even a partnership arrangement of such blatant ethical "Knechtschaft" was humiliation enough to satisfy the new regime in Germany. This was a decisive moment for Viertel. In a letter to Salka Viertel from Berlin dated 15 February 1933 he describes his precarious situation, announces his impending return "home" to Santa Monica and adds:

> Es war notwendig, Bescheid zu wissen, dazu mußte das alles mit eigenen Augen gesehen, mit eigenen Ohren gehört werden! Nun ist die **Richtung** im Leben, Arbeiten, Schreiben festgelegt.[5]

It is as if Viertel had intentionally stuck his head into the lion's den, had sought out this confrontation with official Nazi anti-Semitism to assure himself of its reality and to give his life and work a clear direction. It was time to leave Germany behind and take up the struggle against National Socialism. From now on he could unabashedly call himself a genuine exile or, as he liked to put it, an emigrant "honoris causa" (D 391). Viertel loves such clever formulations fraught with significance. Like the slightly ironic and ambiguous image of the "dethroned king" with its varied associations of luxurious decadence, faded glory, powerless pride, old age abandonment and abject misery, the term emigrant or exile "honoris causa" is iridescent with multiple meanings. "Honoris causa" or "h. c." is the phrase used to mark honorary doctorates or other distinctions that are not earned in the "regular" way but by virtue of unusual public service and achievement. The context of Viertel's use of the term emphasizes the fact that he was not a typical exile because he left Germany voluntarily years before being forced to do so. Other possible aspects of the phrase "honoris causa" are: 1) that he considers it an honor to be exiled by the Nazis; 2) that he has taken up the cause of preserving his honor and that of a "better" German nation or culture in the face of Nazi atrocities; 3) that he has earned his title of exile by unusual circumstance or special service to the exile community, and finally, 4) that he is a life-long "expert" on exile and emigration of many kinds.

Viertel took his self-assigned honorary title to heart, he followed the path he had chosen. He could not and would not relax in sunny California but went back to London, the outpost closest to the frightful events on the Continent, events which he eagerly monitored on the radio and in the newspapers. While he worked as a film director for Gaumont British and later as a stage director in the Shaftesbury Theatre, he used every quiet moment and many a sleepless night to write several dozens of articles and hundreds of poems of protest and warning and calls to action, of which many were published in exile magazines such as *Das Neue Tagebuch* and *Die Neue Weltbühne*.

Viertel's most important contribution to German exile literature are two sizable volumes of poetry, *Fürchte dich nicht!* (1941) and *Der Lebenslauf* (1946) with a total of 233 poems, the large majority of which are not only written in exile but also on exile and thus primarily intended for his fellow emigrants, his "Gefährten im Exil" (L 9). The poems are to give aid and reassurance in their struggle against the forces of darkness within and without. The title *Fürchte dich nicht!* quoted from Isaiah vii, 4, a call of encouragement from God to the beleaguered King of Judah, vividly evokes − as well as it calms − the ever mounting feeling of terror during the years of Nazi rule and expansionism. As Viertel states in his introduction, he searches for the roots of such evil not only in the enemy but also in his own self, his own conscience, his national and social background.

Appropriately, the first cycle of poems in this volume, "Österreichische Elegie," harks back to Viertel's childhood years in Vienna — with highly ambivalent results. "Zurück, zurück, ein Kind zu sein! / Schon hüllt das graue Tuch mich ein", exclaims the author in "Das graue Tuch" (F 11). He literally gets wrapped up in a security blanket of warm memories associated with the grey cloth or scarf of Marie, the cook, who sang all the German folk songs with him. Marie was Catholic, and that was fine as far as it represented the great cultural traditions of Vienna. But Catholicism was dangerous when it represented rigid conservatism, bigotry and anti-Semitism, as expressed in the poem "Österreich":

> Zwischen katholischen Hügeln
> Mit ihren grünen Waldflügeln
> Sitzen
> Dürre Kirchturmspitzen,
> Die den Himmel anritzen.
> Österreichisch bellen die Hunde.
> So ging eine Welt zu Grunde. (F 11)

It is a bitter, spiteful little doggerel, where the word "sitzen" occupies a whole line by itself to show how firmly, immovably the scrawny church steeple spires are "set" in the landscape so that they will "score" the sky. And the dogs bark with an Austrian accent conjuring up images of aggression and persecution. In the eyes of the exiled poet, the scenic Austrian landscape has turned into a foreboding nightmare.

A similar though more gradual shift from nostalgic memory to nightmare occurs within the poem "Schultafel" (1934) — where the year is part of the title. It starts with the loving recollection of a school blackboard neatly filled with the teacher's carefully written words and sentences: all of them designed to initiate the schoolboy into a well-established, securely structured adult world. "Erst war das Wort," the poet says in obvious allusion to the Gospel of John. But soon he discovers that words can be manipulated — playfully or purposefully — and now, in retrospect, he curses this pliability of the "Word":

> Verfluchte Hexerei! Denn alles Elend
> Stieg aus dem Wort, die große ewige Lüge,
> Betrug der Völker, jedes Recht entseelend!
> Und daß sich jeder Satz dem Unrecht füge —:

> Ein langes Leben hat es uns gelehrt!
> Schultafel! Gebt
> Mir einen Schwamm, der naß darüber fährt:
> Da greif ich's, daß der Schwamm vom Blute klebt! (F 12)

The old established trust in the "Word" — the Bible, the Classical tradition, the ethical values, the conventional wisdom — is severely shaken; in fact the "Word" is seen as the root of all misery, of the "eternal lie", of the betrayal of nations. Its propensity to yield to misuse, to lend itself to every injustice, makes it highly suspect. Thus, the author's attitude to his literary and linguistic tradition is completely reversed from admiration and respect to distrust and rejection. He is ready to erase the blackboard, to start with a clean slate. And here comes a final nightmarish twist: the sponge that he grasps for, to erase the writing, is "sticky with blood." This last image is quite enigmatic and ambiguous. It is more like a dream symbol rather than an intellectually conceived metaphor and allows for several interpretations: 1) the poet is risking his life blood when trying to erase his literary and linguistic heritage; 2) the poet bears some of the guilt and responsibility for corrupting his language; as soon as the poet, the master manipulator, gets involved, he risks getting his hands bloody (guilt) or bloodied (punishment); 3) millions of people have (had) to die for the sake of the "Word."

In his earlier volumes of poetry, *Die Spur* (1913) and *Die Bahn* (1921),[6] Viertel has included many nostalgic poems recollecting his childhood and school days. Some of them tell of nightmares, anxiety and fear of the dark, of adolescent guilt and even suicide, but none of them are as bitterly ironic and resentful as the ones discussed here. Homesickness and nostalgia are legitimate emotions for anyone living away from home, but for the person in exile they are bound to be mixed emotions of love and hate, of affection and rejection. For non-Jewish political exiles like Brecht it was possible to focus their hatred on the Nazi leaders and their ideology rather than on the German people as a whole. Brecht sees Germany as a victim, not a perpetrator, of Nazi atrocities: "Das erste Land, das Hitler eroberte, war Deutschland, das erste Volk, das er unterdrückte, das deutsche."[7] A similar argument could be made for the Austrian people. Viertel, however, exiled because he was Jewish, realized that Nazism merely legitimized a wide-spread ingrained anti-Semitism that had already been present in the population and culture for many generations. It was not as easy for him to divide up his mixed feelings of hate and love so neatly between the "evil" leaders and the "good" common folk. Even the simple working man is not without flaws. In "Der Valentin" (F 16), Viertel shows how even a good citizen like the upright Valentin, a craftsman and true "Biedermann" who sings the famous "Hobellied" in Ferdinand Raimund's play *Der Verschwender*, would now be corrupted by Nazi ideology. "Wird Gott dir helfen, Valentin, / Wenn keiner dich beschützt?" the author asks, and he must conclude: "Es überließ dich Gott und Welt / Dem Dritten Reich" (F 16). The common man's major flaw is his passivity, his acceptance, his silence in the face of outrageous acts. In "Das Wiener Schweigen" (13. März 1938) (F 23) this silence is used as a bitterly ironic symbol. On the occasion of the declaration of Austria's "Anschluß" to Germany, two minutes of silence are observed before the celebrating choruses speak the "prescribed" text, i. e., they keep their mouths shut until they are asked to speak Hitler's praise.

According to Viertel, silence certainly is not and ought not to be the poet's response to the frightening events of Hitler's strife for dominance in Europe. While many fall silent in pain, in shock, contempt or desperation, Viertel's production of poems increases in volume and intensity. He does ask himself often, as in the very first poem "Legende": "Darf man Gedichte schreiben / Heute noch . . .?" (F 7). And the answer, from the mouth of Tolstoy, is: "Wenn es denn sein muß — Freund — / Schreiben Sie — / Ihre Gedichte" (F 8). He admits in "Der Schmuggler": "Was jetzt geschieht, entzieht sich allem Sagen," i. e., the present events are "unspeakable," and that it might take a century to recover and rethink these events, "Doch, jetzt schon, heute, brauchen wir ein Wort, /... / Ein Kennwort" (F 103). Finally, in "Das zu Sagende," he stresses: "Gleichgültig, beinahe gleichgültig, **wer es sagt**; /... / wichtig ist nur, / **Daß es gesagt wird**, — nicht, von wem!" (F 101).

And so Viertel follows his urge — his duty — to speak out in protest against brute force, to express his deep compassion with the persecuted, to sound warnings of the impending catastrophe. These poems, typical of the years of Hitler's expansionism, are to shake up complacent citizens into awareness, move them to tears, shock them into action. The urgent need to communicate these messages tends to break up the traditional poetic forms that Viertel had used with virtuosity in his earlier poems. Stanzas, lines, meters become irregular. Dramatic and narrative modes of poetic diction dominate the lyrical. Monologues, dialogues, diatribes, tirades, lamentations, ballads, anecdotes, legends and sagas, all available means of expression are employed in this epic struggle of the "word" against the ruthless jackboots of Hitler's armies. One of the most effective poems in this struggle, "In Schritt und Tritt," uses this very image of military boots marching in step and crushing everything in their way:

> Tritt aufs Herz, tritt aufs Herz, tritt aufs Herz,
> Deinem Feinde, dem Menschen, aufs Herz,
> Seiner Ehr, seiner Würde aufs Herz,
> Der Milde, der Gnade aufs Herz,
> Dem Mitleid, dem Herzen aufs Herz. (F 78/D 38)

This is but the beginning of 34 lines of parallel structure giving incessant commands to step on the "heart" of enemies and other human beings, young and old, on parts of the body, and precious things, on moral and cultural values, anything that may be dear to the human heart. The command form of the sentences is a taunting attempt to put us in the boots of the soldiers or even the commanding officer. The heavy, drum-roll, anapestic meter enforces the relentless, merciless marching in step. The many repetitions of words, phrases and structure are typical for Viertel's urging, pleading style of that time. As soon as the repetitions threaten to become monotonous, a new variation or convergence of repetitions stirs up our attention, as for instance in the last line quoted, where the command is to step on "the heart of the heart" (i. e., on the compassionate heart) or further down in the poem where a line reads "Auf Liebe, die lieben muß, tritt," a line which, unlike any other, reappears verbatim one more time. This "love that cannot help loving" in spite of being stepped on obviously relates to the exile's love for his homeland even though it has rejected him.

A special effort of identification or empathy with the suffering victims of this world pervades many of Viertel's poems. The poem "Gemurmel in schlafloser Nacht" (23. Mai 1940), written at the time of the German invasion of France, begins with a passionate invocation of human suffering:

> Die in den Tanks lebendig verbrennen,
> Deren Pein die großen Kanonen überbrüllt,
> Hängen sie nicht ihren Fluch über die Landschaft? (F 118)

The author cannot help but wonder whether the screams of soldiers burning in their tanks will have a lasting effect on the world around them. What he does know is that world events, even if removed in space and time, can affect him deeply; as he says in "Wachsein" (1936):

> Wachsein: ich höre das eiserne Näherrollen
> Des Großen Krieges. Die Flüsse der Erde, von Blut geschwollen,
> Steigen in meinen Adern, brausen in meinen Ohren. (F 79)

Not only can he predict this coming war, he can literally feel it rising in his own blood.

In fact, Viertel's personal crises often seem to mirror major turns of world events as they happen around him. For instance, the love poems that we find scattered among the activist pleas and apocalyptic visions of *Fürchte dich nicht* are predominantly expressions of an unhappy, imbalanced, almost compulsive love relationship. Thus, in "Der Weinende" (F 136), a new lover weeps already in advance in anticipation of sorrows to come. Similarly, in "Langsam zu sprechen" (F 139) happy love is seen as a prelude to unhappy love. "Das Dunkel der Nacht" (F 151/D 72), tells of resistance and yielding, sadness and consolation and ends with the line: "Ich brach das Brot deiner Liebe, es weinend zu essen". In "Die Uhr schlug eins" (F 158/D 62), the lover is alone in the night, begging for forgiveness, but he receives no clear answer except for the ominous striking of the clock. All these poems of strained, ambivalent love relationships appear at a time when Viertel says of the exile's love of his homeland: "Auf Liebe, die lieben muß, tritt!"

Both emotional spheres, the political and the personal, seem to come together in a farewell poem entitled "Ich werde nie dich wiedersehen" from the cycle "Auswanderer":

> Unendlich wie der Bogen
> Der Sterne, die am Himmel gehen,
> Komm ich, um dich betrogen,
> Dir ewig nachgezogen.
> Ich werde nie dich wiedersehen.
>
> Wie ist um dich mir bange.
> Wie konnte das vorübergehen?
> Sah ich dich denn zu lange?
> Ich werde nie dich wiedersehen.
>
> Ich werde nie dich wiedersehen
> Und muß zum Tode niedergehen.
> Ich fühl dich atmen in der Ferne
> Und zieh dir nach wie Stern dem Sterne. (F 29/D 40)

This deeply moving lament of leave-taking from a lover — of physical separation that is final although the one-sided emotional bonds will remain forever — can also be read as a painful good-bye to a beloved homeland that one has to leave as an exile, perhaps forever, even though he cannot help feeling attached to it. Both lover and exile do feel "deprived" ("betrogen") of and "worried" ("bange") about the object of their love. The powerful image of the star eternally following another distant star in the firmament's daily cycle emphasizes the fatefulness of these love constellations.

Viertel's final departure from Europe for New York and Santa Monica almost coincided with the outbreak of the Second World War. Thus, a greater physical and emotional distance to his homeland was created; visions of doom were replaced by the reality of war and by hopes for a successful outcome. Viertel's narrow focus on Hitler's Germany widened to allow him to observe his exile environments more closely and to develop a more detached, contemplatory realism in his poetry. As he did so, it became clear that he would never feel quite comfortable in the seemingly "unreal" atmosphere of California, which he aptly describes in his poems "Der schöne Herbst" (Santa Monica, November, 1939) (F 81-85) and "Kalifornischer Herbst" (L 37). He moved to New York to be closer to Europe and to the cultural and professional possibilities of this cosmopolitan city. Many plans and special efforts in his various areas of expertise met only with limited success. Soon he found himself "swallowing the bread of poverty" like most of his comrades in exile. A young emigrant actress from Austria, Elisabeth Neumann, whom he later married, supported him in many practical ways, and helped him overcome his self-destructive pessimism. She is the "emigrant" referred to in "Geschenk der Emigrantin":

> Sie schenkte ihm mit ihrer kleinen Hand
> Den großen Fluß. Besaß sie sonst auch nichts,
> Die Ausgewanderte, die Landvertriebene.... (F 37)

The author continues to describe in loving detail the home by the lake that she had to abandon, and the wide and busy (Hudson) river with its boats and bridges that she has decided to make her own instead. While the river reflects the colorful neon signs of the city, its black waves also seem to entice her with a cool "peace offer". But, instead of accepting the suicide offer from the river, she resolves to present her new friend with "das all und eine, das sie noch besaß: / Den Fluß und sich" (F 38). Viertel has obviously accepted the invitation to make this new exile environment his own. The city of New York is the subject or backdrop of dozens of his poems of that time and, like London and Vienna, remains a source of inspiration for the rest of his life. While London often has to serve as a background for eerie stories or apocalyptic visions, the image of New York in Viertel's work is usually that of a city full of life, dangerous perhaps, but always strong and vibrant. Viertel is obviously a creature of the big city, and New York is for him the metropolis par excellence.

Despite Viertel's new appreciation of his exile environment, he has by no means forgotten his homeland and the war raging over it. But, as evident in *Der Lebenslauf*, he considers it no longer his duty to describe its horrors in graphic detail — a job now better done by the news media — but to expose and fight the root causes of war. Here he dutifully and ambivalently mentions the standard "good" reasons a few times: the struggle for freedom, justice and bread — so in "Die Frage" (F 97) and "Gedenkstein" (L 68) — but for Viertel the true culprit behind all war and agression is "der Haß", i. e., plain hatred, bigotry and prejudice. It is "der Haß" that drives people away to become "Auswanderer" (F 27) and makes "the dogs bark with an Austrian accent" (F 11). In "London da drüben" (November, 1939), air raids are described as "Eisensaat ... gesät ... [von] dem Massenhaß der Rassen und der Klassen" (F 88). In "Der Haß des Bürgers," petit-bourgeois hatred is described as particularly long-lasting:

> Der Haß des Bürgers ist der längste Haß,
> Der Bürger kaut ihn ohne Unterlaß.
> Wer einmal in die Krone ihm gefahren,
> Dem wird er seinen treuen Haß bewahren. (L 19)

If you ever insult such a righteous citizen, he will "faithfully" preserve his hatred forever, "chew" on it relentlessly. Another poem just entitled "Der Haß" (L 15) describes a young woman with hollow cheeks as the veri-table personification of hatred. Unpublished diary entries of 7 November 1939 indicate that Viertel was thinking of some unusually vengeful attitudes among the emigrants, which he felt to be counterproductive for the exile community. Especially when it came to the discussion of the "collective guilt" (and punishment) of the German population, Viertel was likely to reject harsh and sweeping judgments.

In fact, it is Viertel's special concern that we should all search for the roots of evil in our own soul before we assign blame to others. In the poem "Der Hitlertod" he admonishes us all:

> Seht ihn genauer an, den Hitlertod! . . .
> Hat er nicht Züge, die uns peinlich vertraut
> Anmuten, manche unheimliche Ähnlichkeit, Züge
> von jedem von uns, die uns äffen?
> . . . .
>   Ihr grabet besser
> Nach den Wurzeln dieses Giftkrauts in eurem
>   eigenen Herzen! (F 91-92)

If we look carefully into the face of Hitler-Death, he says, we can recognize its close kinship to each of us. It it is our first task to combat the evil in our own heart. Besides that, we were not vigilant enough, we did not want to see what was visible to our bare eyes, Viertel contends in the poem "Denen, die nicht sahen, was sie sahen" (F 113).

Generally, in Viertel's poems feelings of guilt and innocence are often linked up with themes of exile and homecoming or homesickness. So, for instance, in "Du kommst heim" (L 90), where a comfortable room has kept its "good character" unchanged while the returning occupant has committed all kinds of little sins and social deceptions during the day, or in the poem "Farewell," where a young man who has "stained" his honor exclaims:

> . . . fahr hin,
> Du Kindertraum vom Ehrenschild!
> Ans Steuer greife, starke Hand!
> Und steuere mutig, denn es gilt
> Die Fahrt durch keines Freundes Land! (L 70)

Driven by an awareness of guilt and error, he makes a conscious decision to leave his childhood behind and set out for an unfriendly country, a kind of voluntary exile. But, unlike returning to an unchanged room after a day's business, it is not possible to return to one's childhood, nor is it always possible to return to one's childhood home. As Viertel says in his epigraph to "Österreichische Elegie": "Ich will nach hause — doch das Haus ist fort!" (F 9). Childhood paradise is lost. Even if the home is still there, it is often no longer the same, or it is not what we imagined it would be. Viertel suggests in "Litanei der Vertriebenen" that many people in exile were looking for a dreamland, a Utopia, the mythical land of Thule, long before they were expelled from their homeland:

> Wir sind nicht aufgewachsen in Thule,
> Nicht im Reich der rechten Gesetze,
> In unserem Lande waren wir nie.
> . . . .
> Ausgewandert, eingewandert,
> Auch das neue Land war alt.
>
> Nirgends war Thule, keine der Inseln
> War das Reich der rechten Herrschaft,
> Nirgends fanden wir unser Land. (L 24-25)

Viertel himself was such a seeker for Thule, a homeland which he never had, but which he strove to attain to the best of his ability. He was a stranger in his own country, wherever he perceived this country to be, and he says so himself in the autobiographical fragment "Exil" that was quoted at the beginning of this paper: "Nirgendwo war ich daheim, mich einzureihen vermochte ich nicht" (D 322). It is this pervasive inner sense of homelessness and alienation which, combined with the outward, Nazi-imposed exile, must have enabled him to articulate the exile experience of a whole generation so effectively.

However ambivalent his feelings toward Austria and Vienna, Viertel never ceased to care about his home country even though he knew it would not be the same when he returned. In fact, as he wrote Salka before his return in 1948, he felt as if he were going into exile for the second time.[8] He did return, and he brought his experience and his inspirations from three great exile centers, London, Hollywood and New

York, where he had not isolated himself but had absorbed as much as he could, and worked tirelessly to transmit them to Austrian and German audiences in the face of much adversity. He was an expert in exile living, an exile *honoris causa* in the most honorable sense of the word.

Notes

[1] D322 = Berthold Viertel: *Dichtungen und Dokumente*, ed. by Ernst Ginsberg. Munich 1956, p. 322. All page references to this volume will be marked (D). Other abbreviations for Viertel's works in this article will be as follows:
F = *Fürchte dich nicht! Neue Gedichte.* New York 1941;
L = *Der Lebenslauf. Gedichte.* New York 1946.

[2] See Joseph P. Strelka: *Exilliteratur: Grundprobleme der Theorie, Aspekte der Gedichte und Kritik.* Berne 1983, pp. 25-26.

[3] Eberhard Frey: "Stilwandlung in Berthold Viertels Gedichten." In: *Modern Austrian Literature*, Vol. 8, Number 3/4, 1975, pp. 124-50.

[4] See Eugene F. Timpe: "Oskar Jellinek" and Uwe K. Faulhaber and Paul Wimmer, "Joseph Wechsberg." In: *Deutsche Exilliteratur seit 1933*, ed. by John M. Spalek and Joseph Strelka. Berne 1976, Vol. I (*Kalifornien*), Part 1, pp. 416 and 635.

[5] See the facsimile in *Viertels Welt*, Catalog of the exhibition "Viertels Welt." Vienna 1988, p. 29; [also published as Number 4, 1988 of *Aufrisse: Zeitschrift für Bildung*].

[6] Viertel: *Die Spur.* Leipzig 1913; *Die Bahn.* Hellerau 1921.

[7] Bertolt Brecht: *Gesammelte Werke in 20 Bänden.* Frankfurt/Main 1967, Vol. 18, p. 219.

[8] See Salka Viertel: *Das unbelehrbare Herz.* Hamburg 1970, p. 447.

Joseph P. Strelka

Joseph Roths politische Exilhaltung im Spiegel seiner Briefe

Es gibt Zeiten, in denen Autoren es sich leisten können, der Politik geringe oder gar keine Beachtung zu schenken. Es gibt aber auch Zeiten, in denen die Politik mit solcher Macht und Ausschließlichkeit nach den Menschen und auch nach den Autoren greift, daß sie sich einfach nicht verschließen können und daß sie förmlich gezwungen werden, Stellung zu nehmen, wenn nicht aktiv zu werden. Der Totalitarismus des 20. Jahrhunderts ist ein Musterbeispiel für letztere Erscheinung, und selbst ein Autor wie Joseph Roth, der zumal in seinen späteren Jahren nach seinem eigenen Einbekenntnis "aktivistische Schriftsteller" perhorreszierte, wurde gleichsam zur Politik gezwungen.[1] Da jedoch solcher Zwang dazu führte, daß sich in Roths Werk — von einigen Texten abgesehen — die Politik nur indirekt spiegelte, wie etwa in seiner *Legende vom heiligen Trinker*, so muß man zum Verständnis seiner direkten Reaktionen auf die Herausforderungen der Zeit und seiner politischen Haltung seine Briefe ansehen.

Wie die Korrespondenz mancher Autoren — etwa eines Rilke oder Hermann Broch — von größter Wichtigkeit für das Verständnis ihrer Dichtung ist, so sind auch die Briefe Joseph Roths weitaus mehr als diejenigen anderer Schriftsteller besonders aufschlußreiche Zeugnisse für seine politische Haltung und darüber hinaus für die politischen Zeitverhältnisse überhaupt. Sie zeigen zudem, wie die Politik keineswegs nur zeitgeschichtliche Ansichten eines Autors mitbestimmen kann, sondern wie sie tief auch in sein im Grunde unpolitisches und privates Leben einzugreifen vermag. Ein Hauptthema, das Roths Briefe von Anfang bis zum Schluß seiner Exilzeit durchzieht, sind die bitteren Klagen über finanzielle Nöte, die Ausbrüche der Angst, nicht zu wissen, wie er für sich und die Seinen in den kommenden Monaten wo nicht Tagen den Lebensunterhalt bestreiten kann. Dabei stand er sich finanziell noch immer wesentlich besser als ein großer Teil der anderen deutschsprachigen Exilautoren jener Zeit.

Die Lektüre seiner Briefe und deren Analyse klärt den scheinbaren Widerspruch zwischen seinem relativen Bessergestelltseins und der Heftigkeit seiner Klagen. In einer gedrängten Selbstdarstellung, die er in einem Brief an seinen Freund Stefan Zweig im Dezember 1933 gibt, schreibt er:

> Ich kann nicht mehr mit fünf Francs in der Tasche leben. Es ist unmöglich, daß ich diese Zeit überlebe. Bedenken Sie, daß ich 20 Jahre gehungert habe, vier Jahre Krieg geführt, weitere sechs "bittere Not" gelitten. Erst seit drei Jahren habe ich halbwegs gelebt. Jetzt dieses sogenannten Weltgeschehen.[2]

Der Autor, der sich in langen Mühen aus bitterer Not endlich herausgearbeitet hatte, wurde durch die politischen Ereignisse und das Exil in die alte Not zurückgestoßen. Die Dinge lägen anders, "wenn nicht Hitler gekommen wäre und mir meinen Lebensunterhalt genommen hätte."[3]

Es sind die Angst und die Qual der frühen Jahre bitterer Armut, die da plötzlich wieder aufleben, nein, aufbrechen. Stefan Zweig sieht zumindest einen Aspekt der tieferen psychologischen Zusammenhänge sehr klar, wenn er Roth schreibt:

> ... fühlen Sie nicht, dass ich leide, weil ich Sie — auch in Zeiten da Sie ein Schwerverdiener waren — immer nur zwanghaft an das Geld denken sah, OHNE *wirklich* GIERIG ZU SEIN. Wären Sie ein Harpagon, so verstünde ich es als eine Lust, bei Ihnen ist es *Qual*, die nur *zum Teil* von den Umständen geschaffen ist, zum Teil von Ihnen selbst.[4]

Die Umstände des Exils haben das alte Phänomen der bitteren Not neu aktualisiert und verstärkt, so daß Roth aus einer geradezu zwangs-neurotischen Angst in die andere stürzt. Gewiß, er sieht durch seine praktische Mitarbeit am Deutschen Hilfskomitee für Flüchtlinge selbst, wie viel elender es noch anderen geht:

> Diese Menschen des Gedankens und der Phantasie haben nicht so viel Bildungskraft, um sich vorzustellen, daß hunderte einfache aber sehr wertvolle Menschen jeden Tag Schlange stehen, um 30 francs für die Arbeitskarte, einen Zettel, für ein freies Essen, einen elenden Betrag zur Beruhigung des Hotelwirts — keineswegs zur Befriedigung — zu bekommen.[5]

Aber Roth selbst hat für acht Angehörige zu sorgen. Dazu kommen noch andere Ausgaben. Als etwa ein bekannter, völlig mittelloser Mann verzweifelt klagt, daß ihm das Geld für die Operation seiner Frau fehle, streckt Roth es ihm vor, obwohl er selbst nicht viel hat. Vor allem aber sind es die frühen Albträume der Not, die neu erwachen und von ihm Besitz ergreifen. Darum finden sich in den Briefen Ausbrüche wie der folgende:

> ... ich kann nicht mehr mit Haut und Haaren und allen Rechten verkauft sein, ich kann nicht mehr Nacht für Nacht mit wahnsinniger Angst vor dem Morgen, vor dem Wirt, vor der Post aufwachen, glauben Sie doch nicht, wenn Sie mir begegnen, daß ich so lebe, wie ich mich zeige, es ist schrecklich, schrecklich, mein Leben. Ich schleiche herum, wie ein Verbrecher, dem man nachstellt, ich zittere an Händen und Füßen, und werde halbwegs sicher, nachdem ich getrunken habe.[6]

Dieses Trinken, das ärger und ärger wird, hat Roth selbst in seinen Briefen als eine direkte und sehr bewußte Reaktion auf das Eingreifen der Politik in sein Leben dargestellt. Er schreibt an Stefan Zweig:

> Sie sind klüger, als ich — das habe ich schon damals in Frankfurt gesehen, d. h., Sie sind ruhiger. Aber zwingen sollten Sie sich zur Unruhe. Denn diese allein kann uns noch zu unseren Lebzeiten zu unserem Ziel bringen. Ich trinke deswegen, wie Sie wissen, eben, um nicht in der tödlichen Ruhe bleiben zu müssen. Denn wir können der Dynamik des Wahnsinns, die diese Zeit erfüllt, nur durch eine ähnliche "Dynamik" begegnen, eine besser intentionierte. Ich habe keine Zeit, ebensowenig wie ein SA-Mann oder ein Bolschewik. *Denn ich muß ihm zuvorkommen.*[7]

Dieses Trinken beginnt mehr und mehr Roths Körper zu zerstören. Schon im Mai 1936 berichtet er seiner französischen Übersetzerin Blanch Gidon, daß er drei Tage mit hochgestreckten Füßen im Bett zubringen muß, jeden Tag einen Liter Milch trinkt, um sich zu entgiften und nicht gehen kann, ohne daß die Beine anschwellen.

Sogar die Schaffensweise Roths wird zu einem großen Teil durch sein Exilschicksal und damit durch die Politik bestimmt. Er schließt aus Geldnot unbedachte Verträge ab, lebt von Vorschüssen, die ein rasches Tempo des Beendigens der Bücher notwendig machen, ist gedrängt, Auslandsrechte zu verschleudern. In einem Brief vom 15. Februar 1935 schreibt er:

> Es war *mein* Fehler, einen billigen Vertrag für sieben Monate abzuschließen. Ich allein bin schuldig. Aber ich habe in der Panik gehandelt, die mein Leben bestimmt und aus törichter Freundschaft für die beiden Jünglinge vom Kurfürstendamm. Mea culpa.[8]

Ein Jahr später klagt Roth aus demselben Grund: "... mein Name ist
erledigt. Durch das schnelle Erscheinen meiner Bücher."[9] Sein kluger
Freund Stefan Zweig sieht auch den weiteren Fehler, daß Roth aus rein
materiellen Gründen in manchen Romanen die Handlung zu breit
auswalzt.

Er meint die politischen Ereignisse, die sein privates Schicksal
hauptsächlich bestimmen, wenn er schreibt: "Das Schicksal bedrängt mich
in einer schrecklichen, allzu billig symbolischen Art, als ob es einen
dummen Romancier nachahmen wollte. Ich schäme mich schon der
Nackenschläge, die es mir erteilt. Geschmacklose Nackenschläge." Und
er faßt alles zu einem seiner "häufigsten Sätze" zusammen: "Ich weiß
nicht, was ich machen soll."[10] Schon ein Jahr zuvor hatte er an Blanche
Gidon geschrieben: "Dieu sait, comment cela finira."[11]

Im Vordergrund von Roths Briefen aus der Exilzeit steht aber ganz
bewußt die Analyse und Beurteilung der jeweiligen politischen
Ereignisse, und er verzeichnet sie nicht nur, sondern ordnet sie in seine
Gesamtschau der zeitgeschichtlichen Situation ein. Dies führt oft zu
grundsätzlichen Schlußfolgerungen und Bewertungen.

Zunächst ist er sich der Schwierigkeit seiner eigenen politischen
Situation durchaus bewußt, die noch weiter reicht, als es die ohnehin
prekäre Exilsituation als solche mit sich bringt. Denn durch seinen
Wandel von einer eher linken zu einer eher konservativen Position und
vielleicht mehr noch durch sein Eintreten für eine unterschiedslos
universale Menschlichkeit auf weiträumiger religiöser Grundlage hat er
sich zwischen zwei Stühle gesetzt:

> Ein paar Leute von "Rechts", die meine jüdische und "linke"
> Abstammung erfahren haben, fangen ebenfalls an, gegen mich zu
> hetzen. In den gleichen Rechtsblättern, in denen man für mein
> Buch[12] geschrieben hat, werde ich jetzt angegriffen. Die Juden
> und Linken sind nicht besser, eher schlimmer.[13]

Einerseits macht er sich in einem Brief über Thomas Mann, Alfred Döblin
und René Schickele lustig und nennt sie die "drei tapferen Schneiderlein",
weil sie 1933 noch versucht hatten, durch eine Art Loyalitatserklärung
ihren Verlag und den Vertrieb ihrer Bücher in Hitlerdeutschland zu
retten; in einem anderen Brief weist er jedoch auf die große Gefahr einer
radikalen Rechtshaltung wie jener Stefan Georges in ihrer Vorläuferrolle
für den Nationalsozialismus hin.[14] Andererseits spricht er von seinem
"alten Feind Tucholsky" oder erklärt Blanche Gidon: "Je ne parle jamais
avec les communistes militants qui parlent dans leur feuilles de moi
comme d'un traitre."[15] Auch was Österreich betrifft, klagt Roth, "die
Reaktionäre halten mich für einen linken Juden und die Linken für einen
'Renegaten.'"[16]

Eine gewisse Abwendung von seiner politisch linken Orientierung hatte Roth bereits vor 1930 vollzogen, rückte aber unter dem Eindruck der Zeitereignisse und seiner Exilerfahrungen nun noch mehr nach rechts. Das wird in seiner Einschätzung der linken Exilzeitschriften besonders deutlich. Was die *Sammlung* Klaus Manns betrifft, so ist Roths Stellungnahme aufschlußreich: "... gegen Goebbels, gegen Mörder, gegen die Schänder Deutschlands und der deutschen Sprache, gegen diese stinkenden Luther-Fürze hat sogar die 'Sammlung' recht."[17] Auf Drängen von Fritz Landshoff, dem Leiter des Querido-Verlages, von dem er abhängig ist, und der zugleich der Verlag Roths und der *Sammlung* ist, setzt er sich sogar gegen das Verbot der *Sammlung* in Österreich ein.[18] Er veröffentlichte selbst gelegentlich in dieser Zeitschrift und versucht auch Klaus Mann den Kopf zurecht zu setzen, wenn er ihm nach dessen positiven Aufsatz über Moskau schreibt: "Ich werde einmal — wenn ich Zeit habe — einen Artikel schreiben: der Okzident und Potemkin. Darin werde ich ausführen, daß ein Westeuropäer, der einmal östlich von Warschau angelangt ist, ein komplettes Kind wird."[19] An Schickele aber schreibt er einmal die knappe Bemerkung: "Im letzten Heft der Sammlung wieder eine skandalöse Glosse über die russische Herrlichkeit. Verbrecherische Dummheit!"[20]

Noch viel schroffer sind Roths Urteile über die *Neuen Deutschen Blätter*. Sie werden mit dem Epitheton "die moskowitischen 'Neuen Deutschen Blätter'" oder mit dem Zusatz, "eine bezahlte Sowjetsache" abgetan.[21]

Als Roth die Entscheidung seines Freundes Stefan Zweig angreift, Herbert Reichner zu seinem Verleger zu machen und als er diesen schlecht machen will, da schreibt er: "Ich kann kleingewachsene Juden mit dieser Art Haar- und Frisur nicht leiden. Es ist das Haar der Weltbühnenleser."[22] Später ist auch Zweig selber von Reichner enttäuscht. Als Gegengewicht gegen den kommunistisch kontrollierten "Schutzverband Deutscher Schriftsteller" im Exil hilft Roth den Autorenclub "Bund freie Presse und Literatur" in Paris zu gründen, dem Schwarzschild, Kesten, Annette Kolb und andere angehören.

In seinen Briefen, in denen er seine private Meinung offen ausspricht, unterscheidet er auch gerne zwischen guten und schlechten Juden. "Es gibt auf dem Schlachtfeld der Humanität," schreibt er einmal, "könnte man sagen, ebenfalls Etappen-Juden. Solch einer darf man nicht werden."[23]

Als die jüdischen Verleger Österreichs die Unterscheidung Hitlers zwischen arischen und nicht arischen Autoren adoptieren und nach Roths Meinung so die arischen Schriftsteller und Verleger verderben, die sich nun mit Recht darauf berufen können, daß sogar die Juden den Anforderungen der Reichs-Schrifttumskammer nachkommen, schreibt er an Stefan Zweig:

Die Juden dürfen eben nicht, weniger, als andere, Antisemiten
und Antichristen werden. Ein jüdischer Verleger, der ein Buch nur
deshalb nicht bringt, weil es keinen Absatz in dem Reich
Goebbels! hat; der nur jene Bücher bringt, deren Absatz nicht
gefährdet ist im Reiche der Antisemiten: solch ein Verleger ist der
letzte aller Würmer, ...[24]

Und sein Zorn steigert sich:

Herr [...], eben eingewandert, Antisemit aus gesicherter Ferne, ein
Judenknecht der Reichs-Schrifttumskammer; die Witwe Tal, die
sagt: wir müssen alle unter *Pseudonym von vorne anfangen*; jener
Horovitz, der sich 'Phaidon' nennt; der Klosett-Fabrikant Zsolnay,
dessen Werfel gestiegen sind; Ihr Chuzpe-Reichner, den Sie, —
für mich unverständlich — wie den Insel-Verlag behandeln: diese
Knechte Pharaos, diese Verräter Mosis, diesen Scheißdreck
verteidigen Sie, jüdischer Dichter, vor *mir*?[25]

Aber auch von seinen eigenen Exilverlegern fühlt er sich ungerecht
behandelt. Ebenfalls an Stefan Zweig schreibt er: "... mein töricht Vertrag
— wie oft haben Sie mich klugerweise vor meinen Freunden L. & L.
gewarnt! — zwingt mich leider, 60% dem [Allert] de Lange-Verlag
abzuliefern."[26] Ja, er schreibt sogar, "Mit Landshoff und Landauer kann
ich nicht mehr Verträge schließen."[27] Zweig versuchte zu vermitteln, und
später behandelte Landauer Roth so gut "wie einen Bruder".

Roths Analyse des Nationalsozialismus — wenn man ein so
anspruchvolles Wort gebrauchen will — seine Faschismus-Theorie wird
gleichfalls in seinen Briefen in aller wünschenswerten Deutlichkeit
sichtbar. Sie geht von der anscheinend paradoxen Voraussetzung aus, daß
man die Gefahr des Nationalsozialismus kaum überschätzen kann, daß
aber die Sache selbst, von der diese Gefahr ausgeht, gerne und sehr
überschätzt wird.

Die Gefahr des Nationalsozialismus sieht er als so groß, weil diese
Bewegung ein Symptom des allgemeinen Wertzerfalls darstellte;
innerhalb dieses Wertzerfalls sei der ideale Boden für den
Nationalsozialismus bereitet, aus dem er wie ein Krebsgeschwür wuchern
könne. Schon 1933 schreibt Roth in diesem Sinn an Stefan Zweig:

Es ist *ganz* gleichgültig, leider Gottes ganz gleichgültig, was in
dieser Welt über uns oder von uns geschrieben wird. Die
Wenigen, die sich auskennen, wissen Alles. Die Anderen sind
blind oder taub ... Das Wort hat gar keine Bedeutung mehr, d. h.
keine aktuelle. Es gibt keine "Öffentlichkeit" mehr. Es ist ja alles
Dreck.[28]

Andererseits findet Roth den Nationalsozialismus als Sache überschätzt: "So dumm die Welt auch ist: von diesem Stall, der jetzt in Deutschland herrscht, läßt sie sich nichts auf die Dauer gefallen."[29] Dennoch billigt er dem Nationalsozialismus ein großes Ausmaß an Macht zu. Aber er selbst, Joseph Roth, hat keinen Respekt vor der Macht, weshalb er das Phänomen des Nationalsozialismus an sich geringschätzt. Die Lösung des scheinbaren Widerspruches liegt nicht so sehr in Roths persönlicher Haltung der Macht gegenüber als in seinem Glauben an die Richtigkeit seiner Ansichten, die sich früher oder später durchsetzen müßten, so lange nur er und einige andere nicht aufhörten, sie bekannt zu machen.

> Aber ich gebe zu, daß es Temperamentsache ist, ob man eingreift oder nicht. Loyalität aber bezeugen wollen gegenüber dieser Bande aus Mördern und Scheißern, aus Lügnern und Trotteln, aus Wahnwitzigen und Wortbrechern, Schändern, Räubern, Wegelagerern: Das ist unverständlich. Überlassen Sie den törichten Respekt vor der "Macht", der Zahl, den 60 Millionen, den dummen Hendersons und Macdonalds, den Sozialisten, den Politikern der Pleite. Wenn *wir* nicht die Wahrheit sehn und *auch* vor Fürzen erschauern: wer soll denn sonst das Wahre sehn?[30]

Die Fähigkeit, die Wahrheit zu erkennen, die Ursache seiner Furchtlosigkeit und das Herzstück seiner politischen Überzeugung ist, liegt in dem Umstand begründet, daß der Nationalsozialismus ein geschlossenes, säkuläres System des Totalitarismus darstellt, das sich gegenüber dem Numinosen und Metaphysischen verschließt, während er selbst, Joseph Roth, auf einer Grundlage des Glaubens an Gott steht. Auf diesem festen Glauben, der die guten Juden und die wirklichen Christen verbindet, beruht die Hoffnung auf die Zukunft.

Es besteht hier eine augenfällige Parallele zwischen den Ansichten von Joseph Roth und Hermann Broch, wobei letzterer im Kernstück seiner Theorie auf das "irdisch Absolute" einer "Ebenbildlichkeit" des Menschen zurückgeht und nicht auf einem herkömmlichen theistischen Gottesbegriff besteht, während Roth dies tut.

In gleichsam komprimierter Zusammenfassung finden sich Roths Überzeugungen in einer Schlüsselstelle seiner Briefe, in einem Schreiben vom 22. März 1933:

> Man konnte das 6000jährige jüdische Erbe nicht verleugnen; aber ebensowenig kann man das 2000jährige *nicht jüdische* verleugnen. Wir kommen eher aus der "Emanzipation", aus der Humanität, aus dem "Humanen" überhaupt, als aus Ägypten. Unsere Ahnen sind Goethe[,] Lessing[,] Herder nicht minder als Abraham Isaac und Jacob. Im Übrigen werden wir nicht mehr, wie unsere

Vorfahren von frommen Christen geschlagen, sondern von
Gottlosen Heiden. Hier geht es nicht gegen Juden allein. Obwohl
sie, wie immer, das schärfste Geschrei erheben. Hier geht es gegen
die europäische Zivilisation, gegen die Humanität, deren
Vorkämpfer Sie [Stefan Zweig] mit Recht und Stolz sind. (Und
gegen Gott.)[31]

Obwohl die letzten drei Wörter in Klammern gesetzt sind, stellen sie die
idée maître des Ganzen dar. Das wurde auch Roth selbst in den Exiljahren
in zunehmendem Maße bewußt.

Wenn sich nur einen Monat später nach dieser Erklärung gleichfalls
in einem Brief an Stefan Zweig der Satz findet: "Was mich persönlich
betrifft: sehe ich mich genötigt, [zufolge] meinen Instinkten und meiner
Überzeugung absoluter Monarchist zu werden."[32] dann erklärt sich dies
nicht zuletzt aus Roths zutiefst religiöser Grundhaltung.

Das Bekenntnis zur alten Habsburger Monarchie und der Wille zu
ihrer Restitution sind als unmittelbare Reaktion auf die Gefahr des
Nationalsozialismus und mehr noch der Exilerfahrung zu verstehen. Für
Roth bedeutete der Katholizismus der Habsburger die stärkste Gegenidee
gegen den säkulären Totalitarismus des Nationalsozialismus. Der Glaube
an Gott und den Kaiser schien ihm das beste und meistversprechende
Gegengewicht gegen Hitler und den Beelzebub.

In solchem Zusammenhang beginnt er nun "die einzige Rettung
Österreichs" in der Monarchie zu sehen.[33] Dies ist einer der ganz
wenigen Punkte, in denen das Wunschdenken mit dem klugen,
skeptischen und ansonsten eher pessimistischen Roth durchzugehen
beginnt.

Im September 1934 glaubt er "Mitteilung" zu haben, daß die
Habsburger bald nach Wien kämen. Zwar fragt er sich, ob aus der engen
Physiognomie des Reiches der Väter, ob aus dem alpenländisch
"Beschränkten" jenes Österreich wieder erstehen kann, dessen "Wesen
eben das geographisch Unbeschränkte" ist.[34] Aber er versucht, daran zu
glauben, daß der Kaiser, einmal vorhanden, von sich aus "das
Übernationale eben schafft, kraft des 'Kaiserlichen.'" Er ist überzeugt, daß
"die Habsburger ... kommen" werden.[35] Er klammert sich an diese um
so mehr, als er fürchtet, der Untergang Österreichs wäre auch sein
innerlicher Untergang.[36] Der Kronprätendent Otto von Habsburg, den
er wiederholt besucht, läßt ihm durch den Grafen Degenfeld nahe legen,
sich den ärztlichen Vorschriften zu unterwerfen und auf seine Gesundheit
zu achten.[37] Nach dem Abkommen von Berchtesgaden im Februar 1938
fuhr Roth verzweifelt noch einmal nach Wien, um den Bundeskanzler für
einen Staatsstreich zur Errichtung der Monarchie als letzter
Rettungsmöglichkeit Österreichs zu gewinnen. Es scheint, daß er gar
nicht mehr vorgelassen wurde, sondern nur den Wiener

Polizeipräsidenten sah, der ihm dringend riet, im Interesse seiner eigenen, Roths Sicherheit, so rasch als möglich nach Paris zurückzukehren.

Roth sah die Gefahren klarer nicht nur als viele andere Autoren, sondern auch als viele Politiker. So undankbar und unklug es im allgemeinen ist, politische Prophezeiungen auszusprechen, gingen doch die meisten Voraussagen Roths in Erfüllung. Die größte Ausnahme und der Punkt, in dem er sich radikal irrte, ist bezeichnender Weise seine im September 1934 ausgesprochene Hoffnung, Deutschland könnte noch durch Christus gerettet werden, ehe ein Krieg ausbräche.[38]

Er prophezeite dem österreichischen Verleger Bela Horovitz schon im Februar 1933, daß er bald andere deutsche Autoren würde kriegen können und er fürchtet bereits im März 1933, daß nur ein Krieg die Situation würde ändern können.[39] Im Mai 1933 sagte er voraus, daß man in hundert Jahren das Wort Jude nicht mehr in der Bedeutung verstehen würde, die es gerade damals besaß. Im April bereits hatte er seinen Freund gewarnt, sich keinem kurzfristigen Optimismus hinzugeben: "Nicht einmal inserieren wird man uns. Auch nicht im Buchhändler-Börsenblatt."[40] In all diesen Fällen sollte er recht behalten. Nur vorübergehend und natürlich im Zusammenhang mit seiner Wunschvorstellung von einer Monarchie prophezeit er unrichtig über Österreich: "In Österreich ist die Lage absolut sicher."[41] Das war im Oktober 1933. Schon im Januar 1934 heißt es: "Ich höre hier ganz schreckliche Sachen über Österreich."[42] Am 18. Februar 1934 aber ist er schon sehr viel vorsichtiger geworden, auch wenn das Wunschdenken noch mitspielt: "Bei aller katastrophalen Tragik sehe ich auch noch nicht Ende oder Anschluß Österreichs."[43]

Zweifellos prophetisch sind alle Voraussagen des Briefes vom 22. Mai 1933 mit Ausnahme der Festlegung von der Dauer des Tausendjährigen Reiches auf vier Jahre. Alle übrigen Aussagen stimmen: Hitler hat im "Disastre" geendet, es gab keinerlei Beziehungen der Exilautoren zum Dritten Reich, es gab fünf Monate später keine jüdischen Verleger, Buchhändler oder publizierenden Autoren mehr in Hitlerdeutschland, es herrschte eine Art "Kriegszustand" zwischen den Exilautoren und dem NS-Schrifttum. Schließlich aber — und hier ist es nicht sicher, ob dies als Prophezeiung oder als Forderung gemeint war: "Solange wir verbannt sind, keine Gemeinsamkeit mit den 'Linken': Feuchtwanger, A. Zweig, Weltbühne. Sie sind mitschuldig an unserm Schicksal. Es ist die Partei der chuzpedigen Trottel."[44]) Nach Roths Ansicht standen eben den alten jüdischen wie christlichen Wertsystemen mit Gott als Mittelpunkt der Welt die geschlossenen, säkulären Systeme des Totalitarismus mit ihrer Gottlosigkeit gegenüber. Nationalsozialismus und Kommunismus waren für ihn lediglich die beiden Janusköpfe des einen und selben Satans.

Von diesem Gesichtspunkt aus werden manche Äußerungen Roths verständlich, wie etwa folgende aus einem Brief an Stefan Zweig:

Wenn Sie wirklich glauben, der "Kommunismus" sei besser als der "Nationalsozialismus", dann besteht Ihr Brief an die Insel zu Recht. Wenn Sie dem Fischer[45] gesagt haben, die Sowjets hätten Recht, dann müssen Sie auch sagen, daß die Nationalsozialisten Recht haben.[46]

Schon vorher hatte er an Max von Hohenlohe-Langenberg geschrieben: "Wenn Sie ein 'weltlicher' Mensch sind, können Sie [s]ich nicht beklagen, daß wir zwischen Bolschewismus und Nationalsozialismus vernichtet werden."[47]

Roth hat versucht, seinen Standpunkt auch Klaus Mann klar zu machen und ihn von der Wahrheit und Richtigkeit der eigenen Auffassung zu überzeugen:

Wenn Sie sich auf die Kommunisten berufen, "radikale Emigranten", wie Sie sagen, die Ihnen gesagt hätten, es sei Ihre Aufgabe, die interessanteren Köpfe der feindlichen Seite genauer zu beschreiben, so wäre das (*für mich wenigstens*) kein Einwand. Für mich sind die kommunistischen Köpfe der Deutschen ... nicht anders als die der Nationalsozialisten.[48]

Seine Haltung in dieser Richtung steigert sich mit den Jahren zu Verzweiflung und Erbitterung. Über eine Feier für den vor dem Ersten Weltkrieg deutschfreundlichen und später kommunistischen Autor Romain Rolland in Paris berichtet er an seinen Freund Stefan Zweig:

Wir sind toll und im Hades, wir sind tolle Schatten, gestorben und immer noch blöd. Das ist die Vorhölle, diese Welt! Bei der Rollandfeier hat man die Internationale gebrüllt, 2000 Leute, ekelhafte Gestalten der Komintern darunter, heute steht in der Zeitung die Hinrichtung von 5 ungetreuen Sowjetbeamten in Petersburg und dieser große Mensch deckt mit seiner Würde den einen Mord, um gegen die andern zu protestieren. Und freut sich vielleicht über eine Feier, die ihm Mörder aus Prinzip bereiten."[49]

Für Roth hängt es mit der Gottesferne zusammen, daß die Allmacht des Staates und einer Afterpolitik die Stelle Gottes in totalitaristischen Staaten einnehmen und die menschliche wie die literarische Freiheit, auf die alles ankommt, einschränken und unterdrücken. Dieses Prinzip sah er vom Nationalsozialismus wie vom Kommunismus in gleicher Weise durchgeführt. Daraus läßt sich der Vorwurf verstehen, den er seinem Freund Stefan Zweig machte, als er ihm schrieb:

Wozu ließen Sie z. B. auf dem Penclub eine Botschaft verlesen? In einem Verein, in dem Kommunisten und Faszisten einverstanden sind mit dem Joch der Politik und des Staates stoßen Sie den Ruf aus: Weg mit der Politik! Das ist unmöglich. Sehen Sie das nicht? So spricht man zu einer Republik der Geister, aber nicht zu einer so greulich zusammengewürfelten Gesellschaft, in der die Arschlöcher Sitz und Stimme haben, wie die Köpfe. Glauben Sie, Sie werden Feuchtwanger ins Gewissen reden? Ach![50]

In durchaus folgerichtiger Konsequenz werden gegenüber den gleich gottlosen totalitaristischen Systemen des Nationalsozialismus und Kommunismus die gottesfürchtigen Haltungen der Juden und Christen einander angenähert, ja verschmelzen fast zu einer Einheit. Darum heißt es in einem Brief an Carl Seelig:

... es gibt gewiß Juden. Aber in einer Zeit, in der Schweinehunde Bücher verbrennen, sind die "Christen" Heiden und die Juden sind Christen. Und in einer Zeit, in der das Wort "jüdisch" mehr als einen Schimpf bedeutet — nicht den Judenohren, sondern den Ohren der Nicht-Juden — kann es Mißverständnisse geben ...[51]

Darum hat er so wenig übrig für die glaubenlosen liberalen Juden wie für jene Christen, die es nur auf dem Papier sind oder nur dem Lippenbekenntnis nach. Aber auch eine andere Art durchaus überzeugter Christen scheint ihm nicht weniger gefährlich. Wie er etwa an den Komponisten Ernst Křenek schrieb, der österreichische Kanzler Dr. Schuschnigg sei ein "katholischer Kulturingenieur":

Ihm hat der Humanismus gar nichts genützt. Das ist einer jener Typen, die aus einem Hexameter eine Betonbrücke machen — und umgekehrt. Produkt einer dem Neuzeitlichen angepaßten katholischen Erziehung. Ich sehe in Frankreich oft Pfarrer auf Motorrädern. Zum Kotzen. Der Vatikan glaubt, naiv, damit könne er den Teufel besiegen. Siehe Konkordate. Goldene Telephone. Kino! Im Vatikan! "Neue Zeit"! Dummköpfe, Esel! Der Antichrist!!![52]

Als eine Art Zusammenfassung der politischen Haltung Joseph Roths, der seinem jüdischen Glauben nie abgeschworen hat, in seinen Exiljahren, können wohl folgende Sätze gelten:

Wichtig allein ist mir Gott — und, vorläufig, auf Erden, als Bereich innerhalb dessen ich arbeiten darf und meine irdische Pflicht erfüllen muß, ein deutsches katholisches Reich. Das werde ich mich, nach meinen schwachen Kräften, durch die Habsburger zu schaffen bemühen.[53]

Diese Haltung hing auf das engste mit Roths fester Überzeugung zusammen, daß "der Katholizismus allein das Dritten Reich heroisch bekämpft."[54] Dies steht zwar in direktem Gegensatz zu den Glaubensbekenntnissen der kommunistischen Volksfrontpropaganda der damaligen Jahre, doch die Zeit sollte Roth recht geben. Denn vier Jahre, nachdem er diese Zeilen geschrieben hatte und drei Monate nach seinem Tod schloß Hitler seinen Pakt mit Stalin.

Ja, daß Roth Hitler genauer und besser durchschaut hatte als viele andere, zeigen die vertraulich gemeinten Gespräche, die Hitler mit Hermann Rauschning geführt hatte und die jener nach Ausbruch des Krieges — und damit nach Roths Tod — veröffentlichte. In diesen Gesprächen enthüllte Hitler nicht nur seine Absicht, nach den Juden auch mit dem Christentum Schluß zu machen — "Aber vom Bauerntum her werden wir das Christentum wirklich zerstören können ..." -- sondern er zeigt von seiner eigenen, Hitlers Sicht her, die tieferen Gemeinsamkeiten zwischen Kommunismus und Nationalsozialismus auf:

> Nicht Deutschland wird bolschewistisch werden, sondern der Bolschewismus wird eine Art Nationalsozialismus werden ... Übrigens gibt es mehr Verbindendes als Trennendes zwischen uns und dem Bolschewismus ... Ich habe diesem Umstand Rechnung getragen und Anweisung gegeben, daß man ehemalige Kommunisten sofort in die Partei aufnimmt.[55]

Der kluge, instinktsichere, abgeklärte Roth der Exiljahre hat einmal erklärt: "Es gibt nur moralische Hierarchie"; ein anderes Mal, "daß Haß mir etwas ganz Fremdes, ja, seitdem ich fromm bin, etwas Sündhaftes ist" und ein drittes Mal: "Unter gar keinen Umständen darf ein aufrechter Mensch die 'Politik' fürchten."[56] Die letzten Zeilen, die er im Exil vor seinem Tod geschrieben hat, war der Aufsatz "Die Eiche Goethes in Buchenwald". Er beschreibt darin die höhnische Ironie, daß eine Eiche, außerhalb Weimars, unter der Goethe Frau von Stein zu treffen pflegte, und die unter Naturschutz gestellt worden war, ausgerechnet auf dem Gelände des Konzentrationslagers Buchenwald stehen gelassen wurde. Für Roth ist dies eine symptomatische Geschichte, welche die Fronten klären hilft. Denn ebenfalls in seinen Briefen betont er: "Daß ich, Jossel Roth aus Radziwillow, gemeinsam mit der ganzen großen deutschen Vergangenheit Deutschland verteidige, ist mir vollkommen klar."[57] Er sollte es nicht mehr erleben, daß nach dem Zusammenbruch des "Tausendjährigen Reiches" in Ostdeutschland die Kommunisten

Buchenwald als Konzentrationslager neu in Betrieb nahmen.[58] Hätte er es aber erlebt, er wäre nicht überrascht gewesen.

Joseph Roth hat sich aus Trauer und Verzweiflung über die zeitgeschichtlichen Ereignisse und sein Exilschicksal buchstäblich zu Tode getrunken. Aber die Verhältnisse, sie hatten nur vermocht, seinen Körper zu zerstören, nicht seinen Geist.

Anmerkungen

[1] Joseph Roth: *Briefe 1911 - 1939*. Hg. v. Hermann Kesten. Köln und Berlin 1970, S. 443.

[2] Ebd. S. 298; vgl. auch S. 438.

[3] Ebd. S. 250.

[4] Ebd. S. 359.

[5] Ebd. S. 433.

[6] Ebd. S. 432.

[7] Ebd. S. 390.

[8] Ebd. S. 402. Die "beiden Jünglinge" sind Walter Landauer und Fritz Landshoff.

[9] Ebd. S. 469.

[10] Ebd. S. 460.

[11] Ebd. S. 401.

[12] Hier ist der Roman *Radetzkymarsch* von Roth gemeint.

[13] Roth: *Briefe*, (Anm. 1), op. cit., 245f.

[14] Ebd. S. 286, 304. Zur Rolle des George-Kreises vgl. Oskar Benda: Die Bildung des Dritten Reiches. Wien und Leipzig 1945. Dieses kleine Buch wurde die "früheste Schrift Europas" genannt, deren erste Auflage von 1931 "durch wissenschaftliche Analyse der Ursprungsideen des Nationalsozialismus die drohende Weltkatastrophe erkannte und prophetisch voraussagte."

[15] Ebd. S. 343.

[16] Ebd. S. 430.

[17] Ebd. S. 286.

[18] Ebd. S. 286, 332f.

[19] Ebd. S. 385.

[20] Ebd. S. 377.

[21] Ebd. S. 334, 285.

[22] Ebd. S. 399.

[23] Ebd. S. 260.

[24] Ebd. S. 508-509.

[25] Ebd. S. 508f.

[26] Ebd. S. 348. "L & L" sind Walter Landauer und Fritz Landshoff.

[27] Ebd. S. 356.

[28] Ebd. S. 283.

[29] Ebd. S. 287.

[30] Ebd. S. 287.

[31] Ebd. S. 257.

[32] Ebd. S. 262.

[33] Ebd. S. 276.

[34] Ebd. S. 376, 388.

[35] Ebd. S. 390, 418.

[36] Ebd. S. 467.

[37] Ebd. S. 524.

[38] Ebd. S. 377.

[39] Ebd. S. 251, 259.

[40] Ebd. S. 263, 261.

[41] Ebd. S. 282.

[42] Ebd. S. 306.

[43] Ebd. S. 314.

[44] Ebd. S. 266.

[45] Ernst Fischer, österreichischer Sozialdemokrat, ab 1934 Kommunist.

[46] Ebd. S. 295f.

[47] Ebd. S. 275.

[48] Ebd. S. 305.

[49] Ebd. S. 449.

[50] Ebd. S. 497.

[51] Ebd. S. 281.

[52] Ebd. S. 391.

[53] Ebd. S. 418.

[54] Ebd. S. 418; vgl. auch 420.

[55] Hermann Rauschning: *Gespräche mit Hitler*. Zürich 1940, S. 56 und 124.

[56] Roth: *Briefe*, op. cit., S. 452, 510, 286.

[57] Ebd. S. 417.

[58] Vgl. Harry Wilde: *Theodor Plivier. Nullpunkt der Freiheit*. München, Wien, und Basel 1965, S. 437.

Lisa Kahn

Österreichische Emigrantinnen schreiben in den USA

Die zahlreichen Werke der Sekundärliteratur über die nach 1933 entstandene deutsche und österreichische Exildichtung befassen sich vorwiegend mit männlichen Autoren. Im Folgenden sollen ausschließlich Dichterinnen[1] behandelt werden, an erster Stelle Österreicherinnen, und zwar aus einem ganz einfachen Grund: Ihre Zahl ist beträchtlich größer als die der deutschen Lyrikerinnen und Schriftstellerinnen. Im Rahmen dieses Aufsatzes ist es natürlich notwendig, die Wahl der zu besprechenden Autorinnen einzuschränken. Sie könnten in drei Gruppen aufgeteilt werden:

1. Emigrantinnen, die sich immer noch intensiv mit ihrer alten "Heimat" beschäftigen, sie in einer Art "Haß-Liebe" betrachten und den Assimilations- und Akkulturationsprozeß an die USA nur schlecht oder mäßig gemeistert haben. Ihre Bindungen an die neue Heimat sind so fragil geblieben, daß die Autorinnen nach all den Jahrzehnten immer noch von Nostalgie erfüllt sind. Einige sind sogar in ihre Heimat zurügekehrt.

2. Autorinnen, die die amerikanische Kultur zwar ursprünglich als Schranke im Anpassungsprozeß erlebten, sich aber mit ihrem Schicksal abfanden, weil es für sie keinen Weg zurück mehr gab.

3. Autorinnen, die sich an ihre neue Umgebung so gut anpaßten, daß sie die USA überwiegend positiv beurteilten oder beurteilen und sich als amerikanische Staatsbürgerinnen fühlen.

Seit Jahrzehnten untersuchen Historiker, Soziologen, Sozialpsycho-logen, Psychiater wie Bruno Bettelheim und Rollo May die Assimilations- und Akkulturationsprozesse, aber es gibt relativ wenige Versuche von Germanisten, diese Entwicklung seelischen Einlebens aufzuzeigen.

Immer schon war der Kulturschock nach der Ankunft in einer von Österreich so andersartigen Zivilisation gewaltig und der Anpassungs-zwang an die "neue Heimat" alles andere als leicht. Diese "neue Heimat" ist zu allen Zeiten von Einwanderern aller Nationen ehrlich bewundert und harsch kritisiert worden. Obwohl die individuellen Erfahrungen sehr verschieden ausfielen, betrachtete die Mehrheit der Autoren und Autorinnen in den Jahrhunderten bis zum Zweiten Weltkrieg Amerika als das Land der "goldenen" und "unbegrenzten Möglichkeiten". Ernst Kapp, ein Texas-Einwanderer vor rund 150 Jahren, drückte es so aus: "Ich werde ein freier Mann auf freiem Boden sein."[2] Aber die Emigranten und Emigrantinnen hatten schon damals auch ambivalente Gefühle; einer der ersten deutschen Dichter in den USA, Franz Daniel Pastorius (1651 bis 1719), stattete Amerika mit den Adjektiven "amorica" und "amarica" aus; niemand beschrieb diesen häufig beobachteten Aspekt des amerikanischen Lebens treffender als die in Düsseldorf verstorbene Lyrikerin Rose Ausländer, die viele Jahre in den USA verbracht hatte. In ihrem Gedicht "Ich vergesse nicht" spricht sie vom "bittersüße(n) Amerika."[3]

Der Grund zur Einwanderung war für Emigranten und Emigrantinnen absolut klar und einfach: Es ging ums Überleben. Erst geraume Zeit, nachdem das Überleben gesichert war, traten zwei weitere Faktoren in den Mittelpunkt — Faktoren, die in der amerikanischen Gesellschaft eine wichtige Rolle spielen: Anerkennung und Geld — jedenfalls genügend vom letzteren, um nicht vom täglichen Lebenskampf erschöpft zu werden.

Betrachten wir nun die erste Gruppe der von Nostalgie geprägten Landschaftserinnerungen. Diese Texte lassen einen an die Pavlow'sche Assoziationstheorie denken. Sobald das Stimulanz einer heimatlichen Landschaft ins Blick- (oder Hörfeld) gerät, kommt es zur Auslösung eines positiv antizipierten Reflexes bei der Autorin — es ist Seelennahrung, Gefühlsnahrung, die antizipiert wird.

"Was du ererbt von deinen Vätern, erwirb es, um es zu besitzen ..."[4] Diese Faust-Paraphrase der Österreicherin Hilde Spiel finden wir in einer Kurzgeschichte, in der sie, die Emigrantin, von einem Besuch bei einem bekannten österreichischen Schriftsteller erzählt, der aber 1936 beim sogenannten "Anschluß" nicht auswanderte. In dieser Erzählung erfahren wir, wie es ihr ganz plötzlich zu Bewußtsein kam, daß das Ambiente von Haus und Garten, die Büsche und Sträucher, das Porzellan, die verblichenen Tapetenmuster, die Nippes, die alten Radierungen, Dinge, die für den in Österreich gebliebenen Mann bedeutungslos geworden, da sie alltäglich waren, starke Erinnerungen in ihr an Kindheit, ihre Erziehung, ihre Familie, auslösten — Erinnerungen, an all das, was ihr geraubt wurde, als sie mit den Kindern von Wien nach Hamburg, und von dort mit dem Schiff nach England fliehen mußte.

In einer Geschichte, betitelt *Ein Kind in Wien*, heißt es:

> Wie die letzten Friedensjahre für mich so fest mit den Ausläufern
> der Stadt verknüpft waren. Die ländlichen Vororte waren noch bis

vor kurzer Zeit Dörfer gewesen, eingebettet in die Hügellandschaft des Wiener Waldes.⁵

Und sie fährt fort, diese winzigen unbekannten Dörfer zu beschreiben:

> Plötzleindorf war das erste, das ich sah, als ich meine Augen öffnete, obwohl ich mir dessen nicht bewußt war; Sievering erlebte ich, aber vergaß es bald wieder, es entschwand, als ich im zweiten Lebensjahr stand. Heiligenstadt, der Kirchplatz, ein Haus und Garten in der Probusgasse, die Landschaft der Kindheit, die sich mir unvergeßlich eingeprägt hatte, als der Krieg ausbrach und das Kind drei wurde.⁶

Sie schildert nicht nur Haus und Garten in allen Details, sondern auch andere Orte ihrer Kindheit, und das in den fünfziger Jahren, als sie nach Österreich zurückkehrte, ein Österreich, das sich so sehr seit ihren Kindheitstagen verändert hatte.

Selbstverständlich litten manche Autoren und Autorinnen mehr unter Heimweh als andere. Vielleicht ist es auch nicht so ausschlaggebend, wie intensiv ihre Nostalgie war, aber es ist wichtig zu vermerken, daß Ausdrücke eines starken Heimwehs kaum bei jenen Dichter und Dichterinnen zu finden sind, die freiwillig aus Österreich fortzogen. Diejenigen, die *novarum verum cupidus* ihr Land verließen, wissen, daß sie jeder Zeit zurrückkehren können, wenn sie es wollen. Keine Regierung wird sie davon abhalten. Die Möglichkeit der Rückkehr macht sie viel weniger empfänglich für Heimweh. Ein freiwilliger *déraciné*, wie es die Immigranten nach dem Zweiten Weltkrieg sind, stürzt sich vielleicht nicht mit Enthusiasmus in das neue Leben auf dem neuen Kontinent, steht dem kulturellen Milieu vielleicht mit Skepsis gegenüber, bewahrt aber eine gewisse Offenheit für neue Erlebnisse, die ihn in neuen Städten mit neuem Lebensstil, neuen Freunden, neuen Kollegen usw. erwarten. Er fühlt sich sicher in der Gewißheit, daß sein Exil aus eigenem Antrieb gewählt ist und jederzeit, wenn er es wünscht, wieder beendet werden kann. Es gehört aber zur psychologischen (und in wenigen Fällen gar zu einer klinischen) Einstellung der Emigranten und Emigrantinnen, die als Flüchtlinge kamen, daß sie nicht in der Lage oder nicht willens sind, solche nonchalante oder pragmatische Ansicht über das Exil zu entwickeln. Für Hilde Spiel wie für viele andere, die schon Erwachsene waren, als man sie zwang, aus Deutschland oder Österreich zu fliehen, wurde das Land der Zuflucht niemals zur Heimat. Der Blick war immer zurückgewandt zum "verlorenen Paradies."

Einer der Gründe, warum es vielleicht für manche Österreicher schwerer als für Deutsche war sich eines gewissen Heimwehs zu erwehren, mag in der landschaftlichen Schönheit des Landes liegen und vor

allem an der so reizvollen Hauptstadt Wien und ihrer lieblichen Umgebung. Maria Weiß gehörte zu den Glücklichen, eine neue Heimat in einer
der landschaftlich bezauberndsten Städte Amerikas zu finden, in Seattle.
Trotzdem heißt es in ihrem Gedicht "Sehnsucht in einem fernen Land":

> Am Wiesenabhang ruh ich aus —
> Wie einst daheim, wie einst zu Haus —
>
> Die Augen, halb geschlossen, sehn
> Dort die geliebten Menschen gehn —
>
> Dann naht ein Nebel grau und feucht,
> Der die Gestalten mir verscheucht.
>
> Kein Vogellied, das lockt und wirbt,
> Die Grille nur im Grase zirpt.
>
> Von einer Axt fällt fern ein Hieb
> Wer kennt mich hier? Wer hat mich lieb?[7]

Nun muß man wissen, daß Marie Weiß eigentlich ein recht privilegiertes
Leben führte. Ich besuchte sie in den sechziger Jahren, als ich noch selbst
in Seattle wohnte. Sie lebte in einem Nobelviertel mit Blick auf den See
Washington und Mt. Rainier, wurde umhegt von ihrem Mann, einem
Arzt, und ihrer Tochter, die Professorin an der University of British
Columbia in Kanada war. Dem Anschein nach blieb also nichts zu
wünschen übrig — und doch, heimisch fühlte sie sich in dieser wunder-
schön gelegenen Stadt nicht.

Mehr als irgendeine andere der österreichischen Autorinnen hat sich
Mimi Grossberg um ihre ehemaligen Landsleute verdient gemacht. Sie
hat in unermüdlicher liebvoller Hingebung Anthologien über Exilautoren
herausgegeben. Nach einem Besuch in Wien in den sechziger Jahren
schreibt sie das Gedicht "Kleiner Park in Wien":

> Ich denke an den kleinen Park,
> wo ich so gern gespielt als Kind —
> ...
> bei Sonne, Regen und im Wind ...
> ...
> Kastanienbäume, schwer und rund
> beschatteten den grünen Grund.
> Die Blütenkerzen schenkten Licht —
> ...

> Noch packt mich das Erinnern stark
> an Spielplatz, Bänke, Bäume, Park,
> der, als ich nach so manchem Jahr
> des Fernseins wieder ihn gesehn,
> ein Parkplatz war,
> auf dem jetzt nur noch Autos stehn ...[8]

Es ist das Wien der Vorkriegszeit, das hier nostalgisch gesucht aber nicht gefunden wird. Sehnsucht nach Kindheit und Jugend werden ausgedrückt. Wie sehr Mimi Grossberg sich noch mit Österreich verbunden fühlte, wird besonders in ihrem Aufsatz *Märchenfee Österreich* deutlich.[9] Als sie die Grenze, mit dem Zug von der Schweiz kommend, überquert hat, bezaubert diese Märchenfee sie im Nu. Mimi Grossberg schreibt:

> Und die Menschen sprachen auf einmal Österreichisch — Mutterlaute, Herzenssprache. Das war doch ganz bestimmt Zauberei. Da war ich hierhergefahren, trotz aller Warnungen, und fühlte mich auch richtig gleich verschluckt und behext. Freilich hatte ich einen Talisman mitbekommen — meinen amerikanischen Reisepaß — und ich hatte mir vorgenommen, ja niemals zu vergessen, daß es sich hier um eine verräterische Fee handelte, die unglaubliche Verbrechen begangen und geduldet hatte. Und ich vergaß es nicht. Aber mit ungeheueren Kräften umfing mich die heimatliche Atmosphäre.

Und so geht es nun Absatz nach Absatz in schwärmenden Tönen weiter. Immer wieder will die Märchenfee Österreich sie einfangen.

> Ja, Österreich ist eine charmante, berückende Fee, die jedoch gelegentlich sehr bös werden kann, man darf das nicht vergessen. Aber gibt es denn **irgendeine** Fee, der man trauen kann? Ich jedenfalls habe ja nur einen kleinen Ausflug in die Vorvergangenheit gemacht.

Sie kehrt nach New York zurück, wo sie immer noch wohnt, und der Titel ihres letzten Buches, 1986 veröffentlich, ist "The Road to America".
Nun könnte der Leser beim Titel des letzten Buches vermuten, Mimi Grossberg sei auf diesem Weg nach Amerika Amerikanerin geworden. Jedenfalls ging es mir so mit dieser Vermutung, die ich ihr gegenüber ausdrückte. Daraufhin schrieb sie mir:

> ... ich habe nie mein Europäertum abgestreift, bin nie Amerikanerin geworden! Wenn ich bezüglich der herrlichen Landschaften dieses Kontinents sagte: "**Das** ist mein Amerika,"

meinte ich damit nicht "Das is **mein** Amerika," sondern meinte,
"das ist das Einzige an Amerika, woran mir liegt." Und wenn ich
amerikanische Gedichte ins Deutsche übersetzte, war das nicht,
weil ich ins Amerikanische einrückte, sondern weil ich hoffte, sie
dadurch für mich brauchbar zu machen. Wäre ich als Kind herge-
kommen, hätte ich wahrscheinlich Deutsch langsam vergessen
und hätte in der neuen Sprache gelebt. So aber, war ich bei
meiner Ankunft hier bereits dreiunddreißig und ein voll ent-
wickelter Mensch, der nicht alles bereits Erworbene im Stich
lassen wollte — der eine vollentwickelte Kultur nicht vergessen
und eine neue, die ihm nur in einem Punkte wichtig erschien (die
Constitution) dagegen eintauschen wollte oder konnte. Und gegen
diese Konstitution wird von den Amerikanern ständig gekämpft
... Ich könnte noch so manches anführen, aber — wozu?

Eine Schriftstellerin, die österreichische Eltern hatte, aber in Moskau
geboren wurde, später jedoch ihre Jugend in Wien (bis zum Studium in
Deutschland) verbrachte, war Lili Körber. Sie ist der zweiten Gruppe von
Autorinnen zuzurechnen, die zwar ein ambivalentes Verhältnis zu den
USA hatten, sich aber doch allmählich der anderen Kultur anpaßten und
nolens volens mit ihrem neuen Mileu arrangierten und nicht unter
Nostalgie litten. Lili Körber war die einzige, die schon 1932 mit dem
Roman *Eine Frau erlebt den roten Alltag* bei Rowohlt debütierte, der sofort
zum Bestseller wurde. Sie war 1930 als überzeugte Kommunistin mit
einer Schriftstellerdelegation nach Rußland gefahren und hatte dort einige
Monate als Bohrerin in einer Fabrik gearbeitet. Ihre Erlebnisse schilderte
sie in diesem Roman. Nach Hitlers Machtergreifung zog sie nach Wien,
nach dem Anschluß nach Frankreich. 1941 erhielt sie eines der Visen, die
Präsident Roosevelt für Kämpfer gegen den Nationalsozialismus zur
Verfügung gestellt hatte.

Obwohl bei der Ankunft in USA nicht so optimistisch wie manch
andere Emigranten, unternahm sie den Versuch, sich anzupassen.

Der Broadway leuchtet. Die bunten Geschäfte,
Die fröhlichen Menschen mit schwingendem Schritt ...

Doch fehlen, um neu zu beginnen, die Kräfte
Die Wunden Europas, man brachte sie mit ...[10]

Als sie merkte, daß sie in den USA nicht als Schriftstellerin und auch
nicht als Journalistin existieren konnte, sattelte sie um und wurde
Krankenschwester. Enttäuschung, aber nicht Verbitterung kennzeichnet
das folgende satirische Gedicht:

Ich sitze zwischen zwei Stühlen,
Der alten und neuen Welt,
Dort bin ich mit meinen Gefühlen
Doch hier verdien' ich mein Geld.

Dort schrieb ich glühende Verse
Und sang "Zur Freiheit, Zum Licht!"
Hier spiel' ich auf der Börse
Und höre den Baseballbericht.

Oh neue Welt, die mir mein Ich zerriß
Mein Selbstbewußtsein und mein Selbstvertrauen,
Du bist wie ein nicht passendes Gebiß,
Doch ohne Dich könnte ich nicht kauen.[11]

Leicht ist der Wienerin Marie Berl Lee die Anpassung an das Leben in
Amerika auch nicht gefallen. Es gab Jahre des Schwankens, in denen sie,
die als Schulmädel mit den Eltern in die USA emigriert war, in denen sie
sich halb dorthin halb hierhin gezogen fühlte. Für sie ist es auch charak-
teristisch, daß sie nicht nur auf deutsch, sondern auch auf englisch
schreibt. Dieses Schwanken drückt sich in ihrem Gedicht "Des
Auswanderers Rückkehr" so aus:

Zwischen zwei Welten
schwanke ich.
Der silberne Stahlvogel flitzt
blitzend ins Blaue —
hin wo die Linde blüht
im alten Hof
und der Leiermann spielt
das altbekannte Lied
von Leid und Vergessen.

Und ich kann dich nicht vergessen,
altgewohntes Haus,
altvertrauten Kummer,
Kindheltswelt.

Wie vom Feuerengel
vertrieben aus dem Paradies
verließ ich dich,
gehetzt auf wilder Flucht.
Eine neue Heimat fand ich,
wollte nichts mehr von dir wissen.

Warum, warum denn
hab ich mich zurückgewandt,
der Salzsäule in Sodom vergessen?

Hin ist die schwererrungene Ruh.
Ach Kindheitsleid,
Du zerrst an mir wie die Nabelschnur,
zerrst mich zurück
von den Glaspalästen überm Meer
in den alten Kummer.

Und zwischen zwei Welten schwankend
gibt's kein Zurück.[12]

Wie Mimi Grossberg so schwankte auch Berl Lee zwischen zwei Welten,
aber sie schwankte doch nicht so sehr, als daß sie nach Österreich
zurückgegangen wäre. In dem sehr ahnungsvollen Gedicht "In die
Catskills gekommen" kontrastiert sie diese amerikanische Hügelkette mit
den Alpen:

Sonnenumzitterte Hügel,
    sanft wie die Mutterbrust
    träumen in blauen Weiten —
fern von Europas Totengebirgen.

Uralter Friede herrscht hier,
wo der Mohawk einsam durch die Ufer zieht
und das Gras noch Siegel trägt
    längstervergangener Stämme.

Kuhglocken tönen feucht-ruhig,
wie die Augen der Tiere,
die grasend nur Frieden wiederkauen.
    Keine Armesünderglocke wimmert.

Du, dem der Tod in den Adern pocht,
bleib stehen mit fliegenden Pulsen:
Schlohweiß gleißen die Farmhäuser
    wie Kindergräber,
wo dein Leben eingescharrt liegt.

Sitzt dir der Tod noch im Nacken?
Vielleicht, in diesen Weiten,
   so groß, so still,
gleitet er sacht zu Boden,
verliert sich im stummen Nicken
   des sensengeweihten
jungen Korns?[13]

Die Catskills sind "sonnenumzittert", sanft wie die Mutterbrust, kein
Totengebirg wie die Alpen. Es herrscht sogar der Friede grasender Kühe,
es wimmert keine Armesünderglocke wie im fernen Österreich. Und die
Dichterin, die vor einigen Jahren an Krebs starb und vielleicht schon um
ihr Schicksal wußte, als sie diese Verse schrieb, empfindet, daß der Tod
in diesen großen stillen Weiten sacht zu Boden gleiten wird. Es wird ein
sanfter Tod sein. In der Heimat wäre es ein gewalttätiger, grausamer
gewesen.

Margarete Kollisch stellt ihre Enttäuschung über Amerika im Symbol
der Freiheitsstatue dar:

Freiheitsstatue im Nebel

Damals war der Himmel märchenblau,
als sie mich empfing, die große Dame.
Leuchtend zog und lockte mich ihr Name,
den ich segnete aus ferner Schau.

Der Empfang war freundlich, aber lau.
Niemals nahm sie mich in beide Arme,
daß mein kranker Mut darin erwärme.
Heute ist sie eine Nebelfrau.

Tiefergraut in sternenlosen Nächten,
Dunst verschleiert ihre Hochgestalt.
Ist sie noch von Hoffnungsgrün umwallt?
Glüht die Fackel noch in ihrer Rechten?

Ach, sie möchte sich wie einst verfechten,
doch lhr Frauenherz ist müd' und alt.[14]

In ihrem Gedicht "Rückblendung," das den Untertitel "zwischen
Semmering und New Hampshire" trägt, drückt sie ebenfalls ihr Leid über
ihre "ungeheilten Wunden" im ersten Vers aus:

In der alten Heimat grünster Grüne
stillesteht mein Atem auf Sekunden,
tropft mein Lebenssaft aus ungeheilten Wunden,
der verbrauchten Tage letzte Sühne.

Warum irrt mein Blick aus grünster Grüne
zu dem jungen Tann an Straßenrändern,
der mir Hoffnung gab in unbekannten Ländern,
den ich herzuzaubern mich erkühne?

Wie sich Grün im Grün in eins verblendet,
Moos und Farn und dunkelndes Gezweige,
weiß nicht, ob ich abwärts, ob ich aufwärts steige,
immer noch der Lichtung zugewendet.[15]

Ihr Lyrikband trägt den Titel dieses Gedichtes, das in seiner letzten
Strophe das Grün der Heimat mit dem Grün der Zukunft vereint.
Obschon die Dichterin sagt, sie wisse nicht, ob sie abwärts, ob aufwärts
steige, so klingt doch die letzte Zeile positiv und optimistich: Sie wendet
sich der Lichtung zu.

Berl Lee und Kollisch stellen − meinem Empfinden nach − den
Übergang zwischen notwendiger Angepaßtheit an das Leben in Amerika
und der ganz betonten positiven Einstellung diesem Lande gegenüber
dar. (Im Falle Berl Lees haben meine persönlichen Gespräche mit ihr dies
bestätigt.)

In die dritte Gruppe der Emigrantinnen, die sich bewußt den USA
gegenüber zugewandt haben, gehört an erster Stelle wohl Franzi Ascher
Nash, die Tochter Aschers, des Wiener Operettenkomponisten, die bis zu
ihrem Ableben November 1991 in Pennsylvanien ansässig war. Lassen
wir sie selbst sprechen. In ihrem Aufsatz, "New York − Ankunft und
Anfang", heißt es:

Meine ersten Wochen und Monate in New York, ab 4. Dezember
1938, waren im Herzen, im Kopf, im Fühlen, im Denken eine
Groteske.... Ich war gerettet in New York. Nicht nur das. Ich war
mit meinen Eltern beisammen. Natürlich hatten wir kein Geld,
aber wir waren beisammen, heil und gesund. Dies sollte den
Grundton meines Empfindens bestimmt haben. Eben dies war
nicht der Fall. Ich fühlte mich versklavt und wütend, weil die
liebliche Ästhetik der Wiener Umgebung mir genommen war. Mir
mißfielen die engbrüstigen Häuser von New York, und es waren
die Fenster, die mir, geradezu körperlich fühlbar, am wehesten
taten.

Und sie fährt nun fort, die Häßlichkeit dieser Fenster zu beschreiben, die als Symbol für alle Häßlichkeiten New Yorks gelten. Dann erzählt sie, wie sie im späten April 1939 die Weltausstellung in New York mit ihren Eltern besuchte. Mit der U-Bahn in Queens fahren sie dann heim. Sie blickt aus dem Fenster des Wagens, langsam nähern sie sich den Konturen Manhattans, dann des Empire State Building. Sie schreibt nun:

> Und während dieser Hochbahnfahrt in der Richtung von Manhattan war etwas in mir, das diesem Anblick zustimmte. Der Zug näherte sich der Insel Manhattan, und in mir war nichts, was mich etwa von dieser Annäherung wegziehen wollte. Im Gegenteil. Es war ein dunkles, namenloses, unerklärliches, warmes Hingezogensein, die erste Vorahnung eines Nachhausefahrens — Nach Hause, nach New York.[16]

Marianne Ultmann, relativ unbekannt, da sie nur wenig veröffentlicht hat, gehörte 1938 zur letzten Gruppe jüdischer Studenten und Studentinnen, die noch an der Universität Wien graduieren durften. Nach ihrer Ankunft 1939 in den USA, mußte sie sich in einer Reihe von z. T. manuellen Berufen durchschlagen, sie paßte sich aber relativ schnell an das Leben in den USA an und wechselte etwa 1960 in ihrer lyrischen Tätigkeit vom Deutschen zum Englischen. "Von 1960-1980 habe ich weitaus mehr englische Gedichte geschrieben als deutsche von 1940-1960," sagte sie. Das Gedicht "Verlor'nes Lied" ist eines ihrer letzten deutschen Texte:

> Wo irrst du einsam in der Welt herum —
> Und bist wie einer, der am Ufer saß,
> In dunklen Stunden seiner selbst vergaß
> Und wirst vom Trauern heimatlos und stumm.
>
> Oh, frag nicht mehr: woher? wohin? warum?
> Erfüllt ist deines Suchens müdes Maß —
> Den Schmerz, von dem die Seele nie genaß,
> Laß hinter dir und sieh dich nicht mehr um.
>
> Kehr heim zu mir, o Wort, das nicht mehr schallt!
> Erweck die Stimme, daß sie nicht verzage —
> Ich harre dein mit jedem Stundenschlage,
>
> Ich bin dein Sinn, dein Ziel, dein Aufenthalt.
> Komm, meiner Hände Kraft gibt dir Gestalt
> Und du wirst singen wie am ersten Tage.[17]

Das folgende Gedicht, "Abschied von Wien," wurde zuerst auf englisch konzipiert, von ihr dann später ins Deutsche übertragen.

> Erinnerung ist lahm —
> Die Zeit ist tot.
> "Einst" ist vorbei und soll nicht mehr ersteh'n.
>
> Gespenstisch weilen Schatten, fremd und stumm,
> Mit Augen schauend, ohne Licht zum Seh'n,
> Mit Händen langend, ohne Kraft zum Griff.
>
> Leblose Formen, einst ein Teil von mir —
> Zwischen "Mir Selbst" und jenen
> Brach der Abgrund.
> Ich weich zurück in Angst,
> Mir graut vor ihnen,
> Mir graut vor ihrem Anblick, drohend nah' —
> Doch ihre Nähe reicht nicht bis zu mir.
>
> Ich wende mich — und eine müde Sonne
> Erhellt für einen flücht'gen Augenblick
> Mit einem Strahl des Mitleids ihre Züge —
> Ein Tal wird sichtbar, ein gewund'ner Fluß
> Sie senden einen schnellen Abschiedsgruß
> An die noch schneller Scheidende
> Mit süß verlockend, tödlich-wundem Ruf.
>
> Dann neige ich mein Haupt,
> um sie zu trauern.[18]

Nicht nur wird aus beiden deutlich, daß Ultmann ihre ursprüngliche Heimat geistig und emotional längst hinter sich gelassen und eine neue lebensbejahende Existenz in der es keine Nostalgie gibt, aufgebaut hat, sie ist auch die einzige der von mir befragten Frauen, die sich von der deutschen Sprache abgewandt hat. Sie sagt: "ich lebe und schreibe in derselben Sprache: Englisch."[19] Ihr Abschied von Wien ist ein endgültiger. Sie ist — meines Wissens nach — nie wieder nach Wien zurückgefahren, auch nicht besuchsweise.

Es wären diesen Autorinnen noch andere hinzuzufügen[20], aber die Fülle der Namen macht dies im Rahmen eines kurzen Aufsatzes unmöglich. Abschließend muß jedoch eine Autorin zitiert werden, eine gebürtige Pragerin, also aus dem ehemaligen k. u. k. Gebiet stammend, weil sie in der Exilliteratur fast nie erwähnt und immer von ihrem Mann überschattet wird. Das ist Gertrud Urzidil. Auch sie gehört in die dritte Gruppe, nämlich derer, die sich überwiegend positiv auf Amerika einstellten. Sie verstarb leider schon 1977.

Großes Geschick

Mein Herzstück blieb in Prag zurück.
In Amerika leb ich auf Reisen.
Das steigert den Alltag zu großem Geschick,
er bewegt sich in neuen Geleisen.

Die Kindheit meldet sich wieder zu Wort:
Lern lesen, schreiben und gehen!
Dann wirst du auch am fernsten Ort
die Proben der Fremde bestehen.[21]

Gewiß ein Herzstück, so gesteht sie, blieb in Prag zurück, aber das Schicksal in der Fremde wird gemeistert, ist man nur willens wieder neu "lesen, schreiben und gehen" zu lernen. Sie hätte noch "sehen und hören" hinzufügen können. Als letztes Gedicht sei Urzidils "Des Dichters Heimat" zitiert, in dem sie auf eine Ansicht Johannes Urzidils zurückgreift, die in mancher Hinsicht richtig ist, obwohl Ultmann sie entschieden abgelehnt hat.[22]

So mancher Dichter ruht im fremden Land,
denk nur an Joyce, Roth, Mann und Urzidil.
Der Tod wird nicht vom Zufall ausgesandt,
Es wohnen solche Geister im Exil.
Ich wiederhole jenes Letzgenannten Satz,
auf daß er immer mit uns bleibe:
Als Heimat gelte nicht allein der Kindheit Platz,
"Denn meine Heimat ist das, was ich schreibe."[23]

Urzidils Beobachtung beschreibt das Schicksal der meisten in diesem Essay erwähnten Emigrantinnen, denen keine so perfekte Integration gelungen ist, obschon sie von etlichen erstrebt und auch bis zu einem gewissen Grad erreicht wurde.

Auf die Frage "Wer bin ich?" gibt es viele Antworten und doch keine endgültige. Der bekannte Psychoanalytiker Erik H. Erikson definierte das Ich als "raum-zeit-bedingt". Wir in unserer Zeit sind fast alle in die Lage gebracht worden, ein neues Leben zu beginnen. Dieser Prozeß ist für viele Menschen heutzutage Grundlage ihrer Existenz. Anthropologen sprechen vom Territorium und vom Menschen als homo territorialis. So verstanden ist das Ziel des territorialen Menschen der Erwerb von

"Heimat." Wenn der Mensch gewaltsam aus der ursprünglichen Heimat vertrieben wird, hängt er mehr an ihr, als wenn er sie freiwillig aufgibt, um sich eine neue Heimat zu suchen. Das war eben bei vielen der österreichischen Autoren und Autorinnen der Fall. Der zweite Grund, warum es für österreichische Emigranten und Emigrantinnen besonders schwer zu sein schien oder scheint, in der neuen Umgebung "heimisch" zu werden, ist wohl ästhetischer Art. Amerikanische Städte können sich — auch wenn sie interessant sind (wie New York) oder landschaftlich von großer Schönheit (wie an der Westküste oder in den Rocky Mountains) — doch nie mit dem Charme und Zauber Wiens messen.

Für viele Autorinnen wurde der subjektiv erlebte Satisfaktionsraum zur "Heimat." Wenn jedoch die Satisfaktion ausblieb oder den Erwartungen, die oft auch viel zu hoch gestellt waren, nicht entsprach, wurde der Mangel an "Heimat", eben die Heimatslosigkeit, umso stärker empfunden. Es kam dann zum Erlebnis der Unbehaustheit, das wir ja schon bei Rilke finden. Bar jeder Utopie wird dann versucht, durch das Schreiben, durch den Text zu existieren. Das literarische Universum ist ein weit größeres Gebiet als ein nationales Staatengebilde. Rilkes Vorstellung von einer "Beheimatung in der Heimatlosigkeit" könnte man die Metapher von einer "Beheimatung in der Sprache" gegenüberstellen, die das Schicksal der hier erwähnten Autorinnen evoziert.

Sicherlich muß abschließend auch die Frage nach dem Wert dieser deutschsprachigen Literatur gestellt werden. Margarita Pazi hat in einem Aufsatz über deutschsprachige Literatur in Israel diese Frage aufgeworfen und dahingehend beantwortet, daß an diese Literatur zusätzliche Maßstäbe zu den rein literaturästhetischen angelegt werden müssen. "In erster Linie ist diese Literatur als Ausdruck geistiger Kraft und seelischen Mutes zu werten; die Tatsache, unter welchen Umständen und in welcher Sprache sie geschrieben wurde — die damit verbunden existentiellen und emotionellen Schwierigkeiten — muß gewürdigt werden."[24] Für die Emigrantenliteratur der Österreicherinnen in den USA trifft das ebenfalls zu.

Anmerkungen

[1] Siehe auch Lisa Kahn: *Reisegepäck Sprache*. München 1979; Lisa Kahn und Jerry Glenn: *In Her Mother's Tongue*. Denver 1983. Vgl. auch Lisa Kahn: *Kleinkunst aus Amerika*. Wien 1965; *Austrian Writers in the United States*. New York 1968; *Österreichs literarische Emigration in den Vereinigten Staaten 1938*. Wien, Frankfurt/Main, Zürich 1970; *Österreichische Autoren in Amerika* (mit Viktor Suchhy), Katalog für das Amerika-Haus, Wien 1970; *Österreichisches aus Amerika*. Wien 1973; *Die k. u. k. Armee in der österreichischen Satire*. Wien 1974; *Amerika im Austro-Amerikanischen Gedicht*. Wien 1978; *1938: Geschichte im Gedicht*. New York 1982.

2   Ernst Kapp: "I will be a free man in a free earth." In: Glen Lich: *The German Texans.* San Antonio 1981, S. 3.

3   Rose Ausländer: *Ein Stück weiter.* Hg. v. Berndt Mosblech. Köln 1979, S. 55.

4   Hilde Spiel: *Kleine Schritte.* München 1976, S. 22.

5   Ebd. S. 9.

6   Ebd. S. 9.

7   Maria Weiß: unveröffentlichtes Gedicht.

8   Mimi Grossberg: *Gedichte und Kleine Prosa.* Wien 1972, S. 58.

9   Mimi Grossberg: *The Road to America.* New York 1986.

10   Unveröffentlichtes Gedicht in einem Brief von Lili Körber an Lisa Kahn geschickt.

11   Ebenfalls unveröffentlichtes Gedicht an Lisa Kahn geschickt.

12   Kahn (Anm. 1), S. 67.

13   Ebd. S. 65.

14   Ebd. S. 185.

15   Margarete Kollisch: *Gedichte und Prosa.* Wien 1981, S. 9.

16   Franzi Ascher-Nash: *Essays aus jüngster Zeit.* Saarbrücken 1975, S. 153-155.

17   Kahn (Anm. 1), S. 363.

18   Ebd. S. 367.

19   In einem Interview in New York mit der Verfasserin.

20   Zum Beispiel Helen Adolf, Ruth Selke Eissler, Anna Krommer, wenn wir uns auf gebürtige Österreicherinnen beschränken wollen.

21   Kahn (Anm. 1), S. 369.

22   Siehe auch *Zeitschrift für Kulturaustausch,* Band 39, 1989.

23   Kahn (Anm. 1), S. 371.

24   Margarita Pazi: *Deutsche Kultur, Sprache und Literatur in Israel.* In: *impressum* Band 4/5, 1988, S.4.

II.

Stefan Zweig und sein Freundeskreis

Stefan Zweig and His Friends

Donald G. Prater

Die letzten Zeugen der dritten großen Austreibung unserer sogenannten Rasse: Stefan Zweig im Exil[1]

Die Vorfahren Stefan Zweigs stammten aus weit auseinanderliegenden Gebieten des kaiserlich-königlichen Imperiums, aus dem Vorarlberg und aus Mähren. Der Großvater mütterlicherseits, Joseph Brettauer, wurde in Hohenems geboren, übersiedelte nach Ancona, wo er über zwanzig Jahre als Bankier und Geschäftsmann florierte und wo seine Tochter Ida, Stefan Zweigs Mutter, geboren wurde, bis er in den siebziger Jahren des vorigen Jahrhunderts als schon reicher Mann nach Wien zog. Der Vater, Moritz Zweig, ebenfalls in jenen Jahren nach Wien gezogen, stammte aus Mähren, hatte aber als Dreißigjähriger eine kleine Weberei in Reichenberg gegründet und sie allmählich durch methodische Leitung und vor allem vorsichtige Geschäftsprinzipien zu einem der größten Textilunternehmen Böhmens ausgebaut.

Aus diesen knappen genealogischen Fakten lassen sich zwei Aspekte hervorheben, die sich als kennzeichnend für Stefan Zweigs Gesinnung und Lebenswerk erweisen: das Kosmopolitische und die Assimilierung. Die Juden dieser wohlhabenden oberen Mittelklasse Wiens, in die er 1881 hineingeboren wurde, hatten sich zu einer Gemeinde entwickelt, deren Assimilierung zur supranationalen, ja europäischen Kultur der Hauptstadt bis zur Jahrhundertwende fast total war — vielmehr also im Sinne eines Hinaufdrängens in die Welt des Adels als Assimilierung im Religiösen. "Wie die meisten Österreicher," bekannte Zweig gegen Ende seines Lebens, "bin ich sehr lax in Dingen des Glaubens erzogen"[2]: wenngleich ein Konvertieren selten in Frage kam, so war der Glaube nicht mehr das Zentrale, gab nicht mehr die Lebensrichtlinie. Reichtum diente ihnen nicht zur äußeren Schau, sondern zur Kultur im weitesten Sinne, zur Literatur, zur Kunst, in einer Umgebung, wo jeder Bürger (wie er rückblickend sagte) "unbewußt zum Übernationalen, zum Kosmopolitischen, zum Weltbürger erzogen" wurde. Mit Recht schrieb er in seinen "Erinnerungen eines Europäers", in *Die Welt von gestern*: "Neun Zehntel von dem, was die Welt als Wiener Kultur des 19. Jahrhunderts feierte, war eine vom Wiener Judentum geförderte, genährte, oder sogar schon selbstgeschaffene Kultur."[3] Das Judentum, das Jude-Sein, wurde nicht vergessen oder gar verleugnet, es bedeutete damals aber wenig in der konzilianten Atmosphäre der francisco-josefinischen Welt, wurde als ein Selbstverständliches hingenommen.

Dreimal aber in seinem Leben stand Zweig vor der Notwendigkeit, sich über dieses Selbstverständliche hinaus mit seinem Judentum und seinem jüdischen Erbe auseinanderzusetzen: um die Jahrhundertwende, als er mit Theodor Herzl zusammenkam und über die Idee des Zionismus nachdenken mußte; im ersten Weltkrieg, als er mit seinem Drama *Jeremias* das rettende Prinzip der Gewaltlosigkeit auf die Fahne erhob; und erst recht in den dreißiger Jahren, als die Weltkrise und der scheinbar unaufhaltsame Aufstieg des Nationalsozialismus eine verhängnisvolle Zukunft für die Juden Mitteleuropas verhieß, und ihn – den pessimistisch Vorausahnenden, durch seine "Witterung für politisches Unheil" wie durch "einen entzündeten Nerv" Gequälten[4] – frühzeitig ins Exil trieb.

Bei aller Bewunderung der Person Theodor Herzls, der ihm als ganz jungem Menschen großes und auch literarisches Vertrauen entgegenbrachte, ihn 1903 seine "branche cadette" benannte[5], konnte er sich nie dazubringen, Begriff und Ziel eines neu aufzustellenden jüdischen Heimatlandes gutzuheißen. Jede nationale Idee, wo sie auch immer entstand, war ihm zuwider, der sich durch das wandernde Leben seiner frühen Jahre die "absolute Freiheit" gewonnen hatte, "zwischen den Nationen zu wählen, sich überall als Gast zu fühlen, als Teilnehmer und Mittler".[6] Sein Judentum hat er bis zum Ersten Weltkrieg eigentlich nur dumpf empfunden, in geradezu mystischer Form im Gedicht "Das singende Blut" 1906 ausgedrückt:

> Im flutenden Dunkel halb erwacht ...
> Hör' ich mein Blut durch die Mitternacht
> Mit kristallenem Singen rinnen: ...
> 'Mich zeugt der Erde tiefste Kraft, ...
> Durch schwindende Gestalten
> Ström' ich zurück zum Mutterschoß ...
> Mein Weg ist lang. Dich streift er bloß,
> Du kannst mich nicht behalten ...'[7]

In den Kriegsjahren aber erlebte er eine innerliche Rettung in jenem "übernationalen Gefühl der Freiheit vom Wahnsinn einer fanatischen Welt", das er sich allmählich angeeignet hatte, und empfand "dankbar, daß es das Judentum ist, das mir diese Freiheit ermöglicht hat"[8]. "Für mich," schrieb er im Frühling 1917 an Abraham Schwadron, "ist es die Größe des Judentums, übernational zu sein, Ferment und Bindung aller Nationen in seiner eigenen Idee."[9] Und an Martin Buber um dieselbe Zeit: Er liebe und bejahe die Diaspora als den Sinn des Idealismus des Judentums:

als seine weltbürgerliche allmenschliche Berufung ... Ich halte nationale Gedanken, wie den jeder Einschränkung, als eine Gefahr und erblicke eigentlich in der Idee, daß das Judentum sich realisieren sollte, ein Herabsteigen und einen Verzicht auf seine höchste Mission. Vielleicht ist es sein Zweck, daß Gemeinschaft auch ohne Erde, nur durch Blut und Geist, nur durch das Wort und den Glauben bestehen kann.[10]

Mit dem *Jeremias* hat er dann, wie er in der *Welt von gestern* schrieb, "unbewußt ... an etwas gerührt, das in mir bisher ungenützt gelegen: an die im Blut oder in der Tradition dunkel begründete Gemeinschaft mit dem jüdischen Schicksal."[11] Nach dem Kriege, in seiner biographischen Studie über Romain Rolland, widmete er ein ganzes Kapitel den "vaterlandslosen" Juden, den "besten Helfern gegen den Nationalismus," wie sie Olivier dem Jean-Christophe gegenüber bezeichnet, und die dieser dann als Wegmacher zum "guten Europäer" erkennt, sie aufnimmt "in den europäischen Traum, dessen fernem rauschendem Rhythmus sein freies Blut sehnsüchtig entgegenschwingt."[12]

Stefan Zweig bekannte sich zur Überzeugung, "daß allein die Anstrengung als wertvoll gelten kann, die die Einigkeit unter den Menschen fördert und das gegenseitige Verständnis zwischen den ... Nationen vertieft." In seinem Werk sei sein Blick immer "auf das Kosmopolitische" gerichtet, seine Gedanken "auf Vorstellungen jenseits des bloßen Nationalismus."[13] Während der zwanziger Jahre, als er auf der Höhe seines literarischen Erfolges stand, schien es für ihn die Aufgabe der Juden, nicht einen neuen Nationalismus zu schaffen und sich dadurch von den anderen Völkern abzusondern, vielmehr in jener geträumten europäischen Gemeinschaft aufzugehen, die er selbst in seiner Arbeit anstrebte — jener "gemeinsamen Kultur", für die seine Heimatstadt Wien, wo man ständig das Gefühl hatte, "Weltluft zu atmen", den "idealen Nährboden" dargestellt hatte.[14] Eine "Gemeinschaft auch ohne Erde" also, wie er es Buber schon 1917 ausgedrückt hatte: nur durch "Blut und Geist," nicht durch "Blut und Boden". Es gehöre zu seinem Wesen, schrieb er später im Exil, "daß mir jeder Fanatismus fehlt, daß ich jede Einseitigkeit und Einlinigkeit ablehne. Deshalb ist mir der Zionismus und Palästina niemals als 'die' Lösung erschienen." Er möge doch nicht, daß das Judentum aus seiner Universalität und Übernationalität sich "ganz ins Hebräische und Nationale" einkrustet:

Ich glaube, daß das Jüdische und das Menschliche doch immer identisch bleiben muß, und jede Überheblichkeit und gewaltsame Absonderung des Judentums ... halte ich für eine große moralische Gefahr. Ich habe mich also niemals auf Programmpunkte festgelegt, sondern habe mich immer nur bemüht, still und

möglichst hintergründig meinen Dienst zu tun, im Werk ... nie
meine Gesinnung verleugnend, aber auch nie sie überbetonend.
Ich glaube nicht, daß wir eine "jüdische", eine nationale Literatur
zu gründen haben, sondern nur das zu schreiben, zu was es uns
drängt. Und da wir eben Juden sind, und es nicht verleugnen, so
wird in sich schon dieses Werk einen jüdischen Charakter
annehmen. Alles Gewaltsame dagegen und bewußt Akzentuierte
scheint mir überflüssig.[15]

Er war in der Tat kein Organisations-Mensch, niemals bereit, sich auf
"Programmpunkte" festzulegen. Bei aller Begeisterung für internationale
Verständigung waren ihm das Kongressieren und die Vereinsmeierei
durchaus zuwider: seine Tätigkeit in diesem Sinne, über das Literarische
und den gelegentlichen Vortrag hinaus, beschränkte sich auf persönliche
Verbindungen, im Kontakt mit den vielen Freunden und Gleichgesinnten
in allen Ländern. Für Rolland, der den Freund schon früh als "einen
dieser europäischen Geister, die unsere Epoche so nötig hat und deren
Ankunft ich seit zwanzig Jahren erwarte" bezeichnete, war es gerade
seine Begabung, "durch Liebe zu verstehen," den "Patriotismus Europas"
mit der "Religion der Freundschaft" zu vereinigen, die zur Entwicklung
seiner Idee einer supranationalen Kultur führte.[16] Seine Bestrebung nach
Verständigung zwischen den Völkern, den Meinungen, den Kulturen, den
Nationen (die er später als das geistige Erbe des Erasmus lobt) läßt sich
wie ein roter Faden durch das ganze Werk erkennen und steht gleichsam
testamentarisch festgelegt in den Erinnerungen der Welt von gestern.
   Im Charakter Stefan Zweigs jedoch paarte sich diese idealistische
Gesinnung mit einem starken Hang zum Pessimismus, der ihm schon in
den zwanziger Jahren ein Gefühl der Aussichtslosigkeit seiner
Hoffnungen einzuflößen begann, sowie mit einem instinktiven
Vorahnungsvermögen, das aus heutiger Sicht erstaunlich wirkt. In den
Memoiren wird ja dieses Kapitel "Sonnenuntergang" betitelt — aber aus
seinen Briefen und Aussagen der Zeit geht hervor, daß er schon damals,
im italienischen Faschismus oder in der Ermordung Rathenaus 1922, das
Heraufkommen der neuen Barbarei gewittert und Europa als nahe "am
Ende seiner Mission" erkannt hat.[17] Zwar erschienen ihm die deutschen
Wahlen des September 1930, die einen überraschenden Aufstieg der
Nationalsozialisten markierten, keinen unmittelbaren Zusammenhang mit
seinen düsteren Ahnungen zu haben, und wie manche hielt er einige Zeit
lang das Phänomen für eine bloß vorübergehende Erscheinung. Doch
bald darauf kehrte die Cassandra-Stimmung wieder, er prophezeite
Hermann Kesten gegenüber einen neuen Weltkrieg, ehe das Jahrzehnt um
sei, in dem man "wiederum schaudernd einen neuen allgemeinen Verrat
der Dichter in allen Ländern" erleben würde.[18] "Das Vorempfinden, daß
wir kritischen, kriegsähnlichen Zeiten entgegengehen" brachte ihn im

Oktober 1931 plötzlich zum Entschluß, wieder Tagebuch zu führen. Unmittelbarer Anstoß dazu waren der Tod Arthur Schnitzlers und die damit verbundenen Erinnerungen; die Zeit aber forderte "documentarische Niederlegung", "sociale Umstürze" seien zu erwarten, in Österreich vielleicht eine faschistisch-heimwehrliche Revolte, in Deutschland "wittern die Menschen Morgenwind und hängen die Mäntel heraus." Im Gespräch schon die Frage: wohin? "Alle Länder sind gleich unmöglich, Europa erst wieder wohnbar, wenn es eins ist."[19]

Zwei Jahre später war es so weit — das heißt, noch nicht eine Emigration, sondern eine Art Erkundungsbesuch in London, wobei er aber schon eine Wohnung mietete, statt länger in einem Hotel zu bleiben. Nach dem Sieg in Deutschland der Gewaltherrschaft, im Januar 1933, rechnete er jeden Tag mit einem ähnlichen Umsturz in Österreich, und wußte sofort, daß er unter der neuen Ordnung als "rassenfremder Schriftsteller" schon als Emigrant galt — als Einzelperson wie die anderen Juden aus dem öffentlichen Leben Deutschlands ausgeschlossen, als Schriftsteller der eigentlichen Heimat schon verlustig, "denn die deutsche Sprache ist doch meine Heimat und unlösbar"[20]. Zwar behauptete sein Verleger Kippenberg noch im November, er werde "in die Lösung unseres Verhältnisses nie einwilligen."[21] Zweig jedoch war es klar, daß *Marie Antoinette* (trotz des großen Erfolgs) sein letztes Buch im Insel-Verlag sein müßte und sicherte sich noch eine vorläufige Heimat in der deutschen Sprache — solange Österreich sich noch würde halten können — mit der Gründung des Reichner-Verlags in Wien. Baldige Heimatlosigkeit sah er für sich voraus, "ich kann in Salzburg nicht bleiben, ohne innerlich gehemmt zu sein"; einziger Trost das kleine Buch über Erasmus, "Tragödie des weichen, schwachen Menschen in der Mitte, erliegend den Fanatikern: damit werfe ich etwas inneres Schicksal in einen Spiegel." Freunde hätten ihn enttäuscht: ob er aber selber recht gehandelt? fragte er sich: "weisestes Wort, was ein Jude heute tut, ist immer falsch."[22] Gegenüber den Ereignissen veröffentlichte er keine Zeile, für ihn hieß es "schweigen und noch einmal schweigen." "Man muß jetzt wirklich die Muskeln anspannen, um sich nicht ... in Politik und Diskussionen hineinziehen zu lassen."[23] Umsomehr, so schien es ihm, was die Judenverfolgungen betraf:

> Speziell für uns deutschschreibende Autoren ist es meiner Meinung nach nicht tunlich, persönlich oder polemisch hervorzutreten, denn die in Deutschland zurückgebliebenen Juden stellen gewissermaßen Geiseln dar, und jede Unternehmung unsererseits, die wir noch frei sind, würde an diesen Wehrlosen gerächt werden.[24]

Und im folgenden Jahr, als er nach den Februartagen in Wien und dem Affront der Hausdurchsuchung in Salzburg endgültig nach London übersiedelte, beharrte er auf dieser Parole.

Damals wie auch später ist er wegen seines Schweigens scharf kritisiert worden, von den Emigranten, die 1933 begreiflicherweise öffentliche Worte des Beistands und eine sofortige Kampfansage dem Hitlerregime gegenüber von ihm forderten, sowie von späteren Besserwissern, die im nachhinein seine Zurückhaltung tadeln und ihm sogar Feigheit ankreiden. Einmal wurde er von jüdischer Seite als einen "Hitler-Juden" bezeichnet, also einen, der durch den Hitlerismus dazu getrieben worden sei, sein Judentum als eine widerliche und unangenehme Tatsache zu akzeptieren, die er lieber vergessen hätte.[25] Man kann wohl sein Schweigen als den Standpunkt eines "weichen, schwachen Menschen in der Mitte" verurteilen, wenn auch das Geiseln-Argument seine Kraft hat. In starkem Kontrast zu Thomas Mann, der sich seit 1917 vom "Unpolitischen" zum dezidiert Politischen entwickelt und bis 1932 in öffentlichen Reden kein Hehl aus seiner Opposition zu Hitler gemacht hatte, drückte Zweig seine dunklen Ahnungen der Zukunft nur privat aus. Dabei, wie Klaus Mann sagte, irrte er sich gefährlich in seinem Bestreben, "auch noch dem Todfeind gegenüber 'objektiv', 'verständnisvoll', 'gerecht' zu bleiben"[26], als er im Wahlsieg der Nazis 1930 eine "durchaus zu bejahende 'Revolte gegen die Langsamkeit'" begrüßte, das "Tempo einer neuen Generation gegen das der Vergangenheit"[27]. Darin scheint sogar ihn sein Instinkt auf kurze Zeit verlassen zu haben: daraufhin aber, wenngleich er die große Gefahr in den Vorhitlerjahren erkannte, hüllte er sich in äußerste Zurückhaltung ein. Er wurde manchmal von jüdischen Organisationen aufgefordert, sich öffentlich zu seinem Judentum zu bekennen, hat sich aber damals — soweit sich feststellen läßt — nur einmal, 1929, in einer jüdischen Zeitung geäußert, ganz allgemein zur "Mission der Juden", wieder einmal auf die frühere Vorstellung von "Geist" anstatt "Boden" zurückkommend: "Seit Verkündung der zehn Gebote hat das jüdische Volk stets eine führende Rolle unter den Menschen genommen. Natürlich bringt eine derart herausgehobene Position auch große Gefahren mit sich, aber diese Gefahren sind integraler Bestand unserer Aufgabe, denn nur in der geistigen Auseinandersetzung wird das Individuum wirklich lebendig und hat die Gemeinschaft Bestand."[28]

Eine tiefe Abscheu vor der Öffentlichkeit hat ihn zeit seines Lebens charakterisiert: das heißt, grundsätzlich nur im Werk war er bereit, sich selbst preiszugeben. Die häufigen *lecture-tours* beschränkten sich auf Vorlesungen aus dem schon Veröffentlichten oder auf Huldigungen bewunderter Persönlichkeiten wie Rolland; seine Antworten auf die in den zwanziger Jahren so beliebten Zeitschriftenrundfragen auf generelle und meist unpersönliche Ausführungen; die spärlichen Vorträge und

Anreden (so im Haag 1929, in Italien 1932) auf jene europäischen Themen, die ihm zu Herzen lagen. Auch blieb diesem friedfertigen Menschen jede Polemik fremd, es sei denn in Affären des Autographensammelns. In politischer Hinsicht ist er nie hervorgetreten, blieb eher Beobachter als Teilnehmer, und wäre nie imstande, wie Thomas Mann seine Ansichten über etwa "Deutsche Republik" öffentlich herzugeben. Selbst im Werk kam er nur indirekt auf die Politik: der Fouché als Andeutung des "Gefährlichen, das der 'brauchbare', der geriebene Politiker für ... Europa bedeutet,"[29] dann im Exil der *Erasmus* als "ein stiller Lobgesang an den antifanatischen Menschen," an Konzilianz und Überparteilichkeit[30], und Castellio als Darstellung "des Problems der Probleme: wie Freiheit und Ordnung vereinen" und der Notwendigkeit eines "Fanatismus des Antifanatismus"[31].

In den ersten Hitlerjahren also wäre nichts weniger als Polemik oder Kampfaufrufe von einer solchen Natur zu erwarten — umsomehr als es ihm wichtig war, erstens einmal Kippenberg, dem Verleger durch ein Vierteljahrhundert, Unannehmlichkeiten zu vermeiden ("Er wird auch seine Mühe haben," schrieb er im Mai 1933, "denn ich bin über Nacht aus einem Pfeiler seines Verlages jener Eckstein geworden, an dem mit Vorliebe das Bein gehoben wird")[32], dann wie gesagt keine Racheakte für die in Deutschland zurückgebliebenen Juden zu provozieren. Wo er noch in deutscher Sprache erscheinen konnte, etwa im Pester Lloyd, oder in anderen Sprachen, vermied er geflissentlich das Politische, selbst in einem "Dank an Romain Rolland," der in der Politik kein Blatt vor dem Mund nahm, zu dessen 70. Geburtstag.[33] Nur aus äußerster Notwendigkeit war er zu einer öffentlichen Bekanntmachung zu bringen. So im Oktober 1933, im Börsenblatt für den deutschen Buchhandel, als er (wie René Schickele, Alfred Döblin und Thomas Mann) seine Mitarbeit an Klaus Manns Zeitschrift *Sammlung* absagte, aufgrund ausgerechnet deren politischen Charakters, und anschließend darauf durch die Jewish Telegraph Agency im November eine Erklärung über seine "persönliche Haltung" an die Presse abgab, wo es unter anderem hieß:

> Nichts steht mir ferner, als mich vom Schicksal meiner Kameraden und Blutsgenossen in Deutschland absondern zu wollen ... Ich habe, dies ist richtig, mich ausdrücklich davon zurückgehalten, irgendwelche polemische Haltung gegen das heutige Deutschland einzunehmen, weil das Polemische niemals die Form war, meine Gesinnung auszudrücken. Aber deshalb denke ich nicht im entferntesten daran, meine Gesinnung zu verleugnen und erkläre klar und deutlich, daß mir das Schicksal meiner Kameraden und Blutsgenossen selbstverständlich tausendmal wichtiger ist als alle Literatur.[34]

Und 1934, ein Jahr vor der Dresdner Uraufführung der *Schweigsamen Frau*, als Emigrantenkritik an seiner "Kollaboration" ihn wieder zu einer Presseerklärung zwang, daß der Vertrag ihn nicht frei ließe, sein Libretto für Strauss zurückzuziehen, daß er aber längst verfügt habe, daß seine sämtlichen Tantiemen zur Unterstützung deutscher Juden verwendet würden.[35] Daß ihn die selbstaufgelegte Verschwiegenheit seelisch tief gequält hat, sah der jüdische Journalist Joseph Brainin im privaten Gespräch ein, nachdem er bei seiner Ankunft in New York Anfang 1935 hartnäckig aber vergebens versucht hatte, ihm "eine druckreife Verurteilung von Hitlers barbarischem Vorgehen gegen die Juden zu entlocken."[36]

Am peinlichsten wurde ihm nach und nach gerade die Judenfrage, und dazu hat er sich während der Exiljahre doch viel häufiger öffentlich geäußert, als gemeinhin bekannt ist — dabei allerdings fast immer auf die schon gehegten Ansichten über das Judentum zurückkommend. Schon am Anfang, Ende 1933 kurz nach seiner Ankunft in London, sprach er auf Englisch zugunsten des Hilfswerks für jüdische Kinder in Deutschland. Ein Jahr später, noch in London, hielt er eine Rede anläßlich eines Empfangs für das Ensemble des jiddischen Theaters aus Vilnius, das sich dort zu Gastspielen aufhielt:

> Wenn es dem Judentum gelungen ist, Jahrtausende der Bedrängnis und der Anfeindung zu überleben so liegt das daran, daß die Juden selbst in Zeiten der Gefahr stets ihr Bestes gegeben haben, weil sie erkannten, daß es zu nichts führt, Haß mit Haß zu vergelten. Es muß daher Aufgabe der Juden bleiben, positive jüdische Werte zu schaffen, zum eigenen Besten und zur Bereicherung der Welt.[37]

Auch im Jahre 1934, bei einem Symposium in London zum Thema "Whither Jewry?," als er nicht gewillt war, persönlich zu erscheinen, wurde ein Beitrag von ihm vorgelesen. Um eine gemeinsame Lösung zu finden, hieß es da, müßte das Judentum "eine soziale, eine nationale, eine religiöse Einheit sein" — aber das sei es leider nicht mehr:

> Wir sind schwächer geworden in der Seele, seit wir nicht mehr gläubig sind. Darum kann der Sinn dieser neuen Prüfung nur sein, daß wir uns eine neue Gläubigkeit erschaffen und damit eine neue Kraft.... Was uns not tut, ist ... die endliche Erkenntnis, daß diese immer erneuten Prüfungen zu unserem Schicksal gehören und daß, was wir sind, wir nur durch dieses Leiden geworden sind.... eine einfache, eine bequeme Formel, was wir Juden heute tun sollen, ... wäre zu leicht für uns ... so billig und so bequem hat

es Gott niemals unserem Volke gemacht, immer hat er uns durch Fragen und Prüfungen über uns hinausgetrieben.[38]

In einer Ansprache — 1936 verfaßt aber, wie es scheint, nie gehalten und später im Jahr zur Publikation im Blatt des Hilfsvereins deutschsprechender Juden in Buenos Aires übergeben — hob er ausführlicher die Assimilierung, den Verlust des Glaubens hervor und die dadurch herbeigezogene Veränderung in der Form des Antisemitismus, der nun das Blut und nicht mehr die Religion als Gefahr proklamierte:

> Trotzdem sind wir kein Volk des Hasses geworden. Wir haben das Land, in dem wir wohnten, geliebt und die Sprache, die wir sprechen ... und ich hoffe, daß auch die heutige geistige Einstellung in Deutschland ... nicht von ewiger Dauer sein wird.... Nicht in der Leistung der Waffen, immer im Geistigen ist unsere Stärke gewesen ... Ich glaube, daß nichts dem jüdischen Volk heute förderlicher wäre und als Haltung geziemender, als eine gewisse Abwendung von der äußeren Welt ... Gerade weil der Verdacht über uns schwebt und zum Teil mit Recht, zu rasch, zu hitzig, vorwärts kommen zu wollen, sollten wir freiwillig jeder Einzelne Zurückhaltung üben ... und vor allem darauf verzichten, die Führer der Nationen, innerhalb deren wir wohnen, im politischen Sinne sein zu wollen.... So kann vielleicht auch aus dieser schwersten Gefahr ... eine innere Erneuerung entstehen; vielleicht wird, was uns zerstören wollte, im höheren Sinne zum Bewahrenden. Diesen Sinn zu erkennen, muß unsere Aufgabe sein.... Wir müssen ... die reinsten Kräfte zur uneigennützigen Leistung in uns zu finden und zu steigern suchen. Aber gerade wer so im Unsichtbaren dient, der dient besser als alle dem Sinn und der Sendung unseres Volkes, nur er erfüllt ganz in sich den Gedanken des unsichtbaren Gottes.[39]

Dem argentinischen Blatt ließ er ebenfalls 1937 die deutsche Originalfassung seines englisch verfaßten Aufsatzes über die "Jews' Temporary Shelter" in London, das "Haus der tausend Schicksale", "dies unbekannte und unvergleichliche Denkmal jüdischer und menschlicher Solidarität!"[40]

In der Legende *Der begrabene Leuchter*, die er 1936 schrieb und von deren "fast ganz imaginärem aber symbolischem Thema", wie der amerikanische Verleger Ben Huebsch notierte, er "tief benommen war"[41], gab er der Hoffnung auf die Zukunft des Judentums einen fast chiliastischen Ausdruck: "niemand weiß, wird er ewig so ruhen, verborgen und seinem Volke verloren, das noch immer friedlos

umherwandert ... oder wird endlich einer ihn finden an dem Tag, da sein
Volk sich wieder findet und er abermals ... leuchten im Tempel des
Friedens."[42] Erstaunlicherweise konnte der erste Teil der Legende noch
im Januar 1937 — also fast vier Jahre nach dem Scheiterhaufen — in Berlin
erscheinen, in der letzten Nummer der *Jüdischen Rundschau* vor dem
endgültigen Verbot der Zeitschrift.[43]

So ganz schweigsam also ist er nicht geblieben. Und da muß etwas
erwähnt werden, was zu seiner Zurückhaltung überwiegend beigetragen
haben wird. Schon in den ersten Monaten des "nationalsozialistischen
Orkans", am 7. Juni 1933, als er noch in Salzburg war, schrieb er an
Albert Einstein über die Notwendigkeit "einer gemeinsamen Haltung",
die sich durch ein "kollektiv auszuarbeitendes Manifest der von
Deutschland zurückgestoßenen Künstler und Gelehrten" an den Tag
gelegt werden könnte. Dies sollte "nicht wehleidig jammern und klagen",
sondern "durchaus positiv", "mit äußerster Ruhe unsere Situation vor der
Welt" klarlegen, gegen den "systematischsten Versuch, uns zu entrechten
und zu entehren, der jemals gegen ein Volk unternommen wurde, unser
Wort" erheben: "ein klassisches und dauerndes Stück deutscher Prosa",
ein "bleibendes kulturhistorisches Dokument, gemeinsam von den Besten
verfaßt und von allen unterzeichnet." Aber schon bei den ersten
Anfragen, so klagte er, habe es sich gezeigt,

> daß die meisten kleinlich fragten, wer dabei sein dürfe und wer
> nicht, und so ließ ich ziemlich enttäuscht den Plan, obwohl ich ihn
> heute noch nach wie vor für richtig halte, daß wir eine magna
> charta hätten verfassen und dem unsichtbaren Parlament der
> Geistigen übermitteln sollen.[44]

Trotz dieser anfänglichen Enttäuschung kam er doch, wie er später
Einstein berichtete, mit "ein paar Kameraden" zusammen und hat einen
ersten Entwurf des Manifestes aufgesetzt, den er schon signiert an Max
Brod u. a. geschickt hat und dessen Text größtenteils unverkennbar aus
der eigenen Feder stammt. In diesem Manifest heißt es:

> Wir verwerfen jeden Rassendünkel nicht nur als eine uns
> persönlich feindselig gemeinte Gesinnung, sondern als eine der
> Wahrheit widersprechende und der ganzen Welt gefährliche
> Ideologie.... Ein Volk, das der Welt das heiligste und kostbarste
> Buch aller Zeiten gegeben, auf dessen religiöse Lehre die ganze
> Sittlichkeit unseres Erdkreises aufgebaut ist, braucht sich nicht zu
> verteidigen, wenn es als inferior erklärt wird und hat nicht Not,
> sich selbst zu rühmen der unablässigen Leistungen auf allen
> Gebieten der Kunst, der Wissenschaft, der denkerischen Taten ...
> Wir verwerfen also ohne Erregtheit, aber mit aller denkbaren

Entschlossenheit den organisierten Versuch unserer Volk-entehrung ... und sind bereit, lieber unterzugehen [denn] diesen Wahn als eine Wahrheit anzuerkennen. Dies soll aber keineswegs besagen, daß wir uns blind stellen gegen das Vorhandensein der sozialen Tatsache eines jüdischen Problems ... Niemand weiß mehr um dieses Problem als wir selbst, die wir es in zweitausend Jahren erzwungener Heimatlosigkeit erlitten. Aber wir weichen ihm nicht aus ... wollen es in Tat und Befriedung verwandeln wie ja schon seit dreißig Jahren unsere besten Kräfte aufopfernd seiner Lösung gewidmet sind.... Darum erklären wir hier öffentlich im Namen des jüdischen Volkes: sosehr wir jeden Versuch einer Entrechtung und Entehrung von Seite irgend einer Nation ablehnen, sosehr sind wir bereit ... an jeder Lösung des jüdischen Problems mitzuwirken ... jedes Opfer zu bringen, um für die Ausgestoßenen den Aufbau einer neuen Heimat zu beschleunigen ... zu allem und allem ... nur zu dem einen nicht, daß wir einen weltgefährlichen rassischen Wahn als gültig anerkennen und Gewalt jemals Gerechtigkeit nennen.[45]

Dieser tapfere Versuch stieß leider offenbar auf kein wirksames Echo. Wir wissen weder wer, außer Max Brod, den Entwurf erhalten hat, noch ob Zweig ihn, wie vorgesehen, an Einstein sandte. Den Plan hat er jedenfalls nicht wiederaufgenommen, und die Entmutigung wird ihn sicher in seiner danach anhaltenden Zurückhaltung bestätigt haben. Fast resigniert schrieb er im folgenden Jahr an Schickele, ihre Aufgabe sei "nicht wie die Journalisten, Polemiker, jede **einzelne** Erscheinung anzugreifen, sondern gegen die **Ursachen** vorzustoßen" — wie er im *Erasmus* versucht habe, der zeigen sollte, "in welche tragische Lage in Zeiten des Rottenwahns der unabhängige Mensch geraten muß." "Ich bin konziliant geboren und muß meiner Natur gemäß handeln ... in der Mitte zwischen den Schützengräben ... Ein geheimes Gefühl sagt mir, daß wir richtig handeln, wenn wir nur dem Menschlichen treu bleiben und dem Parteilichen entsagen."[46] Die Zermalmung der deutschen Literatur, hieß es Ende 1937 an Felix Braun, sei eine vollständige, man müsse nur "wie in biblischen Tagen die Hände im Gebet hochhalten, daß Österreich sich erwehre. Wenn dieser letzte Stein aus der Mauer fällt, muß sie einstürzen."[47]

Den Einsturz sah er aber klar voraus, eilte im November 1937 auf einem kurzen Besuch nach Wien — zum letzten Mal, wie es sich erwies — wo er über den scheinbar unerschütterlichen Optimismus der Freunde staunen mußte. An Salzburg vorbei nach London zurückkehrend, wußte er, daß dies der Abschied für immer von Österreich war, wie für Lot "alles hinter mir Staub und Asche."[48] Von dem darauffolgenden Anschluß, im März 1938, wurde er zutiefst niedergeschlagen, zu allererst über das Geschick der vielen Freunde, auch der Frau Friderike, die an

seinen Cassandra-Warnungen vorbeigehört hatten und nicht rechtzeitig
dem Terror entschlüpft waren, noch mehr aber über den endgültigen
Verlust seiner Heimat in der Sprache. Lähmend nun für den "ex
Austriacus"[49] "il senso di scrivere in tedesco per il vuoto,"[50] der
Gedanke, daß seine Bücher nur mehr "schraffierte Unterlagen für
Übersetzungen" sein sollten; wie Franz Werfel fürchtete er auf die Dauer
im Exil an Sprachkraft zu verlieren.[51] Ausgerechnet in Salzburg fand die
erste Bücherverbrennung, einschließlich seiner eigenen, statt. Im Roman
Ungeduld des Herzens, der im Entwurf fast fertig war und nunmehr,
nach dem Versagen Reichners, doch deutsch in den Exilverlagen von
Allert de Lange und Bermann-Fischer erscheinen würde, drückte er
seinen Abschied von Österreich aus, von der "Vielfalt und Noblesse
seiner Kultur,"[52] das Heimweh des Europäers und Weltbürgers doch
nach der Heimat, mit der er mehr verloren habe, als "einen Fleck
umgrenzter Erde."[53] Er hätte nun Lust, sagte er — erste Andeutung der
späteren Memoiren — eine Geschichte seiner Jugendzeit in Wien zu
schreiben. "Schließlich sind wir die letzten Zeugen eines tausendjährigen
Reichs und auch der dritten großen Austreibung unserer sogenannten
Rasse[54] ... Für uns kommt kein Morgenrot mehr, diese Nacht wird
unendlich lang dauern und nur der Feuerschein eines Krieges sie
vielleicht teuflisch erhellen."[55]

Wie er nun in London nach Kräften versucht hat, der neuen Flut der
Emigranten eine erste Hilfe anzubieten, ist bekannt: wie seine Wohnung
in ein Wohlfahrts- und Unterstützungsbüro verwandelt wurde, zu
Arbeitsvermittlungen, Einreisegenehmigungen, Verlagsverbindungen,
Geldversorgung. Wohl weniger bekannt ist aber, daß er einen "Aufruf für
die österreichischen Juden" verfaßt hat, einen Aufruf an die Londoner
jüdische Gemeinde zur Solidarität mit den Hunderttausenden, "die der
vernichtende Schlag innerhalb einer Woche, eines Monats aus ihrer
Existenz gerissen und dem furchtbarsten Elend gegenübergestellt" habe.
"Eine Aufgabe steht dem Judentum bevor, wie es in den zwei Tausend
Jahren seiner Geschichte kaum eine schwierigere gekannt.... Die Ehre der
Gemeinschaft fordert von der Ehre jedes Einzelnen, daß er aus voller
Kraft gebe und sogar über seine Kraft." Die erste Pflicht sei, "uns selbst
vor allen andern aufzurufen und ... das Äußerste an Aufopferung zu
fordern."[56]

Im Dezember 1938 schrieb er einen Beitrag für die neue jiddische
Zeitschrift Oifn sheideweg in Paris, zur Rundfrage, ob Juden am
allgemeinen politischen Leben teilnehmen sollten. Da argumentierte er
wie früher für "Zurückhaltung als äußerste Pflicht":

> Wer heute ... das Glück und die Gnade hat, durch seine Werke
> Weltwirksamkeit zu erreichen, möge seine Person möglichst im
> Hintergrund halten.... Das einzige Entgelt und der einzig

erdenkbare Sinn des ungeheueren Leidens ... müßte sein, ihn innerlich zu erziehen. Nur dann wäre diese fürchterliche Prüfung nicht völlig vergeblich gewesen, wenn sie den jüdischen Menschen vom äußeren Wirken in die innerliche Leistung zurückführt.[57]

In einem ähnlichen, englisch erschienenen Artikel "Keep out of Politics", wies er darauf hin, daß nichts den Antisemitismus so sehr gefördert habe, als das Hervortreten von Juden in den verschiedenen politischen Parteien, allzuoft als Führer. Als Beispiel dafür zitierte er die Anfänge der Hitler-Bewegung in München, als Reaktion gegen die von den Juden Eisner, Levine und Landauer geführte Revolution, die selbst keine eigentliche Beziehung zum Lande hätten und in ständigem Streit untereinander gewesen seien. Die Juden hätten zwar dieselben Rechte wie andere Bürger, dabei jedoch eine unermeßlich größere Verantwortung. "Tact and restraint is the imperative command and the innermost wisdom."[58]

Noch immer also das alte Plädieren, an dem er noch bis nach Ausbruch des Krieges festklammerte, für Innerlichkeit, für geistige statt kämpferischer Kraft, vor allem für Zurückhaltung. Schweigen, wie 1914, sei noch immer das Richtige, konnte er im Januar 1939 behaupten, bei einem Gespräch mit den Studenten des Hebrew Union College in Cincinnati. Die Juden sollten nicht unter ihren Prüfungen ausschreien, sondern Stärke in ihren inneren geistigen Kräften finden: der Jude leide für die Welt. Der Rabbiner Alfred Wolf, der dabei war, hörte ihn gegen jeden Versuch sprechen, die Juden in Deutschland durch Massen-geldlösung zu befreien: besser, so meinte er, daß ein paar hunderttausend Juden vergingen, als daß andere Länder ermutigt seien, dem Beispiel Hitlers zu folgen. Er war ein Pessimist, der an Wunder nicht glauben konnte, schrieb Wolf später: "he failed to grasp one of the elemental lessons of the Jewish experience, in Simon Wiesenthal's words 'a Jew who does not believe in miracles is not a realist.'"[59]

Für ihn ging das Geschick des Judentums in das allgemeine Leiden einer ganzen durch Krieg verwüsteten Welt auf. 'Soll ich mich nicht ebenso tief betroffen fühlen von dem Los der geschlachteten Armenier', fragte er Otto Zarek, 'von dem Tod hunderttausender Kulis, von all dem Elend, das eine Welt aus den Fugen auf die Menschheit gebracht und noch immer bringt?'[60] "Die Leute reden so leicht von Bombardements," schrieb er 1941 in einem seiner letzten Briefe, "wenn ich aber lese, daß die Häuser zusammenstürzen, stürze ich selbst mit den Häusern zusammen."[61] Nicht nur Verzweiflung über sein verlorenes Europa war es, die ihn zum Entschluß brachte, "still und würdig zu entschwinden", sondern auch dies durchdringende Mitgefühl für das allgemeine Leiden der Menschheit.

Vor etwa zehn Jahren begann in New York eine Serie "Masterworks

of Modern Jewish Writing," unter Mitarbeit eben jenes Hebrew Union
College-Jewish Institute of Religion, Cincinnati. In der Einleitung zu
einem 1987 dort erschienenen Stefan Zweig-Band *Jewish Legends* (der
neben den eigentlichen Legenden auch die Novelle *Buchmendel* brachte)[62]
spricht der Präsident des Bard College, Leon Botstein, gerade von jener
Gemeinde "assimilierter und stolz sekulärer mitteleuropäischer jüdischer
Intellektuellen, die vor 1939 gegen den Zionismus" Stellung genommen
und sich an einem Traum des kommenden Triumphes ihrer
"kosmopolitischen europäischen Kultur" über die entzweienden ideo-
logischen und stark nationalistischen Tendenzen der modernen Politik
geklammert hätten. Dieser "Glaube an die Kraft von Sprache, Vernunft
und Kultur", für den das Leben und das Werk Stefan Zweigs für Botstein
als "mächtiges Symbol" stehen, wird aber von ihm mit starken Worten
herabgesetzt: ihm zufolge sei das bloß der Wunschtraum einer
"entschwundenen Gemeinde". Zugegeben: die Gemeinde an sich ist in der
Tat entschwunden. Friedrich Torberg, ihr späterer Repräsentant — "einer
der letzten aus Kakanien" — 1908 geboren, 1938 auch emigriert, aber 1950
nach Wien zurückgekehrt, schrieb vor seinem Tode, es mögen "möglichst
viele Nichtjuden den Tod des letzten deutsch-jüdischen Schriftstellers als
Verlust empfinden: ob trauernd oder aufatmend ist mir gleichgültig, sie
sollen nur merken, daß etwas zu Ende gegangen ist, wofür sie keinen
Ersatz haben."[63]

Für Professor Botstein aber, erregen heute die Traditionen und Ideen
dieses "vergessenen Milieus" wenig Sympathie: nicht Mitleid, sondern
eher Ambivalenz und Unbehagen. Auf solche Weise die Bedeutung
Stefan Zweigs gering zu schätzen, seine Ideale als unerreichbare
Phantasien abzutun, finde ich abwegig und äußerst ungerecht. Wenn
auch jene Gemeinde Intellektueller, jüdisch wie nichtjüdisch, für die er
sehr wohl als Paradigma steht, durch das zwölfjährige Dritte Reich und
einen zweiten Weltkrieg samt ihren Wunschträumen verstreut und
zerstört wurde, so ist ihr Ideal einer umfassenden europäischen Kultur
doch durch all die Jahre seit 1945 nie verlorengegangen. Das Werk des
Dichters hat sich — trotz einer manchmal gewiß ambivalenten Rezeption
— durchaus bewährt und besonders in dieser letzten Dekade des
zwanzigsten Jahrhunderts überhaupt nichts an Aktualität verloren.

"Ich weiß, daß jede Welle, so gewalttätig sie sich bäumt, in sich
zusammenfallen muß"[64], hat er gesagt, dem eigenen Pessimismus zum
Trotz, in den Tagen des tausendjährigen Reichs. Heute, fünfzig Jahre
nach seinem Tode (gleichzeitig auch fast genau fünfzig Jahre nach der
berüchtigten Wannseekonferenz, die die sogenannte "Endlösung"
vorbereitete), leben wir in einer Welt, die das Ende nicht nur jenes
Reiches, sondern auch der viel länger dauernden kommunistischen
Herrschaft über einem unermeßlich weiterausgedehnten Imperium erlebt
hat. "Eine neue Weltordnung", so heißt es jetzt, steht uns bevor. Was

Stefan Zweig aber, der Kosmopolit und Weltbürger, in der menschlichen Gesellschaftsordnung immer am meisten verabscheut und nach Kräften bekämpft hat — der Nationalismus — erlebt nun trotz allem ein neues Aufblühen und bedroht überall in der Welt den Frieden, der nach dem Ende des kalten Krieges gesichert sein sollte. Am Londoner Symposium, das vor drei Wochen der Wannseekonferenz und dem Holocaust-Thema gewidmet war, fragte Gerhart Riegner beunruhigt, ob die Menschheit jene Tragödie wirklich verstanden habe: "überall in Europa, besonders im Osten, ist ein neuer, aggressiver Nationalismus im Entstehen, voll Fremdenhaß und mit einer tiefen antisemitischen Unterströmung.... Die Welt benimmt sich, als ob Hitler nie existiert hat." Tatsächlich, nicht nur in Afrika, in Asien, sondern selbst in Europa, das nun endlich zu einer Form der Einigkeit vortastet, die Zweig geträumt, erhebt sich die neue Parole "Ethnizität": Schotten, Basken, Moldavier, Litauer, Kroaten, alle wollen ihr Recht zu einem eigenen unabhängigen Staat erheben und reizen dabei die Majoritäten zu entsprechenden Reaktionen. Auch — das muß gesagt werden — sehen sich seine Bedenken dem bodenbedingten jüdischen Nationalismus gegenüber im manchmal starren und sogar reaktionären Benehmen Israels bestätigt. Die Hoffnung auf eine neue Weltordnung, in der der Nationalismus in friedliche Bahnen gelenkt werden könnte, beruht auf den verstärkten Kräften der Organisation der Vereinten Nationen, die sich aber nur auf Abschrecken und letzten Endes — wie im Golfkrieg — auf Gewalt stützen können.

Soll es also keinen Platz mehr geben für die Ideale Stefan Zweigs? für die Gewaltlosigkeit, für den Humanismus, nach Ernst Waldingers Wort für "jene ausgeglichene Weltliebe und erasmische Konzilianz, die zum Wesen des großen Kulturvermittlers gehört"[65], schließlich für ein übernationales Judentum, das im Unsichtbaren in einer "weltbürgerlichen allmenschlichen Berufung"[66] als "Ferment und Bindung aller Nationen in seiner eigenen Idee"[67] dienen kann? Ganz im Gegenteil, möchte ich behaupten. Die großartigen Schlußworte seines *Erasmus* dürfen wir getrost als unsere Lehre nehmen: "Die Menschheit wird nie und niemals leben und schaffen können ohne [den] tröstlichen Wahn eines Aufstiegs ins Sittliche," schrieb er dort,

> ohne [den] Traum einer letzten und endgültigen Verständigung.... Immer werden die vonnöten sein, die auf das Bindende zwischen den Völkern jenseits des Trennenden hindeuten und im Herzen der Menschheit den Gedanken eines kommenden Zeitalters höherer Humanität gläubig erneuern.... Denn nur was den Geist über den eigenen Lebensraum ins Allmenschliche weist, schenkt dem Einzelnen Kraft über seine Kraft. Nur an den überpersönlichen und kaum erfüllbaren Forderungen fühlen Menschen und Völker ihr wahres und heiliges Maß.[68]

Anmerkungen

[1] Vortrag gehalten in München am 26. Februar 1992, anläßlich des 50. Todestages von Stefan Zweig; Münchner Stadtbibliothek/Kulturzentrum der Israelitischen Kultusgemeinde.

Die Werke Zweigs werden nach den *Gesammelten Werken* in Einzelbänden (Frankfurt/Main 1981–1991) zitiert, jeweils unter dem dort angebenenen Titel mit Datum der Ausgabe.

[2] Zweig an Rabbi Dr. Lemle. Petropolis o. D. (Sept.) 1941.

[3] Zweig: *Die Welt von gestern*, S. 27, 37f (hiernach Wvg).

[4] Zweig an Joseph Roth, o. D., April 1938. In: *Joseph Roth, Briefe 1911–1939*. Köln 1970, S. 467.

[5] Herzl an Zweig, 2. 11. 1903. Jewish National und University Library, Jerusalem.

[6] Zweig an Martin Buber, 25. 5. 1917. In: MAL 14: 3/4, 1981, S. 326.

[7] Zweig: *Silberne Saiten*, 1982, S. 140.

[8] Wie Anm. 6.

[9] *Briefe an Freunde*. Hg. von Friedenthal. Frankfurt/Main 1984, S. 71.

[10] Wie Anm. 6, S. 325f.

[11] Zweig: Wvg, S. 291.

[12] Zweig: *Romain Rolland*, 1987, S. 229f.

[13] Zweig: Autobiographische Notiz. London o. D. (ca. 1936). Londoner Nachlaß.

[14] Zweig: "Das Wien von gestern". In: *Auf Reisen*, 1987, S. 395.

[15] Zweig an Alfred Wolf, 4. 2. 1937. Vgl. Wolf: "Stefan Zweig and Judaism." In: *Judaism*, Band 31: 2, 1982, S. 241-4.

[16] Rolland an Zweig, 4. 3. 1915; Widmung seines *Jeu de l'amour et de la mort*, 1924. Vgl. auch Rolland: *Zwischen den Völkern*. Stuttgart 1955, Bd. II, S. 934.

[17] Robert Braun: "Erinnerung an Stefan Zweig." In: *Spiegelungen einer schöpferischen Persönlichkeit*. Hg. v. Fitzbauer. Wien 1959, S. 79 (hiernach *Spiegelungen*).

[18] *Der große Europäer Stefan Zweig*. Hg. v. Hanns Arens. München 1956, S. 171.

[19] Zweig: *Tagebücher*, 1984, S. 343f.

[20] Zweig an Ebermayer, 15. 7. 1933. In: *Buch der Freunde*. Hg. v. Baedeker u. Lemke. München 1960, S. 55.

[21] Kippenberg an Zweig, 13. 1. 1933. Reed Library, SUNY, Fredonia.

[22] Zweig an Rudolf Kayser, 30. 11. 1933. In: *Spiegelungen*, S. 75f.

[23] Zweig an Kurt Frieberger, 27. 3. 1933. Ebd. S. 75.

[24] Zweig an Joseph Leftwich, 12. 6. 1933. Frdl. von Dr. Leftwich zur Verfügung gestellt.

[25] Vgl. Leftwich: "Stefan Zweig and the World of Yesterday". In: *Leo Baeck Institute Year Book*, Band III, 1958, S. 90.

[26] Klaus Mann: *Der Wendepunkt*. Berlin und Frankfurt/Main 1960, S. 249.

[27] Zweig: *Die schlaflose Welt*. 1983, S. 174 und 179.

[28] Vgl. Leftwich, S. 92.

[29] Zweig an Emil Ludwig, 2. 5. 1928.

[30] Zweig an Richard Strauss, 17. 5. 1934. In: *Briefwechsel*. Hg. v. W. Schuh. Frankfurt/Main 1957, S. 63.

[31] Notizblatt. In: *Katalog zur Gedächtnisausstellung*. Salzburg 1981, S. 81; Zweigs Brief an Rolland, 4. 7. 1936. In: *Briefwechsel 1910–1940*. Berlin 1987, Band II, S. 632.

[32] Zweig an Karl Heinrich Waggerl, 8. 5. 1933. In: *Auktionskatalog*. Stargardt 1971.

[33] Pester Lloyd, 26.1.1936. In: *Romain Rolland*, 1987, S. 409ff.

[34] 'U. a. *Arbeiterzeitung*. Wien, 15. 11. 1933. Vgl. Leftwich, S. 93.

[35] Leftwich (Anm.25), S. 93.

[36] Joseph Brainins Anmerkungen. In: *National Jewish Monthly*, April 1942, S. 254, 285.

[37] Leftwich (Anm. 25), S. 93.

[38] Handschriftl. Entwurf im Londoner Nachlaß. Vgl. Leftwich, S. 93f.

[39] *Mitteilungsblatt vom Hilfsverein deutschsprechender Juden*. Buenos Aires, Jg. 3, Nr. 32, 1. 10. 1936, SS. 7–16. In: *Die schlaflose Welt*, 1983, S. 211ff.

[40] *Auf Reisen*, 1987, S. 363.

[41] *Huebsch Tagebuch*, Mai 1936. Library of Congress, Washington.

[42] Zweig: *Rahel rechtet mit Gott. Legenden*. 1990, S. 191.

[43] *Jüdische Rundschau*, Jg. 42, Nr. 1, 19. 1. 1937.

[44] Vgl. Jeffrey B. Berlin: "The Unpublished Correspondence between Albert Einstein and Stefan Zweig", S. 331-357 dieses Bandes.

[45] Beilage zu Brief an Max Brod, o. D., DLA Marbach.

[46] Zweig an René Schickele, 27. 8. 1934. DLA Marbach.

[47] Zweig an Felix Braun, 13. 12. 1937. Wiener Stadtbibliothek. Vgl. Jeffrey B. Berlin, "Briefwechsel Stefan Zweigs und Felix Brauns". In: *Germanisch-Romanische Monatsschrift*, Neue Folge, Bd. 41, 1991, S. 322.

[48] Zweig: Wvg, S. 459.

[49] Zweig an Huebsch, 14. 3. 1938. Library of Congress, Washington.

[50] Zweig an Lavinia Mazzucchetti, März 1938. Mazzucchetti Mailand 1959, S. 271.

[51] Zweig an Felix Braun, 3. 6. 1939. Wie Anm. 47, S. 332.

[52] Zweig an Walter Landauer (Allert de Lange), 2. 8. 1939. International Instituut voor Sociale Geschiedenis, Amsterdam.

[53] Zweig: Wvg, S. 469.

[54] Zweig an Felix Braun, 25. 7. 1938. Wie Anm. 47, S. 335.

[55] Zweig an Felix Braun, 21. 3. 1938. Wie Anm. 47, S. 328.

[56] Handschriftlich korrigiertes Typoskript im Londoner Nachlaß. Nachgedruckt im Katalog der Salzburger Zweig-Ausstellung 1992, S. 85.

[57] Handschriftlisch korrigiertes Typoskript im Londoner Nachlaß, datiert Dezember 1938. Vgl. Leftwich, S. 86f.

[58] Stefan Zweig: "Keep out of Politics!" In: Query, Book 3, 1938, S. 77f.

[59] Wie Anm. 15, S. 243f.

[60] Otto Zarecks Bericht, der auf einem Brief Zweigs an Zareck beruht; Sammlung Prater.

[61] Zweig an Franz Werfel. Zit. nach Arens (Hrsg.), S. 280.

[62] Leon Botstein: "Introduction." In: Jewish Legends. New York 1987.

[63] Vgl. Neue Zürcher Zeitung, 6. 2. 1992, S. 27.

[64] Zweig an Alfred Wolfenstein, 15. 10. 1938. In: Spiegelungen, S. 86.

[65] Zweig: Spiegelungen, S. 108.

[66] Wie Anm. 6.

[67] Wie Anm. 10.

[68] Zweig: Triumph und Tragik des Erasmus von Rotterdam. 1981, S. 188.

Donald G. Daviau

The Friendship of Stefan Zweig and Felix Braun

The friendship of Stefan Zweig and Felix Braun, which extended over a thirty-five year period from 1907 to 1942, was an important one in the lives of both writers. Their correspondence, the principal legacy of their association, is particularly valuable, for it enriches our understanding of both men, and complements and supplements the images of them conveyed in other correspondences and documents. Letter writers normally display a tendency to present a different persona or aspect of their personality in their various correspondences, one adapted to the specific recipient. Such is the case here, and it is this personal note that contributes importantly to our deeper understanding of these two lifelong friends, united by their shared values, exile experience, and their dedicated commitment to turn-of-the-century Vienna, the world in which they had grown up, which shaped their character, *Weltanschauung*, and artistry, and which they never outgrew.

Stefan Zweig (1881-1942) and Felix Braun (1885-1973) met casually in 1907. Their friendship formed a bond that survived all differences of opinion and artistic outlook until it was ended by Zweig's death. Both poets had attended the Wasa (formerly Maximilian) Gymnasium and also the University of Vienna, although at different times and without ever meeting at either school, since Zweig was four years older than Braun. Zweig completed his degree in philosophy in 1904, and Braun his doctorate in art history in 1908. They became aware of each other through their early published poems and were finally introduced in a coffee house, where Braun was looking for Franz Karl Ginzkey, another youthful poet, in order to thank him for the kind words about one of his poems. Zweig, who happened to be with Ginzkey, soon ascertained that Braun shared many of his literary views as well as goals, and he invited Braun to visit him in his apartment in the Kochgasse. Zweig's apartment was lavish by Braun's standards, complete with original art works and manservant. Braun's autobiographical description reveals how Zweig's affluent lifestyle impressed him.[1] Similarly, Zweig held Braun in high regard as this diary entry shows: "Nachts mit Felix dem lieben, einem der besten Menschen, den ich überhaupt kenne ..."[2] Thus began an eventful friendship that despite distance, two wars, the pressures of exile, and personal and literary differences remained intact until Zweig's suicide on 22 February 1942. It is, however, a telling characteristic that this relationship, like all of Zweig's closest friendships, was experienced through letters more than through personal association.

Their correspondence consists of the 49 letters, 6 notes, 2 postcards, and 1 poem ("Der Sechzigjährige dankt") Zweig wrote to Braun and the 114 letters and 2 poems Braun wrote to Zweig.[3] The letters cover primarily the period from the 1920s to 1942, with the exception of Zweig's few early postcards. Emile Verhaeren's signature appears on these postcards, indicating that Zweig could have sent them sometime between 1908 and 1914, when Zweig visited Verhaeren every summer and was occupied with translating three volumes of the Belgian master's works.[4] During the early years of their acquaintance, Braun and Zweig saw each other regularly and had little need to correspond. Only when Braun accepted a teaching position in Palermo in 1924 for lack of an adequate job in Austria, did the poets exchange letters on a regular basis. The majority of these letters date back to the late 1930s, when the friends tried to sustain each other and offer mutual moral support during the tribulations of exile.

The letters, Braun's essay on Zweig, passages from his autobiographical comments, and a few book reviews, provide the information that we possess about these two loyal and true friends. Zweig appreciated Braun, who shared his dedication to literature and the life of pure beauty, and Braun held Zweig in high regard as a successful writer and as a generous human being. But he recognized even at his first meeting with Zweig that they viewed the artist's responsibility differently. Braun felt that the artist should describe the world, while Zweig remained focused on time, an approach Braun found unsuitable:

> Was er [Zweig] über die zeitlichen Aufgaben der Dichter äußerte — wie Verhaeren müsse der moderne Dichter die Gestaltung der Zeit, vor allem ihre technischen und gesellschaftlichen Errungenschaften feiern —, erachtete ich als dem Sinn der Poesie entgegen. Ich verharrte bei meiner Auffassung eines zwar nicht zeitlosen, was unmöglich wäre, auch nicht zeitfernen, aber überzeitlichen Dichteramts. Welt, nicht Zeit ist der Gegenstand des Dichters.[5]

But despite this difference in literary outlook, which continued to create tensions between them, their personal friendship continued unchanged and unchangeable, as Braun often reiterated in his letters.

The two friends came from different social strata of the same class: Zweig from a wealthy upper middle-class family of factory owners and Braun from a lower middle-class background of merchants and workers.[6] Throughout his life Zweig never experienced material want but could live in relative luxury according to his own tastes. By contrast, Braun was raised in meager to modest circumstances and even in the best of times never achieved a comfortable life without material worry. As he describes in his autobiography, *Das Licht der Welt*, which covers his life in considerable detail up to 1910, and as he writes to Zweig in a letter of 30 June 1931, he believed he would never achieve a worry-free existence: "Den Sorgen entkomme ich nie im Leben. Meine Kindheit war von ihnen mitbestimmt, und noch immer bleiben sie mir treu, aber sie sind wenigstens erträglich." Unfortunately, his view became a self-fulfilling prophecy, and he lived virtually at the poverty level much of his adult life.

Braun knew from the beginning that he could never offer Zweig anything more than personal friendship. There were two reasons for this: Braun felt that Zweig, who was four years older, held an advantage over him. Moreover, Zweig had a superior financial position and literary reputation. Indeed, he claimed that over the thirty-five years of their friendship, Zweig always maintained an attitude of superiority toward him, which at times resembled paternalism. The letters bear out this assertion, for Zweig clearly plays the dominant role. Braun accepts his part and usually writes in a polite, almost deferential tone. At the same time, however, he maintains his integrity and reacts sharply whenever he feels Zweig misunderstood him. He also never refrains from giving Zweig honest and candid opinions about his works. Braun knew that his criticisms did not matter to Zweig anyway and had no effect on him. As with other friends, Zweig simply ignored such remarks and did not let them disturb him or the friendship.

Braun was no blind admirer of Zweig, and occasionally criticized him, but usually lavished praise and gratitude on his generous friend, who did so much for him in giving him moral support, personal and literary advice, financial assistance, and tried to help place his works with publishers, although without much success. Like other friends of Zweig, such as Ernst Weiss and Paul Zech, Braun repeatedly expressed his longing for Zweig's visits and for exchanges of ideas, the kind of stimulating conversations that they had held so often in their early years. He felt that no other could carry on a discussion as well as Zweig (24 April 1930) or possessed the "Bildung" to be the conversational partner that Zweig was (23 November 1931): "Mit wem kann man denn so sprechen wie mit Dir?" (24 April 1936). From the beginning they had found each other to be exciting conversational partners — conversation was elevated to a high art among the writers of this generation.[7] Braun recalled in letters of 25 October 1931 and 22 August 1935 how they used to keep walking each other home during the early years of their acquaintance in Vienna because they could never conclude their discussions. Toward the end of the correspondence Braun extols the animation and stimulus that Zweig gave not only to him, but also to all of his other friends: "Deine bloße Gegenwart war belebend! Was Du sagtest, auch wenn's nicht stichhaltig blieb, riß doch Nebelwände von den Augen ... Du bist ein Illuminator und wirst es, das wünsche ich Dir, immer bleiben" (22 December 1941).

Braun never earned any significant income from his writings or from his work as a journalist, and his teaching position in Palermo, which took him into voluntary exile from 1924 to 1937, barely sustained him at a minimal existence level. Zweig generously sent him money from time to time, as he did to a number of other impoverished exiled writers such as Ernst Weiss in Paris and Paul Zech in Buenos Aires.[8] Braun felt that what Zweig did for so many people could never be properly acknowledged.[9] But even with Zweig's financial assistance, Braun in Palermo was at times reduced to finding patrons to invite him for meals. He had a meager income from which he helped his mother who was in dire circumstances in Vienna. Braun's situation improved when he obtained a better paying position in Padua in 1937. The war soon put an end to this opportunity and forced his move to England in 1938. There, at first, he felt like a prisoner and again lived on the edge of poverty, sharing his limited financial resources with his mother and his sister, the artist Käthe Braun-Prager, whom he held in the highest regard. Later he supported himself by tutoring and teaching, but his income was augmented by continued gifts from Zweig and occasionally also from their mutual good friend Raoul Auernheimer.[10] Upon his release from Dachau after six months imprisonment for opposing the Anschluß, Auernheimer was permitted to emigrate to the United States, where he enjoyed better circumstances in Oakland, California, where he was supported by his son-in-law and daughter who had emigrated in 1929 and were already well established.

Braun's entire life illustrates the existence of an individual who idealistically devoted himself to the higher life of the spirit and the intellect and who consequently lived in material want. He can be considered one of the "purest" writers of modern times, fulfilling in the noblest terms what he perceived as his God-given poetic calling at the price of poverty and austerity. Occasionally, Braun would express some doubt about his calling when his works lacked recognition, but he never wavered in his course and never complained about his financial status or want of material things. He found contentment in pursuing the goal he had chosen: to be a "pure" poet in the strictest classical sense. Like Zweig, he was fascinated by the myth of the poet, frequently making the poet's life a theme of his works. It was only with the rise of National Socialism in Germany and the resulting difficulties in publishing his works, that Braun, who had been so devoted to his profession, wondered whether he had chosen the right career. The calling of a writer had been so much more attractive at the turn of the century when he had decided to devote his life to literature. At that time literature, and above all the theater, represented the pinnacle of achievement for young intellectuals.

In contrast to Braun, Zweig, born into affluence, enjoyed a life of ease and comfort without ever knowing financial need or want, a life that he could devote totally to pursuing his own interests. His literary success lead to wealth and popularity, enabling him to travel and to surround himself with original art works and manuscripts of illustrious people. The only demands he knew were those he imposed upon himself, and these were substantial where his work was concerned. In fact, he adhered to a strict bourgeois work ethic. Money he had in abundance, but never enough time, and he therefore always struggled to maximize its use. Whereas Braun, the epitome of patience, languished in solitude in Palermo and had nothing but time on his hands, Zweig was under constant time pressure. He became the "Ungeduldige," as Braun characterized him in both an essay (*SZ* 196) and a letter to Guido Fuchs on 4 March 1942.[11] Indeed, the impatience that aptly characterized Zweig's life and his literary style kept him on the move and, toward the end, caused his life to quicken its pace until he lost his balance like Dr. B. in *Schachnovelle*. Zweig recognized this "Ungeduld" in himself, mentioning it even in his farewell note to his friends.

Both writers similarly committed their lives to literature at an early age. Braun believed that he had been destined to be a poet from birth, and he vowed to fulfill this role, which in his view included celibacy, without compromise:

> Mir, dem Dichter, war verwehrt, was die anderen von Gott aus durften. Und ich ahnte, daß es mir durch mein ganzes Leben so verwehrt bleiben würde. Wie dem Priester war dem Dichter das Zölibat auferlegt. Nicht jedem Dichter — hatten nicht die meisten Frauen und Kinder ihr eigen genannt? —, aber einem von meiner Art, der nur darum dichtete, weil er nicht lebte.[12]

During their student years Zweig and Ginzkey often embarrassed Braun through their frequent discussions about women, causing him to blush. By his own standards he felt that he had once violated the purity of his calling briefly in 1912 by being lured into marrying a young woman named Hedwig. He suffered dearly for this "Frevel," and from then on he knew that he was not destined ever to have a wife or child. After this experience the only women in his life were his mother and sister. When Ginzkey once remarked, "Ja, mein Lieber, es ist nicht alles heimliches Lauten," Braun insisted, "daß durchwegs alles heimliches Lauten zu sein habe, daß zwischen dem Dichter und dem Menschen kein Zwiespalt geduldet werden dürfe."[13] Braun, who never felt torn apart, could later find satisfaction in the feeling that he had fulfilled his single-minded commitment to literature. Zweig, on the other hand, suffered much of his life from his divided soul.

Braun had studied art history and German literature at the University of Vienna and was drawn to the world of the Greeks and Romans as well as to the classical humanistic German tradition of Goethe and Schiller. At an early age he began writing lyric verse, in particular, classical odes, sometimes also verse dramas. He published individual poems, and wrote for the *Neue Freie Presse* and the *Österreichische Rundschau*. After his graduation in 1908 he worked for the short-lived journal *Erdgeist* and from 1910 to 1911 in Berlin as feuilleton editor for the *Berliner Nationalzeitung*. His first volume of *Gedichte* appeared in 1909. While success was never easy, it did come, albeit slowly. Zweig's view of Braun's early poems is expressed in a 1913 review of the lyric volume *Das neue Leben*. He begins by praising the early poems yet ultimately dismisses their beauty as unfelt because they were not based on experience but on the anticipation of life. These early verses "dürften uns bei aller Liebe nur Verheißung sein."[14] Zweig acknowledged that the poems in *Das neue Leben* feature "die seltene Stärke des Empfindens und seine innere Aufrichtigkeit ...,"[15] expressing general feelings that should appeal to everyone.

Zweig's career began similarly with the publication of an early volume of verse, *Silberne Saiten* (1901), followed by a second, *Die frühen Kränze* (1906), the title of which prophesied and characterized the early laurels that he reaped with his writings. Ironically, he later repudiated these volumes of lyric poetry and preferred that they not be reprinted. He, too, worked as a feuilletonist for the *Neue Freie Presse*. Unlike his less successful friend, Zweig, on whom good fortune never ceased to smile, achieved immediate acclaim. By the outbreak of the First World War he was an internationally recognized writer, while Braun still patiently awaited his breakthrough in his native city.

Both men joined in the war enthusiasm that engulfed all of Austria in 1914, but the carnage soon sobered them and caused them to react negatively. While Zweig, along with Rainer Maria Rilke, Franz Karl Ginzkey, and Franz Theodor Csokor, was summoned for duty in the War Archives, Braun was declared unfit for service and worked instead for the *Kriegsfürsorgeamt*. There Braun met Hugo von Hofmannsthal, and for a time was his secretary. The two kindred *Altösterreichler* developed the idea of an *Österreichische Bibliothek* (1915-1918), an attempt to revive the best of the Austrian literary and cultural tradition to enable their contemporaries to draw strength from the country's illustrious past. But, as Braun confessed to Zweig, he never overcame his awe and reverence for Hofmannsthal which caused him later to neglect the poet.[16] Braun expressed this admiration in a poem about Hofmannsthal that he wrote, however, for Zweig. The latter, too, esteemed Hofmannsthal, even though he was aware that Hofmannsthal did not return the feeling and held Zweig's writings in low regard.

It was the major ambition of every young writer of their generation to have a play performed in the Burgtheater, so both Zweig and Braun wrote dramas, but neither achieved any great or lasting success on the stage. Zweig's plays were almost all plagued with production problems and, as an exception to the general rule of his life, were cursed with plain bad luck. Inexplicably, none of the seven plays — *Tersites* (1907), *Der verwandelte Komödiant* (1912), *Das Haus am Meer* (1912), *Jeremias* (1917), *Legende eines Lebens* (1919), *Volpone* (1926), and *Das Lamm des Armen* (1929) — by this master dramatist have remained in the repertoire, although they were all performed successfully in their own day. Ironically, not one of his original works has proved to be his most enduring and engaging drama, but rather his felicitous adaptation of Ben Jonson's *Volpone*.

Braun, too, turned to drama and in 1915 completed *Tantalos*, a tragedy in five scenes, which represents his major work for the theater. Zweig greeted the work enthusiastically when Braun read it to him, noting in his diary that the tragedy *Tantalos* was "ein Meisterwerk, großzügig, menschlich und von einer sprachlichen Vollendung, die neidvoll machen könnte."[17] Zweig persuaded his publisher Anton Kippenberg to print the play and was also instrumental in gaining Braun the Bauernfeld Prize, which he shared in 1917 with Franz Werfel. Despite this honor Anton Wildgans rejected the play for the Burgtheater, and Braun had to wait until Hermann Röbbeling performed it on 29 April 1932, with Ewald Balser in the leading role. The play was not well staged, according to a letter from Max Mell[18] and closed after two performances. Of his other plays, only the tragedy *Kaiser Karl der Fünfte* (1936) was performed in the Burgtheater on 3 April 1937.

Braun scored his greatest literary success with the novel *Agnes Altkirchner* (1927), which glorifies the days of the Austrian monarchy and follows the pattern of works that perpetuate the Habsburg myth. Zweig likewise set his novel *Ungeduld des Herzens* (1938) in the era prior to 1914. Braun and Zweig both recognized that their world was a *Welt von gestern*, but both continued to remain true to its shimmering, glamorous image until the end of their lives. The exiled Zweig could no longer find publishers for any of Braun's texts. He admonished Braun to write more up-to-date books for a broader audience, but Braun stubbornly continued to celebrate the classical past. Regardless of the outer circumstances of his life, Braun continued to write poems and essays, edited collections of works, revised his earlier works, and produced a considerable body of work without ever writing the one book that could carry him to prominence and lasting fame, not to mention financial security. Despite his lack of success, and despite Zweig's urging and scolding, he persisted on his initial course and refused to change his themes to address more contemporary issues or to alter his leisurely, classical, apollonian style, often in verse, which put him so completely out of step with the world around him. As later events proved, Braun in fact was more willing to accept the world's changed reality than Zweig, who could afford to insulate himself against practical pressures.

Zweig reaped widespread success with his psychological studies of major literary and historical figures, and then even greater acclaim with his major series of biographies beginning with *Joseph Fouché*, followed by *Marie Antoinette, Maria Stuart, Castellio gegen Calvin*, and *Magellan*. Braun's praise and critiques in his letters uncover their different approaches to writing. Like Ernst Weiss, the Prague writer who likewise lived in exile most of his adult life, first in Berlin and then in Paris until his suicide in 1940, Braun urged Zweig to write novels or dramas rather than biographies, implicitly criticizing him for not using his talent properly. Zweig's outward success failed to impress Braun, for he attributed it to his friend's quality as a mediator, citing his brother, Robert, who labelled him the "Schriftsteller des Interessanten." Braun was delighted when Zweig finally acceded to his wishes and completed the novel *Ungeduld des Herzens* in 1938.

On 14 February 1931, Braun wrote to Zweig about the novel, cautioning him, as on other occasions about the danger of being overly explicit, of removing the secrecy from things. In addition, Braun did not like "Mitleid," the original title of Zweig's novel which Erwin Rieger judged to be no novel at all, rather a gigantic novella: "Sein Roman ist kein Roman, vielleicht eine gigantische Novelle, abermals eine Verwirrung des Gefühls, diesmal auf der Ebene zwei an sich unbedeutenden nicht sehr sympathischen Menschen" (7 March 1939), wrote Rieger, who was at that time languishing in Tunesia. Ernst Weiss, praised Zweig's novel despite his own difficulties with it. Initially he believed it was a plagiarism of his own novel *Der Verführer* (1937). Yet Zweig was able to persuade him that the similarities were only superficial and that the two works were indeed quite different.[19]

Braun's letters to Zweig about his works illustrate his inherent sense of honesty. They allow us also to trace the changing relationship of the two friends, for in later years Braun no longer felt in awe of Zweig, but instead rather superior to him in literary matters, although he continued to defer to him in his letters. Never content with simple praise, Braun always added his honest criticisms, which demonstrates his sharply diverging literary outlook regarding form and style. He lamented what he called Zweig's "aufgepeitschten Stil" or his "Amokstil," driving, pulsating, energetic, and lapsing at times into purple prose. Zweig's tendency to create new words also disturbed Braun to the point that he asked his friend to let him go over his works and polish the language for him. Clearly, Braun felt that he was the purer writer, the defender of high principles, of stylistic and artistic integrity regardless of public response.

In *Das Licht der Welt* Braun notes that the differences in artistic outlook between him and Zweig surfaced in the early years of their friendship. Zweig joined with Ernst Lissauer in rejecting purity of form, feeling that content was more important. Braun disagreed and maintained his defense of form over content, even though Zweig's enormous success and his own lack of public echo might have caused another to rethink this principle. Braun firmly believed that he had been placed on earth by God to be a pure poet, and a pure poet with uncompromising standards he would remain. Braun represented the Apollonian and Zweig the Dionysian concept. Braun emulated the classical tradition in theme and form, emphasizing the idea of moderation, while Zweig followed Balzac and the concept of fullness and pulsating life as his model.

Braun, by his own declaration, desired nothing more than to be an Austrian writer, while Zweig embraced world literature, choosing Balzac, Romain Rolland, and the Belgian writer Emile Verhaeren as his trinity. Balzac served as his literary model, the pacifist Rolland as his spiritual mentor, and Verhaeren as his symbol of idealism, although Verhaeren's hatred of Germany during World War I diminished Zweig's respect. Zweig's relationship to Balzac becomes particularly evident in his final major work, an uncompleted biography of Balzac. His relationship to Rolland is captured in their published correspondence, while his enthusiasm for Verhaeren is shown in Zweig's devoting three years of his life to translating almost all of his works into German, an uncommon gesture of regard by one writer for another. Zweig's models failed to impress Braun, because, as humanists, they all emphasized man at the expense of God: "Nicht ging ihm [Zweig] die Idee des Lebens, nicht einmal seine Entelechie auf" (SZ 198). He felt that Verhaeren, one of Zweig's most revered friends, acted as a bad influence on him: "Verhaerens Lehre, Lust am Zeitgeist zu fühlen, bekam ihm [Zweig] nicht gut" (SZ 198).

It is emblematic of their *Weltanschauung* that Braun would work with Hofmannsthal on an *Österreichische Bibliothek*, while Zweig would edit a *Bibliotheca Mundi*. Although both men devoted their lives to literature, they could not reconcile their different approaches which caused estrangements between them. In England, Zweig, who was trying to help place Braun's works, grew impatient at Braun's unwillingness to try to help himself by writing works more attuned to the times and the interests of the reading public, but Braun could not be budged to alter his poetic approach. Braun reminds one of Kafka's *Hungerkünstler* more than any other writer. *Don Quixote* was one of his favorite works, and his life as well as his appearance displays qualities of that figure.

At one point, the differences resulted in an angry exchange when Braun mistakenly felt that Zweig accused him of desiring to make money from his writings. Zweig, on 30 August 1938, had merely indicated that Braun's plan to move to a northern country and live from his writings was unrealizable. Braun, aghast at being so misunderstood by one of his oldest friends, used the occasion to explain himself as a writer. He protested that he had never written a line of non-literary character and had paid for his dedication with a life of almost unbroken poverty (30 August 1938). He justified himself by insisting that he was maintaining the tradition uninfluenced by contemporary events, the very practice that Zweig normally complained to him about. Ironically, this exchange came just four days after a letter from Braun reporting how happy he felt that their relationship had been restored to the way it had been at the beginning. On 1 January 1940, Zweig annoyed Braun by telling him to think more of others. Zweig argued that his own endeavors to help others prevented him from constantly asking questions as to whether his poetic existence was useful, thus avoiding Braun's self-torture.

Zweig's and Braun's literary and stylistic differences caused the only major problems between them; but minor differences existed too, illustrating their contrasting personal outlooks and religious views. Although both poets came from observant, but not orthodox Jewish families, Braun converted to Catholicism, while Zweig remained loyal to his Jewish faith. Braun represented a perfect example of assimilation, for he felt himself to be completely Austrian with no desire to be anything but a representative of the Austrian literary tradition. By contrast, Zweig became a humanist with no overt religious ties.[20] In Braun's view: "Obschon nicht religiös gläubig, hielt er [Zweig] seinem Volk die Treue" (SZ 203). But like Braun he did not belong to any Jewish organizations while growing up and later, in exile, did not join any Jewish groups. Under the pressure of events in the 1930s, Zweig made an attempt to display some solidarity with Jews persecuted by the Nazis, but his published efforts were few and without strong inner conviction. As a guest in England, which was attempting to stay neutral, he felt obligated not to publish writings that would antagonize the Nazis. He also worried about making things more difficult for the Jews still in Germany and Austria, including his mother in Vienna. Although he wrote a moving tribute to the Jewish spirit in *Jeremias* (1917) and another tribute in *Der begrabene Leuchter* (1927), one of his finest narrative works, his essays during the 1930s failed to contribute anything meaningful to the combat against the rabid anti-Semitism that flourished not only in Germany and Austria. In general he reaped only criticism for failing to take a more aggressive stand while Braun sympathized with Zweig for being so unfairly attacked.

Perhaps not surprisingly, politics is virtually absent from their correspondence. Even the Anschluß passed by with minimal comment. On 24 February 1938 Zweig, showing how he had adapted to circumstances, writes about how happy they can be that they both have secure homes when they no longer have a homeland. On 19 March 1938 Braun responds, beginning his letter with the words: "Laß uns gar nichts sagen, Worte sind nichts mehr, nicht einmal Verstummen ist etwas mehr." The remainder of his letter deals with his plans to leave Italy.

In his reply on 21 March 1938 Zweig agreed: "Nein, sprechen wir nicht darüber, es ist zu furchtbar." He doubts that he can continue to support everyone he has been helping and plans to limit himself to assisting Jews: "denn denen hilft niemand. Bisher war mir dieser Standpunkt widerlich, aber noch nie seit Beendigung der Sklaverei hat man Menschen in einen solchen Zustand der Rechtlosigkeit hinabgestoßen."

Zweig's rediscovery of his ties to Judaism caused him to react sharply when he learned of Braun's intention to conceal his Jewish identity. Braun, as a Jew who converted to Catholicism, felt even less bound to his Jewishness than Zweig. On 26 August 1938, when he was being forced to emigrate from Padua, he mentioned that he would prefer to have a "stateless" passport rather than indicate Israel as his homeland. Zweig displays annoyance with Braun's use of "das scheußliche Wort Streicherischer Prägung 'nichtarische Christen.'" He tells him not to expect a welcoming reception in England: "ein böses Land für den, der ohne Geld, ohne sichere Stellung hier leben will. Grauenhaft teuer, unwirtlich, ohne Sonne und ewig fremd" (27 August 1938). He cannot hope for any help from the Jewish Committees either. It is also virtually impossible for Jews to move on to the United States. For his part, Braun rejected all of the "isms" of his time: atheism, Fascism, Marxism, and Zionism, all of which he regarded as manifestations of materialism. He discarded psychoanalysis for the same reason and continually warned Zweig against using its methods in his works. Since he felt guided by the hand of God who dictated his career, Braun felt that he should witness life from the outside and report on it without participating in it. In his view, poets can never say "Wir." He suffered from loneliness, but he knew God's will for him and accepted it (20 April 1934). Small wonder that Zweig, with his indifference to religion, could grow impatient with such piety. Zweig may not have appreciated Braun's unbending faith, but his religious beliefs sustained Braun through the many trials of his life. Zweig, with his personal wealth, literary success, and acclaim, possessed more material means of survival than Braun, but ultimately the latter prevailed precisely because of his religious conviction, infinite patience, and perseverance. Braun could never have committed suicide as Zweig did.

As the letters to Zweig and also to other friends such as Auernheimer, Guido Fuchs, and Erwin Rieger show, Braun held Zweig in the highest regard, even while conscious of his flaws. He never envied Zweig's success or wealth, and his frequent congratulations to Zweig on the publication of his most recent books or on birthdays always sound heartfelt. Zweig in turn respected Braun, did not take his friend's criticisms to heart, did not change his literary approach or style, and did not let such disputes with Braun affect their friendship. Braun accepted that nothing or no one could influence Zweig, but did not let Zweig affect him either. Nothing Zweig said could alter Braun's opinion. When Zweig lectured him in a manner and tone not found in any other correspondence between friends, Braun defended himself and simply shrugged off the comments.

In a sense it is ironical that Braun, who was barely surviving, attempted to give moral support to Zweig, who ostensibly had everything and was infinitely better off than Braun in every way. In a letter to their mutual friend, Guido Fuchs on 7 August 1941, Braun describes Zweig as follows: "Von Stefan kam ein zu Herzen gehend trauriger Brief. Was nutze ihm Ruhm und Reichtum, da nichts ihn mehr froh macht? Er denkt daran, nach Südamerika wieder zu reisen. Mit den Freunden in New York ist er wenig zufrieden: nur Beer-Hofmann nimmt er aus." Braun considered that Zweig had long ago lost the capacity for happiness because he simply had too much.

Their correspondence traces a number of ups and downs in this friendship. Braun could not wait to visit Zweig in Salzburg, but on his return to Palermo he wrote on 19 November 1930 that he found the visit unsatisfactory, adding, however, that nothing could disturb their relationship. On 14 February 1931, Braun indicates how much he learns from Zweig and how his "Bildung" would be incomplete without him. On Zweig's fiftieth birthday, Braun thanks his friend for all that he has done for him and concludes: "Ohne dich — wo stünde ich heute?" On 27 August 1935 Braun again notes three occasions on which Zweig had helped him. Without Zweig, his works would never have gone beyond their private circle. Zweig did intercede with publishers on Braun's behalf but with little success. On 28 December 1935 Braun thanks Zweig for the money he sent and for his "unermüdliche Güte, Hilfsbereitschaft und Freundschaft."

On 22 August 1935 Braun expresses his pleasure that Zweig approves of his book on Thomas à Kempis. He is happy to draw Zweig into this realm and away from the psychoanalytic approach, which Braun rejects. Zweig's letter, Braun comments, brings them back closer to the days of their youth. On 26 August 1938, Braun reports that things between them are as they were during the first days of their friendship. But on 8 January 1939 Braun feels that they have grown apart, have gone in opposite directions, and no longer understand each other well. Nevertheless he still feels closer to Zweig than to those he agrees with. He understands Zweig's problems, he claims. Zweig is like Carossa's Doctor Burger, who suffers from "Die Qual, nicht helfen zu können" (28 April 1939). Braun amplifies this characterization in his later profile of Zweig, stating that "zu fordern, zu helfen, zu wirken," were the mainstays of Zweig's existence. Just prior to this letter, Braun had heard from Erwin Rieger in Tunis (7 March 1939): "Von Stefan hab ich einen sehr netten Brief aus Amerika bekommen: Er gondelt durch seinen Ruhm. Sei nicht zu streng mit ihm: man muß die paar Menschen, die uns im Schiffbruch geblieben sind, nehmen wie sie sind."

Braun consistently praised Zweig's writings as masterpieces but always added some reservation or criticism. In his review of *Der Kampf mit dem Dämon*, Braun praised the fact that Zweig, who spent his early career discussing foreign writers, such as Verhaeren, Lemmonier, Rolland, Desbordes-Valmore, Verlaine, and Balzac, now turned to German literature.[21] Yet Braun also warned his friend of involving himself too much with the theme of restlessness, which drove Hölderlin, Kleist, and Nietzsche to madness and death. He stressed that Zweig failed to touch on the religious problem in his analysis.

Concerning *Kleine Chronik*, Braun complained about the use of language, "die an den lebendig-bewegten Stellen leider oft in Irrungen und Eigensinnigkeiten fällt ... Darf ich nicht einmal den Philologen spielen und dir vor dem Druck über gewisse Kleinigkeiten die Augen öffnen?" (5 December 1929). He praises the drama *Das Lamm der Armen* but criticizes its explicitness which reminded him of old, outdated naturalism. He also disliked Zweig's psychoanalytical approach in his play. Zweig needed to restore the element of mystery to literature (6 May 1930). By contrast, Braun considered *Joseph Fouché* to be one of Zweig's best-written books but again objected to the use of psychoanalysis, which he had explicitly rejected (19 November 1931). Braun liked "Mesmer" as a fully realized work, but criticized "Mary Baker Eddy" for its "aufgepeitschten Stil," its "Amokton" (14 February 1931). *Marie Antoinette* Braun deemed as Zweig's greatest work; no historian could have presented her better. Braun especially liked the new style of *Maria Stuart*, and commended Zweig for avoiding psychoanalysis. He praised *Castellio gegen Calvin* but criticized the many allusions to the present. He felt the material was so dramatic that Zweig should have recast the it for the stage. Braun's tempered view of *Castellio* stood in sharp contrast to that of Ernst Weiss, who wrote in an unpublished letter of 25 May 1936 that the work changed his life and that everyone should read it:

Ich habe während des gestrigen Sonntags Ihr neues Buch von morgens bis spät in die Nacht ausgelesen. Sie haben ungeheuren Mut gehabt, (nämlich den, auch der Gegenseite nach Möglichkeit gerecht zu werden,) und Sie haben einen ungeheuren Wurf getan. Ihr Buch ist die erste Antwort aus unserer Geisteswelt. Sie haben die Gegenseite getroffen. Sie haben sie erfaßt. Man kann ihr Buch ungelesen beiseitelegen. Wenn man es aber begonnen und ausgelesen hat, kann man die Welt nicht mehr so sehen wie bisher. Sie greifen in das innerste Getriebe der Historie und der Tiefe der menschlichen Seele ein, Sie sind in diesem Buche zum erstenmal der große Erzieher geworden. Wenn heute Bücher überhaupt noch wirken könnten, (ich weiß es nicht, sage nicht ja noch nein), müßte auf dieses Buch ein gewaltiger welterschütternder Schrei kommen, von beiden Seiten. Eines scheint mir sicher: Hätte man ein Buch wie dieses vor dem Machtantritt der Diktatoren, (besonders in Deutschland) besessen, wäre es nicht so weit gekommen, denn niemals hätte sich der Friedensgeist in seinem Größenwahn so sicher, so unangreifbar, so historisch notwendig geglaubt, ohne es zu sein. Was Sie zeigen, ist nicht eine Ausnahme, es ist die eine Seite des ewigen dialektischen Gesetzes. Solche Bücher müssen unsterblich sein, weil ihr Gegenstand unsterblich ist.

This praise notwithstanding, Weiss, like Braun, urged Zweig to stop writing biographies altogether and to concentrate on producing "Dichtung."

Braun considered *Der begrabene Leuchter*, Zweig's "schönste Dichtung" but nevertheless criticized the language, particularly the "Neuerungen," which he considered philologically impossible. He offered to go through the text prior to a second printing and polish the language. Especially noteworthy is Braun's assessment that, despite his early fame, Zweig's literary development had been slow, and he still hoped for its fulfillment (21 October 1936). Again Braun felt able to lecture Zweig on the first rule of writing, but did not say anything too directly. It is one of Zweig's major flaws, but at the same time probably one of the keys to his wide readership (he is the most translated Austrian author) that he always acts as the omniscient author and thoroughly explains the psychology of the characters to the reader.

The majority of Zweig's preserved letters were written in the years from 1938 to his death in February 1942, and here Zweig more clearly than in any other correspondence presents the growing pessimism and feeling of weariness that corroded his will to live. He seemed more willing to confide in Braun than in others. In late summer 1939 Zweig, who always felt he could see more clearly than others (witness his departure from Austria in 1934) commented that it is foolish to continue to believe that Germany will collapse: "Haben wir durch den Mut, uns zugestehen, daß wir (nicht minder als unser Ideal) etwas Erledigtes, etwas Historisches sind, unfähig die Zeit zu lenken, weil nicht mehr gläubig, weil ermattet, abgeschunden ..." He tries to dash Braun's dreams of returning home, pointing out that their familiar homeland no longer existed. Zweig, more pacifistic than ever, claimed that he would not use his gas mask in an attack: "Ich *will* keinen zweiten Krieg mehr sehen und überleben." When Braun replied with an optimistic report that Hitler's horoscope ends in 1940, Zweig urged him to forget such "Altweibergeschwätz." In view of his own impetuousness, it is ironical to hear Zweig lecture Braun on the need for patience: "Geduld, sie ist es, die wir brauchen, unendliche, demütige Geduld. Ich habe sie, weil mir das Leben und mein Leben schon im wesentlichen weggelebt erscheint ..." (Herbst 1939). It was Zweig's lack of patience and his inability to live up to his own advice that caused his final tragedy.

Zweig lamented that he had used up so much of his sympathy that he had little left; he had seen too much and heard too much. But he recommended that Braun began writing works as difficult and elaborate as his own book on Balzac: "Nur das Schwere in der Kunst kann uns das Leben leichter machen!" (5 August 1935). Although still regretting his inability to help, he admitted to Braun that they had less to complain about than most other exile writers.

Both Zweig and Braun suffered a major disappointment when they learned that Carossa, whom they and the other members of their circle held in the highest regard, had reached an agreement with the Nazis. Zweig complained that Carossa even shook hands with Hitler and Mussolini. He was appalled that Carossa celebrated holidays with the Nazis: "eine Woche lang den Tisch der größten Verbrecher bei allen 'nationalen' Festen geteilt — unverzeihlich, so tief ich ihn liebe, so sehr ich ihn bedaure!" (15 September 1939). Braun tried to defend Carossa, but unsuccessfully. In August 1939 Zweig wrote that he did not want to receive any more letters from Carossa, calling Braun's attention to a saying, "Schwäche ist Schuld," which he included in his novel *Ungeduld des Herzens*.

In a poignant letter of 16 October 1939 Zweig says that they have experienced too much and that:

> unser Gleichgewicht wird, besonders bei uns, Juden, lebenslänglich gestört bleiben. Wir sind lebendige Anomalien, in einer Sprache schreibend und denkend, die uns entzogen wird, in einem Lande lebend und an dessen Schicksal gebunden, dem wir nicht ganz verbunden und in dem wir bloß geduldet sind, Juden ohne den religiösen Glauben und den Willen, Juden zu sein,

Pacifisten, die nicht widersprechen dürfen, wenn man gegen das
Untier rüstet und kämpft — wann war eine Generation innerhalb
der Geschichte so dem Widersinn preisgegeben!?

While Zweig's feelings of discouragement and pessimism kept growing,
he sustained parodoxical views. He worried about losing his facility in
writing German, and on 16 December 1939 claimed he would no longer
speak or write English because of his concern about its harmful effect on
his German:

Du wirst verstehen, daß ich plötzlich aufgehört habe, Englisch zu
lesen und Englisch zu sprechen. Ich finde nämlich, daß es stört,
in einer fremden Sprache zu viel zu denken — man verliert damit
Farbe seiner eigenen und oft spürte ich, daß bei einem Attributiv
mir das englische sich dem deutschen Ausdruck vordrängte. Ich
lese mit Absicht wieder viel Deutsch ...

At the same time, he had a growing sense of his Jewishness, to which he
explicitly referred but, as noted above, without increasing inner
commitment. Still, in his letter of 4 November 1939 he admitted how
deeply the Jewish tragedy affected his life: "Zu diesem Schicksal noch das
Plus des Jüdischen, Tragödie in der Tragödie (die erst ein spätes
Geschlecht wird formen können)." In the same letter he described his
feeling of uprootedness: "Wie sonderbar! Dreißig, vierzig Jahre fühlte ich
mich vaterlandslos und lebte in der Welt als in dem mir gemäßen Raum;
aber kaum daß man das Recht auf das Vaterland verliert, empfindet man
sich als Verlorener." This letter is more positive than most and concludes
with Zweig reminding Braun that if he needs him he will always be
ready with his support.

Although the friendship had deteriorated considerably, Braun was still
shattered by the news of Zweig's death, which he learned when a letter
he had sent on 12 February 1942 was returned with "deceased" written
on the envelope. How this represented a major loss in his life, Braun
understood only then, as he expressed in a letter to Guido Fuchs on 4
March 1942:

Wie sehr ich Stefan brauchte, sehe ich erst jetzt. Die Welt ist mir
nicht mehr dieselbe, seit er sie verließ. Ich denke immer an ihn
und bejammere ihn. Was muß er verschwiegen haben! Vielleicht
litt er immer und war nur zu stolz, es uns zu sagen. Kanntest Du
seine Frau? Nie schrieb er mir über sie. Ich hoffe er war glücklich
mit ihr.

As he had previously noted, Braun mentioned again his view about Zweig's greatest flaw:

> Stefans größter Fehler, auch als Schriftsteller, war seine Ungeduld. Warum, warum wartete er das Schicksal nicht ab? Offenbar hatte er nicht das mindeste Vertrauen mehr zu England. Oder war er krank im Gemüt? Ich sorge mich um seine Seele und möchte alle Heiligen und Engel anflehen, ihr beizustehen.

Finally, Braun, reflecting his metaphysical inclinations, added that he felt Zweig's soul had gone to Fuchs, whom Zweig always admired a great deal.[22]

Impatience was a dominant quality of Zweig, as he acknowledged in his farewell letter to Braun, the epitome of patience. Zweig's poem "Der Sechzigjährige dankt," made clear that he had accomplished what he wished in life and could renounce the rest. Also, something the religious Braun could not fathom, Zweig, an admirer of Kleist, had no reservations about suicide. Braun saw his death as proof, "daß in einem Streit großer Mächte, Glaube an den Menschen allein nicht zureicht" (SZ 204). Humanism without religion is inadequate. Like others, Braun saw the struggle in Zweig between his genius and the demon, but no one expected the demon to win: "Stefan Zweig schien dazu bestimmt, alt zu werden. Er starb nicht seinen 'eigenen Tod'" (SZ 204).

Zweig was used to being in control of his life, the center of importance in all relationships. His circumstances enabled him to bring his inner wishes into reality. Confronting a power that he could not control and that had destroyed the only world that meant anything to him, made suicide no difficult choice. To serve as a moral leader, to use his reputation and position to help others through the difficult time, as Thomas Mann did in the United States was not a responsibility Zweig could assume, although Braun and Ernst Weiss urged him to do so. Auernheimer, who had spent six months in Dachau before being released to emigrate to America, lamented Zweig's death in a letter to Braun, but he remained critical of the escape Zweig had chosen. With Braun, he vowed that they would never relax in the fight against National Socialism.

Braun returned to Austria in 1951 but played no role in the postwar scene although he did serve as an example of the Austrian tradition at a time when every effort was being made to restore the link to the pre-Anschluß period. Many of Braun's essayistic writings were devoted to recollections of authors he had known or to "Würdigungen" of major writers of the past. Even while still alive in postwar Austria, he was already relegated to literary history. For example, his play *Ein indisches Märchenspiel* (1935), which had premiered in Basle in 1936, was performed after the war in the Vienna Kellertheater *Die Tribüne* "als bewußter Kontrast zum avantgardistischen Spielplan."[23]

Particularly instructive in understanding Braun's appraisal of Zweig is the essay "Stefan Zweig," which provides an excellent portrait of his friend from the perspective of twenty-one years after his death. Here Braun repeated many of the views contained in the letters, but the tone is now sharper and more objective, the criticism more direct and more biting. Braun more openly deplored Zweig's superficiality in life as well as in his works. Braun questioned whether he neglected his friend in later years, but he felt that the guilt did not lie entirely with him — Zweig's attitude of superiority had put him off in later life. His older friend's inflexibility, which nothing or no one could change, caused Braun to despair. After Zweig's death, Braun felt helpless because he could in no way repay his friend for all that he had done for him. Braun praised Zweig for helping so many without much return in gratitude: "Ich weiß nicht, ob Stefan Zweigs großmütiger Sinn um das Ausmaß der Undankbarkeit gegen ihn gewußt oder ob er es übersehen hat. Er war zu stolz, um der leisesten Anwandlung von Ranküne nachzugehen" (SZ 196). He had many visitors, but mainly people who were not seeking him out for himself but who wanted something from him. Braun writes: "Fähigkeit zur Begeisterung, Bedürfnis nach Verehrung, edle Neugier nach der Wahrheit des Menschen waren die Voraussetzungen seiner Persönlichkeit" (SZ 194). Like Braun, Zweig had been fascinated by the secret of great men, an attraction that motivated his collection of autographs and manuscripts.

As a writer, Braun felt that Zweig was conscious of being an epigone who knew his limits: "Er war ein Jünger, nicht ein Schüler" of the masters, "ihn zu beinflussen könnte niemand hoffen" (SZ 203). Zweig was divided inwardly and tormented by a demon. The struggle with this inner phantom must have exhausted him. Braun believed that the poem "Du bist erkannt" expressed Zweig's inner truth, showing that it was the inner demon that caused his flight at the end: "Ein Amokläufer ohne Waffen — wußte er auch, wohin der blinde Hang ihn trieb?" (SZ 205).

Although he traveled widely, Zweig was not a "Wanderer," but a "Schweifender": "Nie ruhte der ahasverische Trieb ihn lang" (SZ 198). And he traveled faster and faster; no longer content with boats or trains, he began to fly to his destinations. Braun symbolized Zweig's final months as a chess game, fitting because it showed how Zweig resembled Dr. B. in *Schachnovelle*, who played chess between his divided selves and intensified the speed of the moves until he collapsed. According to Braun, Zweig, after the fall of Singapore, believed he could not see any way to a future that mattered to him. He was convinced he was checkmated: "Der Dämon der Ungeduld war es, der das Spiel umstieß" (SZ 206).

Notes

1   Felix Braun: *Das Licht der Welt*. Vienna 1962, p. 251.

2   Stefan Zweig: *Tagebücher*, ed. by Knut Beck. Frankfurt/Main 1984, p. 17.

3   I wish to express my appreciation to the Stefan Zweig Archive at Fredonia University for supplying copies of the Braun letters to Zweig and to the *Handschriftenabteilung* of the Vienna Stadtbibliothek for copies of the Zweig letters to Braun. In addition, I thank the Williams Verlag for permission to publish the Zweig letters and Mrs. Ulrike Popvic for the Braun letters. An edition of the full correspondence is being published to mark the fiftieth anniversary of Zweig's death (1992).

4   For bibliographical information about Zweig, see Randolph J. Klawiter: *Stefan Zweig: An International Bibliography*. Riverside, California 1991.

5   Braun (Note 1), p. 252.

6   The best biography to date is that of Donald Prater: *Stefan Zweig, European of Yesterday*. Oxford 1972. Expanded German version: *Stefan Zweig. Das Leben eines Ungeduldigen*. Munich 1981. See also Donald Prater and Volker Michels: *Stefan Zweig. Leben und Werk im Bild*. Frankfurt/Main 1981.
    For Braun the most detailed source is his autobiography *Das Licht der Welt*. To date there is no biography. For the most complete bibliography, see Klaus Peter Dencker: *Literarischer Jugendstil im Drama. Studien zu Feliz Braun*. Dissertation. Vienna 1971.

7   Cf. Erhard Buschbeck: "Bahr und Hofmannsthal im Gespräch." In: *Hugo von Hofmannsthal. Der Dichter im Spiegel seiner Freunde*, ed. by Helmut Fiechtner. Bern 1963, pp. 332-335.
    Bahr and Zweig were neighbors in Salzburg and conversed frequently while hiking over the Gaisberg.

8   Cf. Donald G. Daviau: *Stefan Zweig/Paul Zech Briefwechsel 1910-1942*. Rudolstadt 1984.

9   Felix Braun: "Stefan Zweig." In Felix Braun: *Das musische Land*. Innsbruck 1952, p. 191. All further references to this text will be cited in this essay as SZ followed by the page number. This essay is also included in Felix Braun: *Zeitgefährten*. Munich 1963, pp. 59-78.

10 Cf. Donald G. Daviau, Jorun B. Johns, and Jeffrey B. Berlin: *The Correspondence of Stefan Zweig with Raoul Auernheimer and Richard Beer-Hofmann*. Columbia, South Carolina 1983.

11 Braun's letters to Guido Fuchs are contained in his "Nachlaß" in the Handschriftensammlung of the Vienna Stadtbibliothek.

12 Braun (Note 1). p. 165.

13 Ibid., p. 253.

[14] Stefan Zweig: "Das neue Leben." In: *Neue Freie Presse*. 16 March 1913, p. 33.

[15] Ibid., p. 34.

[16] Cf. Felix Braun: "Begegnungen mit Hofmannsthal." In Braun: *Zeitgefährten*, pp. 7-40.

[17] Zweig, *Tagebücher*, p. 237.

[18] The letters of Mell to Braun are found in the Nachlaß in the Vienna Stadtbibliothek.

[19] Cf. Zweig's letter of 1 November 1937 to Weiss, one of the very few preserved. In it, Zweig disclaims any similarity between the two novels. See *Brief an Ernst Weiss*. In: *Ernst Weiss*, ed. by Peter Engel. Frankfurt/Main 1982, p. 116.

[20] For a controversial but provocative view of Zweig's ties to Judaism, see Leon Botstein: "Stefan Zweig and the Illusion of the Jewish European." In: *The World of Yesterday's Humanist Today*, ed. by Marion Sonnenfeld. New York 1983, pp. 82-110.

[21] Felix Braun: "Der Kampf mit dem Dämon." In: *Die Tat*, Vol. 17, 1926, pp. 791-793.

[22] Letter to Guido Fuchs in the Braun Nachlaß in the Vienna Stadtbibliothek.

[23] Franz Pater, ed., *Felix Braun 1885-1973 — Franz Theodor Csokor 1885-1969*. Vienna 1985, pp. 17-18.

Jeffrey B. Berlin

The Unpublished Correspondence
between Albert Einstein and Stefan Zweig
(with an unpublished Zweig Manifesto of 1933 and
letters to Max Brod, Ben Huebsch, and Felix Salten)[1]

> *Wie soll ich Ihnen für Ihre so getreue Gefolgschaft für Stefan
> Zweig und mich danken? Worte können es in Kurzem nicht
> ausdrücken.*[2] (Friderike Zweig. Letter of 19 November
> 1951 to Harry Zohn.[3])

Throughout his lifetime Stefan Zweig (1881-1942) assumed the
self-appointed role of a *Vermittler*, a position that especially Harry Zohn
has clarified in many discerning and informative studies. As such, Zweig
brought himself into contact with many of the most important figures of
this period; at the same time, Zweig initiated and furthered numerous
projects.[4] Importantly, he also assisted other lesser known figures.

Zweig rightfully remained proud of his accomplishments and always
maintained a strong sense of commitment to the individuals and
programs he supported. Through his efforts much was achieved that
might otherwise not have been undertaken. In the bleak period when
Hitler challenged the Jews and the world, Zweig bravely supported
oppressed people to the best of his capabilities. Not only did Zweig
thereby save lives, but he also provided a spiritual refuge for those who
were torn and suffering, even at a time when, we must emphasize, he too
was in exile and greatly tormented. As Zweig's contemporaries have
always acknowledged, his interest, generosity, and connections were
invaluable. It is therefore no exaggeration to state that while Stefan
Zweig's literary writings remain of supreme importance, his capacity as
a *Vermittler* clearly merits, on a different scale, equal significance.

Sometimes Zweig's "epistolary friendships" lasted a lifetime and
resulted in the exchange of hundreds of letters. Even when he exchanged
only a few letters with a friend, his correspondence is of great value.
Although not voluminous, the extant Einstein/Zweig letters are of crucial
importance. These still unpublished documents, spanning a sixteen year
period from 1920 to 1936, contribute to our further understanding of the

times, especially by calling attention to important issues that demand further elucidation.

In this regard, a 1933 manifesto that Zweig discusses with Einstein warrants special attention, particularly because of its historical importance. Although 1933 marks such a dramatic change in the German political scene, the critical literature entirely ignores this manifesto. Yet it is imperative that we not only further examine this period, but also, when available, provide still unpublished documents relating to it. Since the Einstein/Zweig friendship is very different from Zweig's association with Emile Verhaeren, for example, we should not expect to see Zweig taking on his full *Vermittler* role here; however, these letters nevertheless do clarify his interaction with the world's most renowned scientist. By contrast, Zweig's other published correspondences reveal very few remarks about Einstein. Furthermore, Zweig's diary does not mention Einstein and, incidentally, contains no entries for the year 1933; in addition, Zweig does not write anything substantial about Einstein in his autobiography *Die Welt von Gestern*.[5] Thus the Einstein/Zweig letters remain our primary source for documenting their relationship.

Of the few scattered remarks about Einstein in Zweig's other published letters, one of the most revealing is a 17 February 1920 statement to Romain Rolland:

> Der einzige neue große Gedanke, der alle Geister bewegt, ist die Idee und Theorie Einsteins von der Relativität (was die reaktionären Berliner Studenten gleichwohl nicht hinderte, ihn aus dem Vorlesungssaal zu verjagen und wild zu pfeifen, während er sprach). Soviel ich ihn verstehe, sehe ich darin eine große Möglichkeit, unsere Sicht der Natur zu verändern: wie schön ist es, wenn ein einzelner eine Idee hat, die das Sehen von Millionen auf Jahre und Jahrzehnte hin verändert![6]

Zweig's words betray his amazement at Einstein's theories and discoveries. Ever attracted to scientific phenomena, it is not surprising that Zweig should respond in such a manner. In this same letter to Rolland, Zweig adds:

> Er und Spengler mit seinem "Untergang des Abendlandes" sind die einzigen, die unsere Hoffnungen in dieser traurigen und trüben Zeit gerettet haben. Welch eine Wohltat solche Männer, die über all diese Traurigkeit hinweg die fernen Horizonte der künftigen Geschichte und die Gestirne schauen, die unsern Blick und unsern Geist aufrichten![7]

Zweig was comforted and guided by the accomplishments and abilities of figures like Einstein, whom he genuinely regarded, as he says in a statement of 24 February 1920 to Rolland, as the "derzeit größten Wissenschaftler Europas."[8] Yet one cannot but reall that years later, when Hitler temporarily reigned, even Einstein's supreme achievements were unable to brighten and transcend the threatening clouds of piercing darkness that fell upon Stefan Zweig, Europe, and the world.[9]

The first available Einstein/Zweig exchange is a telegram dated 31 August 1920. From Salzburg, Zweig, along with a few colleagues, signed the following telegram from Joseph Chapiro to Einstein. It was sent to his Haberlandstraße residence in Berlin, which in 1933 would be confiscated by the Nazis:

> entruestet ueber die alldeutsche hetze gegen ihre hervoragende persoenlichkeit versichern wir sie im wahrhaft internationaler gesinnung der sympathie aller freien menschen die stolz sind sie in ihrer reihe zu wissen und zu den fuehrern der weltwissenschaft zu zaehlen (oscar die) herzlichst joseph chapiro werner krauss andreas latzko in herzlichster freundschaft drueckt ihnen waermst die haende alexander moissi johanna tervin helene thimig max reinhardt stefan zweig[10]

The "alldeutsche hetze" refers to the "Antirelativity Company," as Einstein had called it, which had announced twenty meetings in Germany's largest towns to demonstrate against Einstein and relativity.[11] Of course, and as Zweig no doubt knew, Einstein's theories were not the actual cause of dispute. Rather it was the ever increasing anti-Semitic fervor that charged Einstein's opponents. Months before, in a letter to his wife, Zweig had characterized the mood: "der Judenhaß zur Raserei gesteigert (auf jedem Klosett, an jedem Tisch Pamphlete, in der Eisenbahn kein anderes Gespräch), der Franzosenhaß ebenso."[12] With headquarters in Berlin, the anti-Einstein movement was led by the *Arbeitsgemeinschaft Deutscher Naturforscher* that was becoming quite vocal. Ronald Clark relates:

> [It] had at its disposal large sums of money, offered fees to those who could write or speak against Einstein ... Its attacks avoided scientific argument; instead they concentrated on the Jewish nature of relativity, and on the personal character of Einstein.[13]

Among its leaders were Paul Weyland and the 1920 Nobel Prize winner Philip Lenard. Thus "to the uninformed public the news that the Study Group was supported by a Nobel Prize winner gave the organization a stiffening of pseudo-respectability it would have otherwise lacked."[14]

Zweig's telegram singles out the "setpiece demonstration" on 27 August 1920 at the Berlin Philharmonic Hall to which Einstein responded in the *Berliner Tageblatt*, noting, among other issues:

> I myself was present. I am very well aware that neither of these speakers are worthy of an answer from my pen, and I have good reason to believe that motives other than a desire to search for truth is at the bottom of their enterprise. (Were I a German national, with or without swastika, instead of a Jew of liberal, international disposition, then ...[15]

The fact that Einstein responded also evoked much discussion, especially among the scientific community. For our purposes, however, it is significant that Zweig (along with the colleagues with whom he sent the telegram) supported his fellow Jew, the scientist *par excellence*. As Zweig characterized Einstein's work in a letter of 28 February 1920 to Rolland: "die Tragweite seiner Entdeckung scheint ungeheuer zu sein" (Rolland/Zweig, 508). Of course we should not have expected otherwise from the author of *Jeremias* (1917), a work that Zweig regarded, as he says in a letter of 9 September 1917 to Hermann Bahr, his own "Flucht und Beichtstuhl"[16] and which, as Donald Daviau maintains, "... encompasses both the strength of the defeated Jews and the tragedy of the man of peace, who foresees disaster but cannot convince his friends and countrymen of the absurdity of war."[17]

The next exchange is related to the above incident. In a letter dated 22 September 1920, Zweig expresses to Einstein:

> Hochverehrter Herr Professor,
>   ich glaube nicht gegen Ihre innere Meinung verstoßen zu haben, wenn ich jene beigelegte Erklärung veröffentlichte (in einer Wiener Zeitung). Jenes Telegramm aus Salzburg hatte ich nur unter der ausdrücklichen Reserve unterzeichnet, daß es Ihnen persönlich zugehe und nicht veröffentlicht werde, was offenbar aber geschah, ehe Sie es selbst in Händen hätten. Zweifellos empfinden Sie eine solche Affichierung einer sehr echten Sympathie ebenso peinlich als ich und sehen in der Aufklärung des Sachverhalts — Außenstehende hätten ja meinen können, die Veröffentlichung sei von Ihnen erfolgt — nur eine Bereinigung.
>   Ich mag mir denken, was Sie unter Zudringlichkeit wie unter feindlicher Gehässigkeit jetzt zu leiden haben: möge Ihnen bald wieder die Stille gegeben sein, in der Sie Ihr Werk weiter ent-

wickeln. Ich nehme den Anlaß herzlich wahr, um Ihnen meine bescheidene aber sehr innige Verehrung zu sagen.

> Ergebenst
> Stefan Zweig

As Zweig's letter indicates, he regretted the publication of something that was meant to remain private. How the mistake happened is more fully explained in Zweig's 10 September 1920 letter to Rolland:

> Zum Glück ist Max Reinhardts Woche hier in Salzburg zu Ende. Chap[iro] ist auch abgereist, nicht ohne wieder mal eine Reklame organisiert zu haben: er bat uns, Einstein wegen seiner Verfolgungen ein Telegramm zu senden, und ich habe es mit Reinhardt, Moissi etc. unter der Bedingung unterzeichnet, daß es nicht an die Öffentlichkeit seinem Namen an alle Zeitungen zu verschicken. Wahrhaftig, er nutzt unsere Schwäche aus — meine Frau und ich hatten alles getan, ihn uns fernzuhalten, sogar Latzko wich ihm aus, aber er läßt sich nicht brüskieren. Ich mache mir den Vorwurf, nicht energischer zu sein, aber ich bin seinem Elan unseligerweise nicht gewachsen.[18]

However, Einstein appreciated such support, as his 10 November 1920 letter suggests:

> Sehr geehrter Herr Zweig:
> Die freundliche Kundgebung der Künstler aus Salzburg hat mich damals herzlich gefreut. Mit besonderer Befriedigung sehe ich aus Ihrem freundl. Briefe und der beiliegenden Zeitungsnotiz, daß wirklich eine persönliche Äußerung nur beabsichtigt war. Ich nehme gerne die Gelegenheit wahr, Ihnen und Ihren Freunden meinen herzlichen Dank zu sagen.
> > Mit herzlichem Gruß
> > Albert Einstein

The next available letter is dated 12 December 1921 at which time Zweig wrote to Einstein:

> Sehr verehrter Herr Professor!
> Gestatten Sie mir, daß ich mich an Sie, obzwar ich schmerzlicherweise nicht das Vergnügen habe Ihnen persönlich begegnet zu sein, direkt auf dem geradesten Wege wende.
> Ein französischer Freund von mir, der Schriftsteller Francois Crucy, der Anatole France auf seiner Reise nach Stockholm begleitete, schreibt mir soeben dringend, daß Anatole France sehr

den Wunsch hätte, Ihnen, sehr verehrter Herr Professor, bei seiner Rückkehr in Berlin zu begegnen und womöglich im engsten Kreise mit Ihnen zu speisen. Crucy bittet mich nun einen Weg zu suchen, Ihnen diesen Wunsch Anatole Frances zu übermitteln. Ich nun glaube der direkte Weg ist der beste und schreibe Ihnen direkt weil ich ja gerade in diesem Augenblick die Begegnung repräsentativer Männer, die im übernationalen Sinn tätig sein wollen für das einzig wesentliche und wirksame halte. Anatole France wird *Freitag Abends* im *Hotel Adlon* eintreffen, vielleicht sind Sie So gütig ihm direkt ein Wort zu übermitteln (falls Ihnen wie ich hoffe sein Wunsch erfreulich ist), wann und wo Sie in Berlin ihn begegnen könnten.

Ich hoffe sehr, sehr verehrter Herr Professor, Sie betrachten diese direkte Übermittlung nicht meinerseits als Anmaßung, sondern empfinden Sie in dem geistigen Sinn der Verehrung dem sie entspricht.

Ihr immer aufrichtig ergebener

Stefan Zweig

Zweig's note to Einstein included a newspaper clipping about Anatole France's 1921 Nobel Prize acceptance speech. In fact, Anatole France had autographed the clipping which was transmitted to Zweig by Francois Crucy. However, Einstein's response to Zweig is not extant. Furthermore, it is unknown, if Einstein and Zweig interacted during the next few years, because the next exchange takes place in 1930.

Kastens Hotel
Hannover
Rathenauerplatz 8-12
Freitag den 14. März 1930

Hochverehrter Herr Professor, ich war sehr beglückt, als mir mein Freund [Otto] Zarek sagte, daß ich Sie Sonntag besuchen dürfe — ein alter und sehr inniger Wunsch, den ich Ihnen nie zu verlautbaren wagte, geht mir damit unvermuteter Weise in Erfüllung. Lassen Sie mich nur dies mit dem Ausdruck aufrichtigster Verehrung sagen. Ihr tief ergebener

Stefan Zweig

Zweig's exuberance about the meeting was expressed to Friderike. Indicating that he was on route to Berlin, Zweig stated to her on 13 March 1930:

und zwar nur weil Einstein erfahren hatte, daß ich da bin und zu meinem Erstaunen ein leidenschaftlicher Leser meiner Bücher ist. Er hat, um eine Begegnung möglich zu machen, eigens eine Einladung abgesagt — so bin ich Sonntag um fünf bei ihm ..."[19]

To be sure, Zweig found the encounter with Einstein fascinating, as comments in Zweig's 17 March 1930 letter to Romain Rolland reveal:

In Berlin hatte ich zwei erlesene Stunden. Einstein wollte mich sehen, und ich hatte ein langes Gespräch mit ihm, ein tiefes und beruhigendes Gespräch. Denn immer ist wahre Größe schlicht. Er ist unendlich bescheiden als Mensch und seiner Ideen ganz sicher; aber er hat die so schöne Auffassung, daß es nicht sein Verdienst sei, sie gefunden zu haben, sondern ein Geschenk der Natur. Dieses Miteinander persönlicher Bescheidenheit und des Selbstbewußtseins des Forschers ergibt etwas Einziges: ich war tief bewegt. "Wenn man ahnte, welche Freude, ja welche Lust es ist, zu denken und zu forschen, würde man uns nicht so bewundern," sagte er, und ich fand große Wahrheit in diesen Worten. Und als ich ihm sagte, daß ich eine hohe moralische Sicherheit darin fände, wie er in einer Sphäre zu schaffen, die so weitab der Menge liegt, daß der Ruhm also einer ist, der nur von einer Handvoll Menschen in Europa verfolgt und begriffen werden kann, bestätigte er mir, daß er darüber glücklich sei. Welch große Schönheit in seinen Augen! Selbst wenn er die kompliziertesten Dinge sagt, bleibt sein Mund lachend, und man spürt keinerlei Anstrengung.[20]

Later in 1930 Zweig expressed the wish to dedicate his *Die Heilung durch den Geist: Franz Anton Mesmer — Mary Baker Eddy — Sigmund Freud* to Einstein, who appreciated the gesture, as his 18 October 1930 letter from Berlin makes clear. In this same letter Einstein also remarks about *Die Augen des ewigen Bruders*, incorrectly referred to by Einstein as *Die Augen des toten Bruders*.

Verehrter Herr Stefan Zweig!
    Ihre Absicht, mir ein Werk aus Ihrer Feder zu widmen, freut mich natürlich sehr. Der Eindruck Ihres Werkchens "Die Augen des toten Bruders" war einer der stärksten, die ich vom modernen Schrifttum überhaupt empfangen habe. Mit herzlichem Dank und freundlichem Grüßen
    Ihr
    A. Einstein

Acknowledged as a masterpiece, this 1922 legend by Zweig shows that "withdrawal from the public sphere, even into the life of a hermit," as David Turner expresses it, "could not prevent entanglement in human guilt and ... bore witness to an overvaluation of the individual self."[21] Or as Friderike Zweig summarizes the meaning of *Die Augen des ewigen Bruders*: "man, in his blindness not knowing whom he strikes and judges, should judge not and strike not."[22]

On 12 January 1931 Zweig responded:

> Hochverehrter Herr Professor!
> Nur eine kleine Zeile. Ich kann das Ihnen gewidmete Buch Ihnen leider nicht persönlich zusenden, weil ich gerade nach Spanien fahre. Aber ich habe den Insel-Verlag beauftragt, es Ihnen zu senden. Mir liegt es ferne, Sie damit inmitten Ihrer Arbeit behelligen zu wollen, aber vielleicht haben Sie auf der Rückfahrt am Schiff dafür einen Augenblick frei, sich ihm zu widmen.
> In herzlicher Ergebenheit Ihr Sie tief verehrender
>   Stefan Zweig

Around this time the following undated note, attributable with much certainty to January 1932, was sent:

> Sehr verehrter Herr Professor, lieber Freund,
> Wir haben die Freude Stefan Zweig bei uns zu sehen — wir denken an Sie — auch heute — und sprechen von Ihnen
>   Antonina Luchaire
>   Jean Perrin
>   In inniger Verehrung
>   Stefan Zweig
>   Paul Valéry
>   Benjamin Crémieux
>   Chana Orloff
>   Rene Jouglet
>   Julien Cain
>   Jules Luchaire[23]

The next exchange takes place in June 1933 (although there may have been some communication between Einstein and Zweig around May 1932.[24] The political environment in Europe had substantially altered since Zweig's last exchange. In January 1933 Hitler of course had become the German Chancellor and by the third week of March had dictatorial power. In an unpublished letter of 3 March 1933 to his American publisher Ben Huebsch, Zweig described the situation:

Lieber verehrter Freund!

Verzeihen Sie, daß ich Ihnen nicht viel schreibe, wir sind jetzt alle, wie Sie sich denken können, durch das Politische im äußersten Grad beschäftigt. Seit zwei Tagen ist in Deutschland die Diktatur und der Faschismus und die Frage ist nur, ob er nicht auch nach Österreich herüberkommt. Wir haben jetzt viele Freunde, die in ihrem Leben und in ihrer Existenz bedroht sind. Toller ist glücklich schon über die Grenze. Literarisch kommt jetzt eine Zeit der schärfsten Reaktion, die überdauert werden muß. Hier pessimistisch, denn in seinem literarischen Geschmack hat sich Deutschland und das deutsche Volk nie betrügen und beirren lassen. Ich freue mich doppelt jetzt mit dem amerikanischen Erfolg, hoffentlich bessert sich dort die allgemeine Lage, was wir an Nachrichten hören ist auch nicht eben erfreulich. Wir haben uns, lieber Freund, die dümmste Epoche der Weltgeschichte für unser kurzes Leben ausgesucht.

Ich bin jetzt für vierzehn Tage in der Schweiz und lese jeden Abend vor. Am 30. März halte ich einen Vortrag in Oslo, am 3. April in Stockholm und wir werden dort herzlich Ihrer lieben Frau gedenken.

Tausend Grüße, lieber verehrter Freund, von Ihrem Stefan Zweig

Fifteen days later, on 18 March 1933, Zweig wrote in another unpublished letter to Huebsch:

Lieber verehrter Freund!

Ich komme eben aus der Schweiz zurück wo ich Vorträge hielt, die mich über die Maßen ermüdeten, denn Sie müssen sich unsere geistige Situation vorstellen! Unsere besten Freunde in Gefahr und bedroht, unser literarisches Werk abgeschnitten und zum Boykott verurteilt, eine Atmosphäre von Haß und Brutalität ohnegleichen; was wirklich hier vorgefallen ist, erfährt man erst nach und nach, alle Zeitungen stehen unter Terror und sogar die Österreichischen und schweizerischen wagen nicht ein Wort, aus Furcht ihre Abonnenten und Inserate zu verlieren.

Es ist nun leider auch möglich, daß ich meine Reise nach Schweden und Norwegen aufgebe, erstens habe ich keine Lust mich auf der Durchreise in Deutschland allerhand Zwischenfällen auszusetzen, ... zweitens kann der österreichische Gesandte schwere Unannehmlichkeiten haben, daß er mich, einen "Fremdstämmigen" Autor eingeladen hat ... Die Verhältnisse sind

also momentan unvorstellbar ... Nun auch das wird
vorübergehen!...
                              Stefan Zweig

P.S. Es handelt sich in Deutschland jetzt um eine völlige materielle
und moralische *Vernichtung* des Judentums — Preisgeben an den
Hunger der Ärzte, Rechtsanwälte, Musiker, Schriftsteller und das
wird mit der ganzen infernalischen Gründlichkeit der deutschen
Organisation besorgt. Wir, die wir schon fünfzig sind, und eine
Stellung im Ausland haben, sind natürlich über das Ärgste hinaus
— aber die Jungen! oder die Alten! Es ist mehr als das Mittelalter,
mehr als Rumänien oder Rußland jemals getan!

At the time, Einstein was in Pasadena as a visiting professor at the
California Institute of Technology. Given the events in Germany, Einstein
knew he could not return, so he went to Le Coq-sur-mer in Belgium
instead (where he spent his last six months in Europe). In March, Einstein
resigned from the Prussian Academy and later renounced his German
citizenship. Only days later, the Nazis confiscated Einstein's possessions
in Germany, including his Berlin bank account, Haberlandstraße
apartment and summer house in Caputh. A caption underneath a
photograph of Einstein that appeared on the front page the publication
of "leading opponents of the Nazi government" sums up the fascist
attitude toward the prominent scientist:

Discovered a much-contested theory of relativity. Was greatly
honored by the Jewish press and the unsuspecting German
people. Showed his gratitude by lying atrocity propaganda against
Adolf Hitler abroad. (Not yet hanged).[25]

The ominous political scene was also distressing to Zweig, who of course
opposed all of what Hitler represented, never even imagining what the
future held. On 10 April 1933 Zweig wrote to Rolland:

ich übergehe mit Schweigen, was wir alle moralisch gelitten
haben, denn selbst in diesem Augenblick will ich, mir selber
getreu, nicht ein ganzes Land hassen, und ich weiß, daß die
Sprache, in der man schreibt, es einem nicht erlaubt, von einem
Volk sogar in seinem Wahn sich loszusagen und es zu verfluchen.
Mir steht jetzt eine tiefgreifende Entscheidung bevor. Soll man
fortgehen? Bleiben heißt: leiden. Bedroht sein. Zum Schweigen
gezwungen sein. Leben wie ein Gefangener. Fortgehen heißt: die
andern im Stich lassen, die nicht vermöge ihrer Arbeit die Chance
materieller Unabhängigkeit haben; wie ein Kapitän das Schiff als

erster verlassen. Aber die Freiheit des Wortes sich bewahren. Bleiben und schweigen (zum Schweigen gezwungen sein) macht der Feigheit verdächtig. Fortgehen riecht noch stärker nach Feigheit. Das ist die Entscheidung, die ich Tag und Nacht hin und her wälze.[26]

In many ways, of course, Zweig immediately felt the impact of the Nazis.[27] One such consequence concerned the libretto of *Die schweigsame Frau*, which he was preparing for Richard Strauss.[28] To be sure, the Nazi dictatorship forbade Strauss to associate with a Jewish librettist. While the ramifications of this affair are many, in short, Zweig, like others, found himself trapped.

As would be expected, then, Zweig's and Einstein's 1933 exchanges react to events in Nazi Germany, as each struggles to understand and deal with the Hitler regime. As fellow Jews, Zweig and Einstein shared a common bond and suffered a common fate. And of these days, Zweig wrote to his friend Huebsch in another unpublished letter of 8 May 1933:

Ja, es ist überall dasselbe, die Politik erschlägt das Interesse am Buch und die Zeiten sind aufregender als sie der kühnste Dichter in einem Roman erfinden könnte. Wahrscheinlich wissen Sie, was bei uns vorgeht, daß auch meine Bücher, obwohl sie mit Politik nichts zu tun haben, in Deutschland öffentlich am Schloßplatz von Berlin am Mittwoch 10. Mai als "undeutsche" verbrannt werden und als Feuerwerk das Auge der Zuschauer erfreuen, statt den aufmerksamen Blick des Lesers. Aber es handelt sich darum, um jeden Preis die Konkurrenz auszuschalten und den Parteigenossen den Weg freizumachen. Vom Standpunkt der Moral, der Gerechtigkeit diese Vorgänge zu untersuchen, hat keinen Sinn. Das wichtigste ist: innerlich festzubleiben. Ich konnte einige Monate gar nichts arbeiten, so sehr war ich von all dem erschüttert und erregt, jetzt fange ich langsam wieder an. Wie es in Hinkunft sein wird, wo meine Bücher erscheinen werden, kann ich noch nicht übersehen, ich denke auch gar nicht soweit. Und auch viele andere Fragen müssen geklärt sein, wahrscheinlich werde ich meine Lebensformen von Anfang bis Ende umstellen müssen — aber immerhin geht es mir noch tausendmal besser als tausend anderen ...

On 10 May 1933 the book burnings had indeed taken place. Around midnight, as William Shirer reports, on a square on *Unter den Linden* opposite the University of Berlin, students ignited some twenty thousand volumes written by so-called "subversive" German authors, such as Albert Einstein, Thomas and Heinrich Mann, Erich Maria Remarque,

Walther Rathenau, Jakob Wassermann, Lion Feuchtwanger and Arnold
Zweig. Foreign authors were not excluded, and the flames also consumed
works by Stefan Zweig, Sigmund Freud, Upton Sinclair, Jack London, H.
G. Wells, Helen Keller, Arthur Schnitzler, Havelock Ellis and others. Dr.
Goebbels watched. And book burnings also took place in other German
cities. As Goebbels defined the book burning mission: " The soul of the
German people can again express itself. These flames not only illuminate
the final end of an old era; they also light up the new."[29] In the chapter
entitled "Incipit Hitler," Zweig later wrote in *Die Welt von Gestern* about
these events:

> Dieses Schicksal völliger literarischer Existenzvernichtung in
> Deutschland mit so eminenten Zeitgenossen wie Thomas Mann,
> Heinrich Mann, Werfel, Freud und Einstein und manchen
> anderen, deren Werk ich ungleich wichtiger nehme als das meine,
> teilen zu dürfen, habe ich eher als Ehre empfunden denn als
> Schmach, und jedwede Märtyrergeste widerstrebt mir dermaßen,
> daß ich dieser Einbeziehung ins allgemeine Schicksal nur ungern
> Erwähnung tue.[30]

Under these conditions Zweig wrote to Einstein on 7 June 1933:

> Hochverehrter Herr Professor!
> Verzeihen Sie, daß ich mich in einer privaten Angelegenheit an
> Sie wende, aber es gilt einen sehr wertvollen und wirklich
> bedeutenden Menschen. Die [illegible words] hat ein
> Preisausschreiben gestellt, bei dem Sie in der Jury sind und ich
> möchte mir erlauben, Sie auf eine wirklich bedeutende Arbeit von
> Dr. Hans Prager[31] hinzuweisen und den sehr wichtigen
> Vorschlag einer internationalen Fakultät — Doktorat des
> Völkerbundes. Er ist nicht mehr Student und könnte sich nur hors
> concours beteiligen, aber seine Erwähnung oder Preiskrönung
> seiner bedeutenden Arbeit wäre für ihn lebenswichtig, er gehört
> zu den zahllosen Existenzen, die durch den nationalsozialistischen
> Orkan beinahe ganz entwurzelt sind, und ist dabei ein geistiger
> Wert hohen Ranges. Und da gegenseitige Hilfe heute mehr denn
> je humane Pflicht ist, erlaube ich mir, Sie auf ihn aufmerksam zu
> machen, falls Ihnen die Arbeit tatsächlich vorgelegt wird.
> Über die Geschehnisse der Zeit denken wir, ich weiß es, in
> gleichem Sinn. Was ich mir wünschte und für wichtig hielte, wäre
> eine gemeinsame Haltung. Ich hatte zu einigen Kameraden
> vorgetastet wie sie sich zu einem gemeinsamen Manifest der von
> Deutschland zurückgestoßenen Künstler und Gelehrten verhielten,
> selbstverständlich ein Manifest, das nicht wehleidig jammert und

klagt, sondern durchaus positiv, selbstbewußt und dabei mit äußerster Ruhe unsere Situation vor der Welt klarlegt. Ich hätte mir ein solches Manifest gewünscht als ein klassisches und dauerndes Stück deutscher Prosa, als bleibendes kulturhistorisches Dokument, gemeinsam von den Besten verfaßt und von allen unterzeichnet — kein Apell um Gnade, kein Hilferuf ans Ausland, sondern nur einen würdigen Epilog, eine granitene Darlesung unseres unverrückbaren Standpunktes. Leider zeigte sich schon bei den ersten Anfragen, daß die meisten kleinlich fragten, wer dabei sein dürfe und wer nicht, und so ließ ich ziemlich enttäuscht den Plan, obwohl ich ihn heute noch nach wie vor für richtig halte, daß wir eine magna charta hätten verfassen und dem unsichtbaren Parlament der Geistigen übermitteln sollen.

Mögen Sie, verehrter Herr Professor, ganz und ungestört sich wieder Ihrer unvergänglichen Aufgabe widmen können, dieser irdisch zerrütteten Welt ihre geistigen Gesetze zu weisen und empfangen Sie in alter Verehrung die ergebene Grüße Ihres

Stefan Zweig

An immediate response to Zweig's letter arrived two days later from Elsa Einstein, Albert Einstein's second wife, whom he had married in 1919 after divorcing Mileva:

Le Coq sur mer, den 9. Juni 1933
Villa Savoyarde

Verehrter Herr Stefan Zweig!

Mein Mann ist augenblicklich in Oxford. Sobald er zurück ist, wird er Ihnen sofort antworten. Dies glaube ich bestimmt, denn ich weiß, wie sehr er Sie als großen Künstler verehrt und ich weiß auch, daß er Ihre Idee, ein solches Manifest zu schreiben, gutheißen wird. Es wäre nett, wenn Sie ihn daran auch ein bissel mitschreiben lassen würden, denn außer seiner Mathematik schreibt er noch einen sehr guten Stil; das wissen so wenige.

Wenn nur die Preisverteilung nicht schon erfolgt ist. Ich habe Angst, es könnte zu spät sein. Lesen Sie bitte inliegenden Brief, Sie sehen, daß der Zeitpunkt beinahe verstrichen ist. Um noch das Möglichste zu tun, schreibe ich heute noch an Schrab und bitte ihn inständig im Namen meines Mannes, alles zu tun, um Ihrem Schützling einen Preis zukommen zu lassen. Diese Verantwortung kann ich wohl übernehmen, nachdem Sie Herr Prager so warm empfehlen.

Führt Sie Ihr Weg nie nach Belgien? Es wäre besonders nett und würde meinen Mann sehr freuen, wenn Sie hier in Coq bei Ostende ein bißchen Station machen würden.

Mit recht freundlichen Grüßen
Ihre
Elsa Einstein

Einstein was at Oxford where he gave the Herbert Spencer Lecture "On the Method of Theoretical Physics." The correspondence with Zweig continued, and on 16 June 1933 the Austrian writer responded to Einstein's wife:

Hochverehrte gnädige Frau!

Ich danke Ihnen vielmals für Ihre gütigen Worte und bitte Sie, mich auch Ihrem verehrten Herrn Gemahl zu empfehlen. Wir leben hier reichlich im unsichern politischen Wolkenspiel und man muß seine Kraft gut zusammenhalten, um überhaupt noch etwas Vernünftiges tun zu können. Für jenes Manifest wollen wir uns einmal ein paar zusammensetzen und einen ersten Entwurf aufsetzen, den wir dann den entscheidenden Männern, so vor allem Ihrem verehrten Herrn Gemahl vorlegen. Es schweben jetzt unermeßlich viel Pläne für eine repräsentative Zeitschrift und einen repräsentativen Verlag, aber die Formen sind noch nicht recht greifbar und "gleichgeschalteten" Deutschland in einer ebensolchen Beschlossenheit und nicht in kraftloser Zersplitterung entgegenzutreten.

Mögen Sie doch oben am Meer helle Tage haben und seien Sie respektvollst mit Ihrem verehrten Herrn Gemahl gegrüßt, von Ihrem

sehr ergebenen

Stefan Zweig

Shortly thereafter Einstein wrote to Zweig:

Le Coq sur mer, den 28. Juni 1933

Verehrter Herr Stefan Zweig!

Unsere jüdischen Intellektuellen sind einzeln genommen prachtvolle Kerle, es scheint aber beinahe hoffnungslos, sie in einigermaßen beträchtlicher Zahl an denselben Wagen spannen zu wollen. So scheinen wir uns in der Hauptsache mit dem unsichtbaren Bande begnügen zu müssen, welches unsere Feinde um uns gelegt haben.

Ich hätte ein heroisch angehauchtes Manifest eingedenk meiner kollegialen Pflichten gewiß unterzeichnet, wenn auch mit zweifelhaften Gefühlen. Denn wenn ich etwas als tragisch empfinde, so ist es der sittliche Niedergang eines großen Volkes und die Leiden der einzelnen Kreatur. Die Wahl meines Aufenthaltortes aber ist für mich nicht mit Gefühlen belastet und das Bewußtsein, deutschen Boden nicht mehr betreten zu können, wiegt für mich nicht schwerer, als dem Quotienten des Flächeninhaltes dieses Landes und der Erdoberfläche entspricht. Es wird gewissermassen ein psychisches Erdbeben auf jungkultiviertem Grunde konstatiert und weiter nichts.

Eine wirkliche Sorge ist nur, daß die Katastrophe einigermaßen lokalisiert bleibt; wer kann dies wissen? Die Liebe und Verehrung für die geistigen und sittlichen Werte scheint wirklich erschüttert zu sein, nicht nur in Deutschland.

Aber unser Volk hat schon vieles durchlebt und die Sonne scheint immer noch warm und die Bäume blühen.

Herzlichst grüßt Sie

Ihr

A. Einstein

P.S. Ich sende Ihnen zur Erbauung eine Einladung des Rektors der Goethe-Universität an seine getreuen Mannen.

Although Zweig discussed the idea with Einstein and other colleagues, the manifesto never materialized as planned. Nevertheless the spirit that sparked Zweig is important, just as is Einstein's response. However, such a significant undertaking should not be summarily dismissed, especially because further information about it is unavailable in the Zweig critical literature and even the manifesto itself remains unknown. In fact, the draft is not among the Einstein/Zweig papers, but a search for it in other Zweig archival collections has proven successful. Indeed, partly hidden, but nevertheless carefully preserved among other unpublished Zweig documents with the Max Brod papers, there exists, with some handwritten corrections, a four page typed statement, which shows itself to be the draft to which Zweig refers in his letter to Einstein. As such, it is not yet the "classical document" that Zweig intended it to represent. Still unpublished, this historic manuscript reads as follows:

Einige *Grundlagen*
zu einem kollektive auszuarbeitenden Manifest[32]

Wenn wir mit einer gemeinsamen Erklärung vor die Welt
treten, so sei es nicht unsere Absicht, Mitleid zu fordern: Es ist
zuviel anderes Leiden in unserer Zeit, als daß wir einen Vorrang
beanspruchten. Ebensowenig ist es unsere Absicht, zum Haß
aufzurufen und Gericht zu fordern: Es ist genug Haß in der Welt.
Wir wollen nichts als klar unsere Stellung zu den Geschehnissen
der letzten Zeit bekunden und gegen den systematischen Versuch,
uns zu entrechten und zu entehren, der jemals gegen ein Volk
unternommen wurde, unser Wort erheben.

Es ist in Deutschland unternommen worden, im Namen einer
Rassenideologie welche weder von der Wissenschaft noch von der
Moral der übrigen Welt anerkannt wird, uns durch organisierten
Haß und offizielle Verfolgung aus einer mehr als tausendjährigen
Verbundenheit loszulösen und zu einer Rasse oder Nation
minderer Art zu erniedrigen. Man hat Gesetze geschaffen um
Rechte zu nehmen, die als Menschenrechte in unserer zivilisierten
Welt sonst unantastbar und unablösbar gelten, man hat
autoritative Bürger, die seit hunderten Jahren dem Lande
verbunden gelebt, als lästige Gäste erklärt. Wir erklären nun, daß
wir niemals eine solche Minderung unserer Menschenrechte auch
in der äußersten Wehrlosigkeit und Bedrängnis als gültig
anerkennen werden, weil wir unbeugsam der Überzeugung sind,
daß Gott die Menschen nicht geteilt habe in obere und untere
Rassen, in Herrenvölker und Sklavenvölker, Edelinge und Parias,
sondern sie alle nach seinem Ebenbilde geschaffen. Wir glauben,
daß weit über unser persönliches Schicksal hinaus eine solche
prinzipielle Proklamierung der ethischen Überlegenheit eines
Volkes über die andern unverweigerlich zu Erbitterungen und
kriegerischen Spannungen führen müßte und die friedliche Einheit
unserer Welt vernichten. Deshalb verwerfen wir jeden Rassen-
dünkel nicht nur als eine uns persönlich feindselig gemeinte
Gesinnung, sondern als eine der Wahrheit widersprechende und
der ganzen Welt gefährliche Ideologie.

Wenn wir so mit aller Entschlossenheit jeden Versuch, uns oder
irgend eine Rasse oder Nation der Erde als eine untergeordnete
und parasitäre zu bezeichnen als verhängnisvolle Überheblichkeit
ablehnen, erklären wir aber gleichzeitig, daß wir durch keine der
Methoden, die jetzt gegen uns im Sinne solcher Erniedrigung
versucht werden, uns entehrt fühlen. Nicht für uns empfinden wir
es beschämend, wenn Frauen mit abgeschorenem Haar durch die
Straßen geschleppt werden, weil sie einem Freunde die Treue

gehalten, wenn ... und ein aufgepöbelter Haß nicht einmal Halt macht vor den heiligen Leichensteinen der Toten; Erniedrigungen dieser Art sind unserer Meinung nach nicht schandbar für denjenigen, der sie erleidet, sondern für denjenigen, der sie vollbringt. Aber was auch geschehen ist und noch geschehen mag, es kann unsere Ehre nicht berühren. Ein Volk, das der Welt das heiligste und kostbarste Buch aller Zeiten gegeben, auf dessen religiöse Lehre die ganze Sittlichkeit unseres Erdkreises aufgebaut ist, braucht sich nicht zu verteidigen, wenn es als inferior erklärt wird und hat nicht Not, sich selbst zu rühmen der unablässigen Leistungen auf allen Gebieten der Kunst, der Wissenschaft, der denkerischen Taten: sie sind eingeschrieben, unauslöschbar in der Geschichte jedes Landes, in dem wir Heimstatt hatten. Und wäre im Raume der deutschen Wissenschaft unter tausend Taten von jüdischen Gelehrten keine andere geleistet worden als die eine Tat Ehrlichs allein, welche die grausamste Geißel der Menschheit, die Syphilis beseitigte und Millionen in Deutschland und Welt zum Segen ward, wir hätten allein schon alle Fehler und Verstöße entgolten, die der Haß uns heute zuschreibt.

Wir verwerfen also ohne Erregtheit, aber mit aller denkbaren Entschlossenheit den organisierten Versuch unserer Volkentehrung, wie er heute von den Rassenideologien unternommen wird und sind bereit, lieber unterzugehen ehe diesen Wahn als eine Wahrheit anzuerkennen. Dies soll aber keineswegs besagen, daß wir uns blind stellen gegen das Vorhandensein der sozialen Tatsache eines jüdischen Problems, das durch den Krieg und die Krise ebenso wie alle andern sozialen und nationalen Probleme eine gesteigerte Schärfe angenommen hat. Niemand weiß mehr um dieses Problem als wir selbst, die wir es in zweitausend Jahren erzwungener Heimatlosigkeit erlitten. Aber wir weichen ihm nicht aus, wir wollen es weiterhin in seiner ganzen Tiefe erleben, in seiner ganzen Schwere ermessen, wir wollen es in Tat und Befriedigung verwandeln wie ja schon seit dreißig Jahren unsere besten Kräfte aufopfernd seiner Lösung gewidmet sind. In diesen dreißig Jahren haben wir aus eigener Energie, aber ohne jede Gewalt, ohne jede fremde Hilfe und doch sieghaft gegen die schwersten Widerstände, uns die alte Heimat erschlossen und großartig aufbauend den Beweis geliefert gegen die Verleumdung, wir seien nur im Zersetzenden tätig; es ist unser eigener Wille, niemandem zur Last zu fallen, der uns nicht volle Brüderlichkeit zuerkennt und keiner, der Palästina gesehen, kann unseren ehrlichen Willen verkennen, selbst die Lösung des jüdischen Problems in schöpferischer Form zu beschleunigen und zu verwirklichen.

Selbstverständlich kann ein zweitausendjähriges Schicksal nicht
mit einem Schlage beendet werden, aber wir sind mitten am
Wege, mitten in der Arbeit, es aus eigener Kraft zu bewältigen.
Was wir nun fordern ist nichts, als daß man uns bei diesem
Werke nicht störe, daß unsere Aufgabe gemeinsam mit uns gelöst
werde und nicht eigenmächtig gegen uns. Das sie beendet werde
im Geiste der Humanität und nicht in der Gesinnung des Haßes
und der Erbitterung.

Darum erklären wir hier öffentlich im Namen des jüdischen
Volkes: sosehr wir jeden Versuch einer Entrechtung und
Entehrung von Seite irgend einer Nation ablehnen, sosehr sind
wir bereit mit allen Nationen und ihrer gemeinsamen Vertretung,
dem Völkerbunde an jeder Lösung des jüdischen Problems
mitzuwirken, sofern sie unserer Ehre und der Ehre des
Jahrhunderts entspricht. Wir sind bereit jedes Opfer zu bringen,
um für die Ausgestoßenen den Aufbau einer neuen Heimat zu
beschleunigen, wir werden jeden Vorschlag dankbar prüfen, jede
Anregung eifrig entgegennehmen; zu allen und allem, was
Energie, Opfer, Hingabe und Gesinnung fordert wird die Welt die
Judenheit freudig bereit sehen, — nur zu dem einen nicht, daß wir
einen weltgefährlichen rassischen Wahn als giltig anerkennen und
Gewalt jemals Gerechtigkeit nennen.

(Dann ein Schlußsatz)

Zweig had also written to Felix Salten[33] concerning the need for such a
manifesto, and a still unpublished letter of 7 May 1933 is instructive:

Lieber und verehrter Herr Salten, ich werde leider nicht zum
Pen-Club nach Ragusa kommen können — unter uns gesagt, halte
ich auch jedes Auftreten und Vortreten jüdisch deutscher
Schriftsteller auf Congressen jetzt für falsch. Die *anderen* müssen
jetzt unsere Sache nehmen, weil es die der Freiheit und der Ehre
des Wortes ist.

Mir schwebt aber eine andere Aktion[34] vor und ich wäre
Ihnen dankbar, wenn Sie diese einmal mit Werfel[35], Beer-
Hofmann etc. besprechen wollten. Ich glaube, wir deutschen
Schriftsteller jüdischer Rasse sollten jetzt gemeinsam ein Manifest
verfassen, ein Manifest an die Deutschen und an die Welt, indem
wir nicht wehleidig über Unrecht klagen, nicht kleinmütig
jammern, nicht gegen Deutschland sprechen, sondern einfach
unsere Situation darstellen. Wir müßten darin sagen, wie wir in
der deutschen Sprache gelebt, wie wir ihr gedient haben, wie weit
wir das Ansehen der deutschen Literatur über die Welt getragen
haben und daß wir durch Jahrzehnte ohne Anfeindung und in

innigstem Zusammenleben mit den besten Deutschen brüderlich gewirkt haben, bis 1933 die Neunzehnjährigen befahlen, wir sollten hebräisch schreiben. Dieses Manifest dürfte nichts fordern — nur *darstellen* und dies in einer Weise, daß es als Meisterstück deutscher Prosa, als Zeitdokument die Zeiten überdauern sollte. Millionen in allen Ländern würden es lesen und je mächtiger je gerechter, je klarer es geformt wäre, umso besser. Ich dächte, wenn wir, Werfel und Sie und Beer-Hofmann und Josef Roth und Wassermann und Döblin uns zusammensetzten, könnte etwas Gültiges und Imposantes entstehen — nur in *dieser*, in einer großen, in einer einmaligen und *gemeinsamen* Form sollten wir das Wort nehmen. Ich hoffe, die andern, Mombert, Feuchtwanger, etc. würden sich dann unserem Text anschließen. Das ist *mein* Vorschlag und ich lege ihn Ihnen vor, weil ich meine, wir sollten heute nichts allein und alles brüderlich-gemeinsam tun. In treuer Verehrung Ihr

Stefan Zweig

Similarly, in an unpublished letter of 9 May 1933 Zweig wrote to Max Brod[36]:

Lieber Max Brod!

Sprechen wir nicht über die Zeiten, man müßte Bücher schreiben. Denken wir nur an Positives.

Erstens, wie denken Sie darüber, daß wir deutsche Schriftsteller jüdischen Stammes, die man jetzt mit dem Rasiermesser absondert, gemeinsam ein Manifest erlassen sollten, das sich an die deutsche Welt richtet? Kein wehmütiges Geklage natürlich, keine Anklage, sondern in klassischer Prosa eine Feststellung unserer Situation und unserer Leistung und unseres für die übrige Welt selbstverständlichen Anspruchs. Ich glaube, ein solches Dokument könnte ein Kulturdokument sein und je ruhiger es gefaßt und je weniger wehleidig und in Gegenteil sicher in seinem Selbstbewußtsein, umsomehr wäre es berechtigt. Ich glaube, wir sollten nichts einzeln tun, sondern mit einem solchen Dokument auf unsere *gemeinsame* Leistung und das gemeinsam erlittene Unrecht hinweisen.

Zweitens, Sie sind an einer Zeitung und haben gute Verbindungen. Wäre es Ihnen moglich, über die Gesandtschaft oder über die Zeitung *baldigst* einige Originalfotografien der morgen in Berlin stattfindenden Verbrennung unserer Bücher zu beschaffen und mir zu senden? Ich könnte sie gut brauchen für

ausländische Zeitungen.[37] Selbstverständlich aber kein Wort, daß
Sie für *mich* besorgen. Strengste Diskretion, ich zähle darauf!
Herzlichst Ihr
S.Z.

Even though Zweig's "classical document" never appeared as he intended
it[38], at least it served to initiate some reaction to the political situation.
In light of the events in Germany, Zweig quickly began work on *Erasmus*
in 1933. In an unpublished letter of 16 December 1933, Zweig described
his literary endeavors to Huebsch:

> Ich habe mit Absicht alles Philologische und Literarhistorische
> darin zurückgedrägt und es gleichzeitig zu einem Programm für
> die humane Weltanschauung und als Kampfbuch gegen jede Art
> von Fanatismus gemacht. Ein wirklich großes Volksbuch wird es
> natürlich nicht werden und will es nicht sein, aber ich glaube, daß
> es ein anständiges Buch wird und bei weitem interessanter als die
> übrigen, die bisher über Erasmus geschrieben werden. Erscheinen
> würde es zunächst in Deutschland als Privatdruck, also
> unverkäuflich, denn in Deutschland möchte ich nicht erscheinen
> wegen der erniedrigenden Bedingungen (Unterschrift, Zensur,
> Genehmigung) die heute damit verbunden sind, ebensowenig in
> einem typischen Emigrantenverlag.

And, in another unpublished letter of 30 December 1933 to Huebsch,
Zweig commented:

> Erasmus schreitet inzwischen fort und wird Ende Januar
> hoffentlich fertig sein, ich glaube, daß es mir gelungen ist, trotz
> des scheinbar Abseitigen des Themas, das Buch für die Zeit
> interessant zu machen. Es wird gleichzeitig ein Traktat gegen den
> Parteigeist und den Fanatismus zur Rechten und zur Linken, den
> Fanatismus per se, als Widerpart der Weltvernunft. Einzelne
> inzwischen veröffentlichte, haben Eindruck gemacht ...[39]

As Daviau rightly says,

> [*Erasmus*] was not only a warning against dictators, but the means
> for Zweig, who felt a close personal bond with Erasmus, to justify
> his reluctance and unwillingness to become embroiled in political
> controversy ... he depicted the suffering and tragedy of the type
> which was powerless to act except through the medium of the
> written word.[40]

Indeed, in another unpublished letter of December 1933 to Huebsch, Zweig, speaking about one of Feuchtwanger's novels, expressed:

> Er ist ein wenig zu rasch gearbeitet, außerdem bin ich privatim der Ansicht, daß Juden nicht zu viele Bücher über die jüdische Frage schreiben sollten, weil dadurch tatsächlich die Absicht Hitlers erfüllt und das Judenproblem zu stark ins Bewußtsein der ganzen Welt getragen wird.

The tragedy is, of course, that neither Zweig nor others could halt the march of the Nazi troops as they tramped through the cities in Germany and then Europe. As we know, the situation in Germany grew worse.

A month after the 1933 exchanges with Einstein, Zweig described the current events to Rolland in a letter of 10 June 1933:

> Die Lage in Deutschland ist schrecklich, die einzige lesbare Tageszeitung, die *Deutsche Allg. Ztg.*, verboten und die Einzelheiten, die man jeden Tag erfährt, abscheulich. Wir sind *sehr* bedroht hier in Österreich, die ökonomische Situation führt den Nazis täglich neue Parteigänger zu. Seit sie gesehen haben, daß in Deutschland Tausende brutal von ihren Stellen verjagt und durch Nazis ersetzt werden, strömt alles zu ihnen in der Hoffnung auf materielles Fortkommen.[41]

Even though history books document other occurrences, the suffering and inhumanity that Einstein, Zweig and hundreds of thousands of other innocent individuals experienced never can be fully recorded. Only brief moments, like those Zweig describes in his letters, can be visualized, but even then the pain and terror defy description. Infinite is the anguish; it is unfathomable, except to its victims who alone know its haunting torment. Nevertheless, even though our best documentary efforts always will be insufficient to the task, it remains our moral responsibility to locate, edit and publish such materials. The last chapter about the Nazi period may never be written, but drafts of it must always be penned. Anguished words like those Stefan Zweig cries out to his colleagues must be heard.

The next available exchange occurs in 1934 when both Einstein and Zweig were in exile:

Portland Place,
London, W.1
21. Juli 1934.

Sehr geerhter Herr Doktor!

Es ist mir sehr leid zu hören, daß Sie ungefähr im selben Zeitpunkt, wo ich freiwillig London verlasse, auch Ihren Aufenthalt infolge der Ungunst der Verhältnisse aufgeben müssen. Leider habe ich hier gar keine Beziehungen zu den Ämtern, durch die ich Einfluß nehmen könnte und weiß auch nicht, ob Sie mit Spanien das Richtige gewählt haben. Es war jüngst Joseph Chapiro hier, der mir zu meinem großen Bedauern erzählte, daß er trotz der besten Beziehungen dort nicht richtig Fuß fassen kann. Hoffentlich haben Sie ein besseres Geschick und ich bitte Sie mir zu glauben, daß es mir aufrichtig leid tut, keinen wirklich praktischen und realisierbaren Rat in dieser Ihrer schweren Situation zu wissen.

Ergebenst

Stefan Zweig

Regarding the 21. July 1934 letter to Einstein, Zweig wrote in another unpublished letter of 8 June 1934 to Huebsch:

... ich [will] im Herbst oder Winter eine Zeitlang außer Europa sein, denn ich will mich von Salzburg loslösen, wo täglich Bomben geschmissen werden, gestern eine gegen das Haus Reinhards, möchte mich aber so loslösen, daß es nicht den Anschein einer Flucht oder Emigration hat. Am besten kachiere ich nun diesen stillen Abgang mit einer Vortragsreise in Amerika oder ähnlichen Dingen.

A two year time gap occurs before the next and last available letter, which is written by Zweig:

[1936]
49. Hallam St.

Lieber, verehrter Herr Professor,

wenn ich Ihnen gleichzeitig ein Buch [*Kaleidoskop*] gesammelten kleinen Novellen schicke, so geschieht es nicht, um Sie mit Literatur zu plagen. Ich habe in einer neuen Arbeit *Der begrabene Leuchter* (Seite 228 u. s. f.) versucht, das jüdische Schicksal in einem dichterischen Symbol zu behandeln und da ich um Ihren Anteil für das jüdische Problem weiß, könnte Ihnen vielleicht diese Legende eine Ablenkung von Ihrer strengen Arbeit in einer freien Stunde sein. Mir bietet sie Gelegenheit, Sie, Verehrter, wieder einmal von ferne auf das herzlichste zu begrüßen. Ihr aufrichtig ergebener

Stefan Zweig

As Friderike Zweig says, *Der begrabene Leuchter* "became for many who despaired, and especially for Jews, an exalting experience. Immeasurable patience is depicted here, and the humility produced by faith and commong destiny."[42]

Although no further Einstein/Zweig correspondence has been located, we do know that Zweig met Einstein at least once in 1938.[43] Otherwise only an exchange between Einstein and Friderike Zweig is extant:

1 Sheridan Sq[uare]
N[ew]. Y[ork]. 14
26. Nov 44

Hochverehrtester Herr Professor,
    nun belästige ich Sie abermals mit der Einsendung dieses Telegramms, wofür meine Rückantwort bezahlt wurde.
    Ich bitte [Sie], sich jedoch nicht um eine Antwort zu bemühen, so gerne ich sie geben möchte, falls es Ihnen an Zeit -- und Lust dazu fehlt.
    Alfredo Cahn war ein Freund meines Mannes und sein langjähriger Übersetzer, der seit vielen Jahren bestrebt ist Argentinien's Intellektuellen ausgezeichnete Bücher zu vermitteln. Er würde Espasa Calpa's Ausgaben gewiß nicht empfehlen, wenn diese nicht höchsten, kulturellen Zwecken entsprächen.
    Ich wäre dankbar für Ihre gütige Antwort.
                In Verehrung Ihre
                ergebene
                Friderike Zweig
P.S. Alfredo Cahn wird demnächst einen wie er mir schrieb sehr vorteilhaften Vertrag Herrn Dr. Kaiser übermitteln (für "Mein Weltbild").

Einstein responded to Friderike Zweig:

Die Herausgabe bedeutender Werke der Weltliteratur als Volksausgaben in der Collection Austral bedeutet nach meiner Überzeugung eine verdienstliche Tat im Interesse der Verbreitung wahrer Bildung.
den 3. Dezember 1944   Albert Einstein

In conclusion, it appears that Einstein and Zweig rarely interacted, and their written exchanges truly are few in number. Nevertheless their contacts encompassed one of the most troubling, momentous periods of history, and given their respective personalities, it is not surprising that their correspondence broaches significant subjects. It is of course possible that Zweig may have hoped that letters from such a renowned figure might enrich his already famous and unique autograph collection; but in fact his approaches clearly arose from a deeply felt commitment to acknowledge the rights of a fellow Jew.[44] To a certain extent each enjoyed the results of the other's research and writing, but their truly common bond was that of Judaism. As we have seen, one of Zweig's first letters to Einstein was to enlist support for a Jewish colleague. Thirteen years later terror and persecution brought them together again. The letters also show that Einstein welcomed and understood Zweig's efforts. It is not surprising that years later, when Friderike asked for Einstein's support, the great scientist should give it. Ever a world celebrity, Einstein never forgot his fellow Jews or other colleagues. In this sense, the last line of Zweig's *Jeremias* summarizes well a keynote theme of their friendship and their heritage: "Man kann ein Volk bezwingen, doch nie seinen Geist" (327).

Notes

[1]   For permission to publish the Einstein letters, I sincerely thank Dr. Otto Nathan and the Albert Einstein Estate (New York). For permission to publish the Zweig letters I also thank Mr. Kurt L. Maschler and the Williams Verlag AG (London), representinq the Stefan Zweig Estate Einstein Estate, the Seeley G. Mudd Manuscript Library at Princeton University, and the Jewish National and University Library in Jerusalem. The Zweig letters to Brod and Salten are privately owned by the Max Brod Estate (Tel Aviv) and Felix Salten Estate (Zurich), both of whom I also thank for making these documents available to me. The Zweig to Huebsch letters are deposited at the Ben Huebsch Archive at the Library of Congress in Washington, D.C. I also sincerely thank Ms. Helen Dukas, Dr. John Stachel (Princeton and Boston), Mrs. Alice von Kahler (Princeton), Mrs. Sonja Dobbins (London), Dr. Donald A. Prater (Gingins, Switzerland), the Huebsch Estate (New York) and the Stefan Zweig Archive at the State University College at Fredonia (New York). All of the above individuals and archives have extended many favors and courtesies to me, especially during interviews and archival visits. Minor errors in the letters have been silently corrected; otherwise the original orthography has been retained in most cases, and any editorial emendations have been so noted by square brackets.

[2]   My 1983 edition of the Richard Beer-Hofmann/Stefan Zweig correspondence carried the dedication: *For Harry Zohn who continues the tradition.* In the intervening years my appreciation of Harry as a true friend and dedicated, genuine scholar

continues to grow. My wife and our children join me in congratulating Harry and his family on the occasion of his seventieth birthday.

3   Harry Zohn: "Aus unbekannten Briefen von und über Stefan Zweig." In: *Modern Austrian Literature*, Number 14, 1981, p. 139.

4   Cf. Berlin/Lindken, *Hofmannsthal/Zweig*.

5   Harry Zohn, in his cogent introduction to the American edition of Zweig's autobiography, calls this work, "a mirror of an age, rather than of a life" (*World of Yesterday*, p. vi).

6   Waltraud Schwarze et. al., eds., *Romain Rolland/Stefan Zweig Briefwechsel 1910-1923*. Berlin 1987, p. 502.

7   Ibid., p. 502.

8   Ibid., p. 508.

9   Cf. my editions of the Zweig/Huebsch letters.

10 Chapior, journalist; Latzko, Hungarian novelist and pacifist; Alexander Moissi, Albanian actor who performed in German and became an Austrian star; Tervin, second wife of Alexander Moissi; Thimig, daughter of Hugo Thimig and the wife of Max Reinhardt.

11 Ronald W. Clark: *Einstein. The Life and Times*. New York 1971, p. 255 ff; cf. Banesh Hofmann and Helen Dukas: *Albert Einstein. Creator and Rebel*. New York 1972.

12 *Stefan Zweig/Friderike Zweig. Unrast der Liebe. Ihr Leben und ihre Zeit im Spiegel ihres Briefwechsels*. Bern 1981, p. 96.

13 Ibid., p. 256.

14 Ibid., p. 256.

15 Ibid., p. 257.

16 Stefan Zweig: *Briefwechsel mit Hermann Bahr, Sigmund Freud, Rainer Maria Rilke und Arthur Schnitzler*, ed. by Jeffrey B. Berlin, Hans-Ulrich Lindken and Donald A. Prater. Frankfurt/Main 1987, p. 49.

17 Donald Daviau: "Stefan Zweig's Victors in Defeat." In: *Monatshefte*, Number 51, 1951, p. 4.

18 *Rolland/Zweig*, p. 576.

19 *Stefan Zweig/Friderike Zweig*, p. 184.

20 *Rolland/Zweig*, II, p. 360.

21 David Turner: *Moral Values and the Human Zoo. The "Novellen" of Stefan Zweig*. Hull 1988, p. 234.

22 Friderike Zweig: *Stefan Zweig*. New York 1946, p. 132-133.

[23] The last signature is illegible; it may possibly be Georges Duhamel's or Leon Bazalgette's. Antonina Luchaire, actually Antonina Vallentin, the Polish-born biographer and literary critic; Jean (Baptiste) Perrin, Secretatry of State and French scientist; Valéry, French poet of the new Impressionism; Crémieux, French literary critic and translator of Pirandello; Jules Luchaire, politician and husband of Antonina Luchaire; Chana (Hannah Orloff, French sculptor; Rene Jouglet (unidentified); Cain, director of the Bibliotheque National.

[24] Cf. *Stefan Zweig/Friderike Zweig*, pp. 209 and 211.

[25] Clark (Note 11), p. 47.

[26] *Rolland/Zweig*, II, pp. 506-507.

[27] Cf. Hildemar Holl and Klaus Zelewitz: "Hausdurchsuchung 1934. Versuch einer Dokumentation über Stefan Zweigs Abschied von Österreich." In: *Zirkular*, Sondernummer 2, 1981, pp. 77=95; Donald A. Prater: "Stefan Zweig und die Neue Welt." In: *Zirkular*, Sondernummer 2, 1981, pp. 137-163.

[28] Donald Prater: *Stefan Zweig. Das Leben eines Ungeduldigen*. Munich 1981, pp. 319 ff.

[29] William L. Shirer: *The Rise and Fall of the Third Reich*. New York 1960, p. 241.

[30] Stefan Zweig: *Die Welt von gestern*. Frankfurt/Main 1985, p. 418.

[31] Zweig had written an introduction to Prager's *Die Weltanschauung Dostojewskis*. Hildesheim 1925.

[32] In the case of this "Manifest," the original orthography was modernized.

[33] An edition of the complete *Stefan Zweig/Feliz Salten correspondence*, which I am editing together with Hans-Ulrich Lindken, is forthcoming.

[34] Zweig uses the spelling "Action."

[35] Cf. Jeffrey B. Berlin: "March 14, 1938: 'Es gibt kein Österreich mehr': Some Unpublished Correspondence between Franz Werfel, Alma Mahler Werfel and Ben Huebsch." In: *DVjs*, Number 62, 1988, pp. 741-763; Jeffrey B. Berlin and Hans-Ulrich Lindken: "Der unveröffentlichte Briefwechsel zwischen Stefan Zweig und Franz Werfel." In: *Modern Austrian Literature*, Number 24, 1991; Donald A. Prater: "Stefan Zweig and Franz Werfel." In: *Modern Austrian Literature*, Number 24, 1991.

[36] An edition of the complete *Stefan Zweig/Max Brod correspondence*, which I am editing together with Julius M. Herz is forthcoming.

[37] Cf. Donald A. Prater and Volker Michels: *Stefan Zweig. Leben und Werk im Bild*. Frankfurt/Main 1981, p. 205.

[38] Cf. Zweig's essay "Die moralische Entgiftung Europas" (1932) in: *Stefan Zweig. Zeiten und Schicksale. Aufsätze und Vorträge aus den Jahren 1902-1942*, ed. by Knut Beck. Frankfurt/Main 1990, pp. 40-56.

[39] Cf. Zweig's letter of 15 May 1933 to Klaus Mann, in Stefan Zweig: *Briefe an Freunde*, ed. by Richard Friedenthal. Frankfurt/Main 1978, p. 228.

[40] Daviau, p. 7.

[41] *Rolland/Zweig*, II, pp. 517-518.

[42] F. Zweig, p. 133; cf. Klara Carmely: "The Ideal of Eternal Homelessness: Stefan Zweig and Judaism." In: *Stefan Zweig. The World of Yesterday's Humanist Today*, ed. by Marion Sonnenfeld. New York 1983, pp. 111-117.

[43] Cf. Prater, *Das Leben*, p. 373.

[44] Cf. Mark H. Gelber: "Stefan Zweig und die Judenfrage von heute." In: *Stefan Zweig heute*, ed. by Mark H. Gelber. Bern 1987, pp. 160-180; Stephen H. Garrin: "Stefan Zweig's Judaism." In: *Modern Austrian Literature*, Number 14, 1981, pp. 271-290; Margarita Pazi: "Stefan Zweig, Europäer und Jude." In: *Modern Austrian Literature*, Number 14, 1981, pp. 291-311.

III.

Brücken im Bau:
Dichtung und Übersetzung als Vermittlungsversuche
zwischen heterogenen Kulturen

Building Bridges:
Literature and Translation as Cultural Mediation

Lola Blonder

Rückkehr (Wien 1956)

Es ist nicht Heimweh, was ich leide,
nur daß es tief im Herzen brennt,
daß ich durch altvertraute Straßen wandre,
und keiner da ist, der mich kennt.
Ist keiner da, der mich mit Augen grüßte,
ist keiner, der mir freundlich gibt die Hand?
Und Amseln singen immer noch die gleichen Lieder,
bezaubernd duftend blüht der Flieder.
Wo ist der Freund, der mich gekannt?

Zuzeiten sitz' ich unter alten Bäumen,
und Vogelruf tönt jubelnd aus dem Grün.
Ich schließe meine Augen zu, ich träume.
Wohin führt mich mein Traum? wohin?
Zum Garten, wo als Kind ich spielte?
Zum Brunnen, draus ich durstig trank?
Kastanien blühn in rot und weißen Kerzen,
darunter träumend steht die alte Bank.

Hier wuchs und blühte meine Jugend
wie Gras in Gottes Garten wächst, wie Strauch und Baum.
Hier in dem Boden war ich eingewurzelt.
Wie tief, wie tief ... ich wußt es kaum.
... und nun ist's so, als wäre nichts geschehn.
Wie rot doch die Kastanienkerze brennt!
Ich wandle durch die Straßen, durch die Gassen,
und nun ist keiner da, der mich beim Namen nennt.

Heimat?

Auf Flügeln die kein Vogel trägt,
schwebend durch die Lüfte zieht der Wand'rer,
über Wolken, die wie Lämmerherden sich
zusammenballen.
Geisterhafte Gletscher heben
traumhaft hoch ihr drohend Haupt.

Nach der Heimat seiner Sprache geht der Flug,
doch nicht zurücke.
Nur zu Gast kommt er, als Künder
längstverscholl'ner Geistesschätze,
in der Sprache, die sein erstes Lallen war.
Ungetreuen ... hält er Treue.
Aus dem Brand, aus Schutt und Asche
rettet er ans sich're Ufer...
kostbarer als Kronjuwelen sind,
          das WORT.

9. Oktober 1984
Mein Brief an Harry Zohn vor seinem Abflug nach Wien

Peter Demetz

Die Legende vom magischen Prag[1]

Als ich unlängst nach vierzig Jahren nach Prag zurückkehrte, in eine, wie mir schien, verwahrloste Stadt, war ich überrascht, von allen Seiten mehr über den magischen Ort des Golem zu hören als über die einstige Residenz T. G. Masaryks. Ich setzte mir damals in den Kopf, eine Streitschrift gegen das magische Prag zu verfassen, gelangte aber bald zur Einsicht, daß eine solche Streitschrift die eine Legende nur durch eine andere ersetzen könnte, und dachte mir deshalb, daß es besser wäre, vorgeformten Thesen zu entsagen, und lieber Proportionen zu definieren und ererbte Gemeinplätze skeptisch auf ihren Kern abzuklopfen. Ich füge hinzu, daß ich in dieser Arbeit sehr viel vom Prager Slawisten Karel Krejčí und seinem Buch *Praha Legend a Skutečností/Prag: Legende und Wirklichkeit* (1967) lernte, das nur sechs Jahre vor Angelo Maria Ripellinos *Praga Magica* (1973) erschien, und im Kontrast zu dem "launischen" italienischen Buch (so seine Selbstcharakteristik), die Traditionen des "phantastischen" Prag mit jenen der königlichen, aufgeklärten, biedermeierlichen, und plebejischen Stadt in lebhafter Pluralität balancierte. Ich will aber nicht nur beschreiben und frage auch nach den Gründen, welche das besondere Bild des phantastischen, magischen, mystischen, unheimlichen oder geheimnisvollen Prag, oder wie man es nennen will, gerade in einer neuen Epoche rationaler Gesellschafts-reformen, in den Vordergrund des Interesses schieben, und nach der Ideologie dieses Interesses, die, indem sie das Eine akzentuiert, das Andere verbirgt und verdrängt.

I.

Ich beginne auf scheinbaren Umwegen mit einem dritten Buch, das ideologische Voraussetzungen klärt, ohne sich ihrer selbst bewußt zu sein. In seinem amerikanischen Buch *Prag: The Mystical City* (1971) streift Josef Wechsberg auf wenigen Seiten die Sage von Libussa und gelangt sogleich, in einem kühnen Sprung, ins siebzehnte Jahrhundert, die Epoche Rudolphs und des Rabbi Löw. In seiner Auswahl der Stoffe und Figuren hält sich Wechsberg an einen kulturkritischen Konsensus, der die Prager Mystik und Magie, allerdings ohne feinere Unterschiede, seit jeher im rudolfinischen Zeitalter lokalisierte und die mittelalterliche und barocke Mystik katholischer Herkunft ignorierte. Die Prager modernen

Geschichtsschreiber, ob Nationale, Erben der Hussiten, oder liberale
Republikaner, waren aus historischen Gründen geneigt, die katholische
Tradition an den Rand zu drängen; und das ist auch bei Ripellino, der
aus der italienischen kommunistischen Bewegung herkommt, nichts
anders. Die Geschichte der Prager Mystik, oder ihrer Ansätze, bleibt noch
zu schreiben; und sie wird sich auch mit der Frage beschäftigen, warum
sich die mittelalterlichen Ansätze im Zeitalter Karls IV und der Hussiten
nicht ebenso entwickelten wie im siebzehnten Jahrhundert, und vor allem
nach der Schlacht am Weißen Berge (1620), welche im Zuge der
Gegenreformation die Spanier und ihre geistlichen Orden nach Böhmen
brachte. Um so wünschenswerter, an einige der frühen Texte und Figuren
der Prager Mystik zu erinnern und ihnen, das Geheimnisvolle
reduzierend, spätes Gehör zu schaffen.

Der erste Prager mystische Text, für lange der einzige, entstand im
benediktinischen Frauenkloster von Sankt Georg auf dem Hradschin, dem
an der Wende vom 13. zum 14. Jahrhundert Kunhuta, oder Kunigunde,
die Tochter des tragischen Königs Přemysl Ottokar II, als Äbtissin
vorstand. Man nennt diesen Text "Kunhutas Gebet," obgleich es durchaus
nicht gewiß ist, daß sie ihn je selbst im Gebete sprach. Kunhuta war
außerordentlich tätig in der Förderung der Künste, sei es der geistlichen
Dichtung oder der illuminierten Manuskripte, die sie aus den Skriptorien
von Salzburg und Bologna importierte, und es hat durchaus historischen
Sinn, ihren Namen mit dem Text zu verbinden (selbst wenn das Brevier,
in dem man den Text fand, einer Laienschwester namens Máňa gehört
haben sollte). In "Kunhutas Gebet," geschrieben in den letzten Jahren des
13. Jahrhunderts, orientiert sich der Prager unbekannte Verfasser an
Thomas von Aquin und Augustinus und hebt das mystische Paradox der
göttlichen Gegenwart in Brot und Wein hervor, die er in aller Sinnlichkeit
umfaßt, Du "*verbirgst Dich ganz in der Gestalt des Brotes ... bist nicht grösser
im Himmel oder kleiner in der Hostie*"; unausdenkbar und unendlich die
Präsenz Christi im Brocken Brot, den jeder Gläubige in der Kommunion
empfängt, der erste, aber auch der zweite, dritte und vierte, ja der
tausendste, der Brot und Wein empfängt. "*Božie tělonenie dvoje ani troje/
ve všěch miestiech vše jedno je/ tako věří srdce moje. Gottes Leib ist nicht
doppelt oder dreifach, er ist an allen Orten überall der eine, so glaubt mein
Herz.*" Man könnte meinen, das Zeitalter Karls IV, in dem die geistliche
Elite, einschließlich des Erzbischofs und des Kanzlers, eine augustinische
Frömmigkeit der innerlichen Kräfte bevorzugte, den möglichen
Entwicklungsprozeß des Ansätze gefördert und genährt hätte, aber das
ist nicht so, zumindest nicht ganz. An internationalen Begegnungen fehlte
es nicht; Johann von Dambach, ein berühmter Professor des Theologie,
den Karl als einen der ersten an die neue Universität berief, war ein
Schüler Meister Eckharts (allerdings ein orthodoxer); und Karl selbst
begegnete dem Mystiker Johannes Tauler in Strassburg, blieb aber,

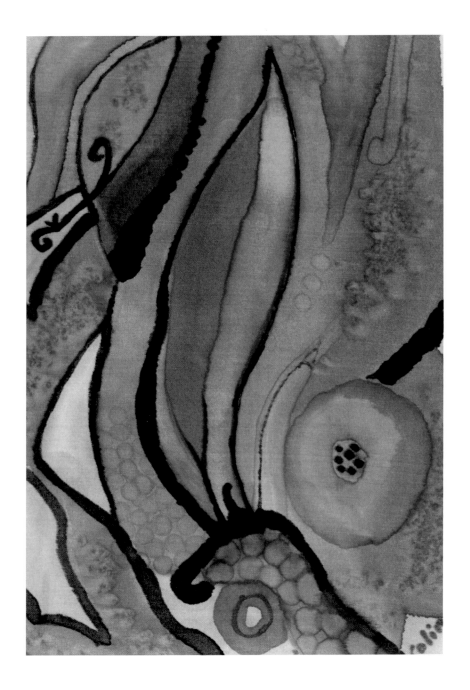

Sabine Colin: Seidenmalerei, Herbst 1993

seinem Temperament nach und aus kirchenrechtlichen Gründen, kühl und distanziert. Ähnliches geschah, als sich der römische Volkstribun Cola di Rienzo hoffnungsvoll nach Prag flüchtete und den Kaiser, unter Berufung auf Joachim de Fiores Visionen von der Herabkunft des Heiligen Geistes, zu einer politischen und militärischen Intervention in Italien zu bewegen suchte; man hörte zu, und setzte ihn dann als potentiellen Herätiker, in Prag und im Rauditzner Schloß des Erzbischofs für zwei Jahre in Haft. Eine mystische Spur führt aber in die karolinische Architektur, die dem repräsentationsbedachten Karl näher stand als das Literarische, und von dort in die Legendenschreibung der Epoche. Karl hatte eine besondere Vorliebe für die gold- und edelsteinstrahlende Vision des "Neuen Jerusalem" in Johanni Offenbarung (21:16-21), und sein Architekt Peter Parler übersetzte den Text, auf Wunsch Karls, in die Architektur des St. Wenzelskapelle (quadratisch im Grundriß, und inkrustiert mit Gold und Edelsteinen) im Veitsdom, und das Gleiche unternahm ein Architekt, der die Hl. Krenz-Kapelle im höchsten Turm der Burg Karlstein für Karl konstruierte. Zu gleicher Zeit schrieb ein tschechischer geistlicher Dichter (vielleicht um die Aufmerksamkeit des Kaisers auf sich zu lenken) eine Legende vom Leben und Sterben der Hl. Katharina (Karls Lieblingsmärtyrerin) und wiederholte, in ihrer Vision vom Verlöbnis mit Christus, den szenischen Entwurf des "Neuen Jerusalem", genau nach dem Text der Offenbarung und der St. Wenzelskapelle. Die Wissenschaft ist sich einig, daß die Legende zu den ästhetisch bedeutendsten alttschechischen Gedichten zählt und fühlt doch einige Hemmungen, sich auf den Text einzulassen, denn der Dichter mischt, auf schon barocke Art, geistliche Ekstasen mit sadomaso-chistischen Elementen, vor allem in seiner Beschreibung der komplizierten Marterinstrumente und der Auspeitschung der nackten Heiligen. Der Prager Hof, der den (im besten Falle) zweitrangigen deutschen Dichter Heinrich von Mügeln zu Gaste lud, tat nichts, um den Katharinen-Dichter zu unterstützen, und selbst Jiří Karásek ze Lvovic, der provozierende Erzmeister der tschechischen Dekadenz, besaß nicht den Wagemut, solche Szenen zu entwerfen.

Die Hussiten, mit ihrem Glauben an die nur symbolischen Präsenz Christi in Brot und Wein und in ihrer Befreiungstheologie, stehen nicht im Rufe Mystiker zu sein, und der späthussitische Text *Praga Mystica* (1505) bestätigt ihre weltzugewandten Neigungen eher als ihnen zu widersprechen. In diesem Traktat interpretiert der Prager utraquistische Prediger Jan Bechyňka das Panorama Prags in stetem Bezug auf das Wirken Gottes. Es geht ihm gar nicht darum, Geheimnisse zu schaffen; er will eher Verborgenes ans Licht bringen und beruft sich dabei auf die Zigeuner, diese ersten Physiognomiker, die Verborgenes aus Handlinien, der Stirn, der Kleidung, in dem Schritt der Menschen zu lesen wissen. Gott selbst hat die Topographie der Stadt geprägt, und Bechyňka will die religiösen Bedeutungen der einzelnen Stadtbezirke und Architekturen zeigen; moderne Leser werden sagen, daß er dabei leicht aus dem Überirdischen ins Religionssoziologische hinabgleitet. Bechyňka zieht einigen Trost aus der engen Nachbarschaft der Alt- und der Neustadt, denn sie bilden den utraquistischen Kern der Stadt, selbst wenn er an dem allzu irdischen Gebaren des Prager Bürgers Anstoß nimmt, der Tag und Nacht seiner Freßlust obliegt, ba i v novi žere a nikdy syt není. Die Kleinseite ist der Ort der katholischen Widersacher, sie hat mehr unbebaute Flächen als Häuser, und ähnelt so der römischen Kirche, die nur in bloßen Worten, und nicht in Taten triumphiert. Der Hradschin, "schön, bunt, kunstvoll aufgebaut," steht leider leer, der Jagellonische König residiert anderswo, und nur der "chaterný Vyašehrad," der verwitternde Vysehrad, erinnert noch an die christliche Urkirche, tugendhaft und ohne weltliche Verwicklungen. Bedřich Smetana, der Komponist, wäre über Bechyňka entsetzt gewesen, denn der Utraquist bezeichnet die Moldau als üblen und giftigen Fluß. Sie fließt von Süden her, aus der Richtung Roms und der Päpste, und es ist nicht von ungefähr, daß die Prager allen Unrat in den Fluß werfen und so ansteckende Krankheiten verursachen. Umso entscheidener die Bedeutung der steineren Brücke, die katholische und utraquistische Stadtbezirke verbindet, und die an sie geknüpfte tolerante Hoffnung, diese beiden Gruppen der Christen würden trotz aller Feindschaft zueinander finden. Die Brücke symbolisert die Basler Kompaktaten, das Minimalprogramm, in welchem sich Katholiken und Utraquisten einig waren, aber Bechyňkas Toleranz bezieht sich nicht auf die böhmische Brüdergemeinde (allzu radikal), oder die Juden, die nicht zu dieser Stadt gehören, obwohl sie dort seit Jahrhunderten wohnen.

Die bedeutendste Kristallisation der Prager katholischen Mystik bildet sich, im Zeitalter des religiösen Barock, in den Klöstern der barfüßigen Karmeliterinnen, und in der Jesusdichtung tschechischer Sprache, ob katholischer oder protestantischer Herkunft. Diese Kristallisation war lange verborgen; das literarische Barock ist ja, auch in Deutschland oder England, eine Entdeckung der Jahre vor dem Ersten Weltkrieg, und in Prag hat sich die jungtschechische, realistische, und republikanische Generation nicht eben dazu gedrängt gefühlt, die Mystik nach der Schlacht am Weißen Berge (1620) zu erforschen, und ihre Historiker, von Bohdan Chudoba bis auf Zdeněk Kalista, fanden sich in einiger Opposition zum Geiste T. G. Masaryks, zur liberalen Staatsideologie der ersten Republik, aber auch des späteren Regimes. Die legendäre Figur des Prager Barock ist die Priorin des Karmeliterinnenklosters Maria Elekta di Giesù, eigentlich Catarina Tramazzoli aus Terni (damals im Kirchenstaat), die mit 22 Jahren die glühende Disziplin der Karmelierinnen in Terni auf sich nahm, 14 Jahre im Wiener Kloster und 13 Jahre als Lehrerin der Novizinnen in Graz wirkte, ehe sie im Jahre 1656 von ihren Oberen, und auf Wunsch der spanischen Gattin Ferdinand II., damit beauftragt wurde, in Prag ein Karmel der Frauen zu gründen; ihm stand sie bis zu ihrem Tode (1663) vor, und wurde dann von ihren Schwestern und von böhmischen Gläubigen weithin verehrt. Ihre Mitschwestern verehrten sie so, daß sie ihren im Garten des Klosters beigesetzten Leichnam ausgraben ließen; und da er wie unverändert war, setzte man sie an den gemeinsamen Tisch (nur mit dem Kopf hatte man ein wenig Schwierigkeiten, denn man hatte ihr bei der Beerdigung das Genick gebrochen), und fand dann für sie eine Stube unter dem Dach, wo viele Gläubige, vor allem Prager Aristokratinnen, herbeiströmten, um das Wunder mit eigenen Augen zu sehen.

Die Historiker wissen nicht viel von Maria Elekta, und die Geschichten, die sich in ihrem italienischen Stammkloster und Prag erhielten, bezeugen, daß Maria Elekta der Theresa von Avila in strengster Observanz diente. Die Gebete, mit denen sie Jesus als Geliebten in der Eucharistie erwartet, zeigen die Tiefe ihres ekstatischen Gefühls, "Komm, oh guter Jesus! Komm mein Geliebter! Komm mein tausendmal und abertausendmal Erwarterer! Komm, den meine Seele liebt; toties te intra me sumere decido. Inveni quem diligat anima mea-tenebo eum et nunquam, nunquam dimittam! ihn will ich in mir haben ... und niemals, niemals, niemals von mir lassen!" Es ist möglich einzuwenden, daß hier mystische Motive spanischer Herkunft über Italien nach Prag importiert werden, aber das Barock ist ein internationales Zeitalter, und ähnliche Motive sind, vor Maria Elektas Ankunft in Prag, in der tschechischen Jesuslyrik des südböhmischen Poeten Adam Michna von Otradovic gegenwärtig, und zu ihrer Zeit in der geistlichen Poesie des Prager Jesuiten Bedřich Bridel, der die Jesuitendruckerei im Clementinum führte, aber auch im Exil, in den Versen Jan Třanovskýs, der bei slowakischen Adeligen Schutz und Zuflucht gefunden hatte.

II.

Den Historikern der Prager Kulturgeschichte ist es immer leichter gefallen, Mystik und Magie im rudolphinischen Zeitalter, am Hofe Rudolphs II, und in der Gelehrtenstube des Rabbi Löw zu finden als früher oder im katholischen Barock. Ich will hier nicht, noch nicht, die Frage aufwerfen, ob Rabbi Löw der rabbinischen Tradition oder einer kabbalistischen Mystik eher zuneigte. Die intellektuelle Geschichte kennt Mischungen und Nuancen, und ich würde ihn eher, mit einem Blick auf sein praktisches und reformatorisches Engagement, als radikalen Konservativen bezeichnen, der die Prager Gemeindeältesten seiner Zeit vor den Kopf stieß (sie lehnten es zweimal ab, ihn zum Gemeinderabbiner zu bestellen) und noch später, gerade weil er so konservativ war, von den Chassidim lebhaft verehrt wurde, und durch ihre Augen sieht ihn auch der einst jugendbewegte Gershom Scholem. Rabbi Löws Verbot, Wein zu benützen, der durch christliche Hände gegangen, ist nur eine, sehr charakteristische Einzelheit seiner Strenge, die sich gegen alle Läßigkeit richtet. Er predigt gegen die Unbildung der jungen Leute, die sich zum Lehrberuf drängen, polemisiert gegen die alltägliche Gewohnheit der Rabbiner, Geschenke für die Ausübung religiöser Pflichten anzunehmen, und kehrt sich mit Abscheu von einer manipulierten Wahl der Rabbiner, mit Hilfe der weltlichen, also nicht jüdischen Obrigkeit (eine solche Berufung ist Angelegenheit der Gemeinde, und nur der jüdischen Gemeinde). Das verbindet sich mit dem Plan einer Jeshiva Erziehung, die sich (wie es auch Comenius gefordert hätte) nach Alter und Auffassungsgabe der jungen Leute richten soll, und mit einer heftigen Polemik gegen die damals herrschende Methode des Pilpul, d.h. einer komplizierten Kasuistik, welche die fundamentalen Texte aus dem Gesichtskreis verliert, und sich mir dem Silbenstechen der Kommentare und Metakommentare begnügt. Auch Rabbi Löw ruft im Geiste der Renaissance nach einer Rückkehr zum Text, vor allem zur Thora, dem zentralen geoffenbarten Text des Judentums, und in der Talmudliteratur eher zum Studium der Haggada, d.h. jener philosophishen und erzählenden Teile des Talmuds, den die Gelehrten des Pilpul sträflich vernachläßigten.

Rabbi Löws Forderungen nach einer rigorosen Reform des Rabbinats, der Erziehung junger Leute und nach einer methodologischen Abkehr von den Metakommentaren leitet sich zuletzt von seinen strengen Gedanken über das Judentum her, das in einem späten Augenblick der Geschichte nicht unvorbereitet von einem messianischen Anruf getroffen werden soll. Merkwürdig, daß sich diese Gedanken, die auf intellektuelle Ausschließung zielen, einer aristotelischen Terminologie bedienen. Für Rabbi Löw ist der Nichtjude ungeformter Stoff, der Jude Form, und von dieser grundsätzlichen Unterscheidung leitet er eine ganze Reihe von Bestimmungen ab, die das Jüdische über das Nichtjüdische heben. Der Nichtjude, biblisch inkarniert in Amalek, ist Materie, Wasser, Zufall und Geschichte; der Jude, inkarniert in Israel, die Sphäre der Form, des Feuers, des Notwendigen und der Ewigkeit; und daraus ergibt sich, und das unterscheidet Rabbi Löw von vielen seiner Zeitgenossen, daß Nichtjuden Juden werden können, denn der Stoff sucht die Form, die sie heiligt und erhöht (so wie die Frau, als Materie, den Mann als Prinzip der Form sucht). Juden, auch wenn sie auch vom Judentum abfallen (so wie es 1492 in Spanien geschah), können dem notwendigen Prinzip der Form niemals abtrünnig werden und bleiben Juden. In einem vor-herderischen Gedanken erklärt Rabbi Löw, jede Menschheitsgruppe habe eine besondere Aufgabe zu erfüllen; deshalb muß sie sich rein und ungetrübt erhalten, in ihrem Glauben, ihrer Sprache, ihren besonderen

Speisen, ja in ihrer Kleidung. Die Abgrenzung, und die soziale Isolation, ist durchaus nicht von Übel, sondern, im Gegenteil, die Vorbedingung jeder Integrität.

Die Frage nach dem Kabbalisten Rabbi Löw, die seit ungefähr 200 Jahren diskutiert wird, verbindet sich zu Zeiten mit dem populären Glauben daran, daß die Prager Judenstadt ein historischer Ort mystischer Lehre und Praxis gewesen sei, aber nichts weist darauf hin, daß Prag je gleichen Ranges mit Safed, in Israel oder Gerona in Spanien, gewesen wäre (in Mosche Edels Darstellung der Kabbalageschichte kommt Prag überhaupt nicht vor). Man wird auch, dem Gedanken entsagen müssen, Rabbi Löw hätte die kabbalistischen Traditionen Prags inkarniert, denn er war drei Jahre lang Oberrabiner von Polen und zwanzig Jahre lang Oberrabiner Mährens und man kann nicht eben behaupten, Posen oder Nikolsburg wären eminent mystische Orte gewesen. Die jüdische Bildung Prags war, institutionell und historisch, tosafistisch, d.h. mit Tosafot, oder der Erarbeitung luzider und in ihrer Art juristischer Talmudkommentare und Metakommentare beschäftigt. In der Epoche des Königs Přemysl Ottokar II, also um 1260, war die Schule der Prager Tosafisten den Schulen in Worms, Regensburg und Paris nahezu ebenbürtig, und Isaak ben Moses or Zarua, der bedeutendste Prager Tosafist, hat zeitlebens an der Auslegung von Talmudkommentaren und Metakommentaren gearbeitet, obgleich er, gelegentlich, zu Zahlenspekulationen neigt, die bei seinem frommen Regensburger Lehrer besonders beliebt waren. Ähnliche Widersprüche unauflösbarer Art sind in den Arbeiten Jom Tov Lipman-Mühlhausens zu finden, des berühmtesten Prager jüdischen Gelehrten und Philosophen der post-karolinischen Epoche, denn er verteidigte den Rationalismus des Moses Maimonides und studierte doch, auf altertümlichere Art, Formen und Bedeutungen des Alphabets, um den Schreibern heiliger Textrollen zu dienen. Rabbi Löw zitiert die Kabbalisten, vielleicht mit Ausnahme seines Zeitgenossen Luria, den er nicht zu kennen scheint, denn sie stehen ihm näher als die neue Rationalität philosophischer Analysen eines Maimonides, den er gänzlich verwirft. Wie selbständig er aber verfährt, zeigt die Art und Weise, wie er mit der Konzeptionen der Sefirot umgeht. Die Kabbalisten glaubten im Zentrum ihrer Lehren, der unsichtbare Schöpfer kehre sich in zehn Mächten und Kräften, oder Sefirot, der Welt des Irdischen zu, und sie definieren diese Sefirot, z.B. Wissen, Herrlichkeit, Majestät verschiedentlich als Essenzen, Instrumente oder gar Offenbarungen einer göttlichen Einigkeit in sich selbst (Ein-Sof). Rabbi Löw besteht auf der Unsichtbarkeit und Ferne Gottes, lehnt die kabbalistischen Theorien der Sefirot als einer Lehre vom Wesen Gottes ab und läßt sie nur anthropologisch, oder gleichsam kantisch, zu. Sie haben nichts mit Gott, wie er ist, zu tun, und sind nichts anders als Kategorien des menschlichen Denkens, das sich die Sefirot als Erkenntnishilfen geschaffen hat. Rabbi Löw sieht die einzige Möglichkeit, sich Gott zu nähern, im systematischen Studium und in der Hingabe an die Thora, und bei einigen wenigen Menschen mag sich diese Hingabe so steigern, daß sie über das übliche Maß gelangt. Das ist genau der Punkt, an dem die spätere chassidische Bemühung ansetzt, die Rabbi Löw in einen **Zaddik** verwandeln will, einen jener wunderbaren Gelehrten und vorbildlichen Heiligen, welche die ungewöhnliche Kraft haben, Gottes Segen auf die Gemeinde herabzurufen.

Das eigentliche Wesen, oder Unwesen, das Rabbi Löw im Bewußtsein vieler mit der mystischen Tradition verbindet, ist der Golem, der durch die Filme Paul Wegeners und Julien Duviviers, oder die Gedichte von Borges und Celan mehr zu einer internationalen Prager Legende beigetragen hat als die Schriften seines angeblichen Konstrukteurs. Die Sage vom Golem, dem Erdkloß, dem Unfertigen oder Unbereiteten (das Wort wird auch von Frauen gebraucht, die noch nicht empfangen haben), ist um Jahrhunderte älter als sein Prager Erscheinen. Sie stammt aus einem gegen Ende des 12. Jahrhunderts in Worms entstandenen hebräischen Kommentar zum *Sefer Jezira (Buch der Schöpfung)* und beschreibt, wie man den Golem aus Erde und durch ein kompliziertes Ritual herstellt, in dem Gesten ebenso wichtig sind wie Zahlen und Alphabetkombinatioen (in der jüdischen Gelehrsamkeit in Worms und Regensburg war die *Gematria*, die Vertauschung von Zahlen und Buchstaben, seit jeher beliebt). In vielen Legenden wird der Golem zum gefährlichen Meisterstück des mit besonderen Kräften begabten Rabbi; einer der frühen Gottesgelehrten, dem er zugesprochen wurde, war, schon im 15. Jahrhundert, der wundertätige Baal Schem in Polen. Nichts deutet aber darauf hin, daß die Zeitgenossen Rabbi Löws von seinem Prager Golem berichteten, auch nicht eine spätere Lebensgeschichte, die eines seiner Familienmitglieder in Prag im Jahre 1718 publizierte. Die Prager Version der Legende von Rabbi Löw und dem Golem erschien zum ersten Male, und in deutscher Sprache, in der Prager Zeitschrift *Panorama des Universums* im Jahre 1841, aus der Feder des deutsch-tschechischen Journalisten Franz Klutschak, der ihn den "Golam" nennt. Das schließt nicht aus, daß Geschichten von Rabbi Löw und dem Golem nicht schon lange mündlich in der Prager Judenschaft und anderswo kursierten, und die Hypothese wird nicht ganz falsch sein, daß es alternative Gruppen wie die Sabbatianer, Frankisten oder vor allem die Chassidim waren, die Rabbi Löw für ihre Tradition in Anspruch nehmen wollten und ihm deshalb einen Golem zuschrieben. Die erste Geschichtensammlung der Prager deutsch-jüdischen Literatur, die *Sippurim* (1847), sind jedenfalls eindeutig und offen in ihrer aufklärersichen Polemik gegen das Kabbalistisch-Mystische, welches das Bild des Rabbi Löw schon zu ihrer Zeit zu überwuchern droht.

Diese *Sippurim* waren eine zuerst in Lieferungen und dann in einzelnen Bänden vom Verleger Wolf Pascheles publizierte Sammlung von Geschichten, Märchen und Biograpien berühmter Juden, und sie sind nicht zuletzt deshalb von historischer Bedeutung, weil sie die ersten Bände einer Prager jüdischen Literatur deutscher Sprache konstituieren, und zwar im Geiste der Halacha, oder Moses Mendelssohns Berliner Aufklärung. Die jungen Schriftsteller, die eben von der Universität kamen, oft Mediziner und Juristen, hatten es nicht einfach, mit dem alten Wunderbaren, das sie erzählen wollten, und wählten verschiedenen Verfahren, um das Interessante zu rationalisieren. Die Sympathien der *Sippurim* sind durchaus auf Seite der aufgeklärten Rabbiner; ihr Ideal ist nicht der gelehrte Silbenstecher, der sich im Foliantenstaub hinter die Talmudschanze zurückzieht," sondern ein hilfreicher Mensch, und ihre Polemik richtet sich gegen "eine der gesunden Vernunft widersprechenden Mystik, die sich wie eine chinesische Mauer von allem Fortschritt, aller Kultur und aller Wissenschaft absperrt." Die **Sippurim** begnügen sich mit kurzen narrativen Hinweisen auf die Golemlegende (sie liegt offenbar unter dem Niveau der Aufklärer); und ihr Rabbi Löw warnt, in einer didaktischen Geschichte, einen Adeligen ausdrücklich davor, die Kabbala zu studieren. Eine andere Szene, die auch in Paul Wegeners Film erscheint, zeigt Rabbi Löw, wie er, auf Wunsch des Kaisers, die patriarchalischen Gestalten der jüdischen Geschichte zur Erscheinung bringt. Der Erzähler denkt aber nicht daran, dem Zauber zum Opfer zu fallen, und er meint in einer skeptischen Bemerkung, Rabbi Löw hätte einfach eine Laterna Magica benutzt und sei also wohl der kluge Erfinder dieses technischen Spielzeugs.

Die Versuche, den Fundamentalisten Rabbi Löw, als Schöpfer eines notwendigen Golem, Jahrhunderte später in einen **Zaddik** zu verwandeln, der magischer Krafte fähig war, und seine Weisheit aus der kabbalistischen Tradition schöpfte, wiederholt sich in den neueren Bemühungen in Amerika und in der Bundesrepublik, den Prager Juristen Franz Kafka als jüdischen Schriftsteller zu interpretieren, der in einiger Ferne von der rabbinischen Tradition, in seiner Epik und in seinen Aphorismen nach einem alternativen jüdischen Glauben sucht, welcher der Kabbala und dem chassidischen Herkommen nahe steht oder gar von ihm abhängt. Ich meine den Essay Harold Blooms, der in seiner fast prophetischen Apodiktik kein Streitgespräch zuläßt, und die nuancierte neue Arbeit Karl Erich Grötzingers über Kafka und die Kabbala ein belesenes Buch, das im Nachweis der Analogien überzeugt, und eben dort, wo es auf die Frage der Quellen und deren Vermittlungen eingeht, den deutlichsten Beweis erbringt, daß Kafka die Mystik der Kabbala und der Chassidim nicht in Prag vorfand, und sie nur durch Freunde kennenlernte, die selbst aus dem osteuropäischen Städtl stammten oder die alternative religiöse Tradition, im Gegensatz zur Prager Assimilation, dort an Ort und Stelle gesucht hatten. Der eine Mittler ist der jiddische Schriftsteller und Schauspieler Jizschak Löwy, der mit dem jiddischen Theater in Prag gastierte und Kafka, der ihn sehr bewunderte, seine Erfahrungen und Geschichten erzählte (wahrscheinlich im Jahre 1911), und der andere war, wahrscheinlich seit 1915, Jiří Langer, der nach Belz in Galizien gegangen war, um dort zu studieren und dann, zum Erschrecken seiner assimilierten Familie, im chassidischen Gewande am Prager Hauptbahnhof einzutreffen. Sein Bruder František war General der tschechoslowakischen Auslandslegionen und ein bekannter tschechischer Dramatiker. Analogien zu chassidischen Volksgeschichten sind in Kafkas Epik gewiß zu finden, aber er hat die Quellen, die selbst wieder der Weltfolklore angehören, nicht in Prag gefunden, und mußte die osteuropäische Tradition eben deshalb importieren, weil ihre Volkstümlichkeit und ihre religiöse Intensität in Prag lange nicht mehr zu Hause gewesen waren.

In den geheimnisvollen Prager Geschichten wirkt Rabbi Löw zugleich mit seinem kaiserlichen Mitmystiker Rudolph auf dem Hradschin. Burg und Judenstadt rücken zueinander, wie in Paul Wegeners Golemfilm; und selbst wenn die persönliche Begegnung des Kaisers (sein Beichtvater Johann Pistorius war ein gelehrter Kenner der Kabbala) mit dem Rabbi im Februar 1592 Fiktion sein sollte, ist sie von notwendig emblematischer Bedeutung. Es ist unmöglich, gegen Rudolphs alchemische und magische Interessen zu polemisieren oder sie gar ignorieren zu wollen; im Alchemistengäßchen wohnten allerdings keine Alchemisten, wie André Breton und die Reiseführer behaupten, sondern bescheidene Kammerdiener, Lakaien und Leibjäger (die Alchemisten hatten ihre Laboratorien in den Häusern und Palästen der großen Herren). Die Macht und das Geld des Kaisers zog eine internationale Elite von ungewöhnlichen Denkern, Künstlern und Wissenschaftlern, im Sinne der Renaissance, nach Prag, die weder vor noch nach ihm ihresgleichen hatte, die problematischen Figuren nicht ausgeschlossen. Die österreichischen Erzherzöge schrieben im Jahre 1606 ein kollektives Memorandum, in dem sie behaupten "Ihre Majestät sei nur an Zaubereien, Alchemisten, Kabbalisten und ähnlichen Leuten interessiert," und Prager Geschichten und Romane haben diese Anklagen stets für bare Münze genommen. Rudolph hatte seine persönlichen Probleme (der Streit darüber, ob er melancholisch, manisch-depressiv oder gar syphilitisch war, dürfte andauern), aber er war keinesfalls von Magie besessen. Er war von einer elementaren Neugier, was die Welt ist und was sie im Innersten zusammenhält, zog Denker an den Hof, die sich, wie er, an der Idee einer "Pansophie" inspirierten (den Glauben an eine Welt immanenter Harmonien erkennbarer Kräfte), und war den religiösen Eiferern und dem päpstlichen Delegaten deshalb verdächtig, weil er eirenisch von einer Grundreligion träumte, die alle Bekenntnisse zu vereinigen vermöchte. Auffällig, wieviele der Ketzerei Verdächtige in Prag Aufnahme fanden, Giordano Bruno, der bedeutendste von ihnen, aber auch der entlaufene Dominikaner Paleologus (in Rom verbrannt im Jahre 1585) und Francesco Pucci, der im Jahre 1597 einen ähnlichen Tod fand.

In der Pansophie des 16. Jahrhunderts verbinden sich magische Gedanken über die Korrespondenz und Verwandlungsfähigkeit aller Weltkräfte und Elemente mit analytischen und systematischen Energien, und die Legendenbildung über Rudolphs Hof verdeckt die zukunftsträchtige wissenschaftliche Arbeit, die internationale und einheimische Gelehrte leisteten. Gewiß: die Engländer John Dee und Edward Kelley, von denen ganz Europa redete, sind merkwürdige Figuren (Kelley mehr als der gebildete Dee), und man sollte jene anderen nicht vergessen, die selbst in der Alchemie die Kenntnis chemischer Elemente förderten, wie den Pole Sendivagius, oder die pansophischen Botaniker und Mineralogen, die in ihren lateinischen, und bald ins Deutsche und Tschechische übersetzten Sammelbänden Pflanzen und Gesteine systematisch beschrieben. Nicht weniger deutlich die Verschränkungen von Alt und Neu als in den Arbeiten der Astronomen Tycho de Brahe und Johann Kepler, denen Rudolph im Schloß Benátky ein wissenschaftliches Observatorium zur Verfügung stellte, das Brahes Uraniborg bei Kopenhagen noch übertreffen sollte. Man sollte die Prager nicht vergessen, die an diesen wissenschaftlichen Arbeiten teilnahmen, in denen sich das Neue allmählich oder rückweise aus dem Netz der alten Spekulationen befreite, so den Mathematiker und Leibarzt Rudolphs Tadeáš Hájek z Hájků, gestorben 1600, der astronomische, geographische und botanische Arbeiten produzierte und an einer Übersichtskarte der Prager Region arbeitete. Ein anderer Gelehrter jener Epoche war der Historiker, Mathematiker und Astronom Rabbi David Gans, ein Lieblingsschüler des Rabbi Löw, der selbst die neuen Wissenschaften in gewissen Grenzen zuließ und legitimiert. Gans nahm dreimal je eine Woche lang mit Tycho de Brahe an den astronomischen Messungsarbeiten im Schloß Benátky teil, verwarf in seinen Schriften die Astrologie der Amateure und Scharlatane, und bekannte sich zu Brahes These von einer Welt der planetarischen Bewegung, in welcher nur mehr Erde, Mond und Sonne aneinander gebunden sind. Ein bedeutender Prager Wissenschaftler der Rudolphinischen Epoche, dem man allerdings magische Interessen nicht nachsagen kann, war der in Breslau geborene slowakische Arzt Jan Jessenius, ein Anatom ersten Ranges, der auch heliozentrischen Ideen anzuhängen begann, eine Schrift Savonarolas edierte und, im Jahre 1606, an der Prager Universität die erste Leichensektion durchführte und sie lateinisch beschrieb. Jessenius, vielleicht ein illustrer Vorfahre Milena Jesenskás, der Freundin Kafkas, war unter der Gruppe der aufständischen Herren, welche man im Jahre 1621 nach der Schlacht am Weißen Berge auf dem Altstädter Ring hinrichtete, und die Legende von der Rudolphinischen Magie ist wenig geeignet, das Gedächtnis solcher Wissenschaftler aufzubewahren.

In der Mythenbildung vom geheimnisvollen Zeitalter des Rabbi Löw, Rudolph II und des Golem, sind spätere Fiktionen des *fin-de-siècle*, die Bilder vom phantastischen Prag entfalten, popularisieren und vermitteln, von besonderer Bedeutung. In Reiseberichten, Briefen und Novellen des späteren 19. Jahrhunderts beginnt sich die neue Legendenbildung vorzubereiten, als Erzählung von einer merkwürdigen, metaphysischen und dunklen Stadt, in der Kathedralen und Synagogen ihre alte Strenge bewahren, und der alte jüdische Friedhof (welcher gar nicht der älteste ist, denn der stammt aus dem 13. Jahrhundert und befand sich am St. Martins-Újezd) auf dem Gebiet der zukünftigen Neustadt) die Phantasie ganz besonders erregt und irritiert. Zu den intelligentesten Besuchern der Stadt zählten im Jahre 1858 George Eliot, die Autorin von *Middlemarch*, und ihr Freund George Henry Lewes, der erste Biograph Goethes, die in ihren Briefen und Niederschriften immer wieder auf Prag und die Judenstadt zu sprechen kamen; und zehn Jahre später schrieb Wilhelm Raabe die wehmütige Erzählung "Holunderblüte" (1868), in welcher ein junger deutscher Student, aus Wien, das schöne Prager Judenmädchen Jemima liebt; auch ein Stück Friedhofspoesie. Im gleichen Jahre bemächtigte sich (wie der amerikanische Germanist Jeffrey Sammons gezeigt hat) der radikale Antisemitismus des Prager Motivs. Der Schriftsteller Hermann Goedsche, Mitarbeiter der Berliner konservativen *Kreuz Zeitung*, begann unter dem Namen "Sir John Retcliffe" seinen historischen Schmöker "Biarritz," über den Fürsten Bismarck und Napoleon III, zu publizieren und beschrieb schon im ersten Bande, wie sich die Delegaten der zwölf israelitischen Stämme, unter ihnen der Ewige Jude als dreizehnter, auf dem alten Prager Friedhof zusammenfinden, um ihre zukünftige Weltherrschaft zu diskutieren und ihre Berichte in einem Dokument festzuhalten, das als "Protokolle der Weisen von Zion" zum Inventar des Antisemitismus und Faschismus gehörte, von der russischen Geheimpolizei bis auf Henry Ford, auch eine unverwelkende Giftblüte der Prager Magie.

Nach dieser Vorbereitung vollzieht sich die neuere Kristallisation des Mythos vom phantasischen Prag in einer Gruppe oder gar kleinen Bibliothek von Romanen des europäischen *fin-de-siècle*, darunter Marion C. Crawfords *The Witch of Prague/ Die Hexe von Prag* (1890), geschrieben von einem populären amerikanischen Unterhaltungsschriftsteller, der es vorzog in Italien oder München zu leben; Rainer Maria Rilkes "König Bohusch" (1899), die erste seiner beiden Prager Geschichten; der Roman *Gotická duše/ Die gotische Seele* (1900) des tschechischen Dekadenten Jiří Karásek ze Lvovic, der die Prager Nationalkleinbürger durch seine sinnlichen Geschichten provozierte; Guillaume Apollinaires "Le Passant de Prague"/ "Der Prager Spaziergänger" (1903), eine Kurzgeschichte von wenigen Seiten, welche die epochalsten Wirkungen in der Sensibilität der französischen und tschechischen Surrealisten nach sich zog, und Gustav Meyrinks *Golem* (1915), ein spätes und eklektisches Kompendium aller möglichen okkulten, mystischen und Kriminalmotive, und ein Welterfolg zugleich. Diese Autoren, ob sie das wußten oder nicht, unternahmen den Versuch, den älteren Schauerroman (man darf ihn auch *the gothic novel* oder schwarzromantisch nennen) in Prag zu lokalisieren. Der Prozeß der Lokalisierung war in Prag einfacher und gründlicher zu bewältigen als in München oder Berlin, denn die Schriftsteller waren in der vorteilhaften Lage, lang tradierte historische und legendäre Motive mobilisieren zu können und ihre Sache durch Antezedenten zu stärken. Prag war ein schauriger Ort, eben weil es schon eine lokale Schauerliteratur gab, und zur alten wie zur neuen gehörten ein fester Personenstand, - der Golem, der Ewige Jude, Rabbi Löw, Rudolph II, und besondere Szenarien und Kulissen, winkelige Straßen, abgelegene Orte, Klöster, Synagogen, Friedhöfe und Gefängnisse, dazu schicksalshafte Begegnungen, melodramatische Todesfälle, okkulte Kräfte und die jüdisch exotischen Ingredienzen, die auch die Antisemiten nicht missen wollten.

Crawfords Roman *The Witch of Prague* (1890), zu seiner Zeit außerordentlich populär in England und Amerika und auch auf dem europäischen Kontinent in einer billigen Tauchnitzausgabe erhältlich, ist ein gutes Beispiel für den Prager *fin-de-siècle* Schauerroman. Ich will die komplizierten Vorgänge nicht nacherzählen, aber auch nicht ganz verschweigen: es handelt sich um einen weltreisenden Gentleman, der seine Beatrice sucht (er hat sie geliebt und verloren), und auf der Suche nach ihr in die Hände und Umarmungen einer Prager *femme fatale* names Unorna fällt (tschechisch *únor* - Februar, die Norne Februaria), die ihm in der Hypnose vortäuscht, Beatrice zu sein. Das könnte auch vom jungen Schnitzler herrühren, aber Crawford kompliziert die Verhältnisse durch einen geheimnisvollen Araber, der mit Mumien experimentiert, und einem blaßem jungen Mann namens Israel Kafka, der die fatale Unorna liebt, die ihm ihrerseits Blut aus den Adern zapft, um dem Araber weiter Experimente zu ermöglichen. Dem Amerikaner ist nicht ganz wohl mit dem allzu wunderbaren Okkulten, und er löst es zuletzt, wie übrigens auch der Tscheche Jakub Arbes, einer der Prager Erfinder der *Science Fiction*, ins Rationale auf, indem er in einer Fußnote erklärt, daß Unornas hypnotische Kräfte rein wissenschaftlich zu erklären seien, wie man bei Professor Kraft-Ebbing im Buche über die Hypnose nachlesen kann. Immerhin: Crawford hat sich in Prag aufgehalten, versteht einige Brocken Tschechisch, und um die atmosphärische Darstellung Prags sollte ihn selbst Gustav Meyrink beneiden, der seine Prager Schilderungen zumeist den Deskriptionen der Londoner Slums von Charles Dickens entnahm, den er ausgezeichnet übersetzt hatte. "Prag," so schreibt Crawford, "ist nach dem Prinzip des menschlichen Gehirnes konstruiert, ein Gewirr von winkeligen Gassen, dunklen Wegen, und düsteren Toren, die alle irgendwohin führen oder nirgendwohin."

Die Prager *fin-de-siècle* Autoren Jiří Karásek ze Lvovic und Rainer Maria Rilke waren miteinander befreundet (Rilke soll mit Karásek sogar tschechisch parliert haben), und das zeigt sich im Roman *Gotická duše/ Die gotische Seele* und in der Erzählung "König Bohusch," die beide, anders als die üblichen Prag-Schmöker, an die mystischen Karmeliterinnen erinnern, in Prag oft Barnabitky genannt. Der junge Rilke schickt seinen bucklingen Träumer Bohusch, der sich in eine geheimnisvolle Konspiration verwickelt, auf Friedhöfe und in Klöster, wo die Karmeliterinnen, so schreibt er, hinter "grausamen Mauern ihr stummes Sterben haben, auch untereinander nie ein Wort tauschen ... und ihre von langen Gebeten zerrissenen Nächte in den Brettersärgen überstehen mußten. Karásek nennt die berühmte Maria Electa di Giesù bei Namen, steigert die Legende ins Mystisch-Erotische, und erzählt eine Szene unerhörter Selbst-peinigungen und Wonnen, "im Wahnsinn ihrer ekstatischen Freuden, die mit Schmerzen vermischt waren, schleppten sich die Büßerinnen zum Kruzifixus, und dann war nichts mehr zu sehen als eine Masse von Leibern, die auf dem Pflaster der Kirche lag." Deutsche Kolporteure der Prager Legenden gehen zumeist auf Gustav Meyrink zurück, aber die neue tschechische Poesie beruft sich, seit 1919 auf Guillaume Apollinaires "Le Passant de Prague" (1903), eine luzide, heitere, fast ironische Reisegeschichte, in der Apollinaire erzählt, wie er *près d'un urinoir*, dem Ewigen Juden begegnet. Der alter Mann ist lebhaft, fröhlich und ge-schwätzig, begleitet den jungen französischen Reisenden auf Spaziergängen durch die Stadt, auch die verrufenen Nachtlokale (eine Ungarin des horizontalen Gewerbes weiß die Manneskraft des Greises nicht genug zu rühmen, *il a marché tout le temps*). Er zitiert alle Autoren, die je über ihn geschrieben haben, und sieht auch den Verhängnissen, die ihm alle hundert Jahre einmal begegnen, mit unverwüstlichen Gleichmut entgegen. Eine ganze Generation der talentiertesten tschechischen Poetisten und Surrealisten hat sich bemüht, diese Prager Spaziergänge geradezu als Ritual praktisch und poetisch zu wiederholen, und Apollinaires Prager Impressionen zu zitieren. Als André Breton im Vorfrühling 1935 nach Prag kam, um seine surrealistischen Freunde zu unterstützen, rühmte er die Stadt Prag, bekannt durch ihren "legendären Zauber," als "magische Hauptstadt des alten Europa" ("la capitale magique de la vielle Europe"), und seine Freunde, die tschechischen Surrealisten, die ja genau wußten, daß er im "Zweiten Manifest des Surrealismus" (1930) Analogien zwischen Alchemie, Kabbala, und Sur-realismus gezogen hatte, fühlten sich in ihrer peotischen Theorie und Praxis gestärkt. Sie vergaßen auch rasch, welche Begrenzungen sein Bild des magischen Prags implizierte — es war die Hauptstadt des *alten* Europa (Paris war die Metropole des neuen), und die Stadt schien nur magisch zu sein wenn man "von allen geographischen, historischen und ökonomischen Erwägungen" absah und sie "aus der Entfernung betrachtete." Die tschechischen Surrealisten interpretierten das Kompliment buchstäblich, aber als Fragment, ohne auf seine Begrenzungen eingehen zu wollen, und wer heute vom magischen Prag spricht, zitiert Breton, oder eigentlich die *productive misreadings* der Prager Surrealisten, und das gilt auch für Ripellinos "Praga Magica."

III.

Von den vielen Eigenschaftsworten, die man mit dem Namen der Stadt verband, ist "magisch" das allerjüngste, dem andere längst vorausgingen, unter anderen das *goldene* Prag, oder "Zlata Praha." Deutschen Ohren klingt das besonders deutsch (z.T. in Erinnerung an einen in den letzten Kriegsjahren gedrehten Ufa-Film), aber die Wendung *Zlatá Praha* ist eng mit einer berühmten Rede (1882) des Prager tschechischen Bürgermeisters Tomáš Černý verknüpft (das goldene, das slawische Prag), mit dem Aufstieg der jungtschechischen Partei im letzten Drittel des neunzehnten Jahrhunderts und zugleich mit dem Titel einer populären Familienzeitschrift analoger Ideologie. Das Wort vom magischen Prag, wie es Ripellino popularisierte, funktionierte jedenfalls auf doppelte Weise, vor und nach der sanften Machtübernahme. Das Buch erfüllte seine, oder eine, besondere Funktion schon vor der Machtübernahme, oder genauer gesagt, in der Epoche der sogenannten "Normalisierung," in welcher die spätstalinistischen Konservativen jede Erinnerung an den "Prager Frühling" tilgen wollten, auf höchst gelehrte, aber auch assoziativ private Weise. Ripellino nannte Prag "eine Brutstätte des Gespensterwesens, einen Tummelplatz der Hexenmeister," aber auch einen Ort der Einsamkeit, Angst und Verlorenheit" und lieferte den nach 1968 verfolgten reformkommunistischen Schriftstellern und Intellektuellen und ihren Freunden, im linken Dissens, einen Kompensationsmythus, der es ihnen gestattete, sich zur Fraktion der Phantasie, und gegen die herrschende Bürokratie zu melden und dabei die internationale Tradition der einst revolutionären Avantgarde gegen die lokale und farblose Literatur des Systems auszuspielen. In die *Praga magica* regredierend, ergriffen die tschechischen Surrealisten die imaginative Möglichkeit, die alte Stadt den prosaischen und rücksichtslosen Planern, die eine Autobahn quer durch die das Zentrum führten, zu entreißen und sie als ästethischen Ort zumindest im Geiste zu restaurieren. Dieser Kompensationsmythus hat aber seine Grenzen, die im Buche Ripellinos deutlich sichtbar sind; die Erinnerung an die authentische Mystik der Kirchen und Religionen ist ausgelöscht, und Ripellino bemüht sich allzu angestrengt, die Konflikte der trotzkistischen KSč Parteiorthodoxie zu verschweigen. In seinem Magischen Prag ist ein Hilfruf der Poeten hörbar, die in der Epoche der "Normalisierung" zu ersticken drohten, und es ist das große Verdienst Ripellinos, die internationale Leserschaft wieder auf Dichter wie Nezval und Holan aufmerksam gemacht zuhaben (von Jan Zahradníček, dem katholischen Dichter, der neun Jahre im Kerker saß, ist weniger die Rede).

Nach 1989 laufen die Bilder vom Magischen Prag allerdings in Gefahr, Barrieren zu bilden und einer Nostalgie zu dienen, die Schwierigkeiten hat, sich im neuen Durcheinander der Ideen zu orientieren. Diese Nostalgie zieht es deshalb vor, sich in eine fiktive Vergangenheit zurückzulehnen, die, gerade in ihrer Enge und Dunkelheit, freundlicher zu sein scheint als eine chaotische, tagesgraue, unvorsehbare, und kalte Gegenwart, die vernüftige Urteile fordert. In allem Reichtum ist das magische Prag eine arme Stadt, denn sie lebt ohne Hussiten, ohne die tschechischen und die deutschen Aufklärer, ohne den liberalen Polemiker Karel Havlíček-Borovský, ohne die deutschen und jüdischen Expressionisten, ohne die kubistische und konstruktivistische Architektur, und ohne T. G. Masaryk, der so lange auf dem Hradschin residierte, und die anderen Prager Philosophen, von Bernard Bolzano bis auf Emanuel Rádl und Jan Patočka.

Die Nostalgie nach dem magischen Prag dient jetzt der Camouflage eines romantischen Anti-Kapitalismus, ist aber zugleich selbst zu einer Ware geworden, die man in Reisebüros, Stadtführungen, Ansichtskarten, Veranstaltungen und T-Shirts die Touristen verhökert, und, indem man die Aufmerksamkeit auf die enge Altstadt und den schmalen Königsweg konzentriert, den Hunderttausenden von Reisenden, den Weg in jene Stadtbezirke versperrt, in der die Prager alltäglich leben. Sie ist jetzt zu einem Mythos der Berührungsängste vor einer wieder offenen, analytischen und beweglicheren Welt geworden, *Rühr mich nicht an!*

Anmerkungen

[1] Für die Genehmigung zum Abdruck dieses Beitrages danken wir der österreichischen Zeitschrift *Transit. Europäische Revue*, in deren Heft 7, Frühjahr 1994, der Aufsatz von Professor Demetz erscheint.

Arno Reinfrank

Pelikan beim Fischfang

Pelikan heißt Schalach auf hebräisch
und ist kein meschuggener Fisch.
Ein meschuggener Fisch aber wird er,
wenn man ihn falsch übersetzt.

Schalach führt zu Schalenuna,
nuna ist mit Fisch übersetzbar,
und ferner kommt auf polnisch
schalai auf meschugge heraus.

Wenn nun der Schalach ein Fisch ist,
was such er zwischen den Vögeln
in jenem Abschnitt der Bibel,
der unreine Vögel behandelt?

Dazu gibt ein polnischer Lehrer
die zweifelsfreie Antwort:
Er such was zwischen den Vögeln,
weil er meschugge ist.

(nach 5. Mose 14:17)

Der gewaltige Frosch

Von Rav Rabba heißt es:
Er sah einen Frosch,
der war wie die Vorstadt
von Hagronja in Babylonien.

Die Vorstadt Hagronja
besaß sechzig Häuser,
so groß war der Frosch,
den er sah.

Eine Riesenschlange
verschluckte den Frosch.
Nun kam ein Rabe,
der verschluckte die Schlange.

Dann wuchs ein Ast
dem Raben zum Sitzen.
Gewaltige Bäume wie dieser
sind selten.

Stark ist der Glaube
an Gewalt und an Wunder.
Und wer nicht dort war,
der hat nichts gesehn.

(nach Babylon. Talmud Bawa batra 73 b)

Sabine Colin: Seidenmalerei, Winter 1993

Sabine Colin: Seidenmalerei, Winter 1993

Herbert Lederer

"Faithful as Well as Beautiful?" Some Notes about Translating: Homage to Harry Zohn

Translators and translations have generally not fared well at the hands of critics. The well-known Italian expression: "Tradduttore-tradittore" is too familiar to comment on here. One of the earliest ironic remarks about adaptations stems from the pen of the eighteenth-century English writer James Howell who says:

> Some hold translations not unlike to be
> The wrong side of a woven tapistry.

In other words, while the translation manages to reproduce the design and general pattern of the original, it does not compare to it in beauty of color, detail, and execution. Unlike other backsides (which shall remain unidentified), the rear of a tapestry can never lay claim to a pert charm of its front.

A contemporary compatriot of Howell, Andrew Marvell, remarked on another shortcoming of translations:

> He is translation's thief that addeth more
> As much as he that taketh from the store
> Of the first author.

Marvell sharply criticizes a common temptation to which translators tend to fall heir: An attempt to *improve* on the primary text, to show some originality, and to add something which — undoubtedly — the author would have liked, if he had only thought of it himself. Goethe, who was no mean translator himself, nevertheless did not hold the kindest view of the task. He once remarked:

> Übersetzer sind als geschäftige Kuppler anzusehen, die uns eine halbverschleierte Schöne als höchst liebenswürdig anpreisen; sie erregen eine unwiderstehliche Sehnsucht nach dem Original.

Thomas Mann, who after all owed his livelihood during his American exile to his translators, above all to Helen Porter-Lowe, was a little bit kinder, although not without his usual touch of irony, when he said:

> Goethe in translation is like a millionaire who has lost most of his money: compared to the rest of us he is still a rich man.

Kurt Tucholsky (not knowing what Harry Zohn would later do with his work), considered that translators needed two main tools to practice their trade successfully:

> Man muß eben nicht nur ein Lexikon, man muß auch Fingerspitzengefühl haben. Die meisten haben nicht einmal ein Lexikon.

One might well argue that the really gifted translator has less need for a dictionary than for his own sensitive feeling for *le mot juste*.

As one of Karl Kraus's aphorisms suggests, the Viennese critic was also not too kindly inclined towards translations:

> ... a linguistic work translated into another language is like someone going across the border without his skin and donning the local garb on the other side.

Kraus's own methods of translation were somewhat unusual, to say the least. Since his English was not solid enough, he relied mainly on someone else's free prose translation which he then rendered into German with his own unerring sense of style. (This technique is not unlike Stoppard's translation of Nestroy and Schnitzler, which can at times result in an unfortunate error, such as equating the title of Schnitzler's play *Das weite Land* with its unmistakable references to the human psyche with *The Undiscovered Country* which — quite incorrectly — echoes back to Hamlet's monologue of "the undiscovered country from whose bourne no traveler returns" — and clearly refers to death.

But undoubtedly the unkindest word of all was spoken by Oscar Wilde, who stated in one of his famous aphorisms, with his customary dose of misogyny:

> Translations tend to be like women: if they are faithful, they are not likely to be beautiful, and if they are beautiful, they are rarely faithful.

With his caustic wit, Wilde at first glance seems to have hit the nail on the head. It is indeed difficult — and possible only under rare and fortunate circumstances — for a translator to have sufficient love and sensitivity for both the original language and the target language, its vocabulary and its sounds, its denotations and its connotations, even its slang expressions and its ambiguities, and in the case of verse, its rhythm, meter, and rhyme schemes. But just because it is hard to have a translation turn out to be both "faithful and beautiful" in its own right, that doesn't mean that it can't be done or indeed hasn't been done.

The original intention of this paper had been to examine Harry Zohn's own masterful translations into English in detail, in particular those of Kraus and Tucholsky, which seemed to fit exceptionally well into the framework of this volume. Unfortunately, my present weakened condition does not permit me to do the research necessary for this task; therefore, I will limit myself to some general remarks, and submit some samples of my own work in dedication to and celebration of Harry's efforts.

I will mention only two outstanding recent examples of Jewish translators who have both served as models for me (as has Harry Zohn himself). Perhaps they inspired him, too. There is for one the unjustly ignored Siegfried Trebitsch, whose ingenious renditions of George Bernard Shaw's works into German I have long admired as inspired examples of how one author who is obsessed with language as a phenomenon can not only be understood by someone of a different native tongue, but can be successfully transferred to another linguistic milieu with all its fine flavor and subtle distinctions intact.

The other role model is the anonymous double personality of Max Knight, whose ingenious, witty, charming translations of Christian Morgenstern are a wonder to behold, whether it is the moonsheep occupying — indeed, being "the center of the cosmic scheme" or the does who meditate at night and who end up by "folding their little toesies, the doesies." This is translation at its inspired best.

And this is what Harry Zohn himself achieves, whether he translates Rudolf Kayser's prose, Viennese folksongs, Kurt Tucholsky's *The World is a Comedy*, and Karl Kraus's selected writings under the titles: *In These Great Times* and *Half-Truths and One-and-a-Half Truths*.

In the introduction to each of these volumes, Harry refers to the essential untranslatability of the authors whom he is about to render into English. One reason is their use of dialect — for Kraus writes in Viennese, Tucholsky in Berlinese. But even more important is the fact that both are satirists who ridicule their society (so that an understanding of their work depends at least in part on a familiarity with the historical background and the social scene which they so mercilessly describe or better hold up to ridicule). But perhaps the most difficult task lies not in the content but in the format: Both Kraus and Tucholsky love puns, plays on words, double entendres; they set deliberate linguistic traps for their characters, and gleefully watch them fall in. (In a way it's like translating Mrs. Malaprop from English into another tongue.) If Harry, in spite of the warning signals he carefully sets out, succeeds so admirably, it is because he shares with his authors their love for language as a means of human expression, capable of so many permutations and combinations, so many unexpected twists and turns, and because like them he is a purist — convinced that precision of thought is identical with and requires precision of speech. Harry has another priceless asset: his musical gift, his finely tuned ear, which picks up vibrations in one language and unerringly transfers them to the target language. It is true, of course, as Harry himself says, that "no translation should ever be regarded as an adequate substitute for the original." But since it is totally utopian for everyone to be familiar with every author's language, we are left only with the choice of remaining ignorant of most of the world's great literature, or of enjoying it second-hand with the help of at least a competent, if not always a gifted translator. And when a fine one like Harry Zohn comes along, we all should be duly grateful. Like Kraus and Tucholsky, Zohn is also by nature a satirist, that is to say a secret idealist, who believes in the perfectability of humankind and in the need of mercilessly exposing our present imperfections and inadequacies. Precisely because I admire his gift, his skill, and his patience (and it takes a lot of that commodity, too), I have been and remain "just wild about Harry."

Lately, I have been moved to attempt a similar undertaking. The University of Connecticut Department of Theater Arts has been anxious for some time to put on an English version of the Brecht/Weil *Dreigroschenoper*. They have, however, been rather unhappy with the quality — or lack of quality — of the existing translations; and that is an opinion which I heartily share. The best-known version (it is called an adaptation rather than a translation) has books and lyrics by the talented American writer Marc Blitzstein. It was premiered at the Theatre de Lys in New York in 1951 and was an immediate success, not least of all because of the presence of Lotte Lenya in the part of "Pirate" Jenny.

But in spite of Blitzstein's undeniable skill and his fine gift for singable, memorable lyrics, he falls into the error mentioned by Andrew Marvell: He often adds material which is not contained in the original. To give just one example, the famous line about all the girls in the cast lining up on the right (Jenny, Polly, Lucy, and even Suky Tawdry), now that Mackie is back in town, has absolutely no equivalent in Brecht. What's more, Blitzsteins sweetens and sugar-coats a lot of Brecht's deliberate cruelty and vulgarity; in keeping with the spirit of the times, the tone is sometimes naughty, but essentially nice. (Even the "Ballad of Sexual Dependency" only ends with the somewhat innocuous line "Once again, he's lying." The whole tone of the production is somewhat too sweet, occasionally too cute and too pretty. Most of the bite, Brecht's deep anger is gone. American society was not in the mood for self-flagellation.

The times and the tone had changed considerably, when the *Three-Penny Opera* was produced on Broadway a second time in the 60s, this time at Lincoln Center in the Manheim translation. Manheim's lyrics certainly captured Brecht's anger and bitterness, and a good deal of his slang. The entire performance was much more in the Brechtian spirit, at least as far as the text was concerned. As for acting technique, the Brechtian style of epic theater was not very much in evidence in either production — but New York was not unique in that (A celebrated production at the Vienna *Staatsoper* unfortunately chose to emphasize the Opera part of the work over the Three-penny aspect, resulting in a kind of *Brecht mit Schlag*.)

The major flaw with the Manheim translation at Lincoln Center, however, lay in a different direction. In its eagerness to conform with Brecht s biting wit, his genuine sense of lyric poetry was lost. Some of the songs, as a matter of fact, became virtually unsingable. It is true that this translation does not descend to the depths of the first, and for a long time only and official translation by that High Priest of the American Brecht cult, who is unfortunately cursed with a tin ear. In one of the songs, he actually makes the words "the cops, those sons of bitches" rhyme with — you won't believe this — "my epidermis itches." When I think of poor Mackie (it is his text) being made to sing words like that on stage, my skin doesn't just itch, it positively crawls.

Be that as it may, all of us at the University of Connecticut thought it was time to try something new. The stage director asked me whether I would like to try my hands at writing a new set of lyrics. Well, a challenge like that cannot go unmet, and I set to work. It was clear to us from the beginning that we wanted to keep the "Ballad of Mac the Knife" in the Blitzstein version. Both the Louis "Satchmo" Armstrong record and the later Bobby Darrin release had made the song and the words so familiar that anything else would have sounded strange to the audience, in spite of the fact that it is also much too cute. Neither in nature nor in Brecht's original did any shark ever have "pretty teath, dear." Nonetheless, that's how we kept it, as a concession to the audience.

We also agreed occasionally to keep another one of Blitzstein's fortuitous turns of phrases, but with few exceptions this was to be a brand-new translation, unfettered by tradition, and adhering as closely as possible to Brecht's intentions, words, and tone. It goes without saying that the new texts also had to match Weill's music tone by tone, syllable by syllable, stress by stress, and rhyme by rhyme. Not an easy task, but one that I launched with eagerness, excitement, and anticipation.

The director and I had agreed to one major change: Instead of setting the production at the time of Queen Victoria, or (as many other shows have done) in the 1920s, we wanted to set it in the present. The milieu was not to be England, but rather the United States, with the beggars replaced by the addicts and the homeless, and the opening scene set in the Port Authority Bus Terminal on 40th Street in New York City. The

Queen's messenger would thus become an envoy from the President's inauguration — perhaps costumed in the full-dress uniform of a Marine colonel with medals hanging all the way down his chest. We felt that for a modern audience, this would enhance, rather than detract, from the spirit of the text.

As a gift to Harry, I would now like to present him with five of my "Three-Penny Arias." I have chosen five songs that deal with the topic of love: The simple declaration of how Polly fell in love with Mac to begin with; for some mysterious reason this music is referred to as "Barbara's Song" in the original, although it is sung by Polly Peachum and there is no character named Barbara in the entire opera. Here is how it goes in the Lederer version:

> POLLY: I once thought when I was an innocent girl —
>   And that's what I was, just like you.
>   Perhaps one fine day someone will come to me
>   And then I must know what to do.
>   And if he's quite rich, and if he's nice to me
>   And his manners are always just so,
>   And if he knows how to treat a lady right
>   Then I will tell him "No."
>   You just have to keep your wits about you
>   And stay rational and cool.
>   Even if the moon shines all night long
>   Even if the dance band plays your fav'rite song,
>   You must remember ev'ry rule.
>   For you simply cannot just surrender,
>   You must never let your feelings show
>   There is so much that still might happen
>   There's simply nothing else but "No."

The first one who came was a man from L.A.,
He was just like a man ought to be.
The second man owned three yachts in the harbor
And the third one was crazy for me.
And they were quite rich, and they were nice to me,
And their manners were always just so.
And they sure knew how to treat a lady right,
But I just told them "No."
I just had to keep my wits about me
And stay rational and cool.
Yes, the moon was shining all night long,
And although the dance band played my fav'rite song,
I remembered ev'ry rule.

> For I simply would not just surrender
> And I did not let my feelings show,
> There was so much that could have happened,
> There just was nothing else but "No."
> However, one day — and the day, it was grey —
> Came a man such as I never knew.
> Hung his hat in the hall, never said please at all
> And I no longer knew what to do.
> And he was not rich, he was not nice to me,
> And his manners were never just so,
> And he did not know how to treat a lady right.
> To him I did not say "No."
> I just couldn't keep my wits about me,
> I did not stay calm and cool.
> Oh, the moon was shining all night long
> And of course the dance band played my fav'rite song,
> > And I simply had to just surrender,
> > Oh, I had to let my feelings show.
> > There was so much that had to happen
> > There wasn't any thought of "No."

Next, the love song between Polly and Mac: taken seriously by Polly, it is a mere travesty of marriage vows as far as Mac is concerned:

> MAC: Do you see the moon o'er the Hudson?
> POLLY: I see it, darling.
> > Can you feel my heart beating, sweetheart?
> MAC: I feel it, beloved.
> POLLY: Wherever you go, that is where I'm going.
> MAC: And where you are, that is where I'll stay.
> BOTH: We don't have a license from City Hall
> > No altar decked with flowers was there
> > Where your/my wedding gown comes from,
> > > I can't recall,
> > And there is no wreath for your/my hair.
> > The wine glass from which we drank our wedding toast,
> > Throw it straight away, leave no trace.
> POLLY: For true love will last
> MAC: Or perhaps it won't
> BOTH: Whether here or some other place!

Polly's naive, innocent faith in love contrasts sharply with her mother's cynical views about sex. Celia Peachum sings the "Ballad of Sexual Dependency":

MRS PEACHUM:

    Some man may think that he is one tough cookie,
    But what he thinks of most of all is nookie.
    He'll kill a man off and he thinks it's boring,
    But what will surely kill him off is whoring.
    He wants to have each woman he can see,
    I call that sexual dependency.
    He doesn't go to church, he goes out on the town.
    He wants to be the boss at any cost –
    Thinks if you love a girl, then you are lost;
    Won't let a woman tie him down.
    He says he wants no billing and no cooing,
    But nighttime comes and once again he's screwing.

    Some men spend afternoons with tea and crumpets.
    Whom do they spend the night with? Mostly strumpets.
    Some men may claim they don't know where the booze is.
    What do they die of? Alcohol and floozies.
    They see a tart, they're ready as can be;
    I call that sexual dependency.
    They go to work each morning each day of their lives,
    They eat a healthfood salad for their lunch.
    They then talk politics with all their bunch,
    Have dinner home with their old wives.
    And they may swear they know what they are doing,
    But nighttime comes and once again they're screwing.

    Here is a man almost condemned to dying.
    The hangman's practicing his noose-knot tying.
    The rope will soon transport him to the next life:
    What is the fellow thinking of? His sex life.
    Beneath the gallows, a horny guy is he,
    That sure is sexual dependency.
    He's already been sold downriver like a slave,
    He's seen the Judas silver in her hand.
    And even he begins to understand
    When he dug her, he dug his grave.
    And well he knows it may be his undoing,
    But nighttime comes, and once again he's screwing.

Next, the bitter-sweet "Whorehouse Tango," in which Mac and Jenny reminisce about the good old days they spent together in the bordello, where Jenny, as Mac himself says, was his favorite among all the women:

MAC: There was a time, and that was long ago,
    When we two lived together, me and she.
    't was paradise, the best I ever knew,
    I pimped for her, and she did tricks for me.
    Things could be diff'rent, but they work this way, too.
    And when a John came, out of bed I'd climb,
    And have a puff of crack, and take my time.
    And when he paid, then I said to him: "Sir,
    You want a girl again, come back to her."

BOTH: I won't forget, wherever I may roam,
    That dear old whorehouse where I made my home.
JENNY:
    During that time, it was so long ago,
    He was my pimp, I was a dumb young thing.
    And when the cash ran out, then he got in a stew
    And he would yell: "Just go and pawn your ring."
    A ring is nice, but you can do without, too.
    But there were times, I thought he went too far.
    I'd ask him: "Who the hell d' you think you are?"
    Then he got angry and his fist just flew
    Across my mouth, knocked out a tooth or two.

BOTH: I won't forget, wherever we may roam
    That dear old whorehouse where we made our home.

BOTH: That was a time, it was so long ago,
    When things were great, that cannot be denied.

JENNY:
    We would make love, almost the whole day through

MAC: Because at night, she was mostly occupied.
    At night it's usual, but by day it's nice, too.

JENNY:
    When I got pregnant once by you, my love,

MAC: I lay below you then, and you above.

JENNY: So's not to hurt the baby on the way

MAC: Which was aborted later anyway.

BOTH: That was the end, and we began to roam
From that old whorehouse which we called our home.

This song clearly reveals Jenny's love-hate relationship with Mac, who
has abused, exploited, and betrayed her as so many other men have
done. Her dreams of revenge are clearly expressed in
the song of "Jenny, the Pirate Bride."

JENNY:
At night I tend bar and by day I make beds
For you men who don't have any feeling.
And you give me a tip and I thank you with a grin,
And you see my poor rags and this joint I work in
// And you do not know with whom you are dealing. //
But one early evening there'll be shouting at the harbor
And you'll wonder why it is that people shout.
And you'll see me smile while rinsing out the glasses,
And you'll say: "What's she got to smile about?"
    And a ship, a four-master,
    With fifty guns shining
    Will make fast at the pier.

And I rinse out the glasses and I fill them again,
And your lousy tip's not worth a damn.
But I take it and make all the beds good and tight
Though I know that nobody will sleep here tonight.
// And you still have no idea who I am. //
But later that evening there's a noise at the harbor
And you'll ask: "What on earth is all that din?"
And you'll see me standing there behind the window,
And you'll say: "Look at her malicious grin!"
    And the ship, the four-master,
    With its fifty guns blazing
    Starts bombarding the town.

Then your laughter will stop as the walls start to fall
And destruction rains down on the city.
On the third day each house in the city is down,
Just this fleabag hotel is left standing in town
// And you ll ask: "How did this dump earn their pity?" //
And during the night there'll be a crowd around this building
And you'll wonder why this house deserved their grace.
And you'll see me coming out the door at sunrise
And you'll whisper: "**She** lived in this place?"

> And the ship, the four-master,
> With its fifty guns silent
> Shows the skull-and-bones flag.
>
> On that day more than hundred men will come ashore
> And the whole town will be very still now.
> And they'll catch ev'ry man who is trying to flee,
> And they'll put you in chains and they'll bring you to me.
> // And they'll ask me: "Which one shall we kill now?" //
> Noon by the clock and it's still on the dock
> As you wonder who will have to die.
> And I'll look at all you men and I'll say: "Kill em!"'
> And when each head falls, I'll shout: "Whoopee!"
> And the ship, the four-master,
> With its fifty guns shining
> Will sail off with me.

By the time I had gotten that far, the University of Connecticut Department of Dramatic Arts asked me to translate not only the song lyrics, but the prose dialogue as well. I accepted willingly, thinking that the job would be much easier. And by and large, it was. I anticipated having to change some place names (Greenwich Village for Soho, the Waldorf for the Claridge), to bring some references up to date (drug dealing, TV, etc.), and to have to Americanize some slang expressions. That, however, turned out not to be quite as simple as I had first imagined. Like Kraus and Tucholsky, Brecht also uses a lot of dialect, a great deal of slang, and many idiomatic expressions. I had to remember that "hops" means "pregnant" and should be rendered as "knocked up"; that "Polente" is police — I used the expression "fuzz" in one place and "pigs" in another; and that "Armleuchter" is a polite euphemism for "Arschlöcher" and thus becomes "assholes." I had before me the horrid example of Bentley's translation of the first scene in *Mutter Courage*, where she shows the recruiting sergeant some of her papers and says: "Hier ist eine Landkarte von Mähren; hoffentlich komm ich einmal hin, sonst ist sie für die Katz." Bentley renders the last phrase as "or else the cat will eat it" — a totally meaningless statement for an American reader or audience. The correct equivalent, of course, is simply "or else it is for the birds."

But Brecht has something else in common with Tucholsky and Kraus. Like them, he was a moralist and an idealist, a radical to be sure, who sharply and satirically attacked and crticized society in order to improve it. Like them, he believed that mankind was essentially good ("Ein guter Mensch sein, ja wer wär's nicht gern?" says Peachum), but is prevented from being so by the social structure in which we live, a society which praises virtue but rewards wickedness. ("Wir wären gut, anstatt so roh, doch die Verhältnisse, die sind nicht so," as the same song continues.) Or, as the Cook says in *Mutter Courage*: "So ist die Welt — und müßt nicht so sein."

Thus Brecht finds himself not only in the company of Kraus and Tucholsky, but also that of Wedekind, Klabund, Ringelnatz, Thoma, Mehring, Fallada, Kästner, and others, who are also still awaiting the translators they deserve, as well as graphic artists like Georg Grosz, Käthe Kollwitz, John Heartfield, or Heinrich Zille, who do not need translators, since they do not have to rely on the printed word to get their message across.

To come back to the main theme of this essay: It is very clear to me that the verses quoted here have no ambition and cannot lay any claim to be regarded as "beauties" in the classic sense of the word. Nonetheless, they are imbued with a fierce faithfulness to the spirit of their ancestor, and perhaps they may exhibit a certain charm of their own. In any case, they were intended for performance, rather than publication. They are here submitted to the print medium for the first and only time as an homage to Harry Zohn, Master Translator.

At the same time, they come with the best wishes for his future. He will soon enter the rank of the "emeriti." If my high school Latin still serves me, the word *emeritus* is composed of the root *e-*, meaning "out of" and *meritus*, which means deserving. In other words, he is "out" and he deserves it. You know it is time to retire when the phrase "getting some action" means "my prune juice is working." But you, Harry, should not fear retirement as a time of enforced idleness. It is rather a time of freedom from dull, routine tasks and freedom for self-directed, creative activity. As for myself, I only find two things wrong with retirement: There is not enough time to do all the things that I want to do, and there are no more weekends. So there is a lot to look forward to. We still expect great things from you, Harry. So Godspeed!

Gespräch mit Harry Zohn
(Boston, Herbst 1993)

Amy Colin: Nach der *Kristallnacht* hast Du Wien verlassen können, bist nach England geflüchtet und später in die USA ausgewandert. Das Trauma der Verfolgung hat Deine Kindheit und Jugend überschattet. Deine Eltern und Geschwister konnten sich retten, aber die meisten anderen Angehörigen starben in deutschen Konzentrationslagern. Hast Du in den ersten Jahren die Fremde als Exil empfunden?

Harry Zohn: Nein, eigentlich nicht. Ich war jung genug, um noch einmal von vorne anzufangen, eine neue Sprache zu erlernen. Verfolgung, Krieg und Auswanderung hatten meine Kindheit, meine Jugend jäh unterbrochen. Ich konnte zweieinhalb Jahre nicht mehr zur Schule gehen und mußte unter anderem in einer *farming colony* hart arbeiten. Als ich in die USA kam, wurde ich aufgrund der Wiener Schulzeugnisse doch so eingestuft, daß ich im Alter von siebzehneinhalb Jahren die *highschool* beenden konnte. Auf diese Weise habe ich die verlorene Zeit wieder aufgeholt.

Amy Colin: War England für Dich ein Exil?

Harry Zohn: Es kommt auf die Definition von Exil an. Solche großen Worte haben wir damals nicht verwendet. "Ich gehe ins Exil", "Ich muß flüchten", "Ich war ein Refugee" — das Wort *refugee* haben wir gebraucht. Ein Flüchtling war ich. Aber die Engländer haben mich prompt als *enemy alien* eingestuft. Die haben alle Fremde mit deutscher oder österreichischer Staatsbürgerschaft — Deutsche, Juden, Nazis, Sozialdemokraten — in einen Topf geworfen. Um der Internierung in einem Lager zu entgehen, mußte ich ab September 1939 *National Service* machen und hart arbeiten. Ich war fünfzehn Jahre alt, durfte nicht die Schule besuchen und sollte nun Landarbeiter werden. Das bekam mir gar nicht. Da wollte ich unbedingt weg und konnte dann mit meinen Eltern nach Amerika weiterwandern, meine Erziehung sofort wieder aufnehmen, die *highschool* abschließen, dann studieren. Also Exil — nein, ich würde nicht sagen, daß ich mich jemals exiliert gefühlt habe.

Amy Colin: Hast Du Dich auch in den USA in den ersten Jahren als ein Flüchtling gefühlt?

Harry Zohn: Eigentlich nicht, denn es gelang mir, eine Stellung zu finden. Ich war Werkstudent, konnte meinen Lebensunterhalt selbst verdienen

und auch meine Eltern unterstützen. Ich besuchte abends und im
Sommer das College. Der Satz "Die Heimat wurde ihm fremd, die
Fremde nicht zur Heimat" trifft für mich nicht zu.

Amy Colin: Empfindest Du die USA als Heimat?

Harry Zohn: Ganz gewiß. Ich bin seit 1945 amerikanischer Staatsbürger.
Vor allem wenn ich in Europa bin, fühle ich mich als Amerikaner. Und
hier, in den USA, bin ich Ex-Österreicher.

Amy Colin: Also lebst Du eigentlich zwischen zwei Welten?

Harry Zohn: Eigentlich schon. Und die jüdische Welt ... Wo ist denn die?
Ich beschreibe mich als ein aus Wien gebürtiger Jude, der seit 50 Jahren
die amerikanische Staatsbürgerschaft besitzt, seit 54 Jahren in Boston lebt.

Amy Colin: Du lebst zwischen Staaten und Kulturen ...

Harry Zohn: Das tun wir doch alle! – wenn wir Germanisten sind und
unsere Muttersprache lehren oder Amerikanern unseren europäischen
Background verständlich machen wollen. Ich bin doppelt beheimatet. Das
ist sehr schön.

Amy Colin: Eigentlich bist Du dreifach beheimatet.

Harry Zohn: Wenn man das kann. Wenn man noch einen Koffer in Berlin
hat, einen anderen in Wien, ... und eine Wohnung in Boston.

Amy Colin: Und wenn man seine Wurzeln in der Literatur hat, dann sind
die Wurzeln portabel. Dann wandern sie mit.

Harry Zohn: Oder wenn man Flügel hat, wie Beer-Hoffmann sagte. Als
man ihn fragte, ob er sich in New York entwurzelt fühlte, antwortete er:
"Wozu brauche ich denn Wurzeln, ich habe ja Flügel". Alle sind
irgendwie beflügelt, auf irgendeine Weise. Und die Flügel – sie können
die Religion, die Literatur, die Sprache, die Kultur sein oder gar die
Rettungen im Lessingschen Sinne, die wir unternehmen – Du mit Deiner
Anthologie Bukowiner Lyrik ... das ist eine Tat.

Amy Colin: Ein Großteil Deines umfassenden Werkes ist der Übersetzung
gewidmet. Du hast sehr viel übersetzt und auch darüber geschrieben.
Welche Rolle spielte die Übersetzung in Deinem Leben? Gibt es eine
Beziehung zwischen der Übersetzung und dem interkulturellen Dasein,
das Du führst?

Harry Zohn: Natürlich. Bereits während des Studiums, durch die Arbeit an meiner Dissertation, habe ich mich mit der Kunst des Übersetzens befaßt. Ich promovierte über Stefan Zweig. Eigentlich hatte das Thema mein Doktorvater, Karl Viëtor, vorgeschlagen. Wir hatten einige Themen besprochen, und da sagte er mir: "Schreiben Sie doch eine Arbeit über Stefan Zweig als Mittler zwischen den Kulturen. Vielleicht ergibt das bereits eine annehmbare Dissertation." Und das tat es auch. Und da entdeckte ich mein eigenes Mittlertum, meine Wahlverwandschaft mit Stefan Zweig, ohne sein Talent überhaupt zu haben. Er war kein Wald- und Wiesenübersetzer. Er hat Emile Verhaeren und Romain Rolland übersetzt und sich an diesen Autoren geschult. Eine Schule des Humanismus. Und bei mir war das auch so. Ich konnte die Schriftsteller wählen, die ich übersetzte. Theodor Herzl, Gershom Scholem, Walter Benjamin. Manchmal ziemlich diffizile Autoren. Ich habe fünfunddreißig Bände übersetzt und habe nicht jeden Auftrag angenommen. Für mich war das Übersetzen kein Brotberuf. Ich brauchte es nicht zu tun, ich wollte es tun.

Mein kulturelles Mittlertum ist auch durch meine Lehrtätigkeit bedingt. Ich wollte meinen Studenten Werke zugänglich machen, die es in Übersetzung nicht gab. Die Übersetzerarbeit kann man von der Lehr- und Forschertätigkeit nicht trennen.

Amy Colin: Die Übersetzung könnte man auch als eine Brücke zwischen der Heimat und der Fremde verstehen. Auch wenn Du diese Fremde nicht als Fremde, sondern als Wahlheimat empfandst, hast Du doch vielen anderen Menschen, die exiliert waren, eine Brücke gebaut. Du hast gleichzeitig dem englischsprachigen Lesepublikum jene Welt nahegebracht, aus der Du selbst wie so viele andere europäisch-jüdische Flüchtlinge kamst. Du hast das Verständnis der Amerikaner für eine untergegangene Welt geweckt und auf diese Weise dazu beigetragen, den Fremden und Exilierten in den USA ein Zuhause zu schaffen. Du baust Brücken.

Harry Zohn: Ja, das mit dem Brückenbau — das stimmt. Aber wenn Du von den Exilanten sprichst, so meinst Du damals lebende oder noch lebende Autoren. Und das sind recht wenige.

Amy Colin: Nein, ich meine Leser, die Flüchtlinge waren. Und ich meine auch die Rettung einer untergegangenen Welt, die nun in Deinen englischen Übersetzungen weiterlebt und neue Leser findet.

Harry Zohn: Ja, ganz bestimmt, vor allem die untergegangene jüdische Welt, die Welt der Satire, das Berlin von gestern, das Wien von vorgestern, Kurt Tucholsky, Karl Kraus, ganz gewiß, aber auch damals noch lebende Autoren, wie Gershom Scholem.

Amy Colin: Aber gerade diese Welt, die untergegangen ist, hat die Katastrophen, in die Europa später geraten sollte, vorweggenommen. So viele Gedanken, die Kraus in seiner *Fackel* aufgezeichnet hatte, gelten nicht nur für seine Zeit, sondern auch für unsere Tage. Seine Kritik an der Presse, am Mißbrauch, den Journalisten und Politiker mit der Sprache treiben. Deine englischen Übersetzungen von Karl Kraus' *Sprachlehre* haben vielen Lesern einen Weg gezeigt, dem Mißbrauch entgegenzuwirken, den man mit ihrer eigenen Sprache treibt. Du hast ihnen Karl Kraussche Waffen in englischer Fassung geliefert.

Harry Zohn: Diesen Vorwurf muß ich auf mir sitzen lassen.

Amy Colin: Das ist kein Vorwurf.

Harry Zohn: Ich weiß.

Amy Colin: Wie war die Rezeption Deiner Kraus-Übersetzungen in den USA?

Harry Zohn: Also Bestseller wurden sie nicht. Aber ich war besonders im Falle von Kraus ziemlich verbohrt, nicht?! Zuerst hatte ich einen Auftrag, ein Buch über Kraus für die Twayne World Authors Series zu schreiben. Und da hatte ich als Anhang einen *Aphoristic Sampler*. Ich begann mit Aphorismen. Ein junger kanadischer Verleger, Ronald Rosenthall, sah dieses Buch und fragte mich: "Could you translate more aphorisms?" Und ich übertrug 450 von den etwa 2500 Aphorismen. Ich habe mir die Rosinen geklaubt. Und dann fragte mich dieser Verleger, "What would be your dream volume of Kraus?" Also ein *Kraus Reader*, antwortete ich. Auszüge aus den *Letzten Tagen der Menschheit*, Prosa aus der *Fackel*, Gedichte, Illustrationen. Und einen solchen Band brachte ich auch heraus. Er erschien in dem besagten, sehr bemühten Montrealer Verlag, Engendra Press, der dann prompt einging. Und ein britischer Verlag, Carcanet Press, nahm sich dieser beiden Bände an. Dann brachte Chicago University Press zwei Taschenbücher heraus. Erst dann wurden diese beiden Bücher für Kurse und Studenten wirklich zugänglich. Mit Tucholsky hatte ich weniger Erfolg. Da habe ich auch drei Lesebücher herausgegeben. Das dritte, das beste, erschien bei Carcanet Press; bisher hat leider kein amerikanischer Verlag angebissen. Es ist schwierig, Verleger für solche feinschmeckerischen Sachen zu finden.

Amy Colin: Wenn man im englischsprachigen Raum lebt und arbeitet, entfremdet man sich allmählich von der eigenen Muttersprache. Wie Kraus sagte, man beherrscht die Sprache nicht, sie beherrscht einen ... Und wenn man so lange im fremden Sprachraum lebt, dann beherrscht einen die englische statt der deutschen Sprache. War die Übersetzung ein Weg, Deine Beziehung zur deutschen Sprache zu erhalten?

Harry Zohn: Zur deutschen Muttersprache gewiß. Aber als akademischer Lehrer haben wir ja alle kleine Museen, wo die deutsche Sprache gepflegt wird.

Ich habe irgendwo geschrieben, daß ich mir meine deutsche Muttersprache nicht vermiesen, nicht rauben lasse. Und ich habe *Dawke*[1] gesagt, und ich habe gesagt, Juden haben immer ein wunderbares Deutsch geschrieben und wurden wunderbare deutsche Dichter, auch Wiener Dichter, haben Wienerlieder geschrieben, und in dieser Tradition sehe ich mich. Und ich glaube, daß dies — psychologisch gesehen — richtig war, an der Muttersprache festzuhalten und nicht zu sagen, ich bin Amerikaner, jetzt spreche ich nur Englisch. Und es ist außerdem schön, eine Sprache ganz akzentfrei zu sprechen. Ich kann auch waschechtes Wienerisch sprechen, so daß die Leute glauben, ich sei gar nicht emigriert.

Amy Colin: Kannst Du eine Kostprobe davon geben?

Harry Zohn: A Kostprobn?! No jo, wos soll i denn sogn? Wie i zum erschtn Mol nach Wean komman bin, hob i mi net guat auskennt, ober i hob a waschechtes Weanerisch geredt, bin amol in a Elektrischen eingstiegen und es wor mir net ganz klor, am Ring, der Justizpalast, des Burgtheata, wos kommt zuerscht? . . . und i hob den Schaffner gfrogt: "Bittscheen, sogn S' ma bis ma beim Rathaus san". "Ja, wos sol i Ihna denn sogn!?" hot er geantwortet. Er hot glaubt, daß i ihn pflanz. Da hob i eam gsogt: Ich bin ein ehemaliger, kein echter Wiener und kenne mich hier nicht gut aus.

Also den Wiener Dialekt lasse ich mir nicht rauben. Ich singe und sammle Wienerlieder. Aber meine Muttersprache war eigentlich weder Deutsch noch der Wiener Dialekt, sondern jenes Gemisch von Wienerisch und polnischem Jiddisch, das Karl Kraus perhorreszierte. Das wurde bei uns zuhause gesprochen.

Amy Colin: Ihr habt gemauschelt???

---

[1] Jiddischer Ausdruck für "trotzdem".

Harry Zohn: Ich weiß nicht, ob ich das Wort "mauscheln" gebrauchen will — mauscheln, also Sander Gilman, der hat es mit dem Mauscheln, mit *the corrupted language of the Jews*, aber ich ...

Amy Colin: Von wem hast Du denn Hochdeutsch gelernt?

Harry Zohn: Von den Lehrern. Ich habe ja die Schule besucht. Noch in der Graduate School in Harvard kannte ich ganze Passagen aus dem Nibelungenlied mittelhochdeutsch auswendig hersagen. Also was man heute nicht mehr lernt, das habe ich im Alter von zehn Jahren gelernt und lernen müssen. Ich konnte ganze Balladen von Schiller, "Das Lied von der Glocke", "Die Kraniche des Ibykus" auswendig. Damals funktionierte das Gedächtnis noch wunderbar. Man merkte sich alles.

Amy Colin: Noch eine Frage zur Übersetzung. Wer waren Deine Vorbilder? Gibt es Theorien, die Dich beeinflußt hatten, nach denen Du auch heute arbeitest?

Harry Zohn: Ich war mit dem Ehepaar Richard und Clara Winston befreundet, mit Abstand die besten Übersetzer aus dem Deutschen ins Englische. Sie haben 150 Bände übersetzt. Die waren insofern ein Vorbild, als ich sie ja gut kannte und auch ein ganzes Wochenende lang interviewte. Das war für einen Artikel, den ich damals schrieb und der den Titel trug "Exilanten als Übersetzer und Übersetzte". Die Winstons haben viele Dichter persönlich gekannt und ihnen den Weg gebahnt. Mit ihnen kann ich mich aber nicht messen. Ein zweites Vorbild war Ralph Manheim, der lange Zeit in Paris und dann in Cambridge lebte, wo er vor kurzem starb.
   Was die Theorie anbetrifft, so ist das eine schwierige Sache. Ich hatte ja Benjamin übersetzt, auch seine Schrift über die Übersetzung. Seine Auffassungen sind sehr wichtig gewesen. Aber die Winstons beispielsweise betonten immer, für sie gäbe es keine Übersetzungstheorie, sondern nur die Praxis. Man setzt sich hin und übersetzt. Entweder man kann gut Deutsch und Englisch oder man kann es nicht — entweder man hat Ehrfurcht vor dem Wort, vor dem Stil eines anderen Autors, oder man hat sie nicht — die Theorie konstruiert man im nachhinein. Das hat einiges an sich.

Amy Colin: Aber Du weißt ja, Karl Kraus, den Du verehrst, vertrat die Ansicht, daß man die Sprache, aus der man übersetzt, ja gar nicht so genau zu kennen braucht, sondern die Zielsprache beherrschen muß. Er hat Shakespeare übersetzt, ohne Englisch zu können.

Harry Zohn: Kraus konnte fast kein Englisch. Er hat bestehende Übersetzungen vor sich gehabt, eine ganze Menge davon; er hat sie miteinander verglichen und überlegt, welcher Ausdruck dem Geist der Werke Shakespeares am nächsten kommen müßte. Und weil Karl Kraus ein Genie war, konnte er Shakespeare auf diese Weise übersetzen. Aber damals gab es in Wien einen Rechtsanwalt, Richard Flatter, der lange Zeit in England gelebt hatte und wirklich gut Englisch konnte. Er hat Shakespeare mit Erfolg übersetzt; eine Zeitlang spielten verschiedene Bühnen seine Übersetzungen. Und dieser Flatter hat es Kraus wirklich gegeben. Der hat aufgezeigt, daß Shakespeare etwas ganz anderes gesagt hatte und daß Kraus kein Englisch konnte. Und Kraus hat geantwortet, Flatters Übersetzungen seien nicht sehr inspiriert. Seine eigenen Übersetzungen seien inspiriert und kämen dem Geist der Sprache viel näher als die des Herrn Flatter. Das ist eine gewisse *Chuzpe*. Kann sich ein Karl Kraus erlauben. Aber das mit der Zielsprache und mit der Quellensprache ... da gibt es verschiedene Ansichten. Es gibt Leute, die mir jede Berechtigung absprechen, ins Englische zu übersetzen, denn Englisch ist nicht meine Muttersprache. Deutsch ist meine Muttersprache.

Amy Colin: Aber gerade deshalb sind Deine Übersetzungen eine besondere Leistung, denn Du übersetzt in eine Fremdsprache, die dadurch, vielleicht gerade dadurch zu einer Wahlmuttersprache wurde.

Harry Zohn: Ich weiß es nicht. Wenn man im Alter von 15 Jahren in ein Land kommt und dann mehr als 50 Jahre später im Englischen noch einen Akzent hat und nicht die schlafwandlerische Sicherheit besitzt, die man in seiner Muttersprache hat ... Aber ich glaube trotzdem, das Recht zu haben, ins Englische zu übersetzen. Denn ich kann sehr gut Deutsch, was manche Leute, die einen viel besseren englischen Stil schreiben als ich, nicht können. Also heute erhielt ich eine Übersetzung zur Begutachtung. Da wird der Satz "er war wenig froh" mit "he was seldom happy" übersetzt. "Wenig froh" heißt aber "he wasn't very cheerful". Ich habe viele dieser Fehler entdeckt. Ich glaube, zweisprachig zu sein, insofern es das überhaupt gibt.

Amy Colin: Elmar Tophoven, der berühmte Übersetzer der Werke Samuel Becketts und Gründer des ersten *Europäischen Übersetzerkollegs* in Straelen, entwickelte eine wichtige Methode, um den kreativen Prozeß des Übersetzens festzuhalten. Er zeichnete die verschiedenen Schritte auf, die er hinter sich legte, bevor er zur endgültigen Fassung gelangte. Zunächst schrieb er die Varianten und die Gründe für die Wahl der einen oder anderen Fassung auf Karteikarten auf, dann auf dem Computer. Ein Übersetzer, der im Jahre 2 500 Beckett noch einmal übersetzen will, kann dann genau verfolgen, warum sich Tophoven für die eine und nicht für die andere Variante entschieden hat. Hast Du das auch gemacht?

Harry Zohn: Du meinst, die Hexenküche der Übersetzung darstellen? Würde man einen Tausendfüßler fragen — auf Englisch *centipede*, also nur Hundertfüßler, immerhin auch eine beträchtliche Zahl — würde man also einen Tausendfüßler fragen, welchen Fuß er zuerst bewegt, dann würde er die Antwort sicherlich schuldig bleiben. Es spielt sich vieles im Unbewußten ab. Und diesen unbewußten Prozeß, der Motor vieler Wortschöpfungen und Einfälle ist, kann man oft nicht festhalten. Das erste Mal, daß ich mich beim Sichtbarmachen einer Übersetzerküche beteiligt habe, war an der McMaster University. Vor zehn Jahren wurde dort ein Kolleg über Übersetzung veranstaltet. Da hatten wir eine Cabarettszene übersetzt, Helmut Qualtingers "Wien wird wieder Weltstadt". Da haben wir genau aufgezeichnet, warum wir uns für die eine oder andere Variante entschieden haben und die Übersetzung mit vielen Fußnoten und Anmerkungen versehen. Zum Beispiel kann man Burenwurst nicht mit *hot dog* übersetzen, das ist zu amerikanisch. *Sausage* wäre hier besser, entspricht jedoch nicht der Burenwurst.

Aber ein Übersetzer, der vom Übersetzen lebt, kann sich das nicht leisten. Also die Winstons haben vier Bücher pro Jahr übersetzt und sind beileibe nicht reich geworden. Glaube mir, ich weiß, was der durchschnittliche Übersetzer verdient. Man kann kaum von literarischen Übersetzungen vollauf beschäftigt sein, muß den ganzen Tag an der Schreibmaschine oder am Computer sitzen, es ist ein harter Beruf. Da hat man keine Zeit, sich so viele theoretische Gedanken zu machen. Ich schreibe die erste Fassung der Übersetzung direkt in die Schreibmaschine und die Entscheidungen über die verschiedenen Varianten spielen sich in meinem Kopf ab.

Amy Colin: Genau dieses "sich Abspielen" des Entscheidungsprozesses im Kopf wollte Tophoven auf Computer festhalten. Und da er die Not der Berufsübersetzer gut kannte, gründete er Straelen, um ihnen eine Möglichkeit zu geben, wenigstens einige Monate in Ruhe zu übersetzen. Straelen bietet ihnen alle Annehmlichkeiten. Später gründete man nach diesem Modell ein ähnliches Kolleg in Arles. Als einzige Gegenleistung müssen die Übersetzer eben diesen kreativen Entscheidungsprozeß, der sich sonst nur in ihrem Gehirn abspielt, für die Nachwelt aufzeichnen.

Harry Zohn: In einem solchen Paradies wäre ich gerne bereit, zu übersetzen und mich sogar mit Elektroden versehen zu lassen, die jede Regung meines Gehirns, jede Verwerfung und jede Annahme aufzeichnen.

Amy Colin: Aber hast Du wenigstens einige Notizen aufbewahrt?

Harry Zohn: Ich habe so viel Erfahrung, daß ich gleich in die Schreibmaschine tippe ... die erste Fassung, dann wird umgemodelt. Im Falle der Winstons war es die Clara Winston, die auch Romane geschrieben hat, die alle Texte stilisierte, dann stritten sich die beiden ... zum Schluß kam noch der *editor* vom Verlag hinzu und hat alles wieder umgeworfen ... ein Übersetzer hat es nicht leicht. Aber manchmal wurden meine Übersetzungen genau so gedruckt, wie sie geschrieben wurden. Das war besonders mit meiner Lieblingsübersetzung der Fall. Ich habe sehr wenig Belletristik übersetzt — also Romane, Erzählungen, André Kaminskis *Nächstes Jahr in Jerusalem* — das hat mich derart gereizt, ich konnte es gar nicht abwarten, mich morgens an die Schreibmaschine zu setzen. Als ich das Buch zum ersten Mal las, schrieb ich sofort an den Rand, wie ich es auf Englisch sagen würde. André Kaminski, der leider gestorben ist, wußte es sehr zu schätzen. "Manchmal hast Du das besser gemacht als ich", sagte er mir. "Du hast Sachen erfunden, an die ich nicht gedacht habe." Sein Buch ist ein komischer Roman, und in Deutschland gibt es nur wenige Romane dieser Art. Er war ein großer Erfolg. Im Amerikansichen leider nicht, denn es erschien in einem kleinen Verlag. Das Buch hat dennoch vielen Leuten Freude bereitet. Kaminskis Buch ist das einzige Exemplar, an dessen Rand ich Anmerkungen gemacht habe — sonst hatte ich nicht die Zeit dazu.

Amy Colin: Hast Du die ersten Fassungen der umgemodelten Übersetzungen behalten?

Harry Zohn: Wenn ich das alles behielte, dann würde es in meiner Arbeitsbude noch viel ärger aussehen, als es jetzt tut. Es ist ja eine Büchergruft! Außerdem habe ich mich nie sehr ernst genommen.

Amy Colin: Hattest Du Mitarbeiter?
Harry Zohn: Nein, ich war mein bester Mitarbeiter.

Amy Colin: Ob Du Kaminski, Kraus oder Tucholsky übersetztest, am schwierigsten muß es wohl gewesen sein, deren Humor, Ironie und Satire ins Englische zu übertragen?

Harry Zohn: Wenn die Englisch geschrieben hätten, dann hätten sie bestimmt so geschrieben wie ich. Denn ich glaube, sie zu verstehen. Im Falle von Tucholsky habe ich manchmal Wortspiele gemacht, die er nicht gemacht hatte.

Amy Colin: Sind Humor, Ironie und Satire eine conditio humana für dich? Eine Brücke über dem Abgrund?

Harry Zohn: Ganz gewiß. Denn ich habe auch eine satirische Ader. In einem seiner Romane schreibt Aharon Appelfeld den tiefsinnigen Satz: 'Karl Kraus was the best Jew. He revived satire, the only art form appropriate to our life.' Und als ich ihn fragte — "Meinen Sie das wirklich?" — da antwortete er mir, "Yes, it is the only art form appropriate to our life." Wir brauchen die Satire. "Die Zeit schreit nach Satire!" schrieb Tucholsky. Aber wo ist heute der große amerikanische Satiriker, der deutsche, der österreichische? Es gibt keinen Karl Kraus, keinen Kurt Tucholsky. Die waren sui generis. Die hätten heute auch noch viel zu sagen. Es vergeht kein Tag, ohne daß ich daran denke, was hätte Kraus gesagt, welches Bonmot hätte Tucholsky gemacht. Aber Kraus starb an der berühmten deutschen Krankheit, an gebrochenem Herzen. Alle waren stumm in ihren letzten Lebensjahren. Heute kann kein Satiriker mehr existieren. Denn das, was geschieht, was hat das noch mit dem Geist zu tun, mit dem Geist der Sprache? Wir leben in einem sprachverlassenen Zeitalter.

Aber als Übersetzer habe ich gehofft, etwas vom Geiste Kraus' und Tucholskys in die englische Sprache herüberzuretten. In dieser Beziehung war es bestimmt therapeutisch für mich.

Amy Colin: Du hast auch vielen anderen Menschen geholfen.

Harry Zohn: Man weiß nie, wer was liest — Kraus war für mich Unterrichtsautor. Wenn ich junge Amerikaner dazu bewegen kann, die Sprache mit anderen Augen zu sehen, Wortwitze, tiefe Geistesblitze zu verstehen, so fühle ich mich schon reichlich belohnt und über die vielen Enttäuschungen getröstet, die man doch auch hatte.

Ich habe mit Vorliebe Judaica übersetzt, jüdische Autoren. Da ist wieder etwas von meinem Gewebe enthalten. Österreichisch-jüdische, deutsch-jüdische Autoren: Alex Bein, Gershom Scholem, Walter Benjamin, Theodor Herzl.

Amy Colin: In Deine Übersetzungen hast Du Dein Schicksal eingeschrieben.

Harry Zohn: Das kommt mir erst jetzt zum Bewußtsein, weil Du es sagst. Ich kann es nicht bestreiten. Es zeichnet sich schon etwas Autobiographisches darin ab. Schon die Wahl der Autoren. Und ich habe viel dabei gelernt. Denn niemand liest so genau wie ein Übersetzer, der jedes Wort auf die Waagschale legt. Das interkulturelle Leben, das Übersetzen, das genaue Lesen, *l'explication de texte*, der Unterricht, das alles gehört zusammen.

Harry Zohn

BIBLIOGRAPHY

I. Books Written or Edited

Liber Amicorum Friderike Maria Zweig. Stamford, Conn. 1952. Editor.

Wie sie es sehen (Intermediate German Reader). New York 1952. Co-editor.

The World Is a Comedy: A Kurt Tucholsky Anthology. Cambridge, Mass. 1957. Editor and translator.

Stefan Zweig: *Schachnovelle*. New York 1960, 1964; London, 1962. Editor.

Wiener Juden in der deutschen Literatur (Essays). Tel Aviv 1964. Author.

What If — ? Satirical Writings of Kurt Tucholsky. New York 1968; New York 1969. Co-editor and co-translator.

Österreichische Juden in der Literatur: Ein bio-bibliographisches Lexikon. Tel Aviv 1969. Editor.

Men of Dialogue: Martin Buber and Albrecht Goes. New York 1969. Co-editor and co-translator.

Karl Kraus. New York 1971; New York 1979. German edition: Frankfurt/Main 1990. Author.

Der farbenvolle Untergang: Österreichisches Lesebuch. Englewod Cliffs, N. J. 1971, 1974; New York, 1984. Editor.

Friderike Maria Zweig: *Greatness Revisited*. Boston 1972, 1982. Editor and co-translator.

Kurt Tucholsky: *Deutschland, Deutschland über alles*. Amherst 1972. Editor.

Marianne Weber: *Max Weber: A Biography*. New York 1975, 1988. Editor and translator.

Half-Truths & One-and-a Half Truths: Selected Aphorisms of Karl Kraus. Montreal 1976; Manchester, New York 1984; Chicago 1990. Editor and translator.

In These Great Times: A Karl Kraus Reader. Montreal 1976; Manchester, New York 1984; Chicago 1990. Editor and co-translator.

Rudolf Kayser: *The Saints of Qumran*. New Jersey 1977. Editor and co-translator.

"Ich bin ein Sohn der deutschen Sprache nur": Jüdisches Erbe in der österreichischen Literatur. Vienna, Munich 1986. Author.

Germany? Germany! The Kurt Tucholsky Reader. Manchester 1990. Editor and co-translator.

Austria and Judaica: Essays and Translations. Berne, New York 1994.

II. Books Translated

Sigmund Freud: *Delusion and Dream*. Boston 1956.

Jacob Burckhardt: *Judgements on History and Historians*. Boston 1958; London 1959, 1965.

Walter Toman: *A Kindly Contagion*. New York 1959.

Theodor Herzl: *The Complete Diaries* (4 volumes). New York 1960-61.

Theodor Herzl: *The Jewish State*. New York 1970.

Theodor Herzl: *Zionist Writings. Essays and Addresses*. New York 1973, Vol. 1 and 1975, Vol. 2.

Giora Josephthal: *The Responsible Attitude*. New York 1966. (Co-translator).

Walter Benjamin: *Illuminations*. New York 1968; New York 1969; London 1970; London 1973.

Walter Benjamin: *Charles Baudelaire*. London 1973.

Arthur Schnitzler: *Dying* (in his: *The Little Comedy*). New York 1977.

Kurt Tucholsky: *Kleines Lesebuch/Little Reader*. Munich 1977.

Gershom Scholem: *From Berlin to Jerusalem*. New York 1980; 1988.

Gershom Scholem: *Walter Benjamin. The Story of A Friendship*. Philadelphia 1982; New York 1988.

Josef Rattner: *Alfred Adler*. New York 1983.

Brigitte Fischer: *My European Heritage: Life Among Great Men of Letters*. Boston 1986.

Ernst Ettisch: *The Hebrew Vowels and Consonants as Symbols of Ancient Astronomical Concepts*. Boston 1987.

André Kaminski: *Kith and Kin*. New York 1988.

Alex Bein: *The Jewish Question: Biography of a World Problem*. Rutherford, N.J. 1989.

Fritz Molden: *The Fires in the Night*. Boulder (Colorado) 1989.

Manès Sperber: *The Unheeded Warning*. New York 1991.

Manès Sperber: *Untill My Eyes are Closed with Shards*. New York 1994.

Hermann Langbein: *Against All Hope: Resistance in the Nazi Concentration Camps*. New York, 1994.

III. Contributions to Books. A Selection

Hanns Sachs: "The Unconscious in Carl Spitteler's Characters," tr. by H. Zohn. In: Hanns Sachs: *The Creative Unconscious*. Ed. Abraham A. Roback. Cambridge, Mass., 1951, p. 324-334.

Dimitry Čiževsky: "Comenius' *Labyrinth of the World*: Its Themes and Their Sources" and N. S. Trubetzkoy: "Introduction to the History of Old Russian Literature," tr. by H. Zohn. In: *Harvard Slavic Studies*. Cambridge, Mass., 1953, 1954. Vol. 1. p. 83-135 and Vol. 2, p. 91-103.

"Stefan Zweig und Amerika." In: *Der große Europäer Stefan Zweig.* Ed. Hanns Arens. Munich 1956, p. 190-196.

Translation of Freud letters. In: *Freudiana,* presented by A. A. Roback. Cambridge, Mass. 1957, p. 21-31, 32-41, 46-52, 57-81.

Consulting editor. *Ferne Länder, fremde Sitten.* Ed. Herbert Lewandowski. Stuttgart 1958.

"Stefan Zweig und Emile Verhaeren." In: *Stefan Zweig. Spiegelungen einer schöpferischen Persönlichkeit.* Ed. Erich Fitzbauer. Vienna 1959, p. 24-31.

"Tucholsky: A Life between Love and Hate" and several translations. In: *Chicago Review Anthology.* Ed. David Ray. Chicago 1959.

Friderike Zweig: "A Biographical Sketch," tr. by H. Zohn. In: George N. Shuster: *A Tribute.* New York 1960, p. 7-36.

"Stefan Zweig's Last Years: Some Unpublished Letters (1935-41)" and "Lion Feuchtwanger." In: *Caravan: A Jewish Quarterly Omnibus.* Ed. Jacob Sonntag. New York 1962, p. 214-220.

Introduction. In: Stefan Zweig: *The World of Yesterday.* Lincoln, Neb. 1964, p. V-XII.

"Franz Kafka." In: *The Jewish Heritage Reader.* Ed. Lily Edelman. New York 1965, p. 227-234.

"A. A. Roback: In Memoriam." In: *Jewish Book Annual.* New York 1966, Vol. 24, p. 55-60.

"The Herzl Diaries as a Self-Portrait of the Man and the Leader" and several translations. In: *Herzl Year Book.* Ed. Alan Steinbach. New York 1962-5, Vol. 3 (1960), p. 207-216.

"Herzl, Hechter, The Grand Duke of Baden and the German Emperor (Documents found by Hermann and Bessi Ellern)," tr. by H. Zohn. In: *Herzl Year Book.* Ed. Alan Steinbach. New York 1962-65, Vol. 4 (1961-62), p. 207-270.

"Participation in German Literature." In: *The Jews of Czechoslovakia.* Ed. Hugo Colman. Philadelphia 1968, Vol. 1, p. 468-522.

"Three Austrian Jews: Schnitzler, Zweig, Herzl." In: *The Jews of Austria.* Ed. Josef Fraenkel. London 1967, p. 67-82.

Articles on Jewish literary historians. In: *Lexikon des Judentums.* Gütersloh 1971, p. 292-293.

Articles on 12 German writers. In: *European Authors.* Ed. Stanley J. Kunitz. New York 1967.

"Die Humanistin Zenta Maurina." In: *Buch der Freundschaft für Zenta Maurina.* Ed. Maximilian Dietrich. Memmingen 1967, p. 131-135.

Hans Ehrenberg: "Elihu The Theologian" and Leonhard Ragaz: "God Himself is the Answer," tr. by H. Zohn. In: *The Dimensions of Job: A Study and Selected Readings.* Ed. Nahum Glatzer. New York 1969, p. 93-100 and p. 128-131.

"Persönliche Erinnerung an Max Brod." In: *Max Brod: Ein Gedenkbuch 1884-1968.* Ed. Hugo Gold. Tel Aviv 1969, p. 239-242.

Articles on 16 German-Jewish writers. In: *Encylopedia Judaica*. Jerusalem, New York 1969.

"Nelly Sachs." In: *Nobel Prize Library*. New York 1971, Vol. 18, p. 63-70.

Introduction. In: Zenta Maurina: *Der Mensch: Das ewige Thema des Dichters*. Memmingen 1972, p. 9-15.

"Herzl's *The New Ghetto*." In: *Encyclopedia of Zionism and Israel*. New York 1971.

"Nelly Sachs." In: *Collier's Encyclopedia*. 1973ff.

"The Teaching of Satire." In: *Geprägte Form: Festschrift für Robert Rie*. Ed. Marion Sonnenfeld. Fredonia, N.Y. 1975, p. 71-82.

Seven articles on German-Jewish writers. In: *Encyclopedia Hebraica*. Jerusalem, 1975ff.

"John Kafka." In: *Deutsche Exil-Literatur*. Eds. John M. Spalek, Joseph P. Strelka. Berne, Munich 1976. Vol. 1, p. 423-432.

Theodor Reik: "On the Effect of Unconscious Death Wishes," tr. by H. Zohn. In: *Psychoanalysis and Old Vienna*. Ed. Murray H. Sherman. New York 1978, p. 38-67.

Introduction. In: *Dictionary of International Slurs*. Ed. Abraham A. Roback. Cambridge, Mass. 1979, p. 5-10.

Introduction. In: Gerhard Fritsch: *Between Evening and Night*. London 1978, p. 5-9.

"Heinrich Heine: A Reassessment." In: *Jewish Perspectives*. Ed. Jacob Sonntag. London 1980, p. 200-222.

"Karl Kraus im Bewußtsein österreichischer Schriftsteller der Gegenwart." In: *Österreichische Gegenwart*. Ed. Wolfgang Paulsen. Berne, Munich 1980, p. 133-152.

Articles on Bauer, Beer-Hofmann, Brod, Canetti, Friedell, Kolmar, Kramer, Sachs, Torberg, Tucholsky, Zweig, Zwillinger. In: *Ungar's Encyclopedia of World Literature in the 20th Century*. New York 1981-84.

Introduction. In: Alfred Farau: *I Long for a New Humanity*. New York 1981, p. 1-4.

"Stefan Zweig, the European and the Jew." *Leo Baeck Institute Year Book*. London 1982. Book XXVII, p. 323-336.

"Aus Theodor Kramers letzten Jahren." In: *Theodor Kramer. Dichter im Exil*. Ed. Konstantin Kaiser. Vienna 1983, p. 1-2.

"The Burning Secret of Stephen Branch." In: *The World of Yesterday's Humanist Today*. Ed. M. Sonnenfeld. Albany 1983, p. 302-312.

"Karl Kraus." In: *Thinkers of the Twentieth Century*. Ed. Elisabeth Devine, et. al. Detroit 1983, p. 302-303.

"Karl Kraus." In: *McGraw-Hill Encyclopedia of the Theater*. New York 1984.

"Fin de Siècle Vienna: The Jewish Contribution." In: *The Jewish Response to German Culture: From the Enlightenment to the Second World War*. Ed. Walter Schatzberg and Jehuda Reinharz. Hanover 1985, p. 137-149.

"Trakl, Kraus, and the Brenner Circle." In: *International Georg Trakl Symposium.* Ed. Joseph P. Strelka. Berne 1984. (French translation in SUD 73/74, 1987), p. 146-153.

"Translating Theodor Herzl: The Zionist Leader and 'Young Vienna' Writer." In: *Silver Tongues: Proceedings of ATA Symposium.* Medford, N.J. 1984, p. 275-282.

"Before and After Your Translation is Printed: Matters Politic, Political, Polemical." *Building Bridges: Proceedings of ATA Symposium.* Medford, N.J. 1986, p. 309-315.

"The Austro-American Jewish Poet Ernst Waldinger." In: *Identity and Ethos: A Festschrift for Sol Liptzin.* Ed. Mark H. Gelber. Berne, New York 1986, p. 253-266.

Review essay on Sander L. Gilman's *Jewish Self-Hatred.* In: *Magill's Literary Annual.* Ed. Frank N. Magill. Englewood Cliffs, N. J. 1987, Vol. 1, p. 440-445.

"Die Rezeption Herzls in der jüdischen Welt." In: *Theodor Herzl und das Wien des Fin de Siècle.* Ed. Norbert Leser. Vienna 1987, p. 97-112.

"Amerikanische Ausstrahlungen Richard Beer-Hofmanns." In: *Sinn und Symbol: Joseph Peter Strelka Festschrift.* Ed. Karl Konrad Polheim. Berne, New York 1987, p. 265-276.

"Das brennende Geheimnis des Stephen Branch oder eine Geschichte mit Moral von einem Arzt, der sich nicht selber helfen wollte." In: *Stefan Zweig heute.* Ed. Mark H. Gelber. Berne, Munich 1987, p. 25-43.

Introduction. In: George E. Berkley: *Vienna and Its Jews: The Tragedy of Success 1880s-1990s.* Cambridge 1988, p. XIII-XVII.

Foreword. In: Peter Fabrizius: *One and One Make Three: The Story of a Friendship.* Berkely 1988, p. IX-XIII.

Articles on Beer-Hofmann, Brod, Canetti, Kraus, Tucholsky, Werfel, S. Zweig. In: *Blackwell Companion to Jewish Studies.* Ed. G. Abramson. Oxford 1989.

"Nelly Sachs." In: *The Nobel Prize Winners: Literature 1962-87.* Ed. Frank Magill. Pasadena, Ca. 1988, Vol. 3, p. 751-759.

Introduction. In: Erich von Kahler: *Israel Among the Nations.* New Brunswick, N.J. 1988, p. 1-4.

Articles on F. M. Zweig, A. Farau, and on translations of and by exiled writers. In: *Deutsche Exil-Literatur seit 1933.* Ed. John M. Spalek and Joseph P. Strelka. Berne, Munich 1990. Vol. 2.

"Schnitzler's *La Ronde.*" In: *Masterplots II: Drama Series.* Ed. Frank Magill. Pasadena, Ca. 1990, Vol. 4, p. 1372-1377.

Introduction. In: Lola Blonder: *Sprache ist Heimat.* Ed. Helga Embacher. Wien 1990, p. 85-86.

Review essay of Ernst Pawel's *The Labyrinth of Exile: A Life of Theodor Herzl.* In: *Magill's Literary Annual,* Pasadena, Ca. 1990, Vol. 2, p. 495-499.

"Karl Kraus in der heutigen englischsprachigen Welt: Kritische Anmerkungen aus der Werkstatt des Übersetzers". In: *Karl Kraus: Diener der Sprache Meister des Ethos*. Ed. Joseph P. Strelka. Berne, Munich 1990, p. 319-329.

Autobiographical article on the experiences of a "Thirty-eighter" in teaching the culture of his native country. In: *Leben mit österreichischer Literatur*. Ed. H. Lunzer. Wien 1990, p. 5-14.

Articles on Max Frisch: *Andorra* (Vol. 1, p. 43-44), Thornton Wilder: *The Matchmaker* (Vol. 3, 988-989), Arthur Schnitzler: *La Ronde* (Vol. 3, p. 1312), Hermann Broch: *The Spell* (Vol. 4, p. 146-61). In: *Cyclopedia of Literary Characters*. Ed. Frank N. Magill. Pasadena, Ca. 1990.

"Das (mitunter verfremdete) Wort als Waffe". In: *"Die in dem alten Haus der Sprache wohnen: Beiträge zum Sprachdenken in der Literaturgeschichte."* *Helmut Arntzen Festschrift*. Ed. Eckehard Czucka. Münster 1991, p. 431-437.

"Franz Theodor Csokor's Allerseelenstück." In: *Immer ist Anfang*. Ed. Joseph P. Strelka. Berne, New York 1991, p. 75-84.

Introduction. In: Alfred Farau: *Aus dem Tagebuch eines Emigranten*. Ed. H. Zohn. New York 1992, p. 1-9.

Review essay on Amy Colin's *Paul Celan: Holograms of Darkness*. In: *Magill's Literary Annual*. Pasadena, Ca. 1992, p. 619-622.

"Heinrich Heine." In: *Magill's Survey of World Literature*. Pasadena, Ca. 1992.

"Karl Kraus" and "Stephan Zweig." In: *Dictionary of Literary Biography: Twentieth Century German Dramatists*, 1992, Vol. 118.

"Werfel's Play *Jacobowsky und der Oberst*: Notes on a Schooltext and Related matters." In: *Unser Fahrplan geht von Stern zu Stern*. Ed. Joseph P. Strelka et al., Berne, New York 1992, p. 191-200.

"Satire in Translation: Kurt Tucholsky and Karl Kraus." In: *The Art of Literary Translation. Proceedings of the McMaster University Colloquium*. Ed. Hans Schulte und Gerhart Teuscher. Lanham, Maryland. 1993, p. 185-199.

"Translating and Transplanting the Viennese Cabaret: A Workshop on Helmut Qualtiger's 'Wien wird wieder Weltstadt'." (co-author) In: *The Art of Literary Translation*. Ed. H. Schulte und G. Teuscher. Laham 1993, p. 201-221.

"The Tragic End of a Great European: Stefan Zweig's Letters from Exile." *Turn-of-the-Century Vienna and Its Legacy. Donald Daviau Festschrift*. Wien 1993, p. 351-360.

"Stefan Zweig's Mittlerrolle." In: *Die Zeit gibt die Bilder: Schriftsteller, die Österreich zur Heimat hatten*. Katalog der Ausstellung. Munich 1992, p. 153ff.

"Der Anschluß in den Autobiographien nach Amerika ausgewanderter Thirty-Eighters." In: *Crisis and Culture in Post-Enlightenment Germany (Peter Heller Festschrift)*. Ed. Hans Schulte. Im Druck.

Introduction. In: Max Knight and Joseph Fabry: *The Peter Fabrizius Reader*. Im Druck.

IV. Contributions to Periodicals. A Selection

"Stefan Zweig and Verhaeren." In: *Monatshefte*, April-May 1951, Vol. XLIII, Number 4-5, p. 199-205.

"Stefan Zweig and Modern European Literature." In: *German Life and Letters*, April 1952, Vol. V, p. 202-212.

"Stefan Zweig, Literary Mediator." In: *Books Abroad*, Spring 1952, Vol. 26, Number 2, p. 137-140.

"Stefan Zweig as a Collector of Manuscripts." In: *German Quarterly*, May 1952, Vol. 25, Number 3, p. 182-191.

"Zweig and Rolland: The Literary and Personal Relationship" (with W. H. McClain). In: *Germanic Review*, December 1953, Vol. 28, Number 4, p. 262-281.

"J. C. Wagenseil, Polymath" (with M. C. Davis). In: *Monatshefte*, January 1954, Vol. XLVI, Number 1, p. 35-39.

"Lion Feuchtwanger und Max Brod." In: *Jewish Quarterly*, Fall 1954, Vol. 2, Number 2, p. 14-23.

"In Memoriam Ludwig Lewisohn." In: *Monatshefte*, January 1956, Vol. XLVIII, Number 1, p. 43-45.

"Stefan Zweig's Last Years: Some Unpublished Letters." In: *Monatshefte*, February 1956, Vol. XLVIII, Number 2, p. 73-77.

"Music in Stefan Zweig's Last Years" (with J. P. Barricelli). In: *Juilliard Review*, May 1956.

"Franz Werfel's *Comedy of a Tragedy*." In: *Jewish Affairs*, February 1958, Vol. 13, Number 2, p. 39-41.

"Schnitzler and the Challenge of Zionism." In: *Journal of the International Arthur Schnitzler Research Association*, Winter 1962, Vol. 1, Number 4-5, p. 5-7.

"The World of Arthur Schnitzler." In: *Jewish Quarterly*, Spring 1963, Vol. 10, Number 1, p. 25-35.

"The Anatomy of Anti-Semitism: Max Frisch's *Andorra*." In: *Jewish Affairs*, February 1963, Vol. 18, Number 2, p. 16-18.

"Franz Kafka, der Jude." In: *Israel-Forum*, May 1964.

"The Jewish Contribution to German Poetry." In: *Judaism*, Fall 1965, Vol. 14, Number 1, p. 437-461.

"The Poetry of Nelly Sachs." In: *Jewish Quarterly*, Winter 1965, Vol. 13, Number 4, p. 20-21.

"Johannes Urzidil." In: *Israel-Forum*, May 1966.

"Jewish Themes in Stefan Zweig." In: *Journal of the International Arthur Schnitzler Research Association*, Summer 1967, Vol. 6, Number 2, p. 32-36.

"The Translation of Satire: Kurt Tucholsky and Karl Kraus." In: *Babel*, Fall 1968, Vol. XIV, Number 4, p. 201-206.

"Krausiana." In: *Modern Austrian Literature*, Fall 1970, Vol. 3, Number 2, p. 25-35.

"Literature in Exile." In: *Jewish Spectator*, Fall 1974, Vol. 39, Number 3, p. 41-43.

"Writers in Exile." In: *Jewish Quarterly*, Spring-Summer 1975, Vol. 23, Number 1-2, p. 37-41.

"The Transformation of a Poet." In: *Germanic Notes*, Fall 1974, Vol. 5, Number 3, p. 34-40.

"Karl Kraus: Jüdischer Selbsthasser oder Erzjude?" In: *Modern Austrian Literature*, Winter 1975, Vol. 8, Number 1-2, p. 1-19.

"Ernst Waldinger - wie ich ihn erlebte." In: *Das jüdische Echo*, September l975, p. 70-73.

"Gertrud Kolmar, German-Jewish Poet." In: *Jewish Spectator*, Spring 1976, Vol. 41, Number 1, p. 43-46.

"The Poetry of Gertrud Kolmar." In: *Jewish Quarterly*, Spring-Summer 1976, Vol. 24, Number 1-2, p. 26-28.

"Translation: American Doctoral Dissertations 1970-74" (with Roy Tinsley). In: *Modern Language Journal*, March 1977, Vol. LXI, Number 3, p. 101-109.

"The Quiet Invaders: A Necessary Supplement." In: *Austria Today*, Spring 1977.

"Aus Max Brods letzten Lebensjahren." In: *Das jüdische Echo*, September 1977.

"F. T. Csokor *3. November 1918.*" In: *Modern Austrian Literature*, Winter 1978, Vol. 11, Number 1, p. 95-102.

"Kraus-Klischees auf Englisch." In: *Kraus-Hefte*, January 1980, p. 28-29.

"Jews and German Culture." In: *Jewish Spectator*, Summer 1980, Vol. 45, Number 2, p. 38-42.

"Und's klingt halt doch so voller Poesie: Versuch über das Wienerlied." In: *Modern Austrian Literature*, Fall 1980, Vol. 13, Number 3, p. 1-23.

"The Stature of Stefan Zweig." In: *Jewish Quarterly*, Summer-Autumn 1981, Vol. 29, Number 2-3, p. 13-15.

"Stefan Zweig: Literatur zur Zentenarfeier 1981." In: *Zeitschrift für deutsche Philologie*, Vol. 101, Number 4, 1981, p. 583-92.

"Thomas Mann's View of the Creative Writer." In: *New American Review*, Fall 1981.

"Poet and Scarecrow." In: *London Times Literary Supplement*, Oct. 16, 1981.

"Germans and Jews Today." In: *Midstream*, October 1981, Vol. XXVII, Number 8, p. 26-40.

Gershom Scholem: "My Friend Walter Benjamin," tr. by H. Zohn. In: *Commentary*, Vol. 72, Number 6, 1981, p. 58-69.

"Aus unbekannten Briefen von und über Stefan Zweig." In: *Modern Austrian Literature*, Winter 1981, Vol. 14, Number 3-4, p. 137-146.

"Stefan Zweig in Fredonia." In: *Das jüdische Echo*, Winter 1981.

"Satire in Translation: Kraus and Tucholsky." In: *New American Review*, Spring-Summer 1982.

"Stefan Zweigs kulturelles Mittlertum: Ein jüdischer Charakterzug?" In: *Bulletin des Leo Baeck Instituts*, Vol. 63, Summer 1982, p. 19-31.

"Eine Hand im Handschuh: Exilschriftsteller in den USA." In: *Das jüdische Echo*, September 1982, Vol. 31, Number 1, p. 99-102.

"Theodor Kramer, wie ich ihn erlebte." In: *Das jüdische Echo*, September 1983, p. 134-138.

"Music in Ferdinand Raimund's Plays." In: *Modern Austrian Literature*, Vol. 17, Number 2, 1984, p. 1-12.

"Lion Feuchtwanger." In: *Jewish Currents*, July-August 1984, Vol. 38, Number 6-7, p. 24-28.

"Friderike Maria Zweig im amerikanischen Exil." In: *Das jüdische Echo*, September 1984, p. 163-165.

"The Vitriolic Viennese: An Introduction to Karl Kraus." In: *Cross Currents*, 1984, Number 3, p. 285-296.

"A Satiric Tale of Two Cities." In: *Colloquia Germanica*, 1985, Vol. 18, Number 3, p. 229-237.

"Judenspott, Journalistenspass und höhere Schusterbuben." In: *Das jüdische Echo*, September 1985.

"Letter from Vienna." In: *Midstream*, November 1985, Vol. 31, Number 9, p. 27-29.

"Three Austrian Aphorists: Kraus, Kuh, Canetti." In: *Cross Currents*. Ed. Ladislav Matejka. 1985, Number 4, p. 365-374.

"The Stature of Karl Kraus." In: *Midstream*, March 1986, vol. XXXII, number 3. p. 42-48.

"The Road to Waldheim." In: *Imprint*, Summer 1986.

"Exil als österreichisches Schicksal." In: *Das jüdische Echo*, September 1986.

"Karl Kraus im englischen Sprachraum." In: *Literatur und Kritik*, April-May 1987, p. 112-121.

"The Bell on the Left." In: *Midstream*, May 1987, Vol. 33, Number 5, p. 12-15.

"Gustinus Ambrosi." In: *Das jüdische Echo*, October 1987, Vol. 36, Number 1, p. 221-224.

"Die deutsch-jüdischen Einwanderer in den USA." In: *Das jüdische Echo*, October 1988.

"German Jewry as Spirit and as Legacy." In: *American Jewish Archives*, November 1988, Vol. XL, Number 2, p. 227-232.

"Gustinus Ambrosi, the Sculptor, the Poet, and the Man." In: *Cross Currents*. Ed. Ladislav Matejka. 1989, Number 8, p. 285-296.

"Als der Adolf über uns kam." In: *Das jüdische Echo*, October 1989, p. 29-34.

"Das Wienerlied als Psychogramm einer Bevölkerung." In: *Literatur und Kritik*. November-December 1989, p. 452-465.

"Three Viennese Vignettes." In: *Cross Currents*. Ed. Ladislav Matejka. Number 9, 1989, p. 365-382.

"Stefan Zweig's Mittlerrolle." In: *Das jüdische Echo*, October 1991, p. 206-212.

"Memorial Address on Wolfgang Amadeus Mozart." In: *Cross Currents*, 1992, Number 11, p. 257-64.

Harry Zohn has published several hundred book reviews and shorter articles in a variety of scholarly periodicals and popular journals, including *World Literature Today* (formerly *Books Abroad*), *German Quarterly*, *Germanic Review*, *Germanic Notes*, *Journal of English and Germanic Philology*, *German Studies Review*, *Modern Austrian Literature*, *Jewish Affairs*, *Jewish Currents*, *Boston Globe*, *World Guild Magazine*, *Boston Herald*, *Jewish Spectator*, *Washington Jewish Digest*, *Modern Lanquage Journal*, *Saturday Review*, *Jewish Advocate*, *Jewish Social Studies*, *American-German Review*, *The Reconstructionist*, *Zeitschrift für die Geschichte der Juden*, *Muttersprache*, *Zeitschrift für deutsche Philologie*, *Neue deutsche Biographie*, and *Shofar*.

These and other journals have also published Zohn's translations of shorter works by such authors as Raoul Auernheimer, Hannah Arendt, T. W. Adorno, Walter Benjamin, Ilse Blumenthal-Weiss, Martin Buber, Franz Theodor Csokor, Herbert Eisenreich, Z. F. Finot, Albrecht Goes, Erich Kästner, Hermann Kesten, Karl Kraus, Arnold Krieger, Anton Kuh, Peter Herz, Theodor Herzl, Else Lasker-Schüler, Heinrich Mann, Zenta Maurina, Alfred Polgar, Helmut Qualtinger, Arno Reinfrank, Eugen Relgis, Nelly Sachs, Oskar Jan Tauschinski, Kurt Tucholsky, Robert Weltsch, Ernst Wiechert, and Stefan Zweig.

Sabine Colin: Seidenmalerei, Winter 1993

Beitragende — Contributors

Siebzehn der vierundzwanzig Beitragenden sind ehemalige Emigranten, davon sind neun einst politische Flüchtlinge gewesen; fünf weitere Beitragende stammen von Emigranten oder politischen Flüchltlingen ab.

Evelyn Torton Beck, University of Maryland
Jeffrey B. Berlin, Holy Family College, Philadelphia
Lola Blonder, Boston
Amy Colin, University of Pittsburgh
Sabine Colin, Düsseldorf
Donald G. Daviau, University of California, Riverside
Peter Demetz, Yale University
Eberhard Frey, Brandeis University
Sander L. Gilman, Cornell University
Lisa Kahn, University of Texas
Edward Kaplan, Brandeis University
Marion Kaplan, Queens College, New York
Herbert Lederer, University of Connecticut
Andrei S. Markovits, University of California
Donald G. Prater, Gingins, Switzerland
Arnold Reinfrank, London
Jehuda Reinharz, Brandeis University
Ritchie Robertson, Oxford University
Julius H. Schoeps, Universität Potsdam, Jüdisches Museum, Wien
Frank Stern, Tel Aviv University
Gerald Stieg, Sorbonne Nouvelle, Paris 3
Joseph P. Strelka, State University of New York, Albany
Elisabeth Strenger, Waltham, Massachussets
Edward Timms, Sussex University

Foto von Harry Zohn (am Schreibtisch)

Tabula Gratulatoria

Evelyn Torton Beck
Ernst Behler
Jeffrey B. Berlin
Lola Blonder
Gerald Chapple
Houchang Chehabi
Amy Colin
Sabine Colin
Donald G. Daviau
Olga Davidson
Peter Demetz
Eberhard Frey
Sander L.Gilman
Karl Guthke
Martha Halpert
Thomas Hansen
Peter Heller
Rosaline Intrater
Lisa Kahn
Edward Kaplan
Marion Kaplan
Herbert Lederer
Leo Lensing
Michael Lützeler
Andrei S. Markovits

Wolfgang Mieder
Gregory Nagy
Eric Offenbacher
Helmut Pfanner
Arnold Reinfrank
Jehuda Reinharz
Ritchie Robertson
Sidney Rosenfeld
Philip Russom
Murray Sachs
Julius H. Schoeps
Lotte Schönherr
Beate Schmeichel-Falkenberg
David Scrase
Edith Silbermann
Frank Stern
Guy Stern
Gerald Stieg
Joseph Strelka
Elisabeth Strenger
Mr. and Mrs. H. Strenger
Edward Timms
Krishna Winston
Leon Zelmann

Österreichisches Kulturinstitut, New York
Österreichisches Bundesministerium für Auswärtige Angelegenheiten (Kultursektion), Wien
Moses Mendelssohn Zentrum für europäisch-jüdische Studien, Potsdam
Jüdisches Museum, Wien
P.E.N. Club: German Speaking Writers Abroad
Wilhelm Fink Verlag

Index